VILLE
RISTOWN
the inch

RIVER

PORTLAND & OGDENSBURG R.R. VERMONT DIV.

H.S.
sey
O. Gates
Res. of
C.C. H.H.Powers
Burke
D. E. Phelps
Eaton
ST.
WOLCOTT
Mrs.
Mrs.A.B. R.Brown
Newton
Res. A.D.
P.K.Gleed
Thomas
Academy
& Graded
SCHOOL O. S. Wm L.
Choate Merriam Cheney McClintock
ST. A.B. A.M.&C.C.Burke H.Smith
Chase
S.F. Mrs.
Spaulding Kelton S.M.Ober
Christ Ch. B. W.W.Cate
Parsonage A.B.
Spaulding Chase J.C. C. C.A. A.M.&C.C.Burke
M.Thomas Robinson Clayton Grout ELMORE ST.
D.P. Mrs.La A.G.West
Hutchinson Plour
Mrs.M.H. J.M.
Mrs. Putman Daniels
W.
Capron J.Trow
M.Peak A.
Bros. Twinell
H.
Bundy
M.Terrill
M.P.Roland L.Bugbee Mrs.
L.E. Hunt
Spaulding J.Noyes F.
Bunker

MORRISTOWN TWO TIMES

History of Morristown, Vermont
Anna L. Mower

More About Morristown, 1935-1980
Robert L. Hagerman

MORRISTOWN HISTORICAL SOCIETY
Morrisville, Vermont
1982

Front Cover Photo: Aiming his camera from an upper floor of the Randall Hotel on Main Street, Arthur L. Cheney "captured" this busy Portland Street scene in 1907. At extreme left is part of the Centennial Block, and at extreme right is part of the Fleetwood Building. Beyond the latter is the Drowne Block, which now houses the Ben Franklin Store. Parked at right at the curb is the popcorn wagon which was a Portland Street fixture for many years. It was then operated by Charles Small. (Photo courtesy of Madeline Smilie) Endleaf Maps: These are reprints of maps in *Atlas of Lamoille and Orleans Counties, Vermont* by F.W. Beers Co., 1878.

Library of Congress Catalog Card No. 81-84221
ISBN C-9607288-0-5

Copyright © 1982 by Morristown Historical Society, Inc.

Writers and reviewers are free to quote from both the Mower and Hagerman works, including extended passages, *provided that credit to author and publisher is given*. The publisher urges writers to use care in summarizing any information contained herein, and prefers to see the text quoted in full, where possible.

Copyright does *not* extend to the extract from "Lamoille River Song" by John Nutting (page 396); to all photographs; and to the following line drawings: Copley Country Club clubhouse by Frank A. Stockwell (page 483); and Red Bridge (page 366), Riverside Cemetery gateway (page 403); former First Universalist Church (page 488), Soldiers Monument, Academy Park (page 520), and town meeting scene (page 524), all by Rosemary G. Mathieu. All of these were used under one-time publication rights granted by their respective owners or creators.

This is copy no. 726 of a printing of 1992 copies.

Printed in the United States of America
Printing by Northlight Studio Press, Barre, Vermont
Binding by New Hampshire Bindery, Concord, N.H.
Design of dust jacket by Cyndy M. Brady
Design of balance of book, excluding the reprint of *History of Morristown, Vermont*, by Robert L. Hagerman

CONTENTS

Foreword v

History of Morristown, Vermont

Foreword ix

Chapters:

    I - Before Man Came 1
    II - Town Beginnings 4
    III - Physical Characteristics of the Town 20
    IV - Early Settlers 24
    V - Churches 39
    VI - Development of Various Sections of the Town 64
    VII - Educational Institutions 78
    VIII - Transportation and Communication 120
    IX - Military Record 130
    X - Morristown Bench and Bar 159
    XI - Medical Profession 169
    XII - Celebrations, Grave and Gay 178
    XIII - Organizations, Fraternal, Patriotic, and Social 196
    XIV - Music in Morristown 226
    XV - The Press, the Postoffice, and Public Houses 234
    XVI - The Incorporated Village of Morrisville 246
    XVII - Industries in Morristown 259
    XVIII - Morristown in Public Affairs 268
    XIX - Miscellany 278

Important Dates and Errata 288

Appendix

    Town Representatives 289
    Pastors of the First Congregational Church 290
    Pastors of the Advent Christian Church 290
    Pastors of the Methodist Episcopal Church 291
    Morristown Soldiers in the Civil War 292
    Morristown Soldiers in the World War 301
    Morristown Sailors in the World War 315
    Worshipful Masters of Mount Vernon Lodge [Masons] 317

Photographs 319

More About Morristown, 1935-1980

Morristown: A Capsule Description of Four Municipalities In One .. 334

Chapters:

1 - Boundaries, Natural Landmarks, And Weather 335
2 - Town and Village: Which Is What and How They're Governed .. 344
3 - Schools 354
4 - Roads And Bridges 366
5 - Morristown Fire Department 374

6 - Morristown Police Department 381
7 - Morrisville Water And Light Department 385
8 - More Town And Village Services................................ 396
9 - Other Town Facilities 403
10 - Other Public Services, High And Low........................... 410
11 - Morristown Centennial Library 414
12 - Population, Land Use And Economy............................. 417
13 - Industries 428
14 - Morrisville Businesses 438
15 - Public Houses.. 451
16 - Transportation And Communication 455
17 - Alexander Hamilton Copley................................... 465
18 - Copley Hospital.. 475
19 - Copley Country Club And Airfield 483
20 - Churches 488
21 - Organizations.. 502
22 - Military Record 520
23 - Politics And Social Issues 524
24 - Prominent People And Buildings............................... 528
25 - Odds And The End 536

Appendix: Principal Officers of Town of Morristown, Morristown
  Town School District, and Village of Morrisville 541

Maps*:
  Morrisville, from *Atlas of Lamoille and Orleans
    Counties, Vermont*, by F.W. Beers Co., 1878............. Front Endleaf
  Morristown, from *Atlas of Lamoille and Orleans
    Counties, Vermont*, by F.W. Beers Co., 1878............. Back Endleaf
  Map No. 1 - Changes In Morristown's Boundaries................... 336
  Map No. 2 - Morristown Original Lotting And
               School Districts Established In 1838 357
  Map No. 3 - Morrisville Suburb, 1980............................ 420
  Map No. 4 - Copley Country Club, 1980 485
  Map No. 5 - Town of Morristown, 1958/1964...................... 546
  Map No. 6 - Central Morrisville, 1980........................... 548
  Map No. 7 - Village of Morrisville, 1980 550

Index 551

*Note About Structure/Landmark Identification Numbers: Most structures and landmarks referred to in the text are followed by a parenthetical identification number, e.g., T6, MS32, V12, C83. Each such number is a key to one or another of four of the seven maps listed here, specifically, Town of Morristown (T), Morrisville Suburb (MS), Village of Morrisville (V), and Central Morrisville (C). Each particular structure or landmark appears, with its number, in its correct location on the appropriate map. Accompanying each of these maps is a roster of its numbers with the respective names of the structures and landmarks so identified. This is intended to aid those who first determine the name of a structure/landmark on a map, and wish, via the index, to find such information as there is about it in the text. Note, however, that information about some structures and landmarks entered on the maps appears *only* in the "first draft" manuscript to *More About Morristown, 1935-80*; see the Foreword for information about that.

FOREWORD

Morristown Two Times, 2,000 copies of which are to be printed, was nearly eight years in the making. During that time this new town history grew a bit like Topsy, and ended as not just one, but *two* publications. Here's what happened.

Members of the Morristown Historical Society (MHS) had their first solid discussion about publishing an updated history of Morristown at a meeting on March 27, 1974. From the outset the plan was to reprint Anna L. Mower's *History of Morristown, Vermont* of 1935 together with a supplement of some kind which would cover the years since then. Initially, Willard K. Sanders was to have prepared the supplement. He was a lifelong Morristowner with a deep interest in local history. His ability to mix good humor with historical information was well-established through his annual reports as the long-time superintendent of the Morrisville Water and Light Department. In early 1975, however, Sanders said that poor health prevented him from taking principal responsibility but that he could assist somebody else in the research and writing. Shortly thereafter, the undersigned volunteered to be the "somebody else." While a resident of Morristown only since 1966, Hagerman did offer professional writing experience, much of that dealing with localized Vermont history.

On November 19, 1975 MHS members made a commitment to sponsor the publishing project. Sanders and Hagerman subsequently made some progress, but their joint effort ended with Sanders's death on August 11, 1977. Hagerman then carried on the project alone.

While the two men had initially planned to limit the update of Anna Mower's work to only very specific subjects with which she had dealt, Hagerman came to feel that many things needed greater development. So throughout 1977-80 his supplement to the Mower work grew, and grew, and grew some more. In the end it was well over 1,000 pages of double-spaced typescript. Its official title: *More About Morristown, 1935-1980: The First Draft Of A Supplement To "History of Morristown, Vermont" By Anna L. Mower, 1935*.

What appears in this book is a major condensation of the *First Draft*. But believing that all the extra information about the town in the *First Draft* should be preserved, together with its detailed listing of sources used, the MHS approved Hagerman's recommendation to actually publish the *First Draft* typescript in a very limited edition. This consisted of 20 copies produced by photo-offset in 1981 plus the original typescript and one carbon copy thereof.

For researchers who would like to consult the *First Draft*, public repositories which have or will have a copy are: Morristown Historical Society, Morristown Centennial Library, Peoples Academy library, Stowe Free Library, Lanpher Memorial Library in Hyde Park, John Dewey Library at Johnson State College, Vermont Historical Society library in Montpelier, and Bailey-Howe Library at the University of Vermont. The remaining copies will be sold.

The undersigned thanks the many Morristowners, both present and former, who helped the undersigned in various ways. Special recognition goes to the following for their significant research assistance on specific subjects: Evelyn H. Shanley (Morristown Centennial Library), Heber Shanley (First Congregational Church), Mary Loati and Barbara King (Puffer United Methodist Church), Rev. George S. Stone (Advent Christian Church), Rev. Bernard Couture and Rev. Donald Ravey (Holy Cross Church), Lester M. Roscoe (Seventh-day Adventist Church), R. Warren Hallsworth (Kingdom Hall, Jehovah's Witnesses), Mary Sanders Mitchell (Morrisville Military Band), and Josephine Sweeney (roster of municipal officers). The undersigned also wishes to recognize the superior professional typing services of Lois Ann McGee.

Individual credits appear with most of the photographs themselves. But special thanks go to Robert S. Jones for making available the negatives from his collection of old photos, and to Lawrence Jay Kennedy of the Village Photographer for his complimentary copy work for some of the photographs.

A final special "thank you" goes to the five Morristown artists who donated their talents in the pen and ink drawings which appear at the beginnings of the chapters in *More About Morristown*. They and their respective initials which appear on the drawings are: Thomas C. (Tom) Bjerke (TCB), Rosemary Gregory Mathieu (RGM), John M. Sargent (JMS) (currently a Hyde Park resident but a Morristown native), Marcia Shafer (MS) and Rett Sturman (RS). The drawings generally are all contemporary renderings of existing subjects. The one exception is the drawing of the Copley Country Club clubhouse. That was produced by Rev. Frank Stockwell, apparently some time in the early 1960's. It is reproduced here by courtesy of the Copley Golf Corporation.

With some exceptions, the information in *More About Morristown, 1935-1980* is current through 1980. The exceptions, which are both earlier and later, are usually noted where they occur.

Anna Mower's *History of Morristown, Vermont* is reprinted almost in its entirety in photo-facsimile of the original book. The following are the few items not included: printed matter: certain front matter items and the index; and photographs: seven of the original 20 (see page 319 for details). While all the other photos are reproduced, they appear together here in a single photo section (some of them resized), instead of being scattered through the text as they were in the original. Also, some of the original identification captions have been expanded. In addition, a list of *errata* to the Mower text appears on page 288; these are keyed by numbers which appear in the margins of the pages where the errors occur.

Finally, the text of *More About Morristown* takes note of the several significant contributions of Miss Mower to her lifelong home town. A more extended biographical sketch appears in the foreword of the *First Draft*. Suffice it to record here that Anna Louise Mower (pronounced "More") was born March 1, 1876 and died December 29, 1966. Presumably, she would be pleased to know that the Morristown Historical Society, for which she did so much, is sponsoring this reprint and update of her own notable work.

Morrisville in Morristown
November 7, 1981

ROBERT L. HAGERMAN

HISTORY

of

MORRISTOWN
VERMONT

by

ANNA L. MOWER

1935

This book is dedicated to the
MORRISVILLE WOMAN'S CLUB
that arranged for its preparation and
made possible its publication

MESSENGER-SENTINEL COMPANY
MORRISVILLE, VT.

Foreword

This History of Morristown is the outgrowth of a meeting of the Morrisville Woman's Club, held on April 4, 1927, at which Miss Lou Rand, great-granddaughter of the first settler in Morristown, presented a paper, "Our Local History," excerpts from which are given in this book.

The Club felt it could engage in no worthier project than to preserve for later generations the story of the men and women who shaped the early destiny of the town.

Macaulay once said, "A people that takes no pride in the noble achievements of remote ancestors will never achieve anything worthy to be remembered with pride by remote descendants."

While effort has been made to avoid errors, the book probably contains inaccuracies and certainly there are many imperfections. But it brings together what has been ascertainable about the founding and development of Morristown.

Heminway's "Gazeteer," Child's "Gazeteer of Lamoille County," Crockett's "History of Vermont," and the material already collected and published by Elisha Brigham and Judge H. H. Powers have been freely consulted and they furnish much of the early history. Thanks are due many people and organizations for their cooperation, but special mention should be made of E. K. Seaver, who gave much of the information about Cadys Falls; of T. C. Cheney, who gave the use of the diaries of his grandfather, S. L. Gates, and his own time in consultation; of Mrs. Mary Cheney, for her interest and information; of D. A. Sanders, for his account of the Morrisville Military Band, and also data on the cemeteries; of Willard Sanders, for his history of the Water and Light Department, and of the Masonic Order; of H. M. McFarland of Hyde Park, who gave access to his complete file of the local newspapers and the index for them which he had prepared; and of Chief Justice G. M. Powers, for his advice and for reading much of the manuscript.

CHAPTER I

BEFORE MAN CAME

SINCE the physical features of a region influence very materially the life of its inhabitants, it seems fitting that the story of Morristown should begin with a hasty glance at those tremendous forces which in the ages long past carved out its valleys and shaped its hills.

Vermont is among the oldest regions, geologically speaking, within the boundaries of the United States, following next after the Archean formation of the Adirondack region; and the Lamoille River, together with the Winooski, are what are termed "antecedent" rivers of great antiquity. In prehistoric times the Labradorian glacier covered all of New York and New England, although the glacial scratches are less plainly seen at the top of Mount Washington. Slowly this huge stream of ice moved southward, crushing and grinding its way along until it extended below New York City, from which point the terminal moraine swung westward south of Chicago, then northward across Montana into northwestern Canada. The thickness of the ice is estimated at not less than 10,000 feet at the northern boundary of Vermont, so it entirely covered the highest peaks of the Green Mountains. At that time the land was much lower than today, partly because of the tremendous pressure of the ice.

As this vast ice sheet began to melt, great bodies of water were created and new channels for rivers were cut out, while the sea level waters followed the retreating ice cap northward. At first these waters formed a narrow strip which the geologist calls the Hudson Inlet. As this mounted still farther north, it became the Hudson-Champlain Inlet. After a time sea level waters took possession of the St. Lawrence Valley, causing what is known as the Champlain Sea. After a long period of time the Gulf of St. Lawrence united with the Champlain Sea and the Hudson-Champlain Inlet became the Hudson-Champlain Strait.

It is thought that at an early stage of the ice front recession one glacial water body covered the Memphremagog, the Lamoille, and Winooski Valleys. The waters of the Memphremagog discharged through the depression now occupied by Elligo Pond into the Lamoille, and glacial Lamoille emptied through the Stowe Strait into the Winooski, which may have flowed through Williamstown Gulf into the White River and eventually into the Connecticut. This occupation by glacial waters seems to have been of comparatively short duration and its existence is deduced from the character of the sand plains which clearly show a water formation. A water level at about the altitude of the highest terrace near Morrisville is necessary to account for the soil and the northerly drainage of the valley of Joe's Brook. A large part of the valley about Morrisville is filled with fertile deposits, but about a hundred acres northwest of the village is of loose gravel, so that it bears little vegetation. This gravel deposit leads the geologist to think it must have been a glacial sand plain, for no other source of such material seems possible. Thus the Labrador glacier of prehistoric times provided the gravel which in this age has furnished the foundation for miles of roads in town.

So the Lamoille Valley first held glacial waters which after a long period were succeeded by an extension of the Champlain Sea. During this time the streams flowing into Lake Champlain formed deep estuaries and their deposits or deltas lay far east of the present Champlain Valley. The Lamoille created a wide delta about Milton, northern Colchester, and southern Georgia and entered the lake farther north than its present mouth. This inlet extended as far east as Hardwick. After the melting of the ice there was a gradual rising and tilting of the land which altered the flow of the rivers.

The region about Morrisville is described by Prof. H. L. Fairchild in the Report of the State Geologist, as follows: "A grand display of delta plains is found at Morrisville and eastward. Here several streams joined the Lamoille waters and the volume of detritus was large and quite filled this section of the valley. Extensive plains indicate the successive falling levels of the static waters. The business part of Morrisville is on a plain with an altitude of 670 feet, taking the railroad station at 646 feet. Passing eastward by the highway a higher plain with abrupt front has frontal elevation of 720 feet, rising to 730 at the back. Another terrace with a bar front is 740 feet. Above this is the handsome plain, with altitude of

750 feet. The village cemetery is on the extensive part of the plain on the south side of the river. The entire width of the valley was probably filled in this section and partly re-excavated by stream erosion. South of Morrisville, along the road to Stowe, the detrital plains, smoothed by the lowering waters of the Champlain Sea, are beautifully displayed. The summit plains lie at the col, or divide, between the Lamoille and Winooski Valleys, with altitude about 740 feet. From these figures it will be seen that while the lower terraces correlate with the summit level of the Champlain Sea the upper terraces are too high. Here again we have complication with glacial waters, as in the Winooski Valley."

On the north side of the river other terraces exist. The buildings of the Lamoille Valley Fair grounds occupy one corresponding to the level of Pleasant View Cemetery, the so-called old fair ground and the high school building. Farther northwest along the St. Johnsbury & Lake Champlain Railroad at Cadys Falls the several terrace levels unite, forming what is said to be the highest formation of that kind in the state.

Thus through the long centuries the waters of the Lamoille deposited rich silt, its course changed, its waters receded until the valleys and plains were made ready for the habitation of man. It was a long time before this section was permanently occupied. No considerable part of Vermont was inhabited by the Indians, but it was rather the hunting and fishing ground for the wandering bands. Tomahawks and other implements have been found in the Lamoille Valley and at a place called Indian Hill in Cambridge there is evidence of a camp-ground, but no settlements were made until Indian Joe and Molly discovered the resources of the Lamoille, or, as the Indians called it, the Wintoak, or Marrow River.

CHAPTER II

TOWN BEGINNINGS

THE years 1780 and 1781 were momentous ones in the history of the United States, for in the fall of the former year began that series of victories in the Southern campaign which included King's Mountain, Cowpens, and Guilford Court House and terminated at Yorktown in October, 1781, and virtually ended the Revolution.

They were also significant ones in the life of the doughty little Green Mountain Republic, which had declared its independence in 1777, and was struggling to maintain it in the face of predatory neighbors, and a Congress which had declared that the acts of Vermont in asserting its independence and continuing its grants of land in violation of the resolutions of Congress in 1779 "are highly unwarrantable and subversive of the peace and welfare of the United States." It demanded that the people abstain from all acts of authority, either civil or military, over those residents in Vermont who preferred to accept the jurisdiction of another state. The young republic accepted this challenge, and the General Assembly of October, 1780, determined to raise an army and to provide revenue for maintaining the same by granting the lands in the state not previously occupied. A printed form of petition to the General Assembly for a land grant was prepared and these petitions were freely circulated, not only in New England, but in the Middle States. Land companies were formed in New Hampshire, Massachusetts, Connecticut, and Rhode Island, and by officers in the Continental Army. Thus the state built up among its neighbors a body of public opinion friendly to the stand it had taken. Some discretion was shown in making these concessions to persons who "will most conduce to the welfare of the state to have such grants." At the session of the General Assembly, held in the autumn of 1780, more than fifty such grants were made by the House, and in most cases the Governor and Council accepted their recommendations, and named the grantees and the terms of the Charter. Among such we find the following:

"Resolved that the proprietors of the Township of Morristown Granted to Mr. Moses Morse & Co. being sixty four in Number, Marked on the plan No. 44, pay £7 L. Money in silver or equivalent in other current money, to be paid by the first day of March next, the terms of Settlement is three years after the War, the reservations are to be Specified in the Charter of Incorporation."

Thus the inception of the Town was closely connected with the early struggles of the state. On that same day, November 7, 1780, grants of twelve other towns were ① made, among them Craftsbury, Coventry and Fletcher, in this section of the state. About nine months later this action was confirmed by the Governor, and on August 24, 1781, the following charter was granted:

"THE CHARTER OF MORRISTOWN

"The Governor, Council, and General Assembly of the Freeman of the State of Vermont
[L. S.]
"To all People to whom these Presents shall come Greeting.

"Know Ye, That whereas, Doct Moses Morse and his associates, our worthy friends have by Petition requested a grant of a Tract of unappropriated Land within this State, in order for settling a new Plantation, to be Erected into a Township; We have therefore thought fit for the due encouragement of their laudable designs & for other Valuable consideration us hereunto moving do by these Presents in the name and by the authority of the Freemen of the State of Vermont, give and grant the Tract of Land hereafter described and bounded, unto him the said Moses Morse and to the several persons hereafter named his associates viz: Timothy Meach, Joshua Morse, Daniel Morse, John Norton, Sarah Morse, Charity Wibon, Gershom Randell, John Kelley, Willard Morse, Elijah Adams, Samuel Cook, Jonathan Cook, John Smith, Daniel Kinney, Nathan Hibbard, Jesse Spawlding, Jacob Kinney, Moses Porter, Simeon Rood, Nathaniel Edwards, Elias Brown, Dennis Mach, Nathan Fay, Joseph Hinsdale, Isaac Kellogg, ② Aaron Hubbel, Robert Cochran, Caleb Bingham, Joseph Hinsdale, Jr., Jedediah Hyde, Jabez Bingham, David Mitchell, Stephen Mitchell, Roger Rose, Ruggles Woodbridge, Noah Goodman, Josiah White, Mary Bingham, Marble Mitchell, Samuel Day, Lois Day, Samuel Day, Jr., Winstone Liberty Day, Gideon Beebe, John Morse, Jonathan Merrick, David Merrick, John Merrick, Eliel Todd, Lucy

Todd, Israel Jones, Marshal Jones, Isaac Searles, Mary Searles, Andrew Alger, Ebenezer Stratton, Luther Rich, William Farrand, Giles Barnes, Enoch Chapen, Thomas Train, Rosanna Farrand, Isaac Whitney, & Jason Wright. Which together with the five following Rights reserved to the several uses in manner following include the whole of said Township viz: one Right for the use of a Simonary or College; one Right for the use of County Grammar Schools in said State; Lands to the amount of one Right to be and remain for the purpose of settlement of a minister and Ministers of the Gospel in said Township forever; Lands to the amount of one Right for the support of the Social Worship of God in said Township; and Lands to the amount of one Right for the Support of an English School or Schools in said Township, which said two Rights for the use of a Seminary or College and for the use of County Grammar Schools as aforesaid, and the Improvements, rents, Intrests, & Profits arising therefrom shall be under the Controul, order, dircetion & disposal of the General Assembly of said state forever; And the proprietors of said Township are hereby authorized and Empowered to locate said two Rights justly and equitably, or quantity for quality in such parts of said Township as they or their Committee shall judge will least incommode the General Settlement of said Tract or Township; And the said Proprietors are further empowered, to locate the lands aforesaid amounting to three Rights assigned for the Settlement of a Minister & Ministers for their Support, & for the use and Support of English Schools in such and so many places as they or their Committee shall judge will least incommode the Inhabitants of said Township when the same shall be fully settled and improved Laying the same equitably, or quantity for quality, which said lands amounting to the three rights last mentioned when located as aforesaid, shall Together with their Improvements, Rights, Rents, Profits, Dues & Intrest remain unalianably appropriated to the uses and purposes for which they are respectively assigned, & be under the charge, direction & disposal of the Inhabitents of said Township forever; which Tract of Land hereby given and Granted as aforesaid is bounded and described as follows, viz. Beginning at the North, Easterly Corner of Stow, Then westerly in the line of Stow (something more than) six miles to an angle thereof, Then carying that Breadth back North 36

Do East so far that to extend a Line north 54 Do West across said Breadth will encompass the contents of six miles square, And that the same be and hereby is Incorporated into a Township By the name of Morristown, and the Inhabitants, that do or shall hereafter inhabit said Township, are declared to be Infranchised and entitled to all the Priviledges, and Immunities that the Inhabitants of other Towns within this State do and ought by the Laws and Constitution of this State to Exercise and Enjoy.

"To Have and to Hold, the said granted Premises, as above expressed in equal shares with all the Privileges and appurtences thereto belonging & appertaining, unto them and their respective Heirs and assigns forever upon the following Condition and Reservations viz that each Proprietor of the township of Morristown, aforesaid his heirs and assigns, shall plant and cultivate Five acres of land, and Build an house at least Eighteen feet Square on the Floor, or have one Family settled on each respective right within the term of three years next after the circumstances of the war will admit of a Settlement with Safety on penalty of the Forfeiture of each respective Right of Land in said Township not so settled and Improved, and the Same to revert to the Freemen of this State, to be by their representatives regranted to Such persons as shall appear to Settle and Cultivate the same, That all Pine Timber suitable for a Navy be reserved for the use and Benifit of the Freemen of this State.

"In Testimony whereas we have caused the Seal of this State to be affixed in Council this 24 day of August AD 1781, in the 5th year of the Independence of this, and 6 of the United States.

"THOMAS CHITTENDEN

"By His Excellency Command
"Thomas Tolman Depy Secy"

It has generally been assumed that the name Morristown was derived from that of Dr. Morse, the chief grantee, being a modification of the somewhat awkward term Morse-town. Judge H. Henry Powers, who investigated the early history of the town so thoroughly, refers to a tradition which suggests a different origin of the name. While the early settlers were struggling for their rights, a man by the name of Morris was a staunch friend of the Vermonters, and the name Morristown was given the new township in his honor. The fact that in both grant and charter the town is always called Morristown makes this explanation plausible. The question who this Morris was at once arises, and a study of the history of the state during that period suggests that it might have been one of two men.

Gouverneur Morris was a delegate from New York to Congress from 1777 to 1780 and served with marked ability. In private correspondence as well as in his public acts he showed that he was opposed to much of New York's policy. In a letter to Governor Clinton he said: "I wish the business of Vermont was settled. I fear we are pursuing a shadow with respect to that matter and every day I live and everything I see, gives to my fears the consistense of opinion. It is a mighty arduous business to compel the submission of men to a political or religious government." Again he wrote: "Let splendid acts of justice and generosity induce these people to submit early to our dominion for prejudices grow stubborn as they grow old."

Naturally these views were not in accord with those of the other leaders of New York and in part because of them Morris was retired from public service by that state in 1780, the year in which the grant of the town was made. He moved to Pennsylvania, where he was chosen a delegate to the Federal Convention and became one of its most influential members. Later he returned to New York and was elected United States Senator. If this tradition is worthy of any credence, it is not impossible that this early friend of the state suggested the name and any citizen of the town might well feel the town was honored by this choice.

Still another Morris whose services to the state were prominent about this time was Judge Lewis R. Morris, a nephew of Gouveneur, who had served in the American Army with distinction and settled here in Tinmouth. He served as Clerk of the Assembly, and in January, 1791, he and Nathaniel Chipman were elected Commissioners to go to Congress and negotiate with it for the admission of Vermont into the Union, which duty was performed to the satisfaction of his fellow Vermonters. President Washington recognized his ability by appointing him the first Marshal of the District of Vermont. It must be conceded, however, that his more notable services to the state were performed after the township had been granted in 1780.

If, as has been generally supposed, the town was named after Dr. Moses Morse, it was connected with a strong and rather unique character. Dr. Morse at the time he became proprietor was living in Worthington, Mass., and so many of the men who invested in the new township were associated with that or adjacent towns that a few words in regard to its history seem in order.

In 1762 this town, together with Patridgefield, now known as Hinsdale, and Cummington were sold at public auction and settlement at once began, many of the pioneers coming from Connecticut. A list of these early settlers, as given in the history of Worthington, reveals the following names of persons who were soon to become proprietors in the new town of Morristown: Jonathan and Samuel Cooke, Samuel and Lois Day, John Kelly, Moses, Joshua, Daniel and Sarah Morse, Timothy Meech, John Norton, and Gershom Randall. In addition to these, Nathan Hibbard and Jacob and David Kinne were from the adjacent town of Patridgefield, now Hinsdale. Isaac and Mary Searles and Andrew Alger were from nearby Williamstown. John Smith came from Hadley, in the same county, and Joseph Hinsdale, who figured so largely in the early meetings of the proprietors, lived just across the state line in Bennington, while Moses Porter, another grantee, was in Pawlet. Other names indicate that still others came from that section of New England, but the ones given are definitely identified by the town records. Thus a third of the proprietors were from the northwest corner of Massachusetts or just over the border in the new commonwealth. Many of the records of the first sales in town were made by Nahum Eager, who served as Town Clerk in Worthington for years, and a study of the history of that town shows that these men who were identified with the new settlement were men prominent in the affairs of that place.

The one of them most vitally concerned with Morristown was Dr. Moses Morse, who was born in Newbury, Mass., in 1721, a descendant of Anthony Morse who came to that town in 1635. Dr. Morse was educated at the University of Cambridge, England, and served his apprenticeship as physician and surgeon in the hospitals of Liverpool and London and then returned to America and settled down to practice his profession in Preston, Conn. About 1765 he moved to Worthington, being the first doctor in the town. In the record of the first town meeting he was elected Surveyor of Highways and later served as Selectman. In 1773 he was Agent to the Provincial Congress, the first man thus to represent the town, and in 1777 he was elected representative to the General Court. From the beginning of the Revolution his sympathies were with the mother country. "By shrewdness and tact, in 1774, he influenced the town to pass a vote making the Non-importation Act in regard to tea, which the town a few years before had covenanted to maintain, null and void." He remained in the session of the General Court of 1777 but a short time, being recalled and censured in the following resolution passed by the town: "Voted that Dr. Moses Morse, for his misconduct in refusing to act in behalf of the town, relative to a petition and saying that he would oppose it with all his might directly contrary to the vote of the town, ought not, in justice to the cause for which we are now contending with Great Britain sit any longer as a Representative in the General Court for this town." The petition referred to was a request made by the town to the Massachusetts Legislature to have its unimproved land taxed to assist in defraying the expenses of the war. "In spite of the ill-will and prejudice which his conduct at this time occasioned he was subsequently appointed by the town to act on important committees, on account of his eminent ability and talents." His financial standing also doubtless increased his influence in the town since his education, his frequent trips to England, and his colonizing activities indicate that he was a man of wealth for that period.

He died in 1783 in a fit of apoplexy and his body was borne to its resting place by Revolutionary soldiers. "The coffin in which he was carried burst open on the shoulders of his neighbors before they reached the grave which was nearly a mile from his residence, causing the corpse to roll upon the ground, and manifesting, as one of the soldier bearers quaintly expressed it, that 'habitual contrariness which was so characteristic of him'."

Whatever may have been the doctor's political views, he entered heartily into the opening up and settling of the undeveloped land. Having made his home in what was then a frontier town, he became interested in the still more remote Republic of Vermont. Perhaps the very independence which the new state had shown in its dealings with Congress and its neighbors appealed to his pugnacious temperament. At any rate, he and his family became closely concerned with one of the new townships. Rights were made out to the doctor himself and to at least four other members of his immediate family. Family names were perpetuated among the Morses so it is impossible to tell whether the Sarah Morse mentioned among the grantees was his wife or daughter. Joshua and Samuel were his sons and Daniel may have been either his son or his brother. John and Willard Morse of the grantees were not in his immediate family, but Willard was at one time a resident of Worthington so was possibly a relative.

The doctor's death in 1783 occurred before the disposition of rights had begun to any great extent, but his son, Samuel, was made the administrator of his estate and the records show he not only handled the lots belonging to his immediate family, but also bought freely from the other grantees. For a time his name appeared more frequently in the real estate transactions than that of any other. At the first meeting of the proprietors he was chosen Moderator and in 1794 he came to inspect the township. He was so favorably impressed with it that during his stay he deeded land to his grandson, Ansell, who later moved to Ohio, and to another grandson, Rufus, who died in Worthington when but a young man. Again in 1804 he and his two sons, Elijah and Elias, were in town to attend to the disposition of some of their property, but in 1812 they gave the power of attorney to their townsman, Samuel Cooke, who had now moved to the new settlement. So far as we know the direct connection of the family ceased soon, but four generations of the family were land owners here and played their part in the development of the township.

So Morristown is probably the lineal descendant of Worthington, Mass., more than of any other one place and if, as generally supposed, it was named from Dr. Morse and his family it was a fitting recognition of their influence in its inception and settlement.

Some time elapsed after the granting of the charter before the proprietors took active steps to develop their new grant, but on May 19, 1784, they called a meeting at Pownal at which they chose Samuel Morse Moderator and

Joseph Hinsdale Clerk and elected a committee "to go and take a view of said town and report at the next meeting the quality thereof, and adjourned to meet at this place at ten o'clock in the forenoon, on Wednesday the first of July next." Various meetings were held either at Pownal or Bennington, at one of which held August 10, 1784, they voted to lay out the town of Morristown under the direction of a committee of three, but no report of such a committee is recorded. Two and a half years later at Bennington they voted to make a division, to lay out 105 acres to each right to make and number the corners and make out a plan. They also voted to give Lieutenant Hinsdale twenty-six shillings for each right, except public rights, to complete the survey. On February 2, 1789, they again met at Bennington and voted to make a second division and that it consist of 200 acres to each proprietor's right and gave Joseph Hinsdale one pound, thirteen shillings on each right to complete the survey. At Cambridge on the first Wednesday of June, 1794, they voted to lay out the third division, consisting of land not included in the other two, the lots of which were of smaller size. They adjourned until the third Monday of July, 1794, at Aaron Hurd's, "in said town of Morristown," the first gathering of the proprietors held within their domain.

Even before the laying out of the rights had been accepted, a sale in grants had begun, the first one occurring on April 1, 1782, when Daniel Kinne of Patridgefield, Mass., sold two rights, to one of which he was the original grantee and the other belonged to his brother, Jacob; and again on March 17, 1784, we read, "I, John Norton of Worthington, Mass. Gentlemen, in consideration of 12 £ do acquit my Rite or Share of land in the town of Morristown in the State of Vermont in County of Rutland being granted to Doct. M. Morse and his associates to John Stone of Worthington, etc."

These first transactions involved no thought of settlement which was not to come for some time yet. They were rather speculative in character and involved some risk for the purchasers, since, in addition to the price paid for the grants, the owners met some expense in connection with the development of the new township. Aside from the taxes levied by the proprietors the state made its demands. In October, 1788, for example, Morristown, together with some other towns, was required to pay twenty-three pounds, three shillings, eight pence for surveying the town lines, which survey was made under the general direction of Ira Allen, Surveyor General. When improvements such as the making of roads and bridges or the building of a state's prison were undertaken, a tax of from one to three cents per acre would be levied. Some of the proprietors were unwilling to meet these recurring assessments and rather than pay the price of progress they let their lands lapse. On June 6, 1805, a vendue was held at Elisha Boardman's tavern for the sale of land to pay such taxes as were not met and such auctions were not infrequent in the early days.

In New England the county as a unit of government does not play the part it does in the South and West, yet some explanation as to why the early deeds place Morristown in four different counties may be desirable.

When the state was organized, it was divided into two counties, Cumberland to the east and Bennington on the west, with the Green Mountains forming the dividing line. This division lasted about two years when the County of Rutland was incorporated from Bennington, while Windsor and Orange Counties were taken from Cumberland, the name of which changed to Windham. When the first deeds were recorded, Morristown was in Rutland County. In 1785 Rutland County, which had extended to the northern border of the state, was divided and Addison County was formed, which in turn was divided to form Chittenden in 1787. Five years later Orleans County was incorporated, which included the towns of Eden, Hyde Park, Morristown and Wolcott from this section. For more than forty years this division remained, but there began to be agitation for the formation of still another county.

At first the movement had little following in the state, then a bill for such a change passed the House only to be defeated in the Council, and years of contention followed. The story of this struggle forms an interesting chapter of local history. While Morristown was only one of the group of towns thus battling for what they thought were their rights, its representatives were instructed to work for the project at the Legislature, and, although opposition to the movement existed in some of the towns, particularly Stowe and Elmore, there seems to have been none here.

In the fall of 1834 a convention was held which drew up a petition to be presented at the coming session of the

Legislature. Previous to this, the towns had acted individually. It was probably the work of a committee, but there is no way of determining who they were. The document is too long to be given in full, but its line of argument is so logical and its language is so characteristic of the century that produced the Declaration of Independence, that excerpts are given at some length as indicative of the spirit of the people who had settled the region and the manner of life they lived. The petition was signed by 234 delegates, of whom fifty-nine were from Morristown and included its leading men from all walks of life:

"To the honorable General Assembly of the State of Vermont to be holden at Montpelier on the second Thursday of October, 1834.

"A portion of your fellow citizens having assembled in Convention as delegates from the towns of Cambridge, Johnson, Waterville, Sterling and Belvidere in the County of Franklin; Hyde Park, Eden, Morristown, and Wolcott in the County of Orleans; Stowe and Elmore in the County of Washington; and Mansfield in the County of Chittenden for the purpose of consulting for the common good and devising means for the redress of grievances which they have suffered in times past and are still oppressed with, beg leave before they separate to address you. And we feel confidence in our cause, inasmuch as the 20th article of our Bill of Rights declares, 'that the people have a right to assemble together to consult for their common good; to instruct their representatives; to apply to the Legisture for redress of grievances by address, petition, or remonstrance'.

"We are instructed by the people of the several towns which we represent, and under whose delegated authority we act, to ask your honorable body to constitute a new County of the foregoing towns with all the rights and privileges of other counties in this state and as reasons therefor we respectfully ask your attention to some of the prominent facts in support of our petition.

"1st The distance from the various county seats to which we belong,

"2nd The natural situation of our territory,

"3rd The inconveniences to which we are subjected in order to obtain the rights and immunities enjoyed in common by the rest of our fellow citizens.

"It cannot be supposed that we shall be able to go very minutely into detail as to the distances, but we deem it necessary previously to remark, that all the towns here enumerated are on the borders, or extremities of four counties (to wit) Franklin, Orleans, Washington, and Chittenden."

Then follows the different distances which each town is from its county seat, which is summed up as follows:

"So that it will be seen that the common distance of the several towns from their various county seats is about twenty-nine miles. We leave these facts without comment here only to add that the distances as here enumerated are on the nearest public roads.

"2nd The natural situation of our territory.

"And to this part of the subject we invite the particular attention of your honorable body. Although the distances from our county seats are great, yet if we may be permitted so to say, the God of nature himself has so formed our situation and shapen our territory, and marked the boundaries of a distinct county, we apprehend that you have only to become acquainted with its situation in order to be fully convinced of the justice of our claims which entitle us to a favorable decision. The river Lamoille passes through the interior of our territory from an easterly to a westerly direction. The north, northeast, south, and south westerly parts of our county are bounded by mountains some of which are totally impassible nearly enclosing a tract of several hundreds of square miles of land of as good a quality we hesitate not to say as any other portions of the state. The most prominent outlets from this territory are by the valley along the banks of the Lamoille on the road that leads from Burlington to Danville. The county lines, as they are now formed, pass through the most fertile part of our territory and instead of giving us a common center for the transaction of our business draw us off four different ways, through a mountainous country and over rough roads thus constantly detracting from our growth and prosperity.

"With these facts thus briefly enumerated, we invite your attention in the third place to the inconveniences to which we are subjected in order to obtain the rights and immunities, enjoyed in common by the rest of the citizens of the state and here beg leave to set forth

"That our County and Superior Courts are so far

removed from us that we are compelled to purchase justice in order to obtain it.

"That our roads to the various county seats are not only rough and impassible, but the face of the country through which they pass is such that it is impossible by ordinary means, ever to make them good.

"That many of our citizens from the great expense which attends it, are compelled to sacrifice their rights rather than attempt to obtain them; thus giving the rich an ascendancy over the poor.

"That jurors and witnesses are compelled to attend courts at considerable pecuniary and personal sacrifice.

"That our inhabitants are obliged to travel from twenty five to forty five miles to attend Probate Courts and obtain the settlement of estates, many times taking a large portion of the widow's substance to protect her in the enjoyment of the rest of it.

"That we are compelled to pay our proportion for the administration of the government while we are denied the common rights and privileges guaranteed to us by the Constitution.

"It is for the purpose of obtaining a redress of these inconveniences under which we are laboring as a community and many others of a lesser consequence that has called us from our several occupations at the busy season of the year, together in convention in order that some means may be devised to get our true situation before your honorable body.

"It is true that this is no new subject to the Legislature; yet we apprehend very many of you have not become acquainted with all the evils that oppress us. For the last seven years this subject has been before the House of Representatives and as many times our rights have been passed by. But our cause has strengthened every year with our fellow citizens, and each succeeding Legislature has contained an increased number in favor of granting the prayer of the people which we have the honor to represent in Convention. This gives us one consolation and furnishes us with a hope that our rights will be eventually regarded. When this subject was first brought before the Legislature, it was generally regarded as chimerical and although it was referred to a Committee, yet it was passed upon almost without examination. We cannot refrain from mentioning the opinion of the Hon.

Henry Olin who was once Chairman of a committee to whom this subject was referred. He says after examining it, 'I have been disposed to think unfavorably of any alteration of our County lines; but the claims of these petitioners are peculiar and striking. Here are county lines formed by the God of Nature and a sense of justice will soon compel the Legislature to grant their request'.

"Thus it was viewed in its primary stages by many more that might be mentioned but so strongly have been our Legislatures prejudiced against any alterations that it was referred year after year to the next session without much examination until 1832."

In 1832, and also in 1833, the matter was again referred to the Legislature and in one case was considered by the Judiciary Committee and in the other by the Ways and Means Committee, both of whom after careful investigation recommended the passage of the bill, thus bearing out the contention of the petitioners that "the facts of our cause need but to be examined in order to convince every impartial mind of its justice."

In answer to the argument brought forward by the opponents of the measure that it would put the state to more expense, the petition states "It would cost no more for judges or jurors. No officers are created in counties with salaries but they are all paid by fees or perquisites and the only possible effect it could have in a pecuniary point of view would be to lessen the state expenses and divide the fees between five instead of four." Then follows a discussion in regard to the saving to the residents of the section under consideration. In answer to the argument that it is dangerous "to alter ancient landmarks," they reply: "Let justice be done and the consequences will not be evil. What then we ask is to interpose and deprive us of justice long sought by an oppressed people? Who would still make us tributary to our more wealthy neighbors? Have we not served long enough in this land of boasted liberty and equal rights now to have our freedom?"

The petition closes with the affirmation that they will not despair so long as the Bill of Rights forms a part of the Constitution, and will persevere in their request until it is finally granted. Whether it was the line of reasoning or the determined and persistent spirit shown that began to weigh with the members of the Legislature cannot be known, but on October 26, 1835, the measure was passed and the county incorporated.

Thus came into being the youngest and, with the exception of Grand Isle, by far the smallest of the fourteen counties. It contains only 431 square miles, which is just half the area of Rutland County and less than half that of Windsor. What it lacked in size and population it made up in other ways, for early in its history it was referred to as "Spunky Lamoille," spunk being a quality to which it owed its existence.

There have been many conjectures as to the origin of this appellation and the following was given in the "News and Citizen" in 1895 by Joshua Merriam, a former resident of Morristown and grandson of Capt. Joshua Merriam, one of the early settlers. He states that in the War of 1812 live hogs and poultry were taken from the Hubbell and McDaniels farms to supply the fleet on Lake Champlain. They were in charge of Jack Virginia, a negro captured from the British when Ticonderoga was taken by Allen. During the battle of Plattsburgh, there came a shot which killed one of the hogs, knocked a hencoop to pieces, thus liberating a rooster which flew into the rigging and stood there crowing loudly. Negro Jack Virginia, seeing the bird, yelled, "Hurrah for Spunky Lamoille." He composed several songs about the Battle of Plattsburg, among others being this one:

"Macdonough on his knees a-crying
While British balls around his head were flying
The river boys, they fear no noise
In the battle hotly going,
Their 'Spunky Bird' was heard
In the rigging loudly crowing,
When every red coat that got loose
Ran for Canada like Joe's moose."

This may or may not have been the reason why the county has been termed "Spunky" Lamoille.

The act which incorporated the county also provided that when some town should erect a suitable courthouse and jail, the county should be deemed organized. There naturally followed keen competition as to which of the towns should have the honor and the advantages which would belong to the county seat. The southern portion wanted Johnson and the northern part favored Morristown. It was left to a committee to settle and partly through the efforts of Joshua Sawyer, a prominent lawyer and influential citizen of Hyde Park, the decision was made in favor of that town. The county buildings were erected at once and Court convened there in December, 1836, for the first time.

Thus it happened that the early deeds placed Morristown in Rutland County, then in Chittenden, later in Orleans, and then in Lamoille.

CHAPTER III

PHYSICAL CHARACTERISTICS OF THE TOWN

ONE wishes that the report of the committee which was appointed in 1784 "to go and take a view of said town" was extant or, better yet, would be diaries in which they recorded their impressions of their new possessions. But only in imagination can one accompany them as they left the older settlements of the south and pressed their way, probably on horseback, into the unbroken wilderness where thousands of acres lay awaiting the woodman's axe and the settler's plow.

Johnson and Cambridge to the west were already settled, Cambridge the year before and Johnson the same season. To the south, Waterbury had received its first family in 1784, but at the most probably less than a half dozen families could have been found in all Lamoille County.

The original grant embraced 23,040 acres and to this was added in 1855 a part of the township of Sterling, which was divided among Johnson, Stowe, Cambridge, and Morristown. In 1898 the boundaries between Hyde Park and Morristown were altered and the net result of these changes has been to increase the size of the town to 29,238 acres. The surface is moderately uneven except in the western part, where the Sterling range of mountains separates it from Cambridge. Here Whiteface Peak rises to the height of 3,715 feet and lies about four miles to the northeast of the Chin of Mansfield. No attempt has been made to develop the scenic attractions of this region except that the Long Trail traverses this mountain barrier and through it thousands of nature lovers from all parts of the United States have become familiar with the beautiful panorama which spreads out, a view very similar to the one obtained from Mansfield.

When this committee saw the district, it was covered with a rich stand of maple, birch, hemlock, and spruce. When cleared, the soil is for the most part fertile and well adapted to agriculture. They must have been impressed by the numerous streams which could furnish power for mills of all kinds. The Lamoille, traversing the northern section, was soon harnessed and put to work. It receives three tributaries from the south, East Brook, or the Ryder Brook; West Brook, or the Kenfleld Brook, flowing west of Morristown Corners through a gorge of great beauty; and Boardman's, or Joe's Brook. The last two streams were soon busily turning mill wheels. In the southern part of the town the Shaw, or Sterling Brook, was to become known as Mill Brook because it furnished water power at four different points. On this stream Luther Bingham built the second saw mill in town on his farm now known as the Coan place. He also ran a starch factory nearby. A short distance above his plant another mill was located just above the Red Bridge; farther west was the site of the Billings mill and still nearer the source of the stream was a mill known in later years as the Gregg mill.

No lakes of any importance lie within the borders of the town, but Joe's Pond and Molly's Pond, situated between the LaPorte and Randolph roads, are rich in interest for the botanist who penetrates their swampy environs. Here in their season abound the Sarracenia purpurea or Side-saddle flower and the Cassandra calyculata or Leather leaf; while the orchid enthusiast will delight in the Arethusa bulbosa or Indian pink, the Calopogon pulchellus or grass pink, and the Cypripedium acaule or pink ladies slipper. Protected by their surroundings which do not invite the casual picnic party, these shy beauties bloom undisturbed.

If the grantees hoped for mineral wealth in the new tract, they were destined to be disappointed, since no deposits of sufficient quantity to warrant their being worked have been found. Thompson, in his "Gazeteer," refers to veins of lead which occur on a hill in the eastern part and promise to be productive, but that promise was never fulfilled, although lead has been found on the farm occupied in 1935 by Carl Mudgett and occurs in some amount on Elmore Mountain.

The geographer has long been familiar with the fact which the average person does not fully realize, that the differences in climate in Vermont are determined not so much by latitude as by the relative positions of the mountain ranges and the Champlain and Connecticut Valleys which effect the rain and snowfall as well as the temperature. Lamoille County, enclosed within in the Y of the Green Mountains, is included in that section of the state where the average snowfall is, according to official records, 126 inches. These same conditions determine the rainfall in the summer so that droughts seldom occur here.

Nothing is more unreliable than general impressions about the weather from year to year, but the following items were taken from the diaries of two of the early settlers and record not later memories, but contemporaneous accounts. It is a well attested historical fact that the year 1816 was one of great hardship in northern New England and New York. There were practically no crops raised because of the unseasonably cold summer and the two years previous were cold and unfruitful. These conditions following the War of 1812 caused sufferings which would have entirely discouraged less persevering settlers. The following extracts taken from a diary kept in the Hadley family in 1816 record local conditions:

June 6. Snow fell to the depth of five or six inches and some sleighs ran.

June 8. Snow fell six inches more.

June 9. Ground froze hard at night.

June 16. Very cold. Began to snow about nine o'clock and snowed all day.

June 29. Killing frost.

Aug. 27. Frost that killed all corn.

This destruction of the corn crop by a frost which greatly injured the potatoes meant that turnips became one of the staple articles of food, while corn and rye were brought in from the southern sections and sold for two dollars and fifty cents per bushel. It is little wonder that the year 1816 was always referred to by the people who experienced its discomforts as "the cold year."

Records of other unusual seasons have been handed down. In 1834 snow fell on May 15 and 16 to the depth of one foot, while seven years later, in 1843, winter began on October 22, with a two days' snowfall which did not entirely disappear until spring. In contrast to these unseasonably long winters, the local paper of January 15, 1885, stated that the heavy rains had taken off nearly all snow and that farmers were ploughing greensward. Mr. S. L. Gates states that "since 1850 there have been several winters when wheels were used more than sleighs." The winter of 1931-1932 was a remarkable one in all the northern part of the United States. The local paper of January 20, 1932, contained the following comment:

"Why go South for the winter when you can play golf in northern Vermont in January? Thursday afternoon of last week an all-time record was established at the Lamoille Country Club with a dozen playing the regular course, and being able to putt on every green." Others recorded the picking of arbutus buds, pussywillows, and lilac buds. The thermometer registered sixty-eight degrees in some places on that date.

As a further illustration of the possibilities of local weather conditions, the following table is given, which was taken from the records of Mr. C. A. Saunders, who was for many years official weather recorder. It covers the period of twenty years, from 1895 to 1915:

	Maximum	Date	Minimum	Date
January	53	Jan. 19, 1900	—39	Jan. 9, 1901
February	50	Feb. 21, 1899	—33	Feb. 5, 1908
March	63	March 25, 1910	—26	March 6, 1912
April	85	April 30, 1903	—10	April 4, 1911
May	88	May 30, 1895	18	May 2, 1903
June	97	June 28, 1901	30	June 8, 1912
July	99	July 5, 1897	35	July 12, 1898
August	95	Aug. 8, 1909	32	Aug. 26, 1914
September	99	Sept. 4, 1898	20	Sept. 29, 1914
October	92	Oct. 10, 1909	10	Oct. 28, 1903
November	69	Nov. 8, 1895	— 6	Nov. 29, 1904
December	59	Dec. 12, 1901	—28	Dec. 26, 1914

These figures show the extremes to which the thermometer went in twenty consecutive years, but do not indicate the average weather which offers a succession of fruitful harvests and beautiful seasons.

CHAPTER IV
EARLY SETTLERS

WHEN the first census was taken, there were twenty-three towns in Vermont that had more than 1,000 inhabitants, most of them in the southern part of the state. Guildhall was the banner town, with 2,422 residents, and Bennington, with 2,350, was a close second. Of the six towns settled in what is now Lamoille County, Cambridge was the metropolis, with 167 inhabitants; Johnson, second in size, with ninety-three; Hyde Park had forty-three; Wolcott, thirty-two, and Elmore, settled the same year as this town, had twelve. Morristown reported ten; namely, Jacob Walker and wife, William Walker, wife and two children, two hired men from Bennington, and Indian Joe and Molly.

Ten years later, at the second enumeration, the number had swelled to 144, and included the following heads of families: Abner Brigham, Daniel Sumner, Micaijah Dunham, John Safford, Crispus Shaw, Cyrus Hill, Lydia Boardman, Elisha Boardman, William Boardman, James Little, Aaron Hurd, Samuel Rood, Samuel Gosslin (probably Joslyn), George Kenfield, Joseph Burke, Sylvans Perry, Stephen Childs, Nathaniel Goodale, Cyril Goodale, Alpheus Goodale, Asa Cole, Ebenezer Cole, Joseph Williams, Asa Sumner, Comfort Olds, John Keyser, Samuel Scrivner, David Scrivner.

This list, taken from the official census files, contains some names which do not appear elsewhere in the town records and omits some which tradition has connected with this first decade of the town's history.

Many of these people were so closely identified with certain phases of local life that brief accounts of them are given elsewhere. Of some of the others a few facts are here noted.

Miss Lou Rand, in a paper, "Our Local History," presented before the Morrisville Woman's Club, gave the following account of the coming of her great-grandfather, Jacob Walker, the first settler of Morristown:

"In 1789 Jacob Walker, a young surveyor, who was living in the home of his brother, William, in Bennington, was employed by Joseph Hinsdale in behalf of the proprietors of Morristown to run the lines of the second division of the allotment of land. Jacob Walker, twenty-four years of age and unusually well educated, was in every way fitted for the task which he performed during the summer months of that year. He received a certain amount of land for his services which he shared with his brother, William, who came to help him.*

"There are many things connected with the history of our town, of which we may well be proud. First and foremost, is the fact that the first settlement was made by a young man whose character was crystal clear, his faith in God steady as the stars, and total abstinence a part of his religion. Steady, true, and brave he came into the wilderness in early June, 1790.

"Each Saturday night found him at the McDaniels home not far from Hyde Park Street, where he remained over the Sabbath, returning each Monday with food supplies. Before the cold weather set in, Jacob Walker returned to the home of his brother in Bennington to formulate plans for the following spring. In January, 1791, he journeyed to Fairfax, Vermont, and on the thirteenth day of that month Phillipa Story became his bride.

"Jacob Walker and his wife did not come alone into the wilderness. William Walker, his wife, and two children, with two hired men, came with them. They brought a few common tools and for live stock had a cow, a dog, and a cat. Thus it was that the log house became a real home in the heart of the forest. Soon potatoes, corn, and a few vegetables were planted and the clearing of the land went forward. That was the summer of 1791. Before severe weather came, they dug a deep hole in the ground and buried the vegetables, then set forth on their journey to Fairfax and Bennington, where they spent the winter. But the winter of 1792 Jacob Walker, with his wife and children, remained in town.

"Mr. Walker built a second cabin in 1801. It was much larger than the first and built a short distance from it in an easterly direction. He built a third house in 1820, where he lived twenty-three years, or until his death in 1843. It is now known as the brick house on the LaPorte Road."

---
*In the records of Brookfield, Mass., are these statistics: Daniel Walker married Hannah Upham January 27, 1763. Children: William born on October 19, 1763; Jacob born on October 20, 1765; James born on August 15, 1769; Metilde born on March 7, 1779.

Comfort Olds, the first of the settlers to winter in town, was born in Brookfield, Mass., on July 29, 1760. Caught by the pioneering spirit, he and his wife and two children left there in March, 1791, and came by ox team to settle on a lot previously bought on the LaPorte Road, afterward called the George Poor farm. After a laborious journey of about 200 miles he arrived to find that there was little prospect of the building of a road near his purchase, so he exchanged it for a lot on the height of land between Hyde Park and Stowe, the farm occupied in 1935 by Mark Kellogg. He shared the log cabin of the Walkers until his own could be built. At this time his nearest neighbor to the south was Joshua Hill of Waterbury, fourteen miles distant. In 1794, Oliver Luce settled in Stowe about three miles away. To the north was only two miles to neighbors.

The following incidents taken from Heminway's "Gazeteer" give an idea of the daily life of these pioneers: Soon after coming to Morristown, it became necessary for Mr. Olds to go to Cambridge to get his grist ground. He set out with his ox team expecting to return by the middle of the week. A severe snowstorm began and, knowing he had left wood enough to last only a short time, he set out for home on foot. Late Wednesday night he arrived to find that Mrs. Olds had burned all the fuel and, alone with her two little ones, was awaiting the consequences of the storm. After replenishing his woodpile, Mr. Olds returned to Cambridge for his grist.

He also had the misfortune to lose his only cow soon after settling here, so started to go to his brother's in Randolph, Vt., to secure another. He went by marked trees through Stowe and Waterbury and then crossed the Hogback Mountains, keeping on the north side of the river, since there were no bridges in Middlesex and Waterbury. He obtained a cow which wore a bell and on his way back called on his neighbor, Mr. Hill. On reaching home he put his purchase in a yard made by felling trees, but Bossy evidently did not like such primitive quarters and a few mornings later he awoke to find her gone. He followed her until he reached the home of Mr. Hill, who, having heard a cow bell the night before and remembering Mr. Olds and his purchase, got up and secured her.

When the town was organized, Mr. Olds was elected Town Clerk, which office he held for six years. He also filled other positions of trust and responsibility. He was a strong church man, serving as class leader in the Methodist Episcopal Church for more than thirty years. He died April 22, 1839.

A distant neighbor of Mr. Olds was George Kenfield, who, in 1793, settled on a farm a short distance west of Morristown Corners occupied in 1935 by Jesse Briggs. Here the following June was born a son, Asaph, the first male child born in town. A son of Asaph was Frank Kenfield, for years one of the leading men of the town who died in 1914.

The first family to settle in Cadys Falls and the fourth to winter in town were the Boardmans, who came here from Canaan, Conn. The head of the family, Ozias, had married Lydia Hinsdale, sister of Joseph Hinsdale, who was one of the most active of the proprietors of the new township. It was perhaps through him that Mr. Boardman was led to purchase land intending to move here with his family, which consisted of his wife and four sons. Mr. Boardman died before the change was made, but his son, Ozias, came in 1793 at the age of nineteen to examine the land his father had bought. He remained during the summer, working for Aaron Hurd, and the March following he returned with his brother, William, making the trip with an ox team by way of Lake Champlain and the Lamoille Valley. They settled on lots sixty-three and sixty-four and the next spring the two other brothers, Elisha and Alfred, came with their mother. From that time on the Boardmans were intimately associated with the development of the town. When the sons were married, they asked their mother to choose with whom she would live. She replied: "Elisha has too much public business and cannot well attend to his home affairs. William is a good son, but careless and will leave the bars down, exposing the crops, but Ozias always puts up the bars." So it seems probable that she went to dwell with Ozias.

The eldest son, Elisha (1773-1826), built the first tavern in town, which also served as a town house for years, was the second Town Clerk from 1802-1812, was the first Town Representative, being elected four years in succession, from 1804 to 1808, and was Captain of the first Militia. His eldest son, Milton Hervey (1799-1834), married Sophia Haskins and later Alice Gates; and Milton's oldest son, Hervey C. (1824-1898), was a farmer and lumberman who for years ran the mill still known as the Boardman mill. He was the father of Maria Boardman Tinker, who died in 1933, and Milton H., who still resides here, although his son, Winfield H., and daughter, L. Alberta Ballard (Mrs. Percy), live elsewhere. The second son of Elisha, Alfred C. (1801-1871), married Mary Holcomb and was Town Clerk from 1842-1871. He was one of the men injured in the raising of the Universalist Church, his leg being so shattered that it had to be amputated.

The first of the family to come here, Ozias (1774-1843), married Lydia Whitney and all of their children except the eldest son, Almond, went West. Almond (1807-1891) married Jemima Goodell and remained on the home place. Of his five children only two grew to maturity here, Cornelia, who married Leander Small, an attorney at Hyde Park, and Ellen, who married Albert L. Noyes of that town.

The third son of Ozias, Sr., William B., married Anna Town of Stowe and had eight children. His oldest daughter, Lydia, married Hiram Earle, whose father came from England and settled on the farm occupied in 1935 by Joseph E. White. This family is now represented by Hiram Earle's two grand-daughters, Mrs. Alice George and Mrs. W. F. Churchill, and by a great-granddaughter, Mrs. C. B. Spaulding. William's youngest son, Charles Wright, married Huldah Cole and spent most of his life here. His grandchildren, Mrs. George Wells and Mrs. Roger Newton and Leslie Boardman, are residents of the town.

The fourth son of Ozias, Alfred, married Lydia Little and left a son, William A., and a daughter, Diantha.

Of two other pioneers, Nathaniel and Cyril Goodale, or Goodell, as the name was often spelled, their descendant, Miss Lou Rand, wrote as follows:

"Nathaniel and Cyril Goodell came from Amherst, Mass.* Nathaniel built a temporary cabin of logs which

---

*From the records in Woodstock, Conn.: Nathaniel Goodell and Abagail Chaffee, both of Woodstock, were married May 29, 1766. Their children: Esther, born September 16, 1767; Nathaniel, born August 21, 1769; Abagail and Alpheus, born February 2, 1771; Cyril, born November 4, 1774.

From records in Amherst, Mass.: Nathaniel Goodell died in Amherst, September 13, 1814, aged seventy-nine years. Abagail, wife of Nathaniel Goodell, died June 7, 1811, aged seventy-four years. Nathaniel, his son, died in Amherst, September 18, 1840, buried in the Union Cemetery at Dwight, Mass.

he occupied three years while he was getting out lumber for the large two story dwelling which he erected on the hill which overlooks the 'Sally Joy' place. After its completion he returned to Massachusetts in 1798 for his bride, Miss Warren. Tradition says she was a niece of Gen. Joseph Warren of Revolutionary fame.

"To this home Nathaniel, when he had reached middle life, brought a second mother for his boys and girls. Her name was Mary Thompson, daughter of Col. Loring and Mary (Whitten) Thompson, of Cornish, N. H., and a direct descendant of Lieut. John and Mary (Cook) Thompson. John came in the third ship to America and Mary's father was Francis Cook who came in the Mayflower."

Miss Rand goes on to say that from this home, with only the education gained in the little red schoolhouse, two of Nathaniel Goodell's sons migrated to Massachusetts. The younger one settled in Boston, took up the trade of a cabinet maker and read law evenings and was later admitted to the Bar and became a successful lawyer. The other built the great dam seen as one enters the City of Lawrence, Mass.

Among the most prominent of the early settlers was Samuel Cooke, who was born in Hadley, Mass., in 1755. He served in the Revolution, being with Arnold in his unfortunate expedition against Quebec where he contracted smallpox. In 1786 he moved to Worthington, Mass., where, like so many other of his neighbors, he became interested in the new township of Morristown, Vt. He bought a lot just south of the Four Corners and began to clear it in 1794, and the year following built a block house. For some reason he did not move his family to their new home until 1805, but from that time on he filled various positions of trust and responsibility. Before leaving Worthington he had served six successive years as Selectman and he was Moderator of the first recorded town meeting in Morristown. He was Town Representative from 1809 to 1814, Justice of the Peace and Assistant Judge while the town was still a part of Orleans County. He died in 1834, leaving a family of seven children.

His oldest son, Dennison, married Margaret Matthews and was Town Clerk for a quarter of a century. Another son, Chester, settled on the Plains, married Lucy Shaw, and had six children, one of whom married Salmon Niles, whose son, Albert A., held many public offices and is survived by two daughters, Mrs. Ila Jackson and Mrs. Lula Spaulding, and an adopted son, Logan A. Niles. Another daughter of Chester Cooke married John S. Chaplin, whose son, Joseph, was a well known figure in the west part of the town for many years. A third son of Samuel, Jonathan, married Sarah Felcher and was one of the leading men on the LaPorte Road. He lived for many years on the Ryder place and his son, Oscar, succeeded him there. No descendants of Jonathan's ten children reside in town, but Oscar, Jr., is a prosperous farmer in Hyde Park. Samuel's daughter, Fanny, married Elisha Brigham and lived to the ripe age of ninety-six, while her sister, Mary, married Jedediah Story of Fairfax, who first came to Morristown with Jacob Walker. That branch of the family is represented by Charles, E. S., and George Story, who live on Morristown Plains.

Another of the substantial men of that early period was Luther Bingham, who was born in Windham, Conn., on April 5, 1778. When a small boy, he moved to Cornish, N. H., and at the age of twenty-two began for himself on a farm in the new settlement of Morristown. He felled the trees on land adjoining the town of Stowe, known for years as the Hale place, which in 1935 is occupied by Max Coan; built a frame house and then returned to Cornish for his bride, Polly Cummings, of that place, and another home was established here. He soon realized the possibilities of the water power in the stream running through his property, and in 1806 he built the second saw mill in town, for which he bought a crank at Starksboro, Vt., and brought it here upon a drag.

The town recognized his ability and at four different terms he represented it in the Legislature. For several years he commanded the local militia, three times he was chosen a member of the Committee to consider Amendments to the State Constitution. In 1812 he was made Justice of the Peace, an office which he held until his death, in 1846. By hard work and good management, he amassed what was a considerable amount of property for that day and more than that he enjoyed the respect and affection of his townsmen. His daughter, Emma, married Clark Boynton and their son, Luther Bingham, or "Bing" as he was generally called, was for years one of the well known business men of the town, being owner and manager of the Morrisville House and also one of the largest maple sugar dealers in Northern Vermont.

Another of the prominent men of the first decades of the town's life was Micaijah Dunham, a native of Southampton, Mass., who possessed more education and more means than did many of the pioneers. He surveyed one section of the town and settled in the eastern part on the farm occupied in 1935 by Owen Douglass. Their large house built by Mr. Dunham is said to have been the first two story house in town. He married Dorothy Pratt, but died in 1812 at the age of forty-seven. His descendants who have remained here were in the line of his daughter, Maria, who married Amasa Spaulding, and lived on her father's place. Her grandson, Calvin Spiller, is a resident of Morrisville.

Another name frequently found in the history of Morristown is that of Shaw. The first of that line to settle here was Crispus, who was born in Nova Scotia in 1763, but when a boy moved to Shutesbury, Mass., and, although young, served in the Revolution. In 1798 he moved here when there were but twelve families in town and remained until his death, in 1845. He was twice married, first to Anna Burke, and later, in 1840, to Fanny Liscomb. Most of his children spent their lives here. Crispus, Jr., settled in Elmore and with his descendants was a leading citizen there. Benoni married Betsey Whitney and their children who grew to maturity here were Benoni, Jr., who married Hannah Travis, and was a mill man in what is still known as Shaw Hollow near the Red Bridge. A second son, Boardman, lived near the Sterling line and was the father of Leslie M. Shaw and also of Dutha, the father of Mrs. Walter Isham. A third son of Benoni, Darwin, married Mary Reed and they were the parents of Carlos Shaw, the father of Ned Shaw, still a resident here, and of Almary, now Mrs. Joseph Bannister and the mother of Mrs. Frank Allen. Darwin Shaw was also the father of a daughter, Marion, who married Jackson Chaffee, the father of Mrs. Frank Strong and Mrs. William Welch.

A fourth son of Benoni was Rockwell, who lived in the southwestern part of the town and had one daughter, Della, who married Levi Gile and only recently moved to Stowe. A daughter of Benoni, Betsey, is represented by Mrs. Wayne Durett.

Crispus Shaw had three daughters whose lives were spent in town. Martha married Baruch Darling and their sons, Alden and Chester, were for many years proprietors of the excellent farm in Mud City, occupied in 1935 by Ernest Inkle. They left no descendants. Another daughter of Crispus was Sally, who first married Jared Spaulding, father of Alonzo Spaulding, and late in life she married Jedediah Bingham. A third daughter, Lucy, married Chester Cooke and her descendants are given in connection with the Cooke family.

Another Shaw influential in local affairs was Ebenezer, who was born in Middlebury, Mass., in 1773, and died in 1866. As a young man he came to Vermont, where, at Woodstock, he learned the tanner's and shoemaker's trade and was the first tanner in Morristown, coming here about 1800. He is said to have been the first Universalist here and was for years one of the pillars of that church. His first wife was Polly Whitney, daughter of Eliphalet Whitney, who was also the father-in-law of three other early settlers, Benoni Shaw, Seth Haskins and Ozias Boardman. Young Shaw and his bride settled on land given him by his father-in-law and kept in his family until after the death of his grandson, Charles. It is occupied in 1935 by W. G. Lepper and Son. His wife, Polly, died in 1835, and the year following he married Abigail Sherwin. His son, Edwin H., born in 1818, married Pelina Gay and their son, Charles, remained on the home place until his death, in 1913. His widow, Helen Bliss Shaw, was a resident of Morristown until her removal to Burlington, in 1932, but they left no descendants.

Another family identified with the town since its early days are the Brighams. Lieut. Abner Brigham came to Vermont from Grafton, Mass., where his ancestors settled at an early date. He was a Revolutionary soldier, being one of them who went with Arnold in his attack upon Quebec. He died at Hartland, Vt., in 1791, leaving a widow and several children. About 1800 Mrs. Brigham and several of the children came to Morristown and from that date until the present (1935) the farm just north of the Tenney Bridge has been occupied by a Brigham, the present owner being Melville, the fifth generation to live there.

Seventeen years after their coming here the family was smitten by a disease much more prevalent then than now, typhoid fever. In July a son, Enoch, twenty-eight years of age, who two years previous had married Lucy

Bingham, died from that disease. The following September, the oldest son, Abner, who had married Anna Safford, died of the same scourge and within three weeks a grandson and a granddaughter were laid away, victims of the same plague. Abner Brigham at the time of his death was Captain of the local militia and was buried with military honors in September, 1817.

Another son of Lieutenant Abner was Elisha (1791-1831), who married Fanny M. Cooke, daughter of Samuel Cooke, and to them were born four children, three daughters and a son, Elisha (1823-1906), who throughout his life was one of the town's leading citizens. He held many town offices and his judgment was respected by everyone. He was deeply interested in local history and many of the facts in this volume were obtained from his research. He married Mary Adela Cole, in 1848, and left two sons, Charles and Albert. The former married Clara Eaton and to them were born two children, Gertrude F., who married Charles Ross, now deceased, and is a Methodist minister in Pennsylvania, and Melville, who married Bernice Guyette and has three daughters, Lucy, Eunice, and Emma. Albert Brigham married Rose Messer and lives in Morrisville.

James Matthews was living in town when the second census of 1800 was taken, on the road leading to Tyndall Hill on the farm long known as the Hill place. He married Clarissa Ketchum and had a family of eight children. He died in 1868. His son, Leonard, born in 1826, carried the mail between the Corners and Morrisville for many years, dying in 1900. Another son, Addison, who was unmarried, for many years owned the farm on the brow of the hill west of the Corners, occupied in 1935 by Harry Fisk. His later years were spent with his brother, Leonard, at the Corners.

Another name familiar to anyone acquainted with the history of the town is that of Cole. Three brothers, John, Asa, and Ebenezer, sought their fortunes in the new township just previous to or in the early years of the nineteenth century. The oldest, John (1752-1842), was a Revolutionary soldier, noted for his huge stature and great strength. Those of his descendants most closely connected with the town came in the line of his son, Harvey, who first married Lydia Pottle, by whom he had three sons, Horace, Hiram, and Heman, and a daughter, Huldah.

Horace married Caroline Wilkins and died in 1863 while serving in the Civil War, leaving two daughters, Lizzie and Laura. The former married Henry Fisher and has two sons, Claude, who has been a clerk in the local postoffice for several years, and Harold of Palo Alto, Calif. Heman left no sons to carry on the family name, but two daughters, Alice, deceased, and Emma, who married Lysander Barrows of Stowe. The daughter, Huldah, married C. Wright Boardman, and her descendants are given in connection with that family. John Cole's second wife was Mary Springer, by whom he had three sons, John, Levi, and Daniel. The last named married Amelia Reed and had four children, Effie, Eulalia, Etta, and Alberto. The son lives on his father's farm in what is still known as the Cole Hill District.

Ebenezer and Asa moved here in 1801 from Cornish, N. H. Ebenezer (1766-1849) married Ruth Pierce and so far as is ascertainable is represented in town now by a great-grandson, Arthur Douglass. His daughter, Sally, married Jonathan Douglass who, with his, son, Albert, lived for years on the farm occupied in 1935 by Henry Ross. Of Albert's children, one son, Arthur, resides at the Corners. Lucy, another daughter of Ebenezer, married Warren Goodell, but their four children, Emmaline, who married Elias Merritt; Lucy, who married Sewell Baker, and the two sons, Bliss and George, have no direct descendants here.

Asa (1772-1852) settled in the northern part of the town by the Hyde Park line on land which remained in his family for a century and a portion of which is still owned by a descendant, Melville Brigham. One of his sons, Daniel (1800-1868), married Lucy Burke. Not all of Daniel's children grew to maturity, but one of them, Charles, married Laura Clark and had two sons, Henry and George, who still reside here. The latter married Winnifred Foss and has been a R. F. D. mail carrier for years. A second son of Asa's was Morris Cole (1801-1890), who married Mary Chaplin and was the father of Albert Cole, a respected citizen of Morristown throughout his life, and of Mary Adela, who married Elisha Brigham in 1848, and her descendants are given in connection with the Brigham family.

A name prominently connected with the early development of Cadys Falls and a familiar one in the history of the town is that of Gates. This family originated in Essex, England, and in the tenth generation came to Hingham, Mass., in 1638. Later they migrated to Preston, Conn., where was born Nathan Gates (1754-1838), the one who came to Morristown. He served as private in the Sixth Connecticut Regiment at the siege of Boston in 1775 and gained the rank of Lieutenant. In 1777 he married Tamerson Kimball. They lived in Plainfield, N. H., for a time, coming from there to Morristown in 1801.

Lieutenant Gates was the father of eleven children and the ones most closely identified with the town through their descendants were Nathan, Jr., Daniel, Lovell and Elizabeth.

Nathan, Jr. (1778-1858), soon after coming to Morristown, married Martha, daughter of Abner and Mary Brigham, and had six children. The oldest was Nathan Brigham Gates, who had one son and three daughters, of whom only two lived to maturity. The son, Benjamin N. (1830-1893), married Delia Whittier and had one son, Calvin Leo, who married Abbie L. Bullard. C. L. Gates was a well known business man, one of the few Democrats whom the town has sent to represent it at Montpelier. He was Postmaster during the Wilson Administration, and his daughter, Mary, the only one of his three children to reside in Morristown, has been clerk in the postoffice for several years.

Nathan B. Gates' youngest daughter, Alice, married Horace Day and they had one son, Clarence, whose family have been residents here much of the time.

The second son of Nathan Gates, Jr., was Daniel F. (1804-1859), who married Lavinia Jordon. One of his daughters, Ellen, was the first wife of Henry D. Bryant, who was prominent in the local business world of the 80's and 90's. A son, Amasa O., was for years the leading druggist in town.

The fourth son of Nathan, Jr., was George Washington (1810-1890), who married Betsey Smith and their grandson, Ernest W., was in business in town for many years and Postmaster from 1924 to 1933.

The fifth son of Nathan, Jr., was Sylvester L. (1809-1897), a life-long resident of the town, who married as his first wife Lydia Ferrin, daughter of John and Hannah Ferrin. To them were born two daughters, one of whom, Mary, married William Cheney, and to them were born a daughter, Winnifred, and a son, Thomas C.

The third son of Lieutenant Nathan was Daniel Gates (1781-1869), who married Sally Spaulding. Of their twelve children, descendants of two have spent their lives here. Susan A. married Truman C. Ryder, father of Elmer Ryder and grandfather of Harold and Bessie Ryder. Sanford (1824-1856) married Diantha Town and their daughter, Sanfordora, married George E. Town. Their four children, Grace (Mrs. Fred Wilson), Gerald, Winifred, and Lila, live in the eastern part of the town.

The fourth son of Lieutenant Nathan was Lovell (1784-1865), who married Hannah Coates. Their oldest son, Irvine, married Hancy L. Pike of Sterling. Of their children the oldest, Celeste, married Eli B. Gile and left no descendants, while their three sons, Elmer, Carroll, and Bert, were well known here in their day. The other son of Lovell was Orsemus, who lived in Cadys Falls until his death, in 1909. His only child, a daughter, Benelia, married A. J. Sherwood, a prosperous farmer in the western part of the town. Lovell's daughter, Harriet Carola, married Danforth Eaton, a long-time resident of Morristown.

The sixth child of Lieutenant Nathan was Elizabeth (1787-1866), who married David Reed. Her great-granddaughter, Ida A. Lilley, married William H. Towne and their great-grandson carries on the line of Lieutenant Nathan to the eighth generation.

JOE AND MOLLY

Jacob Walker is always referred to as the first settler of Morristown, but years before his coming and before the charter was granted, Indian Joe and Molly had explored this region and found it good.

Joe was born in Nova Scotia, but his tribe was practically annihilated by the English at the siege of Louisburg and he was brought up by the St. Francis Indians and served with Capt. John Vincent's Indian Company in 1777-1778. This early experience of his probably accounted for his hatred of the English and led him to serve as scout for the colonists during the Revolution. Thus he became familiar with Northern Vermont and about 1780 selected the Lamoille Valley for his fishing and hunting ground and for a time established his wigwam on Butternut Island on the bank of this river a short distance below Morrisville. It was during his stay here that he and Molly visited General Washington at his headquarters on the Hudson, where they were received with respect and given many presents in return for Joe's services to the patriot cause.

The pioneers of this and other towns were indebted to him for many kindnesses, and many stories are current of his helpful acts and also of his quick wit. Miss Lou Rand related hearing her grandmother tell of the many ways in which he befriended Jacob Walker. Once when a panther menaced the Walker home, the Indian warned the occupants, and himself shot the beast. Again the first winter this family spent in town, when their supply of food was almost exhausted, Joe shot a moose and shared the meat with his white friends before he took any to his own wigwam. It is told that he and Molly were once starting on a season's hunting and trapping and called at Esquire Taylor's tavern in Wolcott. He asked for a glass of rum, for which he was charged six cents. When he returned in the spring, he stopped for another glass and laid down six cents as before, but Taylor demanded ten, saying it cost as much to winter a barrel of rum as a horse. Joe drew himself up, looked at the esquire a moment, and said: "Ugh, it don't take so much hay, but heap more water."

Many years before his death it seems he was beginning to lose his skill as a hunter, for, on November 7, 1792, the State Legislature in response to a petition, appointed John McDaniel of Hyde Park his guardian and authorized McDaniel to purchase such supplies as were necessary not to exceed three pounds per year. Later the state granted him a pension of seventy dollars annually. Joe's troubles increased as the Saffords built a dam across the river, and their mill began to pour forth sawdust which interfered with his fishing. Then, too, neighbors were encroaching too closely on every side. So he left the valley to spend the remainder of his days in Newbury, Vt., where he died in 1819. He is buried in the Ox Bow Cemetery there, and the marble slab marking his grave bears the simple inscription, "Joe, the Friendly Indian."

At the session of the Legislature of 1886 an attempt was made to secure funds to erect a monument to him, but it was not successful. Many years later it was proposed to name a portion of the new cement highway after him, but that was not done.

Morristown has preserved his name and that of his wife in the two bodies of water lying between the Randolph and LaPorte Roads and similar memorials occur in the towns of Cabot and Danville. As the State of Washington honors Chief Tacoma, and Massachusetts perpetuates the name of Massasoit, so the Lamoille Valley may well keep alive the memory of Joe and Molly.

CHAPTER V
CHURCHES

IT IS a well known principle of physics that water seeks its own level. It is equally true that the intellectual and spiritual life of a community will rise no higher than its schools and churches, which, of course, have their origin in the lives of its citizens.

These first settlers in Morristown were as sturdy and strong in their religious convictions as in their physical bodies. Unlike many others this town was settled by men from many different sections of New England instead of a band from one locality, and this fact may account for the diversity of religious beliefs held from the first. Within thirty years after the first settlement, four different denominations had established churches, while others have been added since, including such short lived sects as the Millerites, who had a preacher here in 1847.

Jedediah Safford, son of the first settler in Morrisville, used to say that he sawed the first log, ground the first grist, and heard the first sermon preached in town. This first sermon has been attributed to Elder Bogue, a Baptist minister, but as early as 1798 the noted evangelist, Lorenzo Dow, held preaching services in John Safford's barn. This man was one of the unique characters in the early religious history of the country. When but nineteen, this Connecticut youth began his career as an evangelist, and during the first years of his work traversed large sections of New England and within fifteen years had traveled on horseback and on foot all over New England, and New York, had gone into Canada, and south as far as Georgia and Mississippi, often preaching four and five times a day. He traveled as an independent preacher, but his sympathies were with the Methodist Church and most of his converts affiliated with that body. His enemies described him as "in habit and appearance more filthy than a savage Indian," but in spite of his harsh voice and uncouth appearance people gathered to hear him, his largest audience being estimated at 7,000. The earnestness of purpose which led him to travel over hills and through valleys in all kinds of weather and over all kinds of roads or with no roads at all; his devotion to a cause which led him to persevere in spite of opposition from the religious leaders of his day, attracted and moved his hearers in spite of his eccentricities. His work, carried on amid such difficulties, bore fruit in some of the neighboring towns and undoubtedly helped to keep religious feeling in this town strong.

At the second town meeting, of which there is any record, held on September 2, 1806, a committee was appointed to arrange for the organization of a religious society and Samuel Cooke, John Cole, and Ralph Tinker were chosen to draw up a subscription paper for signers to form a Congregational Society. Just how much this committee did is not known, but the vote was in line with the law passed by the Vermont Legislature in 1798 requiring every person of adult age and a legal voter to help support some religious body. It is a fact that the Congregational Church was the first one organized and its records have been kept much more fully than any of the others, so it is possible to give its story more in detail for that reason.

Its earliest records were burned, but the account of its founding was contained in a historical sermon preached by the Rev. Septimius Robinson in 1859. From this sermon the following facts are taken, the first record begins thus: "At a conference holden at Jacob Walker's barn Saturday, July 13, 1807 several persons came forward and manifested a desire to unite in church covenant. After the examination of some persons relative to the subject the meeting was adjourned until nine o'clock in the morning of the Monday following. At the time appointed meeting began with prayer, the Rev. J. Hovey, pastor of the Cong. church in Waterbury." After further examination the church was organized and the following officers were elected: Moderator, Crispus Shaw; Clerk, Dr. Ralph Tinker. Dates are not given in the list of members at first, but it seems evident that thirteen people constituted the newly organized body. One man stands out prominently in these early years, Deacon Cyril Goodale. Though no date of his election is recorded, he seems to have been the first deacon and he held that office until his death, in 1854. For a series of years the church depended upon him mainly to conduct religious services. Meetings were held in private houses until 1815, when the first town house was built east of Jacob Walker's and then gatherings were usually held there.

It was customary for the Congregational Church of that period to have an Ecclesiastical Society in connection with the church, and in 1823 such a body was organized with the following officers: Moderator, Samuel Cooke; President, Elisha Brigham; Vice-President, Dennison Cooke; Secretary, James Tinker; Treasurer, Samuel Cooke; Collector, Ira Edwards; Chaplain, Cyril Goodale. The first record of any preaching service is as follows: "Preaching and sacrament Lord's Day April 13, 1817 by Rev. Mr. Parker." It is uncertain how much regular preaching was enjoyed during this period, but in June, 1817, occurs the following record: "Rev. Nathan Rawson began to preach with us June 8, 1817. June 24th at a conference at the Town house agreed with Mr. Rawson to preach with us four months or one third of a year for which we are to give him one hundred dollars next winter, one half in money, the remainder in grain."

This first settled pastor in Morristown was a man of recognized ability, who was born in Mendon, Mass., in 1780, of a long line of distinguished ancestors. One of them served as Secretary of Massachusetts for thirty-five years, another was so influential in the affairs of that colony that "he was complimented as being the General Court's oracle." Another of his more distant forbears was Archbishop of Canterbury in the reign of Queen Elizabeth, and Bacon called him "the greatest and gravest prelate in the land." Still another was an evangelist among the Indians, and Cotton who preached his funeral sermon said of him, "We usually took it for granted that things would be fairly done when he had a hand in doing them." The same missionary spirit which led him doubtless influenced young Rawson to come to the new settlement of Vermont about 1809. He first located in Hardwick, in 1811, as the first Congregational pastor and served there acceptably for more than six years. Then he came to Morristown, but the struggling church here was too weak to support a settled minister and he left to fill other pastorates in other sections of the state.

On September 8, 1824, a call was extended Rev: Daniel Rockwell, which ran in part, as follows: "We do now agree to give you a small piece of land near the meeting house and build upon it a comfortable dwelling house. House is to be built and said land and house to be legally conveyed to you within the term of two years from your settlement to be yours and your heirs forever. We also agree to pay you on the 15th day of January $150 annually one third of which is to be paid in money the remainder in grain. We also further agree to pay you said Society's share of public ministerial money which we suppose will be at least $20 annually. Until the parties shall otherwise agree we expect that you will appropriate one half of the time, every other week only. We also agree that you may appropriate two weeks out of said time to visit your friends.

"Signed
"Cyril Goodale
"Ebenezer Cole   Com.
"Crispus Shaw"

In addition to the advantages set forth in the above call another inducement for Mr. Rockwell was the fact that he could occupy a fine modern church. Some years previous a Baptist Church had been organized, and these two denominations became the joint proprietors of what was undoubtedly the finest church ever erected in the county. It was a brick structure with a two story pulpit reached by winding stairs and galleries on three sides, and stood on the brow of the hill just east of the brick house occupied in 1935 by Mr. Hadlock. Its towering spire was a landmark for a long distance around. It was built by popular subscription, and it speaks volumes for the devotion of these people that they would undertake such a task with their limited means. They were certainly building for the future since the edifice was capable of seating 1,000 people, while the population of the entire town, according to the census taken two years previous, was less than 800. It must have been a grievous disappointment to them when, ten years later, the building was declared unsafe and it was torn down in 1849.

The first Congregationalist minister to preach in the brick church was the Rev. Jotham Waterman, who came here from Connecticut. His term of service was short. According to the records "the funds for the support of preaching the present year being nearly expended a vote was passed that it be not advisable to employ the Rev. Mr. Waterman any more at present." Tradition says he was so intemperate in his use of liquor that some of the church members called a meeting and drew up a temperance pledge which was signed by some fifty people. Mr. Waterman failed to appear at this meeting and was not engaged for a longer period.

Mr. Rockwell accepted the call as given and on October 19, 1824, an ordination Council was held at the home of Ebenezer Cole on West Hill. It was a stormy day and after the examination the whole Council spent the night at Mr. Cole's, and the following day the ordination service was performed. Because Mr. Rockwell was the first minister to be really settled in town, he received the ministerial lot not far from Jacob Walker's. He was a man greatly beloved by his church and respected by the townspeople. He shared his time with the Congregational Church of Johnson, where he was equally liked. He set a worthy example for the long line of ministers who have succeeded him in the different pulpits in town. He remained here after the close of his pastorate, preaching for short periods at different places, and in 1835 moved to the Western Reserve and later to Illinois, where he died.

With the downfall of the splendid brick church, it became necessary to plan for a new edifice, and the Congregational Church decided to change its location to the new village of Morrisville, although "at the time of building the meeting house not one member of the church lived in the limits of this large school district nor but four, all females, in the territory north, east, and south of us." But in 1832 and 1833 the LaPorte Road was opened and soon settled by thrifty prosperous farmers, whose names figure largely in the history of the church of that period. Deacon Horace Felcher owned the farm later known as the Malvern Stock Farm, or New York Farm, Wingate Webster the Rand place, Frederick Powers the old poor farm, and John Ferrin the farm just north of that; and for all these Morrisville was more convenient to reach than the Corners. The change seems to have been effected without any friction which may have been due, in part, to the wise leadership of the Rev. Septimius Robinson, whose pastorate deserves more than a passing word, for his guidance, both in church and in the affairs of the town, was wise. More than any other one person he was the founder of Peoples Academy, and was for many years president of its Board of Trustees. He was diplomatic, both in and out of the pulpit. Judge H. H. Powers relates that once while at the Corners the choir, without his knowledge, introduced a violin into the musical part of the service. It was expected that he would not approve of the innovation, but he made no comment. The first hymn was sung with violin accompaniment. In announcing the second one Priest Robinson, for thus he was called by everyone, simply said, "the choir will please sing and fiddle Hymn number 48."

Septimius Robinson was the sixth in direct descent from John Robinson of Pilgrim fame, and was born in Dorset, Vermont, in 1790. Not until he was thirty-one did he begin to study for the ministry with several clergymen of the Rutland Association. Licensed to preach in 1823 and ordained pastor at Underhill in 1824, he conducted a revival service in which the church was nearly doubled. Then he went to Fairfax, where he preached half the time and divided the balance between Fletcher and Waterville. For six years previous to his coming to Morristown he was acting pastor at Milton, where about eighty were added to the church. During his stay here about 100 joined the local church. In addition to his eight children, several of whom settled here, he adopted his niece, Emily Redington. One son, William Albert, followed his father in the ministry and came from Homer, N. Y., to deliver the sermon in connection with the Centennial of 1890.

Mr. Robinson gives the story of his call and first impressions of the church here as follows: "On returning from a journey into the state of New York, I found a messenger from the Church inviting me to visit the place and preach the next Sabbath. I complied, found a large meeting house not rendered very comfortable for winter meetings. Spent two Sabbaths with a people evidently in earnest to obtain the stated administration of the Gospel yet evidently in the lot of churches unable to sustain the ministry without aid from the Home Missionary Society. Before leaving town on Monday a regular call in due form was presented me to settle in the ministry here. With some misgivings I consented to bring my family here and subsequently accept the call to settle here as pastor."

Thus was begun a quarter of a century of fruitful service. In 1856 it became necessary to enlarge the church, which fact is recorded as follows: "The pastor would here record with gratitude to God, His smiles and His good hand upon the Congregational Society in making them enlarge and improve their house of worship so as to render it commodious and tasteful by the addition of sixteen feet to the length of the house so as to add twenty four more seats, by the erection of a new and beautiful pulpit, by removing the old gallery and forming a new orchestra for the choir and by rendering the walls beautiful by tasteful paper, by making the house warmer and more pleasant both for speaker and hearers. It was completed about the sixth of September and on Wednesday the eighth as the whole interior was new was dedicated to the worship of Almighty God, Father, Son, and Holy Ghost. Sermon on the occasion by Rev. Charles Parker of Waterbury. Prayer by the pastor. To the Triune God be the Glory."

A review of the church records emphasizes the fact that in those early days church membership meant something. A Committee on Church Discipline was elected annually and for years they were no mere figureheads. In 1859 the following rules of discipline were adopted at the annual meeting:

"Article I. Disciplinable offences are Walking disorderly II Thess. 3.6
  (which see)
    Neglecting Gospel institutions, Heb. 11:25
    Private injuries to the members of this Church or others Matt. 18:15
    Heresy, Titus 3:10
    All open and gross offences against the laws of God.
"Article II The general rules of procedure in all cases of gross offence or scandal shall be that laid down by our Savior in Matt. 18:15.
"Article III If any brother be offended with any other, he shall go and tell him his fault in a humble, private manner; and if this step be not successful, he shall take with him one or two brethren, and labor for a Christian settlement of the difficulty previous to any public steps of discipline in the case by the Church.
"Article IV Every complaint brought before the Church shall be exhibited in writing (a copy of the same containing charges and specifications with the names of witnesses having been previously left

with the accused) signed by the accuser and also accompanied by a certificate recommending this course, signed by his associates in the labor. Whenever a complaint is lodged against a member of this Church, in his absence from Church meeting, it shall be the duty of the Moderator to send a copy of the complaint to the member accused and also to notify him of the time appointed for his trial.

"Article V No complaint shall be exhibited before the Church except at a Church meeting duly warned which it shall be the duty of all members to attend, when the charge shall be read by the moderator and if no good reason is offered to the contrary, trial shall proceed.

"Article VI The accused may have the liberty of naming witnesses and mentioning evidence of the fact on charge but not of acting in the decision of the church; the accused may be heard in answer of the charge brought against him either by himself or any other person a member of the Congregational church whom he may choose as his counsel but he shall not act on the deciding of the question proposed for the decision of the Church.

"Article VII After a full hearing of both parties the question proposed for the decision of the Church shall be, 'Is he guilty or not guilty' and the mind of the Church on the question shall be taken by yeas and nays.

"Article VIII When any member is convicted by the Church of the charge brought against him, he shall be considered as disqualified for and suspended from communion; he shall be called upon to give in the presence of the Church glory to God by confession and if satisfaction be not given, a letter of admonition from the Church shall be transmitted to him at the time of the next Communion following his trial; and a second letter at the time of the second Communion; and if he shall still continue obstinate, a letter of excommunication shall be publicly read on the Sabbath. Provided that this course may not be averted by the calling of a new trial council; for the offending brother shall in all cases have the privilege of calling one new trial ecclesiastical council."

Such trials were not unknown, and excommunication was sometimes the result. In 1855 two men were excommunicated; in one case, because the accused was "a profane and wicked man, guilty of great severity and unkindness to his family." The charges related sometimes to business and sometimes to the personal life. In either case they were investigated according to regular rules of procedure and very fully. In one instance we read that the vote was taken at 2:00 A. M. We smile at such procedure today, but it was an honest attempt to keep the life of the church pure and above reproach, though it could hardly have been conducive to church harmony.

But the interests of this early church were not merely local. In the report of the annual meeting in 1875 we read: "Voted that our contributions for the next year be 1st Freedmen's Bureau, 2nd Vermont Domestic Missionary Society, 3rd A. B. C. F. M." This placing of the foreign missionary interests last is rather strange since the church of that day had several close personal contacts with the foreign field, and many interesting missionary events had occurred within its walls. In August, 1863, Mr. Giles Montgomery of Walden was ordained for foreign work here. The reason the service was held in this church was because on that day he married the niece of Priest Robinson, Miss Emily Redington, who lived in her uncle's family and accompanied her husband to his work in Marash, Turkey. On August 19, 1863, an Ecclesiastical Council was called which was presided over by Rev. Benjamin Labaree, D. D., of Middlebury College, who also preached the ordination sermon, and Rev. Daniel Bliss of Syria extended the right hand of fellowship. The young couple started at once for their life work in Turkey, where Mr. Montgomery died at Adana, in 1888.

Four years later Priest Robinson's successor, Rev. Lyman Bartlett decided to take up work in the foreign field, and on July 21, 1867, a council was called and his relations with this church were severed, and Mr. and Mrs. Bartlett afterwards left for his chosen field of work in Caesarea, Turkey. In 1884 they were removed to Smyrna, and here in 1892 Mrs. Bartlett died. At her request she was buried in the Protestant cemetery there, the only American to lie among the Armenian, Greek, and Jesuit converts. In 1884 their daughter, Cornelia, who had completed her education in this country, joined her parents and started a kindergarten, the first mission kindergarten in Turkey. In 1904, because of his daughter's ill health, Mr. Bartlett returned to this country, and resided in California until his death, in 1912.

On July 1, 1880, still another Council was called in this church to ordain the Rev. Henry Otis Dwight to foreign work in Turkey. Mr. Dwight had previously married a Morristown girl, Miss Della Griswold, a member of the local church and this fact doubtless led him to take a letter from the Edwards Congregational Church of Northampton, Mass., to this church. At this Council the sermon was preached by Rev. N. G. Clark, D. D., Secretary of the A. B. C. F. M. It is interesting to note that Mr. Dwight's name remained on the church roll here until his death, in 1917, in spite of his long years of distinguished service in Turkey and his last years spent in this country. His daughter, Adelaide, who was a teacher at Peoples Academy for a short time, joined this church and retained her membership for some time after she, too, took up foreign work in Turkey, where she is still engaged.

In 1875, under the vigorous leadership of the Rev. V. M. Hardy, the church building was again remodelled, being raised up and a furnace added to make better heating facilities, also a ladies' parlor, a vestry, and a kitchen equipped to make possible the serving of meals. The building was rededicated in December of that year, Rev. M. H. Buckham, President of the University of Vermont, preaching the sermon. In the winter of 1885 and 1886, the pipe organ, the first one in town, was added at a cost of $1,425 with a dedicatory service under the direction of Prof. W. F. Whipple. Local talent, consisting of Professor and Mrs. Whipple, Miss Mellie Slayton, Mrs. H. P. Munson, Miss Kate Healey, and Mrs. P. K. Gleed, presented the program, assisted by S. D. Hopkins and Professor Davis of Burlington.

For twenty years this edifice met the needs of the congregation, and then agitation for a new church was begun. So hearty was the response that in less than a year from the time the building committee was appointed the present structure was dedicated. No small part of this efficient work was due to the building committee, consisting of H. A. Slayton, Chairman, H. P. Munson, E. S. Robinson, Rev. G. N. Kellogg, Mrs. P. K. Gleed, and Mrs. G. M. Powers. The new church was a memorial to the

Rev. G. N. Kellogg in more ways than one. Not only did he create the sentiment which made its erection possible, but he designed the building, the architect simply carrying out his ideas. On January 21, 1897, the structure was dedicated, the Rev. Smith Baker of Boston preaching the sermon.

In 1880 the Church and Society voted to purchase a parsonage and the debt thus incurred was assumed by the Ladies' Industrial Society. The house at the corner of Main and Summer Streets opposite the Soldiers' Monument served for a time, but was exchanged for the house adjoining on Summer Street. This proved too large and not well adapted to the purpose and was later sold. When the death of Mrs. Martha Safford made the lot adjacent to the church available, it was purchased and an attractive, modern, Dutch colonial house was erected and opened in 1927.

In June, 1898, the facilities offered by the new church made possible the entertainment of the General Convention of the Congregational Churches of Vermont, at which Rev. V. M. Hardy, pastor here ten years before, was Moderator. In October, 1912, the twenty-seventh annual state Christian Endeavor Convention was held here. Rev. Fraser Metzger of Randolph, candidate for Governor on the Progressive ticket, was President of the State Association that year, and among the high spots of the convention were the addresses by Rev. George L. Cady, D. D., later Executive Secretary of the American Missionary Association; Rev. Paul Moody, then at St. Johnsbury, now President of Middlebury College, and A. J. Shartle, long associated with "The Christian Endeavor World," the official organ of the society.

Among the men who have gone out from this town to serve as Congregational ministers were: Wm. A. Robinson, 1840-1910; Herbert M. Tenney, 1850-1924; Samuel Luman Vincent, 1851-   ; Josiah Wood-   ; Wilbur Rand, 1856-   . Dr. H. M. Tenney, after thirteen years of fruitful service as pastor of the First Congregational Church of San Jose, Calif., resigned in 1903 to become the Secretary of the American Board for the Pacific District, and was serving in that office at the time of his death.

THE BAPTIST CHURCH

The second organized church in town was undoubtedly the Baptist, since on January 19, 1811, this church was received into fellowship by a council, in which the Johnson and Fairfax churches were represented. The Articles of Faith previously prepared were then examined and after slight changes were found satisfactory, and in 1812 the church joined the newly organized Fairfield Association. The Covenant accepted by the Council was a long, but a very clear statement of their belief as Christians and as Baptists. From it the following characteristic articles are quoted: "Baptism and the Lord's Supper are ordinances of Christ and to be observed in the church until His second coming and that no person has any right to the Lord's Supper until he has received baptism and that baptism is to be administered by burying the body in water and that in the name of the Father, Son, and Holy Ghost and this is to be done on the profession of the candidate's faith and that the administrator must be one who has been authorized according to Christ's appointment. . . . . A church thus gathered have power to choose and call to ordination those officers that Christ hath appointed in His Church viz. Bishops or Elders and Deacons and also to depose such officers as evidently appear to walk contrary to the Gospel and to discipline their members though in some cases it is common and profitable to request the advice of sister churches. . . . . We believe that brother ought not to go to law with brother but all differences should be settled in the Church according to the rule given by Christ in the 18th of Matthew and elsewhere."

That this Covenant was made the rule of their daily life is shown by the church records. Elder Thomas Brown was called in 1814 and seems to have been their first pastor, but, applying their right as an independent church, three years later they withdrew fellowship from him, and in thus excluding him were sustained by a regularly called Council. Nor did they neglect the discipline of their own members, as their records show: "Voted to send a letter of admonition to Bro. Rankin for neglecting to meet with the Church and refusing to abide his own agreement." In another instance the church was called upon to settle a dispute between father and daughter, the former complaining the latter had spread a report about the extravagance of her mother-in-law in using 200 weight of sugar, while the daughter said she had been neglected when sick, and that her father had not paid her for work done before he married a second time. Votes were taken upon all charges. In 1819 it was "Voted to raise six cents on the dollar on the Ratable Property for the purpose of hiring preaching." In 1823 Elder Spaulding was called and they "Voted to assist Elder Spaulding to move to this town and get up his wood and pay him $125. for a compensation for preaching one half the time for one year." Again we read, "The Church was then called to express their mind in regard to Br. Dulcive's gift whether they thought he had a preaching gift. The majority thought he had not and could not approbate him." Another brother, Joel Hayford, was more fortunate, for in 1826 a Council was called to set him apart by ordination to the work of an evangelist.

The Church Covenant was signed by twenty-four people, Earl Wingate and Miriam Wingate heading the list. The fifth name recorded was that of Jacob Walker, but in point of service and influence in the church his name might well have come first. He not only served as Deacon, but was Clerk for a quarter of a century. Church meetings were often held at his house, and he was generally included in any committee elected, and to him fell the lot of writing letters of admonition to recreant church members.

After the fine brick church already referred to was declared unsafe the Baptists shared the newly erected Methodist Episcopal Church, but much of the time they were without regular preaching service, and again they had a supply for a fourth or a half of the time. One does not wonder at the entry which appears, "Feelings generally low." That they met these discouraging circumstances with a brave spirit is indicated by the last entry in their first and only record book, which is extant: "Church met at Br. Hocomb's on Sat. 20 of June, 1835. Meeting was opened and some remarks made on our situation and it was proposed to leave all old difficulties, say nothing about them and make one effort to travil on and a prayer meeting was appointed every Sabbath evening at 5 o'clock at Br. Hocomb's. Jacob Walker, Clerk."

Ten years later, in 1845, Rev. J. B. Hall moved into town from Waterbury Center. He was not a close-communion Baptist, so from that time on the character of the church changed somewhat, and in the "History of the Baptists in Vermont" it is later listed as a Free Baptist Church. In 1873 the local paper contained the following item: "The Baptists of the western part of the town have been making strong efforts to raise the means to engage the services of Rev. Mr. Stevens of Waterbury for a year, but on account of the smallness of their numbers have failed. Mr. Stevens has officiated in the church at the Corners for a few Sabbaths." Ten years later Rev. Lyman Sargent was preaching there, and the pulpit was occupied more or less regularly until 1892. After that date there was no resident pastor, though services were held at different times by various denominations until 1922, when the church was burned in the disastrous fire which destroyed the large barn on the Hadlock place, and the blacksmith shop.

THE METHODIST CHURCH

But little is known of the very early history of this church. At a town meeting, held in September, 1813, the subject of dividing rent money due for the support of the Gospel was discussed, and it was voted that the Selectmen be empowered to make the division among the different denominations "when either of them shall provide a preacher on the Sabbaths at the most convenient place agreed on, they shall have their proportion of the money." At the March Meeting following, these officers reported that there was a balance of $78.94 unexpended, and recommended that under the former vote it be divided among the Congregationalist, Baptist, and Methodist Societies, and it was so voted. So they were holding preaching services here as early as 1814. The town was probably a part of the Stowe or Wolcott circuit, with no resident pastor until 1865, when Benjamin Cox was appointed to Morristown, Hyde Park, and North Hyde Park, and since that date it has been a regular conference appointment, sometimes alone and at other times as of late years with Elmore.

After the brick church at the Corners was condemned for use, the people began to plan for another building, and the second church erected was another Union Church, this time at Morrisville, on the site of the present Universalist Church. It was completed about 1836. Like the first edifice the money was raised by general subscription, and no one denomination had a controlling voice in its construction or management. There were fifty-two pews and the same number of pew owners, and each owner, according to these articles of organization, had the right to dictate the kind of preaching for one Sunday in the year. If these early churchmen thought in this way to settle the troublesome question of church rivalry, events soon proved they were mistaken. Human nature was still too selfish, and soon a sharp contest for the control of the church was on. Proxies were solicited from pew owners; in fact, they were bought, as each denomination struggled to maintain its hold. The Universalists were successful in gaining domination, and the Methodists began to work for a church of their own at the Corners.

In June, 1839, a meeting was held which was recorded as follows: "We the undersigned inhabitants of Morristown do hereby agree to bind ourselves our heirs, and assigns to pay the sum affixed to our names for the purpose of building a house for the worship of God, to be located near the south line of the land now owned by Horace Powers in James Tinker's garden. Said house is to be for the use of the Methodist Episcopal Church and Society of Morristown and occupied for no other purpose than religious worship. The expense of building above the foundations is not to exceed the sum of $1,000. When $500. shall have been subscribed, said subscribers shall meet and choose such officers as shall be necessary to constitute them legally qualified to carry into effect the above design. Said house shall be completed in the month of October next or before if possible."

In less than three weeks the contract had been let, the pews had been sold at public auction, and over $1,200, or enough to pay for the church building, had been raised. Thus was built the structure, which for almost a century was a familiar landmark at the Corners. For more than thirty years it was the home of the Methodists. Then they yielded to the trend of population and in 1872, during the pastorate of Rev. J. H. Wallace, moved to Morrisville. Services were held in the Town Hall for a time, then they purchased the Christian Church and occupied it for two years, but sold it back because they could not secure a clear title to it. Plans were already under way for a house of worship of their own. In June, 1874, a committee was appointed by the Quarterly Conference to build a chapel on the present lot and the following November it was completed and served for more than a decade. In January, 1888, a meeting was called to consider building again, and under the direction of Rev. W. F. Puffer this was done. Mr. A. F. Whitney was one of the foremost workers, and offered to build and complete a church ready for use for $3,000 and to give $300 towards it. Others gave freely, and the project was pushed forward. The chapel was moved back to serve as a vestry and the present edifice was built. On November 22, 1888, the dedication was held. Rev. E. W. Culver was presiding elder, and the dedicatory sermon was by Rev. C. B. Pitblado of Hartford, Conn. The exercises closed with pledges sufficient to cover all indebtedness.

The new edifice made possible the entertainment of the State Conference, which opened its forty-fifth session here on April 18, 1889, with Bishop Ninde of Topeka, Kans., presiding. Again, seventeen years later, the local church was host to the state body, when on April 17, 1906, the sixty-second annual conference assembled, with Bishop Hamilton of San Francisco, Calif., presiding. It was during this gathering that news came of the disastrous San Francisco earthquake. In addition to the regular meetings of the Conference the local Board of Trade, of which D. H. Lamberton, editor of "The Morrisville Messenger," was president, tendered a banquet to the bishop and other invited guests to the number of 100.

Twice since this church was built it has been necessary to enlarge it in order to accommodate growing numbers. During the pastorate of Rev. W. T. Best, in 1912, the choir loft was added and in the pastorate of Rev. Wm. J. MacFarlane, in 1928, a large addition was built on to the vestry, and it was newly equipped throughout, making very fine convenient Sunday School rooms.

One of the unique contributions of this church was its support of the local camp-meetings, which were held here for many years, the story of which is told elsewhere.

THE UNIVERSALIST CHURCH

The fourth religious body to formally organize here was the Universalist Church, which has continuous records of its annual business meetings since 1828. Tradition says that Ebenezer Shaw was the first Universalist in town, and that he took the lead in calling a meeting which convened in a barn at the Corners. If its beginnings were thus humble, the men who organized it possessed clear reasoning powers, and were actuated by lofty purposes as the following constitution which they drew up at that time shows:

"That religion is the most important subject that can engage the mind in the present state of existence is abundantly evident both from reason and revelation. It teaches us to contemplate God as our Creator, our Father, and bountiful Benefactor. That His designs of mercy are unlimited and although as children we have gone astray like the Prodigal and abused His Goodness, yet His arm is not shortened that it cannot save, neither is his ear heavy that it cannot hear but in accents of mercy is calling to us in the language of Scripture 'Look unto me all the ends of the earth and be ye saved for I am God and there is none else'. 'I have sworn by myself, the word has gone out of my mouth in Righteousness that unto me every knee shall bow, and every tongue shall swear, Surely shall one say, in the Lord have I Righteousness and Strength'. To accomplish this glorious design the only begotten Son of God, left the bright abode of immortal glory, and condescended to take upon him human nature, to suffer and die as a propitiatory sacrifice for the sins of the world. That this atonement was as extensive as Creation is evident from testimony incontrovertible. 'For as in Adam all die, so in Christ shall all be made alive'. That he came 'to seek and to save that which was lost. That he is the propitiation for our sins and not for ours only but for the sins of the whole world'. That Repentance towards God and faith in our Lord Jesus Christ are prerequisites to Salvation is also evident from the preaching of Christ and His Apostles. 'Without Repentance there is no remission of Sins'. 'Repent ye therefore and be converted, that your sins may be blotted out when the times of refreshing shall come from the presence of the Lord. And He shall send Jesus who before was preached unto you Whom the Heaven must receive until the time of the Restitution of all things which God hath spoken by the mouth of all the Holy Prophets since the world began. And without Faith it is impossible to please God'.

"To the end that sinners may be converted from the error of their ways and come to the knowledge of the truth, it is necessary that the Gospel should be preached in its purity—unshackled by metaphysical Subtelties, or Sophistical reasoning. That Holiness and Happiness in contrast with sin and its attendant misery should be brought to view, and that the unbounded love of God, His goodness and His mercy, clearly exhibited as an inducement for them to forsake the way of the transgressor which is hard, and walk in Wisdom's which are ways of pleasantness and all her paths are peace.

"With these views, we the subscribers, inhabitants of Morristown, in the County of Orleans and State of Vermont do hereby voluntarily associate and agree to form a Society by the name of the First Universalist in Morristown for the purpose of supporting the Gospel according to the first section of an act entitled An Act for the support of the Gospel passed Oct. 26, 1797. In witness whereof we hereunto set our hands. Dated at Morristown, Vt. the 29th of March, 1828."

John Walker heads the list of 110 men who signed this document and he was elected President of the society, with E. A. Burnett, Scribe, and Daniel Pierson, Treasurer. Among the signers are many well known in the early history of the town, including David P. Noyes, Calvin Burnett, Milton and Alfred Boardman, the Spauldings, Burkes, Giles, Chaffees, Gates, and others. Thus the liberal faith was launched.

While the records give the officers of the society, they say comparatively little about the early pastors. There was doubtless preaching before the above organization was made. S. L. Gates says the first Universalist sermon was by Elder Palmer of Barre. The early business meetings were often held in the schoolhouse at Mill Village, or Cadys Falls, as it was later called. The first mention of hiring a preacher was in 1832 and in 1834 it was voted "that the superintending committee be authorized to hire Mr. Fuller one fourth part of the time for the year ensuing." That his services were acceptable may be inferred from the record made three years later: "Voted that a sum sufficient to pay Mr. Fuller for preaching one fourth part of the time the present year be raised by a tax on the Grand List of such members of the Society as the superintending committee shall suppose willing to pay in that proportion and that the Society rely on their generosity for the payment of the same."

This society later shared with the Methodists in the use of the union church built in 1840, and, as previously related, gained control of it only to have it destroyed by fire on February 23, 1852. Various places of worship were then used, especially the Town Hall, until in 1865 the present structure was built and dedicated during the pastorate of the Rev. George Bailey. Among the leaders who made the new building possible were S. M. Pennock, Orlo Cady, Hiram Kelsey, Harrison George, H. H. Powers, and others, and later, in 1883, Mr. Pennock conferred a rare distinction upon the church by presenting a town clock to be placed in its belfry. Various changes have been made in the interior, and in the season of 1924-1925 a large addition was made to the vestry, furnishing adequate room for Sunday School and social purposes.

In September, 1919, this church entertained the annual convention of the Universalist Churches of Vermont and Quebec, the most interesting event, of which, for local people, was the sermon by the Rev. I. P. Booth of Stafford, Conn., minister in the local church for sixteen years and well known in other parts of the state, having held pastorates in various other towns.

Several interesting ordinations have been held here. In 1893 was the joint ordination of Mr. and Mrs. Alfred Wright. Again in 1906 there was a similar service for the Rev. Otto Raspe; in 1911 for Mr. John Porter; in 1913 for R. D. Cranmer; in 1917 for the Rev. F. A. Stockwell, and in 1926 for the Rev. Donald K. Evans. Mr. Stockwell's service was particularly impressive since he was about to take up war work, serving first as Y. M. C. A. Secretary at Camp Devens and coming here each week for Sunday services, and later he was accepted to serve as Chaplain overseas.

On June 24, 1928, a little more than one hundred years after its establishment, the church observed its centennial. Special exercises were held, which were participated in by the pastor, the Rev. Donald K. Evans, and the Rev. George F. Morton, pastor from 1923 to 1926, and the sermon was by the Rev. Otto Raspe of the First Universalist Church of Cambridge, Mass., pastor here from 1923 to 1926. In the evening a reception was held with exercises which included a history of the church by Mrs. H. J. Fisher, from which many of the facts in this sketch were obtained; greetings from former members and from the other churches in town. This centennial was enjoyed not only by the people of the town, but by several from other parts of the state, for the two days following, the annual state convention was in session here. making the last week in June, 1928, one of the red letter weeks in the calendar of this church.

THE CHRISTIAN CHURCH

The year 1928 also marked the hundredth anniversary of the organization of another religious body, the Christian, since Heminway's "Gazeteer" is authority for the statement that on November 13, 1828, Jabez Neuland, John Orcott and Royal Haskell met and established this denomination here. There was also quite a body of believers of this order in the southern part of the town, but they did not affiliate with the Morrisville group to form a strong church. It is believed that the Rev. J. P. Hendee, father of the Hon. G. W. Hendee, was the first pastor of the local church, but it had no settled place of worship until the Civil War when, largely through the efforts of A. G. West and B. B. Hawse, the structure occupied by the Advent Church was built.

Indirectly the Civil War made its contribution, for the bell placed in its belfry at the building of the church was one of the many captured by Gen. B. F. Butler at New Orleans. Early in the Civil War the need of the Confederacy for some kinds of supplies was desperate, and in March, 1862, General Beauregard issued an appeal to the planters of the Mississippi Valley to contribute the bells in their possession to the common cause that they might be cast into cannon. These bells were used on the large plantations to call the slaves to and from their work. After the capture of New Orleans by General Butler, these bells were sent to Boston and sold at auction. Most of them were sold to junkmen and foundry men to be melted, but a few were bought by churches, and one of them found its way to this village, where it still performs its task of calling men, but it summons free men to Divine Worship instead of slaves to drudgery. The casting bears the date 1859, and the bell itself is a work of art, being profusely embellished with many designs.

The Rev. A. A. Williams was the first pastor installed, and it was under his leadership that the church was built. Two of the more important ministers of the earlier period were Elder Isaac R. Pettingill, who was here most of the time from 1836 to 1847, and died here the latter year, and is buried in the Cadys Falls Cemetery; and the Rev. John A. Capron, a well known preacher of this denomination, who preached here from 1854 to 1858, and died here in his eighty-seventh year. Pastors are credited to this church until 1879, but that it was not functioning regularly is proved by the fact that in 1872 it was sold to the Methodist Church, who two years later sold it back because they could not get a clear title to it. In 1901 A. G. West and his heirs deeded the building to trustees of the Advent Christian Church.

THE ADVENT CHRISTIAN CHURCH

This body was organized on July 19, 1892, with twenty-six charter members, and the month following a Sunday School, with thirty-two scholars, was formed under the leadership of the Rev. A. P. Drown. The early members were largely residents of Morristown and the meetings were held at the homes of the members bi-monthly. Then the church at the Corners was used for a time, but in April, 1893, its present church home was leased from Mr. West and later purchased. Extensive repairs were made on the building in 1907, while the Rev. L. L. Chase was minister, and a re-dedication service was held with a sermon by a former pastor, the Rev. Daniel Gregory. Further repairs were made in 1916, while the Rev. J. J. Bennett was serving the church, and these improvements were celebrated by a mortgage burning service.

On July 19, 1932, the church observed its fortieth anniversary with appropriate exercises. Addresses were made by visiting clergymen, including former ministers, a history of the church was given by the Clerk of the church, L. Grace Prior, and recollections of early church events were offered by some of the older members. Such events as this indicate the loyalty which characterizes this body.

THE ROMAN CATHOLIC CHURCH

There is no record of any Roman Catholics among the early settlers in town, and the first followers of this faith were obliged for years to attend religious services at Hyde Park. It was not until the fall of 1911 that the Rev. W. P. Crosby, who had recently come to Hyde Park, began to say mass in Morrisville. He is authority for the statement that at the first service there were thirty-five present. Meetings were held in the Grange Hall, the G. A. R. Hall, etc., and the interest and numbers steadily grew so that the project of building a church began to be agitated. Encouragement was received from the townspeople, even though they were not of that faith, and Judge H. H. Powers was especially friendly to the idea, and in 1913 the Church of the Holy Cross was built on Brooklyn Street. Begun in the summer of that year it was completed so far as to permit holding the first service in it on November 23, 1913. On June 10 of the year following the formal dedication was held. The service was conducted by the Rt. Rev. J. J. Rice, D. D., of Burlington, assisted by the Rev. E. C. Droulin, P. P., of St. Johnsbury and the Rev. Napoleon La Chance of Fairfield. Solemn high mass was celebrated by the Rev. E. M. Salmon of Swanton, and the sermon was preached by the Rev. P. J. Barrett of Poultney. The service of dedication was followed by the confirmation of a class of seventeen.

During 1918 and 1919 the influx of French Canadians into this section of the state greatly increased the number who attended this church, and the need for a larger structure began to be felt keenly. So in the summer of 1931 extensive alterations were made in the building, and the grounds were improved by grading and the setting out of shade trees, removal of the horse sheds in the rear of the church, etc. An addition which doubled the seating capacity of the auditorium was built, and the altar was enlarged to nearly twice its former size, and a new and larger heating plant was installed, the interior was tastefully decorated and the exterior freshly painted. Thus there was provided an attractive place of worship for a large body of attendants. The priests thus far have been residents of the adjoining parish at Hyde Park.

THE SPIRITUALIST SOCIETY

During the early days of Spiritualism, it was considered more as a religious belief than as a matter of psychical interest, and its followers were grouped together into Associations which met at stated intervals to listen to lectures and exchange experiences.

The adherents of this faith in this and the adjacent towns were banded together in the Morristown and Hyde Park Spiritualist Association. As there are no records of this Association available, the date of its organization cannot be obtained, but it was doubtless in existence during the Civil War period, perhaps before. It was the custom to engage a speaker for a month at a time, and the meetings were held at different places, sometimes at the Town Hall, or in the hall which formerly was found on the second floor of the building now occupied by the Morrisville Fruit Co.

Prior to 1869, this Association secured the union church at Cadys Falls, where they held preaching services more or less regularly for about twenty years. In the autumn of 1870, Mr. Henry Houghton was hired and conducted services for two or three years. Then Mrs. Emma Paul, who had in the meantime moved to Morrisville and had previously filled some shorter engagements, carried on the work for about twenty years, dividing her time between this Association and those in other states.

At least five state conventions were held under the auspices of the Morristown and Hyde Park Association, one at Cadys Falls, two at Hyde Park, and two at Morrisville, which brought distinguished speakers from other states as well as local talent. Among the pioneer workers in this organization were Mr. and Mrs. Edwin H. Shaw, Mr. and Mrs. George Brewster, Mr. and Mrs. Charles Burke, Mr. and Mrs. Samuel Clark, Mr. and Mrs. William Thomas, and others who supported the movement loyally for many years.

With the decline in interest, the hall at Cadys Falls remained closed for several years until it was bought by the Cadys Falls Hall Society, in 1894, and has since been held and used by it for public purposes.

THE EPISCOPAL MISSION

The Episcopal Church has never been strong in this part of the state and its adherents in Morristown have always been few in number if firm in their loyalty to that faith. As no local records have been kept, the following facts in regard to the mission have been obtained by the present priest-in-charge, the Rev. F. W. Burge.

The first services of the Episcopal Church in Morrisville were probably held by the Rt. Rev. Arthur C. A. Hall early in his episcopate, beginning February 2, 1894, and have been continued by the different priests-in-charge at Hardwick, including the Rev. George R. Brush. The present minister, whose pastorate in Lyndonville dates from July 1, 1925, ministered here for the first time on the second Sunday in October, 1927. During these years meetings have been held in different halls, the Grange Hall having been used of late until the purchase of the property on Bridge Street, formerly known as "The Castle," the acquisition of which was due to the initiative of Mr. Burge. At the last service held in the Grange Hall the name of Chapel of the Resurrection was adopted by unanimous vote of the congregation present.

The $1,500 required for securing the property from Mr. George Prior was obtained as follows: $500 from a gift to the priest-in-charge by George T. Adee and Mortimer N. Buckner of New York, classmates of Yale, '95; $500 from the Missionary Committee of the Diocese of Vermont; $250, the loan of a fund at the disposal of the priest-in-charge; $250 the gift of the American Church Building Fund Commission, New York.

After gaining possession, the barn and woodshed in the rear were torn down and other improvements in the appearance of the property were made. The two rooms constituting the temporary Chapel of the Resurrection were ready for use and the whole site dedicated on the evening of September 19, 1931, including the altar for the permanent basement chapel from the former Universalist Church of Lyndonville. The Holy Eucharist was celebrated for the first time in the new property the following day, September 20, 1931.

Services are held here regularly once a month.

THE CHRISTIAN SCIENCE SOCIETY

During a period of about ten years prior to 1917 a few persons became interested in Christian Science and began meeting in private homes, usually on Sunday afternoons, studying and reading the Christian Science lesson sermons. From this small beginning the interest grew, and the numbers increased until the winter of 1917 when regular meetings were held in the G. A. R. Hall and the present order of services was established.

This continued until April 1918, when the use of the rooms over the old Brick Store on Main Street was secured and they were appropriately furnished. On January 2, 1919, a group of interested Christian Scientists met and decided to form a Christian Science Society. A set of by-laws was adopted and on January 21, 1919, at an adjourned meeting, formalities were completed, and the first officers were elected as follows: President, H. A. Slayton; Clerk, Mrs. H. A. Slayton; Treasurer, Mrs. M. C. Greene; Readers, Mr. and Mrs. E. W. Gates.

The Society consisted of nineteen charter members and became an authorized branch of the Mother Church during the year 1919.

CHAPTER VI

DEVELOPMENT OF VARIOUS SECTIONS OF THE TOWN

WHEN Jacob Walker chose the geographical center of the town as the spot on which to build his log cabin, he doubtless thought he was fixing the business center also, and well he might. The highway which linked his home with the outside world was surveyed in June, 1800, and ran from Waterbury through Stowe past his door and on to Hyde Park. Near him Elisha Boardman built and kept the first tavern and in a room finished off at the end of it was convened the first school in town taught by Eunice Pratt and attended by six children. This tavern also was the civic as well as the social and educational center, for here the town meetings were held until 1814, when it was voted to build a Town House and two cents on a dollar of the Grand List was appropriated for that purpose. The committee in charge, which consisted of Joseph Sears, Luther Bingham, and Crispus Shaw, may have proved poor financiers, for the year following one and one-half cents additional was voted to complete the simple one story structure which stood on the east side of the highway and served as both town house and church for eight years. In 1802, Dr. Ralph Tinker, the first physician in town, had settled a little farther south, and a blacksmith by the name of Samuel Huggins began to ply his trade nearby; and, on the road to Stowe, Comfort Olds and Cyril Goodale, two of the leading citizens, had built their homes, while the ministerial lot given to Daniel Rockwell, the first settled minister, was not far distant. Mr. Walker utilized the power furnished by the brook running north of his property by erecting a saw mill, and an oil mill in which flaxseed was ground. This making of linseed oil from flaxseed sounds like a strange proceeding today, but a study of the industrial life of scores of Vermont towns shows it to have been one of the earliest industries. The oil mill flourished along with the pearlash and the potash. The Center seemed to be the heart of the town.

But about 1809 Dr. James Tinker, the second physician, came here and proved to be an important factor in the development of the town. The record of his professional career is given elsewhere, but now it is noted that he settled on the level plain to the south of the Center. (7) The fine old brick house opposite the store is a monument to his good taste and judgment. When the postoffice was established, he secured its location at the Corners and was the first postmaster, being appointed about 1812. About this time, the first general store in town was opened here by Robert Kimball, who also operated a "Potash."

The making of potash and pearlash was an important industry in those days. Before the era of barrels a huge hollow log was placed upon a platform and filled with hardwood ashes mixed with quicklime, and wet down. The resulting lye was drawn off and evaporated and the residue was the salt of lye or potash. To form pearlash these salts were again dissolved and filtered through straw into a barrel. The liquid was again evaporated, and the resulting substance, broken into small lumps of a pearl white color, contained a considerable percent of potassa. These factories were found in different parts of the town and the brook running through the village back of Cherry Avenue, and known as Potash Brook, received its name from this industry. The market value of the salts ranged from $3.00 to $5.50 per hundred pounds, and they were some of the few products that could be sold for cash when barter was the ordinary method of trade.

To the Corners came the first lawyer, Charles Meigs, who may have been the prosecuting officer in what is said to have been the first lawsuit in town. Samuel Town was complained of because he traveled on horseback on Sunday to Stowe. He was tried before Justice Elisha Boardman and was fined one dollar and costs. When the fine brick church was built in 1822, the people decided it should be located at the Corners. A tannery was built by the Cole brothers; Joseph Sears opened a tavern and also did cabinet work; Giles Rood, who built the first house at the Corners, opened a saw mill and also a grist mill. Thus a variety of interests and industries met here, and it was but natural that at the 'March Meeting, held in 1833, it was voted "that individuals may without expense to the town remove the town house to the Four Corners if they will provide a suitable spot to set it on, then the town will finish off said house in convenient manner." The spot chosen was one near the brick church, and perhaps the clay soil was responsible for its being abandoned in a comparatively short time, for in 1850 there was an article in the warning to see if the town would build a Town House. It was dismissed, but in May, 1853, the old building was put up at auction and bid off by John West for $19.50.

In 1853 and 1854 the town meetings were held at the Methodist chapel at the Corners. If one follows still farther the fortunes of this center of our civic life, he finds that on March 7, 1854, the town voted to build a Town House at Morrisville, which village furnished the site which was acceptable to the selectmen and gave $300 towards the erection of the building. John West, Fabius George, and Benjamin Howard were elected a committee to superintend the construction. In passing, it is interesting to note that the Four Corners did not meekly submit to losing this symbol of its importance, for on March 23, 1854, an adjourned meeting was called to reconsider the vote taken two weeks before to place the new Town House in Morrisville and to vote to place it "on the land now owned by widow Marshall near where the old store used to stand." This article was passed over, the die was set, and in 1855 the annual meeting was called in the new structure, which, with alterations and additions, is our present building.

CADYS FALLS

In the northwestern part of the town another hamlet sprang up which was at one time the leading industrial center. The magnet was the excellent water power furnished by the Lamoille River, and the little village was known as Lower Falls, Little Falls, Gates' Falls, Mill Village, and finally, with the establishment of the postoffice in 1858, as Cadys Falls, after Elisha Cady, who then owned most of the mills there. Around this water power was centered a greater variety of industries than existed elsewhere in town. A saw mill, tannery, grist mill, shingle mill, carding mill, starch factory, wagon and sleigh shop, butter tub factory, woolen mill, and forge for the manufacture of iron were among the industries which depended upon the river for their maintenance. A short distance from the Lamoille on what is known as Ryder Brook there was a factory for the manufacture of shoe pegs, operated by the firm of Wilder and Patten. After the local manufacture of shoes was discontinued, it turned to making tubs and pails. This mill was carried off in the high water of October, 1869, and not rebuilt.

With Cadys Falls are connected a few names which have always been associated with the history of the town, and descendants of the Gates family, the Boardmans, the Terrills, the Watermans, and the Towns still play their part in the Morristown of today. Something of their story is told elsewhere and here is noted only their part in the development of the village. We are indebted to Mr. E. K. Seaver for most of the facts in regard to this hamlet.

The first settlement here was made in 1794 by the Boardmans, who located on lots sixty-three and sixty-four. In 1801 or 1802 Nathan Gates came and was evidently impressed with the possibilities for water power, as he purchased lot sixty-one, a 200-acre lot, which included all of the water power and most of the present village, together with a considerable area that was flooded when Lake Lamoille was formed. He constructed a dam across the river and built the first saw mill here and sold water rights to John Cook, who operated a woolen mill for several years. This building was later occupied by a planing mill and job shop run by E. B. Reed. A tannery was soon established which supplied leather for the boots and shoes which were made in the first place by a Mr. Lewis and later by Frank Pettingill. In 1826 Mr. Gates sold to Joshua Sawyer of Hyde Park and others the privilege of taking water from the pond to run an iron forge. This plant was a little south of the present electric power house. The iron ore was obtained in Elmore on the east side of the mountain near the head of the pond, and also on the west side, and was of good quality so that edged tools could be made from it. At first the project suffered from the inexperience of the workers, and the material would not weld because of a lack of cinder in the ore, a deficiency which was later remedied. In August, 1828, a serious reverse came in the shape of high water, which swept away the forge and its equipment. There was no insurance on the property and as Mr. Sawyer had recently suffered heavily from a fire which destroyed his home and contents, the forge was never rebuilt. Some years later a starch factory was built on the site by V. W. Waterman and Orlo Cady, and that was burned.

Mr. Gates operated his saw mill until 1830 when he sold it, together with the water power, to Elisha Cady of Stowe, from whom the village was named. Mr. Cady built a new saw mill and a grist mill containing three runs of stone which served the citizens of the town for years. After Mr. Cady's death the property passed in 1881 into the hands of Napoleon Manning, who conducted the business along the same lines as his predecessor and also manufactured chair stock. Ten years later George Brown bought the property and improved the saw mill by changing the old upright saw, the last one in this section, to a circular saw. T. S. Seaver then became the owner of Mr. Brown's interests and they were managed under the name of the Cadys Falls Mill and were enlarged by the addition of a shingle mill. With the construction of the municipal dam the property came into the possession of the Village of Morrisville, and the buildings were torn down.

At an early date a shop for the manufacture of carriages and sleighs was located here, which was managed at one time by Truman Ryder. In later years the products of the Lilley Wagon Co. were well known in this section, but that business was eventually moved to Morrisville.

For a time one of the largest enterprises of the town was situated near Cadys Falls, namely, the hide business of the late United States Senator Carroll S. Page. This industry was started by Mr. Page and his father, R. S. Page, in a small way in Hyde Park village. After the railroad was built, it was moved near the track to be more convenient for shipping and receiving stock. This location was in Morristown. Because of Mr. Page's business ability the enterprise grew to be one of the largest in green hides and calfskins in the world. He bought and sold in many foreign countries and employed over a hundred men. Sheepskins and wool were also handled and bone meal, poultry feed, and fertilizer were by-products of the business. In 1898, when the town line was changed, the district occupied by this plant was given to Hyde Park.

In addition to the business enterprises cited the village was supplied with all the other industries which characterized that period, blacksmith shops, hotels, etc.

Mention of the hotel calls to mind another family long connected with Cadys Falls, the Towns. Samuel

Town, Sr., settled on a part of lot number sixty-two, purchased of the Boardmans in 1819, and built himself a plank house, one of five such which were constructed here, and for a short time was associated with Mr. Sawyer in the iron business. He raised a family of seven children and his descendants of the sixth generation still live here. One son, Edmund, popularly known as "Mun" to distinguish him from his twin brother, Edwin, built a hotel at an early date. It was a two story building with ell and dance hall in the second story of the ell. Mr. Town managed it during his life time, but after his death it was bought, in 1883, by Fred and Ullie Dow, and has since been used as a dwelling house. Another son, Hiram, was the father of George Town, who long served the county as Deputy Sheriff and Sheriff, and has left children to carry on the family name and traditions. A daughter, Jennette, married Hiram Kelsey, a well known citizen here for many years. Another daughter, Clarissa, first married Hiram Town of Stowe and later Allen Terrill, and died in 1898 at the ripe age of ninety. Another son, Nehemiah, was the father of Eli and Samuel C., whose son, William, has carried on the occupation of his great-uncle, Roswell, and of his father, that of stone mason.

Another man prominent not only in Cadys Falls but also in a wider field was Vernon W. Waterman, who was born in Johnson, Vt., July 30, 1811, the son of Aurunah and Rebecca (Noyes) Waterman. An an early age he went with his father to Montpelier to live, where he remained until he was nineteen. He then came to Morristown, and entered the employ of his uncle, David Noyes, who was engaged in the mercantile business. When he became of age, he went into partnership with Mr. Noyes and continued it until eight years later when he went to Cadys Falls and went into the mercantile business for himself, and engaged in other business enterprises. He was active in securing the charter of the Waterbury Bank and upon its organization in 1854 he was one of its directors, a position which he held until the establishment of the Hyde Park Bank, when he resigned to become associated with that institution.

Mr. Waterman held many public offices, being Town Representative in 1844 and 1845, Assistant Judge two terms, Sheriff for two terms, Court Auditor for nearly thirty years, and a Delegate to the State Constitutional Convention at Montpelier in 1857.

Through his family his influence was perpetuated as his son, George, was a prominent lawyer in the county for many years, and his daughter, Caroline, became the wife of H. H. Powers.

Another name long associated with Cadys Falls is that of Terrill. Timothy Terrill, born in East Canaan, Conn., came there in 1817 from Fletcher, Vt., with his son, Moses, and settled on the river farm occupied by his descendants for more than a century. Moses soon found his bride here in the person of Matilda Weld, to whom were born three children. After her death he married Minerva Calkins, who bore him seven children. "Uncle Moses," as he was familiarly called, held several town offices and died in 1883.

His son, Moses Weld Terrill, was born in 1826 and in 1849 entered the general mercantile business, but his keen commercial instincts led him to seek a broader field, and in 1861 he moved to Middlefield, Conn., where he became president of a firm making washing machines, wringers, and other laundry utensils. Mr. Terrill was a successful man in the highest and best sense of the word. His daughter, May, returned to her father's native town as the wife of T. C. Cheney.

Another son, Newton, remained on the home farm and married Mary Cheney. Three of his children became well known educators, Flora being a teacher of German until her retirement to California; Herbert filled responsible educational positions in New England and New York, and Bertha has been head of the Home Economics Department at the University of Vermont for many years. Another son, George, remained on the home farm, filling many important local offices until 1923, when he moved to California.

School District No. 3 was organized in the early days of the village, and the first schoolhouse was not far from the present one, only nearer the road. The earliest records to be found are in 1872 when the officers were: Moderator, David Drown; Clerk, H. J. Town; Collector, S. B. Clark; Treasurer, A. V. Wiswell; Committee, S. C. Town. Article 5 of the warning that year was to see if the district would vote to build a new schoolhouse, but it was passed over. In 1878 a similar motion was carried, and it was voted to build, the cost not to exceed $1.50 on a dollar of the Grand List of that year; one-half to be collected that year, the remainder when the building was completed. When Morristown began to standardize its schools, this was one of the largest in town, and in 1930 the necessary alterations, including better lighting, heating, and toilet facilities were made, and the building received its plate as a superior school that year from the State Department of Education.

Although affected by the hardships due to the Civil War, the people of this locality realized their community life was not complete without a church, and in 1865 and 1866 one was erected at a cost of about $2,000. At first it was used as a union church, and later was taken over by the Spiritualist Society, which occupied it more or less regularly until about 1887. It remained closed for several years, and in 1894 the Cadys Falls Hall Society purchased it and moved it to its present position, where it is used as a public hall.

MORRISVILLE

As the coming of Jacob Walker marked the beginning of settlement in Morristown and the rise of the Center, so the name of John Safford is forever connected with the early history of Morrisville.

He was born in Norwich, Conn., on August 14, 1738, and at the age of twenty-four married Sarah Plumb of Stonington, Conn. From Connecticut the Saffords moved to Windsor, Mass., but in 1796 migrated from there to Morrisville, and were for six years the sole residents of this part of the town. The family consisted of Mr. and Mrs. Safford; a son, Jedediah, and three daughters. One daughter, Lydia, married Darius Felcher and died in 1799, her's being the first adult death in town. On Christmas Day, 1803, another daughter, Anna, married Abner Brigham and some years later, while mentally deranged, drowned herself. The third daughter, Sabria, married Gardner Clark of Milton, Vt., and the son, Jedediah, chose as his wife Miss Eunice Pratt, who taught the first school in town.

The Saffords were attracted by the water power afforded by the river at what was called the Great Falls, and here, in 1798, they built the first saw mill in town and later, in 1812, the first gristmill. The following description of the river taken from Thompson's "Gazeteer" gives a vivid picture of the Falls as they then appeared:

"The river at this place (the Falls) pours itself into a channel cut directly across the stream twenty feet deep and thirty feet broad. On the west side of this chasm the rocky side rises perpendicularly thirty feet and the beholder standing upon the verge of this precipice, sees the whole volume of the river at his feet plunged into this boiling cauldron, from which it escapes through a channel cut at the south end and immediately spreading itself out, encircles numerous islands, whose high jagged points are covered with a thick growth of cedar and fir and altogether present a scene of grandeur and beauty seldom found surpassed."

No wonder that Indian Joe chose one of these islands for his home and today in spite of all the changes it is still a place of beauty.

John Safford died in 1813, leaving his son, Jedediah, to carry on the business enterprises which they had established, and these mills were kept in the Safford family for more than a century, for it was not until 1899 that the grist mill was purchased from Hiram Safford by H. A. Slayton.

Others were attracted by the natural advantages of the place and soon there grew up the different kind of industries that characterized the village of that day. A clothing mill was established by David P. Noyes, one of the leading men of the village; a tannery was opened by Calvin Burnett; a cabinet shop by Daniel Gilbert; a general store by Clark Noyes; and a blacksmith shop by William Brockway. Soon a doctor, Robert Gleason, located here, and a lawyer, George Mason, was prepared to settle any legal difficulties; and steps were taken to educate the children. The first school was held in David Noyes' barn, with Sarah Gates as teacher, while the winter term was housed in more comfortable quarters in Mr. Safford's back kitchen. In the winter of 1822 a small schoolhouse was built on Randolph Street near the site of the house so long occupied by William Howard. This building was afterward moved up near the building which was the home of Peoples Academy for so long a time and was used as a primary school building.

Another factor contributing to the growth of Morrisville was the development of the Randolph and LaPorte Districts. The first settlers in the former section were the Smalls, who were not only the first here, but were pioneers in the United States as well. William Small, the progenitor of the family in this country, came to Salem, Mass., on the third trip of the Mayflower, in 1634. Among the household goods which he brought was a comb back chair, which is now in the possession of his descendant, Fred M. Small. More than a century later, a Small fought in King Phillip's War and received in return a grant of land in Amherst, N. H., to which his descendants moved, about 1750. From that town in June, 1811, came William Small, Jr., and a cousin, Levi Secombe, to Morristown, built a house which in 1935 is still standing on the farm owned by his great-grandson, Fred M. Small. In the fall they returned to New Hampshire, but came back in the spring with William's two brothers, George and Luther, built a house, and cleared a few acres of land. The following February, 1813, their father, his wife and six children came to take possession of their new home. They exchanged their place in Amherst with Levi Secombe for his lot here, thus adding to their original holdings and forming the fine farms which their descendants have occupied for a century and a quarter.

William Small, the elder, married Patience Lovejoy, granddaughter of the first William Bradford, and perpetuated her family name in that of his oldest daughter, Patience Lovejoy Small, and another daughter, Nancy Bradford Small. The latter, familiarly known as Aunt Nancy, was a well known figure in town, a school teacher, who died in 1894, having lived more than eighty years in the same house. Of William's eight children who came to Morristown, three of them, William Milo, George, and Sarah, married and settled here. Sarah married Amherst Palmer in 1823 and had four children, two of whom, Luther and Sylvester, were well known residents of the southern part of the town. The latter married Rosepha Cleveland, the granddaughter of Oliver Luce, the first settler in Stowe, Vt.

William Milo Small married as his first wife Loretta Dyke, and as a second, Harriet E. Bennett, and by the latter union had two children, William H., who died unmarried, and Fred Milo, who occupies the home place and has two sons, William D. and Wayne A., to carry on the family name.

The second son of this early settler was Levi S. Small, who married Martha Harris, and left four children,

Walter, Henry, Frank, and Allen. Two of them, Henry and Allen, are prosperous farmers in "the Small neighborhood."

The only daughter of William Small to grow up was Viola, who married John M. Campbell and had five children who grew to maturity. Their oldest daughter, Arlie M., became the wife of Harry D. Neuland and they have one son, Paul, and occupy one of the best farms in this Randolph District.

The youngest son of Mr. and Mrs. Campbell, Hugh, married Mary A. Johnson, and remained in his home neighborhood, and has three children, James, Lois and Lucy.

Another son, who came from Amherst, N. H., to help found the new home, was George F. Small, who took as his bride, Orpah Wilkins, from his native town. They had ten children, two of whom were life-long residents of Morristown. George F., married Caroline Keeler and is survived by one son, Albert G., a merchant here for many years, who has two daughters, Dorothy and Barbara. Hiram M. took as his wife Laura Edson, and had one son, Charles, who married Ella Spaulding and still resides here, as does his son, Charles Lyle.

While this settlement was made in the southern part of the town, farther to the north came David Thomas, in 1825 or 1826, and made a beginning on the farm owned in 1935 by Mrs. Stillman Ring. He replaced his first log cabin by the brick house which is still used. As was the custom in those early days, he returned to Tunbridge, Vt., for the winter, but the following spring came with his family. His five children, William, Martha, Almon, Norman, and Henry, were born here, with the exception of the oldest, and resided here as respected citizens throughout their lives. William's son, Don, with his two children, Donald and Maurice, still live here, as does Mrs. Elizabeth Thomas, the widow of Henry, while Henry's son, J. Frank, has but recently moved to the neighboring town of Hyde Park.

At about the same time came James Kibbie, Mr. Thomas' nearest neighbor, and several other settlers, so many of whom were from the town of Randolph, Vt., that they gave that name to the locality.

The LaPorte District was first settled by Stephen Spear, who built his house on the LaPorte Dairy Farm, but later sold to Isaac Allen. This road received its name from the fact that in early days a settler by the name of LaPorte lived there. He was a great wrestler and the neighbors used to speak of going over to LaPorte's for a wrestle and gradually the name became attached to the entire locality. This district was soon occupied by thrifty, prosperous farmers, such as Frederick Powers, John Ferrin, Wingate Webster, George Poor, Moses Weld, Jonathan Cooke, and others. The most convenient trading center for them and for the Randolph District was the hamlet at Morrisville.

In 1840 the mail route which had run from Waterbury to Hyde Park and beyond, via the Four Corners, was changed to pass through Morrisville. So marked was the trend towards the younger village that in 1840 the Congregationalists in building their new church located it at the new metropolis, and the union church of the Methodists and Universalists was also erected there.

Some years previous to this, steps had been taken to define the bounds of Morrisville as the following entry in the Town Records shows:

"Whereas applications in writing has been made to the undersigned selectmen of the town of Morristown in Orleans County, state of Vermont, signed by more than seven freeholders of said town requesting us to lay out and establish bounds and limits to the village near Safford's Mills in said Morristown, we hereby certify that in compliance with said application we have layed out and established limits and bounds to said village as follows: viz. beginning at the bridge below Jedediah Safford's mills and running up the Lamoille river on the south side thereof to the east line of Jedediah Safford's land and running thence south on said Safford's line to the south east corner of said Safford's land thence west on said Safford's south line to the brook that crosses the road near Calvin Burnett's; thence down said brook to the river thence up said River to the Bridge or bound begun at.

"Given under our hands at Morristown the 18th of Feb., 1829.
    "LUTHER BRIGHAM
    "ISAAC ALLEN Selectmen"

The Calvin Burnett house was the one on East High Street now owned by George Cole.

76 HISTORY OF MORRISTOWN

From the bounds thus laid out considerable growth had been made. Local advertisers in the "American Observer" of 1852 and 1853 included D. Gilbert, with a supply of readymade coffins constantly on hand; Thomas Tracy, carriagemaker; Joseph Somerby, mason; C. H. Fox, fashionable tailor; shoe shop, W. F. Hutchins; a co-partnership of Jos. Somerby and M. W. Terrill to carry on a mercantile business; Morrisville House, F. L. Matthews; Charles Robinson and Leander Small, attorneys-at-law; S. L. Gilbert, straw bonnets, artificial flowers, etc.; Thomas Gleed, attorney and counsellor-at-law.

Twenty years later, in 1873, the following business cards appeared: Dr. C. A. Jackman, homeopathist; C. W. Fitch, architect and builder; C. C. Rublee and E. J. Hall, physicians and surgeons; A. M. Burke, Geo. W. Hendee, Powers and Gleed, A. A. Niles, lawyers; D. Gilbert, furniture and caskets; O. Hitchins, painter and paperhanger; B. H. Dickinson, millinery and ladies' furnishings; B. B. Hawse, practical house builder and mechanic; A. O. Gates, apothecary; D. C. Hardy and D. L. Eaton, auctioneers and deputy sheriffs; C. R. Page, wholesale and retail dealer in flour, feed, etc.; Dunham and Spaulding, boot and shoemakers; Geo. P. Hardy, gent's furnishing goods; Merriam and Jockow, foundry; B. S. Wilson, Morrisville House; J. A. George, H. H. Elmore, and C. A. Rich, groceries; W. M. Clark, barber; R. G. Gilbert, dentist; Geo. J. Slayton & Co., D. A. Gilbert, Stoughton & Tift, general merchandise; Dodge and Shaw, insurance; Danforth & Stone, marble works; W. F. Moulton, water tubing, and G. W. Doty, carriages and wagons.

Thus a variety of professions were represented, together with a few business activities, although the village consisted for the most part of High and Main Streets with scattering houses in other sections. With the survey of the proposed railroad, land near that took on new value. Portland Street, now the principal business street of the village, was laid out and built up, and in 1873 we read that a movement was on foot to extend Portland Street from the depot across the flat bridging the river. This would open up the section known today as Brooklyn. The foundry, one of the oldest business enterprises, was built near the railroad, and Morrisville became the center of a brisk lumber trade, fostered by the mills scattered throughout the town, as well as a shipping point for agricultural products.

HISTORY OF MORRISTOWN

Centennial year brought something of a boom, the results of which are evident in the village of today. In 1890 the Centennial block was erected through the enterprise and initiative of Dr. E. J. Hall and the professional skill of C. W. Fitch, the architect and builder. The tannery, which has been on the whole the leading manufacturing plant in town, was built in 1889 by Webster and Stafford. In 1891 the Union Savings Bank & Trust Co. opened its doors, with G. W. Hendee, President; C. H. Stearns, Vice-President, and a strong board of directors, and has been an increasingly vital factor in the business life of the community since. At first it was located in the rooms now occupied by the Water and Light Department, then the present home was built, with the bank occupying the first floor and the library the second. These quarters were soon outgrown, and in 1913, when the present library building was completed, the second floor was taken over by the bank. That does not provide sufficient room and the lot adjacent on Main street has been purchased with the idea of building. The stability of this institution is shown by the fact that in the crisis of March, 1933, when supposedly solid banks all over the country were closed for months, if not permanently, the Union Savings Bank & Trust Co. was ready to carry on business in a normal way except as it was obliged to meet the statewide requirements, and local business was but little hampered by this financial emergency.

In 1892 the Waite block was erected at the foot of Portland Street, while at its head the old Morrisville House was moved back and the new Randall arose. In 1896 the Congregational Church was moved back to form the vestry of a handsome new edifice. There was a general spirit of progress.

The village bounds have been enlarged several times since its incorporation, the last addition being in 1923 when the section near the Fairground was included.

CHAPTER VII
EDUCATIONAL INSTITUTIONS

THE winter of 1792 and 1793 Comfort Olds, with his wife and two children, occupied their new home on the height of land on the hill road to Stowe and these children were the vanguard of that army of youth who have since made possible and necessary the public schools. They must have been instructed at home for a time, since it was not until 1799 that Eunice Pratt, who, afterwards married Jedediah Safford, taught the first school in a room finished off in the Boardman tavern at the Center. Here six children formed the nucleus of the system which has since been such an important factor.

In 1797 the State Legislature passed a law giving the several towns in the state power to raise such sums of money on the list of their polls and ratable property as they thought proper to be used for the support of English schools, and the money thus raised was divided among the several districts according to the number of pupils between the ages of four and eighteen years. In 1810 an advance step was taken when one cent on the dollar of the list of polls and ratable property was levied by the Legislature for the purpose of schooling for a term of two months. In 1824 the amount was raised to two cents, and, as the school movement gained impetus, the rate was increased until in 1842 it was nine cents. One-fourth was distributed equally among the districts and the remainder according to the number of children between four and eighteen years of age. The part of the cost of schools not furnished by towns was provided by the different districts, and the bone of contention was, "Shall the money be raised by a tax on the grand list or a tax upon the scholar?" Just how serious a matter this was may be seen from the following extract taken from the records of the Baptist Church: "Church met at Bro. Hocomb's the last Friday in Jan. 1831 agreeable to appointment on account of some difficulty about supporting the school. Some thought there was no morral right to injure one to benefit another but that we should do by others as we should wish to be done by and not do evil that good might come. Others thought it was right to support the school on the Grand List and that brethren ought not to have any trial on that account. After much conversation it was agreed that we would not as brethren vote to support the school on the Grand List to the grief of any of our brethren."

In September, 1806, it was voted to appoint a committee to divide the town into school districts and lay a plan before the town at their next meeting. Jacob Walker, Crispus Shaw, and Samuel Joslin, Jr., were chosen thus to act. The boundaries of the districts then laid out were very flexible and scarcely a town meeting passed but that some family was set from one district to another. At first these units were named according to their location as Center District, North District, etc. Later numbers were given to designate them. Morrisville was number one, Morristown Corners two, Cadys Falls three, etc.

Nineteen such school units have been organized at different times. Changes were made in the location of the schoolhouses, and in time some of the first districts were combined. In 1873 the district formerly known as number twelve was given up, and a part of it was set off into number six, or the Elmore Road, and a part into the North Randolph District. This schoolhouse formerly stood at the junction of the road leading past the George Town homestead to the Mountain Road, and one going by the Dodge place to the Randolph Road. The year following, 1874, numbers ten and eleven were combined, and the schoolhouse in number ten, which first stood on the D. J. Cole farm on a road now abandoned, but once intersecting the Stowe Road near the Dyke farm was moved up to its present location; and the present road past the schoolhouse, built that year, better accommodated all the pupils. The number eleven building was on the highway not far from the Eli Gile homestead and the farm owned by the Douglass brothers. In 1883 H. R. Burke, a well known contractor of that day, constructed the new building on the Elmore Road and changed the site somewhat to better accommodate the pupils from the southwestern part of the district. In 1895 a new plant became necessary in the North Randolph neighborhood and in 1896 the schoolhouse at the Corners was relocated and rebuilt. It formerly stood on the road leading past the old Center to Stowe at the foot of the hill below the store, but was changed to the flat opposite the cemetery.

When the movement for standardizing rural schools began in Vermont, Morristown gradually fell into line in places where it seemed practicable and made a superior school at North Randolph in 1925, at South Randolph in 1926, and at the Corners in 1927. Schoolhouses are maintained in a condition suitable for occupancy at No. 1, Morrisville; No. 2, Corners; No. 3, Cadys Falls; No. 4, South Randolph; No. 5, South LaPorte; No. 6, Elmore Road; No. 7, Plains; No. 8, Lamson; No. 9, North Randolph; No. 10, Cole Hill; No. 13, North LaPorte; No. 14, Cheney; No. 15, Mud City; No. 16, Tyndall Hill; No. 19, Billings. But not all of them are used, since the number of pupils in each varies from year to year. Numbers seventeen and eighteen have long been discontinued. In one case only a cellar hole marks the site of the former building. One was situated on the old County Road that lead from Mud City to Sterling past the foot of Judd Hill, and the other was on the Wolcott Road not far from the Tenney Bridge on the farm occupied in 1935 by Leo Edson.

The trend towards centralization has led to the transportation of some pupils to the village school or to other districts, but some sections offer problems which make such a plan unwise, and the town probably maintains more rural schools than most others in the state.

If the tax for the support of the early schools was paid with reluctance by some, effort was made to render the process of paying as easy and painless as possible. In December, 1811, the following item appears in the town records: "Voted to pay the cent tax for the support of schools in grain if paid on or before the first day of February and, if not by that time, to be paid in money. Voted that said tax shall be paid to the several trustees of each district or some one of the committee for said districts if paid in grain as aforesaid otherwise to be paid to the Town Treasurer. Voted that after said tax shall be collected and a dividend made by the selectmen that the balance due from any district shall be paid to the Town Treasurer to be paid to such districts as shall have a ballance in their favor. Voted that the price to be allowed for grain shall be as follows viz: $1 per bushel for wheat, .75 per bu. for rye, and .50 per bu. for corn. Voted that said tax shall be made up on the present year's list to be averaged according to the return of the Schollars made last March."

From the records of District No. 5, the following copy of one of the returns thus made is taken:

Heads of Families	Names of Children from 4 to 18	No.
Nelson Slocumb	Sanford, Calista, Harriet	3
Seth Sherwin	David	1
Seamon Lewis	Chauncey, Clarinda, Adeline, Mary	4
Jonathan Powers	Lester	1
Hiram Bingham	Susan, Sarah	2
Horace Felcher	Horace, Harriet, Erastus	3
Alanson Stow	Cordelia, Baron, Solomon, George	4
Wingate Webster	Laura	1
Isaac Allen	Samuel, Nancy, Louisa	3
John Ferrin		
Frederick Powers	Martha, Henry, Charles	3
Joseph Sears	Julia, Margaret, Hannah, Albert	4
Isaac Alger	Lucien, Emily	2
John Spaulding	Francis	1
Sylvester Gates	Maria	1
Edwin Dunham	Milton, Lisander	2
Nathan Ferrin	Collins	1
Rufus Wheeler	Mary, Nathaniel, Fidelia, Susan	4
Dotham Goodale	Weltha Ann	1
Archibald Fuller		3

No. of scholars who have attended school   45
No. of weeks   13 taught by a male at per mo. $12.50
No. of weeks   16 taught by a female per mo.   4.00
Received and appropriated of public money $47.95

"I certify the above to be the true returns of Dist. No. 5 as required by law.
    "Attest   RUFUS WHEELER, District Clerk
"Morristown Jan. 1, 1845."

This roster of names is interesting for many reasons. It shows the fine old Yankee stock which formed the backbone of the town, and the fact that almost every family was represented by from one to four pupils accounts for the size of the schools of those early days, while one familiar with local history recognizes in almost every name people of sterling character who played an honorable part in the life of the town.

Perhaps no better idea of this phase of those early days can be obtained than by copying the report of one of those most democratic of all assemblies, the district school meeting:

"Morristown, Vt. Nov. 1, 1847.

"The legal voters in District No. 5 met according to notice and were called to order by the Clerk. The warning read. Wingate Webster was chosen Moderator and the following business transacted: Namely

"1st Voted to have three months school the following winter

"2nd Voted to spend two thirds of the public money to support the school and the remainder to be raised on the poll of the schollars according as each one shall send.

"3rd Voted to prepare eight cords of good hard wood split and prepared for the stove two feet long and put under the shed by the first day of May 1848. Sold to Isaac Allen at $.49½ per cord.

"4th Voted to repair the house suitable to teach school in the ensuing winter.

"5th Voted that if any schollar shall break a light or lights of glass in said schoolhouse said schollar, his parents or guardian shall replace the same forty eight hours after being notified or shall forfeit and pay to the committee the sum of twenty five cents.

"6th Voted that the repairs of the house shall not exceed $5.

"7th Voted to pay the wood on the poll of the schollars as each shall send.

"8th Voted to adjourn without date.

"HARRISON FERRIN, District Clerk"

At a following meeting they voted to appoint a committee of three to visit the school once in every month. That this act was prompted by a sincere interest in the school is indicated by the following resolution which was passed at the March Meeting in 1867: "Whereas the prosperity and advancement of our common schools depend upon the interest taken in them by the parents and guardians of the scholars attending such schools and whereas it is the duty of all of us to visit such schools while in session, Therefore Be it Resolved that we individually pledge ourselves to visit the school in this district at least once during the summer and winter term of said school the ensuing year." This resolution passed by an unanimous vote. That the rising tide of expense was felt even then is seen in the fact that this year the wood was bid off at $1.65 per cord. At this meeting it was also voted "to board teachers on the Grand List of the district, the teachers boarding round the district having a rate bill of the time made out by the Prudential Committee before commencing the school, said board to be estimated at a reasonable rate at so much per week and those who do not choose to board shall pay the money to the Prudential Committee."

Later the teacher boarded around in the summer, but had a steady boarding place in the winter term. This was auctioned off to the lowest bidder and in 1883 the winner received $1.20 per week.

To one who has ever attended a district school of the olden times, there comes a vivid picture of the bare room with its huge box stove, its uncomfortable seats whose desks bore the marks of the jackknives of many former occupants. In the earliest days there were no blackboards and no slates. Instead on rough unbleached paper the ciphering was done with a plummet, the predecessor of the lead pencil, made by running melted lead into a groove. When cooled, it was whittled off to point. The pen of the earliest period was a goose quill. As the first steel pens cost twenty-five cents apiece, one may be sure the children of Morristown did not indulge in such luxuries until they were reduced in price, about the middle of the century. Here, by the laborious alphabet method, the pupils learned to read and thus unlocked the treasures of The American Preceptor, being a New Selection of Lessons for Reading and Speaking, Pike's New Complete System of Arithmetic, Dwight's Short but Comprehensive System of the Geography of the World, Wells' Grammar of the English Language, Childs' First Book of History, or other textbooks equally ponderous in title and contents.

The Vermont Legislature of 1827 enacted a law that "it shall be the duty of the Town Committee or some one of them to visit each of the district schools in said town for the purpose of making a careful examination thereof; of seeing that the scholars thereof are properly supplied with books, of inquiring into the regulations and discipline of such schools and of the habits and proficiency of the scholars therein; such visits to be made on the first or second week after the commencement of each school, and also once a month afterwards during the continuance of such schools, without giving previous notice of such visit to the instructors of such schools; and also once during the last week of school."

We have no way of knowing how faithfully these officials carried out the law, but in time they delegated a part of their duty and in 1857 Charles H. Heath was elected "Superintendent of Common Schools," but it was voted that the Selectmen attend the examination of school teachers in connection with the Superintendent, and the town as a body kept a watchful eye over its schools as is indicated by the fact that in 1879 a textbook committee was elected. At first the Principals of Peoples Academy added the duty of supervision to their duties in connection with that institution, but the office of Superintendent was seldom filled by one man for any length of time. The Rev. I. P. Booth, who acted in that capacity from 1877 to 1882, was perhaps the longest incumbent of that early period and it was most often filled by the ministers or lawyers of the town. P. K. Gleed, H. H. Powers, G. W. Hendee, O. W. Sturges, G. M. Powers, and F. G. Fleetwood have represented the legal profession in that capacity, while among the clergymen Lyman Bartlett, V. M. Hardy, and I. P. Booth served.

No town ever fought harder against adopting the town system than Morristown. In 1885, by a vote of 240 to four, they rejected the plan and it seemed to gain little following in the succeeding years, but in 1893 they yielded to the inevitable and C. H. Slocum, A. O. Gates, and J. M. Campbell were elected the first School Directors. When the property was turned over to the town, there were fourteen district schools and the property was appraised at $7,742.75.

THE QUIMBY SCHOOL

No account of the early attempts at education in town would be complete without mention of the select school kept by Miss Jennie Quimby at the Corners in the late 50's. It was a co-educational institution maintained during that part of the year when the brief terms of the public schools were not in session. While it gave instruction in the regular school subjects, it specialized in music and it was that feature, doubtless, that attracted pupils from Hyde Park, Waterbury, and other neighboring towns. For a time its sessions were held in the last house on the right-hand side of the main street as one goes south, a house which was burned some years ago. The large dwelling house owned in 1935 by Frank Shippey was also occupied by Miss Quimby and furnished rooms for the out-of-town students.

Miss Quimby was an accomplished musician, a student of the Boston Conservatory of Music, at one time connected with Peoples Academy as Instructor in Music, and in 1858 the school was included in the list of educational institutions in Morristown given in "The Vermont Register" under the name of the Morristown Seminary, Jennie F. Quimby, Principal.

In addition to her work as teacher, Miss Quimby used to give concerts. The following advertisement, taken from "The Mountain Visitor," a short lived publication appearing in Stowe, August 17, 1858, indicates that her company had more than a local reputation: "The Green Mountain Bards, consisting of two Ladies and two Gentlemen, are visiting all the principal parts of New England giving concerts in Vocal and Instrumental music. The attention of the musical public and all classes of citizens who are fond of music, new, popular, and edifying is respectfully solicited.

"Morristown, Vt. 1858

"E. QUIMBY, Agent."

The agent mentioned was Mr. Elisha Quimby, her father.

Miss Quimby was, in many respects, a unique character who left Morristown for Johnson in her later years and there died.

PEOPLES ACADEMY

For the first half of the nineteenth century the rural schools satisfied the educational needs of the community except in rare cases. Occasionally a lad was ambitious to continue his studies beyond what they offered, and was sent to the Lamoille County Grammar School, established at Johnson in 1830, or to the Bakersfield Academical Institution, which was founded only seven years before. But the desire for broader educational advantages was working like leaven in the community. The Rev. Septimius Robinson, himself an educated man in the best sense of the word, coveted for his children and those of his parishioners better opportunities and to him perhaps as much as to any one man Peoples Academy owes its inception. Other pioneers in the project were Thomas Tracy, at whose shop at the lower end of Main Street the first meeting to plan for it was held; Dr. D. W. Putnam, Judge Calvin Burnett, F. T. George, the Rev. J. P. Hendee, Dr. Horace Powers, Frederic Powers, and others. It must be remembered that Morrisville at that time contained about 400 inhabitants and unfortunately most of the wealthy men of the community were opposed to the whole idea and fought it vigorously.

The plan agreed upon at the preliminary meeting of raising $1,500 by subscription was easier to frame than to carry out. Only about $700 was pledged and the idea was temporarily given up. Nothing daunted, Mr. Tracy started a second paper in which the subscribers pledged notes payable in six and twelve months. In this way about $700 was raised, of which less than $100 was cash. The money was used to buy nails and glass, and Mr. Tracy took the contract to build the structure for $750 and take the notes in payment. The work was started in earnest and within forty days the building was completed. Anyone who contributed one dollar or more was a proprietor of the institution. No wonder the name first chosen for the school was "The Poor Peoples Academy," and the struggle and real sacrifice which entered into its founding perhaps account in part for the loyalty with which it has always been regarded. Surely no school in the country had a more romantic conception and institution than this one.

The first recorded meeting of the proprietors was held June 1, 1847, with Jonathan Cooke, Chairman, and the

Rev. J. P. Hendee, Clerk, Pro Tem. Three important committees were chosen. John West, D. W. Putnam, and Thomas Tracy formed a committee to draft a constitution; John West, Robert Parcher, and Thomas Tracy were the Building Committee; while the Rev. Septimius Robinson, Josiah Atkins, Abel Camp, Jr., and Horace W. Gates were to obtain subscriptions for raising funds to buy apparatus.

The constitution reflects the aims and ambitions of those sturdy men. It could be amended with the exception of the eighth, eleventh, and twelfth articles. These three were its "Bill of Rights." Article eight read: "No person shall be compelled by law to pay any tax or assessment for the benefit of this institution in any case whatsoever." Article eleven stated that, "Any person who is not a deist or atheist and sustains a good moral character and has all the necessary qualifications for teaching all the different branches of learning usually taught in Academies shall be eligible to the office of preceptor or preceptress." Article twelve guaranteed religious equality in these words, "There is not to be taught or inculcated any particular religious creed or sectarianism in the Academy."

The year following by-laws were added which were changed from time to time. The first ones required among other things that all students should attend public worship on the Lord's Day unless excused by their parents or guardians, and that no exercises should be attended in the Academy building except under the direction of the principal, and no evening meeting of students, even a lecture or lyceum, should last later than 9:30 except by special permission of the Prudential Committee. Later, in 1852, were added the study hour regulations in force for more than sixty years, which required the students to be in their respective rooms by 7:30 o'clock unless excused by the principal. No doubt this general oversight of the life of the pupils was prompted by the fact that many of the students came from surrounding towns and even distant ones. For the first few years the boarding places of the students are given in the catalogues, and it is evident that the best homes in the village were open to them, and every precaution was taken to make their stay here both pleasant and profitable. That it was never a purely local institution is shown by its roll of students and its trustees. When it opened in 1847, its officers were as follows: The Rev. Septimius Robinson, Chairman; L. P. Poland, Secretary; Calvin Burnett, Treasurer; Hon. Nathaniel Jones of Wolcott, Hon. Nathan H. Thomas of Stowe, Hon. Lucius P. Noyes of Hyde Park, Deacon Abel Camp of Elmore, Frederick Powers and John West of Morristown, Trustees. In 1851 its trustees included men from Hyde Park, Elmore, Stowe, Waterville, Waterbury, Woodbury, Hardwick, Walden, Lowell, Eden, Cambridge, and East Montpelier. Men well known in all walks of life have served in that capacity. Among such are the Rev. Edwin Wheelock of Cambridge, P. K. Gleed, H. H. Powers, G. W. Hendee, George M. Powers, and T. C. Cheney of Morrisville, Frank Plumley of Northfield, Harland P. French of Albany, N. Y., C. P. Hogan of St. Albans, Benjamin F. Sanborn of Boston, and Mason S. Stone of Montpelier.

In 1847 the doors of the new institution swung open to a body of students numbering thirty-six young men and forty-eight young women, representing eleven different towns. The faculty consisted of: Ozias C. Pitkin, A. B., Principal; Mrs. Julia Bliss, Assistant Teacher; Miss Elizabeth D. Pitkin, Assistant Pupil; Azro B. Robinson, Teacher in Penmanship; Nathan D. Thomas, Lecturer in Anatomy and Physiology.

We can imagine the satisfaction with which the trustees made the following statement in their first catalogue: "The Peoples Academy was established for the purpose of supplying in part the demand for an increased number of schools, occasioned by the interest awakened by the late movements in the cause of education. This institution, as its name implies, is intended expressly for the People. The Trustees, in presenting their first catalogue to the public, take pleasure in stating that they have been confirmed in the opinion that the Institution was needed by the full attendance of this their fall term. And this serves, also, to confirm their opinions that Morrisville is the place for an Academy. The trustees would farther say that, without disparagement to any other school, they consider the advantages here offered to the scholar, as unsurpassed by any in the state. The Academy Building is new and convenient and occupies a delightful place, which will soon be rendered more delightful by the improvement of the grounds. The village is small and is pleasantly located on the Lamoille River, which here makes a great fall, adding much to the romantic and picturesque scenery of the place. Board can be obtained on as reasonable terms as at any other place in this section—at present $1.25 per week. Tuition for common English branches $3. per term. Higher English branches $3.50. Languages $4. Drawing and Painting $2. Penmanship $1. A regular examination of the pupils will take place at the close of each term and all friends and patrons of the Institution are respectfully invited to attend. Textbooks— The following textbooks have been selected for the subjects to which they respectively relate: Crosby's Greek Grammar, Shurtleff's Governmental Instructor, Olmstead's Philosophy, Cutler's Physiology, Wood's Botany and Worcester's Dictionary. Upon other subjects the textbooks are those in common use.

"Winter term will commence on Thursday, Nov. 25th; Summer term, Thursday, May 20th; Fall term, Thursday, Aug. 21st. Vacations, the first of one week, at the close of the Fall term; the second of two weeks at the close of the winter term; the third of one week at the close of the spring term; and the fourth of four weeks at the close of the Summer term."

Thus Peoples Academy was launched, and the sacrifices and aspirations of its founders must always be a challenge to its friends of later years.

In 1851 the catalogue contained the work of the Classical Course:

FIRST YEAR

1st Quarter	2nd Quarter
Andrews & Stoddard's Latin Grammar	Grammar reviewed
Andrews & Stoddard's Latin Reader	Latin Reader continued
3rd Quarter	**4th Quarter**
Latin Reader finished	Caesar's Commentaries
Exercises in writing Latin	Exercises in writing Latin

SECOND YEAR

1st Quarter	2nd Quarter
Caesar's Commentaries	Virgil commenced
Greek Grammar	Greek continued
3rd Quarter	4th Quarter
Greek-Anabasis	Virgil completed
Virgil continued	Anabasis cont.

THIRD YEAR

1st Quarter	2nd Quarter
Anabasis continued	Anabasis continued
Cicero's Orations	Cicero's Orations
Extra studies	French-Ollendorf's
Telemaque	Grammar
	Oeuvres of Jean Racine

3rd and 4th Quarter
Review of Latin continued
Review of Greek authors
Boyer's Dictionary
Corinne

Declamations and compositions once in two weeks throughout the year

"Young ladies wishing to pursue the ornamental branches will have an opportunity of so doing every term of the year under the instruction of a well qualified teacher. Thorough instruction in Oil Painting given."

They who pursued the "ornamental branches" were required to pay a little more for the privilege as the tuition for music "with the use of the piano $8, on Melodeon $5, on Aeolian $5, Oil Painting with use of Patterns $8, Drawing and Water Paints, each $2."

While in accordance with the spirit of the age, the Classical subjects were stressed, the Trustees were not unmindful of the so-called practical studies, and in 1855 a Scientific Department was added, and in the catalogue of that year they stated it was their purpose to make it correspond to the Scientific and Agricultural schools in various parts of the country. It included Arithmetic, Algebra, Trigonometry, Surveying, Chemistry, Agricultural Chemistry, Geology, Botany and Mineralogy, in addition to

History and English. The school was doubtless as well equipped to teach these subjects as most of the schools of the state.

In the second year the number of students had increased to 169, or more than doubled, thus farther justifying the faith of the founders.

In the catalogue of 1852 was included the following letter from Ex-Governor Horace Eaton, first State Superintendent of Schools:

"To the Trustees of the People's Academy, at Morrisville, Vt.,
"Gentlemen:

"In accordance with your request I attended the examinations held on the 11th and 12th inst. in the above named institution under charge of Mr. Baker and his able assistants and while I would carefully avoid speaking more favorably than strict truth would warrant, I should on the other hand be doing less than justice if I did not say that I was highly pleased with the evidence presented that a judicious and faithful system of instruction had been pursued; for the character of the system was clearly manifested in its results. Indeed the indications of accurate and thorough scholarship both in the languages, Latin and French, and in Mathematics including Arithmetic, Algebra, and Geometry, were, I am free to say, extremely gratifying and such as I did not expect to see exhibited by pupils of such age as those examined had attained to.

"At the closing exhibition also, the original productions in the form of Orations, Compositions, and Dialogues displayed generally—and some of them in a very eminent degree, a power of discrimination, an accuracy in the use of language, a correctness of taste, and a reach of thought, which were not merely creditable to their authors, but such as would be not unworthy of those who had reached maturer years.

"Briefly and finally, I can freely say, that I believe the People's Academy under its present teachers is doing a noble service in the cause of education.

"Yours truly,
"H. EATON.

"Middlebury, Vt.
"May 14, 1852."

One can appreciate the satisfaction this letter brought to both friends and students of the institution, but his sympathy must go out to the students who had to pass through the ordeal of such a public examination. One year the Examining Committee consisted of the Rev. Septimius Robinson of Morrisville, the Rev. Edwin Wheelock of Cambridge, Prin. C. H. Heath of Plainfield, the Rev. R. H. Barton of Morrisville, the Rev. Eli Ballou of Montpelier, P. K. Gleed, A. B., of Waterville, and Hon. George Wilkins of Stowe. When to such a board was added an ex-governor of the state, together with a company of interested friends and relatives, one may well believe that each student would do his utmost to acquit himself with credit.

It must be remembered that the students of that day received much practice in public speaking. It was a day when oratory was at its height. In the second catalogue it is stated that Rhetorical Exercises are attended to weekly and also the fact that "there is connected with the school under the immediate supervision of the principal a flourishing Literary Society, called the Society of Social Friends; the exercises of which consist of written and extemporaneous discussions, declarations, essays, Letters of Friendship, of Recommendation, of Introduction, billet doux, etc., calculated to promote the advancement of general literature in the mind of the student, and at the same time prepare him for the relations of active life."

For a time the organization was known as The Society of Literary Improvement and following is a report of one of its weekly meetings:

"Sept. 22, 1852

"Pursuant to adjournment, the Society of Literary Improvement assembled at the People's Academy and was called to order by the President. The Secretary being absent, C. Swasey was appointed Sec. Pro Tem. The proceedings of the last meeting were then read. The Society then listened to an oration by C. Herrick next listened to a ladies essay by Julia A. Raymond. The following question was then discussed, Resolved that the literature of the past fifty years has been more favorable than unfavorable to Christianity. Discussed in the Aff. by Messrs. Aiken and Durkee. Neg. by Messrs. Swasey and Allen. Not decided by the President. The Emblem was then read by the Editors followed by the reading of the Rising Star by the Editress. The Emblem, for the first one, had a very encouraging appearance. The Rising Star, though it has but lately made its appearance in the Horizon, shone with almost dazzling brightness. The following question was then chosen for discussion in one week, Resolved that war is conducive of more evil than intemperance. Disputants, Aff. Messrs. Durkee and Davis, Neg. Messrs. Gleed and Robinson. C. Swasey was appointed to write the gentleman's essay for one week and Sarah Somerby the Ladies essay. George Waterman delivered an oration. No other business before the society voted to adjourn one week.

"C. D. SWASEY, Sec. Pro Tem."

Other questions that claimed their attention about that time were: "Resolved that the Maine liquor law ought to be introduced into Vermont. Resolved that the principles of the Whig party tend more to advance the prosperity of the United States than those of the Democratic party. Resolved that a monarchial form of government has more permanence than a republic." And in 1853 they debated the following: "Resolved that women ought to be allowed the right of elective franchise." It was decided in the negative by the President, but in the affirmative by the House.

These meetings of the S. S. F., as the society was popularly called for most of the time, were kept up for more than sixty years, and many a man and woman all over the country can testify to the value he or she derived from these lyceums where training was given in presiding over a public gathering, in debating, and various other forms of self-expression.

In 1855 and 1856 two other literary organizations were formed, the A. D. A. and the V. E. A., the former for the boys and the latter for the girls. At the close of each term these societies held public exercises consisting of music, recitations, essays, etc. At first these associations had the added attraction of secrecy, although always under the control and supervision of the principal. Later the societies were discontinued, but the custom of holding exhibitions at the end of the fall and the winter terms, usually by the Junior Class, was kept up until 1913.

The prosperity of the school continued until the Civil War curtailed its activities. In 1860 over 200 students were registered, but the war clouds which were then piling up cast their shadow even over this remote village. In 1861 one of the boys at the closing rhetorical exercises took as the subject of his oration, "The Horrors of Civil War." Soon the care-free lads, then students, were to know from actual experience what those horrors were. The story of their splendid achievements is told elsewhere in this record. It is enough to say here that when Prin. A. J. Blanchard answered the call to a higher service, resigned as head of the school and marched away as Captain of Company E of the Third Vermont, he took with him a goodly number of his former students.

Soon after the war an important change was made in the management of the Academy. In April, 1866, the following resolution was adopted: "Resolved that B. L. Rand, President of the Board of Trustees, be directed to lease the Academy Building, library, apparatus, and the appurtinences to school district Number One in Morrisville so long as wood grows and water runs upon the terms and conditions that said school district Number One shall during said term keep and maintain a High School or Academy and in all respects carry out and fulfill the stipulations of the lease of said premises by Jedediah Safford to The People's Academy and with the further consideration that said school district shall at all times keep said Academy buildings in suitable repair and well insured and said district shall have the right to repair, enlarge, or alter said buildings in such manner as they may deem advisable for the purpose above set forth and in consideration that said district accept the lease of said property as above set forth, the treasurer of The People's Academy is hereby directed to pay annually to the treasurer of said district all moneys received by him during said time for rents of public lands or otherwise." Thus was closed a picturesque period in the history of the institution when it passed out of the private control of its Board of Trustees whose duties from henceforth were largely honorary.

This transfer of the management was followed by some changes in the policy of the Academy. For example, in 1868, diplomas were granted and the first class was formally graduated with the following program and members:

Class motto—Finis coronat opus
Music
Prayer
Music
Oration, Destiny   A. P. Grout
Oration, The Worker and His Work   C. H. Slocum
Oration, Literature and Its Influence   H. M. Tenney
Oration, Memory of the Past, its Lessons for the
    Future   H. E. Carter
Oration, Vermont and Her Defenders with
    a valedictory address   A. A. Niles
Presentation of Diplomas
Music
Benediction
    Music by the Morrisville Silver Cornet Band

District Number One was keenly alive to the educational needs of its children, and both Academy and graded buildings were proving inadequate. So in 1874 the Academy building, erected at so much sacrifice by Thomas Tracy and his associates, was moved to Pleasant Street, where it is now occupied by the Lamoille Grange and Lanpher's feed store, and the building used for more than fifty years was constructed with the idea of housing both grades and Academy in the same structure. The grades occupied the first floor, the Academy students the second floor, while on the third was a commodious hall in which all public exercises were held.

These enlarged facilities were naturally emphasized and the catalogue for 1875 and 1876 was quite elaborate. The classes are listed as Senior Class, Middle Class, Junior Class, and Preparatory Class, which included the sixth and seventh grades. The course of study for the grades was included and the teaching force consisted of A. J. Blanchard, Principal, with a preceptress, teacher of vocal and instrumental music, teacher of penmanship, and three grade teachers. The class of '75, the first to be graduated from the new building, numbered seven, four boys and three girls. It is indicative of the type of student and of the character of the school that all of the boys went to college, three to Dartmouth and one to the University of

Vermont. Thus the Academy was the head of the school system of District Number One, the catalogue emphasized the fact and the diplomas were granted from Peoples Academy and the Morrisville Graded School.

By a change in the state law in 1892 the districts were abolished and the year following H. H. Powers, P. K. Gleed, and J. C. Noyes were elected by the trustees a committee to confer with a similar committee from District Number One to arrange for the management of the Academy under the new system. Tuition for the pupils from without the district was done away with and the entire town has been free to enjoy its advantages in return for the payment of the town school tax.

In 1895 the Lamoille County Summer School was established and its two weeks' sessions were held in the Academy. This was made possible through the increase in state aid to summer schools which the General Assembly of 1894 granted, and such sessions were held for several years. Thus the Academy contributed to the larger educational life of the county.

In 1912 and 1913, in order to keep in line with similar movements in other High Schools in the state, the curriculum was expanded to include a Teacher Training Course, a Home Economics Course, and a course in Agriculture. The latter never seemed to be in great demand and was dropped after a few years. The Teacher Training Course was popular, but its close proximity to the Johnson Normal School led the State Department to give it up.

In line with the policy quite general throughout the state, in 1919 seventh and eighth grades were abolished and a Junior High School established in their stead. These various changes and additions would have been impossible had not more room been provided. In 1899 the town voted to build a graded school building and a pleasant four-room structure was erected, which left the entire building free for the use of the Academy. This new graded building was soon outgrown, and in 1917 money was appropriated for enlarging it; and a $25,000 addition was made which doubled its capacity. In the basement of this new building were located the Home Economics Department and the science laboratory, while the Junior High rooms were on the second floor except for a short time.

The year 1927 marked another epoch in the history of Peoples Academy, for at that time the gift of its beautiful new home was made.

The story of poor boys who have gone to the city and there won fame and fortune is not unusual in this country, and often they have remembered their birthplaces with generous benefactions, but it is doubtful if any of them ever made any more practical manifestation of their love for their birthplaces than did Mr. A. H. Copley, donor of Peoples Academy-Copley Building and Copley Hospital. Alexander H. Copley was born in 1856 in the old hotel, the first Morrisville House, his mother being the widow of Mr. F. L. Matthews, so long its proprietor. At the age of ten he was left an orphan without resources and went for a time to live with relatives in Elmore and elsewhere. When old enough to plan for himself, he returned to Morrisville and learned the drug business in the A. O. Gates store. Then, like many another Vermont lad, he left his native state for Boston. There in addition to his drug business he began to deal in real estate. His industry, frugality, and foresight were rewarded and manhood found him successful in the best sense of the word.

But his home town still kept its grip upon his heart strings. To it he returned for his bride, Miss Lucy Page, daughter of Charles R. Page of the Malvern Stock Farm, and he bought the height of land known as Thomas Hill, which, as a boy, he had coveted because of the wonderful view to be obtained from it. The death of his wife changed the plans he had made for erecting a summer home upon the plateau, and in time he began to think of making some large benefaction. At first he considered erecting a hospital, but a study of local conditions led him to the conclusion that one such as he had planned was inadvisable, although the idea of a hospital was not given up as his later donation proved. At length he decided that in no better way could he serve the community than by improving the facilities of Peoples Academy. At first he intended to give a sum of money toward the erection of an adequate schoolhouse on the site of the building then standing. It soon became evident there was not room enough to construct such with sufficient grounds, so he offered to build, at his own expense, a modern building on the hill, and present it to the town on the condition that the town would remove the old Academy, and construct and maintain a suitable approach and connect it with the village lighting, water, and sewerage systems. At a special meeting the town gladly complied with his conditions and during 1928 and 1929 the building was in process of construction.

On September 11, 1929, it was opened for use, but its formal dedication was not held until Commencement of the June following, which was a gala event for the entire town. All the business places and many private residences were decorated with P. A. colors, Green and Gold, and pennants of the same color outlined the approach, now called Copley Avenue, and Main Street.

The event had called together a large number of Alumni and they, together with townspeople, filled the auditorium and halls long before the hour set for the opening exercises. The following program was carried out:

DEDICATION EXERCISES
PEOPLES ACADEMY-COPLEY BUILDING
MORRISVILLE, VERMONT
MONDAY, JUNE 16, 1930
EIGHT P. M.

PROGRAM

Hon. Frederick G. Fleetwood, Presiding

Music	Peoples Academy Orchestra
Invocation	Rev. G. E. Goodliffe
Presentation of the Building	Mr. Alexander H. Copley
Acceptance for the Town	Mr. C. H. A. Stafford
	Chairman of the Board of School Directors
Music	Peoples Academy Orchestra
Acceptance for the State	Mr. Clarence H. Dempsey
	Commissioner of Education, State of Vermont
Vocal Solo	Miss Grace Limoge
Dedication Address	George M. Powers, Class of '79
	Chief Justice of the Supreme Court of Vermont

Acceptance for Peoples Academy Students
Leon Morris White
President of the Senior Class
Benediction   Rev. G. A. Coburn
Reception to Mr. A. H. Copley

The building is a beautiful structure, 60x145 feet, constructed of tapestry brick with granite trimmings and pillars of Indiana limestone at the entrance. On the first floor there is an auditorium capable of seating 450, with study and recitation rooms; on the second floor are the laboratories, drafting room, commercial rooms, sewing room, etc., while in the basement the cooking rooms, manual training department, locker rooms, lunch room and a modern gymnasium are found. The building is equipped with all the modern appliances, such as humidifiers, automatic heat control, telephones in each room, electric clocks, and adequate fire protection.

The large tract of land permitted laying out a large athletic field north of the building, while the beautiful lighting of the avenue, the terracing of the embankments on either side of the approach, and the grounds at the brow of the hill have made a beauty spot of this height and have given the school a home worthy of its past and an inspiration for its future.

PEOPLES ACADEMY ALUMNI ASSOCIATION

The present Alumni Association was the outgrowth of a meeting held on December 29, 1892, to which all graduates of the school had been invited. At this gathering, which was largely attended, a permanent organization was effected by the election of the following officers: President, Mr. Thomas C. Cheney; Vice-President, Miss Lillian J. Leach; Secretary, Miss Mellie M. Slayton; Treasurer, Miss Alice C. Doty.

The object of the Association was "for the purpose of helping the Academy in every possible way and of annually bringing together the former students, thereby renewing old acquaintances and forming new ones."

The class of 1892 probably originated the idea of the Alumni Banquet, for as a feature of their commencement they held a class banquet. The June following the first annual banquet of Peoples Academy Alumni Association was held on the night of graduation at The Randall, with the following program:

Toastmaster, Hon. H. Henry Powers

President's Welcome	T. C. Cheney
The School and the Town	Hon. G. W. Hendee
Our Students in the Rebellion	Hon. U. A. Woodbury
Poem	Lavinia L. Plumley
The Legal Fraternity	Hon. P. K. Gleed
Prophecy	M. S. Stone
The Academy and U. V. M.	Hon. R. W. Hulburd
Oration	Geo. M. Powers

Thus was inaugurated a custom which has proved one of the pleasantest features of each succeeding Commencement, and has proved a strong factor in stimulating loyalty to the school. At first the banquets were always held at the hotel, but as the numbers increased, the hotel was unable to accommodate them and they have been held in the vestries of the different churches. The Alumni Association has meant much in the life of the school and doubtless will continue to in the future.

PRINCIPALS OF PEOPLES ACADEMY

The high reputation which Peoples Academy early established and has since maintained has been due in part to the hearty support of the town, in part to its housing and equipment which have always been abreast of the times, but most of all to the excellent character of its teaching force and especially of its principals. Some of them, as was the custom in early days, taught in order to secure money with which to fit themselves for other professions, but most of them chose teaching as a life work, and many went from this school to important fields of educational endeavor.

It is impossible at this time to gather data concerning all who have guided the destiny of the institution, but a brief survey of the ones whose records can be obtained seems fitting.

This educational infant, brought forth at so much sacrifice and effort, was entrusted to the care of Ozias C.

Pitkin, who came from a well known Montpelier family, being the son of Alfred and Orpha W. Pitkin of that town. He was born in 1827 and twenty years later was graduated from Dartmouth College and at once took up his duties at Peoples Academy. After two years, he went to Taunton, Mass., where he taught five years and found his bride in the person of Caroline Muenscher. In 1854 he went to Chelsea, Mass., where he was principal of the High School for sixteen years. Then on account of growing deafness he gave up teaching, and moved to Syracuse, N. Y., where he went into business as an analytical and manufacturing chemist. In 1905 he had a stroke of paralysis, from which he never recovered, and died at the home of a daughter in Elmira, N. Y., in 1906.

The second principal, Melvin Dwinell, was unique in that he was the only head of this school and one of the few Vermonters who wore the Confederate gray. He was born at East Calais, Vt., in 1825, fitted for college at Montpelier Academy and received his degree from the University of Vermont in 1849. He came to Morrisville that fall. After two years he went south to Georgia, where he taught for three years, and then bought "The Rome Courier." When the Civil War broke out, he was pro-Union until Georgia seceded. Then, like so many other Southerners, he placed his allegiance to his state above that to the Union, and enlisted in the Eighth Georgia Volunteers and finally attained the rank of captain. He was wounded in the service, and at the close of the war returned to Rome to find that his printing plant had been wrecked and that he must begin at the bottom if he would again build up his business. Of that new beginning he says: "I soon got type enough to print small circulars, hand bills, etc., using a planer and mallet for lack of a press." "The Courier" was re-established and he was its publisher for more than a quarter of a century. In his later years he traveled extensively, both in this country and abroad, and published a volume, entitled "Common Sense Views of Foreign Lands." His death occurred at Rome, Georgia, in 1887.

Of Mr. Dwinell's successor, A. C. Baker, who taught in 1851 and 1852, nothing can be learned, and in 1853 two principals are given, J. Gilbert and E. Wheelock, but nothing has been ascertained about their subsequent careers.

Charles Henry Heath, the sixth principal and the first alumnus of the school to be called to head it, was one whose interest in the institution was of long duration and of great value. He was born in Woodbury, Vt., in 1829, and educated in the public schools of that town and at Peoples Academy. After completing his studies here, he went to the University of Vermont and was graduated in 1854 and received his Master's degree three years later. For four years after his graduation he acted as principal, at the same time studying law with Thomas Gleed. He was admitted to the Lamoille County Bar in 1858, and settled at Plainfield, Vt., practicing there until 1872, when he moved to Montpelier, where he continued to practice until his death, in 1889. One of the ties which bound him to Morrisville was his marriage to Sara Putnam, daughter of Dr. David W. Putnam, of this town. After leaving he served as trustee for many years, was a member of the Board of Examiners, and was the speaker on different occasions in the history of the school.

Malcolm McKillop was a westerner by birth, being a native of Inverness, Calif., but he entered the University of Vermont from Northfield, Vt., and graduated with the class of 1861. He taught here the year following, and then returned to his native state, where he taught and studied law and was admitted to the bar in California in 1865. He acted as County Superintendent of Schools, and filled different political offices, but later came to Missouri, where he entered the banking business, and was active in politics. He died at Rock Port, Mo., in 1899.

George B. Cochran was a native of Northfield, Vt., and a graduate of the University of Vermont in the class of 1862. He taught at Peoples Academy the year of 1862-1863 and then in Stowe, Vt., and in Gouverneur, N. Y. He decided to enter the medical profession and received his degree of M. D. from the University of Vermont in 1867. He began to practice in Newbury, Vt., but later moved to Massachusetts.

George P. Byington, who succeeded Principal Cochran for a year, was a native of Hinesburg, Vt., who came to Peoples Academy following the completion of his studies at the University of Vermont in 1863. He later studied for the ministry and held pastorates in several Vermont towns, later going to Massachusetts.

HISTORY OF MORRISTOWN 103

The period of the war were years of stress for the school. Each year saw a change of leadership. Mr. Byington was succeeded by Preceptress Almira Benton, and she in turn by C. A. Vorce, who, in the middle of the year, gave place to George Bliss. When A. J. Sanborn took over the school in September, 1866, its fortunes were at a low ebb. He restored its morale and the confidence of the community in it, but in 1869 he left to take charge of the newly opened Green Mountain Seminary at Waterbury Center, started under the auspices of the Freewill Baptists.

The loss which the school suffered in the retirement of Mr. Sanborn was met by the appointment of Fernando C. Hathaway, who came in the fall of 1869 and remained until his death, on July 6, 1873. He was the son of Loam Hathaway of Calais, Vt., and after completing his preparatory course at Hardwick he entered Dartmouth College in 1864, and was graduated among the first of his class four years later. Being a thorough student, it was natural that he should choose teaching as his life work, and he spent his first year out of college as head of Hardwick Academy. Here he married Miss Hattie Woodbury in 1869. Then he became principal of Peoples Academy, to which he gave the remainder of his brief life in conscientious service. The type of work he did is indicated by the fact that in the fall of 1872 he was appointed a member of the State Board of Education. His death at the early age of twenty-nine cut short a promising career.

Mr. Hathaway was succeeded by a man later to be known in all parts of the United States as an efficient educator. George Augustus Gates, born at Topsham, Vt., was educated at St. Johnsbury Academy and Dartmouth College. Immediately after his graduation from the latter institution, he came to Peoples Academy with all the vigor and enthusiasm of a well balanced youth. He had decided to enter the ministry, so after two years here he went to Andover Theological Seminary. His first pastorate was in Upper Montclair, N. J. After seven years of fruitful service there he accepted a call to the presidency of Iowa College at Grinnell, Iowa. To this institution he gave thirteen of the best years of his life, proving himself to be an able administrator and a constructive educator. He received flattering calls to the presidency of Dartmouth College and another eastern college, but he remained at Grinnell until the serious illness of his wife made a change of climate necessary. When he was called to be the head of Pomona College at Claremont, Calif., he accepted because the change promised to be good for Mrs. Gates.

This young institution was heavily burdened with debt and Mr. Gates at once started upon a financial campaign, and gave himself for eight years to the difficult task of building up all departments of the institution. In 1909 he felt obliged to resign because of his own health. As soon as it became known, the trustees of Fisk University at Nashville, Tenn., renewed their invitation for him to become president of that institution. When arrangements were made so that he was relieved from most of the financial burden, Dr. Gates accepted, for he felt it represented one of the greatest opportunities for service in the country. After two years of successful work there he received injuries in a railroad accident, from the effects of which he never recovered, and he died in 1912. Of his work at Peoples Academy his wife in her life of him says: "He proved himself an able administrator and an especially inspiring teacher and won friendships which lasted to the time of his death."

Andrew J. Blanchard, who was twice principal, was born in Cabot, Vt., in 1828, and came to take charge of the school in 1858. With the outbreak of the Civil War he resigned and enlisted as Captain of Company E, Third Vermont Regiment, in May, 1861. After his term in the army was ended, he went to Illinois, where he remained some years, but came East again and was principal of Peoples Academy in 1875 and 1876. In the autumn of 1876 he returned to Sycamore, Ill., and entered upon a long and successful career as principal of the High School of that city, serving for more than twenty-five years. Mr. Blanchard died in 1903.

Dartmouth College has furnished a large number of principals for this school, and among the best loved of them was Charles Darwin Adams. Born at Keene, N. H., in 1856, he prepared for college at Lawrence Academy, Groton, Mass., and received his degree from Dartmouth in the class of 1877. He came to Morrisville at once, and remained here until 1879, when he entered Andover Theological Seminary, where he studied for two years. Professor Adams himself said: "I had not expected to make teaching my life work, but the boys and girls at Peoples Academy made the work so delightful that I had to keep on but never with finer response from students."

At any rate instead of entering the ministry he became teacher of Greek and Physical Science at Cushing Academy for three years, until he received an offer to become Professor of Greek at Drury College, Springfield, Mo. After nine years of successful work there, President Tucker of Dartmouth invited him to come back to his Alma Mater as head of the Greek Department, where he taught from 1893 to 1927. In the latter year Dartmouth conferred upon him the degree of Doctor of Literature and he became Professor Emeritus. He also received the degree of Doctor of Philosophy from the University of Kiel, Germany, in 1891.

His ability as a teacher is attested by this long and honorable career in the class room; his scholarship by the fact that he was chosen to edit several texts in the Loeb Classical Library, and also in the series, "Our Debt to Greece and Rome," and was editor of the "Classical Journal" for five years. The large place he held in the hearts of his students, both at Peoples Academy and in his later career, show the strength and excellence of his character.

Professor Adams was succeeded by D. M. Weld, who, after one year, gave place to Dana M. Dustan, who received his education at Kimball Union Academy, at Meriden, N. H., and was graduated from Dartmouth College in 1880. He began a successful teaching career at Peoples Academy in September, 1880, remained here two years, and for twenty years more followed that profession in different Massachusetts schools. In 1902 he became special agent for the Connecticut Mutual Life Insurance Co., with headquarters in Worcester, Mass., a position which he held until his death in that city, in 1928.

Another brilliant man who presided over the destiny of Peoples Academy was Hollis S. Wilson, who was a native of Johnson, Vt., a graduate of Peoples Academy in the class of 1877 and of the University of Vermont in 1881. He began his teaching career at Hyde Park, but came to Morrisville in 1882, and acted as principal, while at the same time studying law in the office of Powers and Gleed. After his admission to the Lamoille County Bar, in 1886, he resigned his principalship, and entered into partnership with George M. Powers, a connection which lasted until 1890. In the meantime he had married Miss Grace Hyde, a pupil of his both at Hyde Park and at Peoples Academy. In June, 1890, the Wilsons went to The Dalles, Oregon, where they remained a few years and then went to Portland of that state, where he gained recognition as the leading lawyer of the state and amassed a considerable fortune. He gave up much of his practice about 1930.

Another alumnus of Peoples Academy, who was called to be its principal, was Mason S. Stone, who was born in Waterbury Center in 1859, the son of Orson and Candace (Mason) Stone. He was educated in the schools of that town and at Peoples Academy, and was graduated from the University of Vermont in 1883. He took up teaching as a profession and after a short period in other towns in the state came to Morrisville in 1886. After three years here, he resigned to engage in supervisory work in both Vermont and Massachusetts.

In 1892 he returned to Vermont as its State Superintendent of Education. He added to his general knowledge and experience by acting as Superintendent of Schools for the Island of Negros in the Philippines for some years, but returned to Vermont in 1905 and again became head of the educational department of the state. During the war he was active in different kinds of war work, holding among other offices that of assistant to the State Fuel Administrator. He also entered into politics somewhat, and in 1918 was elected Lieutenant-Governor. His continued interest in Vermont and in the cause of education is shown by his generous gifts to the University of Vermont.

To be connected with the same school for more than a quarter of a century and to be a strong moulding force in the lives of more than 300 young people who received their diplomas from his hand was the fortune of Mr. William A. Beebe, who was principal from 1889 to 1912.

Mr. Beebe was a native of Malone, N. Y., and came to Morrisville immediately after his graduation from the University of Vermont. His first graduating class numbered three, his largest one twenty-eight. During his administration the teaching force was more than doubled, and the curriculum was so enriched that the graduates of the school were admitted to the leading colleges of the East without examination.

Mr. Beebe was a thorough student, a firm disciplinarian, and a natural teacher who left a permanent imprint upon all who came under his care. He was also a strong influence in the community. The soldiers' monument is a testimony of his artistic ability, since he designed it. He was a trustee of the local library and a member of the building committee when the present structure was erected. He was an active member of the Congregational Church, and a worker for all worth-while causes.

In 1891 he married Miss Cora Mudgett of Cambridge, who was a helpmate in every sense of the word. After leaving Morrisville he carried on supervisory work in Proctor, Vt., and Bristol, Vt., and upon retiring from active educational service he went to Underhill, Vt., to reside, where his death occurred, in 1933.

Arthur W. Ruff, who succeeded Mr. Beebe for two years, fitted for college at the High School of Schenectady, N. Y., and was graduated from Yale in the class of '09, and had three years' teaching experience before coming to Peoples Academy. His coming marked a change both in the management and the curriculum of the school. Courses in agriculture, home economics, and teacher training were added and the teaching force was increased to meet these new features. These changes met with some opposition, and Mr. Ruff was confronted with a difficult situation which he faced with tact and ability.

Mr. Ruff's successor was Rollo G. Reynolds, a native of Cambridge, Vt., who received his High School training at Brookline, Mass., and was graduated from Dartmouth College in 1910. Following his graduation, he taught in Juniata College, Huntingdon, Penn., where he met and married Miss Alice MacCarthy. He was principal of the Cambridge High School and of the Stowe High School before coming to Peoples Academy. Early in his second year here, he resigned to become Executive Clerk in the office of the State Superintendent of Education at Montpelier. During the World War he was Director at Camp Vail at Lyndon Center, where the boys of the state were given intensive training in farm work. He later began teaching in the Horace Mann School in New York City, of which he is now principal, and also Professor of Education at Columbia University.

J. Thatcher Sears, who filled the vacancy caused by Mr. Reynolds' resignation, came from five years' experience as head of a private school in Stamford, Conn. Mr. Sears was a Harvard graduate, and embodied many of the traditions of that institution, and went from here to continue his educational work at Glens Falls, N. Y.

Lyman C. Hunt, who came to Peoples Academy in September, 1917, was a graduate of the University of Vermont and had taught three years in Champlain, N. Y., prior to coming to Morrisville. It was with genuine regret that after he had taught one year the School Board received his resignation, and he went to head the Spaulding High School at Barre, and later was called to be Superintendent of Schools in Burlington, Vt.

In the stress of the World War period Mary Jean Simpson, who had previously taught here and knew local conditions, was called to the principalship. She studied at Mt. Holyoke College, but received her degree from the University of Vermont and had had a varied teaching experience before becoming head of the school. The fine response which the students made to the unusual demands of that memorable year was due in no small degree to her leadership. After one year she resigned, and later served several years as Bill Clerk of the United States Senate, and in 1933 and 1934 was Director of Women's Work, Civil Works Administration, for the State of Vermont.

Miss Simpson was succeeded by Lucian H. Burns, a graduate of New Hampshire State Agricultural College. He had taught two years at Leominster, Mass., before coming to Peoples Academy. During his principalship the change was made from the seventh and eighth grades to the Junior High School, a change which was made in many other schools of the state. Mr. Burns was principal for two years and has continued his educational work in other towns in the state.

Willis R. Hosmer, who succeeded Mr. Burns, was a graduate of Williams College in the class of 1902 and came to Morrisville from Fair Haven, Vt., where for a long period of years he had been principal of the High School and later district superintendent. His ability, both as teacher and administrator, was generally recognized, and after one year here he was called to head the Spaulding High School of Barre, Vt. Thus twice within five years the largest High School in the state came to Peoples Academy for its principal.

During the school year of 1922 Robert R. Morrow was the principal. He had received his Master's degree from Columbia University and came from Poultney, Vt., where he had been a district superintendent.

Mr. Morrow's successor was Paul E. Pitkin, a westerner by birth, who prepared for college at Goddard Seminary, Barre, Vt., and was a graduate of Middlebury College. Previous to coming here he had been principal of McIndoes Academy, McIndoes Falls, Vt., and after leaving here was for two years supervising principal of the Charleston High and Rural Schools in West Charleston, Vt. He then took up the insurance business, with headquarters at Bennington, Vt.

The school was especially fortunate in having associated with it for several years so fine and rich a personality as that of Maude M. Chaffee. Born in Morristown, she received her education in its rural schools and at the Academy, from which she was graduated in 1902. After completing her studies at the University of Vermont, she taught at Bellows Free Academy, in Fairfax, Vt., for five years and then went to the Edmunds High School at Burlington, Vt., as teacher in mathematics. Sickness in the home obliged her to resign, and she came back and entered upon her work at her Alma Mater. For seven years she was instructor and assistant principal, and in 1925 became its head.

To the school she literally gave her life, since the year 1929 in which the change from the old building to the new was made proved a serious tax upon her strength, and in the summer of 1930 it was found tuberculosis had developed. She was given a leave of absence for a year, with Ralph E. Noble, who had been head of the English Department since 1925, as acting principal. She was never able to resume her work and died on November 21, 1931.

Probably no teacher ever enjoyed the love and respect of her pupils more fully than did Miss Chaffee, and this esteem was the result of the love and confidence she bestowed upon them. She was an inspiring teacher and a rare woman who left an abiding influence upon the school.

One of the sad pages in the history of the principals of Peoples Academy is the record of the career of James Greig. He was born in Aberdeen, Scotland, in 1901, and came to Barre, Vt., when five years of age. He was graduated from the University of Vermont in 1924, and came to Peoples Academy as instructor in 1930. He proved his worth and ability so quickly that, when it became evident that Miss Chaffee would not be able to resume her duties as head of the school, he was made its principal in 1931. During that year he gained the love and respect of both students and townspeople, and both shared in the general sorrow at his death, which occurred in July, 1932.

To fill the vacancy caused by Mr. Greig's death the school turned to the man whom it had previously tested in various ways and had not found wanting. Ralph E. Noble had been instructor and assistant principal for five years and acting principal one year and then was elected superintendent of the Lamoille South District. When Peoples Academy again faced an emergency, Mr. Noble responded by becoming its head.

He is a native of Randolph, Vt., and a graduate of Dartmouth College. Before coming to Morrisville he had been principal of the Underhill High School at Underhill, Vt. Mr. Noble is a man of the highest character and a teacher of the first rank, as well as an able administrator, and under his direction the school enjoyed a high degree of prosperity.

Once again Barre looked to Morrisville for educational leadership, and in the spring of 1934 elected Mr. Noble Superintendent of Schools in that city.

Mr. Merwin Forbes, a graduate of Norwich University in the class of 1932, who, as teacher of science for the two years preceding had made an excellent record, was promoted to fill the vacancy caused by Mr. Noble's resignation.

PEOPLES ACADEMY STUDENTS

The record of the lives of many of the students of Peoples Academy has been given elsewhere in connection with their services to the state, but it has always been characteristic of Vermont to contribute freely of her best to other states. Thus many of the students of this Academy have done their life work far from the scene of their school days. The following are some not included elsewhere whom the Academy is proud to claim as Alumni:

HISTORY OF MORRISTOWN 111

Among the students attracted to Peoples Academy in its early days was Constans Liberty Goodell of Calais, who was graduated from the University of Vermont in the class of 1855, a Phi Beta Kappa man. He then attended Andover Theological Seminary and was ordained to the Congregational ministry in 1859. His first pastorate was in New Britain, Conn. In 1872 he was called to the Pilgrim Congregational Church of St. Louis, Mo., where he stayed until his death, in 1886, being one of the leading ministers west of the Mississippi River.

From Westfield, Vt., came Carroll S. Page, a student here in 1857. He became a well known figure in both the business and political worlds. For years he was president of the Lamoille County National Bank and the Lamoille County Savings Bank & Trust Co., but was better known for his business in green calfskins, the largest of its kind in the world. He was equally successful in his political career, being Governor of Vermont from 1890 to 1892, and United States Senator from 1909 to 1923.

A fellow student of Mr. Page was Urban A. Woodbury, who was born in Acworth, N. H., in 1838, but came to Vermont when he was two years of age. He was educated in the public schools and at Peoples Academy and was a graduate of the Medical School at Burlington, Vt. Mr. Woodbury had a fine record in the Civil War, and was later a prominent business man in Burlington, Vt. He was Mayor of that city and in 1888 was elected Lieutenant-Governor of the state and was its Governor in 1894.

John W. Simpson of East Craftsbury was the first of that family to be connected with this institution. He afterwards became a member of the well known law firm of Simpson, Thacher, and Bartlett of New York City. His niece, Mary Jean Simpson, was teacher and principal, while his nephew, John W., was a graduate in the class of 1909. The latter received his degree from Amherst in 1913 and from the Harvard Law School, and after being admitted to the bar entered his uncle's law office in New York City. He saw service in the World War and after his return from France resumed the practice of law with the firm of Gleason, McLanahan, Merritt, and Ingraham of New York City.

Harlan P. French, a student here in 1859, was a familiar figure in educational circles as the manager of the Albany Teachers' Agency. The school had no more loyal alumnus than Mr. French, who established the prizes which bear his name, awarded each Commencement to the young man and the young woman who write the best oration and essay.

Among the students of the 60's to give a good account of himself was Don D. Grout, a native of Morristown, who was to become one of the best known physicians and surgeons in the state. Dr. Grout was in charge of the bill providing for a State Hospital for the Insane and was the Superintendent and Treasurer of that institution at Waterbury for the last fifteen years of his life.

Another student of that period was Frank Plumley, who was born in Eden, Vt., in 1844, studied at the Academy and also in the law office of Powers and Gleed. Later he completed his law studies at the University of Michigan. He began the practice of law at Northfield, Vt. He was elected to various legislative offices and in 1902 was elected Chief Judge of the Vermont Court of Claims. President Roosevelt appointed him umpire in the Mixed Claims Commission in the case of Great Britain and Venezuela, of Holland and Venezuela, and of France and Venezuela. In 1908 he was elected a Representative in Congress and was re-elected twice, but declined further nomination.

J. C. Fremont Slayton was born in Calais, Vt., but received the greater part of his education in this town, being a student at Peoples Academy from 1869 to 1871. He was engaged in the wholesale produce business in Boston for more than forty years, and was also associated with large real estate enterprises in that city. He was a member of the Governor's Council during the term of office of John L. Bates, and at his death, in 1922, both Gov. Channing B. Cox and Ex-Governor Bates paid tribute to his services to the city and state.

Benjamin H. Sanborn, for years a well known figure in the publishing world, was a native of Morristown and an active factor in its life during his school days. Like many other Vermont lads he went to Boston to seek his fortune, and obtained a position with the publishing house of Robert S. Davis & Co. In 1883 he became a member of the firm of Leach, Shewell, and Sanborn, and fifteen years later withdrew from it, and organized the firm of Benj. H. Sanborn and Co., with which he was connected until his retirement from active business, in 1912. Mr. Sanborn showed his continuing interest in the school by presenting it with a flag and by offering the prizes given for years in connection with the Sanborn Prize Speaking.

Jesse Eugene Thompson was born in Jericho, Vt., in 1853, but his parents moved to Morristown when he was a boy, and he completed his studies at Peoples Academy in 1875. He studied at the Medical School in Burlington and received his degree of M. D. from the City of New York Medical College. For forty years he was a prominent physician in Rutland, Vt., specializing in diseases of the eye and ear. He died in Rutland, in 1922, one of the most beloved and respected citizens of that city.

Another successful physician is Willis A. Tenney, who was graduated from the Medical College of the University of Vermont in the class of 1877, and has made a large place for himself in the life of the people of Granville, N. Y.

Roger W. Hulburd entered Peoples Academy from the neighboring town of Waterville, completed his studies in 1876, and was graduated from the University of Vermont in 1882. He was principal of Lamoille Central Academy several years before taking up his life work as lawyer. He was Lieutenant-Governor of Vermont from 1917 to 1919, and was generally recognized as one of the best orators and after dinner speakers in the state.

Had anyone prophesied as to the future of the members of the class of 1881 he probably would not have selected Charles Waterman as the one to attain the highest position, yet such was the change which the years brought. Born in Waitsfield, Vt., in 1851, he studied here and received his degree from the University of Vermont in 1885. He taught several years and then was graduated from the University of Michigan Law School. He settled at Denver, Colo., and became a member of the law firm of Wolcott, Vaile, and Waterman. As council for the Great Western Sugar Co., the Chicago, Rock Island and Pacific R. R., the Denver and Rio Grande R. R., the Great Western R. R., and other corporations he amassed a fortune which enabled him to retire from active practice and enter politics. In 1927 he was elected Senator from Colorado, which position he held until his death, in 1932. His love for his native state was shown by his making the University of Vermont the ultimate recipient of the bulk of his property.

Alice H. Bushee, P. A. 1886, is one of the students of whom her Alma Mater is proud. After graduation from Mt. Holyoke College, she taught in Spain at the Colegio Internacional. She was then invited to Wellesley College, where she is chairman of the Spanish Department. She is a corresponding member of the Spanish-American Academy of Science and Arts in Cadiz. Her election in 1924 to the Hispanic Society of America, a distinguished international organization limited to 100 members who are outstanding in their various fields, is a tribute to her work as a scholar and teacher. In addition to her work as teacher, Miss Bushee has contributed to various leading magazines and written a Spanish textbook for college students.

Thomas C. Cheney is a descendant of Nathan Gates, one of the early settlers at Cadys Falls, and has proved to be a most helpful citizen in both town and state. He was graduated from Peoples Academy in 1886 and from the University of Vermont in 1891, and began the study of law in the office of Powers and Gleed, and was admitted to the Lamoille County Bar in 1895. He entered into partnership with George M. Powers, a relationship which lasted until the latter was made Judge. Mr. Cheney has probably had a longer direct connection with the Legislature at Montpelier than any other man in the state. From 1894 to 1898 he was Assistant Clerk of the House of Representatives and Clerk for the next eight years. The four years following he was Speaker of the House and from 1915 to 1923 he was Legislative Draughtsman. He gave up the practice of law for the insurance business, and is a director of the Vermont Mutual Fire Insurance Co., and Chairman of the New England Advisory Board of Insurance Agents. He has served as Trustee of the University of Vermont for several years.

Another student of that period was Carroll B. Merriam, whose father, E. B. Merriam, went to Topeka, Kans., and became a prosperous banker. The son followed his father's business and in the recovery efforts introduced by the Roosevelt administration in 1933, Mr. Merriam was made head of the Deposit Liquidation Board.

Bert E. Merriam, a native of Elmore, was graduated from Peoples Academy in 1889. For years he was engaged in school work, but with the outbreak of the World War he volunteered for Y. M. C. A. work overseas and continued with that organization after 1918, serving for several years past at Manila, Philippine Islands.

Fred B. Thomas, born in Stowe, was a graduate of Peoples Academy in 1892 and of Norwich University in 1898. He studied law in the office of George W. Wing of Montpelier. He was Collector of Customs at St. Albans, Vt., until 1934, when he returned to Randolph, Vt., to resume the practice of law. At the outbreak of the Spanish-American War he enlisted and during the World War he was Colonel of the First Vermont Infantry, which was redesignated the Fifty-Seventh Pioneer Infantry and remained until that organization was broken up for replacement purposes. He served throughout the war and has been Department Commander of the American Legion of Vermont.

Bert L. Jennings of Elmore, P. A. '94, has held pastorates in several important Methodist churches, among them in Worcester, Mass., and in Venice and in Sinis, Calif.

Hollis Gray of Cambridge, P. A. '94, worked his way up to the presidency of the Winooski Savings Bank, one of the oldest institutions of that kind in the state.

C. Francis Blair, of the class of '95, is a prominent lawyer in Buffalo, N. Y., and a Trustee of the University of Vermont.

Hugh Tyndall, of the class of '05, is a successful surgeon, who has been connected for several years with St. Mary's Hospital, Hoboken, N. J.

Harold H. Fisher, P. A. '07, engaged in the teaching profession until the outbreak of the World War when he served overseas. Then he was one of the group of men who administered relief in famine stricken Russia under the direction of Herbert C. Hoover. Upon his return to the United States he became Vice-Chairman of the Hoover War Library at Leland Stanford University and Associate Professor of History in that institution. He is also Curator of the American Relief Archives and has charge of the research work on the Russion Revolution and has published two volumes on that subject.

H. Clifford Bundy, P. A. '09, is chief surgeon of the Bangor & Aroostook Railroad at Milo, Maine.

Lillian Thompson, née Fisk, has won on enviable reputation as a portrait painter. While in Washington, D. C., several of the prominent people of that city posed for her. She afterwards went to Japan and for several years has resided in Paris.

Ruth Mould, née Greene, P. A. '12, studied and taught art before her marriage to Willis Mould, P. A. '11, who is manager of the Johnson branch of the Eastern Magnesia Talc Co. She has participated in several art exhibitions and has a reputation more than local for her portraits in oils and crayons, landscapes, and block prints.

William M. Meacham, P. A. '15, after teaching in various schools in Vermont, was called to the head of the Farm and Trades School on Thompson's Island, Boston, Mass.

These men and women are only a few of the Alumni of Peoples Academy, who, in all walks of life, have been an honor to themselves and to the school.

THE MORRISTOWN CENTENNIAL LIBRARY

Whatever the education and culture of the early settlers of Morristown may have been, the toil and hardship of their life here made books and reading matter a luxury, and it is probable that few books except the Bible were found in their homes. That they did not forget them, however, is shown by the following article found in the Constitution of the Congregational Society, adopted in October, 1823: "That a library shall be attached to this Society as soon as a majority of the members shall judge it practicable, when a Constitution shall be formed for that purpose."

There is no record of any further action on the part of the Society, but a Sunday School library in connection with each of the different churches was established at an early period, and ministered to the needs of the younger members of the community.

When Peoples Academy was established, a library was collected for use there and the early records of the institution point with pride to the additions made and its excellence.

These collections were not public libraries, however, and it was not until 1885 that there was any general agitation for one. Then there appeared items in the local newspaper setting forth the advantages of such an institution. In that year there came to Morrisville a woman who was not only interested in this project, but capable of executing it. There is no more fitting place in which to pay tribute to the influence of Mrs. Laura Gleed in the community than here.

HISTORY OF MORRISTOWN 117

Laura Kinney Gleed was a native of Bethlehem, N. H., the daughter of William Kinney of the place, but after her marriage to Mr. Henry Fleetwood, in 1863, she went to St. Johnsbury to live, and it was here she married Mr. Philip Gleed, in 1885. Upon coming to Morrisville, she identified herself actively with its life and development. An Episcopalian by birth and belief, she adopted the church of her husband and loyally supported all its activities. She was interested in the material progress of the place, such as better sidewalks and better lighting of the streets, but she was concerned even more with its cultural development. For that reason she hailed the Woman's Club as a means by which women everywhere might broaden their outlook. She was not only the founder of the local club, but for years she was its president. For most people, however, the printed page is the great educator and Mrs. Gleed soon began an active campaign to crystalize sentiment in favor of a public library, giving freely of her time and effort until the project was completed. A survey of the books purchased to launch the undertaking testifies to the soundness and excellence of her literary taste. Any sketch of Mrs. Gleed, however brief, would be incomplete without mention of another dominant characteristic, her hospitality. Her home was always open to the school, the church, or the club, and she loved to gather her friends about her own table for the interchange of ideas. Her death occurred in 1912, but during the quarter of a century she spent here she left a distinct imprint upon the life of the town, and the Woman's Club and the public library are her best memorials.

The Centennial year of the town seemed a favorable time to launch her campaign for the money necessary to start the undertaking. Letters to former residents and interviews with local people brought in the sum of $350 in sums varying from one to fifty dollars. Then Mrs. Gleed applied to Mrs. H. O. Cushman of Boston, daughter of Hon. Luke P. Poland, who began the practice of law in Morrisville, and received from her the generous sum of $1,000. Thus encouraged, a special town meeting was called, at which the town voted to appropriate $1,000, the interest of which should be paid on January first each year. The Resolution of Thanks adopted at that time mentions as donors, besides Mrs. Cushman, J. C. F. Slayton of Boston, E. B. Merriam of Topeka, Kans., R. E. Jennings of New Jersey, the Rev. W. A. Robinson of Homer, N. Y., Mrs. Emily Montgomery, formerly missionary to Turkey, Dr. W. H. Stowe of Palmer, Mass., the Rev. George W. Bailey of Springfield, Vt., B. F. Sanborn of Boston, C. S. and J. W. Gleed of Topeka, Kans., Mrs. Gov. Fairbanks of St. Johnsbury and, Col. D. J. Safford of Augusta, Me.

The Morristown Centennial Library Association was formed the same month, with Allen B. Smith of the Corners its first president. According to its constitution any person of lawful age who is a resident of the town is a member of this Association which meets annually and elects two trustees who hold office for five years. The management of the library is in the hands of this Board of Trustees. Of the money raised $400 was set aside as a permanent fund and the remainder invested in books and the simple furniture required. On April 19, 1891, the library opened for use in the right-hand room in the so-called "Matthews Block," the small building just below the Drowne block.

That the institution met a recognized need is shown by the librarian's report at the second annual meeting of the Association, when there were 518 borrowers and, although it was open only on Tuesdays and Saturdays, 5,081 books were circulated. It at once outgrew its quarters and was moved in June, 1892, to the second floor of the bank building, and a reading room was provided in connection with it. In addition to the interest on the town order already mentioned, the town appropriated $125 for some years, and the balance needed to run it was raised by entertainments. People became more interested and the second year the G. W. Clark fund of $200, later raised to $300, was added to the endowment. In 1901 the D. J. Safford fund of $500, in 1906 the Lucene Louisa Slayton fund of $500, in 1913 the E. J. Hall fund of $368.91, in 1923 the Wheelock fund of $500, in 1925 the Willard Stowe fund of $5,800, and in 1928 the Lucretia Campbell fund of $6,560.61 were added to the permanent endowment.

It was always the purpose of the Association to have it serve the community in every way, and, according to the constitution of the Association, its object is "to disseminate useful knowledge and to contribute in every proper way to the literary, moral, and educational welfare of the community."

Before long the pleasant rooms over the bank were outgrown, and as early as 1910 we find in the minutes of the Association discussion of methods for securing a new building. Mrs. Gleed went about that task in her characteristically vigorous fashion and obtained from the Carnegie Library Foundation a grant. In 1911 the town voted not less than $500 for the maintenance of the library in case the gift of a building could be secured and the year following the village voted $200 annually to supplement the town appropriation, so that $7,000 was obtained from the Foundation. In 1912 the Kelsey lot was purchased as a site, its proximity to the schools making it especially desirable for the purpose. In 1912 and 1913 the present building was erected and opened for use in July, 1913.

The improved facilities and increased income made possible an increase in service to the community. It is now open six days in a week, instead of two, more books and magazines are available, and it is the meeting place of the Woman's Club and other organizations.

CHAPTER VIII

TRANSPORTATION AND COMMUNICATION

INDEPENDENT and self-supporting as these early settlers were, they had to have some means of carrying on intercourse with their fellow pioneers, but the road over which Jacob Walker carried his grist to Cambridge and brought back his needed supplies might more correctly be termed a trail.

The first road in town worthy of the name was surveyed under date of June 11, 1800. So for nearly ten years the settlers had made their own way in a very literal sense. This first road from the Stowe line to the northern boundary of the town, going past Jacob Walker's and through the Corners, was known as the "North and South" road in the records. Another referred to as the "East and West" road began on the Sterling line and extended in a southeasterly direction for seven miles. This may have been the one which intersected the North and South road at the Corners, ran past the Hadley place, the Farr place, and the Wheeler Cemetery. A study of the earliest maps of the town bears out the truth of the traditions that many roads formerly existed which have long since been abandoned.

People speak of the building or opening of the Randolph Road or the LaPorte Road and do not always remember that the process of road building and maintenance was quite different then from what it is today. It was a neighborhood affair, with the school district as the administration unit. Within a certain section one man was appointed highway surveyor, and it was his job to work as overseer while the remaining citizens of the district under his direction "worked out their road tax." This was done in the spring or early summer, and the modern engineer would find little scientific knowledge of grading or drainage displayed.

The spirit of that early method has been caught and expressed by Daniel Cady, in his poem, entitled

"WORKING ON THE ROAD" IN VERMONT

Surveyors, yes; highway surveyors—
    That's what the statutes used to call 'em,
But looking back, that legal title
    Appears too all-fired long and solemn;
They didn't handle much surveying,
    But 'bout the time the pie plant blowed,
They'd get the men and boys together
    And go to fooling with the road.

'Twas great to see the "workers" gather
    With plows, whips, jugs, stoneboats and shovels;
The 'Squire was always on the docket,
    And all the Baxters, Bucks, and Lovells;
They'd bring the same old wooden scraper
    That wouldn't hold but half a load—
But what the Dickens did it matter
    To Freemen working on the road?

They'd hitch a plow to Barret's oxen
    And give the roadsides ripping battle;
Then spread the sod upon the roadway
    And make it soft for sheep and cattle;
And every ten or fifteen minutes
    You'd hear that Highway Boss explode—
"Stick in a waterbar: Gol Darn It
    Can't any of you fix a road?"

They always "worked" the sandy stretches,
    But might as well have hoed the ocean;
They brushed and stoned the Perkins clay bank
    Year after year with deep devotion;
They 'lowed they'd build no "railroad 'bankments,"
    However swift the river flowed—
They knew they'd be there in a twelve-month
    A-working on the same old road.

The following page from an account book of 1881 shows the financial side of the enterprise:

May 16	George Atwood work on road, self, team, and hired man	$3.75
May 17	George Atwood self and man	$2.50
May 16	C. W. Boardman work on road	$1.06
May 16	Nathan Cross work on road	.53
May 16	Heman Cole work on road self, team, and man	$3.75
May 17	Heman Cole work on road self, team, and man ½ day	$1.25
	Heman Cole Plough 1½ days	.75
	Heman Cole, Log for sluice	.60
May 16	Daniel Cole work on road	$2.63
May 16	V. W. Rand work on road 1½ days	$1.87
	V. W. Rand work on road 2 days	$2.50
May 16	W. D. Thomas work on road 1 day	$1.25
May 17	M. C. Mower work on road 3 days	$3.75
	M. C. Mower work on sluice 1 day	$1.25

In the winter the roads were made passable after the heavy storms by ploughing out the snow. Where it had accumulated to any depth, it was necessary to make "turn outs" where teams might pass each other. Under this method there would be a period in the spring when travel was almost impossible, and in 1888 the town purchased and put into use the first roller. The advantage of rolling over ploughing, as stated in the local newspaper, was that it made it "easy to turn out with teams and there is usually a solid bottom till late in the spring."

The advent of the automobile has made desirable the policy of scraping the roads throughout the winter on the main traveled thoroughfares.

Communication with the remote world outside was an even more difficult undertaking, In an article written for the local newspaper several years ago, the daughter of Jacob Walker states that about 1803 her father built a potash and took the product, pearlash, by team to the mouth of the White River, where he exchanged it for hardware, salt, calico, and those other necessities which had to be imported. Other tradesmen probably traded with other centers.

In 1849 the Central Vermont Railroad was built to Waterbury, and that became the source through which the local merchants obtained their stock of goods. The building of the LaPorte Road, much more level than the old North and South road, had simplified the problem a great deal, but the hauling of all supplies eighteen miles was a laborious proceeding, and the town hailed the prospect of more direct contact with the outside world, and was ready to do its part to establish such connections.

At first it seemed that this union might come by way of Waterbury. There was talk of building a railroad from that place to Morrisville, and in 1866 at a special town meeting the selectmen were authorized to subscribe $10,000 for shares in the Mount Mansfield Railroad Company. It seems there may have been some doubt in the minds of the citizens whether it would be a going concern, for they specified that the money should not be expended for surveying, but for actual construction of the road between Stowe and Morrisville. There was also a growing sentiment for a railroad across the state to connect Portland, Maine, and Lake Champlain. In 1867 a convention was held at Montpelier to discuss such a plan, and among those present was George J. Slayton of Morrisville, who conceived the idea of such a road down the Lamoille Valley to the lake. He interested Col. E. B. Sawyer, editor of "The Lamoille Newsdealer," in the plan, and Mr. Sawyer gave it publicity in the columns of his paper. At St. Johnsbury a group of men, the most prominent of whom was Horace Fairbanks, later to be Governor of the state, was pushing the project. In spite of scepticism and opposition its promoters worked unceasingly, and in December, 1869, the first dirt was dug for the Portland and Ogdensburg Railroad.

To hasten construction and to raise funds, several different organizations were formed, and the road from Cambridge Junction to Hardwick was financed by the Lamoille Valley Railroad Co., of which Hon. Waldo Brigham of Hyde Park was president. At a town meeting, held on February 12, 1868, it was voted to accept the act of the Legislature enabling the towns to aid in the construction of the railroad, and also "that the Commissioners to be named by said town subscribe for five hundred fifty shares of the stock in the name of the town, said shares being one hundred dollars each, and the inhabitants also voted that the said commissioners be instructed to subscribe for ten thousand more shares of the stock in said railroad, the shares being one hundred dollars, amounting to one hundred shares of said stock whenever the liability of the town shall cease to build a road from Waterbury to Morristown which $10,000 was voted by said town." V. W. Waterman, George W. Hendee, and A. B. Smith were elected the commissioners to act for the town.

It was more than seven years before the road was completed. The last rail was placed in the town of Fletcher on July 17, 1877. A special train left St. Johnsbury that morning and met another train from Swanton, and Gov. Horace Fairbanks, president of the road, drove a silver spike, the last act in uniting the Connecticut River and Lake Champlain. The road had reached Morrisville by December 28, 1872, and the following extract from "The Lamoille Newsdealer" describes the event:

"Last Saturday a large number of citizens gathered at Morrisville to witness the arrival of the first locomotive, and see the track-layers iron the road. The work was accomplished about 4:30 P. M., when the engine 'St. Johnsbury', with the supply train attached, on which was quite a crowd, backed down to the depot and was greeted by three hearty cheers, and responded with a whistle that echoed far up and down the valley and filled the people with enthusiasm."

Governor Hendee sent the following dispatch:

"Morrisville, Dec. 28, 1872

"Hon. Horace Fairbanks:

"At 4:30 this P. M. our town was joined to the commercial world by 'new ties' and the iron rail at 5:15. The noble engine, 'St. Johnsbury', ran majestically to our depot amid great excitement and cheering. Our entire community send greeting and wish you a long life of happiness, for to you more than any other do they feel indebted for this great event and the consequent prosperous future that is to follow.

"GEO. W. HENDEE"

Which was replied to as follows:

"St. Johnsbury, Dec. 28, 1872

"Hon. Geo. W. Hendee:

"You have my warmest congratulations. A new railroad is a most fitting Christmas present for your community.

"HORACE FAIRBANKS."

In the issue of January 10, 1873, the following report is given:
"Nearly a week and a half now have regular trains been bringing passengers into this valley. The regular train was put on January 1 as previously advertised, and took a full load of passengers to St. Johnsbury under charge of S. W. Parkhurst of Cavendish, conductor, and F. N. Keeler of Hyde Park, baggage master, drawn by the engine 'Hyde Park'. No formal demonstrations were made along the line. At St. Johnsbury a crowd had collected at the depot to welcome the train and three cheers were given at the call of N. P. Bowman, as the passengers got out."

The transfer of freight was soon provided for, and in 1884 the present freight depot was built.

In 1879 the town refunded its indebtedness and issued negotiable bonds for not over $60,000, payable after five years and within twenty years, bearing semi-annual interest at five percent. This burden of extra taxation, no small one for a town with no larger grand list than that of Morristown, was rolled off before the twenty years had elapsed. No wonder at the town meeting of 1890 they "gave three rousing cheers and a tiger in view of the payment of the Town Bonds." With great enthusiasm the meeting voted $500 for the Centennial Celebration.

The road since its inception has had a checkered career. The cost of construction and the upkeep exceeded expectations and its indebtedness increased. After passing into the hands of a receiver it was reorganized under the name of the St. Johnsbury & Lake Champlain Railroad, in 1880. Five years later it passed into the control of the Boston & Lowell Railroad and still later was taken over by the Boston & Maine. The annual deficit incurred by its operation became so great that it was about to be abandoned. On January 1, 1925, it came into the hands of a group of Vermont men who were willing to put work and thought into its management for the sake of the prosperity of the towns through which it ran. The increased business which followed was due in part to good management and to the economies which could be introduced since the road lay entirely within the confines of the state and was not bound by the restrictions of the labor unions. Perhaps the most important factor was the spirit of cooperation which was aroused since the towns realized the seriousness of the situation and the desire to serve the district which the new officers manifested. It was under the efficient management of Mr. E. S. French of Springfield, Vt., the vice-president and manager, whose ability was later recognized by his election to the presidency of the Boston & Maine Railroad. The first year it paid operating expenses, something which had not happened for a long time before; the second year it paid operating expenses and $66,000 interest. In 1927 it had done even better when on the fateful November third the flood struck the state, and the angry waters of the Lamoille began their work of destruction.

No trains came into the station from noon of November third until Monday, December 26. For ten weary disheartening weeks no car whistles regularly echoed through the valley and for a time it seemed they never would again. At the first inspection of the road, it was estimated that it would require $500,000 to restore the system as 160 washouts, twelve bridges, six culverts, and twenty-four landslides wrought havoc with the line. In this town the long bridge between here and Wolcott was swept away, and three deep washouts between here and Hyde Park were nearly as difficult to restore. Unsuccessful attempts were made to get help from the Boston & Maine and the Canadian National roads. In despair the road then turned to the state for help and at the special session of the Legislature, due in no small degree to the efficient work of T. C. Cheney and Justice G. M. Powers of this town, a loan of $300,000 was obtained.

With new courage and vigor the work on the road was taken up and on December 26 the people of Morristown gathered at the station to welcome the first train since November 3. Supt. J. A. Cannon and Assistant Superintendent Darling accompanied the train, the engine was specially decorated and amid the din of whistles from the industrial plants and the cheers of the crowd the train pulled in. Ex-Congressman F. G. Fleetwood voiced the thanks of the people for the work done by the officials, and the Morrisville Military Band contributed its part to the occasion. The following Saturday night the Rotary Club gave a banquet in honor of the men of the pile driving crew who worked every day, including Sundays, from five o'clock in the morning until eight o'clock in the evening for more than a month under most trying weather conditions; also in honor of the large crew who, under the same trying conditions, labored on the roadbed between the station and the Jones Bridge. Gov. John E. Weeks and several of the officials of the road were present on this occasion, and Justice George M. Powers acted as toastmaster.

After ten weeks' time the normal train schedule was resumed. At a cost of $234,000, temporary work had been done which made the road passable. To restore it to normal conditions required more than $215,000 additional.

Thus the road has been maintained in the face of obstacles of all kinds, although in later years its train schedule has been limited, and its freight service is its important source of income.

THE TELEPHONE

Of all the steps in the development of communication none was more important than the introduction of the telephone, which came to Vermont in 1877. One of the pioneer lines in the state was at St. Johnsbury. That they were slow in coming into general use is seen from the fact that, although introduced there in July, 1877, there was no regular exchange in that town until 1880.

Two years later the Bell Telephone Exchange was inaugurated in Morrisville. An item in the issue of "The News and Citizen" of April 20, 1882, reads as follows:

"The telephones are working satisfactorily. The exchange includes four offices at Hyde Park and the following here viz. Judge Powers and A. O. Gates, both places of business and house; H. A. Slayton and Co., P. K. Gleed, B. A. Calkins and Hendee and Fisk, places of business. Morrisville is connected with Hyde Park depot, the bank, and Page's office at the Park. The central office is located in Gates' store. In time the telephone will be the general means of communication between towns."

From this simple beginning has grown the present intricate system which, since 1908, has been housed in its present quarters on the second floor in the Centennial Block and its eight subscribers have increased to 800. The prophecy of the newspaper has been fulfilled within a half century.

As revolutionary a step in the history of transportation as the introduction of the railroad was the invention of the automobile which came to Morristown in 1903 when A. R. Campbell bought his first model, which was the first one in the county. Previous to that C. C. Warren, who was the owner of the first one in the state, had made use of his in coming from his home in Waterbury to attend to his business here in connection with the Warren Leather Co. Thirty years later the main roads in town are kept open to motor traffic the year round and cars from all parts of the country frequent our highways.

AIRPORT

The latest step in transportation has been that of aviation, and in this Morristown has had an interest. Early in 1934, as a result of investigations by the aviation section of the Federal Civil Works Administration, Morrisville was selected as the site of an airport if the town would furnish the site. Again Morristown's generous benefactor, A. H. Copley, of Boston, showed his interest in a tangible way, and purchased thrity-eight acres of land lying between the Elmore Road and Maple Street, most of which is included in the tract known as the old fairground. Workmen began at once to clear the tract and make it suitable for aviation purposes.

The selection of this site was a part of the government policy to construct airports at strategic points throughout the country.

This tract was an ideal location for a golf course as well as an airport and Mr. Copley soon interested himself in developing it along these lines. With the help of local devotees of the game and through the cooperation of the federal government he had constructed a fine nine-hole course with a beautiful club house which commands a view of eight of the nine greens and also the panorama of mountains to the east, south and west.

The house can be heated so is available for winter sports and is built and equipped with all the completeness that has characterized Mr. Copley's other gifts to the town.

CHAPTER IX

MILITARY RECORD

ALTHOUGH Morristown has given to the nation no military leaders of high rank, a careful study of her part in two of the major wars of the country shows that her military record forms a glowing page in her history because of the honorable service of the rank and file of her citizens.

Since Morristown was a trackless forest until after the Revolution had closed, it had no direct contact with that event as did the settlements in the southern part of the state. Indirectly, perhaps, it was affected, for it is a fact that many men from Massachusetts, Connecticut, and New Hampshire, gained first-hand knowledge of this region during their military service, and it may well be that this was true of some of the pioneer settlers in the town. At any rate it is known that several of the early settlers had engaged in the Revolution previous to coming here.

The roll of revolutionary pensioners who received ninety-six dollars a year for their services to the nation included eight names. They were Crispus Shaw, Barzilla Spaulding, John Cole, whose great size (he was six feet, seven inches according to tradition), and ability as a story teller contributed to make him a valuable soldier; Josiah Roberts, who served as a drummer; Moses Weld, also musical, who took his singing book into the army; Samuel Cook, one of the men in Arnold's ill-fated expedition against Quebec; Nathan Gates, who served two years and gained the title of lieutenant; and James Little, who came here in 1800 from Litchfield, Conn., and was said to have been one of three who survived a British prison experience in which several hundred lost their lives. To this list of participants should be added the name of William Small, and probably that of Joseph Safford, Asa Little, Alpha Goodale, and perhaps others.

The military spirit which these men exemplified led to the organization of the Morristown Militia early in the history of the town, with Elisha Boardman the first captain of the body and David Freeman later serving in that capacity. Doubtless this company increased the military efficiency of the town; at any rate, it gave meaning and zest to the annual June Training Day, held on the first Tuesday of that month, when our ancestors laid aside their usual cares and enjoyed wrestling, pitching quoits, and other sports in addition to the military drill.

THE WAR OF 1812

The War of 1812, termed by Woodrow Wilson "a clumsy, foolhardy, haphazard war," was never popular in New England, and in Vermont it was largely the instinct of self-preservation which led to participation in it. As soon as war was declared, the selectmen of several towns in the northern part of the state furnished and supported a small number of men to act as guards in the frontier towns, and Morristown was one of this group. From the Roster of Soldiers in the War of 1812-14, it seems probable that Jonathan Cook, Harvey Olds, and Adam Sumner composed the town's contribution to this body. Both Cook and Sumner saw later service with the United States troops. Joseph Burke enlisted for one year in Capt. James Taylor's Company, in the Thirtieth Regiment, as well as in the company raised in town in 1814. James Sanderson saw service in the Thirtieth Regiment for more than a year as well as in the local company. Heminway's "Gazeteer" states that Clement and Thompson Stoddard enlisted for the war, but their names do not appear in the official roster.

When the British advance on Plattsburg exposed all of Vermont to attack, volunteers from all parts of the state started for Burlington without any regular call. According to the Roster many of them never reached Plattsburg, and still others did not get to Burlington, and their term of service was limited to three or four days. The company organized in Morristown to help in this crisis is credited with eight days' service and was under the command of Capt. Denison Cook. Its roll contains the following names: Lieut. Abner Brigham, Thomas Brown, Asahel Burke, Joseph Burke, Corp. Lyman Carter, Second Lieut. Enos Cole, Samuel W. Cole, Chester Cook, John Felcher, John Hovey, Samuel Joslin, Calvin Keiser, John Keiser, Robert Kimball, Joseph Marshall, Amos Paine, John Parish, James Sanderson, First Sergt. Peleg Scofield, Sergt.

Joseph Sears, Bennoni Shaw, Corp. Crispus Shaw, Sergt. Joseph Sinclair, Luther Small, Musician Alva Spalding, Barzilla Spalding, Equilla Spalding, Sergt. Levi Spalding, Ozias Spaulding, Adam Sumner, Samuel Town, Samuel Warren.

This limited experience doubtless gave greater efficiency to the local military organization which, under the leadership of Denison Cook, was known as the Morristown Light Infantry. This in turn gave way to the Green Mountain Rangers and later to the Morristown Artillery.

The war with Mexico was a matter of little concern to local people, but they came to have a vital interest in one of the questions involved, that of slavery. The Compromise of 1850, especially the Fugitive Slave Act, was very unpopular. This feeling about the great problems of the day was reflected in the local press, the columns of which were filled with accounts of the seizure of escaped slaves in northern states and with speeches which the congressional giants of those days, Seward, Sumner, Everett, and others were delivering. The feeling entered into local politics in the choice of Town Representative, and in 1843 and again in 1846 Moses Terrill, who opposed the extension of slavery, was elected on a Third Party ticket.

It will be remembered that the constitution of the state drawn up in 1777 was the first in the United States to prohibit slavery, and it is safe to say that it fairly represented the attitude of most Vermonters. On the question of the constitutionality of the right of secession, the technical and legal questions involved, the average citizen was not greatly concerned, the possibility of such an act was too remote for him to consider.

Veneration for the Union and the Constitution based upon the principles enunciated by Daniel Webster in his famous reply to Hayne thirty years before had been his heritage.

According to the census, Morristown contained 1,751 inhabitants in 1860. Of this number, 168, or nearly one-tenth of her entire population, went to the front. When one stops to think that this number was recruited entirely from her virile young men, he realizes what it meant to the life of the town. The statistics gathered at the time of the erection of the Soldiers' Monument credited the town with 172 volunteers. According to the Roster of Vermont Volunteers in the War of the Rebellion, published by the state in 1892, one of the men thus assigned, Charles Dodge, enlisted from another town, and this statement is confirmed by members of his family. Two others, Charles Rowell and George Levigne, are not found among the Vermont troops, but may have served with the soldiers of other states. Horace Elsworth is credited to Morristown in the Memorial Volume of the Soldiers of the Civil War and in Heminway's "Gazeteer," but to Underhill in the State Roster. C. W. Boardman, a native of Morristown, was first credited to Stowe, but upon his re-enlistment in December, 1863, was changed to Morristown.

Of this body of soldiers, one attained the rank of lieutenant-colonel, three became captains, six first lieutenants, three second lieutenants, five sergeants and fourteen corporals. This is no unusual record, but that most of them discharged their duties honorably is attested by the fact, reported in the official records, that fifteen men were wounded, seven died of wounds, and six were killed in action; that is, one-thirteenth of the whole number gave their lives for the Union cause, while the ratio for the Northern Army as a whole was one-twenty-fifth. Sixteen died of disease, while nine suffered the horrors of imprisonment and one of this number died at Andersonville.

Men from Morristown were found in eleven different Vermont regiments, in the Second Battery Light Artillery, the Second Regular United States Sharpshooters, the Frontier Cavalry, and the First Vermont Cavalry, but the Third, Fifth, Eighth, Eleventh, and Thirteenth Regiments contained more soldiers from here than the other organizations. So in briefly reviewing the town's contribution to the cause of the Union, the history of these regiments is given more in detail.

It is no exaggeration of the truth to say that the Northern Army contained no better troops than the famous "Old Brigade," the First Vermont Brigade, which was composed of the Second, Third, Fourth, Fifth, and Sixth Regiments, which were joined in May, 1864, by the Eleventh Vermont. The roll of its battles is the record of the major engagements of the Civil War from Lewinsville to Petersburg, and in its splendid achievements the soldiers from this town bore an honorable part.

Company E, of the Third Vermont, was the first company organized in Lamoille County, although individuals had volunteered previous to its formation. Into it flocked twenty-one of the youth of the town, influenced in part by the fact that its first captain was Andrew J. Blanchard, principal of Peoples Academy, whom many of them had come to know and respect in that capacity. The rendezvous of the Third was at St. Johnsbury on the grounds of the Caledonia County Agricultural Society. The "Lamoille Newsdealer" thus briefly records the beginning of their great adventure:

"On June 12th the Lamoille Company left Morrisville for St. Johnsbury. Their friends gave them a ride most of the way and Col. Earle of this town, Mr. Whipple of Morrisville, Mr. Rankin of the Corners and others went along with teams to help them."

They received their baptism of fire at Lewinsville on September 11, 1861, and from that time on they participated in all the battles of this famous brigade. Of the twenty-one who marched away that bright June day, five never returned. Two of them, Sergt. Amos White and Edwin Burnham, were killed at the Battle of the Wilderness, and the other three, George R. Powers, Thomas F. Sawyer and Moses Sawyer, died of disease.

The Fifth Vermont, raised in response to Governor Holbrook's proclamation, was composed of ten companies, one of which was recruited at Hyde Park, and naturally contained many from this and adjacent towns. It had its rendezvous at St. Albans, and left for the front on September 17, 1861. According to Benedict's "Vermont In the Civil War," this regiment showed a larger percentage of killed and mortally wounded in action than any other Vermont regiment, and at the Battle of Savage Station it suffered the greatest loss in killed and wounded ever sustained by a Vermont regiment in action. Morristown gave one son, John Davis, to the Union cause on that battlefield. To the Fifth was accorded the perilous honor of leading the final assault on the enemy's line at Petersburg, and its colors were the first planted on the enemy's works.

The Eighth Vermont, recruited in January, 1862, together with the Seventh, was a part of Gen. Benjamin F. Butler's New England Division. Owing to the unhealthful conditions prevailing around Baton Rogue, the latter regiment had the dubious glory of losing more men by death from disease than any other regiment. One out of every three of the original number died from that cause, and Morristown's loss was in just that proportion, as three out of the nine from here fell victims to the unsanitary surroundings, while one man, Joseph O. Kimball, was killed at the storming of Port Hudson. Later, in 1864, to their great joy the Eighth was sent north to join the Army of the Potomac. Company D, of the Eighth, was one of the companies which formed a permanent organization after the war, and as late as 1914 held its eighth annual reunion in Morrisville, with about sixty veterans present.

The Eleventh Vermont was the largest regiment sent from this state and contained the largest number of volunteers from this town. Between the twelfth and fifteenth of August, 1862, ten companies were recruited for it, and Company D, organized at Hyde Park under the captaincy of Urban A. Woodbury, contained twelve from this town, two of whom, Chester Dodge and D. J. Safford, were destined to have a colorful military experience. The lieutenant-colonel was Reuben C. Benton of Hyde Park, a rising young member of the Lamoille County Bar.

A little less than a year later, on July 11, 1863, the regiment was increased by the addition of Company L, under Capt. D. J. Safford of Morristown, which group was mustered in at Brattleboro with nine men from here, and in October of that year Company M, with its quota of local men, joined their comrades at the front. In all twenty-five men from this town fought in this regiment, whose losses in action in proportion to the time it served exceeded those of the other five regiments of the brigade.

Aroused by the reverses which the Union Army sustained in the Peninsular Campaign, in August, 1862, President Lincoln issued a call for 300,000 militia to serve for nine months. According to the General Order there would be no recruiting officers, but the town officials and patriotic citizens would be expected to handle the details of enlistment. The Morristown Company, formed in response to this appeal and containing men from Stowe, Eden, Cambridge, Wolcott, Johnson, and Westford also, was completed by September 8 and became Company E of the Thirteenth Vermont. Joseph J. Boynton of Stowe was its captain and afterwards was promoted to the rank of major. It was assembled at Brattleboro, and in October was sent to the front where it was joined with the Twelfth, Thirteenth, Fourteenth, Fifteenth, and Sixteenth Regiments to form the Second Vermont Brigade.

The most notable work of this body of troops was their

part in the repulse of Pickett's charge at the Battle of Gettysburg, an event which many a man of Company E counted the most important event in his military career. They returned to Brattleboro and were mustered out on July 21, 1863, only, in many cases, to re-enlist. In fact a surprising number of men who had tasted the realities of war upon the expiration of their term of enlistment re-entered the service, thus proving beyond question their devotion to the cause for which they had already suffered.

The victories of Gettysburg and Vicksburg led many to look for a speedy termination of the war. They little dreamed of the stubborn defense by the enemy which made the final surrender of Lee such a bloody affair. In August, 1863, Governor Holbrook issued an order for recruiting a new regiment. But enlistments were slow. The glamor of war which had tempted many adventurous boys to volunteer was gone. In addition the bounty for recruits in the new regiment was only $100, a third of the sum offered to such as enlisted in the older organizations. Naturally any who were willing to enter the army preferred to fill vacancies in the existing regiments. Finally the War Department remedied the situation by equalizing the money paid, and early in 1864 the work of completing the companies of the Seventeenth Vermont was finished. Morristown was especially interested in Company C, which consisted of men from this and adjacent towns, and was commanded by Capt. Frank Kenfield, who had already learned the game of war in Company E, of the Thirteenth Vermont.

The company, consisting of eighty-six officers and men, was organized at Burlington, and went from there directly to the terrible Wilderness Campaign, where the list of the killed and wounded of the regiment exceeded that of some of the larger regiments. It joined the Brigade on the twenty-fifth of April, and on May 5 took an honorable part in the Battle of the Wilderness, where Captain Kenfield was shot through the left arm. From here they went to Petersburg, leaving two men, William Bassett and Corp. Lucian Bingham, on the battlefield of Cold Harbor. In the first attack on Petersburg, Morristown lost Corp. James Glines and Lieut. Guy H. Guyer, whom Benedict called "one of the bravest officers in the regiment." His death was deeply felt by his comrades, with whom he was very popular. He had first enlisted in

Company H, of the Ninth Vermont, and was promoted to the rank of captain in it. This regiment had been captured at Harper's Ferry, but as Stonewall Jackson could not hold or transport so large a number to Richmond, they were sent to a parole camp at Chicago to wait until exchanged. Later, much to their disgust, they were detailed to guard a body of Confederate prisoners sent to that city, and this no doubt led to Guyer's resignation. In February, 1863, he re-enlisted in Company C, Seventeenth Vermont, and fell early in the charge at Petersburg, shot through the left breast. Had he remained with the Ninth Regiment, he would undoubtedly have become its colonel.

On July 30, in the Battle of the Mine at Petersburg, Captain Kenfield, with others, was captured and the entire regiment suffered terribly, only one line officer and a few more than half the men surviving. In the final assault on that city and the lesser battles following this company was a credit to their state.

The men who enlisted in the other regiments and other branches of the service did their work as honorably as did they whose record has been given.

As the share of Morristown in the struggle was not unlike that of hundreds of other places, so the experiences of the following citizens from the town were typical of many others, but they are narrated because they were of local interest and they befell men whose families were long and favorably known here and give an idea of what participation in that conflict really involved.

One of the most varied experiences which befell a citizen of Morristown came to Frank Kenfield. Captain Kenfield, as he was always called in later years, was born in Morristown in 1838, the son of Asaph Kenfield, the first male child born in the town. After completing his education, Mr. Kenfield taught school for a year in Massachusetts, and then traveled through the South and West with the idea of locating there. He returned to his native town, however, where he engaged in the lumber business at the Corners. In response to the call for service, he enlisted in Company E, Thirteenth Vermont, one of the nine months regiments which formed the Second Brigade. In the repulse of Pickett's Charge at Gettysburg, Mr. Kenfield was wounded and later in the month he was mustered out by reason of the expiration of his term of enlistment. Like many others of his company, he did not leave his country in its time of need, and was soon active in recruiting Company C of the Seventeenth Vermont, of which he was made captain.

The company left the state on the eighteenth of April, and in less than three weeks were in action at the Battle of the Wilderness, one of the bloodiest engagements of the war. Captain Kenfield, with two other Morristown men, was wounded and taken to the Georgetown Hospital. When able, he came home on a furlough, but returned to his regiment in time to participate in the ill-fated mine disaster near Petersburg. It was proposed to run a mine or gallery, blow up the works, and pave the way for a general assault on the city, but these plans miscarried and after the explosion the northern troops found themselves in the huge crater made by the explosion, unable to advance and the target for the murderous fire of the enemy. When the order to retreat finally came, Captain Kenfield was one of many captured by an Alabama regiment.

Colored troops had been used in the Northern Army in this engagement, and the story was current in Petersburg that, if the Union assault had been successful, the city would have been given over to the negroes for plunder. This enraged the Southerners so that these prisoners were treated a little worse than was the average captive. The officers were marched through the streets of the city the next day in a column formed of white officers and negro privates in alternate ranks amid the jeers and jibes of the enemy. "Birds of a feather flock together" greeted their ears, and some were even wounded by their guards. All their valuables were taken from them, but Captain Kenfield saved his gold watch and chain by concealing them in his boot.

He and one other officer were taken to Danville, Va., and later to Columbia, S. C., where they were confined in the Richford County jail. Here their lot was pitiable. Their rations consisted for the most part of corn meal and sorghum, and as Captain Kenfield could not eat the latter he would probably have starved had he not met a Southern officer who was a brother Mason. This friend in need pawned the gold watch and chain of his adversary for $700 Confederate money, and with that Captain Kenfield managed to secure food until seven months later, on March 1, 1865, he was exchanged and six weeks later was mustered out.

Following the war Captain Kenfield engaged in farming and stock and produce raising and buying. For four years he was president of the Vermont Sugar Makers' Association, and represented the town in 1884 at Montpelier, where he was active in securing an appropriation for the Soldiers' Home at Bennington, of which he was a trustee at the time of his death, in 1914. He served as Senator from Lamoille County in 1894, besides filling a variety of local offices, but he was never too busy to be a loyal and active member of the local G. A. R. Post.

Another son of Morristown who reflected honor upon himself and his community was Darius J. Safford, whose family was long and favorably known in this section of the state. Mr. Safford enlisted as a private in Company D, of the Eleventh Vermont, in response to the call issued by Governor Holbrook in July, 1862. The government was at that time in special need of heavy artillery to garrison the forts, and by order of the Secretary of War this regiment was made a heavy artillery regiment, its official designation being First Artillery, Eleventh Vermont Volunteers, with orders to increase the companies from ten to twelve. On the eleventh of July following, Company L was mustered in at Brattleboro, with D. J. Safford as its captain.

The first serious fighting in which it engaged was in the Wilderness campaign, in 1864. At Spottsylvania one of its number, Stephen R. Wilson, was fatally wounded, and a few days later at Cold Harbor this company, with others, suffered heavily, and Captain Safford was mentioned in the official report as conspicuous for gallantry and good conduct. A few days later on, June 23, 1864, occurred the affair of the Weldon Road, the saddest day in the history of the regiment. In the attempt to cut the railroad at this point the troops were supported and guarded by certain companies of the Eleventh. Captain Safford was in charge of one section of the skirmish line and his account of the affair is quoted from Benedict's "Vermont in the Civil War":

"About one hundred and fifty yards before I reached the line, I found Major Fleming in a hollow surrounded on three sides by some rails. His orders to me were 'Extend the line to the left till you connect with the Fourth Vermont, and hold the line at all hazards, reporting to me every half hour'. I found the men busy covering themselves with rails, logs or whatever they could find. I extended the line until I made it as thin as I dared, but found no connection with any troops on the left. I did find a much stronger line, of the enemy, than our own, a short distance in front of us, and quite a brisk firing was kept up. I returned leaving Lieut. J. H. Macomber in charge of the left, and reported to Major Fleming, and about that time the Fourth Vermont, under Major Pratt, came up on our rear, instead of on the left of our line, and there remained so far as I know until the surrender. Finding there was to be no connection on the left I then drew in the line somewhat to strengthen it. About this time Captain Beattie came in from the front with the division of sharpshooters. He said: 'Captain, if you don't get out of this you will catch h—l', adding that the enemy were in force at the front. Soon after this I met Lieut.-Colonel Pingree, division officer of the day, on or near the left of our line and suggested that the line be drawn back nearer to supports; he replied, 'The orders are to hold the line at all hazards'. I think previous to my seeing Colonel Pingree one attack had been made upon us and after a while another was made, but the men being well covered, we suffered little from either. Soon after the second attack I became aware that a force was working around our left flank. Upon stating these facts to Major Fleming, and that we must retreat or be captured, he said he was ordered to hold that position and must be captured rather than abandon it. At five o'clock P. M., our ammunition was almost exhausted, and we were covered by the enemy in front, on our left flank and partly in our left rear. The enemy then began to cover our right flank, and when at last, about sundown, the Major gave me permission to see if I could find a place where I could take the command out, I personally saw the circle completed and the enemy's left and right unite in rear of our right flank."

Gen. L. A. Grant afterwards stated he did not know why this small force was kept at the front or if kept there why it was not supported, but, through no fault of their own, the regiment sustained the greatest loss of any Vermont regiment in one action. Nine men were killed, thirty-one wounded and 261 missing. Among the missing was Captain Safford, who, with seventeen other officers, was taken prisoner. They were carried to Petersburg, and the day following were sent to Richmond, where they were confined in Libby Prison until June 30, when they were sent by railroad to Macon, Georgia.

The men were naturally on the alert to escape before they were carried still farther into the enemy's country. At a point near Lynchburg, Va., the railroad track had been torn up in a Union raid so the prisoners were marched to the Roanoke station, and halted under guard for the night on the banks of the Roanoke River. Here Major Safford and two associates made their escape by dodging into a clump of willows, and crawling off through the bushes. After swimming the river, they lay in the woods until dark and then started to the northwest, traveling by night and resting by day. They were fed and directed by negroes. At one point they were hunted by a provost guard with bloodhounds, and one man was captured and taken back to Libby Prison. The other two, by separate ways, traversed the Alleghany Mountains and reached the Union lines at Beverly, West Virginia, within twelve hours of each other, having traveled on foot about 350 miles.

Both men were granted furloughs to visit their homes, but returned to their regiment in time to participate in the Battle of the Opequon, where both were wounded. Captain Safford recovered sufficiently to have an honorable part in the final assault at Petersburg on April 2, 1865, being in command of one of the battalions. As a reward for his bravery he was appointed major.

In June, 1865, the original members of the regiment and the recruits whose term of service would expire before October first were mustered out, and the remainder were consolidated into a battalion of four companies of heavy artillery under the command of Major Safford, who was promoted to the rank of lieutenant-colonel and stationed at Fort Foote, Md., for the defense of Washington. The following August these troops were mustered out and Lieut.-Colonel Safford returned home to his duties in connection with his father's gristmill, which he had dropped upon enlisting.

About 1883 he entered the government employ in the pension department, and was stationed at Augusta, Me., and later in Concord, N. H., Washington, D. C., and Minneapolis, Minn. When obliged to give up active work, he came back home to die after a painful lingering illness from cancer. He testified to his love for the place by remembering the First Congregational Church and the Morristown Centennial Library with legacies.

Another incident in many respects typical of hundreds, but in one feature unique, was that of William Preston Gates, who received his discharge by direct order of President Lincoln.

Mr. Gates was the grandson of Lieut. Nathan Gates, one of the pioneers of Cadys Falls, and at the outbreak of the Civil War had recently passed his fourteenth birthday. Like other boys he was swept away by the martial spirit of the period, and finally persuaded his reluctant mother to permit him to enlist. When Company D, of the Fifth Vermont, left for the front in September, 1861, he was in its ranks as a fifer. The year following, his widowed mother lost her only other child, a daughter. Thus bereaved, she began to think of securing his discharge, basing her appeal upon the ground of her lonely condition, his extreme youth, and the fact that he had already served more than two years. She left for Washington and attempted to see Secretary Stanton, but being only one of a large group there for that purpose and without influential friends, she was unsuccessful. She then decided to appeal to the President himself and to her surprise soon gained admittance to him.

She told her story which, after all, differed only in details from the many he was hearing daily. But it struck a sympathetic chord in Lincoln's great heart, and he told her if she would go before the Secretary of War and take oath to the facts she had told him, he would order her son's discharge. So he wrote his order addressed to Secretary Stanton and when she told him of her fruitless attempt to obtain an audience with that official, Mr. Lincoln wrote on the lower left hand corner of the envelope which is now a prized possession in the Gates family, "Please see this lady. A. Lincoln."

Thus armed, Mrs. Gates was soon able to see the Secretary, secure her son's discharge, and start for home. In January, 1865, Mr. Gates re-enlisted in the Frontier Cavalry, and served until the end of the war. In after years he went to the Middle West, and his death occurred at Wakefield, Kans.

Back of the men at the front there must always be the united support of the citizenry at home if successful

HISTORY OF MORRISTOWN 143

war is to be waged. Let us now turn to this phase of Morristown's war record.

It is a matter of history that Vermont's response to the call of President Lincoln was prompt and generous. At the special session of the Legislature, convened on April 25, 1861, eleven days after the fall of Fort Sumpter was known and the first call for volunteers reached the state, that body appropriated one million dollars for war expenses and provided for the organizing and equipping of six more regiments in addition to the one already called, for two years' service. Each private was to receive seven dollars per month of state pay in addition to the thirteen dollars offered by the United States government, and the relief of the families of volunteers was provided for in cases of destitution.

But the townspeople who had just given twenty-one of the best of their youth to the Third Vermont were not content to let the pecuniary side of the transaction rest there. At a special town meeting, called on September 2, 1862, they voted to pay fifty dollars as a special bounty to each volunteer who served in the armies of the United States for nine months, one-half payable when he was mustered in and the rest when mustered out and "extra pay of seven dollars per month if the present law did not secure the same or the state pay it."

It will be remembered that following the victories at Vicksburg and Gettysburg the recruiting for the Seventeenth Vermont lagged somewhat, due in part to the hope that the war was nearing its end and partly to the action of the government in offering larger bounties to the men who re-enlisted in the old regiments. To stimulate enlistment, at a special town meeting, called in December, 1863, the town voted to pay a bounty of $300 to all recruits in order to fill the quota of the town, and a tax of fifty cents on a dollar of the Grand List was raised to meet this additional expense.

Once again after the terrible Wilderness Campaign had depleted the ranks of the men at the front and sapped the courage of the non-combatants at home, a meeting was held on July 2, 1864, and it was voted to pay a bounty of $500 to each recruit and the following resolution was passed: "In view of the coming call for soldiers and to the end that a draft may be avoided in this town we earnestly desire and request the selectmen to use all and every effort to raise a sufficient number of men to fill the quota of the town for the next requisition that may be made." A tax of eighty cents on a dollar of the Grand List was voted to meet this demand. Thus loyally the town aligned itself with others throughout the state and nation to care for her sons at the front and to support the government.

Women played a much less prominent part in the Civil War than in the World War, and there was no such carefully organized activity as that of the Red Cross. Yet an Auxiliary to the Sanitary Commission was formed which met to prepare bandages, to knit socks, and to make those little toilet articles which testified to the continuing love and interest of the dear ones at home.

Among other contributions of the town to the war may well be mentioned the services of Dr. Horace Powers, to whom fell the happier task of saving human life than of taking it. Following the terrible Wilderness Campaign in May, 1864, the wounded were taken to Fredericksburg, which was soon taxed to its utmost by the influx. Its churches, public buildings, and larger dwelling houses were filled to their limits with thousands of victims of the struggle. The regular surgical force was entirely inadequate, and Governor Smith and Surgeon-General Thayer went there in person to see what could be done for the welfare of the Vermont troops. As a result of their personal investigation, fifteen or twenty of the best surgeons and physicians in the state were sent to assist, and among this number was Dr. Powers. Later the wounded were brought home to army hospitals at Burlington, Brattleboro, and Montpelier, where more than 2,500 were cared for.

MORRISVILLE HOME GUARDS

(11) In the fall of 1864, about the time of the Fenian Raid, military feeling rode high and a company known as the Morrisville Home Guards was organized, with George W. Doty, just returned from splendid service at the front, as its captain; P. K. Gleed, first lieutenant, and D. K. Hickok, second lieutenant, but this martial spirit soon died down, and was dormant for more than a half century until once more aroused by the exigencies of the World War.

HISTORY OF MORRISTOWN

THE SPANISH-AMERICAN WAR

Although a Vermonter, Senator Redfield Proctor, by his speech in the Senate crystallized public opinion in favor of intervention in Cuba, and two other sons of the state, Admiral Dewey and Capt. Charles Clark, were among the most popular heroes of the Spanish-American War, that conflict aroused little enthusiasm in Morristown. According to the official records none enlisted, although Glenn W. Raymond, a native of the town but then residing in Johnson, served in the ranks. On the whole this struggle left the town untouched and not until two decades later did its citizens once more feel the urge to take up arms again.

THE WORLD WAR

When the World War broke out, the interest of the citizens of Morristown was the general concern with which any intelligent people follow an event of such tremendous significance as this promised to be. Their most direct contact with it came through the letters printed in the local papers from George W. Drown, Jr., whose family resided in Morrisville. This young man, though not a native of the place, had visited here and was known locally. While working in Alberta, he enlisted in August, 1914, and saw five years' service under the Canadian colors and his letters home conveyed more intimately than newspaper accounts could what life at the front was like.

As the months passed and America's relations with Germany grew more critical, it became evident that we were being drawn into the whirlpool of war. The same spirit which had animated their forefathers led at least fifty-six young men to volunteer for active military service. With the advent of April, that month so fateful in America's history, and the formal declaration of war on April sixth, the number who went to Fort Ethan Allen to enlist increased, since many hoped thus to form a part of the First Vermont Infantry Regiment, an organization which might exist as a distinct unit and represent Vermont in this gigantic conflict as the various state regiments did in the Civil War. Their disappointment can well be imagined when on August 18 orders came from the Northeastern Department to transfer about 350 men and officers from the First Vermont Infantry Regiment to the newly formed Twenty-Sixth Division, and in less than a week's time they entrained at Fort Ethan Allen for Camp Bartlett. With similar groups from the northeastern states they combined to form the famous "Yankee Division," the pride of all New England. Later in the season still others joined the various units of this organization, and as a result this division contained more men from Morristown than did any other. But it is significant of the magnitude and complexity of the war machine and the strain upon the morale of the men that these twenty-two soldiers served in seven different branches of the division. Thus that comradeship which would have meant so much in a distant land amid the hardships of war was largely lacking. The sixty-three men who served overseas were connected with twelve different branches, viz.: Infantry Regiments, Field Artillery, Machine Gun Battalions, Pioneer Infantry, Depot Brigade, Coast Artillery Corps, Motor Transport Corps, Engineers, Sanitary Squadron, Ammunition Train, Ordnance Department, Repair Unit of the Motor Transport Corps, and Supply Company, to say nothing of the different phases of the work in the navy. War had become a complex and terrible thing.

According to the official records, the first Morristown lad to go overseas was Perley Laird, who had enlisted at Fort Ethan Allen in June and arrived in Europe on September 16, 1917. A week later, on September 23, Eugene Burroughs, Edward Emmons, and Percy Sweetser landed, the vanguard of that larger group which found their way across the submarine infested Atlantic and took their places beside the Allies.

It is not possible to tell in detail the story of the Twenty-Sixth Division, which has an honorable place in the history of the World War. It may be said in brief that in October these troops were assigned to a winter training area in the vicinity of Neufchateau, in the Province of the Vosges. Here, through the bitter winter of 1917-1918, the boys became proficient in target practice, bayonet drill, trench digging, trench warfare and the other forms of modern combat. In January, 1918, the training became more intensive, for the division was soon to go to the front. Early in February it was sent to the Chemin-des-Dames sector, where for six weeks they became acquainted with the horrors of battle. Scarcely had they returned to their former training ground when they were sent to occupy the

Toul sector, where they remained until called to participate in the Champagne-Marne defensive, the Aisne-Marne offensive, and at last in the Meuse-Argonne offensive, where up to eleven o'clock of November 11 they were in action. It is a matter of record that the Twenty-Sixth was chosen to form a part of the Army of Occupation and march into Germany, but it was so weakened by the rigorous service of the last three weeks that the honor had to be declined.

The story of the Twenty-Sixth has been given more fully than that of any other division since it contained the largest percent of local men, but the record of the other units is no less worthy. Of the three men killed in action, the first, Smith Warren, who was killed in the Aisne-Marne offensive, belonged to the Fourth Division; the second, Ernest Ward, was in the Twenty-Sixth; the third, Morton Stiles, was in the Seventy-Eighth. A fourth, Eugene Burroughs, who was wounded in the Muese-Argonne offensive and died from the effects, belonged to the Twenty-Sixth.

It will be remembered that almost as deadly as the shells and poisonous gas was the influenza. While it took heavy toll from the civilians in their homes, it was especially fatal to the men in the crowded training camps, and it was here that three others from Morristown were vanquished by disease. The first was Claude Chaplin, who was credited to Rochester, N. H. He had been a resident here; his grandfather, Joseph Chaplin, had a fine record in the Civil War. While living here, he had tried to enlist at Fort Ethan Allen, but was rejected. About a year later the family moved to New Hampshire and he tried again, was accepted, and sent to Camp Greene, Charlotte, N. C., where he died of pneumonia. The remains were brought to Morristown for interment in the family lot at Mountain View Cemetery. The second victim of disease was Karl Kramer, who was stationed at Camp Colt in Pennsylvania. He had been assigned to the Medical Corps of the Tank Service. When the epidemic of influenza broke out, he volunteered to care for the sick, contracted the disease, and died on October 5, 1918. His remains were brought home and interred in Riverside Cemetery. Four months later Herbert Wright, who is officially accredited to the Town of Cambridge, but had been for a considerable time a clerk in the Rexall Drug Store, died of disease at Staten Island.

This war was a world war in every sense of the word. Not only did it include nearly all the civilized nations, but, more than any other struggle, it involved the entire civilian population who were organized and grouped together to back up the men at the front.

The first of these various organizations was the Committee of Public Safety, which was formed even before war was officially declared. On March 22, 1917, Governor Graham, in accordance with a plan adopted by the other New England States, appointed such a committee to cooperate with the Federal Government in recruiting soldiers, speeding up production, and aiding in conservation. Hon. F. G. Fleetwood of this town was a member of this committee, serving on the important sub-committee of publicity. Both Mr. Fleetwood and Justice G. M. Powers were among the public speakers which this organization furnished as they were needed. The state was subdivided into districts, each with its own local directors, and, in this district, Justice G. M. Powers, Lieut.-Gov. R. W. Hulburd of Hyde Park, J. M. Kelley of Morristown, M. C. Lovejoy of Stowe, with F. M. Small of this town as secretary and treasurer, formed this local body.

On May 18 the Selective Service Law was signed by the President who designated June 5, 1917, as the day upon which all males between the ages of twenty-one and thirty-one, inclusive, should present themselves in the town which was their legal residence or the town in which they could vote, and register. The local Registration Board consisted of Moderator T. C. Cheney, Town Clerk A. A. Niles, Health Officer W. T. Slayton, together with F. G. Fleetwood, M. P. Maurice, L. M. Munson and J. M. Kelley. Dr. C. W. Bates served on the County Exemption Board. One hundred and ninety-nine young men, about seven percent of the population of the town, thus registered.

Registration was quickly followed by the first of the Liberty Loan drives, in which the town went "over the top" by a subscription of $64,500. Had someone told its citizens that five times in succession they would buy bonds to the extent they did, the statement would have been greeted with incredulity to say the least. Nearly a half century had elapsed since they had been called upon to sacrifice in a common cause such as this.

VERMONT VOLUNTEER MILITIA

When it became certain that the National Guard would be called into active service, thus leaving the state without any form of military protection, the Governor caused an executive order to be issued asking for the formation of a force of twelve companies of not more than fifty-three men each, to be called the First Regiment Vermont Volunteer Militia. The men must be American citizens or aliens who had declared their intention of becoming citizens who were at least thirty-one years of age and not more than fifty, or men between the ages of twenty-one and thirty-one who had been rejected from the draft because of slight physical disqualifications or dependent relatives. While they served without pay unless brought into active service, they received such clothing and equipment as was necessary. So generous was the response to this call that within a month after the executive order was issued the companies were established and the commissioned officers appointed.

Company F was located at Morrisville and included men from here and a few from adjacent towns. The following officers were appointed: Captain, L. M. Munson; First Lieutenant, J. M. Kelley; Second Lieutenant, Craig O. Burt of Stowe. A school of intensive instruction for the officers was held at Norwich University, Northfield, from July 5 to 14, and the men returned to the business of drilling the recruits who took up the work with enthusiasm and aptitude. Some months later, in May, 1918, Company F acted as host at the first May muster of the Second Battalion of the Vermont Volunteer Militia, which included Company E from St. Albans, Company G from St. Johnsbury and Company H of Newport. The fair ground was the site of the rendezvous, and the manoeuvres executed there indicated that the state was not without military protection should an emergency arise. The grim background of war gave the occasion a seriousness which the old June training lacked. This organization was not demobilized until June, 1919.

PUBLIC MEETINGS

The World War as fought was unique in many respects and especially in the different factors which entered into the contest. Never before had printers' ink and propaganda played so important a part. Millions of dollars was spent in this country alone in advertising matter sent out in connection with the Liberty Loans and the various drives, while public meetings in every little hamlet throughout the country aroused the people to the white heat of sacrificial giving.

The first public meeting held in this town for any of the various organizations which served throughout the war was a union gathering held at the Methodist Church for the purpose of raising funds for books for the soldiers. This movement was sponsored by the American Library Association, which undertook, according to its slogan, to raise "A million dollars for a million books for a million soldiers." Books were recognized by all the nations as one of the best aids for keeping up the morale of the troops and besides this first campaign for money the March following a drive for books was made in which the local library participated by collecting and forwarding them to the state headquarters, from which they were sent to the various training camps. This first mass meeting of October 7, 1917, was addressed by local speakers only, and $126 was raised.

Ten days later a War Convention for Lamoille County was held at the town hall, which building proved entirely inadequate to accommodate the crowd which came, and an overflow meeting was held in the Congregational Church At this meeting the people were given the opportunity of hearing men who had a wide outlook upon the situation and the events which led up to it. Prof. W. B. Guthrie of the College of the City of New York; Hon. W. W. Gilbert, former governor-general of the Philippines; Col. C. S. Bigelow, representing food control; and Joseph O'Toole of Washington, D. C., were the speakers who aroused the patriotism of their hearers to a high pitch.

FOOD REGULATION

By the time the United States had entered the war it was evident that the struggle had become a process of gradual wearing out the contestants with victory on the side having the strongest reserves of supplies and men, and that one great service in which everyone could engage was to produce and conserve food. As the months passed wheat, meat, and sugar became of the greatest importance.

So October 21-28, 1917, became Food Crusade Week. The Food Administration force from Herbert Hoover, who had been appointed in August, 1917, down to the local officers had been completed. J. M. Kelley and Mrs. Harriet Ide of this town had been made chairmen of the county and the Rev. W. T. Best and Mrs. Charles Chapin had charge of the campaign in the town. The Campfire Girls and Boy Scouts distributed the cards throughout the town, and by the end of the week 488 families were enrolled in the food conservation campaign and were offering to abstain in a large measure from the foods which had always been their staple diet.

The menu as planned by the National Food Administration was as follows:

Monday and Wednesday	Tuesday and Thursday	Friday
Wheatless day	Meatless day	Wheatless meal
Meatless meal	Wheatless meal	Meatless meal

Saturday	Sunday
Porkless day	Wheatless meal
Wheatless meal	Meatless meal

With the purchase of each pound of wheat flour it was necessary to buy an equal quantity of substitutes such as rye, buckwheat, oatmeal, etc. Recipes for the use of these substitutes were freely circulated and housewives began to adapt themselves to a new type of cooking. In some cases where there were invalids or semi-invalids these regulations worked a real hardship, but for the most part they were generally observed.

In July, 1918, the sugar ration cards were introduced, limiting the amount of sugar to from two to five pounds per person per month, and the disagreeable task of handling these cards was given to the Rev. W. T. Best. Later the cards were changed allowing three pounds to a person and the purchase of a month's supply at one time was permitted. Hooverizing had become a part of the daily routine of life and the slogan "Food Will Win the War" had become an accepted truth.

Less than three weeks after the County War Convention, came another union service at the Congregational Church to open a drive for funds for the Y. M. C. A. This meeting was addressed by Congressman Frank L. Greene of St. Albans and D. M. Claghorn of Boston, who was state campaign director. T. C. Cheney was chairman for Lamoille County, and so heartily did both young and old respond that over $1,700 was raised for this branch of war work. It will be remembered that one feature of this drive as later developed was the enlisting of the boys to earn and give ten dollars each. This matter of organizing the boys for this effort was left to the Rev. Frank Stockwell and fifty-three boys from Peoples Academy and the upper grades pledged and turned in the required amount.

The work of the Y. M. C. A. was of especial interest here since several people well known to local residents were engaged in that form of war work. Supt. B. E. Merriam, a native of Elmore but a graduate of Peoples Academy, and then residing in Bellows Falls, was among the first to volunteer for service overseas. Later J. M. Kelley from here and M. G. Morse, a Peoples Academy graduate; the Rev. C. C. St. Clare, a former pastor of the Congregational Church, who had recently gone to New York State; and M. S. Stone, graduate and former principal of Peoples Academy, saw duty overseas, while the Rev. Frank Stockwell of the Universalist Church served in Y work at Camp Devens and later entered the Chaplain's Training School at Louisville, Ky., received his commission as chaplain, and was prepared to go over when peace was declared.

The campaign for the Y. M. C. A. was followed at once by the Second Liberty Loan drive, when through posters, newspapers, and speakers the way was prepared for the canvass conducted by willing workers.

THE FUEL SITUATION

As November advanced people became aware of the fact that they were face to face with another serious problem, that of winter weather, and a shortage of fuel. While this lack doubtless aggravated the consciousness of the cold, still that it was not simply a state of mind is proved by the weather reports. The following extracts from the local newspaper speak for themselves: "December 31st local thermometers registered from 40 to 50 degrees below zero and all records for forty-seven years were broken. On January 27th, 1918, thermometers registered from 20 to 50 degrees, according to kind, condition, make, and location. On February 4th and 5th there was a regular western blizzard. The thermometers registered from 24 to 38 degrees below in the morning and 23 degrees below at noon while the wind blew a gale. The evening train from the east was cancelled and the first mail from Burlington came at 9:00 P. M." Again on February 9 there was another blizzard which tied up train service. On March 10 another blizzard nearly broke all March records. This was perhaps the last struggle of winter, for mild weather came on and the ice went out of the Lamoille River on March 31. In the weeks following people began work on the land, eager to do their part in raising food. In the village, lawns were plowed up, and on the farms all available land was tilled, and everyone started work on their "war gardens." But it seemed as though the forces controlling the weather were on the side of the enemy when people awoke on the morning of June 20 to find there had been a killing frost which ruined corn, beans, and in some instances potatoes. At Northfield, Vt., the official record was twenty-eight degrees and weather bureau reports indicated that it broke all June records since 1816.

A diary, whose record was unofficial but probably fairly accurate, reports that there were fourteen days in December, seven days in January, six days in February and three in March when the mercury went below zero. Such an unprecedented winter as this would have meant careful planning on the part of many to avoid suffering under normal economic conditions. With the fuel shortage that faced the country, it was appalling. The unusual demand for coal to supply battleships and auxiliary craft, for the manufacture of war supplies, and for heating the military cantonments, together with the reduction of the number of men working at the mines and the difficulties in securing transportation made the problem of securing coal for the state a serious one.

In September, 1917, the State Fuel Administrator, H. J. M. Jones of Montpelier was appointed, and in each town where there was a coal dealer a local fuel committee was designated who should regulate the local price and distribution of wood and coal, and conduct a local campaign to secure economy in the use of all fuel. The

Morristown committee consisted of L. M. Munson and C. A. Slayton. When on November 1 an appeal was made to supplement coal with wood, the village bought one woodlot and the stumpage on another and held a supply of four-foot wood on hand which was sold out at a reasonable price in small lots. This was not meant to interfere in any way with those farmers who brought in their regular amounts which were quickly bought up. It was rather an emergency measure which prevented real suffering. Sometimes as many as thirty cords a day were distributed, and over 2,000 cords were sold in all.

There was some coal available. The local newspaper reports in December that "coal has been doled out during the past week to families having babies and no wood stoves for heating their houses, 300 to 500 pounds to a family." In the meantime everyone joined in conserving fuel. All rooms in private houses not necessary for daily use were closed; beginning with the last of December the library was open only one day per week; services were held in the vestries of some of the churches instead of the auditoriums; and in common with other towns, schools did not begin after the Christmas vacation until January 14. On January 28 came the first of the "heatless Mondays," when all manufacturing plants, business offices, etc., were forbidden to use fuel unless the nature of the business made it necessary. The winter following, the supply of coal was limited, and many became acquainted with the peculiarities of soft or bituminous coal and buckwheat coal, but the wood situation was well in hand and there was no suffering, only inconvenience.

In February, 1918, through a new ruling of the Provost Marshal General, men not physically fit for the army but able to perform other duties were called and this order took fourteen more youths.

On March 5 a Win-the-War meeting was held in connection with the town meeting in response to a request sent out by Governor Graham. In common with other towns throughout the state, at eleven o'clock all other business was suspended, the Governor's letter was read and Justice G. M. Powers read a patriotic address prepared by the State Committee of Public Safety.

April brought the Third Liberty Loan, the campaign for which was opened on April 26 with a rally and a parade which included the school children. Morristown's quota was $60,100, and over $65,000 was subscribed. In this campaign a Woman's Committee functioned for the first time and secured $15,500.

In June, twelve more boys who had become twenty-one since the last date of registration were enrolled preparatory to entering the service. June and July also saw the development of the drive to purchase War Savings Stamps and Thrift Stamps. Justice G. M. Powers was county chairman and the Rev. W. T. Best, Mrs. Harriet Ide and Miss Lou Slocum had charge of the local work. The allotment for the state was $20 per capita and an intensive campaign to attain this goal was put on. A committee of thirty young people canvassed the town and the campaign closed with a rally at the town hall, in which the school children participated. The town did not reach its quota as it did in the various Liberty Loans, but it did raise over $34,500 in these small sums, which was an average of $13.03 per capita. This was less than the average of $13.90 for the state, but in excess of the per capita of $9.64 for the nation.

In September, the possible duration of the war was brought forcibly home by a further registration of all men between the ages of eighteen and twenty and between thirty-two and forty-five. This undoubtedly gave momentum to the Fourth Liberty Loan drive, which started on September 28. W. M. Sargent, who had conducted the three previous campaigns, had been made county chairman, so Charles M. Chapin succeeded him as local manager in the last two drives. The "Fighting Fourth Liberty Loan" had added impetus from the War Relic train which visited Morrisville on October 1. It consisted of two flat bottom cars, one box car, and one sleeper, and the flat cars were mounted with guns, bombs, shells, parts of airplanes and other implements of war. It arrived at 8:30 A. M. and remained here three hours. By actual count 4,267 persons passed through the cars and inspected their contents. Speeches were made by A. J. R. Helmus of the New England Liberty Loan Committee; William H. Kenney, an American, who volunteered as an ambulance driver; Private Ketchum of Putney, Vt., a member of the 101st Ammunition Train, who had been gassed; County Chairman W. M. Sargent, and Lieut.-Gov. R. W. Hulburd of Hyde Park. Two Frenchmen, decorated with the highest military emblems of the French army, accompanied the train. The

Morrisville-Stowe Band was in attendance, and the Home Guards were on duty at the station. As a result $6,500 worth of bonds were subscribed for on the spot. The Woman's Loan Committee also put on a Community Sing which was a success both in numbers and enthusiasm. The Morristown quota for the Fourth Loan was $120,200 and the amount actually raised was $145,200, of which over $24,000 was raised by the women. It is a significant fact that there were 686 subscribers to this fund, or practically one in four of the entire population of the town.

In September, also, the organization of the War Work Council of the Y. W. C. A. was completed. Mary Jean Simpson, then principal of Peoples Academy, was county chairman, and Mrs. T. C. Cheney was local chairman. In this campaign the girls between the ages of ten and twenty were enrolled and pledged to earn five dollars each. In the meantime it had become evident that all the different welfare organizations were in need of money with which to continue their work and were about to launch a drive for funds. At the wise suggestion of President Wilson, it was decided to combine these various appeals into one intensive campaign. In this United War Work Campaign, T. C. Cheney was county chairman and W. M. Sargent county treasurer and M. P. Maurice town chairman. The highspot in this drive was the rally held on the evening of November 7, the day on which the great peace hoax swept the country. The mass meeting was addressed by Guy Potter Benton of the University of Vermont and others. By that time, the peace report was denied and the necessity of continuing the welfare work was stressed even though peace came soon. There was pledged for this work $5,200.

Early in the afternoon of November 7, the citizens were startled by the ringing of the church bells. One after another they joined the chorus, not tolling as if to announce some calamity, but ringing joyously as if telling good news. The bells were soon joined by the blowing of whistles and as people rushed out to inquire the cause of the outburst they were met by the joyful news that the armistice had been signed. An excited throng soon gathered at the Randall Hotel, where soon there blazed a huge bonfire fed by boxes, old wagons, hayracks, anything the excited crowd could get hold of.

Four days later when the great deed was actually consummated another celebration was staged, less spontaneous, but no less joyful. This time the bonfire was made at the junction of Park and Main Streets and music by the band, speeches, and a parade all gave expression to the happiness which everywhere prevailed.

THE RED CROSS

The World War brought to public attention an organization which had been functioning for some time, but had not been fully appreciated before, the Red Cross. Miss Mary Moody was president of the local chapter throughout the war and gave untiringly of her time and strength to direct its activities. The bank directors gave up the second floor of the bank for a work room, and here day after day groups of busy women met to make surgical dressings, bandages, knitted sponges, and all the other articles necessary for use in the hospitals, while at home young and old worked on socks, sweaters, mufflers, helmets, and other articles used to bring comfort to the men at the front.

The treasurer of the society reported for the year beginning in October, 1917, receipts of $4,000, aside from the labor contributed, while this branch had the proud distinction of not paying out a cent for overhead expenses. Fuel, trucking, rent and all such expenses were freely given. The women on the Randolph Road, at the Corners, on the LaPorte Road, and on West Hill were organized and did splendid work. From the girls in the Junior Red Cross in the lower grades at school to the oldest residents in town, all were proud to have a part in the service. Three of the valued workers were Mrs. Esther Spaulding, who was eighty-six years old; Mrs. C. M. Boynton, eighty-nine; and Mrs. Alma Shaw, ninety-five.

The latter days of the war were marked by one of the most severe epidemics which ever swept the world, the influenza. While Morristown was extremely fortunate in being comparatively free from its ravages, it greatly affected the activities of those closing weeks of the war. That the loss of life was not greater here was undoubtedly due to the prompt action of the local Board of Health, which closed all places for public meetings, all churches, schools, clubs, etc., on October 2, an action which was taken by the State Board of Health a few days later. At that time there had been only three cases in town and only one death, but Barre, Montpelier, Waterbury, Stowe and Hardwick were severely afflicted and the week following an embargo was laid upon travel to and from these towns, such persons being kept in quarantine six days. These measures proved so effective that after a month the ban was lifted, and schools reopened after all the pupils had been immunized. The latter part of November saw a return of the disease which led to the resumption of the quarantine, which lasted some time longer, and the following January the Red Cross secured the vestry of the Congregational Church and fitted it up as a temporary hospital to care for those victims who could not be cared for at home, and here several patients were housed.

In the April following came the last, or Victory, Loan. Once again committees were arranged, the thermometer which registered the progress of the campaign was on display, and another War Relic train came to try to bring to people the realization of what war really was. This time the town responded to the amount of $87,000.

The total amount subscribed by residents of this town cannot be obtained exactly since the official report included some money raised in Stowe, which was sent in through this bank, but the Union Savings Bank & Trust Co. stands on record as forwarding $623,000, which was divided as follows: First loan, $74,000; Second loan, $93,000; Third loan, $109,000; Fourth loan, $215,000; Fifth loan, $132,000. Of this amount nearly a half million dollars was from Morristown.

The World War naturally invites comparison with the Civil War in its immediate effects upon the town. The number of soldiers engaged was smaller, for in the '60's one in every ten persons here shouldered his musket and marched to the front; in the World War, one in twenty fought from trench or dugout. Whatever glamor may have rested upon the battlefields of '61 was lost in the later struggle which had become more scientific, more deadly, but less romantic. The convalescent in the Civil War was able to return to his family to recuperate, but thousands of miles of ocean intervened between the boys of 1917 and their homes. The organizations back of the soldiers in the earlier conflict were simple in comparison with the various agencies, like the Red Cross, the Y, the Salvation Army, etc. Both wars left their imprint upon the lives of millions and in 1917, as in 1861, the town played with credit its part in the great drama.

CHAPTER X
MORRISTOWN BENCH AND BAR

IN the life of Abigail Adams, wife of John Adams, it is said that her family was opposed to her marrying the future President of the United States on the ground that he was only a farmer's son and a lawyer, a profession which was not then comparable to the ministry in social prestige. Whatever may have been the status of the law in the middle of the eighteenth century, a hundred years later it was recognized as one of the learned professions which many a farmer's son aspired to enter.

The law school is a comparatively modern institution, as it was formerly the custom for the young attorney-to-be to study in the office of some well known barrister, where he not only became familiar with the contents of Blackstone and Coke, but also with the practical side of preparing and presenting cases. In this way, in addition to the young men who were born or settled here to practice, a large number received their training in whole or in part here in the offices of such well known attorneys as Thomas Gleed, Luke P. Poland and Powers & Gleed. Some of these students have occupied such conspicuous places that they will be discussed elsewhere, but here are brought together several who in this state or elsewhere have reflected credit upon their chosen profession and upon Morristown as the place of their birth or training.

The first member of the legal profession in town was Charles Meigs, of whom little is known except that he settled at the Corners as early as 1818, possibly sooner. A contemporary of his was George Mason, who came to Morrisville from Craftsbury, but remained only a year or two. Another attorney of that early period was Edward L. Mayo, who settled here in 1827 and served for a time as postmaster.

The first lawyer to become prominent in his profession was Samuel A. Willard, who studied in the office of Isaac Fletcher of Lyndon, was admitted to the bar in Caledonia County early in 1828, and moved to this town in June of the same year. He was a nephew of Daniel Cahoon, the first settler of Lyndon and of William Cahoon of that town who was a major-general in the War of 1812. and a member of the national House of Representatives from 1827 to 1833. Mr. Willard lived in Morrisville about twenty years, during which time he was judge of probate for the district of Lamoille in 1838, 1840, 1841 and 1843, and was register of probate in 1838. It was a distinct loss to the community when he decided to return to the northern part of the state. After moving to Barton Landing, as it was then called, he served as representative, as state's attorney, and as a member of the Constitutional Convention of 1857. He died in 1864, and he and his wife are both buried in Riverside Cemetery in this village. It was in his office that Luke P. Poland, who may be considered his successor, got his professional training.

Judge Poland's most conspicuous services to the state and nation were rendered subsequent to his residence here, yet the town has always been proud of the fact that the foundation for his successful career was laid in Morristown. Mr. Poland was a splendid example of a self-made man. Born in Waterville in 1815, he attended the district schools of his native town until he was twelve years old and when seventeen went to the Academy at Jericho for five months. The rest of the time he clerked in a store in Waterville or worked in his father's saw-mill or on his father's farm. Yet he improved his meager opportunities to such an extent that he was hired to teach the winter term of school in Morrisville and was so successful that he was engaged to teach it again the following winter. In the meantime he had entered Judge Willard's office and showed such aptitude for the law that before he was admitted to the bar he was sent to take charge of an office in Greensboro. He was admitted to the Lamoille County Bar at the December term in 1836, the first term after the organization of the county.

For three years he was a partner of Judge Willard and then he was in business alone, his office being on the site of the Sweet & Burt filling station, north of the Drowne block. He was register of probate for Lamoille District in 1839 and 1840, member of the State Constitutional Convention in 1843, state's attorney in 1844 and 1845. In 1848 he was a candidate for the office of lieutenant-governor on the Free Soil ticket. His election as judge of the Supreme Court at the age of thirty-three was a personal triumph since the majority of the Legislature was of the opposite political belief. He served as judge until 1865, when he was elected senator to fill out the unexpired term of Senator Collamer and later was a member of the House of Representatives. As a legislator and as a jurist Judge Poland was undoubtedly one of the most gifted men the state has produced.

The greatest work of his congressional career was the revision and consolidation of the statutes of the United States. "The ultimate decision of what was and was not law, the sifting out of statutes that over-lapped, the construing of difficult phrases, and the re-arrangement of the Statutes by subject were all guided by him."

He left Morrisville for St. Johnsbury in 1850, but the virile years of his young manhood were spent here; here was gained the legal training which served him so well in later life; and he was elected a judge, the beginning of his broader public career, while a resident of the place. In later years his daughter, Mrs. Isabelle Poland Rankin, testified to her continued interest in the town by giving generously for the establishment of its public library.

Judge Poland's successor was J. Charles Robinson, who was practicing here as early as 1849. He was educated at Peacham Academy and studied law with William Baxter of Brownington, who was one of the leaders of the Orleans County Bar for the first part of the nineteenth century. Mr. Robinson was one of a family long and vitally associated with the town and for years was a prominent figure, acting as postmaster as well as attorney.

Among the successful lawyers who got their legal training in Judge Poland's office was Levi Underwood, one of the leaders of the Chittenden County Bar of his day, and lieutenant-governor of the state from 1860 to 1862.

Another brilliant student in the Poland office was Thomas Gleed, who, with his brother, Philip, made the name of Gleed an honored one in the town and county. Born at Lyme Regis, Dorset County, England, in 1826, he came to Canada when only a small boy. In 1837 the family moved to Vermont, where the father preached for a time in Berkshire and then settled at Waterville. His formal education was meager if judged by the standards of today, but he improved the opportunities given to such a degree that in 1844 he came to Morristown to teach school. Having made up his mind to follow the legal profession, he studied with W. G. Ferrin of Wolcott and in the office of Judge Poland and was admitted to the Lamoille County Bar in 1849. He first began to practice in Waterville, but upon his election to the office of state's attorney, in 1853, he moved to Morrisville, where he remained until his death in 1861. During those few years he was a member of the Council of Censors in 1855, county senator in 1856 and 1857, and represented Morristown in the General Assembly in 1859 and 1860.

In politics he early identified himself with the cause of freedom so associated himself from the first with the newly formed Republican Party. His untimely death from typhoid fever in August, 1861, cut off a man of brilliant intellect, sound judgment, and rich personality. No greater tribute could have been paid him than the fact that it was estimated that 2,500 people attended his funeral, and the members of the Lamoille County Bar met informally after that service to express their sorrow at the passing of "a man who was an honor to himself and his profession."

Two sons, Charles S. and J. Willis, both born in Morrisville, carried on the legal prestige of their father. The former not only practiced law, but was interested in a variety of other activities. For a time he was editor of the "Denver Daily Tribune," president of the "Kansas City Journal," a director of the Atchinson, Topeka & Santa Fe Railroad, and associated with the Bell Telephone Co., besides serving his home city, Topeka, and his adopted state in many ways. James Willis, besides being a practicing attorney, did considerable literary work and was professor of law in the University of Kansas.

Another student in Thomas Gleed's office was Charles Heath, who was admitted to the Lamoille County Bar in 1858, but his connection with the town was closer through his work as principal of Peoples Academy, and a brief sketch of his life is given in connection with that institution.

Still another young man who proved a credit to his training in the Gleed office was LaFayette Wilbur, who was born at Waterville in 1834 and attended the public schools of that town and the Academies of Fairfax, Bakersfield, Underhill Center, and Morrisville. Through his untiring efforts he gained a liberal education and, having decided upon law as his profession, came to the Gleed office. He was admitted to the bar in 1856 and followed his profession for the most part in the town of Jericho and for a time in Burlington. In addition to his success in law he was a historian of merit, having written a work of four volumes, entitled the "Early History of Vermont." He was also one of a committee to prepare the comprehensive history of Jericho.

In Philip K. Gleed, younger brother of Thomas, the town had one of its outstanding attorneys and citizens. Born in Granby, Quebec, in 1834, he came to Vermont with his family and after his brother settled in Morrisville he came here as a student at Peoples Academy and later attended Bakersfield Academy and Troy Conference Academy. In 1859 he was graduated from Union College, New York, and came to Morrisville to teach and to study in his brother's office. His first term of school was in District No. 8, or the Lamson District.

After his admission to the bar he practiced for a time in Richmond, until the death of his brother in 1861, when he moved to Morrisville. The year following he formed a partnership with H. Henry Powers, which continued until 1874, when Mr. Powers was elected judge. The firm of Powers & Gleed was one of the best known in Northern Vermont, their practice extending far beyond the bounds of this county. For more than a decade these two men were associated, Mr. Gleed preparing the cases while Judge Powers did the trial work. In addition to his law practice, Mr. Gleed was given many positions of trust and responsibility, as a list of the different offices which he held shows. He was state's attorney in 1867-1868 and again in 1880-1882; representative to the General Assembly in 1868-1869; trustee of the Reform School in 1869; assessor of internal revenue, 1870-1874; president of the Vermont Bar Association in 1888; senator from Lamoille County and president pro tem of the Senate in 1880-1881; member of the committee to revise the state laws in 1893-1894; and yet he was never too busy to serve his own town in different ways. For years he was a member of the School Board and one of the selectmen, also one of the first village trustees. He was a director of the local bank as well as of the two banks at Hyde Park. Yet he never allowed business and public cares to take precedence of his duties to his God. For sixteen years he was a deacon in the First Congregational Church and for twenty-six years superintendent of its Sunday School. Many a man and woman carry a distinct mental picture of his slight form and refined student's face as he came into church, his Bible in his hand, and made his way to the Gleed pew well in the front of the structure.

It is said that his father intended that his son should follow his own calling, the ministry, and without doubt he would have been eminently successful in that profession, but he also worked effectively as a layman, and the town and state were distinctly the poorer with his passing in 1897. In his remarks at the funeral Judge Wendall P. Stafford of St. Johnsbury spoke of Mr. Gleed as the representative type of the general all-around lawyer who relied upon his own investigations, whose cases were always thoroughly prepared and were tried on their merits. As a public speaker he was much sought after as his remarks were clear, direct, logical, eloquent, and enlivened with apt quotations and illustrations.

The Gleed brothers have a distinct and honored place in Morristown history.

Joseph Burke came here from Westminster, Vt., in 1800 and settled on a farm on the Wolcott road beyond the Tenney Bridge, where he lived until his death, in 1846. He had a family of twelve children and his oldest son, Samson, who married Levisa Haskins, raised a family of ten so that for more than a century the name of Burke was a common and honored one. Three Burkes were admitted to the Lamoille County Bar, O. S. and A. M. in 1860, and Carlos C. in 1862. The second of the above mentioned was so closely connected with town affairs that more than passing mention should be made of him.

Asahel M. Burke was educated in the public schools of the town and at Bakersfield Academy. In 1857, like so many other young Vermonters, he went to Kansas and, together with George W. Doty and C. W. Fitch, helped to organize the town of Mapleton and served as its first town clerk. In two years' time, however, he returned to Vermont and took up the study of law in the office of W. G. Ferrin of Johnson. Directly after his admission to the bar he settled in Craftsbury, but soon moved back to Morristown. In 1870 he was elected town treasurer and in 1871 town clerk, which office he filled very creditably until he had rounded out a quarter of a century, when he resigned, in 1896, and his death occurred seven years later.

HISTORY OF MORRISTOWN 165

Another Morristown attorney was Charles J. Lewis, a Civil War veteran with a gallant war record, who was admitted to the bar in 1869 and settled in Morristown to practice his profession. He soon entered into partnership with the Hon. George W. Hendee and in 1869 was elected state's attorney for Lamoille County. Some years later he left the state for Hannibal, Mo., where he spent the remainder of his life.

George L. Waterman, a leader of the Lamoille County Bar for twenty years, was the son of Vernon and Adaline Cady Waterman and a brother of Mrs. H. Henry Powers. Born in Morristown in 1838 he received his education in the public schools, at Peoples Academy, and the University of Vermont. He pursued his legal studies in Hyde Park and settled there to follow his profession.

C. Herbert Slocum was a native of Morristown and was educated in its public schools and at Peoples Academy and was admitted to the Lamoille County Bar in 1869, but, like many other Vermont boys, decided to try his fortune in the West. He went first to Kansas and later to Colorado, where he was engaged in mining for eleven years. Then he returned to Morristown and kept a store for several years until he sold out to become associated with C. C. Warren and H. C. Fisk in the tanning industry, under the name of the Warren Leather Co. This business was sold in 1926, and Mr. Slocum retired from active participation, although he remained a director in the new firm. Mr. Slocum was a member of the Water and Light Board from the organization of that enterprise until his death and held many other local offices, and was one of the town's most respected citizens when he died, in 1934.

Still another man connected with the bar and with other activities also was Henry C. Fisk, who was born in Morristown in 1852 and was educated at Peoples Academy and at Peacham Academy. He was admitted to the bar in 1875. After being connected for two years with the United States Patent Office as an examiner of interferences he returned to Morristown and in 1877 entered into partnership with his half-brother, George W. Hendee. Mr. Fisk served as register of probate for the district of Lamoille and was representative for both town and county at Montpelier. He also became associated with his brother-in-law, L. H. Lewis, in the Lamoille Publishing Co., producing in the "News and Citizen" an excellent

(13) country newspaper. In 1869 President Harrison appointed Mr. Fisk consul at St. John, New Brunswick, where he remained until 1893.

After his return he resumed his law practice and his business connection with other enterprises, such as the Warren Leather Co., of which he was treasurer. After going to Florida for the winter a few years, he took up his permanent residence there in 1921. He later moved to California, where his son, Carroll, was located, and died there in 1928.

One of the lawyers long and closely associated with the later history of the town was Albert A. Niles, son of Salmon Niles, who lived at the intersection of the roads near the corner of the fairgrounds. Born in 1842, Mr. Niles was in school at Peoples Academy when the Civil War broke out and enlisted in 1862, serving until the close of the war.

Upon his return to Morristown he completed his studies at the academy, graduating in 1869, and at once entered the law office of Powers & Gleed. He supplemented his studies there by a course in the law school at Ann Arbor, Mich. He was admitted to the bar in 1870 and began his practice in Johnson, but with his election as state's attorney he moved to Morrisville, where he resided until his death, in 1922.

While the Hon. G. W. Hendee was serving as representative at Washington, Mr. Niles occupied his office and in 1876 Edgar Thorpe, who was admitted to the Lamoille County Bar the year previous, formed a partnership with him. Mr. Thorpe was state's attorney in 1876, but later went West, and died in Jamestown, N. D., in 1904.

Mr. Niles remained here and became more intimately associated with the life of the town than as a lawyer. He filled most of the local offices, but his peculiar contribution was his clerical services. He was secretary of the Lamoille Valley Fair Ground Co. more than twenty-five years, secretary and collector of the trustees of Peoples Academy more than twenty years, secretary of the Board of Village Trustees, town and village clerk, and treasurer from 1900 to 1918, in addition to his activities, in the G. A. R., and the local Methodist Episcopal Church.

Among other students in the office of Powers & Gleed was Charles P. Hogan, a student at Peoples Academy until he enlisted in Company E, Seventh Vermont. After being mustered out of the service he studied at Johnson for a time, then came to this office. He was admitted to the bar in 1868 and settled in St. Albans, where he was a prominent attorney until his death, in 1915.

At the same session of the Lamoille County Court there was admitted a fellow student of Mr. Hogan, M. A. Bingham, who, for a time, practiced at North Hyde Park, but in 1873 moved to Essex Junction.

Another young student with Powers & Gleed was Frederick W. Baldwin, a native of Lowell, who was admitted to the Lamoille County Bar in 1872 and settled in Barton, where he held many local offices and became known as a man of letters.

After Judge Powers withdrew from the firm the Gleed office was no less popular with students, among whom was Frank S. Rogers of North Troy, who was admitted to the bar in 1880 and settled in his home town.

Hollis S. Wilson studied in this office while acting as principal of Peoples Academy and was admitted to the bar in 1886 in the same class as Chief Justice George M. Powers, with whom he entered into partnership here.

Melvin G. Morse, a native of Elmore, was educated at Peoples Academy, being a member of the Class of 1897. He completed the law course at Boston University in 1899 and then studied with Mr. Gleed and also with Bates, May & Simonds of St. Johnsbury. Besides carrying on his legal work, Mr. Morse has filled many state offices, having represented his town and county in the State Legislature and served as commissioner of taxes.

Melville P. Maurice was a native of Cambridge, Vt., and studied law in the offices of P. K. Gleed and of L. F. Wilbur of Jericho, and was admitted to the bar in 1898. He settled at Montgomery for a time, but in 1907 he moved to Morrisville, where he practiced for twelve years. During his residence here he held many local offices, was state's attorney from 1908 to 1919 and senator from Lamoille County in 1919. He resigned this position and moved to Brattleboro to enter the law firm of Harvey, Maurice & Fitts.

This does not complete the roll of men who in the earlier days studied here and then went away to be an honor to themselves and their profession. Among such might be included Chief Justice Dixon of Wisconsin, Ex-Governor Glick of Kansas, and Levi Vilas of Wisconsin.

Mr. Vilas was the postmaster here and after completing his studies moved to Johnson, then to Chelsea and in 1851 to Madison, Wis. He was mayor of that city and democratic candidate for governor and for United States senator. Henry E. Boardman, son of Ralph Boardman of Cadys Falls, was admitted to the bar in 1878, but went elsewhere to practice his profession.

In later years the following admissions to the bar from Morristown have been made: F. G. Fleetwood in 1894; Leon J. Thompson in 1894; Thomas C. Cheney in 1895; Preston A. Smith in 1908; Dean A. LaFountain in 1912; Leon E. Ellsworth in 1923; Helen L. Anair in 1927.

Of this number Mr. Thompson maintained an office here until failing health compelled him to give up practice. Mr. Ellsworth practiced here a few years before going to Enosburg Falls, while Miss Anair opened an office here, but later returned to her home in Hardwick. The Rev. P. A. Smith never practiced law and Mr. Cheney gave up the law to enter the insurance business. Mr. Fleetwood, Mr. LaFountain and Clifton Parker represent the legal profession here at present.

Since the organization of Lamoille County the following residents of Morristown have been state's attorney: Luke P. Poland, 1844-'46; Thomas Gleed, 1853-'55; George W. Hendee, 1857-'59; H. Henry Powers, 1861-'63; P. K. Gleed, 1863-'65, 1882-'84; Charles J. Lewis, 1867-'69; Albert A. Niles, 1872-'74; Edgar W. Thorpe, 1876-'78; George M. Powers, 1888-'90; Frederick G. Fleetwood, 1896-'98; Leon J. Thompson, 1898-'00; Thomas C. Cheney, 1900-'02; Melville P. Maurice, 1908-'16; Leon J. Ellsworth, 1924-'28.

CHAPTER XI
THE MEDICAL PROFESSION

WHEN one considers the vigor of the pioneer stock and their scattered location, he wonders that a physician should ever have had the courage to try to earn a living in one of the new towns. Yet before the first resident minister had been called or the first lawyer had sought a client, Dr. Ralph Tinker had settled near the old Center on a lot which afterwards became the first ministerial lot, known for many years as the Collins farm, now owned by Mr. Elmer Gallup. This was in 1802 when the population of the entire town could scarcely have exceeded 200 people. Here he remained for at least eight years, and here three sons and one daughter were born to him.

Dr. Ralph Tinker was the son of Elihu and Lydia Huntington Tinker of Worthington, Mass., and was born in 1778. Unpromising as the opening here must have seemed when viewed from the present day standpoint, there seem to have been some encouraging features, for his younger brother, James, having studied here for a time later returned and entered into partnership with Dr. Ralph. This business relation lasted a few years and was then dissolved, and the senior member of the firm removed to the still more remote settlement of Ashtabula, Ohio, where he died.

His brother, Dr. James, however, elected to cast in his lot permanently with Morristown. He was born in Worthington, Mass., in 1785, and lived there with his parents until he was twenty-one years of age and ready to start on a career for himself when he chose to come to study with his brother in the new settlement. He later returned to Massachusetts and completed his medical studies with Dr. Holland, the father of Dr. J. G. Holland, the author. After a year and a half with Dr. Holland he returned to Morristown about 1809 and began to practice medicine first, as previously stated, with his brother and then alone. He became a skillful and successful physician whose services were in demand, not only here, but in the neighboring towns. His native ability supplemented by wide experience and his strong personality made him a well known figure in the early days.

He set out the beautiful maple trees which still surround his former home at the Corners. It is told that he was annoyed by the practice, common among the attendants at the neighboring church, of hitching their horses to his young trees. One Sunday he went out and cut loose all the horses. This resulted in some interruption to the Sabbath service and a confusion of vehicles, but put an end to the custom of using his maples as hitching posts.

In 1813 he married Miss Anna Town and to them were born one son, Albert Byron, and four daughters. To his descendants he transmitted his love for his profession and each succeeding generation has furnished one or more physicians. His success in his chosen field enabled him to retire from active practice and his last few years were spent in farming at his pleasant home at the Corners, where he died April 19, 1860. His great-great-grandson, Charles Tinker, Jr., still carries on the family name here.

The third physician to locate at the Corners was Dr. Horace Powers, who was born in Croydon, N. H., in 1807, and was educated at the academy in Newport, N. H. When he decided to study medicine, he followed the custom which prevailed at that time of reading with a practicing doctor and located with Dr. J. B. McGregor of Newport, N. H., and was able to attend medical lectures at Dartmouth College. He received his degree of M. D. in 1832, from the "Clinical School of Medicine" at Woodstock, Vt., which had been established a few years before and later was known as the Vermont Medical College.

The next year, with his diploma and his newly wedded wife, Miss Love Gilman, of Unity, N. H., he moved to Morristown, where for more than thirty years he served his town, not only professionally, but in a variety of other ways. For twenty years he was a member of the Board of Civil Authority, was sheriff for a long period, a member of the Constitutional Convention of 1850 and senator from Lamoille County in 1853-1854.

With the outbreak of the Civil War he was made the examining physician for Morristown, and one of the veterans whom he examined related the following anecdote which illustrates his dry wit. After testing the prospective soldier's heart and lungs, the doctor remarked: "Now let me look at your feet, for they will probably be what you will use most in your first engagement."

Dr. Powers not only served as examining physician, but was one of several called to the front for special duty in the hospitals at Fredericksburg following the bloody Wilderness campaign of 1864. He died at a comparatively early age, in 1867, leaving one son, Horace Henry, to carry on and add honor to the family name.

The first physician to locate at Morrisville was Dr. Robert Gleason, who came from Claremont, N. H., in 1822, and was here about three years. He was followed by Dr. D. W. Putnam of Montpelier, who, for a half century, was a well known figure in town and died in 1879.

Dr. Almerion Tinker, youngest brother of Dr. James (14) Tinker, began to practice in Johnson, to which place he came about 1830. After a few years he moved to Morrisville, where he continued to live until his death, in 1880. He was not engaged in active practice the latter part of his life, but held many town and county offices.

One of the most typical doctors of the old school was Dr. E. J. Hall, who for more than thirty years traversed the hills and valleys of this and neighboring towns in all kinds of weather and over all kinds of roads. He and the roan mare which he drove in later years were familiar and beloved figures.

Dr. Elmore John Hall was born in Beansville, Ontario, on February 28, 1834, a son of the Rev. J. P. Hall. When he was six years of age, his family moved to Waterbury, Vt., where they lived for six years, and then came to Morristown. He was educated at Peoples Academy and in Castleton and taught school here and in other towns. Having made up his mind to follow the profession of medicine, he studied with Dr. Horace Powers, and was graduated from the Medical College at Burlington. Later he took post-graduate courses at Burlington and New York.

Having completed his studies, he married Miss Ophelia Titus of Wolcott and began practice at Waterbury Center. He soon moved to Highgate, where he remained until August, 1862, when he enlisted as private in Company L, First Vermont Cavalry, and was promoted to the rank of assistant surgeon within a few months. In 1866 he decided to move to Morrisville and from that date until one week before his death, on May 1, 1897, he gave himself unsparingly to the demands of his calling.

Aside from his professional work he was influential in the life of the town. He served as village trustee, was for many years a trustee of Peoples Academy, acted as United States pension examiner for more than twenty years, and was an influential member of the Congregational Church. In 1890 he entered into partnership with Arthur L. Cheney, having bought out the Woodward drug store, and took the initiative in building the three-story Centennial block in the corner store of which the drug business was located. He was survived by his wife, who died in 1929, and an adopted daughter, A. Belle Hall Donaldson, a talented musician, who passed on in 1927. No one carries on his name, but his influence upon the town will long be felt.

Another physician who for a generation ministered to the sick and afflicted of this locality was Dr. Charles C. Rublee, who was born in Montpelier in 1852, the son of Dr. Chauncey M. Rublee of that city. His mother was the daughter of Dr. Charles Clark, a veteran physician, of Montpelier, and his paternal grandfather was a doctor, so it was a matter of both inheritance and training that he should follow medicine as his life work.

Dr. Rublee was educated in the public schools of Montpelier and at Barre Academy when Jacob Spaulding was its head. He attended Dartmouth College one year, but in 1869 he began the study of medicine in the office of Dr. J. E. Macomber of Montpelier. He also attended medical lectures at Harvard and at Burlington, and in 1873 was graduated from the College of Physicians and Surgeons of New York City. While at Burlington and in New York, he acted as assistant to Benjamin Howard, professor of surgery. When it came time for him to settle, he decided upon the small town rather than the city and cast his lot in Morristown, where he spent the remainder of his life, with the exception of a year in Montpelier and six months in the West. In 1873 he married Miss Kate Spicer of Waterbury, who died in 1897, leaving four children, Sarah J., who married Fred M. Pike of Stowe and is now deceased; Edna S., wife of Walter M. Sargent of Morrisville; Emily, who married Bloomfield Palmer of St. Johnsbury; and George, who is a successful doctor in Rochester, N. H. In 1898 he married Miss Lou Mooney of Burlington, who survives him.

In addition to his regular practice Dr. Rublee served as health officer several years, was for eight years chairman of the Board of Pension Examiners, and at the time of his death was president of the Lamoille County Medical Association. He was a man of fine physique and seemed to radiate health as he entered a sick room. At the time of his death in 1905 he was the senior doctor in town and a generation who had grown up under his care regarded him as a personal friend.

Dr. Thomas J. Holbrook, although he did not practice in town so long as the others mentioned, was one of the old type of family physicians who made a large place for themselves in the life of a community. He was born in Hyde Park in 1835 and was graduated from the Medical College at Burlington, Vt. During the Civil War and before he received his degree of M. D., he was a hospital steward. In the Seven Days' campaign before Richmond he received injuries, from which he never fully recovered. Upon his return from the Civil War he settled in Wolcott, but in the fall of 1890 he moved to Morrisville, where he practiced until his death, in 1899.

Dr. William Taft Slayton will be remembered not simply for his professional work, but because he was an active force in town affairs for many years. He was born in Elmore, Vt., in 1870, the son of Capt. Aro and Lucy Slayton. He was graduated from the Laconia, N. H., High School and received his medical degree from the University of Maryland in 1894. He did post-graduate work at Harvard Medical College the year following while maintaining an office in Boston and served his internship at Guy's Hospital, London. Upon his return, in 1896, he settled in Hyde Park, but soon afterwards moved to Morrisville.

Dr. Slayton was an enthusiastic supporter of the development of the electric power in town and after the construction of the municipal dam at Cadys Falls in 1907 and the subsequent formation of Lake Lamoille, he conceived the idea of developing a summer resort on the new lake. The shores were improved and on the western side he built twenty charming cottages, together with a central dining hall, a club house, etc. He succeeded in attracting a fine type of summer residents. The first cottage was rented to Prof. Durant Drake of Vassar College, while W. J. Henderson of New York, dramatic and musical critic; Dr. William Hanna Thomson, physician and author; Prof. T. Leslie Shear, lecturer on art and archaeology at Princeton University; Dr. David G. Downey, general editor of the Abingdon Press; Dr. Frederick Whiting, New York surgeon, and others well known in their spheres have been connected with the colony.

During the World War Dr. Slayton volunteered for medical service and was stationed at Camp Meade, Md., with the rank of captain. In 1918 he was elected representative to the General Assembly and four years later he was senator from Lamoille County. While representative, he introduced an important health measure which divided the state into ten health districts, each in charge of a whole time health officer. The measure passed and made Vermont the first state in the Union to be entirely covered by trained health officers. From a professional point of view this was a distinct advance, but it proved to be somewhat more expensive than the old method, and after four years the appropriation for carrying out the provisions was refused. Dr. Slayton remained a member of the State Board of Health until his resignation in 1923, when he went to Miami, Florida, and became interested in the development of the city and made it his winter home until his death.

Dr. George E. Woodward was a well known figure for many years. He was born in Danville, Vt., in 1853, and was a graduate of Boston University, receiving his degree as a homeopathic physician. He came to Morrisville in 1874, and, at the time of his death, in 1907, he had practiced here longer than any other doctor in the county had been working in one town. For several years he was also engaged in the drug business, but in 1890 he sold that to Hall & Cheney. The fact that for years he was the only homeopathic physician in a considerable district extended the circle of his practice.

Dr. Charles W. Bates was born in Colchester, Vt., although his parents moved to Morristown when he was a youth. He was a graduate of Rush Medical College in the class of 1881 and after completing his studies settled in Wolcott, Vt., but moved to Illinois in 1891. After nine years in the Middle West he returned to Vermont, locating in Hardwick. He remained there until 1905, when he came to Morrisville, where he was in active practice until his death, in 1919.

PRESENT PHYSICIANS

At present there are six doctors in town, of whom the dean in point of service here is George L. Bates, who is a native of Morristown and a graduate of the Medical College of the University of Vermont in the class of 1897. He began to practice in Morrisville that year and has been here since with the exception of the years from 1925 to 1929, which were spent in Florida, and one year in the late war. At the outbreak of the World War he volunteered and was called to service in the Medical Corps in August, 1917. He was stationed at Fort Benjamin Harrison, Indiana, and Camp Grant, Illinois. In August, 1918, he was sent overseas, where he remained until the following June when he was discharged with the rank of major and resumed his practice in Morrisville.

Dr. William M. Johnstone was born in Thompsonville, Conn., and was a graduate of the Medical College of the University of Vermont in 1906 and began to practice in town the year following. Since that time he has served his profession and the community in various ways. He has been secretary of the Lamoille County Medical Society for twenty-five years and secretary of the staff of Copley Hospital since it was opened; he was health officer for several years, village trustee five years, and was president of the Vermont State Medical Society in 1931-1932.

Dr. Archibald J. Valleau was born in Selby, Lennox County, Ontario, and was graduated from Queen's Medical College at Kingston, Ontario, in 1890, and from the Ontario Medical Council the year following. He specialized in diseases of the eye, ear, and throat; and his study abroad was along those lines. He came to Morrisville in 1908 after some years of practice in Wolcott, Vt.

Dr. Anthony M. Goddard is a native of St. Armand, Quebec, and a graduate of the Medical College of the University of Vermont in the class of 1897. Two sons, Glendon and Philip, have also received the degree of M. D. from there, Philip being the fifth of the family to be graduated from that institution. Dr. Goddard began practice at Albany, Vt., but moved to Morrisville in 1918.

Dr. Philip Goddard, after completing his internship, spent several months studying in Vienna and in the autumn of 1934 returned to Morrisville to take up his profession, having specialized in surgery.

Dr. Seth H. Martin is a native of Alburgh, Vt., and was educated at the University of Minnesota and the University of Maryland, and studied in Vienna in 1927-1928. He specialized in genito-urinary surgery and urology and has been on the staff of the Mary Fletcher

Hospital in Burlington for several years and lecturer on those subjects at the Medical College of the University of Vermont. He joined the staff of the Copley Hospital in 1932 and came to Morrisville to reside in 1934.

COPLEY HOSPITAL

The agitation for a hospital in Morristown began as early as 1908 when the local newspapers contained communications from the doctors pointing out the advantages of such an institution and suggesting ways by which it might be financed. There was considerable interest shown and a Hospital Association was formed to promote the project. The Woman's Club conducted a Tag Day for its benefit and some money was raised in different ways, but the amount secured was not sufficient to warrant pushing the enterprise and it was dropped.

When Mr. Alexander H. Copley first thought of remembering his native town by large benefactions, he intended to erect a hospital on the plateau east of the village which he had owned for some years. When he investigated the expense of maintaining such a building as he proposed to construct, and discovered the need for a new high school, he abandoned his first plan and gave instead the beautiful edifice which now dominates that part of the village. However, the thought of a hospital was not entirely forgotten. Learning there was still interest in the project and that the Wheelock place had possibilities of development, he finally bought that property. Located on a plateau southeast of the village, it contains about fifteen acres and is ideally situated for such an institution. The house, built by Mr. A. P. Wheelock of Dorchester, Mass., as a summer home and later occupied as a permanent residence, was well adapted to the uses of a hospital. Near the house was a large barn which was moved up and connected by a passage way with the house.

The work of reconstructing and equipping the building was completed so that on September 26 and 27, 1932, the building was open for inspection and nearly 1,200 people, not only from Lamoille County, but from outside the state, passed through. On September 28 the Lamoille County Medical Association was host to a large gathering of physicians from all parts of the state. Following the inspection of the hospital, a banquet was served at the Masonic Temple.

When opened, five rooms had been endowed as follows: The Jane M. Copley Room, by the ladies of the Universalist Society, in honor of the donor's mother; the David Randall Room by Mrs. Ellen Child, in memory of her father, a well known physician of Lamoille County; the Mr. and Mrs. F. H. Hickok Room by these summer residents of Morrisville; the Carrie Powers Room by Miss Powers, and a room by the Morristown Post, No. 33, American Legion and Auxiliary.

In 1933 an Auxiliary was organized with committees in the different towns in the county, which carry on an annual drive for members and supplies, and meet to sew as occasion demands. Opened when the depression was at its height, the hospital exceeded the expectations of its friends by the way in which it met its financial and working problems, and it soon won for itself a large place in the life of the county. Increased space became necessary in 1934 and was secured by further donations from Mr. Copley. No small part of its success was due to the efforts of Mr. C. H. A. Stafford, who had charge of the remodelling and equipping, and to its first superintendent, Mrs. Vivian Greene Isham.

CHAPTER XII

CELEBRATIONS, GRAVE AND GAY

WE are apt to think of the lives of our forefathers who lived before the days of the automobile, the motion picture, and the radio as dreary and colorless; but it is probable that we have entirely over-estimated the dullness of that period. While no ceaseless round of social engagements claimed their strength and time, they often came together for work and recreation. The old-time quilting party, singing school, husking bee and apple parings have been celebrated in song and story and no doubt did much to relieve the monotony of life. No small part of their pleasure in the religious services was due to the social contacts which they offered, and other occasions were also seized as opportunities for merry making.

One of the annual events looked forward to by young and old alike was the Lamoille County Fair. Its early history has to be gathered for the most part from newspapers. From that source we learn that the officers and board of managers met to select not only the time, but also the place of the gathering and reports are extant of fairs held in Johnson, Hyde Park, and Elmore, as well as Morristown. Doubtless other towns of the county were included as well.

The fairs of that early period were devoted solely to the interests of the farmers and artisans of the district. The exhibits were held in the town hall or other public buildings, the cattle were hitched beside the road, and the racing, which was purely local in character, was held in the main street of the village. The "American Observer" of September 22, 1853, contained the following editorial: "We are anxious to see 'Spunky Lamoille' en masse at Johnson next Wednesday to take part in as well as to see the exhibition. It will be recollected that the Seventh Annual Exhibition and Fair of the Lamoille County Agricultural Society takes place at Johnson on the 28th inst. Let it be recollected that the best way that our County can be made still more prosperous is to take hold individually and collectively and sustain our Agricultural Society and it will certainly Sustain Us. Suppose We dont all get a Premium. Are we too small souled to give the paltry sum of fifty cents (the price of membership) to an institution whose only aim is to increase, improve, and beautify all that pertains to our industrious and thriving population? Who believes it? We wont anyway."

If these gatherings were held each year, this would indicate that as early as 1847 the movement began when the county was only a lusty youngster. Perhaps the exhortation quoted might have produced results had not the weather man taken a hand in the affair. The "American Observer" of September 29, 1853, contains the following account of the event:

"About dark on Tuesday night it commenced to rain and continued almost without intermission until sometime Wednesday night after the Fair. Rain and mud were more plentiful than specimens of industry or spectators; but considering the disadvantages labored under, it was the most promising Fair ever held by the Society. There was a large number of excellent cattle and the best apples, or as good as can be found in or out of Vermont. Notwithstanding the weather five hundred people were in attendance, one third of whom were females. The female department contained but few articles but those presented were very creditable to their fair manufacturers —some very well executed drawings, specimens of millinery, bed quilts and spreads and a rug, all as good as if made in Paris. Mr. J. L. Whittier's gloves were as good as the best. Some brass fastened rakes—an improvement. Nice onions, watermelons, and pumpkins and a large crookneck squash were presented. We shall publish the premiums soon."

Heminway's "Gazeteer" gives no date for the organization of the society, but states that interest in it had almost died out so that in 1862 Elmore was the only town that still clung to the custom of exhibiting its products at a fair. Later Morristown joined with Elmore, and we find the Morristown and Elmore Agricultural Society and Farmers' Club holding its Sixth Annual Fair on the grounds at Morrisville on September 20 and 21, 1865, showing that the war had not entirely absorbed the strength and energy of the people. It is an interesting side light on changing agricultural conditions to note that on this occasion there were forty-eight yoke of oxen on exhibition.

The advantages of a race track and distinct place of meeting had become apparent by this time and the level plateau east of Maple Street, owned by J. C. Noyes and still known locally as the "Old Fairground," became the regular place of meeting from 1865 on. Here a race track was laid out, a hall for exhibits was built and everything necessary for staging a real fair was provided. The management was reorganized and here was held on September 25 and 26, 1866, what was proudly announced as the First Fair under the direction of the following officers: President, Hon. John West of Morristown; Vice-President, Edmund Phelps of Morristown; Recording Secretary, J. W. Bryant of Elmore; Corresponding Secretary, H. D. Bryant of Morristown; Treasurer, H. S. Kelsey of Morristown; Marshal, G. W. Doty of Morristown.

An address formed one of the main features of these early fairs, and on this occasion the Hon. H. H. Powers was the orator of the day. Following are some of the regulations which governed the organization:

"All members of the Society and all who become such by the payment of one dollar have certificates of membership which admit family to the grounds.

"Tickets to single persons are .10 only.

"A purse of $50 open to all for the best trotting horse three to enter and two to start and a second purse of $20. All competitors pay entrance fee of 10% of the purse contested for."

There was a long list of premiums on cattle, horses, sheep, butter, fruit, vegetables, grain, mechanical devices and on articles in the woman's department.

The fair of 1866 was marred by what is probably the only fatality in the history of the organization. At that time John B. Seaver of Stowe, a well known resident of that town, who married the sister of the Hon. George Wilkins, was thrown from his sulky while driving a trotting horse on the track and struck the wooden instrument used in smoothing the track and was fatally injured.

The high spot in the history of the old fair ground was undoubtedly reached in 1869 when Horace Greeley, one of the well known figures in American life, soon to be a candidate for the presidency, was secured as the orator of the day. The "Lamoille Newsdealer" of September 28, 1869, gives the following account of his visit:

"Mr. Greeley arrived about eleven o'clock on Friday and after an hour's rest, dined in company with the officers of the fair and a few invited guests at the Morrisville House after which he was taken to the Fair Grounds in a large wagon drawn by thirty yoke of fine oxen. The wagon also contained the officers and invited guests and the Morrisville Cornet Band. The oxen seemed inspired by the occasion and the music and took a lively pace for oxen, and the novel train made the circuit of the ground in order that all might witness the spectacle." Mr. Greeley then delivered an excellent address along agricultural lines for the edification of his large audience. Many white haired men and women remember the day when Horace Greeley, drawn by thirty yoke of oxen, came to the fair.

A few years later another reorganization took place, and in 1872 the Lamoille Valley Fairground Co. was formed. It was decided that the Old Fairground, which had seemed so commodious and satisfactory when leased, should give way to a more convenient place. In May, 1872, Salmon Niles deeded to the new company a tract containing a little more than seventeen acres, upon which a race track was laid out, a floral hall built and other buildings added as they were needed. This move was made in the face of bitter opposition. Many questioned the advisability of making the change, and the local merchants felt they would lose greatly by it as the new grounds were too remote for them to receive any patronage. On the other hand, there was the greater accessibility of the new grounds; a fine spring of water, which later failed them; and, above all, the proximity of the new railroad which was then rapidly approaching Morristown.

Since 1872 many changes have been made in the management. In 1885 the length of the fair was increased to three days, and in 1928 to four days, but in 1932 it was changed back to the three-day period. In 1901 the grounds were sold to a stock company, consisting of O. M. Waterman, George M. Powers and Walter Churchill of Morrisville and Orlo Luce and J. J. Vearen of Stowe. Another change was made in 1926, when a new stock company, composed of Lamoille Valley men, took it over, and that year the first night programs were given, with fireworks and vaudeville forming the chief attractions.

No fairs were held in 1890 or 1900, in part because of financial conditions, and in the later instance because of the prevalence of smallpox in this section.

On August 30, 1912, came another red letter day in the history of the organization, for on that day Theodore Roosevelt was the guest of honor. The Colonel was making his whirlwind tour of the state in his famous Bull Moose campaign, and the management found he would be able to stop here for a short time on his way to Barton. So they voted to continue the fair another day in order to secure him. The Colonel and his party arrived in town about 3:00 P. M., and were escorted to the west end of the grounds, where Mr. Roosevelt and his secretary and a small party took seats on a big float decorated with bunting, pictures of Washington, Lincoln, and Roosevelt, and a fine bull moose head at the front. This float was drawn by fourteen yoke of oxen and the procession, headed by Capt. S. B. Waite of Hyde Park and the Morrisville Military Band, moved around the track to the grandstand. Here for about a half hour Mr. Roosevelt addressed an audience of 6,000 people, defining his idea of progressive principles. He then left for his next engagement. While Lamoille County voted Republican as usual in November the Colonel had many warm admirers here who welcomed the opportunity to listen to him.

The country fair has reflected the changing life of the people as clearly as any other institution. At first it was purely agricultural in character. The exhibits and attractions were local, and it made a pleasant diversion to go for a day or more and see what one's neighbors were doing in the line of fancy work, cooking, raising stock, or dairying. The day in the open, visiting with friends from neighboring towns, was a relaxation enjoyed by all. Gradually other attractions were added. Among the first of them was the balloon ascension and many a person can remember the thrill with which he saw Bonnette or some of his successors soar away into the distance in his balloon and the eagerness with which the news of his safe descent was awaited. Then came the addition of Fakirs' Row, the merry-go-round, the midway and the aeroplane. To secure this entertainment and to ensure good trotting the fairs have been obliged to arrange their dates so that these attractions can make the circuit; and the fair, especially since the night performances, has more of the nature of a carnival than the old time country gathering. But one thing here remains unchanged, namely, the beautiful panorama which lies before the spectators standing on the height. To the east, west, and south is the rim of mountains with the green valley in the foreground.

Certain men have given untiringly of their time and strength for the maintenance of this institution, and among them should be mentioned O. M. Waterman, who was secretary and director for twenty-three years; A. A. Niles, who acted as secretary for more than twenty-five years, and the Hon. George W. Hendee, who was president of the association for about thirty years.

SOLDIERS' REUNIONS

The fair ground has served as the gathering place for many other bodies, among them various soldiers' organizations. The first of these meetings was in 1886 when, on October 5 and 6, the veterans of the Civil War assembled to renew old associations. An organization was perfected known as the Lamoille Veterans' Association, though its membership was not confined to this county. In fact, several of its officers were from beyond the borders of Lamoille County. The principal features of this first reunion were the campfire in the evening, with speakers from a distance, and the sham battle which was staged. "Black Betsy" was taken over from the village to participate, and the old soldiers once more listened to the crack of muskets and breathed the smoke of battle.

"Black Betsy" perhaps deserves a word in passing. This cannon was secured for the town soon after the Civil War, probably by Col. D. J. Safford, and for many years every celebration of any importance was ushered in by a salute from her. Of late years she has been mute, and with the erection of the Soldiers' Monument in Academy Park she was placed there to keep guard over it and the memories of the soldiers of 1861-'65.

The eleventh of these annual reunions was held here in 1896, but after that date they seem to have been held at the G. A. R. halls in the different towns until finally the thinning ranks of soldiers led to their being discontinued. The last one recorded was at Johnson in 1915.

During the World War the first muster of the Second Battalion of the Vermont Volunteer Militia, including companies from St. Johnsbury, St. Albans and Newport, as well as the local company, was on the fair ground. The American Legion has also held county meetings there and it has served as an athletic field from the days when the No-Names, Morristown's famous baseball team, were at their height to the present. The State Firemen's Association met here in 1909 and the level fields adjoining have been used as a landing place for airplanes in connection with the fairs and also for air meets held here at different times.

Another occasion for merrymaking of quite a different character is reported in the "Vermont Weekly Tribune" of March 9, 1854, as follows:

"The one hundred and twenty second anniversary of the birth of him who was 'First in war, first in the hearts of his countrymen', was celebrated at Morrisville on the 22d inst. The 'Morrisville House' was full to overflowing at an early hour. 'Our host' with his usual urbanity and good nature gave us a hearty welcome. The wants of every guest were more than anticipated; they were supplied. We were summoned to the Hall at half past six o'clock, where we found that indispensable requisite to every festival, Music, in the persons of friend Eastman and his accomplished band. Age was there—side by side with blooming youth, manhood with its strength; childhood in its helplessness—wives, sweethearts, daughters, all were there.

"J. Miles, Esq. now brought forward and introduced Dr. .... as Chairman of the meeting, after which Mr. L. F. Warner introduced as orator Geo. W. Hendee of Morrisville and as Poet, Freeman O. Hodge of Lowell. Music by the band, after which Mr. Hendee in a most happy and masterly manner gave us an intellectual treat. Subject—Washington. A feast to the soul. It was good to be there. Then followed the poem, by Mr. Hodge, entitled "Vermont" which is herewith transmitted to you and speaks for itself.

"Music, dancing, supper—and such a one, it was one of Matthews' best; toasts, music, dancing-rain-snow-blow; morning; and we all went home.

"Your's truly,
"ONE OF THEM."

The poem referred to didn't speak loudly enough to the editor to cause him to print it, but as this issue of the "Tribune" contained poems by Whittier and Alice Cary, Mr. Hodge could hardly have hoped to compete with them.

HISTORY OF MORRISTOWN 185

It is interesting to compare this celebration with the one held a little more than three-quarters of a century later when, together with the rest of the United States, Morristown devoted February 22, 1932, to commemorating the bi-centenary of Washington's birth. The observance began at sunrise with a salute given by the firing squad of the American Legion, followed by a fife and drum corps which paraded the principal streets playing patriotic music. At 11:30 o'clock the public were invited to meet at the town hall, where they engaged in singing patriotic music until President Hoover's address at Washington was brought by a radio installed for the occasion at the hall.

The climax of the event was the evening meeting which was enjoyed by a crowd so large that not all were able to secure seats in the hall. A brief appropriate musical program was the prelude to a short colonial play. But the main feature was a scholarly historical address by W. A. Beebe of Underhill, former principal of Peoples Academy. At the close of this the memorial trees planted in honor of the Father of His Country were dedicated and turned over to the village trustees. The American Legion then gave a costume ball at the Barracks. The celebration was sponsored by the Woman's Club, and achieved the distinction of being reported in the "New York Tribune".

On March 4, 1865, a jubilee meeting was held at the town hall to celebrate the recent victories of the Union army and the inauguration of President Lincoln. The Hon. G. W. Hendee was the presiding officer and P. K. Gleed, "Father" Gleed, as the Rev. John Gleed was affectionately termed, Dr. Horace Powers and others appeared on the program. The general rejoicing of that occasion was turned into mourning in a few short weeks when word was brought by a messenger on horseback from Waterbury of the assassination of the beloved President.

CAMPMEETING

Another important event in the community for a good many years was the annual campmeeting, which was usually held the second or third week in August. Before the summer vacation had become so common, this occasion filled the need for change and relaxation.

At just what date the first campmeeting was held in Morristown cannot be definitely ascertained, but in 1868 and possibly a short time before, such services were held in the grove by the river at Cadys Falls. It was probably a gathering of local people who were attracted by the charm of the place. Just when and why the change was made to the beautiful maple grove near Morrisville is not certain. Doubtless many things contributed to bring about the removal. Salmon Niles, who owned the new site, was one of the prominent members of the local Methodist Church and may have been influential in bringing it about. As the movement grew in popularity, quarters larger and more centrally located may have seemed desirable. It will be remembered that the new railroad had reached Morrisville by 1872 and may have been the determining factor in making the transfer.

In 1882 Salmon Niles leased to the Morrisville Campmeeting Association "a certain piece of land known as the old M. E. Campground in the Salmon Niles sugar place adjacent to the fair ground, it being a strip of land running from the St. Johnsbury & Lake Champlain Railroad to the fair ground, where meetings have been held for the last ten years." If the period stated was accurate it fixes the date as 1872 and in "The Vermont Citizen" of August 28, 1873, we read of the extensive preparations for the gathering to be held in the Niles grove that year. The grounds were enlarged, a boarding house run by H. H. Elmore was added and tickets on the Portland & Ogdensburg Railroad were sold at half-price.

That the meetings increased in popularity is shown by the fact that in 1880 a new preacher's stand was built, and arrangements for seating 2,500 people were made, and preliminary steps were taken to make it the recognized campmeeting of the St. Albans district. In 1882, the association took a twenty-year lease of the grounds and expended $500 in repairs. The new preacher's stand, built only two years before, had been burned, but was now replaced, the seating capacity was increased, and it was the only campmeeting in the district.

While the officers were in the main local they were not confined to this town. In 1883 there was the following slate: President, B. F. Morse of Elmore; Vice-President, Newton Terrill of Morrisville; Secretary and Treasurer, A. A. Niles of Morrisville; Railroad Agent, W. H. Hyde of West Berkshire; Assistant Agent George Story of Hyde Park; Executive Committee, Rev. M. P. Bell of Morrisville, Newton Terrill of Morrisville and A. F. Whitney of Morrisville.

Towns as far distant as Essex and Sheldon had built cottages which were the headquarters for their residents while many individuals owned camps or pitched their tents for the week. The presiding elder of the district took charge of the services. In 1886 it was estimated that there were 1,500 teams on the ground on Sunday.

During the 80's the temperance movement was prominent and this campground was chosen as the place for the annual State Temperance Campmeeting, which was usually held during the first two days of the regular period of gathering. From its platform were heard temperance speakers of national repute, such as Mrs. J. K. Barney of Rhode Island, Bishop Hamilton of Boston, Gov. John P. St. John of Kansas, Mrs. Ellen Foster of Iowa, Neal Dow of Maine and Mary Livermore of Chicago and Boston, while prominent Methodist divines from all parts of the country participated.

Today one looks in vain for any sign of the old campground, and the question arises why this change. Various reasons contributed to bring about its abandonment. Chief among them was the change in the spirit of the age which has caused the campmeeting everywhere to lose its hold on people. There was a decreased interest and attendance, and the depredations of the tent caterpillars injured the grove so that it was finally cut down. So with the expiration of the lease the meetings were given up. On August 17, 1902, the last hymn was sung, the final benediction given, and the property was later disposed of at public auction. Thus a chapter of the town's history was closed. But in imagination one can still see the speaker's stand with its rows of singers and ministers, the wooden seats filled with an audience, part of which were under a canvas roof, but most of them under the blue dome of heaven, the circle of tents and cottages which enfolded the seats, the fagots which cast a wavering light upon the assembly, and in the background the stillness of the forest.

The campground also served as an ideal place for holding political rallies and here county gatherings were often held. These rallies were always Republican in complexion as no opposing party in Lamoille County was ever strong enough to stage such pretentious ones as were put on here. On this platform have appeared the candidates for the highest offices of the state, supplemented by spell binders of national repute from beyond its borders. In 1896 Gen.

P. J. Conlon of Boston and Governor, later Senator, Dillingham were the main attractions. In August, 1902, Morristown welcomed her native son, the Hon. Leslie M. Shaw, then secretary of the treasury, together with Governor McCullough and Fletcher Proctor. Professor Maxam, the popular campaign singer of that period, contributed to the entertainment his well known musical hits. From this platform have been expounded the cardinal Republican doctrines of protection, "the full dinner pail," and sound money, doctrines almost as important in the minds of the assembly as the ten commandments and the moral precepts which were enunciated during the campmeeting.

The political gatherings were not always held on the campground, for in 1888 a big meeting was staged to celebrate the victory of Harrison and Morton. Black Betsy, which figured in so many gala days, was taken to the old fair ground to contribute its part to the occasion, a huge bonfire was laid up there, and a procession lead by the Morrisville Drum Corps and the Hyde Park Band paraded the principal streets. The culmination of the event was the speech-making which consisted of remarks by P. K. Gleed, G. W. Hendee, G. W. Doty and D. J. Safford of Morrisville, R. W. Hulburd of Hyde Park, and C. H. Stearns of Johnson. This array of talent leaves no doubt of the high grade of eloquence and the genuine wit which enlivened the occasion.

Another diversion of quite a different character which flourished, especially in the 80's, was the squirrel hunt. These events were nominally in the interests of protecting game and destroying animal pests such as red squirrels, owls and other animals which were predatory by nature. Two teams, which included everyone who had any interest in hunting, were selected and staged their contest in the late fall, usually in October. In '82 the captains of the opposing forces were Benjamin H. Sanborn, later to be the founder of the well known publishing house of B. H. Sanborn & Co., and L. B. Boynton, for many years hotel keeper and dealer in real estate here. The year following George M. Powers, later chief justice of the state, and E. E. Boomhower, a well known blacksmith, led their respective sides to victory or defeat. Again F. B. Livingstone, a prominent business man who later went to California, and C. C. Rublee, one of the leading doctors in the county, led the opposing forces. On one occasion the scores reported were 21,040 to 10,070. The rating of the different animals cannot be determined, but it would seem that many a squirrel or other pest met his fate that October day.

As a reward for their prowess the victors were entertained at some public eating place.

CENTENNIAL CELEBRATION

Undoubtedly the high spot in the history of gala days in Morristown was the Centennial Celebration, held on July 4, 1890. At the March meeting of 1889 a committee consisting of H. Henry Powers, G. W. Hendee, P. K. Gleed, I. N. LeBaron, and M. C. Mower were appointed to lay plans for it, and the year following $500 was appropriated and an executive committee was elected to carry out the details of the affair. G. W. Doty, Frank Kenfield, A. O. Gates, O. D. Matthews, and R. L. Fairbanks were the men upon whom fell this task and they entered into it with enthusiasm and ability and secured the hearty cooperation of the townspeople. The grounds were on the south side of Harrison Avenue, which was not built up at all then. Here on the lots now occupied by Mrs. George A. Morse was erected a tent capable of holding 2,000 people. The whole village was gay with flags and bunting, but the centerpiece of the decorations was the arch which spanned the head of Congress Street, designed and built by C. W. Fitch. Upon one side, it bore the inscription "Grateful for the Past—Hopeful for the Future," and upon the other side, "One Hundredth Anniversary of Settlement."

The event really began on the Sunday before, with a sermon delivered by the Rev. W. A. Robinson, a native of Morristown, whose father, the Rev. Septimus Robinson, was pastor of the local Congregational Church for twenty-six years. On the evening of the third the Sherman Military Band of Burlington gave a concert in the tent and at sunrise on the Fourth, Black Betsey ushered in the momentous day by a ringing salute. Already on every hillside people were astir about their tasks so as to reach the village in time to secure a good position from which to view the parade which started at 10:30, with G. W. Doty as chief marshal. It contained several bands, the Burlington Cadets, the local G. A. R. Post, together with posts from several neighboring towns, floats representing Joe and Molly, the Walkers riding in an ox cart, Uncle Sam and the States, and various organizations. At 1:30 the audience gathered at the tent where the following program was presented:

Music
Prayer—Rev. W. E. Douglass, Pastor of the M. E. Church
Address of Welcome—
    Hon. G. W. Hendee, President of the Day
Music
Historical Address—Hon. H. H. Powers
Music
Centennial Poem—
    Rev. P. B. Fisk, Pastor of the Congregational Church
Song—Sermon from the Mountains—
    Music by Prof. W. F. Whipple
    Words by Rev. P. B. Fisk
Toasts and Responses

Hon. P. K. Gleed was toastmaster and in his inimitable manner presented a group of men particularly qualified to discuss the subject assigned them. Gov. W. P. Dillingham responded to the toast, My Green Mountain State; the Rev. W. A. Robinson spoke on The Churches of Morristown; Lieut.-Gov. U. A. Woodbury addressed the G. A. R. in particular; the Rev. Edwin Wheelock, who held an unusually long pastorate at Cambridge and was for years a trustee of Peoples Academy, paid tribute to the influence of this institution in this section of the state. The Hon. M. W. Terrill of Middlefield, Conn., a former business man here, whose ancestors were pioneers at Cadys Falls, responded to "The Merchants of Morristown"; the Hon. Leslie M. Shaw of Iowa, later secretary of the treasury, spoke of the great West and its future; the Rev. George H. Bailey of New York, pastor of the Universalist Church when the present structure was dedicated, took as his theme, "The Ministers of Morristown"; the Hon. George Wilkins of Stowe, himself a well known attorney, responded to the toast, "The Lawyers of Morristown."

To entertain such frivolous ones as did not care for the intellectual feast provided by these toasts, a ball game between the No-Names of this town and a team from Johnson was staged, and the Burlington Cadets gave an exhibition drill. At nightfall many of the "men-folks" had to return home to do the chores, but came back for the fireworks which were to afford the climax of the event. Rain injured some of the set pieces, yet they presented a spectacle which was to linger long in the memories of the boys and girls who were allowed to sit up to see them.

It was estimated that more than 10,000 people were present, and the entire event was a distinct credit to the town. Not the least of the permanent benefits coming from it was the historical address of Judge Powers. From the lips of men and women whose fathers planted the town, he gathered the facts which have formed the basis for all subsequent records of our early history.

MEMORIAL EXERCISES FOR PRESIDENT McKINLEY

On September 19, 1901, this town, in common with thousands of others throughout the country, held memorial exercises for President McKinley, recently assassinated. The citizens assembled at the Congregational Church, where a selected quartette presented suitable music and the Rev. I. P. Booth, pastor of the Universalist Church, had charge of the program. Different phases of the lamented President's life and work were presented by H. P. Munson, George J. Slayton, Frank Kenfield, Prof. W. A. Beebe, George W. Doty, F. G. Fleetwood and Congressman H. H. Powers. Thus was added another note to the chorus of love and sorrow which arose from all parts of the land.

DEDICATION OF SOLDIERS' MONUMENT

Morristown has always been proud of the military record of her sons and has shown her pride by electing individual veterans to high office and by supporting the work of their organizations. So the project of erecting a Soldiers' Monument, while discussed for some time before undertaken, when finally launched met a hearty response.

At the March meeting of 1910 Col. G. W. Doty, a tireless worker for the memorial, made an earnest appeal to the voters and Mr. C. H. A. Stafford presented the following resolution which was adopted:

"Resolved, that the Selectmen are hereby instructed to draw their order for one thousand five hundred dollars to be paid when a Soldiers' monument is erected on Academy Park to cost not less than two thousand five hundred dollars, the balance to be raised by subscription. W. A.

Beebe, H. A. Slayton, and F. G. Fleetwood are appointed to act as a building committee for the town in conjunction with a committee appointed by the G. A. R. Post, and said committee are to select kind and style of said monument." The committee elected by the G. A. R. consisted of Frank Kenfield, A. A. Niles, and Austin Wilkins, who at once started out to raise the required amount. The G. A. R. raised about $1,400, and the balance of the $4,000 spent for the memorial was secured from townspeople and persons interested in the project.

So efficiently had the committees worked that on May 30, 1911, the semi-centennial of the outbreak of the Civil War, the beautiful memorial was dedicated. It is twenty-five feet six inches high, cut from Barre granite, and is surmounted by a bronze figure twelve feet three inches high. The tablets on the first die bear in relief the names of 172 Morristown Volunteers and of eighty-five members of J. M. Warner Post, No. 4, G. A. R. Nature smiled upon the exercises, and on that bright May afternoon a large gathering of people assembled in Academy Park, where the following program was carried out:

Music	Band
Invocation	Rev. W. T. Best
Reading of National G. A. R. Order	A. A. Niles
Lincoln's Gettysburg Address	Clifford Chase
Barbara Frietchie	Mrs. Ila Niles Jackson
Presentation of the Monument to the Town of Morristown and to J. M. Warner Post, No. 4,	
	Prin. W. A. Beebe
Acceptance of Monument for the Grand Army,	A. A. Niles
Acceptance for the Town	Dr. George L. Bates
Dedicatory Ode	Chorus
(Composed for the occasion by Rev. V. M. Hardy, D. D.)	
Address	Hon. Frank Plumley, M. C.
Music	Band
Remarks	Hon. U. A. Woodbury
	Hon. H. H. Powers
America	Band

While the monument is a credit to all who participated in its erection, it speaks particularly of the interest and artistic ability of Prin. W. A. Beebe, who not only worked untiringly as chairman of the building committee, but designed it and drew the plans from which the contract was let.

CELEBRATION IN HONOR OF THE WORLD WAR VETERANS

On July 4, 1919, the town was the seat of a big celebration in honor of the Lamoille County World War Veterans. Though the gathering was held in Morrisville, most of the towns of the county participated in it, thus ensuring its success.

The village was gaily decorated with the national colors and with four honor arches, one over Main Street at The Randall, one on lower Main Street, one on upper Main Street and one on lower Portland Street. The great event of the day was the parade, which started from Waban Avenue, with Major G. L. Bates as chief marshal. The center of interest was the service boys of the county under Capt. Harold J. Fisher, but other interesting features were the floats of the G. A. R. veterans who were represented by forty-six men, the Boy Scouts, the Camp Fire Girls, the Red Cross float and floats of different business houses from here and surrounding towns, with two bands and two drum corps to supply music for the occasion.

In the afternoon excellent sporting events were staged on Main Street and in the evening from eight o'clock until nine a community sing was held. On a platform erected at the foot of Academy Park a chorus of over 300 voices, assisted by the two bands and the Thousand Islands Orchestra, gave a patriotic concert which was enjoyed by a crowd which completely took possession of that part of the village. The event closed with a ball at which, as throughout the day, the veterans were the guests of the town.

It was a perfect July day and evening, and the program was enjoyed by everyone, but especially by the guests of honor, the boys in khaki, to whom the county thus gladly paid tribute. Other places may have put on a more elaborate welcome, but nowhere was there one more sincere.

PEOPLES ACADEMY ANNIVERSARIES

So secure has been the place held by Peoples Academy in the hearts of the citizens of the town that each milestone in its history has been appropriately marked. In 1872 its twenty-fifth anniversary was remembered in connection with the completion of the year's work. May 6 was devoted to examinations, conducted by the Rev. Edwin Wheelock, Hon. C. H. Heath and F. M. Baldwin. On Tuesday evening Mr. Heath delivered an address before the alumni, as a result of which an association known as the Associated Alumni of Peoples Academy was formed, with the following officers: President, Charles Heath of Plainfield; First Vice-President, George Waterman of Hyde Park; Second Vice-President, Mrs. P. K. Gleed of Morrisville; Secretary, A. A. Niles of Morrisville.

This association seems to have been rather ephemeral, for we read nothing of its subsequent activities.

Twenty-five years later the post-prandial exercises at the Alumni Banquet featured the fiftieth anniversary.

But it remained for the seventy-fifth anniversary to call out a fuller expression of loyalty on the part of the alumni, and June 12, 1923, was a gala day in the history of the school and the town.

For months the officers of the Alumni Association, together with a special committee, had been planning to make the celebration worthy of the occasion. The committee on decorations had erected at the foot of Academy Park an arch spanning both Park Street and Main Street, outlined with electric lights and bearing the inscription 1848-1923 and surmounted by a replica of the old belfry and bell. Practically every business place in town and many private residences were gay with Green and Gold, the school colors, and even the weather man cooperated by giving a pleasant day for the event.

In the forenoon, class picnics at Lake Eden, Elmore, or some other point of interest were in order, but at one o'clock all gathered at Academy Hall for the business meeting of the Alumni Association. Following this they marched by classes, headed by Mrs. Maria Tinker of the class of '75, to the Congregational Church, where W. A. Beebe, for twenty-three years the beloved principal of the school gave a scholarly and interesting address.

The banquet was held in the gymnasium which had been artistically decorated for the event, and here about 350 guests sat down by classes to renew old acquaintances, enjoy the fine repast, and listen to the post-prandial exercises.

Hon. R. W. Hulburd, '77, of Hyde Park was toastmaster and with inimitable grace and wit introduced R. R. Morrow, principal of the school; Marion Brooks of the class of '23; Hon. H. M. McFarland of Hyde Park, who spoke along reminiscent lines; Dr. R. G. Reynolds of Columbia University, N. Y.; Mary J. Simpson of Craftsbury; Dr. C. D. Adams of Dartmouth College, and Hon.

M. S. Stone of Montpelier, all former principals, who spoke of conditions and experiences during their years of teaching here. The program closed with remarks by Justice George M. Powers and the singing of an ode written for the occasion by the Rev. V. M. Hardy, D. D. The event closed with a ball held at the town hall, which was gaily decorated, and contained, among other unusual features, pictures of nearly all the graduating classes of Peoples Academy.

Seven former principals of the school, representing a considerable part of its life time, were present, and the loyalty of its graduates is attested by the fact that New York and all the New England States, except Rhode Island, were represented by graduates, many of whom came for that day only. The generous cooperation of the citizens of the place, many of whom had never been connected with the academy, showed their appreciation of the influence and value of the institution.

WILSON MEMORIAL SERVICE

Although Morristown, like the rest of Vermont, has always been strongly Republican in politics, she appreciated the idealism and sacrifice of the great war president, Woodrow Wilson, and on the evening of February 6, 1924, a memorial service was held which was simple but genuine. It was presided over by Major G. L. Bates, who thus honored his former commander-in-chief, and the following program was presented:

Prayer	Rev. E. E. Pender
Vocal Solo	Mrs. George M. Powers
Address	Rev. W. J. McFarlane
Address	Rev. George F. Fortier
Song, "Nearer, My God, to Thee"	Audience
Taps	Harold Ober
Benediction	Rev. George F. Morton

The Rev. Mr. McFarlane spoke of the late President's early political career, when, as governor of New Jersey, he surprised both friends and opponents by demonstrating that there was a place for idealism in politics, an attitude which attracted to him the speaker, together with thousands of other young men.

Mr. Fortier spoke of Mr. Wilson's larger service to the United States and to the world in his work as president and as moulder of public thought during and after the World War.

CHAPTER XIII
ORGANIZATIONS, FRATERNAL, PATRIOTIC, AND SOCIAL

WHILE the church was the first organization in town, it antedated but a few years the oldest of the fraternal bodies, the Masons. That Masonry has played a large and honorable part in the life of the town is shown by the men who have been prominent in its work and in the history of the community. Among its members during the early period were Robert Kimball, the first merchant in Morristown; Ralph Tinker, the first doctor; Charles Meigs, the first lawyer; David P. Noyes, the first general merchant in Morrisville; Charles H. Heath and A. J. Blanchard, early principals of Peoples Academy, and since that day its ranks have included the leading business and professional men of the town.

The following history of Mount Vernon Lodge, No. 8, Free and Accepted Masons, gleaned largely from the records of the lodge, was compiled by Willard K. Sanders, worshipful master, in 1931-1933.

In the early days, Masonry was not exalted in this section by imposing temples or other beautiful edifices, nevertheless members took their Masonry more seriously then than many do today. When we remember the poor facilities for travel and the meager forms of entertainment, it is easy to see why interested members should devote a great deal of time and energy to their Masonic work. Masonry and religion were nearly synonymous. We find that a lodge congregated at ten o'clock in the morning of the date set and many times lasted until late in the evening. It was even customary to have a by-law which made it compulsory to close the lodge at 9:00 P. M. Even with those long hours, it was not unusual to have much unfinished business which had to be held over for the next communication. We find records of Masons driving regularly twenty or thirty miles once a month to attend lodge meetings, and at that time it was an offense punishable by suspension or expulsion, if a member neglected to atttend regular meetings more than three times in succession without reasonable excuse.

Records do not give us the Masonic history of the men who became the charter members of the lodge, but it is probable that they migrated here from the south and formerly belonged to some lodge, either in southern Vermont or in the southern New England States.

HISTORY OF MORRISTOWN

However, in 1812, eight Masons residing in the town of Hyde Park, namely, Thomas Taylor, John McDaniels, Nathaniel Sawyer, Christopher Huntington, Russell Hyde, Joel Burnam, Joseph Waterman, and A. Waterman, Jr., applied to the Grand Lodge of Vermont, and on November 5, 1812, Grand Master John Chipman awarded the following dispensation, which appears on page one, book one, of the records of Mt. Vernon Lodge: (While under dispensation, the lodge was known as Orange Lodge.)

"L. S. To Thomas Taylor, John McDaniels, Nathaniel P. Sawyer, Christopher Huntington, Russell B. Hyde, Joel Burnam, Joseph Waterman, and Araunah Waterman, Jr.:

"In virtue of the power and authority in me vested, I, John Chipman, Grand Master, of the Grand Lodge of the State of Vermont, do authorize and empower you to assemble in due form when a constituted number of you shall convene and open a Master Mason's Lodge at Hyde Park by the name of Orange Lodge and to do and transact all business appertaining to that degree and the lower degrees until the Monday next preceeding the second Thursday of October next.

"And I do hereby constitute and appoint my worthy Brother Thomas Taylor to be Master, Christopher Huntington, Senior Warden, and Araunah Waterman, Jr., Junior Warden thereof and for the purposes herein mentioned this shall be your sufficient Letter of Dispensation.

"In Testimony whereof I have hereunto affixed my signature and private seal this 5th day of November, Anno Lucis 5812 (1812).

"(Signed) JOHN CHIPMAN, Grand Master"

The records of the first meeting of Orange Lodge are given as follows:
"Orange Lodge convened at Hyde Park, Dec 16th 1812.
Present: R. W. Thomas Taylor M.
W. Christopher Huntington, S. W.
W. Araunah Waterman Jr, J. W.
Brothers: Nathaniel P Sawyer
Joseph Waterman
Russell B. Hyde
Daniel Griswold
John McDaniels
John Griswold
Abel Smith
Nathaniel Merrill, Visiting brother.

"Lodge opened on the first degree of Masonry and proceeded to ballot for Treasurer and Secretary when Nath'l P. Sawyer was chosen Treasurer and Joseph Waterman Secretary.

"Appointments by W. Master
    Russell B. Hyde Senior D.
    Daniel Griswold J. D.
    John McDaniels Steward
    John Griswold Tyler.

"The ballots were taken for Gamaliel Taylor who was proposed to the Lodge as a candidate for initiation and found clear he was accordingly initiated. Fees $10.00 paid $8.00.

"Lodge opened on second degree of Masonry and passed Brother Abel Smith to the degree of Fellow Craft. Fees $2.00 paid.

"Opened on the third degree of Masonry when Brother Daniel Griswold was raised to the sublime degree of a Master Mason. Fees $3.00
                                2.00
                                1.00

"Joseph Farrar of Eden was proposed by Bro. C. Huntington as a candidate for initiation at our next regular communication and Bro. Huntington became accountable for the deposit. Bro. Joseph Waterman proposed Joseph Hadley of Hyde Park as a candidate for initiation at the next regular communication and becomes accountable for the deposit. Bro. N. P. Sawyer proposed Jonathan Merrill of Sterling as a candidate for initiation and became accountable for the deposit. Bro. John McDaniels proposed Jacob P. Hadley for initiation at our next regular communication and paid deposit $2.00.

"Descended and closed on the first degree of Masonry.

"JOSEPH WATERMAN, Sec'y."

From the above we note that Orange Lodge's jurisdiction covered a great deal of territory since at this first meeting there were proposed candidates from Eden, Hyde Park, and Sterling (later the town of Sterling was divided between Morristown, Johnson, and Stowe). In later records we find candidates from Elmore, Wolcott, Stowe, Johnson, Cambridge, and Kelleyvale (later Lowell); also many from Morristown.

Other interesting facts show the difference in Masonic procedure from that of today. At that time the lodge

HISTORY OF MORRISTOWN   199

was opened on the first degree of Masonry and the business of the lodge transacted in that degree, except the exemplification of the higher degrees when the lodge was later opened on the second or third degree. Today, the lodge must do all its business on the third degree and only Master Masons (third degree) are eligible to take part in voting or other business of the lodge. We also learn that the ballot had to be passed for each degree, and it was not at all uncommon for a Mason not to take more than the first or second degree.

The by-laws under which this lodge worked are interesting and are found in the front of book one immediately after the copy of the dispensation:

"BY-LAWS OF ORANGE LODGE

"Article 1. This Lodge shall hold their regular communication on the Wednesday's preceeding the full of the Moon unless the moon shall full on that day in which case the communication shall be one (illegible) Wednesday at the full of the Moon in each month at one o'clock P. M. except in the month of June and December, and then unless the Lodge should conclude to celebrate the Festivals of the St. Johns, in which case the communication shall be holden on Festival days, the Lodge on such days shall convene punctually at 10 o'clock A. M. If the Festival should fall on Saturday or Sunday, the Monday following shall be the regular communications. (Note: There are many lodges who still adhere to this old rule of dating their meetings from the full of the moon.)

"2nd. All regular communications and also at all meetings of the Lodge called in cases of emergency it shall be the duty of each member residing within a reasonable distance for attendance, of which distance the Lodge shall judge, to attend punctually at the hour appointed unless prevented by some unavoidable necessity or unavoidable excuse of which the Lodge shall be informed and judge of sufficiency of excuse.

"3rd. The officers of the Lodge shall be chosen at the first regular communication in December annually unless to supply vacancies.

"4th. During Lodge hours every brother shall attend in the Lodge room and not absent himself therefrom without the leave of the Master and then not more than five minutes unless from necessity.

"5th. Every brother desiring to speak shall arise and address the Master and having obtained leave shall speak during the Master's pleasure.

"6th. No brother shall speak more than once to the same question unless to explain himself nor shall any brother interrupt the brother speaking.

"7th. All questions of order shall be decided by the Master.

"8th. A candidate for initiation shall be nominated by a Brother Master Mason and at least one regular communication previous to that in which the ballots shall be taken on the question of his admission. At the time of his nomination such candidate shall advance two dollars to be put into the treasury. If he withdraw or neglect to pursue his application the money shall be forfeited to the Treasury, if he should be balloted for and not admitted it shall be returned to him but if he be admitted it shall pass to his account as part of initiation fee.

"9th. The Master and Wardens shall be with Secretary and Treasurer a standing committee of Charity for this Lodge.

"10th. No member of this Lodge can be absent more than two regular communications unless he assigns reasons satisfactory to the authority of the lodge for such absence and such absence without reasons assigned as aforesaid must be considered as grounds for censure or suspense.

"11th. No brother during hours of business shall in the Lodge room drink spirituous liquor unless by a general order from the Master. (Note: There is a heavy black line drawn around article 11 and underneath it appears the notation "Expunged by unanimous vote".)

"12th. Every brother and member of this Lodge shall behave himself discreetly and orderly in and out of the Lodge so that he may thereby obtain a good report. And if any member shall in or out of the Lodge at a meeting of the Lodge or at any other time be guilty of profane swearing; or drinking spirituous liquors to excess, he shall for the first offense receive a severe reprimand from the Master in open lodge and shall for the second offense be liable to suspension or expulsion. And it shall be the duty of and every member is hereby required to make complaint to the Master against any Brother whom he shall know to be guilty of intoxication such complaint may be public or by private communication to the Master who shall be permitted to disclose the name of the complainant without his consent.

"13th. No brother shall disclose the name of a brother voting against a candidate upon pain of expulsion.

"14th. It shall be the duty of the Master and Wardens to examine and decide on the validity of all claims or demands against the Lodge and no account shall be paid by the Treasurer until it has been passed or allowed by them. They shall have power at all times to examine the books of the Secretary and Treasurer to order all furniture and clothing as they shall find necessary and to report from time to time to the Lodge such things as they may think proper and sufficiently important. And it shall be their duty to report the state of the Lodge at the first regular communication in December annually.

"15th. When any brother shall desire to remove his relation from this to any other Lodge he shall apply for liberty assigning his reasons and upon his request being granted he shall receive a certificate thereof from the Secretary and an entry shall be made on the Lodge Book of his regular dimission.

"16th. Every brother shall sign his name to the By-laws before he shall be permitted to exercise the privileges of a member of this lodge.

"17th. No brother shall be allowed to cast his vote for any candidate for initiation passing and raising until he shall have been raised to the sublime degree of a Master Mason.

"18th. The Lodge shall close by nine o'clock in the evening unless unfinished business remains before the lodge or in some case of emergency. And no member shall remain in the Lodge room more than one hour after the Lodge is closed without being liable to a severe censure from the Master in Open Lodge."

At the annual communication of the Grand Lodge in October, 1813, a charter was duly awarded to this lodge and the name changed to Mount Vernon Lodge and registered as Number 36, it being the thirty-sixth lodge chartered under the Grand Lodge of Vermont. This charter was dated October 12, 1813.

One of the major problems confronting the lodge in its early years was the collection of dues. We are unable to discover just how much the dues were at that time, but the earliest allusion to dues some years later is $1.25 per year, and at that period even that sum was much more of a burden than a greater amount would be now. At this period, however, a needy brother was promptly assisted if in distress. We find that in October, 1816, "Voted three dollars from the funds of the Lodge as a donation of Charity to alleviate the distress of sickness of a son of William Whitney of Wolcott." In July, 1817, we find "Proceeded to call Brother G——— W——— to answer to a charge preferred against him for un-Masonic Conduct and after a humble confession, was excused from his charge."

Another instance of the munificence of the lodge appears under date of August 8, 1821: "Voted that after the present dues of this lodge are paid that the sum of fifteen dollars be taken from the funds of this Lodge for F——— S——— to purchase him a cow."

In May, 1822, the lodge received "and read from certain individuals (Mason) at the City of Washington concerning the formation of a Grand Lodge of the United States." This was only one of a number of attempts to bring about such an organization, but each attempt has failed since the feeling was that more good could be had by each state operating under its own Grand Lodge rather than being subject to a national organization.

If a brother was expelled the word was broadcast by having the fact published in the "Northern Sentinel" at Burlington.

We now come to an unsavory part of the history of the lodge and of Masonry in general. To understand the situation, we shall have to study facts in other places the more clearly to understand the situation in this lodge during the so-called Anti-Masonic period.

At Batavia, N. Y., there lived a man by name, William Morgan, dissolute and shiftless, intemperate in his habits and irresponsible in his obligations, a man shunned by his neighbors and respected by no one. Formerly he came from Canada, where he was in the brewery business, but his plant burned and he drifted into New York State. Masonically, he claimed to have been made a Royal Arch Mason at some former time and there were certain credentials to prove it, but it is extremely doubtful if he ever received any of the six preceeding degrees. Through some weakness he was admitted to the Royal Arch degree without care being taken to see that he had been invested with those which precede it. He was one of the signers of a petition for a Royal Arch Chapter at Batavia, but owing to his character, the others interested refused to have anything to do with him and would not admit him to the new chapter.

This fact, and the influence of unscrupulous friends, influenced him to write an exposé of the degrees and lectures pertaining to Freemasonry. Had he been permitted to publish this work unmolested, it would have undoubtedly soon died an early and natural death, but unfortunately several Masons acting without authority of any lodge sought to thwart his attempts with the result that the whole nation was placed in turmoil.

Two attempts were made to burn the printing office where this work was in preparation, both of which were unsuccessful. Soon after this (1826) Morgan was spirited away mysteriously and never seen again. He was traced to Fort Niagara, but no clue could be found of him farther. This was sufficient grounds for the story that he was kidnapped by Masons, taken in a boat into the Niagara River, tied, weighted, and drowned. A year later a body was found upon the shores of Lake Ontario and positively identified as being that of Morgan and was buried as such. Soon after, a family, a member of which had been drowned, hearing of the incident, had the body disinterred and found that it was not Morgan at all, but an entirely different person. By this time, however, the incident had become a national issue socially and politically, and the anti-Masonic feeling was growing fast as it was said that Masonry was responsible for the death of Morgan.

Forty-three years later, after the excitement was all over, a true account of the incident came to light which was as follows: A man (and a Mason) met Morgan and entered into an agreement with him whereby he would destroy all copy of the exposé, stop drinking, clothe himself decently with money donated, provide for the immediate necessities of his family and go to Canada, where he would be set up in business and given a new start and in due time bring his family to live with him. This he agreed to. They left Batavia on the night of September 12, 1826, and upon arrival at Fort Niagara, were rowed across the river to Canada, where they were met by a committee of men who were to see that he was safely taken care of. However, plans had not been completed in Canada, so he was taken back to Fort Niagara and kept there a week and finally turned over to the Canadians who took him to Hamilton, Ontario, gave him $500 and took a receipt for it and left him.

Arrangements were made to transport his family to him, but upon investigation it was found that he had boarded a ship and left the country never to be heard from again.

It is a strange fact that following this disturbance that feeling against the Masonic Fraternity should crystallize in Vermont. The "North Star," a newspaper published in Danville, was the chief aggressor. This paper was the whip-lash which kept Vermont completely stirred up over this event for many years. Many strong Masons were as intent upon continuing the organization as were others to destroy, but many who were easily swerved by public opinion denounced the fraternity as a veritable invention of the devil and freely made statements (mostly false) about the oaths and obligations of Masonry. Lodges all over the state lost in membership and many had to give up their meetings altogether. Others struggled on, meeting occasionally. At the session of the Grand Lodge at Montpelier in 1831 the following resolution was passed:

"Resolved that the secular lodges under the jurisdiction of this Grand Lodge be recommended to hold but two communications during the year; one for good order and discipline and instruction in Masonry and the other for the yearly choice of officers."

We have the following quotations from the "North Star":

July 19, 1831: "The organization and government of the Grand Lodges, Chapters and Grand Encampments must be totally annihilated and forever; subordinate branches must fully participate in the general dissolution of the Sorceress and Cheat; and an evidence must be given to the American freemen that masons, one and all, have simultaneously and with united voice absolved themselves, not only from masonic government but from the aristocratic and treasonable obligations of their illegal and murderous oaths."

October 25, 1831: "The result of the Grand Lodge and Chapter at Montpelier, for the ostensible purpose of giving up their charters, is such as we anticipated. Masonry will never give up its usurped power and exclusive privileges. Tyrants never do this but by coercion. It must be destroyed by inches."

The lodges struggled on for about two years longer, many making known their desire of surrendering their charter and disbanding. So many of these requests were made that the Grand Lodge in 1833 enacted the following resolution:

"Resolved that the Grand Lodge is ready to receive and revoke the charters of such secular Lodges under its jurisdiction as are desirous of surrendering them at the present time, and that the representatives of secular lodges who are authorized to make such surrenders are now requested to deposit their said charters with the Grand Secretary and that each and every secular lodge be and is hereby authorized to surrender and deliver its charter and records to the Grand Secretary aforesaid at any time previous to the next annual communication of this Grand Lodge, and that all the funds, jewels, furniture and property of such Lodges be left under their control respectively, to be appropriated to such objects as they may think proper and that the Grand Lodge recommend to said Lodges to appropriate their funds and the avails of their property to the common schools fund of this State."

Now, what effect did this feeling have upon the local lodge?

We find that from 1828 to 1833 the meetings were more and more poorly attended, at times there being only two or three present. The presence of these few, however, shows the spirit with which many persisted in their views of the righteousness of Masonry.

March 14, 1832, we read:

"Mt. Vernon Lodge convened at Hyde Park.
Present: Joseph Sears
          Jonathan Merrill
          Sewell Newton
          David McDaniel
          Breed Noyes

"Lodge opened on the first degree of Freemasonry without form. Lodge closed in same form.
"JOSEPH SEARS, Sec'y Pro tem."

And on Dec. 25, 1833, the last meeting we have any record of prior to the discontinuance of operations shows that:

"Mt. Vernon Lodge convened at Hyde Park Dec 25, 1833.
Present: Sewel Newton
          Ralph Hill
          Ariel Newton

"Lodge opened on the first degree of freemasonry without form. Voted that the old officers serve the year ensuing. Lodge closed without form.

"RALPH HILL, Sec' pro tem."

No record exists as to whether any attempts were made to meet between the years 1833 and 1850. We only have it handed down by tradition that during these years, different members met clandestinely in different places, gathering after dark and traveling singly or by two so as not to arouse suspicion. At this time a Mason was shunned by the majority and very few would admit membership in the fraternity. One favorite rendezvous, we hear, was in one of the large vats in the tub shop on the Lamoille River, in Morristown. As to how much degree work was done or other activities attended to, we know nothing. It shows the spirit which prevailed during the craft at that period. We do know, however, that the charter of this lodge was never surrendered.

In 1846 the Grand Lodge convened in Burlington and opened for business in ample form for the first time in ten years. The attendance was much better since by this time the feeling against the fraternity had grown less intense. Plans were made for the re-establishment of Masonry and for the investigation of the condition of those subordinate lodges still under charter.

At the annual session in 1849 notice was served upon all lodges that they must organize within one year. Accordingly we find Mt. Vernon Lodge convened at Hyde Park December 16, 1850, for reorganization. Officers were elected for the first time in seventeen years and the lodge was represented in Grand Lodge.

At this point owing to the small number of the original seventy-three lodges then holding charters it was necessary to renumber them. Mount Vernon Lodge being the eighth oldest lodge then in existence, its number was changed from thirty-six to eight, by which number it has been known ever since.

At the regular communication, held September 10, 1851, "Chose Bro. J. Tinker and J. Sears a committee to furnish a suitable place for Lodge meetings."

This committee evidently functioned, for we find that the next communication was held at Cadys Falls under date of February 4, 1852.

A few pages later the following appears:

"Mt. Vernon Lodge convened at Morristown November 4th 1852 to celebrate the centennial anniversary of the initiation of Brother George Washington into the secrets of freemasonry.

"A. NEWTON, Sec'y."

Under date of November 1, 1854, we find a record of the lodge in which it states that it was voted to remove the furniture of the lodge to Morrisville at the next regular meeting. As the meetings at that period were all held at Morristown, we may infer that heretofore they had been held at Morristown Corners. The records show that November 29, 1854, the lodge opened at Morrisville, so that this is probably the first time that a Masonic Lodge opened in the present village of Morrisville.

January 5, 1855, it was "voted to meet at Morrisville the succeeding six months and the subsequent six months at Hyde Park and alternately so in the future." In May, 1855, it was also voted that "Brothers Burnet and Noyes are a committee to remove the Lodge Furniture to Cleveland's Inn, at Hyde Park."

This is the first record that shows definitely just where the lodge meetings were to be held. In June, 1855, we find that Mt. Vernon Lodge convened at Hyde Park, where they met regularly until December, 1855, when they again returned to Morrisville.

An interesting note appears in the records of the meeting December 19, 1855: "The following ladies were initiated into the degrees of Daughters of Zion as Master Masons Wives: Lucy Wheelock, Cornelia Gleed, Anna M. Burnet and Lydia Earl." This degree was conferred while the lodge was open on the first degree. No record seems to exist as to the nature of the order of Daughters of Zion nor what they stood for. Only one more record appears (June, 1856) when this degree was conferred upon Ruth Allen, so it would appear that this organization was short lived and of little consequence.

By this time it was undoubtedly unsatisfactory to the members to have their meetings held in Morrisville for six months and in Hyde Park for the remainder of the year. Accordingly at the meeting March 4, 1857, we read "That the Worshipful Master be requested to summon a special Lodge and that every Brother have notice thereof and information be given that the matter of Permanent location will be presented for the consideration of said meeting at 3 o'clock P. M."

July 1, 1857, the Grand Lodge issued a dispensation enabling the lodge to meet at Morrisville. From this we would judge that even though they had been meeting in Morrisville they had no legal right to do so under their charter, as the place of meeting had not been approved by the Grand Lodge.

The following year the members decided that they wanted a hall of their own, so in August, 1858, a committee was appointed to investigate the possibilities of either renting a hall or building one. Several different ones proposed to build a hall suitable for the use of the lodge and then rent it to the lodge, but this plan did not appeal to the members, so in September, 1860, it was voted "to appropriate $150.00 to the building committee in building a hall for the Lodge on the Ground occupied by Mr. Gleed's office and the motion passed unanimously." Mr. Gleed's office was located on the lot where the building occupied by the Peck Pharmacy now stands. A committee was appointed to see to the building of the hall and funds were raised by subscription and the sale of stock to finance the project.

There were several innovations in force at about this time which are interesting. Of course the country was in the midst of the Civil War at this point and many wanted to become Masons before entering the service. Working under special dispensation August 31, 1861, several candidates came forward and were invested with the three degrees all at one session.

At that time it was customary to call the lodge from Labor to Refreshment from one meeting to another, or, in other words, the lodge was never closed from month to month. This is strictly illegal now, but at that time Masonic law was not so strict.

December 3, 1862, "The petition of members of the 11th Regiment Vermont Volunteer Militia, to the Most

Worshipful Grand Lodge of Vermont for a charter for a regimental Lodge was presented to Mt. Vernon Lodge requesting their influence at the next Grand Lodge meeting in their behalf." Other records show that there were many such lodges in the army working under the authority of different Grand Lodges of the United States.

On March 26, 1863, the new lodge room was first opened for business and we read "the Most Worshipful Grand Lodge of Vermont came in and dedicated the Hall with proper ceremonies. Then formed in procession with the Grand Lodge and proceeded to the town hall and listened to an address by L. B. Englesby, Esq. Grand Master of the Grand Lodge of Vermont. Then formed in procession and returned to the hall and the lodge was closed in due form." Thus it seems that the lodge room must have been rather small and not ample to care for the large crowd which attended the dedication.

From this time onward for a year or more there were many Masonic funerals of members who had lost their lives in the war, whose bodies were sent home for interment, and many pages of book two of the records of the lodge are inscribed to the memory of these members.

In 1865 interest was aroused in the organization of a chapter of Royal Arch Masons and it was voted to make such alterations to the hall as was necessary to accommodate the chapter. The chapter was not officially chartered until October 2, 1867, and was chartered under the name of Tucker Chapter, as it now stands.

An interesting bit of reading is found under date of December 27, 1865, as follows:

"Voted to pay the Tyler $1.50 for his attendance on every regular and special communication and it shall be his duty at the hour of the meeting of the Lodge to have the hall warm and swept and to have the care of the Jewels and in short to give a general evidence of good housewifery."

In 1868 the Grand Army of the Republic was organized in Morrisville and the lodge voted to rent to the Grand Army the ante room for use in holding their meetings.

Following the war, new lodges began to spring up in the smaller villages and where before, Mt. Vernon Lodge covered the whole county, now there were new lodges being formed in Cambridge, Johnson, Eden, Stowe, and Wolcott. The charter members of all these lodges were largely formerly from Mt. Vernon Lodge. Mt. Vernon Lodge having become settled in Morrisville with a new building, the members of the lodge from Hyde Park felt that they should have a lodge of their own so they petitioned Mt. Vernon Lodge for permission to form such a lodge, and the permission was readily granted. However, we find no record that the matter went any further, so it evidently was given up for lack of membership.

No sooner had the lodge begun to be prosperous than once more it was destined to endure another hardship, for on the first day of March, 1869, their new hall was totally destroyed by fire. Thus we see that they only occupied this lodge room for seven years. At this point the Vermont spirit stood uppermost, for on the sixth of March the lodge convened at the Morrisville House and made plans for a new hall to be erected as soon as possible. Several plans were presented and the matter was left for further consideration at the next meeting.

March 24 the lodge opened for work in Cadys Falls and George's new factory (this is the building that was later used as a pulp mill and stood on the spot where the little power house now stands). At this meeting D. J. Safford, P. P. Roberts and J. A. George were appointed a committee to provide jewels, furniture, and aprons.

In the fire which destroyed the lodge room, the original charter was also destroyed, together with the furniture, jewels, and other paraphernalia. It is indeed fortunate that the records of the lodge up to that time were not also lost, but for some reason they were saved, probably being in the hands of the secretary and not kept in the lodge room.

Being without a charter, they were not legally entitled to meet as Masons in lodge so application was made to the Grand Lodge and the following dispensation was granted pending the awarding of a new charter:

"To whom it May Concern:

"Greeting: The permission of the Grand Master is hereby granted to the Officers and Brethren of Mount Vernon Lodge No. 8 at Morrisville, Vt. to meet in accordance with their usual custom as Masons, and to perform their regular duties as such and in capacity of a Regularly Chartered Lodge of Free and Accepted Masons. Said Lodge having lost its Charter by fire and everything pertaining to the Lodge, except its Charter. This Permission or dispensation to be, or remain in force until such time as said Lodge shall receive from the usual proper source a duplicate of the Charter lost by fire the 1st Day of March 1869 unless for cause sooner revoked.

"GEORGE M. HALL, Grand Master."

In April, 1869, U. A. Woodbury presented the following plan to the lodge:
"that this Lodge build another story on the Town Hall, provided that we can get the consent of the Town and that they will pay in what it will benefit said Town."

Arrangements were therefore made for a special town meeting, which was held April 24, and the town agreed to the plan and appropriated $250 to assist in the work.

That the lodge lost no time is evidenced by the fact that on December 4, 1869 (only nine months after the fire), they moved into the new hall over the town hall, which was to be their permanent quarters for the coming sixty-one years. At this first meeting it was voted to give the Morrisville Silver Cornet Band the use of the dining room for rehearsals as long as the band would agree to play for Masonic funerals.

The new hall was formally dedicated June 24, 1870 (on the anniversary observance of St. John the Baptist), beginning in the morning with a parade consisting of the Morrisville Silver Cornet Band; Mineral Lodge, Wolcott; Waterman Lodge, Johnson; Mt. Norris Lodge, Eden; Warner Lodge, Cambridge; Meridian Sun Lodge, Craftsbury; North Star Lodge, Richmond; Lamoille Lodge, Fairfax; Mt. Vernon Lodge; Stowe Silver Cornet Band, and the Grand Lodge. A series of exercises were held in the town hall, and after dinner and another parade, the lodge room was dedicated by the Grand Lodge.

For the next few decades, there appears little in the records that would be of general interest. Most of the time there was little beside degree work and routine business to occupy the attention of the lodge. Therefore we will touch upon a few high-lights briefly.

May, 1883, it was voted to allow the Eastern Star Chapter, about to be organized in Morrisville, the use of the Masonic rooms for their meetings.

November, 1883, we read that the entire indebtedness incurred from the building of the rooms over the town hall was cancelled.

In November, 1891, agreeable to recommendation of the Grand Lodge, the date of the annual meeting was changed from December to April. There are a few lodges, however, who still hold their meetings in December.

By 1892 it was felt by the lodge that the quarters were not large enough to accommodate the several bodies so a committee was appointed to investigate the possibility of enlarging the hall. This is but the beginning of a series of attempts at expansion which cover a period of nearly forty years.

In 1907 Lamoille Commandery was organized and was given the use of the Masonic hall for their meetings.

December, 1915, a committee was appointed to investigate the possibilities of the erection of a new Masonic Temple and the following month a committee composed of C. H. Slocum, C. H. A. Stafford, A. H. Slayton, W. I. LeBaron, and C. A. Spiller was appointed.

In May, 1916, this committee began to function and in July, agreeable to recommendations of this committee, the lodge voted to purchase the Matthews lot on Portland Street as a site for a new hall This is the lot where the Sweet & Burt filling station now stands. The plan at that time was to proceed with the building immediately, but by April, 1917, the United States became engaged in the World War and the matter of a new temple was dropped.

July 11, 1917, the lodge voted to present the sum of $10 to each new initiate who should receive the three degrees and who was enrolled in the Army of the United States. There were many young men already enlisted who took this opportunity to become Masons, and many were the occasions when the lodge was in session until the early hours of the morning working the three degrees upon those who were soon to leave for France. July 18, 1917, nine members received the Master Mason degree, having received the first and second degrees at a special meeting held under dispensation of the Grand Lodge the previous week. The lodge procured a service flag upon which were many stars showing that the lodge was well represented in the great national catastrophe.

After the war the matter of building was again brought up, but owing to the unsettled condition it was dropped.

With the boom times of 1929 the matter was once more brought up, the old committee discharged, and a new one appointed, consisting of C. A. Spiller, E. W. Gates, A. M. Adams, P. J. Liberty, and J. H. Eaton, to report at the next communication as to the possibilities of building. They reported favorably so a building committee was appointed, consisting of W. M. Johnstone, M. B. White, W. K. Sanders, R. B. Woods, and the Rev. D. K. Evans.

February 12, 1930, the committee reported and the lodge voted (1) to empower the master and wardens to sell the lot then owned by the lodge on Portland Street; (2) to empower the master and wardens to sell the property then used by the lodge as soon as a new temple should be built; (3) to purchase the W. T. Slayton property which was then available and well suited to the use of the lodge. The master and wardens purchased the Slayton property and sold the old lot to Sweet & Burt, Inc., of Stowe, immediately after this meeting.

March 12, 1930, the lodge, after examining plans unanimously, voted that the committee proceed with the building immediately. The Rev. D. K. Evans having moved away, O. E. Blodgett was appointed to serve on the committee in his place.

Thus we find that after a period of nearly forty years a long cherished desire for more comfortable quarters for the lodge and other orders was about to materialize, for on the morning of May 27, 1930, the work of excavating the new cellar was started. Work progressed rapidly and on Thanksgiving Day, 1930, the furniture was moved from the old hall to the new.

On the morning of December 3 the temple was thrown open to the public until noon. At three o'clock that afternoon, with a large number of members and friends present, the Grand Lodge of Vermont, Grand Master Aaron Grout, presiding, dedicated the new temple to the use of Masonry. A very inspiring address was given at this time by the Rev. G. E. Goodliffe, a member of Mt. Vernon Lodge. In the evening, Past Masters' night was observed with the working of the Master Mason degree, George G. Morse, presiding, and Philip A. King was the first candidate to receive a degree in this new hall.

Very soon after, the old hall was sold to James M. Warner Woman's Relief Corps, and the proceeds of the sale used to help defray the expenses of the new building.

Also the Pastime Club, most of the members of which were also members of Mt. Vernon Lodge, disbanded and donated all of their furniture to the lodge to furnish its club and recreation rooms with.

Thus we find that Mt. Vernon Lodge has quite an unique history since it has existed through the War of 1812, the Civil War, the Spanish-American War, and the great World War, or over a period of 120 years. What the future years will bring to Mt. Vernon Lodge we can only guess, but we hope that it will continue to spread the gospel of Truth, Charity, and Brotherly Love as it has in the past.

ORDER OF THE EASTERN STAR

The dispensation for the inauguration of the Order of the Eastern Star was granted in May, 1883, upon petition of Mesdames Cleora V. Carner, Calista M. Burke, Addie A. Wood, Esther A. Fitch, and Deette F. Woodward, and the body was designated Coral Chapter, No. 16, O. E. S. Its first worthy matron was Mrs. Cleora Carner, its associate matron Mrs. Calista Burke and Carlos C. Burke was its first worthy patron. At the annual session of the Grand Chapter, held the month following, the charter was granted and the order started with eighteen members. Since that time it has been one of the leading organizations of the town.

During these years it has played its part in the work of the order in the state and its members have filled many of the lower offices in the Grand Chapter. In 1886 William G. McClintock was elected worthy grand patron of the Grand Chapter and was re-elected the year following, while Mrs. Edna Billings worked up through the various chairs and became grand matron of the Grand Chapter in 1934.

In 1889 the Grand Chapter meeting was held here. The growth of the order in the state may be seen from the fact that at this meeting there were forty-two voting delegates, while today there would probably be 400. The following account of the exemplification of the work of the order by Coral Chapter was printed in the Transactions of the Sixteenth Annual Convocation of the Grand Chapter:

"The work of the order was finely exemplified, in some respects better than had ever before been witnessed, with the Grand Chapter as audience."

The order has shared the pleasure of the Masons in their new quarters and has taken its part in the activities common to both bodies.

The temple is also the meeting place of Lamoille Commandery, No. 13, Knights Templars, which was chartered in 1907, and includes in its membership sir knights from Hyde Park and Stowe as well as Morristown. One of its members, Thomas C. Cheney, served as grand commander of the state Order of Knight Templars in 1930, at which time the annual conclave was held here.

Morrisville was never host to a more colorful gathering than this Eighty-Eighth Conclave, held on June 22-24. The convention opened on Sunday evening with a musical program presented by local talent and a sermon by the Rev. William J. Ballou of Chester, grand prelate. On Monday, a banquet was held at Samoset-on-Lake Lamoille, the most largely attended past commanders' meeting ever held in the state up to that time. The business session was held Tuesday morning, and in the afternoon the parade started from Peoples Academy, and marched through the principal streets of the village. The striking uniforms of the knights, representing fourteen different commanderies, and the varied uniforms of the five bands made it the largest and most beautiful parade ever seen here. The conclave closed with a concert, reception, and ball held in the auditorium of Peoples Academy.

GRAND ARMY OF THE REPUBLIC

Next to the Masons in point of time was the James M. Warner Post, G. A. R. The loyalty which prompted the men of Morristown to volunteer at the time of their country's need led them to establish and maintain a strong and active G. A. R. post. It was first organized on May 6, 1868, the same year in which the Department of Vermont was established, and was the fourth post in the state. Its first commander was Capt. C. J. Lewis, an officer with a gallant war record which caused the State Department to select him as its first assistant adjutant-general. The post was named after Gen. James M. Warner, a native of Middlebury, Vt., a graduate of West Point, who was made colonel of the Eleventh Vermont Volunteers at the outbreak of the war and was promoted for gallant and meritorious conduct until he was brevet brigadier-general in 1865.

The new post had eleven charter members at first, but interest lagged and in September, 1870, their charter was surrendered. This indifference was only a passing phase, however, and in 1878 the post was reorganized with forty-one charter members and George W. Doty its commander. From that time until death depleted its ranks to the point of extinction it was one of the leading influences in town. A perusal of the local newspapers shows it to have been instrumental in arranging lecture courses and public entertainments; it was the prime mover in the Soldiers' Reunions held on the fair grounds for many years; it was influential in securing the Soldiers' Monument; and its members were leaders in the civic life of the town for many years.

This post furnished three of the commanders of the Department of Vermont. In 1893 and 1894 George W. Doty served in that capacity and during his term of office A. A. Niles was assistant adjutant-general and Frank Kenfield assistant quartermaster-general. At the annual encampment, held in Burlington that year, Colonel Doty was able to report that the local post included seventy-four members. There were then 111 posts in the state, with a membership of 5,308.

Ten years later the state again honored the local post by electing Capt. Frank Kenfield its department commander. As an indication of the decreasing ranks of this body throughout the state, the official reports gave 101 posts and 2,838 members. This, the Thirty-Seventh Annual Encampment, was held in Morrisville on February 25 and 26, 1903. Preliminary to the opening of the business sessions of Wednesday the local W. R. C. gave a reception, at which about 250 guests were greeted by the receiving line which included among others several of the past presidents of the corps and past department commanders of the G. A. R. Hon. Hugh Henry of Concord, N. H., Gen. O. O. Howard of Burlington, Governor McCullough of Bennington, Gen. T. S. Peck of Burlington Ex-Congressman H. H. Powers of Morrisville and others well known throughout the state and beyond. At the public campfire, held in the town hall on Wednesday evening, F. W. McGettrick, then of St. Albans, acted as toastmaster and presented among others Dr. T. H. Murphy of New York City, Mrs. Kate Jones, also of New York, then national patriotic instructor, Ex-Lieut.-Gov. Z. M. Mansur of Newport, H. H. Powers of Morrisville, Pension Agent Hugh Henry of Concord, N. H. Thus was brought to an end an event of much interest to the soldiers of the town.

In 1911 and 1912 the state again selected its department commander from the local post in the person of A. A. Niles, and the Forty-Sixth Annual Encampment, over which he presided, was held in Rutland June 6 and 7, 1912. The number of the posts in the state had then been reduced to eighty-seven, with a membership of 2,131. The passing years have taken their toll in the local order until this organization, which once included the leaders of the town, in 1935 has but one member.

WOMAN'S RELIEF CORPS

Closely connected with the Grand Army of the Republic is the Woman's Relief Corps and James M. Warner Relief Corps, No. 57, was organized in December, 1889, largely through the efforts of Frank Kenfield, then commander of the post. It had twenty-five charter members and chose Mrs. Florence Gates its first president and Mrs. Clara Niles its second. This body has always been a strong ally of the G. A. R., and since its membership is not confined to the wives or close relatives of the veterans of the Civil War, it is not limited in numbers as are the other affiliated orders and still maintains its strength. That its membership has been of a high order is shown by the contributions this corps has made to the work of the order in the state.

Mrs. Gates, the first president of the local corps, was elected president of the Department of Vermont in 1897-'98.

Mrs. Clara B. Niles was elected senior vice-president of the state body in 1898 and president in 1899-1900. She was renominated for a second term, but refused to serve.

Again in 1925 and 1926 the state body came to Morrisville for its president and Mrs. Annie Wallace served in that capacity.

There have been many red letter days in the history of the two organizations. On one occasion Capt. and Mrs. C. J. Lewis, then residing in Hannibal, Mo., visited the post, of which he had been the first commander. He presented it with a gavel, the head of which was of mahogany shaped from a piece taken from the historic battlefield of El Caney near Santiago, while the handle was of oak from the noted cave of Mark Twain at Hannibal.

Another interesting event was the visit of Mr. and Mrs. James Van Metre, which occurred in September,

1915. Mrs. Van Metre was the Unknown Heroine of L. E. Chittenden's novel by that name and the story of her services to a Vermont soldier is the theme of that book. They are also related in brief form in Benedict's "Vermont in the Civil War." In September, 1864, Lieut. Henry Bedell of Westfield, Vt., a member of the Eleventh Vermont, was seriously wounded near Berryville, Va. His captain, Charles J. Lewis, of this town, and Capt. Chester Dodge, also from Morristown, took care that he was removed to a dwelling and money and medicine left for his care. But the only attention he received was from a faithful colored man who finally went to Mrs. Van Metre and begged her to do what she could for the sufferer. One of her brothers was supposed to have been killed and another mortally wounded in the conflict and her husband was even then confined in a northern prison. If she had been a woman of less noble character, she would have let the thought of what she had personally suffered at the hands of this man's comrades check her natural impulses to succor; but, instead, she called in her own family physician and at considerable danger to herself nursed him back to such a state of health that he could be brought back to his Vermont home and she herself accompanied him there. While all Vermonters were glad to honor Mrs. Van Metre, and the state later did so officially, the local G. A. R. was especially pleased since Lieutenant Bedell had several warm friends among its members who were glad to express in person their gratitude for her heroic kindness to a comrade.

In 1931, after the new Masonic Temple was completed, the corps bought the former Masonic hall and has been comfortably installed in it since that date.

SONS OF UNION VETERANS

An offspring of the G. A. R. was the G. W. Doty Camp, No. 50, Sons of Union Veterans, which was organized in 1888 largely through the efforts of Colonel Doty, who presented the camp with two beautiful silk flags and in many other ways showed his interest in its welfare. The camp began with twenty charter members and George F. Earle, for many years a well known business man in town, was its first captain. Since Colonel Doty was not only interested in its progress, but was the first man to enlist from

HISTORY OF MORRISTOWN 219

Morristown in 1861, it was fitting that this camp should bear his name. The fortunes of the order have waxed and waned. Twice it has been disbanded, but in 1902 it was reorganized, with A. N. Camp as its captain, and since that time has maintained its standing.

Its companion order is the Sons of Union Veterans' Auxiliary, which first bore the name of the Ladies' Aid Society of G. W. Doty Camp. It was the seventeenth of such groups in the state and was formed with fourteen charter members and Mrs. Emma Cheney its first president. At least one of its number, Mrs. Florence Wilson, who afterwards moved to Burlington, was division president of the Department of Vermont. This order at length disbanded, but later reorganized under its present name.

DAUGHTERS OF THE AMERICAN REVOLUTION

The next patriotic organization in point of time is the Capt. Jedediah Hyde Chapter of the D. A. R., which was formed on February 23, 1914. Its membership is not confined to this town, but includes residents of Hyde Park, Stowe, Johnson, and Elmore as well. It took its name from Captain Hyde, the first settler of Hyde Park. Its membership is limited to fifty and its first regent was Mrs. Lou Slocum Fleetwood of Morristown. This body has marked the graves of the Revolutionary soldiers within its territory, has presented pictures of George Washington to the standard schools in its district, and participated in the other activities which characterize that society.

In September, 1933, this chapter was hostess at the Thirty-Fourth Annual Vermont State Conference of the Daughters of the American Revolution. The meetings convened at the Congregational Church, with the exception of the reception and banquet, which were held at the Masonic Temple. The guests of honor at the conference were Mrs. William H. Pouch of New York, vice-president-general, and Mrs. Henry Bourne Joy of Michigan, recording secretary-general, and over 150 delegates were registered.

AMERICAN LEGION

Morristown American Legion Post, No. 33, was organized in 1919, with Dr. Lloyd C. Robinson as its first commander, and has grown into an active influential body. At first its meetings were held in the Grange hall, the gathering place of the other patriotic orders, but in 1931 it took over the old gymnasium, thoroughly renovated it and now, as The Barracks, it serves as an attractive hall for social gatherings of all kinds as well as for the post meetings. This body furnished the state vice-commander in 1932 in the person of R. R. McMahon, while Dr. G. L. Bates and Carroll Silloway have both served on the state executive board, the former in 1932 and the latter in 1933.

One member of this post, Percy Sweetser, received the medal of the Order of the Purple Heart for bravery displayed and wounds received while carrying a message in the Meuse-Argonne offensive.

AMERICAN LEGION AUXILIARY

The Auxiliary of the Morristown American Legion Post was organized on January 13, 1921, with Helen Robinson as its first president, and since that time has offered efficient aid in the charitable and patriotic work of the post. From its membership have been elected the presidents of the Department of Vermont for three terms. Mrs. Irving L. Potter was department president in 1923 and again in 1926, while Mrs. James M. Kelley filled that office in 1930.

NEW ENGLAND ORDER OF PROTECTION

The New England Order of Protection is a fraternal and benevolent order which was started here in the late 80's with Walter Pike, a local marble dealer, its first warden. It has provided a maximum insurance at a minimum cost and for many years was one of the most flourishing orders.

GRANGE

The present Grange dates from 1893. Previous to that time, Malvern Grange, No. 24, was organized in the late 70's, functioned a few years and disbanded. Later the farmers, realizing the value a live branch of the Patrons of Husbandry might be to them, reorganized under the name of Lamoille Grange, No. 233. Clement Smith was its first master and was also active in the state Grange, serving as state master in 1909. Mr. and Mrs. Smith attended the meeting of the National Grange, held that year in Des Moines, Iowa, where they were elected national chaplain and lady assistant steward, respectively, the first time that two national offices had been given to one state.

On February 7, 1917, the order fittingly observed its twenty-fifth anniversary with an all-day session, which included dinner and post-prandial exercises.

THE ROTARY CLUB

The Rotary Club is one of the more recent organizations, having been formed in 1927 with Levi M. Munson its first president. Since that date it has shared in the various activities which characterize that movement.

PARENT-TEACHER ASSOCIATION

Attempts had been made to form a Parent-Teacher Association for some time, but not until 1930 was it placed on a permanent basis. It now contains a representative section of the parents of the village and similar organizations exist in several of the rural schools.

Other orders like the Modern Woodmen of America, the Independent Order of Good Templars and others have come and gone, showing that the town has never lacked for fraternal organizations.

THE MORRISVILLE WOMAN'S CLUB

Among the town organizations which have been influential in shaping the life of the community is the Woman's Club, whose name has been linked with most of the worthwhile projects which have been undertaken locally or by the State Federation.

It had its inception in a little reading club organized by some of the young ladies of the village who, as early as 1884, began to meet weekly at the homes of the members and to study the lives and works of different authors. Often times they put on a public musical and literary entertainment and sponsored lectures of a cultural nature. This type of club was maintained for several years until some members felt the time had come for a little broader field of work and more varied lines of activity.

(18) In 1892, under the able leadership of Mrs. Laura Gleed, the Morrisville Woman's Club was organized. Its object, according to its by-laws, was "the mutual improvement of women and the securing of all benefits arising from organized effort." For the first eight years of its existence Mrs. Gleed was its president and she laid its foundations broad and deep enough to sustain a progressive, growing body whose methods have changed with new conditions and expanding interests. Its modest membership fee of twenty-five cents was raised to fifty cents, to a dollar and then to two dollars, thus reflecting in part the changes in living conditions, but quite as much the varied demands that are made today of such organizations.

The meetings were at first held at private houses in the afternoons, then they alternated between Saturday afternoons and Monday evenings, but for a good many years they have been held regularly at the library on Monday evenings, and that date is generally recognized as "Woman's Club Night" in planning social gatherings. The character of the programs has changed greatly through the years. At first a definite line of study was undertaken in art, literature, travel, etc., and current topics kept the members in touch with present day conditions. The programs consisted for the most part of papers prepared by the club members. Gradually, as the work of the different committees increased in importance, it became necessary to give them a place and the intensive study of one subject gave way to the presentation of all kinds of questions of social, political, and economic interest and competent speakers from outside brought the club views of the larger groups of women or of state and national bodies.

To recount the story of its local activities would reveal its manifold interests. In 1900 it equipped and sent out the first traveling library in the state, a line of work which was taken up and maintained by the State Federation as long as the need for such existed. In 1901 it erected the drinking fountain for man and beast at the foot of Academy Park, which was for many years a great convenience until changing conditions and the alteration in the streets made advisable its removal, in 1929. It also placed the granite watering trough on Watering Trough Hill. For years it maintained an excellent lecture course which brought to the town a high grade of musical talent, and such well known lecturers as Adirondack Murray, Thomas Dixon, Jr., Newell Dwight Hillis, and others. That the club entertained lofty ambitions is seen from the fact that in October, 1906, it sponsored a Tag Day to raise funds for a local hospital and the $250 raised then was turned over and used for that purpose a quarter of a century later. In 1913 it gave an entertainment to raise money for an opera house and the money secured is still available for that end. During the winter of 1919 an evening school was held under the immediate direction of Supt. C. D. Howe, which was attended by thirty-four different adult students and the club was interested in this project both financially and otherwise. It employed a district nurse during the winter months for two years, 1919-1920, until that work was taken over in part by the Public Health Department of the Red Cross. During the war it was engaged in every form of relief work as it raised money for the Belgian Relief Fund, the War Children Relief Fund, Furlough Homes for Soldiers, etc., and bought Liberty Bonds, and assisted the Red Cross and engaged in all the other activities that characterized that period.

As its founder was the prime mover in establishing the town library, it was only natural that it should be closely identified with that institution. Its meetings have usually been held in the library and in return it has contributed money for the purchase of books and magazines and, when the Carnegie building was erected in 1912, it bought chairs and tables for the new rooms and placed the shrubbery on the grounds. It has also been instrumental in beautifying other parts of the village and has made many contributions to the public welfare of the village.

It was identified with the State Federation from the latter's inception in 1896. When that body was organized at St. Johnsbury by delegates from six clubs, the local organization was one of the six, and Mrs. Gleed was the first vice-president of the larger group. In 1922 it joined the General Federation of Woman's Clubs and it has been privileged to share in the work of both of the larger bodies. For eleven years one of its members, Miss Mary Moody, was chairman of the education committee of the State Federation, whose great work was raising money for scholarships in the Normal Schools, and thus helping to build up the rural schools of the state. Mrs. Gertrude Powers has been chairman of the music committee of the State Federation and also vice-president of the Northwestern District. Mrs. Augusta Slayton was president of the State Federation, 1921-1923, and later General Federation director. Mrs. Diadama Greene was vice-president of the Northwestern District, 1933-1934.

When the local club was less than ten years old, with an average attendance of only a dozen or so, it had the temerity to invite the State Federation to meet with it. The convention assembled on October 16 and 17, 1901, with the meetings held in the Congregational Church, and thirty-one delegates representing eighteen of the twenty-seven clubs then federated were present. The chief items on the program were addresses by Mrs. Sally Joy White, who spoke on some important phases of the labor question, particularly of women wage earners; and by Helen Winslow, daughter of the neighboring town of Johnson, residing in Roxbury, Mass., who took as her subject, "What the Club Should Mean." On Wednesday evening Mrs. Gleed entertained the gathering at an enjoyable reception at her home.

On October 13, 1920, the local body entertained the clubs of the Second District, at which time it was estimated that there were 200 visitors.

On May 20-22, 1924, this club again acted as hostess to the Federation. During the lapse of years its member ship had grown to 115 and it was assisted by the Uplift Club, organized by the women living in the eastern and southern part of the town and of Elmore, numbering thirty-one members, and the Unity Club of the Congregational Church, which had just federated. If the resources of the club had grown during the lapse of years, the task which they had undertaken had also increased in magnitude since the official records showed a total of 366 present, the largest attendance at any state meeting up to that date. The enlarged scope of the interests of the Federation is shown by the program which, aside from the reports of the various departments, included an address on "Illiteracy" by Augustus O. Thomas, then commissioner of education in Maine; on "Better Homes in America" by Miss Helen Risdon of New York; "What Is the Greatest Danger in America Today?" by Chancellor C. S. McGown, president of the International College of Springfield, Mass.; and

"Traffic in Opium and Other Dangerous Drugs" by Mrs. John W. Moorhead of New York. Gov. Fletcher D. Proctor, Rep. F. G. Fleetwood and other well known people took part in the meetings in one capacity or another.

For many the climax of the convention was the presentation of Mendelssohn's oratorio, "Elijah," on the second evening of the gathering. But one joint rehearsal was held, yet this splendid production was worthily presented. This feature has been followed in successive Federation meetings.

CHAPTER XIV

MUSIC IN MORRISTOWN

MOST towns and cities claim consideration either because they have certain natural advantages or can do some one thing better than most others of their class. It has been the boast of Morristown that it was a musical town, and it has been fortunate in the number of talented musicians within its borders who have given generously of their time and talents. Certainly any study of local history shows that it has always been a music loving place and its standards of excellence have been high.

The first evidence of this is seen in the singing schools which flourished a few generations ago. We often read of the paring bees and huskings which constituted so large a part of the social life of our ancestors. With them should be included in this town, at least, the singing school and the neighborhood sing. In Sterling, Mud City, District No. 10, Cadys Falls, the Corners, as well as at Morrisville, these singing schools are known to have flourished and they were probably just as common in the southern and eastern part of the town. These gatherings were usually held at the schoolhouse, thus anticipating the modern idea of making the schoolhouse a social center. At the Corners the church was the natural meeting place, while sometimes a private house was used. In most cases there was no musical instrument, but the tuning fork served to give the pitch. At a little later date the organ or melodeon was found in many homes largely because of the love for music, which was fostered at the singing school. Usually at the close of the term, a public exhibition was held at which schools in two or more districts united in putting on a program in which both old and young had a part. Stored away in the attic of many a home in town is a worn copy of "The Morning Star," with scales, exercises, two part, three part, and four part songs or some other singing book highly prized by earlier generations.

It is not known that John Flanders taught singing, but for years he led the singing at church when the services were held in the old town house at the Center and also acted as drum major on public occasions. Doubtless the custom of lining the hymns which prevailed in colonial times had long since been given up, yet the responsibility of leading the singing, when there was no musical instrument to assist, must have been no slight one.

The distinction of teaching the first singing school probably belongs to Moses Weld, a Revolutionary soldier, whose love of music was so great that it is said that he carried his singing book into the army with him. It is not possible to make a complete list of these old time musicians, but among them were E. R. Ober of Eden, who conducted singing schools throughout the county; George Story of this town, whose entire family were musical; Lucius Hadley, a well known resident on the LaPorte road; Mr. Wilkins and A. H. Cheney of Stowe; W. F. Whipple, whose contribution to the musical development of the town deserves a more extended notice; Enos Fletcher of Waterville, probably the last of the itinerant singing masters; and others, who, through their love for this art, helped to relieve the monotony of the busy lives of our forefathers. One likes to linger over the picture of these families, young and old, gathering together week after week to enjoy the ministry of music. There naturally arises a comparison of those days with the later period, when the victrola and radio bring the work of great artists to most homes. However much the quality of the product may have improved, does the individual receive equal benefit by the change?

Successive years of singing schools had trained a body of musicians capable of more advanced work, and during the late 60's and 70's there flourished the Morristown Musical Association. It included not only local talent, but members from Elmore and Hyde Park. An orchestra, consisting of violin, flutes, and cello, augmented the voices and each year this organization presented a very creditable program. The first public concert was held in February, 1867, before an audience, gathered from the entire county. The local paper speaks of the contributions of Miss Cora Clement and Prof. Wilbur F. Whipple as "among the most interesting features of the program." This shows that previous to that date Prof. Wilbur F. Whipple had come here from East Hardwick. His natural musical ability had been cultivated by years of study in Boston and he not only possessed a rich baritone voice, but was a skilled performer upon the organ, the piano, the pipe organ, and violin, and gave lessons on them. Under his leadership the Morrisville Silver Cornet Band was organized and flourished. He was active in securing for the Congregational Church the first pipe organ in town and arranged two public concerts, the proceeds of which were given to the organ fund. For twenty-five years he was organist and choir leader at that church and for five years never missed one Sunday, even though in those days there was a church service fifty-two weeks in a year. For many years he was associated with his brother-in-law, Joseph Clement, in the mercantile firm of Clement & Whipple, but his lasting contribution to the life of the town lay in the more than thirty years he gave freely of his time and talent to enrich and elevate its musical ideals. Mr. Whipple died in 1901.

THE CHORAL UNION

In 1893 George M. Powers brought to Morrisville as his bride, Miss Gertrude Woodbury of Burlington, whose sweet, natural voice, perfected by careful training, had already given her a recognized standing in the musical circles of that city. Mrs. Powers at once took an active part in the musical life of the town. Its singers rallied to this new leadership and the operetta "Pinafore" was presented in 1897 and was followed in 1903 by "The Mikado." As an indication of the popularity of these entertainments, it is noted that "The Mikado" ran three nights to crowded houses and the call for its repetition was so insistent that in a short time it was given two more evenings.

In 1913 the musical interest in town crystallized in the organization of a Choral Union with a membership of one hundred, and this organization has been maintained down to the present time (1935). That it had high aspirations and ambitions is shown by the fact that May 6, 7 and 8, 1913, it staged a Musical Festival with only seven outside artists assisting. Selections from Wagner's "Lohengrin" and "Tannhauser," Donazetti's "Lucia," Gounod's "Redemption," and "Faust," as well as modern compositions, such as Anderton's "Wreck of the Hesperus" and Coman's "Rose Maiden," were successfully presented at four concerts under the able direction of Mrs. Powers. Enthusiastic audiences and a satisfactory financial showing testified to the popularity of the effort. This success was repeated in 1914. Since its organization the union has participated in all but two of the oratorios which the State Federation of Woman's Clubs has presented in connection with their annual conventions, besides giving several worthwhile concerts at home.

When the Vermont Federation of Woman's Clubs sent a group of eight women and a director to participate in the national musical contest, held at Atlantic City in 1926, the local Choral Union furnished the director, Mrs. Powers, and one of the members, Mrs. Ila Niles Jackson. Mrs. Jackson was already favorably known beyond the borders of her own state, for in 1901, as a member of the Alice Neilson Opera Company, she has toured in England as well as this country.

Mrs. Powers has not only been the leading spirit in this work, but for twenty-two years she was leader and director of the choir at the Congregational Church. Thus in a very literal way she carried on the torch laid down by Professor Whipple.

MORRISVILLE DRUM CORPS AND BAND

Another proof of the statement that Morristown is a musical town is found in the fact that for the greater part of more than sixty years an excellent band has been functioning. The following data in regard to its membership and activities has been furnished by D. A. Sanders, who has been secretary of the organization for more than twenty-five years as well as serving as leader and playing on a variety of instruments.

Before following the story of the band, mention should be made of the Morrisville Drum Corps, which flourished during the late 80's. This organization, composed of school boys under the leadership of "Rob" Barnes, a Civil War drummer of North Hyde Park, was in great demand. From a photograph of the corps its personnel is given as follows: Robert Barnes, leader; Horatio N. Cram, drum major; fifers, Henry S. George, Charles Goozey, Walter Fitch, William Whipple; snare drums, Ellis E. Foster, Leon E. Brackett, Walter Gilbert; bass drum, Wallace Gilbert; cymbals, Horatio Barrows and Edward Cram.

It seems certain that the first band owed its inception to the enthusiasm and ability of Mr. W. F. Whipple and as early as 1868 the Morrisville Silver Cornet Band furnished music for the first graduating exercises at Peoples Academy, and Mr. Whipple was its leader. Other references are made at later intervals to Mr. W. I. Paul, for many years well known as a violinist and orchestra leader, as the director of its activities. There is still in the possession of the present organization one of the old "over shoulder" instruments which were in use soon after the Civil War. In 1883 its personnel was as follows: Leader, Charles Spaulding; treasurer, C. A. Gile; secretary, Charles Hadley; members, George Woodward, J. A. Robinson, Fred Spaulding, A. O. Gates, Percy Stone, A. B. Munson, H. Drown, John Morgan, E. S. Robinson, W. E. Field, S. Town, A. W. Spaulding, and George Collyer. That year the first of the band stands was erected in Academy Park. But the tide of its fortunes ebbed and flowed as the enthusiasm of its members waxed and waned and on the great gala day of the town, its hundredth anniversary, it is noted that the bands were all imported, only the Morrisville Drum Corps appearing from this town. Perhaps this led to the activity recorded in the "News and Citizen" of July 17, 1890: "Morrisville has a brass band. An organization was effected Saturday evening. C. A. Gile was elected leader, J. J. Burdick, assistant leader, and D. A. Sanders, secretary and treasurer. It is expected that there will be fourteen players, and next week we hope to publish the names. With the musical ability in the band we may be sure of excellent music. It should be liberally sustained." After a few meetings in the town hall this attempt was discontinued and a juvenile drum corps furnished music as occasion required.

On July 10, 1895, another attempt was made with better success and the Morrisville Military Band was organized, with the following officers: President, C. A. Gile; secretary, D. A. Sanders; treasurer, C. B. Greene; leader, W. E. Dufer. This organization functioned for about two years, but upon Mr. Dufer's leaving town it gave up for want of a leader. Two or three years later Mr. James Simms, a very fine cornetist, organized another band, made up for the most part of younger players, and this was well under way when he, too, moved away. Mr. James Winn took up the reins and kept up the interest for some time and was succeeded by D. A. Sanders, who held the position of leader until 1905, when another reorganization took place.

In 1905 Morristown held a grand Fourth of July celebration, music for which was furnished by the Morrisville Military Band and the Peconic Band. The latter was a Morrisville Foundry production, consisting of a homemade truck propelled by a gasoline engine and having a platform large enough to hold the band, consisting of C. P. Greene, C. B. Greene, C. A. Gile, F. L. George, Eli B. Gile, and others. That fall a reorganization took place and these officers were elected: President, J. M. Kelley; leader, C. Porter Greene; secretary and treasurer, C. H. Crane. Mr. Crane held the office about a year and then was succeeded by D. A. Sanders, who is still serving in that capacity.

The band was sadly in need of new instruments, but had no money in the treasury. It was decided to hold a band fair. As the instruments were needed for use at the fair, two sets were ordered to be sent on trial, one from the C. G. Conn Co. and the other from the Boston Musical Instrument Co. The former came in due time, but a fire in the factory of the latter delayed their shipment. However, permission was obtained from the Conn Co. to retain their instruments so that the two sets might be compared. And the band found itself with about $1,500 worth of instruments in its possession and an empty treasury. But the fair which was held for five evenings, with concerts, the drawing of prizes, and dancing each evening was a financial success so the instruments were paid for and a balance left in the treasury. These new instruments were deeded over to the village of Morrisville, so they could be used only by local bands and could not be disposed of without the consent of the trustees of the village. Several of these band fairs have been held and always with profit to the band and, in addition, concerts, dances and plays have been held to raise money.

At the next March meeting the town appropriated $200 for the band, provided it furnished music for Memorial Day and gave at least ten outdoor concerts during the summer. This amount was later increased and the village has also given a sum annually.

In 1913 the band lost one of its best players in the death of Channing B. Greene, the first of its members to pass on; there was a lack of interest and no concerts were given that summer, but in the latter part of the year, through the efforts of Mr. Walter C. Ward, the organization was revived. A few of the old players came back, but the majority were new men, some of whom had never played before, and they were mostly of high school age. D. A. Sanders was the leader and two meetings a week were held, one for the beginners and the other for the whole band, and when the concert season opened there were thirty-one members. They tried to carry on the same routine as previous bands, but owing to the World War were greatly handicapped. In 1918, as the Stowe band was in the same plight, the two organizations united, the Stowe boys coming here for rehearsals. The following summer the united band gave concerts in both villages, and played for several patriotic meetings, including the celebration at the end of the war when the the soldiers returned home.

In 1920 another reorganization took place. A subscription paper was circulated among the business men to raise funds to hire a leader and Mr. C. P. Greene was hired for the position. Soon afterwards the town increased its appropriation to $500 and the village voted a like sum. Since 1926 the band has been on a commercial basis, each member receiving fifty cents for attending rehearsals and one dollar for each concert given during the summer.

Since 1905 this has been one of the best equipped bands to be found among country organizations. At the present time another change is taking place, with the addition of several new members from the high school. In 1930 Mr. Greene, with the assistance of Mr. J. O. Reed, organized a band in the village schools. It was a success from the first and has been a fine thing for both school and band. At the present time it is under the able direction of Willard K. Sanders.

The band has had many different meeting places, in the Tift block at the foot of Main Street and in the adjoining building, in the town hall, over MacDonald's blacksmith shop on Bridge Street, over the H. A. Slayton & Co. feed store, etc. In 1921 the room over the fire station was secured and meetings have been held there since.

In 1930 the Rotary Club gave the members of the band a banquet at the Randall Hotel in commemoration of the twenty-fifth anniversary of its organization, and presented Mr. Greene with a gold mounted baton and Mr. Sanders with a gold trimmed desk set. That the band has been a source of enjoyment, not only to the people of

Morristown, but to those from surrounding towns, is evidenced by the crowds which attend the concerts given during the summer months. These concerts were formerly given in Academy Park, where during the past forty years four wooden stands were built. Then one of cement was constructed and used until 1931, when an up-to-date "shell" type stand was built on the school grounds not far from Peoples Academy and given by Mr. A. H. Copley. At the dedication of this stand on July 2, 1931, Justice Powers, in the course of his remarks, called upon C. P. Greene, J. O. Reed, H. E. Woodbury and D. A. Sanders, pioneer members of the organization, to rise as he publicly expressed the gratitude of their fellow citizens to these men who, by their loyal support, have done so much to maintain an institution which has added greatly to the pleasure of the music loving citizens of this locality.

In September, 1933, Mr. C. P. Greene resigned as director and no meetings were held for three months. Then they reorganized with Willard K. Sanders as leader, and the keen interest of the younger members indicates that the reputation of the town for having one of the best bands in the state will be maintained.

CHAPTER XV

THE PRESS, THE POSTOFFICE, AND PUBLIC HOUSES

IN this age when the radio has been added to the mammoth daily as a means of disseminating news, it is difficult to picture a day when knowledge of the outside world was confined to the visits of the weekly newspaper which told not merely the important local events, but of occurrences of national and world-wide interest. Without doubt the press of that day, inadequate as it seems, was a potent factor in shaping public opinion, and the quaint sheets issued from many small towns bore fruit in political action. The fourth estate was a significant element in the early history of Vermont and the story of its beginnings in any town is worthy of consideration.

The first newspaper in the county was published at Stowe in 1830 by the Rev. J. P. Hendee, father of Governor Hendee, and was called "The Christian Luminary." It was a semi-monthly which appeared less than three years and was followed by a series of papers issued under different names at Johnson. It was not until 1848 that the hamlet of Morrisville could boast of its own publication.

The "North American Citizen," published every Thursday in Morrisville and Waterbury by Joseph A. Somerby, began its career in 1848. It bore the inscription, "The Vermonter's Own Paper; devoted to news, education, morality, agriculture, science and art, literature and general miscellany—independent in politics." Mr. Somerby had served his apprenticeship in the newspaper world in Waterbury, where he had published "Excelsior" in partnership with Melvin Stow, and "The Free Mountaineer" of Waterbury and Montpelier. As his slogan indicates, this was a general newspaper and except for its advertisements contained little which was of more interest to Morristown than to Montpelier. No file of these papers is extant, but if there was it would reflect American thought and interest rather than local life.

This publication was succeeded in 1852 by "The American Observer," published by Mr. Somerby and

Charles Scott. The prospectus of the "Observer" makes the following statement of its conception and purposes: "A desire from the Weslyan Methodists in all parts of New England, having been repeatedly expressed that a weekly anti-slavery newspaper devoted to the interests of the Weslyan Methodist denomination should be permanently established within our own borders has induced the subscribers to commence the publication of such a newspaper. We rejoice at one thing especially, that our denomination is not based upon men or names, but upon principles. Principles that were laid down and established by Orange Scott, whose name will always be associated with the cause of the oppressed, and Popular Rights, and will live in the affections of the good, when his pro-slavery opposers will be remembered only to be despised. We must expect to meet with opposition, endure reproach, and make sacrifices; but these we can cheerfully bear, in the cause of God, justice, mercy, and humanity. Let the strength of our principles support us—let the magnitude of the cause in which we are engaged stimulate our exertions—let the true spirit of Christianity give direction to all our efforts, and the glowing prospects of success which brighten upon the not very distant future, inflame our zeal. What have we to fear so long as we are conscious of doing right. And while our enterprise commends itself in its high moral aspect more particularly to our own Denomination, it must be a question of absorbing interest to the philanthropist and Christian—to all who desire the perpetuation of Free Institutions and the universal prevalence of those principles of Christian Morality without which freedom is but a mockery and a name. It will be our endeavor to make in every respect a Good Family Newspaper. Every thing of an immoral tendency will be carefully excluded and we shall give it a somewhat general character, that those who take but one paper may have a summary of all the important news.

"SOMERBY AND SCOTT."

From this it is evident the paper had high ideals and great expectations. It had its authorized agent for receiving subscriptions in Philadelphia and its men to receive advertisements in Boston and New York.

The year following Somerby was carrying on the enterprise alone with an enlarged paper bearing the slogan,

"Free Discussion, Free Land, Free Education, Cheap Postage, and a Free Press for a Free People." He worked manfully for the success of the Free Democratic ticket which included among other nominees for county offices Horace Powers for senator, Samuel Pennock for assistant judge, and Thomas Gleed for state's attorney.

Perhaps these different papers had not received the support he expected, at any rate it would seem the project had not proved as profitable as he hoped, for his business card as a mason appears, and later he was one of the firm of Somerby & Terrill, general merchants. In the year 1854 there appeared "The Vermont Weekly Tribune," published at Burlington, Morrisville, and St. Albans, by Somerby & Sampson, with the former acting as local agent and editor, but this, also, was short lived. After a few years the local field was covered by "The Lamoille Newsdealer," established at Hyde Park in 1860.

In the spring of 1873 "The Vermont Citizen" was started at Morrisville by A. A. Earle, who four years later purchased "The Newsdealer" and combined the two sheets. During the time that newspapers have been published in the town at least three well known figures in this field of work have been associated with them and not the least of them was Mr. Earle.

Araunah Augustus Earle was a native of Lamoille County, having been born in Hyde Park in 1826. Later his family moved to New York, where at the age of sixteen he began his journalistic career in the office of the Essex County Republican. He soon returned to Vermont and worked as journeyman in several different offices, but, restless by nature, like so many other young men of the period, he was attracted by the opportunities of the West and set out to seek them. While there, he had the unique experience of walking from Kansas City, Mo., to the Pacific Coast. Starting in April, 1852, he arrived in Portland, Oregon, in August and resumed his work as a newspaper man in Oregon and later in Washington, but returned to his native state after two years.

Here he set out upon a career of establishing newspapers. "The Orleans Independent Standard" and "The National Opinion" at Bradford were founded by him and he was editor and proprietor of the "St. Johnsbury Times" before coming to Morrisville. In all these papers he maintained a unique reputation because of his sharp tongue and caustic wit. His locals were breezy and unconventional and not infrequently gave offense to the persons mentioned, but he pushed everything he thought contributed to the progress of the town, and the modern publicity agent would delight in his originality. As an example of his style the following excerpt from his report of the races and balloon ascension on July 3 and 4, 1873, is given:

"We are not much of a trottist. Fast horses are not our delight. Of the two we much prefer a campmeeting; but will confess to getting just a little excited when we witnessed the last race, for our favorite 'Jerry Drew' was in it and he struck out so grandly on the home stretch that it seemed as if he had wings. If he could only score as well as he can fly over the home stretch we would bet on him against any horse in New England. Utton, too, is a good driver; cool headed, self possessed, temperate and virtuous.

"But the balloon was what called the crowd together, and was the all absorbing object of interest during the day. About 8000 tickets were sold on the second day, including team tickets; of people there were about 5000. The ascension was made at 1.40 P. M. It rose to an altitude of about a mile and rested over Morrisville like a luminous globe, for some fifteen minutes, when it once more took a heavenward shoot and went nearly a mile and a half higher, and then sailed off slowly, gracefully to the northeast—all eyes intently watching it until it passed into the clouds. The view was magnificent and grand beyond description. Jay Peak, Montgomery Mountain and Notch, Mansfield, and Camel's Hump, the White Mountains, the Adirondacks, Champlain, Memphremagog, the St. Lawrence—all these were seen or dimly outlined below or beyond him. They will stay upon the map of his memory like so many flowers plucked from the garden of paradise. The balloon was up a little more than an hour when it descended into a thunder storm; it then rose higher and met a storm of snow which sent it down into the wilderness near the line between Eden and Hyde Park, landing we think, upon land owned by George Waterman. Mr. King landed in a tree safely, exploded his balloon and commenced to ransack the wilderness for an outlet to the promised land. Being city bred and not used to the woods, he took the wrong direction, got lost, wandered about for a while and when dark came went to bed supperless on the wet ground. No breakfast, no dinner, no supper on Saturday, but plenty of travel all day, while the midgets, mosquitoes and black flies by their constant nips and bites satisfied him that he was mortal, but that if that kind of fun was continued a great while longer he would be immortal. He thinks he would rather liquidate any other bill than a mosquito's. He rose at three A. M. on Sunday, said his prayers (we hope) and commenced tramping again, went down a stream and found the Jewett mill at eight o'clock. Here he met a few of the hundreds searching for him and went with them to the Haskin's house where he took something to eat and drink for the first time in two days and a half."

His notices of marriages appeared under the heading Sailed and deaths under the caption Wrecked, and every issue could be depended upon to contain something unusual and entertaining.

The "News" was established in Hyde Park in 1877 to succeed the "Newsdealer," but four years later this too was combined with the "Citizen"; and, for a score of years, "The News and Citizen," published jointly at the two towns by the Lamoille Publishing Co., consisting of L. H. Lewis and H. C. Fisk, was the local paper for Lamoille County. In time Mr. Fisk withdrew from the partnership, and in 1922 Mr. A. A. Twiss bought out Mr. Lewis.

Then there appeared a newcomer in the shape of "The Morrisville Messenger" which was started by J. E. Harris in January, 1901. "Jack" Harris, as he was called, was a well known newspaper man, who had gained his experience on "The Burlington Clipper" and "The Hardwick Gazette" and had made his reputation as a writer who, in a very caustic semi-humorous style, commented freely on the political affairs of both state and nation. In fact, it is said that he started his new venture because certain officeholders were dilatory in helping him to a position. The paper offered him a medium of reminding them of his continued existence. It seems to have been efficacious, for in October he was appointed doorkeeper of the Senate.

While Mr. Harris was publishing the paper, it had been printed by the press of "The Burlington Clipper" which had been moved to Essex Junction by L. P. Thayer. When Mr. Harris settled with Mr. Thayer, he gave him "The Messenger" subscription list, remarking

that it ought to be kept going as it had paid well. To
a natural newspaper man like Mr. Thayer, who was then
controlling several papers, this was a challenge which he
did not refuse. He had just sold "The Vergennes Vermonter" to R. W. McCuen and according to the terms of
sale the printing plant had to move out of town. He
found a desirable location, the Currier store was vacant,
and the plant was soon lodged in the quarters which it has
since occupied.

F. W. Sault was the first manager, but was succeeded
by D. H. Lamberton, who was responsible for starting the
Cambridge, Bakersfield, Stowe and Wolcott editions.
After Mr. Lamberton left, Mr. Thayer came in person to
run the paper with and for his son, H. S. Thayer, until
the World War broke out and the young man enlisted.
For twenty-two years Mr. Thayer resided in Morrisville. In
1920 A. B. Limoge of Burlington, who had received his
training in the Free Press office, came as business manager.
At length poor health compelled Mr. Thayer to spend his
winters in a warmer climate and Mr. Limoge purchased
the paper and has since run it.

THE POSTOFFICE

In the early days the presence of the postoffice in a
village gave official recognition to its importance as a
center of influence. So when Dr. James Tinker secured
the location of the first postoffice in town at the Corners
rather than at the Center, it gave the former hamlet prestige quite out of proportion to the importance of the few
pieces of mail which were left there by the stage on its
way north from Waterbury and Stowe. First established
about 1812, this office was in use about ninety years.

Dr. Tinker was its incumbent for many years and
among his successors were Joseph Sears, about 1850;
Samuel Olds, in the late 50's; Orrin Lyman, in the early
60's; A. B. Smith, in the late 60's; Bishop Ashe, in the
early 70's; M. C. Mower, in the late 70's, and then Eben
Douglass, who had the longest term except Dr. Tinker.
He was succeeded by James Hill, who soon gave way to
M. W. Carleton, who was acting at the time the office was
discontinued, in 1901. Located at various places in the
village, it was fixed at the store when Mr. Ashe assumed
the office of postmaster and remained there ever afterwards.

For a time after the stage from Stowe was routed by way of the LaPorte Road, the mail was left at the Hadley farm, but later was taken to the Morrisville office. At first the postmasters carried the mail to and from the office, but later regular carriers took it. Among the men who were well known figures in that capacity were Moses Rankin and Leonard Matthews, who, with his handsome horse, Comet, made the trip for many years.

THE MORRISVILLE POSTOFFICE

The official recognition of the status and importance of the village of Morrisville came with the establishment of the postoffice here in 1833. Its first incumbent was Levi B. Vilas, who held the position less than a year and then moved to Johnson and later became a well known figure, both in this state and in Wisconsin, to which he removed. This vacancy was filled by the appointment of S. A. Willard, who entered upon his duties about March 14, 1834. On that date he received his first letter which was brought from St. Albans bearing ten cents postage. During the last half of that month thirteen letters were received and in the month of April twenty-four.

When comparing this volume of business with what is done today, one must take into account the difference in the rates of postage. Then a single letter composed of one sheet of paper if carried thirty miles or less required six cents in postage, when taken from thirty to eighty miles the amount was ten cents, from eighty to 150 miles twelve and one-half cents, from 150 to 400 miles eighteen and three-fourths cents, and over 400 miles twenty-five cents. If the writer was very diffuse and wrote two sheets, the rate was double that of a single sheet and a triple letter paid triple postage.

The office in that early day was "the little red shop" formerly standing on the Miles property now owned by the bank. Judge Willard was succeeded by Edward L. Mayo, another lawyer. The task of caring for the mail was not arduous and the small salary was doubtless a welcome addition to their remuneration as lawyers. During Mr. Mayo's term the office was on the second floor of what was later to become the Morrisville House.

On December 1, 1841, Daniel Gilbert became postmaster and in the Christmas rush of that first month received sixty-four letters and mailed eighty-one. Mr.

HISTORY OF MORRISTOWN 241

Gilbert added these duties to his regular work as a cabinet-maker and the office was in his furniture shop, later occupied by Doty's furniture store, now a garage on lower Main street. Mr. Gilbert held the office for twenty years, with the exception of four years, when J. C. Noyes served and moved the equipment to his home in the brick house on the corner of High and Main streets, now occupied by James Eaton, where it was located in the room now used as a rest room.

In June, 1861, Thomas Gleed, another attorney, was appointed, and upon his death his term was filled out by his widow, and the office was in the Masonic Temple on the corner now occupied by Peck's Pharmacy. This building was burned in 1869 and the office was moved temporarily to the saddle and harness shop on the Miles place until the corner block was rebuilt. Another attorney, J. C. Robinson, then secured the position and served for twenty years until a turn in the political wheel placed the Democrats in power, and Charles Rich became their nominee.

In 1873 it became a money order office and the increasing business demanded the full time and attention of some one rather than the use of the position as an adjunct to some other profession. Also, it was desirable to have larger and more convenient rooms. In 1889 the building now occupied as a milliner's shop by Mrs. Ella Warren was built and equipped expressly for a postoffice and George F. Earle with his wife as assistant was the fortunate occupant of the new plant. With the return of the Democrats to power Daniel C. Spaulding succeeded to yield place in 1900 to H. J. Fisher.

During the latter's administration another important change was made in postal matters, the introduction of rural free delivery. This necessitated more space than could be provided in the rooms then in use and with the building of the Drowne block in 1901 the office was moved into its present quarters. Mr. Fisher was succeeded by C. L. Gates, who benefitted by the Wilson regime. With the return of the Republicans to power E. W. Gates was appointed, who was succeeded by John E. Stewart. The force now consists of the postmaster, an assistant postmaster, two regular clerks and an auxiliary clerk.

The office soon outgrew its facilities and the year 1928 saw extensive changes. A long term lease of the present quarters was taken, and new lock boxes and new equipment throughout was added. During the flood rehabilitation period this office was the center from which huge truck loads of mail sent in from surrounding places was sorted and re-routed to different districts.

Probably the government has undertaken no activity which brought richer returns to the rural population than free delivery of mail. Today the automobile, the telephone, the radio and frequent trips to the creamery bring the farmer into touch with the outside world; but formerly his weekly trip to the village to dispose of his farm products, to lay in his supply of groceries, and get his mail was almost his only point of contact. When Uncle Sam's agents brought his mail to his door, it made possible access to the daily newspaper and easy communication with distant sections. In 1901 two rural free delivery routes were established in Morristown, and W. W. Fairbanks and E. S. Robinson were appointed carriers. The former soon resigned and was succeeded by I. N. LeBaron, Jr. When this work had to be carried on entirely with horses, the job was no sinecure, but it brought returns in increased enjoyment in living. Since that date two additional routes have been laid out so that now practically all sections of the town are reached by the carriers and the offices at the Corners and Cadys Falls have long been discontinued.

CADYS FALLS OFFICE

The office at this place was opened in 1858 with V. W. Waterman postmaster. The office was in his house and the mail was delivered by the stage running from Waterbury to Hyde Park. After the railroad was built the mail was brought from Hyde Park until in 1892 a mail catch was installed beside the track and the sacks were deposited there. That year C. B. Terrill was appointed postmaster, and the office was moved into the store where it remained until it was discontinued in 1906. Later postmasters have been Erwin Lilley, Fred Waterbury, and A. H. Calkins.

PUBLIC HOUSES

The tavern of the olden days was quite a different institution from the modern hotel and met quite a different need, but both have played an important part in the development of our civilization. From its settlement Morristown has been well supplied with such houses of entertainment.

There is no doubt that the first tavern keeper in town

was Elisha Boardman, but some question has been raised as to where his hotel was located. His descendants maintain that it was north of Cadys Falls, where the roads fork, one leading to Johnson, the other continuing to Hyde Park. This was the point at which the Boardmans located upon coming to town and unquestionably a house of entertainment for man and beast was kept there and is so reported in Heminway's "Gazeteer." But according to Mr. S. L. Gates, Judge H. H. Powers and other authorities on early local history, Mr. Boardman first settled at the Center opposite the cabin built by Jacob Walker, where his hotel served as town house and schoolhouse for a time as well as a hostelry. Here was hung out the oblong sign bearing, besides the name Boardman's Inn, the suggestive picture of a tankard and glasses. This sign is still in the possession of his great-grandson, Milton H. Boardman.

When it became evident that the Center was only a geographical point and not the place at which the population would focus, it was natural that a tavern should be opened at the Corners, and Joseph Sears, son-in-law of Jacob Walker, combined the occupation of hotel keeper with that of cabinet maker, and here in the house later known as the Rood place now occupied by Eli Fisk he ministered to the needs of any traveler who passed by what was then the main highway from Waterbury and Stowe to Hyde Park and points farther north.

Near Cadys Falls the Boardmans had served the traveling public for some time when Edmund Town built a two-story structure at the village in 1853, which, for thirty years, was used for hotel purposes and later served as a dwelling house.

The construction of the LaPorte Road, which diverted the Stowe travel from the Corners, made feasible the opening of some place of entertainment for teamsters and others along that route. Here Mr. William Clement built a large house with a dance hall on the upper floor which he maintained for some years. Anticipating by several decades the present day of unique names for such places, he termed it the Call-and-See House. When he sold this property to Lyman Woodworth, the dance hall was retained and served as a social gathering place for a time. Then the dwelling house became just a roomy farm house until the advent of the automobile once more created the need for the over-night lodgings and it is again used in that capacity.

The rise of Morrisville naturally led to the establishment of a tavern there and Mr. S. L. Gates is authority for the statement that E. V. Herrick was its first hotel keeper, but how early in its history is not known. Some time before 1853 the Morrisville House, standing on the site of the present Randall Hotel, was christened. Here for many years its proprietor, F. L. Matthews, was a well known figure and the hotel was the scene of many banquets, oyster suppers, dances and general good times as well as a home for the traveling public. Perhaps Mr. Matthews' successors lacked his capacity to serve as a host, at any rate for years there was an almost annual change of managers. Among them were A. S. and M. T. Whipple, E. O. Hammond in 1870, Munroe Jocelyn in 1871, George Orcutt in 1872, B. S. Wilson in 1873, Foster Brothers in 1875, and E. C. Carpenter in 1878. In 1879 a Mr. Robbins of Swanton bought the property only to have it totally destroyed by fire in April of that year. The hotel was rebuilt, however, and for several years L. B. Boynton was connected with it as owner and sometimes as manager.

In 1891 this property was purchased by Carroll F. Randall, who moved the Morrisville House back to serve as dining room and kitchen of the new structure, while facing Main Street, he erected a three-story building. Thus the old Morrisville House, after a half century of existence, was succeeded by the Randall Hotel. For more than thirty years Mr. Randall was proprietor of this hostelry, and was one of the best known hotel men in the state, his genial personality making him an ideal landlord. Since his death, the property has changed hands several times, but it still seems to retain something of the imprint of his personality.

For years the village supported two or even three hotels at the same time. The Exchange Hotel, the Union House and others appeared and disappeared from the stage of action, but among the most important of them was the Lamoille House, which occupied the building where Aiken's market and the Quality restaurant are now housed. In March, 1909, this was burned and when rebuilt was made into a business block.

The most important competitor of the Morrisville House was the Vermont House, built and managed by A. G. West, who had served his apprenticeship in the hotel business as proprietor of the Morrisville House. Mr. West came here from Northfield in 1837 when the village contained but sixteen dwelling houses, and few citizens contributed more to its growth than he. This hotel was situated on Portland Street on the site of the Kelley block now occupied by the Ben Franklin Stores. It was intended to cater particularly to railroad patrons, and its destruction by fire in 1893 was one of the largest conflagrations which has ever visited the town.

The changed modes of life have revolutionized the hotel business. The restaurant, the tea room, and the over-night lodging place have grown up to meet the needs of the automobilist, and they may have for future generations the same glamor of romance which now surrounds the old tavern.

CHAPTER XVI

THE INCORPORATED VILLAGE OF MORRISVILLE

EARLY in the 80's some of the more progressive citizens began to discuss the advantages to be gained by having the village incorporated so that better streets and sidewalks might be secured, and other civic improvements obtained. On November 26, 1884, the act of incorporation was passed by the state Legislature, having been introduced by H. C. Fisk, then senator from Lamoille County. But then, as always, other residents weighed the effect such a step would have upon their pocketbooks and fearing the advantages of a corporate existence would be overbalanced by the increased cost of maintenance at a meeting held the February following they refused to incorporate. Not until seven years later when the enthusiasm of the coming centennial was already leavening the prevailing indifference did they agree to take that step. In June, 1890, upon motion of Governor Hendee the act of 1884 was accepted and the following village officers elected: President, Frank Kenfield; clerk, W. H. Robinson; treasurer and collector, A. M. Burke; trustees, P. K. Gleed, Seymour Harris, O. D. Matthews, A. F. Whitney, and H. P. Munson.

Within the next few weeks various steps were taken to promote the welfare of the village. The fire department was enlarged; Dr. C. C. Rublee was appointed the first health officer; street lamps were authorized; provisions for sprinkling the streets were made; and at the first annual meeting a survey of the village for a sewer system was ordered; and action looking towards a more satisfactory water system was discussed; and, truth compels one to add, arrangements were made for a "lock-up," showing that human nature even in an incorporated village was still faulty.

One of the most far-reaching improvements of the period was the beginning of the development of the municipal electric plant. The Lamoille River has always contributed materially to the beauty and prosperity of the town. To the present generation "Pulpit Rock" is but a name sometimes applied to the narrow ridge of rock which rises almost perpendicularly from the river below the power house. Years ago at the end of this lofty crag there was a rock shaped like an old-fashioned pulpit, into which one could step and obtain a splendid view of the falls. Long years ago this rock fell because of the action of the frost, but the name still clings to the place. Beautiful as the spot was, it was the practical side of the falls which interested men. From the railroad bridge to the point where the stream from the south joins the main river there is a fall of seventy-five feet. Here the Saffords threw the first dam across and at least two others were built before the big municipal dam of 1924 was constructed. Various industries, such as grist mill, pulp mill, tub factory, and others have utilized this power. Tradition says the Fairbanks family were impressed by the possibilities of the place, and attempted to locate here before establishing their scale works at St. Johnsbury, but were unable to make satisfactory terms with the Saffords.

But with the progress of invention, water power gave way in a measure to electrical power; and it is as a source of electricity that the Lamoille River has contributed most generously to the development of the town. Because it was undoubtedly the most important act in the life of the village the resolution, passed on August 21, 1894, which inaugurated the municipal electric plant, is given in full: "Resolved that a committee consisting of G. M. Powers, C. H. Slocum, G. W. Doty, H. A. Slayton, and H. P. Munson be appointed and authorized to contract for and establish an electric light plant for the incorporated village of Morrisville with full power to purchase for and in the name of said village such power as they shall deem wise and to develop the same for said purpose and to make all contracts pertaining to the establishment of said plant and do all things necessary to complete and put in operation said plant and to borrow money on the credit of said village corporation to an amount not to exceed $18,000 to carry the purpose of this resolution into effect."

How wisely the committee discharged its duties constitutes the story of the Water and Light Department, for a more adequate water system was as important as better lighting facilities.

Willard K. Sanders, from the office of the Water and Light Department, gives the history of these undertakings as follows:

THE WATER SYSTEM

At the time that the village was incorporated there was no municipal water supply in operation, the water being furnished by a Waterbury firm, by the name of Warren & Somerville. This firm had established water lines running from springs on the Elmore road about two miles above the village, to a reservoir which was located in a field near the farm now occupied by R. L. Barrows, and from there the water was piped to the different customers in the village. Under this arrangement, there were times when in spite of the small number of customers connected the service was quite limited and very little fire protection afforded. Naturally this led to quite a bit of discontent among the patrons and a village committee immediately began to look about for a supply of water which could be used for a municipal water system, and in 1894 such a supply was found on the Bugbee farm three miles east of Morrisville on the Wolcott road. At that time, Col. George W. Doty was on the board of trustees, and not wishing to wait for action on the part of the village, personally purchased the entire farm for its water supply and later the village authorized the purchase for the sum of $1,800. The land immediately around the spring was fenced in to avoid pollution, and the balance of the farm re-sold. This water supply was constant during rainy periods or extremely dry periods and bubbled forth from the foot of a steep bank with a capacity of nearly 300 gallons of clear, pure water every minute. A line of pipe was run from this spring to the farm now occupied by R. H. Sharrow and thence through the Woodward pasture over the hill to the reservoir which, though not in use, is still standing just above the residence of T. J. Stewart. The water line was not completed that fall, but seeing that competition was sure to come, the firm of Warren & Somerville sold their entire system to the village, January 2, 1895, thereby forming the nucleus of our present system. Finding that by improving the springs on the Elmore Road, a larger supply of water could be obtained, it was decided to discontinue the old reservoir which the private company had built and to build a larger one on the site of the present one at the village limits, this being done in 1895. Thus a constant supply of water was assured from two sources which would be adequate for domestic use and for fire protection. Following this, the business of the department steadily grew until in 1897 it had 275 water customers and in 1906 represented an investment of $37,631.

By this time the reservoir built in 1895 was beginning to show the effects of the weather, it being a wooden building with a pitch roof, and a little later, half of the roof was blown off, exposing the village water supply to the elements and laying it open to contamination, so that plans were made to replace the old reservoir. In 1912 plans were completed and the present reservoir was built. It was of concrete construction, 100 feet long, fifty feet wide, and thirteen feet deep, and had a capacity of 450,000 gallons; the cost of construction being $4,448.05.

For a time this new reservoir had ample capacity for the needs of the village, but a little later the demand exceeded the supply, caused by the growth of the manufacturing establishments and creameries so that a survey of the system was made and it was found that by moving the intake of the Bugbee line down stream about 200 feet, the water supply at that point would be doubled, so in 1916 a concrete dam thirty feet long and four feet high was placed across the brook 200 feet below the old intake and a new intake installed, thereby forming a small pond about forty feet in diameter whereby the supply of water could be conserved during the night when the demand was low and held in reserve for the larger day time demand. A small building was erected over the intake in such a way that all water entering the intake was filtered through fifteen inches of sand and gravel before entering the pipe line. Also at this time an electric pump was installed in the basement of H. A. Slayton's store. This pump had a capacity of 250 gallons per minute and was used to pump water from the little reservoir line into the big reservoir line.

The next real improvement in the water supply took place in 1919, when it was found that the water in the Bugbee spring was only about twenty feet higher than the water in the little reservoir, so it was decided to discontinue the old line over the hill through the Woodward pasture and run it down through the "Dugway" and in on Park Street. This was done and the little reservoir discontinued. In 1921 the old pump in Slayton's store was also discontinued, and a new pump of 350 gallons per minute capacity installed in a specially built fire-proof room under the town hall so that the water could be pumped directly from the Bugbee line into the reservoir line at their intersection at Park and Main Streets. The motor on the pump was driven through an electric line crossing Main Street at the town hall and operated at 2,300 volts, thereby eliminating the use of transformers for stepping the voltage down and the possibility of transformer damage through lightning. In 1924 a duplicate pump of 450 gallons per minute was installed in the pump room and as a further protection the old electric line across the street was discontinued and a new underground line run under the street so that today we have a pumping station which is fire proof, has duplicate pumping equipment to guard against failure of one pump and a source of power for the motors that is as dependable as it is possible to obtain.

There are a number of customers in the village who still take water from the old reservoir line which gets its supply directly from the Bugbee spring without going through the pumps, but in recent years a large number of these customers have changed their connections onto the new high pressure line, thus insuring better service.

The water system at this time comprises seven springs on the Elmore Road near district school No. 6, which empty directly into the reservoir on the farm occupied by Mrs. Pope. From the reservoir a twelve-inch pipe leads down into Main Street about one-half mile into the mains of the water system and from there the water is distributed all over the village. At the town hall, as explained above, the water from the Bugbee springs enters the reservoir line through the pumps which are kept in operation at all times. Under this arrangement the reservoir is kept nearly full all of the time as the water furnished to the mains is largely taken from the pumps, and water is taken from the reservoir only when the demand exceeds the capacity of the pumps. In this way adequate water for fire protection is assured at all times.

A few statistics will not come amiss at this time. The water system to 1929 represented an investment of $64,826.22, all of which is paid for, and the department is entirely out of debt. In recent years the department has shown a yearly profit of approximately $4,500, which has been used by the trustees to purchase fire fighting equipment and for maintenance of streets.

There are fifty-three hydrants connected with the high pressure line for fire protection, with a pressure varying from forty to 100 pounds per square inch, depending upon the location. There are also two hydrants connected with the Bugbee line which are used for street sprinkling service only. There are approximately 600 residences taking water from the water system, all operating under a flat rate. There are twenty industrial plants and creameries taking water through meters.

Owing to the number of flat rate services, the income from one year to another is practically constant, the only variation being caused by the differences in amount of water used by the industrial plants.

THE ELECTRIC DEPARTMENT

The history of the electric department is more colorful than that of the water department, owing to the many improvements which have been made in electricity in the last thirty-five years. Electricity first became a commercial possibility when George Westinghouse, founder of the Westinghouse Electric & Manufacturing Co., introduced in 1885 machinery which could generate and utilize alternating current; whereas previous to that time direct current only had been used with the attendant prohibitive cost of distribution. Another factor contributing to the commercial use of electricity was the invention of the incandescent lamp by Thomas A. Edison in 1879.

Thus it will be seen that in 1894 the electrical industry had not reached any great degree of perfection when the people of Morrisville began to talk about electric lighting for the streets, oil lamps being in use at that time. Interest was aroused to such an extent that a committee was appointed, consisting of G. M. Powers, G. W. Doty and C. H. Slocum, to investigate the situation and make a report. Their report was evidently favorable, as H. P. Munson and H. A. Slayton were added to the committee to install and operate an electric plant. To that end the village voted to bond for $45,000 to take care of the expense of the development and a contract was awarded to Almon & Sargent of Boston to build the first electric plant. Work was started on the project in September, 1894, and on May 15, 1895, the plant was placed in operation. The power house was located at Cadys Falls, the north portion of the present station being the original power house. The dam was located only a few rods upstream from the power house and was connected with it by a penstock leading to the water wheels, or water motor, as it was called.

There were two generators installed in the power house connected with the water wheels by a complicated system of line shafting, clutches, and belts. One of these generators was used to furnish power for the domestic lighting and the other for the street lighting system. The domestic lighting generator had a capacity of 1,050 incandescent lamps, or, in other words, had a capacity of about eighty horsepower, which was then considered ample for all time to come. The street lighting generator had a capacity of thirty arc lamps, which furnished power for twenty-one street lights in the village. The switchboard was made of oak, there being two vertical members to which slats were attached crossways to which were hung the various switches and instruments. At that time, as there were no electric motors in operation in Morrisville, it was the custom to start the plant just before dark and run until morning if there was sufficient water to last through the night. There were occasions when there was not enough water to last all night, so that the plant would be forced to shut down and the village left in darkness. However, in those days people were accustomed to such service and were perfectly satisfied. Only one man was required in the operation of the entire system as he could trim the arc lights and repair trouble during the day and in the evening run the plant. At that time it was not an uncommon occurrence for a customer to have only one light in the house, this being on a long extension cord so that it could be carried from one room to another.

The following item taken from the Village Report of 1897 shows that the electric plant was quite successful: "Our electric plant has run very smoothly with no serious breakdowns during the year, showing efficiency as well as good luck."

By 1901 so many additions had been made to the system that it became necessary to install a new generator of double capacity in place of the old one for domestic lighting, and, as before, this generator was then considered adequate for all time to come, but within five years it was again overloaded so it was decided to build a large concrete dam about one-fourth mile upstream and form what is now Lake Lamoille, so a contract was awarded to Douglass & Varnum for this construction and the work was completed in 1907. Also at this time a new generator of 350 horsepower capacity was installed and the generator purchased in 1901 discarded. The new generator was the very latest type and furnished three phase sixty cycle current in place of the old two phase current which had been previously supplied.

Also by this time several customers had begun to use electricity for power purposes so the plant was kept in continuous operation.

The report of 1908 shows that $3,425.79 was received for lighting service and $614.05 for power.

At this time there was in operation in Stowe the Mt. Mansfield Electric Railroad, which had its own steam power plant between Stowe and Waterbury, but evidently the cost of generating power was excessive, as they began to talk of buying power from some other source. Also at this time the village of Stowe began to think of public improvements and naturally electricity was one of the first things mentioned, so it immediately began negotiation for securing power. Finally arrangements were made whereby Morrisville would furnish power for Stowe and the railroad, and a line was built and suitable transformers installed in 1910, and again our plant was taxed to its capacity.

With the ever increasing load it was soon evident that something must be done to increase capacity, so in 1913 the plant was enlarged to its present size, a surge tank erected, and a 1,000 horsepower wheel and generator installed, giving the plant a total capacity of 1,350 horsepower.

For the next six years no great improvements were made except for the natural growth of the system, owing to the war which made any material change excessive in cost.

In 1920 the American Mineral Co. of Johnson was in the market for power and appealed to Morrisville to furnish it and after due deliberation a line was built connecting with the mine and mill of this company and also giving the village of Johnson emergency service in the event of breakdown. Naturally, this, coupled with the normal growth of the system, made it necessary to add to the capacity of the plant, but owing to the high prices no large development could be made, so the Slayton grist mill power with its seventy-five horsepower generator was purchased, and a small plant of 250 horsepower capacity erected on the site of the old pulp mill to help out until prices were lower so that a large development could be made at that point.

In 1922, in order to obtain a greater water storage, the water rights to Elmore Lake were purchased and also during the year a line was built to connect with the Hardwick plant at Wolcott providing for an exchange of power and conservation of the water supply.

By 1924, prices were down to normal so a contract was awarded to J. M. Swan & Son of St. Johnsbury to build a concrete dam and power house capable of developing 2,500 horsepower. Work on this project was started in May, 1924, and the small unit was placed in operation January 10, 1925. This plant automatically did away with the grist mill power and pulp mill power, but gave the system a total capacity of 3,850 horsepower, which is the capacity of the system today.

In 1926, in order to make the system more efficient, an outdoor sub-station was erected on the grounds of the new station and a large bank of transformers installed to take care of the outside villages. This work was not much more than completed when the flood of 1927 descended and carried away the sub-station, and did considerable damage to the two electric plants. Through desperate effort, the Morrisville plant was again started only two days after the flood and the Cadys Falls plant placed in operation in about a month.

In spite of its crippled condition, the plants put out more power immediately following the flood than ever before, thus making the income for the year larger than it had previously been.

In 1928 a group of influential business men in Waterville formed a corporation, built a line to Johnson connecting with the Morrisville system and installed lights throughout the village, and have entered into a contract with Morrisville to furnish them with power. Also, during the latter part of 1928 a contract was made between the Green Mountain Power Corporation, operating plants in Hardwick, Marshfield, Danville, Montpelier, Bolton, Burlington, and Vergennes, and the village of Morrisville whereby the Green Mountain Power Corporation agreed to take $550 per month of prime power at a primary rate and as much more as the village could furnish at a secondary rate. Accordingly a line was built to Green River to connect with this company and to date this has made a very satisfactory arrangement, as the power sold to this concern is generated from water that would otherwise run over the dam and be wasted.

The sub-station which was carried away by the flood has been replaced and three transformers of double the capacity of those in the former station installed.

A few figures are here given to show the progress which the electric system has made.

The gross income by decades is as follows: 1899, $3,574.32; 1909, $8,755.42; 1919, $23,170.89; 1928, $75,549.09; 1934, $83,970.41.

The capacity of the plants by decades: 1899, eighty horsepower; 1909, 350 horsepower; 1919, 1,350 horsepower; 1928, 3,850 horsepower.

The village has now a demand of approximately 1,600 horsepower during the day and 500 horsepower during the night, as compared with no load during the day and 100 horsepower during the night in 1898. This demand includes only what the village is obliged to furnish and not what they do furnish when selling power to the Green Mountain Power Corporation.

The village now serves the following regular customers: Village of Stowe, Village of Elmore, Morristown Corners, Cadys Falls, Waterville, and the Eastern Magnesia Talc Co., besides its own domestic and rural customers. It furnishes emergency power to the Villages of Hyde Park and Johnson, and is connected for mutual benefit with the Village of Hardwick, and the Green Mountain Power Corporation.

An idea of the progress made in the two departments can be gained from what has been written about them and the success of them is due in large part to the public spirit which has prevailed among the men who have served as Water and Light Commissioners. During the nearly forty years of its existence, the commissioners have not received any remuneration whatever for their services, but have given freely of their time and advice.

Other factors contributing to the success of the enterprise are the fact that a municipal plant is exempt from taxation, can borrow money at low interest rates, and has no large salaries. All bills are a lien on the property and collectable the same as taxes, so there are no lost accounts.

One of the advantages which has come from the municipal lighting system has been the cement streets which the village enjoys. In 1929 it was voted to adopt a plan of permanent road construction to cover Copley Avenue, Main Street from Maple Street to its foot, Portland Street, Bridge Street, Park Street and Congress Street to Union Street. The roadways, curbings, gutters, and sidewalks were to be of cement, constructed according to plans prepared by competent engineers, and all the expenses for the same were to be met from the profits of the Water and Light Departments.

In accordance with this vote Copley Avenue was completed in the fall of 1929, a thirty-two foot roadway being constructed with grass plots and sidewalks on either side. In 1930 a forty-foot road was laid on Portland and Bridge Streets, and in 1931 a fifty-foot road was laid on lower Main Street and a forty-foot one on upper Main Street to the foot of Academy Park. Cement was also placed on Park Street, with grass plots on either side, thus giving a beautiful entrance to the village from the east.

In connection with this work the sewers were relaid as the ones originally installed were now inadequate and the water pipes, where the cement was used, had to be replaced by more permanent ones of copper. All of this work entailed an outlay of more than $172,000, which would never have been met by taxation, but is one of the fruits of the foresight of the citizens of yesterday.

At the annual village meeting of 1933 a resolution was passed setting aside $15,000 from the profits of the Water and Light Department to be represented by a promissory note bearing interest at five percent for the benefit of the Copley Hospital. The note was paid the year following and became a part of the permanent endowment. Thus once more this department acted the part of the fairy godmother to one of the worthwhile institutions of the town.

At the annual village meeting in 1934 it was voted not to levy a village tax that year, but to meet the current expenses from this department, thus helping to relieve the tax situation which was acute because of the business depression.

THE FIRE DEPARTMENT

Another step taken soon after the village was incorporated was that of increasing the fire protection. Up to that time the water supply had been inadequate and the equipment, although as good probably as most small towns enjoyed, consisted of a hand cart and a hook and ladder team. The installation of the village water system marked a distinct advance, for hydrants were located at different points. In 1897 there were thirty-three such, with pressure sufficient to drench the highest points. As the village grew this number was increased until at present there are more than fifty.

In 1900 the fire department was reorganized under the direction of George W. Doty, chief engineer, and since then its chief engineer and two assistants have been elected by the village and its members by the company. Weekly practice meetings are held during the summer months and in the winter they meet monthly. The department includes twenty-five men. In 1924 a new Maxim combination pump and fire engine was bought from the profits of the Water and Light Department and this, together with added hose and the hook and ladder equipment, gives adequate protection.

The first fire alarm was the ringing of the Universalist bell, and for years the key to that church hung on the outside of the building to permit entrance for the purpose of ringing the alarm. In 1910 it was decided to make the tannery whistle, a particularly sonorous one which was audible for a long distance, the official alarm. This served until 1922, when a new siren, also purchased by the Water and Light Department, was installed on the engine house and the village was divided into districts with different signals for each.

Among the men who have been long and honorably connected with the department are C. W. Fitch, Horatio Cram, George W. Doty, E. W. Webster, E. M. Davis, A. J. Smith, W. H. Towne, and J. S. Bannister, who have served as chief engineers or assistants. In addition to these men many others have given freely of their time and strength and deserve praise for their public service.

The most serious fires in the history of the village have been the burning of the Universalist Church with an adjacent dwelling in 1852, the Morrisville House in 1879, the Vermont House in 1893, and The Lamoille House in 1909. The fact that these fires did not spread is due in large part to the efficiency of the fire company. Its fire protection is one of the great assets of the village as a place of residence or of business.

CHAPTER XVII

INDUSTRIES IN MORRISTOWN

A GLANCE at the industrial life of this country town in the early part of the nineteenth century reveals an amazingly independent, self-supporting community. The various enterprises were small, but ample to meet the needs of the citizens which was all they thought of doing. They were concerned only with a local market.

If a settler wished to build a house, the mill of a neighbor prepared lumber in case he didn't use logs; if he preferred brick, a local brickyard could supply that material from the clay which prevailed in and near the Corners. Tanneries which were established early in the history of the town provided leather for the shoe and harness maker. A carding and woolen mill furnished heavy cloth for the busy housewife whose dye came from the butternut tree and sumac bush. Grist mills ground the corn and wheat raised by every farmer whose meat was grown on his premises, and his sugar came from the abundant maples. Cabinet makers could shape furniture from woods as beautiful as grew anywhere, while the cooper fashioned pails, tubs, and such utensils from the timber at hand. The affairs of the world outside the circle of their lives were a matter of interest, but not of vital concern. A war in Europe or a decline in the stock market, had there been such, would not have affected the fortunes of any one here.

Mention has been made of many of the early industries in connection with the development of different sections of the town and the enumeration of the principal ones is made here to show their diversification in regard to both character and location.

The first saw mill was erected by John Safford at Morrisville, but not many years later Luther Bingham had built a saw mill and starch factory in the southern part of the town near the Stowe line on the Shaw or Mill Brook, Nathan Gates was operating a saw mill at Cadys Falls, Samuel Rood at the Corners, and Jacob Walker on Cook's Brook. Potashes on Potash Brook and near the Corners supplied pearlash.

The Saffords at Morrisville and Nathan Gates at the Falls were running grist mills; tanneries were established by Ebenezer Shaw on the Plains, by Calvin Burnett at Morrisville and Walter White on the brook above the Corners, while later in the 60's George Eddy was manufacturing leather at Cadys Falls; starch factories both at the Falls and at the Corners flourished and disposed of the surplus potato crop. In fact, the abundant water power in all parts of the town was early utilized to produce a variety of products.

In the half century following the Civil War, which may be called the middle period, one notes some changes that indicate the passing of the old order. Better means of communication with the outside world had made possible the bringing in of many of the necessities of life more cheaply than they could be produced locally.

The following account taken from the 1869 daybook of M. C. Mower, who kept a general store at Morristown Corners, shows that the modern department store does not offer a much greater variety of goods than did the old general store. It also makes an interesting record of the prices then prevailing and of the needs of the average family of the period:

MOSES WOOD

1	bbl. flour	$9.50
½	lb. tea	55
1	lb. soda	08
1	plug tobacco	56
2	qts. oil	20
1	lb. candles	15
1	spool thread	04
2	lbs. nails	14
¼	lb. snuff	22
1	oz. indigo	15
2	30 wgt. tubs	60
1	lamp chimney	10
1	bottle linament	25
1	paper navy clippings	11
¼	lb. pepper	10
	matches	06
1	scythe and two rakes	1.95
2	doz. crackers	16
2	lbs. loaf sugar	30
1	rake	25
1	50 wgt. tub	50
8	sticks candy	08
1	lamp wick	01
1	box pills	25
1	hammer	12

The candles, snuff and indigo speak of bygone days and some of the other articles would find little market there today.

A page from the daybook of Curtis Mower, shoemaker at the Corners at this time, shows that the boot and shoe problem, even with a family of growing children, was not a serious one:

A. B. TINKER, Dr.

Mar. 13	To mending 1 pr. boots	.17
Mar. 26	To taping and caping 1 pr. boots	34
Mar. 27	To mending 1 boot	17
Apr. 12	To mending Albert's boot	06
Apr. 19	To mending boy's boot	13
May 30	To taping 1 shoe	17
May 31	To mending 1 shoe	20
Je. 20	To mending boy's shoe	17
Jy. 18	To mending 1 shoe	17
Aug. 17	To taping and heeling 1 pr. boots	50
Sept. 23	To taping 1 pr. boots	50
Nov. 29	To mending 1 pr. boots	58
Dec. 14	To mending boy's boots	17

We hear no more of the potash and except for one subsequent attempt to manufacture brick for a short time on the Ryder farm, they are imported, while some of the smaller mills have disappeared. Little manufacturing is found at the Corners. A clothes rack factory did business for a time and the starch factory, situated on the brook not far from the schoolhouse, was run by W. S. Cheney until carried away by high water, after which it was not rebuilt.

Cadys Falls still keeps its cluster of mills, grist mill, chair stock and fulling, carding, and dressing mill. In the southern part of the town in the 80's by far the most important industry is the clapboard mill established by James J. Billings on the Shaw Brook, while farther north near the base of Sterling Mountain W. W. Peck's steam saw mill is doing a thriving business.

At Morrisville, three-quarters of a century after the wheels of the first mill were set in motion, the Saffords were still running a grist mill and turning out chair stock, house furnishing stock, etc., and above them Clark & Daniels were manufacturing sugar and butter tubs. George Elmore for some time met more than local needs for wagons, carriages, and sleighs.

The local newspaper of December, 1881, contains an item to the effect that the first specimen of pulp was run off at the pulp mill which, under the management of the Lamoille Valley Pulp Co., did a good business for some years. This plant was taken over by the National Fibre Board Co. about 1890, and for several years was one of the leading industries in town. The fibre board was made from the screenings of pulp mills. The material was ground in the basement of the three-story building and pressed into the desired thickness; on the second floor the sheets were cut into boot and shoe counters and on the third floor was the drying room. The main office of the company was in Boston, with plants in different parts of the country and most of the time Mr. H. M. Gordon was their local manager. The factory was located at the junction of the Boardman Brook and the Lamoille River near the site now occupied by the power house, and was destroyed by fire.

The manufacture of monuments, headstones and cemetery memorials of all kinds has been carried on in town for a long period of years. Among the early dealers were Josiah Trow, E. E. Foster, and W. W. Pike, while at present F. M. Ober & Son handle this line of work, and set and letter monuments. In addition to this, granite sheds have operated here many years. The first sheds were built in 1895, with Mr. John Brechin of Barre as manager, and the company was known as the Arnold Granite Co. Later they were taken over by Stearns & Daniels, who moved here from Hardwick and employed a considerable force. They in turn gave place to Mould & Davis, and in 1908 Mr. F. M. Mould bought out his partner, and the business was carried on by him alone.

In 1911 another granite shed was built near the railroad track on Waban Avenue by the Wallace Brothers, Robert, William and George, who moved here from Hardwick, and for nearly twenty years they had one of the largest payrolls in town. One by one these brothers died, Robert being the last survivor, and in the depression of 1929 these sheds were closed down.

As has been noted, the tanning industry was connected with the earliest history of the town, but in pioneer days it was only a local market that was supplied. In 1889 the business was reopened on a larger scale when Messrs. Edward Webster and C. H. A. Stafford of Stowe came here and built north of the station in the bow of the river a plant which has since been one of the most stable industries of the town. In 1900 this firm sold out to Mr. Charles Warren of Waterbury, with whom were associated H. C. Fisk and C. H. Slocum, and the firm name continued to be the Warren Leather Co., even after Mr. Warren withdrew and Mr. Slocum became the manager. Later the business was sold to a group of men from Worcester, Mass., with Mr. J. G. Parks of that city as manager. For many years the firm specialized in the manufacture of leather for harness. When the demand for that declined, they made leather for belting and the lacings of belts which was shipped in the rough to Worcester, Mass. This plant was badly damaged by the flood which was later followed by the depression so that it suspended operations, and in December, 1932, the property was sold at public auction to a New York firm who operate under the name of the Vermont Tanning Corporation. At a special town meeting, called early in 1933, the business was exempted from taxation for a period of years, and then the buildings were repaired and business resumed.

The oldest business in town which has been carried on at the same place is that of the Morrisville Foundry Co. Soon after the coming of the railroad was an assured fact, in 1872, Mr. E. B. Merriam erected a building near the proposed site of the road to house a small foundry business. Mr. H. H. Morgan became proprietor of it in 1874, and different ones managed it until 1889 when the property was bought by a group of men incorporated as the Morrisville Foundry Co., of which Hon. George W. Hendee was the president.

In 1893 the company engaged as foreman Mr. Channing B. Greene, who came from St. Albans, where he had been employed in the shops of the Central Vermont Railroad. Mr. Greene was not only a practical workman, he also had a great deal of inventive genius. His brother, C. Porter Greene, is a skilled pattern maker and a son, Morris, succeeded his father as manager. The foundry proper is only a part of their work, as jobbing and general repair work is done for a large section of northern Vermont, while plows and drag saw rigs are among their regular products; and novelty lathes, shoe last lathes, machines for making clothes pins and many others are made. One of their most ingenious pieces of work was the dome of the astronomical observatory, the gift of Mr. George G. Grout to the town in 1930.

Many of the industries of Morrisville center around the timber supply of this and surrounding towns and among the concerns of this character is the G. A. Morse Lumber Co. Mr. G. A. Morse, the founder of the company, came to Morrisville to reside in 1893, and at that time had mills located in Wolcott, Elmore and other towns. In 1907 he established his hardwood dressing mill here that furnishes a product which the firm ships to all parts of New England.

Another industry dependent upon the hardwood supply is the manufacture of veneer or plywood. The local plant was built by C. H. A. Stafford & Sons, but was bought by the Atlas Plywood Co. in 1925 and is one of the many units operated by this company in New England and in the South. All kinds of hardwood are used in making the plywood packing cases which are used for shipping textiles, radios, and heavy articles like refrigerators, pianos, etc. When operated at capacity, this firm has employed the largest force of any industry in town.

Another woodworking industry is the last block factory of C. H. A. Stafford & Sons, which was built on Wabun Avenue in 1917. For a time this firm owned and operated a similar factory in Bristol, and their business connections extend beyond the limits of the United States.

Other shops, dependent in part upon the waste products of these larger establishments, have been maintained which have manufactured novelties and small wooden utensils, such as bread boards, rolling pins, towel racks, etc.

The chief industry in this section of Vermont has always been agriculture with dairying its main factor. For many years each farmer kept his herd, for which he raised his grain, set his milk in pans, skimmed off the cream which he churned into butter, and used the skimmed milk for feeding his stock. The quality of the butter produced depended upon the individual maker. But the business of dairying has been revolutionized. The introduction of the silo and more scientific methods of feeding, of the milk separator, and of the milking machines were all significant steps, but the greatest change has been the coming of the creamery.

Hood and Whiting, both leading factors in the distribution of milk in Boston as well as local men began in the early 90's to maintain plants here for manufacturing butter and cheese and pasteurizing milk. Among the resident firms were C. H. A. Stafford & Sons and H. Waite & Sons.

The largest factor is the United Farmers' Cooperative Creamery Association, Inc., which was established in 1920. It began in a small way with 200 patrons doing a business of less than $100,000, which has grown to one of more than $3,000,000 and 1,900 patrons. While the main plant is here and the business is done through the local office, it has plants in Wolcott, Johnson, Hardwick, and Troy, and in March, 1933, the stockholders of the Franklin County Cooperative Creamery voted to join it. The enterprise began in a small inconvenient building, but it now owns a modern plant equipped with all modern devices while three tank cars each with a capacity of 6,000 gallons transports its milk to Boston and a plant at Charlestown, Mass., looks after the marketing. Thus it has become a real factor in the milk, cream, and ice cream business of New England.

The town has always been generous in exempting new industries from taxation and the very low rates for electric power and for water are two factors making Morrisville a desirable place in which to locate manufacturing plants.

So gradually do changes come in the life of a community that it is only by surveying a period of years that they become apparent. Of the business firms now operating here most of them are comparatively recent.

The firm of H. A. Slayton & Co. was in the feed and grain business more than fifty years ago and is the oldest enterprise doing business under the same name. In this case the son, A. H. Slayton, has succeeded his father, now deceased, as manager of the firm.

The Munson Store has been operating since the late 80's with the son, Levi, succeeding his father, Harlan P. Munson.

The next oldest business house is that of H. Waite & Sons, whose founder, Mr. Henry Waite, came to Morrisville in the late 80's and first ran a bakery, then he opened a grocery store to which he added a wholesale produce business. Before his death, one son, Arthur, took over the grocery department, while the second son, Jesse A., remained with his father in the produce business, which is continued under the old firm name.

The Campbell Jewelry Store still retains the original

name, although it has passed entirely out of the hands of the family which managed it so successfully for more than a quarter of a century.

At one period in its history, Morristown was known throughout the state and well beyond its borders because of the trotting horses which were trained here in the Utton Stables. In 1871 the Utton brothers, John and Thomas, came here from Worcester, Vt., purchased adjacent lots on Maple Street, then containing only a few dwellings, and built their homes and large barns for the accommodation of the handsome blooded horses which were brought here from all parts of New England for training. At times twenty to twenty-five trotters were handled by these men and their assistants and made the circuit of Vermont Fairs and of races outside the state. While the stables were supported largely by outside patronage, there was much interest in blooded horses among residents of the town. Ex-Gov. G. W. Hendee, after the press of public duties allowed, pursued the raising of fine carriage horses, especially of the Morgan breed, as a hobby and at one time Charles R. Page, for some years the owner of the Malvern Stock Farm, was engaged in raising them and built a race track on the level field in front of his residence for their training.

Another horse lover of the 80's was James M. Joslyn. While running a grocery store was his business, the keeping of blooded horses was his avocation.

John Utton usually drove the trotters until he was thrown from his sulky while racing on the local fairground, and fractured one hip, which practically ended his career as a driver, though he recovered enough to train young horses. Later both brothers died and John's son, William, moved to Barton, Vt., where he still carries on his father's calling.

That the stables had more than local reputation is shown by items such as the following taken from the "News and Citizen" of August, 1883: "The horse, George C., owned by Utton and Clark, has been sold to Philadelphia parties for $1,300." Some idea of the range of their clientele can be gained by a survey of their stables in the spring of 1897. At the beginning of the season the string included two belonging to Governor Hendee of this place, three owned by H. R. C. Watson of the Forest Park Farm, Brandon; three belonging to Thomas A. Lake of Rockville, Conn.; two of H. H. Peck's of Waterbury, Conn.; one of A. P. Wheelock's of Boston; one owned by G. L. Clark of Hartford, Conn.; and one owned by E. F. Carpenter of Ramsay, N. J. Many of them already had fast records to their credit.

The Smalleys, E. A. and H. A., father and son, are among the men who have maintained an interest in racing and the names of Utton and Smalley have been given to two of the stakes at the local fair. In 1929, after the death of Mr. E. A. Smalley, his son, Herbert, donated a silver cup to be presented to the winner of the Smalley stakes at this annual event.

Thus they and Dr. A. M. Goddard, C. H. A. Stafford & Sons, and W. C. Tripp, who also trains horses, and a few others have carried on the traditions of the town in this respect, even though the automobile has so largely supplanted the horse.

CHAPTER XVIII

MORRISTOWN IN PUBLIC AFFAIRS

IT is a well known fact that the majority of the country's leaders in the business and political worlds have come from the smaller centers of population. A survey of the men who have gone from Morristown into different fields of activity indicates that the town has furnished its quota; in fact, it is doubtful if many places of less than 3,000 inhabitants have sent three of their residents to Congress.

The first of these men to represent the town and state in the broader field of national politics was George Whitman Hendee, who was born in Stowe, Vt., in 1832, the son of Jehial P. and Rebecca (Ferrin) Hendee. His father tried to supplement his meager salary as minister by publishing the first paper in Lamoille County, the "Christian Luminary," a short lived periodical; and it was necessary for the boy to work on a farm and later to teach school in order to obtain his education. After the removal of the family to Morrisville, the son attended Peoples Academy, and then went to study law in the office of his uncle, W. G. Ferrin, of Johnson, and afterwards completed his studies with Thomas Gleed of Morrisville.

The year 1855 marked his admission to the Lamoille County Bar and his marriage to Melissa Redding, who died six years later. He began to practice his profession at Waterville, but in the spring of 1858 moved to Morrisville, became a partner of Thomas Gleed, and entered upon his political career by being elected state's attorney. He also represented Morristown in the Legislature in 1861 and 1862. During the Civil War he was deputy provost marshal, and after a warmly contested election was chosen senator from Lamoille County in 1866. He was unanimously elected president pro tem of the Senate and his election as lieutenant-governor in 1869 was a natural consequence of his service in the Senate. A contemporary, writing of him, said: "Nature had anointed him a presiding officer." Upon the death of Gov. Peter T. Washburn, in February, 1870, Mr. Hendee took the oath of office as governor, thus gaining the title by which he was commonly known the rest of his life. In less than a month he was seriously ill of lung fever, and for a time it looked as though the state would face an unprecedented condition so far as its chief executive was concerned. However, Governor Hendee lived to complete his term, and did it so acceptably that he was a prominent candidate to succeed himself, but he withdrew his name in the interests of party harmony. Political gossip said he had his eye on a larger stake, that of representative from the Third District, but he refused to be considered for that office, preferring to wait until he had united party support.

In 1873 he was elected representative to Congress by a good majority, succeeding Worthington C. Smith. For three terms, from 1873 to 1879, he served at Washington, where he had the reputation of being a hard working, conscientious congressman. He was a member of the committee on private land claims and the District of Columbia, and was instrumental in drafting and securing the passage of a bill changing the form of government of the district.

After his return from Washington, he was national bank examiner for six years; and, although he continued to maintain his law office, having entered into partnership with his half-brother, H. C. Fisk, in 1877, business claimed more and more of his attention. He had been one of the prime movers in securing a railroad through the Lamoille Valley and the stiffest local opposition for office that he ever received was due to differences of opinion in regard to building the Portland & Ogdensburg, now the St. Johnsbury & Lake Champlain road, of which he naturally became a director. For many years he was president of the Montreal, Portland & Boston Railroad of Canada. He was closely identified with the Union Savings Bank & Trust Co., having been a director from its establishment, its vice-president, and for the last nine years of his life its president. He loved a good horse and during his later years owned many and this interest doubtless led him to give freely of his time and thought to the affairs of the Lamoille Valley Fairground Association, of which he was president more than a quarter of a century.

After the death of his first wife he married Viola S. Bundy in 1863, who shared his success until her death in 1901. On January 10, 1906, he married Mary Watts of Stowe, but in less than a year's time he died, thus removing one who for nearly half a century was a familiar and honored figure here.

It has been said of him that, "As an advocate at the bar he had but few equals in the state, but his great good nature so overcame his lawyer's natural craving for popularity and pelf that his clients were frequently brought to a compromise advantageous to themselves and honorable to their attorney." He was an impressive looking man, tall and portly, but the kindliness of his manner dispelled any diffidence which he might naturally have inspired. The much abused word genial accurately described him.

HORACE HENRY POWERS

Another man destined to be known beyond the borders of his native state was Horace Henry Powers, born on May 29, 1835. His father, Horace Powers, was that most useful citizen, a country doctor, who had also served the community in various public offices after coming here from New Hampshire with his young wife, Love E. Gilman.

The son, H. Henry, was given the best educational advantages which were available, studying at Peoples Academy and then entering the University of Vermont, from which he was graduated in the class of 1855, a class which contained an unusually high percentage of young men who were highly successful in various walks of life. Among them were Charles Heath and Benjamin F. Fifield, well known Vermont lawyers; Benjamin L. Benedict, clerk of the United States Circuit Court and United States commissioner more than twenty years; Moses Parmalee, well known missionary to Turkey, and author; C. Liberty Goodell, a clergyman of national reputation; Norman Williams, Chicago lawyer, first president of Crerar Library and known to Vermonters through his gifts of the Norman Williams Library at Woodstock, Vt., and the Williams Science Building at the University of Vermont.

After graduation Mr. Powers taught for a few months at Huntington, Canada, and then became the first principal of Lamoille Central Academy at Hyde Park. He was at the same time carrying on the study of law, at first under the direction of Thomas Gleed of Morrisville and later in the office of Child & Ferrin of Hyde Park. The year 1858 marked his admission to the Lamoille County Bar, his marriage to Miss Caroline Waterman of Cadys Falls, and his election to the General Assembly from

Hyde Park, where he was the youngest member of that body. In 1861-1862 he served as state's attorney and in the latter year he entered into partnership with P. K. Gleed at Morrisville, forming a firm which soon gained an enviable reputation throughout northern Vermont. In 1869 he was one of the twelve men composing the thirteenth and last Council of Censors, a body which was at that time peculiar to this state. The year following he was a member of the Constitutional Convention, being chairman in the committee of the whole of that body. Among the changes made by this body was the abolition of the Council of Censors and the adoption of biennial elections. In 1872 he was senator from Lamoille County and two years later represented Morristown in the General Assembly and was elected speaker, serving as such until his election to the Supreme Court Bench. He held this position until his election to Congress in 1890.

On his career as lawyer and judge the following comment is taken from Crockett's "History of Vermont":

"In the practice of his profession Judge Powers took high rank, and the firm to which he belonged was one of the leading ones in northern Vermont. Judge Powers had unusual grace and power as an advocate; he possessed a wealth of wit and sarcasm; was well equipped in the law, and had a personality that was winning. He was a handsome man, and would attract attention in any public gathering. Besides these elements of advantage, he had good business judgment, and an assurance that made him fearless on the firing line. He inspired his clients with confidence, and knew how to acquire and hold an extensive clientage. In the legislative duties which he performed he was naturally in places of leadership, and commanded attention and respect whenever he spoke. His speeches in political campaigns were careful and convincing presentations of the issues that were before the public.

"When he came to the bench in 1874, he was at the right age, and had had the right preparation in every way for a useful career as judge. His studies and his practice had qualified him for the service, and his temperament was ideal for the discharge of his duties. He looked the judge in every way, and this lent not a little to his charm as a presiding officer. He was personally an attractive and interesting man, and it is natural that he should have enjoyed the confidence and warm personal friendship of the bar.

"In the Supreme Court he wrote opinions in 161 cases. These are his permanent monument. They show clear thinking, careful examination of authorities, good reasoning and simplicity and beauty of diction. In his capacity for direct statement in plain and perspicuous terms he was exceptionally happy. His personality was such that his influence was bound to be felt strongly whether he sat around the counsel table as an attorney, or with the judges in chambers. He saw a point quicker than most others and led for the adoption of his views with a great deal of insistence."

Previous to Judge Powers' election in 1890, he had received scattering votes for the office of both United States senator and representative, but he had declined to be a candidate. So when he did enter the contest, he was nominated without opposition. He was early appointed a member of the judiciary committee, a position which his experience made him particularly well qualified to fill. In the Fifty-Fourth Congress he was chairman of the committee on Pacific railroads. No question came before that session that involved more money than this one. The Union Pacific and Central Pacific Railroads at the time of their construction had not only received large land grants, but also subsidies ranging from $16,000 to $48,000 per mile. In spite of the assistance given, the roads were at this time unable to pay the $190,000,000 owed, and there were many difficult legal problems involved. Yet the help of the roads in developing the country had enriched the government far more than the amount at stake, and justice demanded the consideration of all these factors.

The "Louisville Courier Journal," in January, 1895, commenting on Congress and its activities, gives the following pen picture of Vermont's representative from the First District:

"He is typical of the state that gave Thad Stevens to Pennsylvania, Stephen A. Douglas to Illinois and Matt Carpenter to Wisconsin. He is one of the few men in public life who has attained a distinguished position in the national councils without uttering a word calculated to ruffle the feelings of a political opponent. His speech in support of the Sibley claim, a southern war claim, gave him the heart of every southern congressman, as all his utterances had commanded their respect. He is a man of massive head and frame—one of the handsomest men in Congress. It is a great pity that there are not more statesmen like him."

After five terms in Congress, he had enjoyed a longer term in that body than has usually been given the representative from this state, and he was defeated in one of the most exciting campaigns and conventions ever held in Vermont, being succeeded by D. J. Foster of Burlington. After his retirement to private life, he resumed the practice of law and acted as counsel for the Rutland Railroad for several years.

One of his marked traits was his independence of thought and action. The fear that he might be on the unpopular side of a question never deterred him from espousing the cause in which he believed. This was true in politics as in other things, but never seemed to diminish the votes he received at election time.

A conservative in politics, he was a liberal in his religious views and a staunch friend of the local Universalist Church, yet this did not prevent his being interested in the building of the Catholic Church, and the priest who had that in charge testified to his council and help. In fact, he was concerned with anything that affected his native town, with whose history he made himself familiar and much of which he preserved. During the last few years of his life he was a familiar and striking figure about the village, and after his death, on December 8, 1913, his townsmen missed one who, in his home, in his state, and in the nation had been an honor to himself and to his community.

LESLIE MORTIER SHAW

Although Morristown can claim little part in shaping the career of Leslie M. Shaw, she has always been proud of the fact that his birthplace was within her borders. In a log cabin on a hillside farm in the western part of the town, on a road now abandoned, he was born on November 2, 1848. His parents, Boardman O. and Louisa Spaulding Shaw, were of that sturdy, sterling stock that made New England and contributed largely to the shaping of the Middle West. When Leslie was but a boy, the family moved to another farm in Stowe, and so thrifty and industrious were they that later his father retired to Morrisville in comfortable financial circumstances. It was at Peoples Academy that he got his education. His own mother died in 1865, and two years later his father married

Susan A. Mason of Morristown, for whom the stepson cherished a strong affection. Upon attaining his majority young Shaw looked about for the best place in which to begin his life work and chose the promising young state of Iowa, settling in Denison. Realizing the importance of a college education, in 1870 he entered Cornell College, Mount Vernon, Iowa, from which he was graduated four years later. He decided to enter the legal profession, and for two years was a student in the Iowa Law School at Des Moines, Iowa. After receiving his diploma, he was admitted to the Iowa Bar and opened his office at Denison. He soon became interested in the banks of Denison, Manilla, and Charter Oak, and later was chosen president of the first two. Because of this connection, he began to make a careful study of the whole question of finance. Thus when the free silver movement swept the Middle West, he was one of the few men who had thoroughly investigated the question. His study led him to align himself with the gold standard forces, and in 1896 he stumped the state of Iowa for McKinley and his forceful, persuasive arguments for the gold standard attracted the attention not only of his adopted state, but of the nation. The following year he was elected governor of Iowa, in which office he served two terms. His election as permanent chairman of the Monetary Congress at Indianapolis in 1898 gave him still more prominence in financial circles. So it was but natural that Theodore Roosevelt, who had heard him speak during the free silver campaign, should call him to be secretary of the treasury, where he served until 1907. Some time after his retirement from this position, business reverses led him in his later years to write and lecture, and for a time he traveled over the country as a lecturer for the American Bankers' Association.

He was a man of varied interests, among which were education and religion. He was responsible for and contributed freely to the establishment of a Normal School at Denison and was for a time its president. He was also a generous supporter and trustee of his alma mater, Cornell College. Brought up in the Methodist faith, Mr. Shaw never departed from it and four times he represented the Des Moines Conference in the Quadrennial General Conference of the denomination. He was a man with a keen sense of humor, strong convictions, and deep loyalties, and at his death, in 1931, he received from the press of the country high commendation for his life and work.

FREDERICK GLEED FLEETWOOD

The third man whom Morristown sent to represent the First District at Washington was Frederick G. Fleetwood, a native of St. Johnsbury, who came to make this town his home when his mother married Philip K. Gleed. He received his secondary school education at St. Johnsbury Academy, studied at the University of Vermont and was graduated from Harvard in the class of 1891. Having decided upon the law as his life work, he began to read in the office of his stepfather, Mr. Gleed, and was admitted to the Lamoille County Bar in 1894 and the year following entered into partnership with Mr. Gleed.

He passed through the different local offices which the political aspirant naturally fills. He was secretary of the Commission for the Revision of the Vermont Statutes in 1893 and 1894, town clerk from 1896 to 1900, state's attorney from 1896 to 1898, represented the town at Montpelier in 1900 and that same year was chosen presidential elector, being the one selected to take the official vote of the state to Washington. From 1902 to 1908 he was secretary of state, and again in 1917 he filled out the term of Guy W. Bailey, when the latter was elected president of the University of Vermont.

During these years Mr. Fleetwood had become well and favorably known in all parts of the state. He was in demand as a public speaker not only within the state, but well beyond its borders, so that it was only natural that when Porter H. Dale was promoted from the House of Representatives to the Senate, Mr. Fleetwood should be a candidate for the position of representative and be elected. He knew the routine work of his office as he had acted as secretary for Congressman H. H. Powers in 1894. Soon after going to Washington, he was struck by a truck, an accident which incapacitated him for some time. After his recovery he performed his duties ably and conscientiously, serving upon the committee on public lands and the committee on insular affairs. At the end of his term he refused to be a candidate for re-election and returned to resume the practice of law in Morrisville.

No better illustration of his standing in the community can be given than the following incident: In 1910 he was a candidate for the office of governor. He was late in entering the contest, to the practical politician he was too much of a "scholar in politics," and he was defeated by John J. Mead. On the evening after the convention a large number of the residents of the village and town turned out to greet Mr. Fleetwood at his Park Street residence. Victorious candidates are often treated thus, but not often is the defeated one the recipient of such a spontaneous expression of the affection in which he is held by his fellow townsmen.

Mr. Fleetwood is a student of world affairs and finds his greatest pleasure at home in his large library. In 1928 he married Miss R. Louise Slocum of this town, thus making the Gleed house once more the center of hospitality.

GEORGE McLELLAN POWERS

Among the many different lawyers who have studied or practiced here, the one most highly honored by the state is George M. Powers, who has for several years served in the highest judicial position in the state, that of Chief Justice of the Supreme Court.

George M. Powers was born on December 19, 1861, the son of H. Henry and Caroline (Waterman) Powers. The year following the family moved to Morrisville, where the son received his education in the graded school and at Peoples Academy. He was graduated from the University of Vermont in the class of '83, and at once took up the study of law in the office of P. K. Gleed. He was admitted to the Lamoille County Bar in 1886 and entered into partnership with Hollis S. Wilson, former principal of Peoples Academy. He served his apprenticeship at Montpelier in various positions which made him thoroughly familiar with laws and the methods by which they are made. He was assistant clerk from 1884 to 1888 and secretary of the Senate for the six years following. He was reporter of the decisions of the Supreme Court from 1902 to 1904, when he was appointed associate judge of the Supreme Court, succeeding Judge Wendell P. Stafford. who resigned. Thus at the early age of forty-three he began his judicial career.

In 1906, when a reorganization of the judicial department was made, the number of the Supreme Court was reduced to four and he was elected a judge of the Superior Court, but in 1909 he again became an associate judge of the Supreme Court. It had been customary to apply the seniority rule in the advancement of judges, but when Chief Justice John W. Rowell retired in 1915, Judge Powers, though one of the younger men, was made chief justice, a position which he held until February 1, 1915. The Legislature of that year restored the succession and he was elected an associate justice of the court, and continued in that position until December 14, 1929, when, upon the death of Chief Justice John H. Watson, he again became chief justice, which office he has filled to his own credit and to the satisfaction of the state.

Although Chief Justice Powers' name has often been mentioned in connection with the office of United States representative and senator, he has not seemed inclined to follow in the steps of his father and give up his judicial career for political honors.

In 1893 he married Gertrude Woodbury of Burlington and to this union were born four children: Horace Henry, who is an attorney in St. Albans, Vt.; Dorothy, who married Warren L. Peck of St. Johnsbury, Vt.; Elizabeth, who is the wife of Donald Cockcroft of Albany, N. Y.; and Roberta, who, after graduation from the University of Vermont, did post-graduate work at Simmons College, and now holds an important secretarial position.

Chief Justice Powers has always been a loyal son of Morristown and keenly interested in its welfare. He has been one of the water and light commissioners since the inception of that department, and has held various town offices. Keenness of mind and wit, eloquence, dignity, conservatism, and integrity—all these and many other qualities—are a part of the composite picture of this well known son of Morristown.

CHAPTER XIX

MISCELLANY

THE FLOOD

THE great flood of November 3 and 4, 1927, which will always be a mile-stone in the history of the Green Mountain State, did not take any toll of life in Morristown, but left scars which can never be effaced. While it was the most disastrous occurrence of this kind in the state, it seems it was not the only one. In September, 1828, the Lamoille Valley, in common with other sections of the state, suffered from a severe freshet which did much damage to the intervales, the roads, and bridges. In Morrisville, Mr. David Noyes was one of the greatest sufferers as his carding mill and clothing mill, situated above the present power house, were carried off, and Mr. Seth Bagley was swept away in the clothing mill. His remains were found three days later on what was known as Joe's Island, a short distance below the falls.

About forty years later another period of high water affected the town, and a special town meeting was called on January 4, 1870, to vote a tax to pay the extra expense of repairs on highways and bridges damaged by the flood; and, at the regular March meeting following, six men who suffered loss either had their taxes abated or were given orders by the selectmen toward the same.

Spring freshets often did damage, but it remained for the flood of 1927 to set the highwater mark in a very literal way. It began to rain in Morristown about nine o'clock in the evening of November 2 and continued with more or less intensity for forty hours. According to unofficial records seven and three-fourths inches fell upon ground already filled by copious autumns storms. The climax was reached about midnight of November 3 when there seemed to be a prolonged and continuous cloud burst. The water was then running over the floor of the iron bridge below the railroad track and four feet of water flowed over the wing wall of the new dam which had a cement core banked with earth. Unable to withstand the terrific pressure it gave way, thus doubtless saving from destruction the new power plant. According to the report of the consulting engineer of the committee appointed by the Legislature to recommend flood control methods, the flood flow per second of the Lamoille at Cadys Falls was 36,600 cubic feet. The night of November 3 will never be forgotten by residents of the town. The electric light plant was disabled early in the evening so the village was in inky darkness. About eight o'clock the fire alarm sounded, calling for helpers; and out into the storm went every able bodied man on some kind of rescue work, either attempting to save Ward's mill, which was threatened, moving goods from houses which were doomed, acting as guard at various strategic points, working to save the electric station, or in some other activity.

When the residents were able to take account of stock, they found six dwelling houses had been swept away and two more undermined so that they were carried off later; the foundry, Morse's mill, and the tannery had been flooded and the latter almost completely wrecked; the Tenney bridge, the bridge across the Lamoille at Cadys Falls, the one across Ryder Brook on the Stowe Road and most of the smaller bridges and culverts all over town were gone. But most spectacular of all was the great gorge cut by the river south of Bridge Street from the north end of the new dam through the pasture and Clark Park, a chasm from forty to sixty feet deep and fifteen to eighteen hundred feet wide where the soil was completely eroded, leaving only huge boulders and debris.

The report sent to the Vermont Flood Survey estimated the losses to private property in Morrisville at $23,200, to municipal property $15,000, to manufacturing plants $75,000, and to bridges and highways $150,000. This does not include losses to farmers from erosion, flooded areas, etc.

One of the most thrilling features of the disaster was the rescue of twenty-seven people who were marooned on the island resulting from the new channel of the river. A rope was stretched across the chasm from tree to tree, and the refugees were brought to safety in a breeches buoy.

One of the landmarks swept away was the Tenney bridge which, the day after the deluge, rested on the meadow north of Park Street. In 1830 there was the following article in the warning for town meeting, "to see if the town will build a bridge across the Lamoille near

Colonel Tenney's to accommodate the road leading from said Tenney's to Safford's mills, if thought best." The article was dismissed and the proposal was voted down again at a special town meeting called in 1831, but on October 5, 1831, after a public hearing at Truman Tenney's, the road commissioners ordered the building of this bridge at a cost of $400, and the construction of a road from this bridge to intersect the road leading from Morristown through Elmore to Montpelier; and on January 5, 1833, the town so voted. The Cadys Falls structure was nearly as old, having been built about 1834 or 1835 with the surplus money deposited by the United States government with the several states in Andrew Jackson's administration. This bridge did away with the necessity of fording the stream at a point a little below the site selected for the bridge, which had previously been the custom.

The most serious blow that threatened the town as a result of the flood was the loss of the railroad, the story of the damage and rehabilitation of which is told elsewhere.

But the flood had its bright side as well, and the spirit of real self-sacrifice with which the citizens aided their more unfortunate friends in Waterbury and Johnson, the alacrity with which the Red Cross shouldered its burden of caring for the homeless here and elsewhere, and the cheerfulness with which all met the deprivations caused by their isolated condition was heartening.

CEMETERIES

Soon after the settlement of the town there came of necessity the sad task of planning for a cemetery or burying ground, as our forefathers termed it. Often in those early days it was the custom to lay the loved ones away on the home place, and doubtless more than one such grave is now unknown and unmarked. Sometimes these private grounds were discontinued and the occupants removed to other cemeteries. For example, the Boardmans at Cadys Falls had their own private place of interment near the Page hide house. When the railroad was surveyed and found to pass through this section, removal was made to Morrisville.

Eight cemeteries have been established as follows: Pleasant View and Riverside at Morrisville, the Wheeler southeast of Morrisville near the farm formerly owned by

Luman Wheeler, Mountain View at the Corners, Greenlawn on the Plains, Lake View at Cadys Falls and LaPorte and Randolph on these roads. A visit to anyone of them arouses admiration for the good judgment and taste shown by the early settlers in selecting such beautiful locations. One is bound to say with the poet

> I like that ancient Saxon phrase which calls
> The burial-ground God's Acre: it is just.
> It consecrates each grave within its walls
> And breathes a benison o'er the sleeping dust.

As one stands in these cemeteries and lifts his eyes to Elmore Mountain or to more remote Sterling and Mansfield, or follows the windings of the Lamoille, in whatever direction he looks, beauty greets him and he feels such a name as God's Acre is not only "just" but fitting.

In June, 1809, Nathaniel Morse deeded "to the inhabitants of Morristown a part of Lot No. 4 in the second division lying on road that leads from Four Corners to Elmore." It must be remembered that the first road from the Four Corners to Elmore ran across the flat past the house occupied in 1935 by R. H. Farr, and then followed very nearly the line of the George Washington Highway past the Copley Hospital, the B. L. Stewart farm, etc. This cemetery was once known as the Burnt Ground Cemetery, and here as early as 1810 Daniel Sumner, the first man in town to die of the dreaded disease, smallpox, was interred. Here rest Nathan Gates, Jr., and his family, many of the Brighams, the Earles, and the Revolutionary soldier, Josiah Roberts.

No deed of the transfer of land for a cemetery at Morristown Corners has been found, but a study of the names and dates of the stones indicates that it was probably the second to be occupied. Here one sees many of the names connected with town beginnings, including Jacob Walker, the first settler, and his family; Comfort Olds, who first wintered in town; the Hurds; the Roods; and the Revolutionary soldiers, John Cole, Samuel Cooke, Crispus Shaw, and Moses Weld. In 1919 this cemetery was enlarged by the purchase of adjacent land.

Greenlawn on the Plains is the smallest of the group and at first seems to be almost a family plot, for here lie Eliphalet Whitney, his wife, and relatives, including the large families of his sons-in-law, Ebenezer Shaw and Seth Haskins. Other familiar names are the Metcalfs, Kimballs and Wheelers.

Not long after the first settlement on the Randolph Road, that burial ground began to be occupied. Here may be found the lot containing Elisha Herrick, Esq.; the Revolutionary soldiers Barzillai Spaulding and William Small, with five later generations of Smalls; Laura Kibbey, wife of one of the first settlers in that district, and others.

In April, 1833, Polly Poor, in consideration of $16 paid her by the inhabitants of Middle School District No. 10 of Morristown, deeded to the town one-half acre of land for a cemetery. Here were interred some of the Websters, the Rands, Deacon Jonathan Powers and others whose names are associated with the opening of this part of the town.

In 1838 land was purchased from the original Gates farm at Cadys Falls for Lake View Cemetery, which was enlarged and improved in 1894. Here are buried the Revolutionary veteran, Lieut. Nathan Gates; the Towns, the Watermans, some of the Boardmans, and others who were pioneers at Cadys Falls.

At the town meeting of 1846 it was voted "to purchase three-fourths of an acre of land of Jedediah Safford for a Public Burying Ground" at Morrisville. This original plot was added to as long as space permitted and here lie the Saffords, including the Revolutionary soldier, Joseph Safford, Judge Samuel Willard, the Felchers and many others who are gratefully remembered for their services to the town.

When this cemetery became so crowded that other accommodations had to be provided, the town bought the plateau south of the village in 1892 which they appropriately designated Pleasant View Cemetery. In 1894 a board of Cemetery Commissioners, consisting of G. W. Doty, C. H. Slocum, G. M. Powers, E. J. Hall and G. W. Clark, were elected. Although no funds were appropriated, yet from the sale of lots, they raised money with which they built a receiving vault, and hired an engineer to lay out roads, walks, and lots to the number of 2,600; and began to beautify the grounds. In 1916 it was thought best to enlarge this by the purchase of additional land to the east.

Beautiful as the natural setting of these cemeteries is, they would doubtless have been as unkempt and neglected as many country yards are, had it not been for the efforts of two associations, the Morristown Cemetery Association, organized in 1907, and the Pleasant View Cemetery Association, in 1915. Before then a few individuals cared for their lots. At Morrisville this was quite customary, but outside the village the grass was mowed only at haying time, grave stones had fallen and there was a general air of neglect. With the establishment of these two associations, a transformation took place. The grounds were put into shape so they could be well cared for, fences were rebuilt, sunken graves filled and stones cleaned and repaired. Now the visitor to any cemetery in town will find it neat and well tended. This has been accomplished through the work of the women who have taken the lead and secured the cooperation of the parties directly concerned. Many lots have been endowed, thus ensuring perpetual care.

STRANGE CUSTOMS

A study of the uninviting looking town records brings to light many strange customs which prevailed among these early settlers. In the first recorded town meetings one notes the election of tithing men, haywards and hogreeves. The tithing men were to maintain suitable decorum in church and one can in imagination see them keeping a watchful eye upon active youths and somnolent adults at the old brick church.

Haywards were men appointed to watch over the growing hay and to see that it suffered no damage from wandering animals. They were paid according to the number of sheep, cows, or horses that they turned out of any field, the owner of the animals being responsible for the fine.

It was the duty of the hogreeves to catch and put in the pound swine found running at large and tradition says the office was usually given to someone who had married since the last March meeting. These officers seem to have been discontinued after 1840.

Judging from the records this matter of the care of stock gave considerable trouble, for in 1816 it was voted that any ram found running at large between September

1 and December 1 should be forfeit to the person finding. Cattle were branded or marked for purposes of identification. Jedediah Safford's mark for cattle and sheep was, "a half penny crop out of upper side of the right ear." In 1868 it was voted that every man's yard be a pound and every man who had a barn be a pound keeper.

In 1813 this entry was made: "To Abner Brigham, 1st Constable of Morristown Greeting:—You are hereby required to summon Nehemiah Randall and family now residing in Morristown to depart the same. Fail not and due return make according to law." This leads one to expect that he has come upon evidence of some undesirable family and the proof of the zeal of the early citizens in ridding the town of such. It is surprising to learn that it was a curious custom in this period of New England's development to warn out every newcomer to a town on the assumption that he might sometime become a town charge. By serving this process our thrifty forebears relieved the town from any subsequent obligation to support him; and such a warning carried no reflection upon the wealth, position, or character of the family.

When the original proprietors failed to pay their taxes, their holdings were disposed of at an auction or vendue. These vendues were conducted strictly according to law as the following record shows:

"Morristown 10 April 1804—The vendue being opened pursuant to the advertisement proceeded to sale.
"DENNISON COOKE, Constable.

"Morristown 10 April vendue adjourned at one o'clock for one hour.
"DENNISON COOKE, Constable.

"Vendue being opened at two o'clock proceeded to sale.
"DENNISON COOKE, Constable.

"Half an hour before sunset vendue adjourned to the second Monday of April at 10 A. M.
"D. COOKE, Constable."

These vendues were usually held at the tavern and no doubt proved profitable to the tavern keeper as well as to the purchaser of land.

Another custom which seems to have been quite common judging from the petitions in the archives at Montpelier was that of asking for remuneration for the catching of thieves, a crime which was a frequent one in spite of the supposed honesty of the early settlers. The petition of David Little presented to the Legislature October 12, 1812, is typical of others from the town. Mr. Little was asking for reimbursement for time and money spent in pursuing two horse thieves who were caught, tried before Justice Dennison Cooke, and convicted. Little petitions, "that he is poor and unable to bear the whole cost and expense that he has been at in proving and detecting said thieves and as it was for the benefit of the government as well as for the benefit of your petitioner that said thieves should be pursued and detected and as the government by means of the exertions of your honor's petitioner has received and will receive more than a complete indemnity for all costs that the State has sustained, your Honor's petitioner prays your honorable body to take his case into his wise consideration and to allow him the whole or a part of the sums he has so expended or from the same as you in your wisdom may judge right."

A similar petition from Asa Cole and others proves that Mr. Little was not unique in thus soliciting pay from the state.

CARE OF THE POOR

There is Biblical authority for the statement that society will always have some needy and unfortunate ones to care for, but the method by which relief is given changes from time to time. The earliest method used in this town is revealed in the record of the town meeting of 1814 when it was voted, "The support of Avis Whitney for one year be set up at auction to the lowest bidder and the same was struck off to William Brockway at .76 per week."

Five years later it was voted that $30 be at the disposal of the overseer of the poor. These items lead one to conclude or at least to hope that the early residents were for the most part self-supporting. For several years this custom of hiring the unfortunates boarded prevailed, but in time some dissatisfaction arose, and in 1859 this town, Johnson, and Stowe formed an association and purchased a farm on the LaPorte Road to be used jointly by the three towns, the expense being shared according to the grand list of each. This farm was pleasantly located with ample accommodations for the inmates and was managed by superintendents of good judgment and character so the plan was generally satisfactory. This house was destroyed by fire and the towns were faced by new conditions. A committee was appointed to see what should be done, with A. B. Smith, E. E. Brigham and P. K. Gleed representing Morristown. It was decided to disband the association, sell the property, and divide the proceeds together with the insurance among the three towns, which was done in 1897.

The farm on the LaPorte Road now occupied by H. E. Kirby was run as a poor farm for a time, but this was not satisfactory, and it became the practice to aid families by grants and to hire the board of individuals in private homes.

With the depression of 1929-1933, the question of poor relief became a vital one everywhere, and Morristown shared in the burdens which weighed upon most communities. The closing of practically all manufacturing plants threw a large number out of employment, many of whom were forced to call for help. The expenditures in this department rose more than 400 percent in the ten years from 1922 to 1932 and public sentiment was strong for a change in the method of dealing with the question.

At the annual town meeting in 1933 it was voted that the selectmen appoint a committee of five to investigate in regard to the purchase of a poor farm. After examining various sites, the committee recommended the purchase of the Milton Boardman farm on the Randolph Road for a town poor farm. At a largely attended special town meeting it was voted to carry out this recommendation. Arrangements were made to build cottages on the place to accommodate families with children and in the summer following the town returned to the system in vogue years ago.

POPULATION

Many of the rural towns of Vermont have shown a decrease in population, but Morristown, except for the period between 1840 and 1850, has shown a small but steady increase. Its population by decades is as follows:

Year	Population
1791	10
1800	144
1810	550
1820	726
1830	1,315
1840	1,502
1850	1,441
1860	1,751
1870	1,897
1880	2,099
1890	2,411
1900	2,583
1910	2,652
1920	2,813
1930	2,939

The grand list is a reflection of the general economic condition of a place and through a period of years it has been as follows:

1849	$ 3,628.21
1860	$ 4,710.10
1875	$ 6,396.59
1890	$ 9,611.40
1905	$11,259.24
1920	$13,956.61
1935	$16,031.50

A study of the listers' figures shows the gradual increase in the property valuation of the village and the changes that have come in farming.

In 1897 there were more than 1,000 sheep in town; in 1907 there were 382; in 1934 there were forty-nine. The earliest appraisal showed over 1,600 cows; in 1907 there were 2,098, and now there are 4,342. The lumber that grew so plentifully everywhere has been cut off, but little reforesting has been done. Agriculture now centers in the dairy cow, but the difficulties which the dairy industry has met during the past few years may bring about other changes in the future.

IMPORTANT DATES

Grant of the town	Nov. 6, 1780
Grant of the charter	Aug. 24, 1781
First settlement by Jacob Walker	June, 1790
First birth, Lemira Walker	Sept. 14, 1792
Organization of town	1796
First death, Mrs. Lydia Safford Felcher	1799
First marriage, Deacon Cyrel Goodale and Jemima Walker	1800
Establishment of first church, Congregational	1807
Incorporation of Lamoille County	Oct. 26, 1835
Opening of Peoples Academy	1847
Arrival of railroad in Morrisville	1872
Completion of railroad	1877
Incorporation of Village of Morrisville	1890
Establishment of Municipal Water and Light Department	1894
Gift of new building for Peoples Academy	1929
Gift of Copley Hospital	1932

ERRATA - MOWER TEXT

1. Page 5 - Upper: The General Assembly action actually came on November 6, 1780, not November 7.
2. Page 5 - Lower: Dennis Mach almost certainly should be Dennis Meach.
3. Page 23 - C.A. Saunders should be C.A. Sanders.
4. Page 24 - Guildhall should be Guilford.
5. Page 57 - Rev. Otto Raspe was pastor from 1906 to 1911, not 1923 to 1926.
6. Page 64 - "south" should be "north."
7. Page 65 - "south" should be "north."
8. Page 70 - Middlefield should be Middletown.
9. Page 88 - Assistant Pupil should be Assistant Principal.
10. Page 113 - 1851 should be 1861.
11. Page 144 - Fenian Raid should be St. Albans Raid.
12. Page 160 - Poland was born in Westford, not Waterville (on November 1, 1815).
13. Page 166 - 1869 should probably be 1889.
14. Page 171 - Almerion should be Almerin.
15. Page 190 - Middlefield should be Middletown.
16. Page 210 - "... opened for work in Cadys Falls and George's new factory ..." should read "... opened for work in Cady's and George's new factory..."
17. Page 215 - While the Lamoille Commandery was *organized* in 1907, it was not *chartered* until 1908.
18. Page 222 - 1892 should be 1894.
19. Page 228 - Donadetti's should be Donizetti's.
20. Page 230 - "soon after" should be "during."
21. Page 247 - The fall of the river is actually 52 feet, not "seventy-five feet."
22. Page 273 - MORTIER should be MORTIMER.
23. Page 277 - 1915 should be 1913.

And this general note: In several places Miss Mower cites, in slight error, "Heminway's 'Gazeteer'" as a source of information. This is a reference to the *Vermont Historical Gazetteer*, edited by Abby Maria Hemenway and published in five volumes in the 1860's to 1880's. Volume II, published in 1871, includes a basic history and description of Morristown on pages 680-92.

A bibliographic note: This page is a partial remake of the original. Without change in content Miss Mower's "Important Dates" was reset in more compact form to make room for the addition of the *errata* discovered in her text. —RLH

Appendix

Town Representatives

Elisha Boardman	1804–1806, 1808
No choice	1805
Samuel Cooke	1809–1814, 1817, 1819, 1820
Robert Kimball	1815, 1816, 1818
Luther Bingham	1821–1826, 1828–1831
Asa Cole	1827
David Noyes	1832, 1833, 1838
Asaph Kenfield	1834, 1835
Joseph Sears	1836, 1837
John Ferrin	1839, 1840
George Small	1841, 1842
Moses Terrill	1843, 1846
V. W. Waterman	1844, 1845
No choice	1847
Julius Hall	1848, 1850
Arad Baker	1849
No choice	1851
Almond Boardman	1852, 1853
Thomas Tracy	1854
M. W. Terrill	1855, 1856
Harrison Ferrin	1857, 1858
Thomas Gleed	1859, 1860
G. W. Hendee	1861, 1862
S. M. Pennock	1863
E. E. Brigham	1864, 1865
Orlo Cady	1866, 1867
P. K. Gleed	1868, 1869
Charles R. Page	1870, 1871

Biennial Sessions of Legislature

G. W. Bailey	1872–1873
H. H. Powers	1874–1875
Alden Darling	1876–1877
S. N. Palmer	1878–1879
I. P. Booth	1880–1881
Charles R. Page	1882–1883
Frank Kenfield	1884–1885
H. C. Fisk	1886–1887
I. N. LeBaron	1888–1889
F. B. Livingstone	1890–1891
W. S. Cheney	1892–1893
C. F. Smith	1894–1895
G. M. Powers	1896–1897
G. H. Terrill	1898–1899

F. G. Fleetwood.................................1900–1901
C. H. A. Stafford...............................1902–1903
Calvin L. Gates................................1904–1905
T. C. Cheney..................................1906–1909
G. W. Clark...................................1910–1911
Glenn Wilkins.................................1912–1913
M. H. Boardman..............................1914–1915
Elmer Smalley................................1916–1917
Dr. W. T. Slayton.............................1918–1919
H. D. Neuland................................1920–1921
L. M. Munson.................................1922–1923
R. C. Stafford.................................1924–1925
G. F. Smith...................................1926–1929
C. H. Raymore...............................1930–1931
E. W. Terrill..................................1932–1933
Frank Allen...................................1934–1935

Pastors of the First Congregational Church

Rev. Nathaniel Rawson, Jr.....................1817–1818
Rev. Jotham Waterman........................1823
Rev. Daniel Rockwell.........................1824–1828
Rev. Elihu Baxter..............................1833
Rev. Septimius Robinson......................1835–1860
Rev. Lyman Bartlett...........................1861–1867
Rev. John C. Houghton.......................1867–1869
Rev. Vitellus M. Hardy........................1870–1877
Rev. William T. Swinnerton...................1878–1879
Rev. William A. Bushee.......................1880–1888
Rev. Perrin B. Fisk............................1889–1892
Rev. Edward P. Seymour......................1892–1894
Rev. George N. Kellogg.......................1894–1902
Rev. Frederick L. Davis.......................1902–1903
Rev. Christopher C. St. Clare.................1903–1910
Rev. Walter E. Baker..........................1911–1918
Rev. George E. Goodliffe.....................1919–

Pastors of the Advent Christian Church

Rev. A. P. Drown.............................1892–1895
Rev. J. A. Reed...............................1895–1897
Rev. Daniel Gregory..........................1898–1901
Rev. George W. Tabor........................1901–1906
Rev. L. L. Chase..............................1906–1907
Rev. S. M. Wales.............................1908–1910
Rev. L. E. Peabody...........................1911–1913
Rev. J. J. Bennett.............................1915–1919
Rev. E. E. Pender.............................1920–1924
Rev. R. W. Linnell............................1925–1928
Rev. George A. Coburn.......................1928–1930
Rev. Alice Bennett............................1930–

Pastors of the Methodist Episcopal Church

Revs. M. H. Stewart and J. Graves	1834
Revs. R. Brown and W. Henry	1835
Rev. W. N. Frazer	1836
Revs. Richard Brown, J. F. Chamberlain, and H. Dun..	1837
Revs. A. Witherspoon and A. C. Hand	1838
Supplied	1839
Rev. G. W. Cottrell	1840
Revs. C. Liscomb and G. W. Cottrell	1841
Revs. C. H. Lovejoy and John Fassett	1842
Revs. C. H. Lovejoy and Sylvester Clement	1843
Revs. John Thompson and David Osgood	1844
Revs. Owen Gregg, G. C. Simons, and A. Campbell	1845
Revs. Owen Gregg and G. C. Simons	1846
Rev. D. H. Loveland	1847
Revs. J. S. Hart and M. F. Cutler	1848
Revs. H. H. Smith and A. H. Honsinger	1849
Rev. B. Eaton	1850–1851
Supplied	1852
Rev. Fernando C. Kimball	1853
Revs. D. W. Gould and W. O. Thayer	1854
Rev. F. Williams	1855
Rev. John Fassett	1856
Supplied	1857–1858
Rev. Wm. C. Robinson	1859
Rev. Jas. O. Longstreth	1860
Rev. B. Haff	1861–1862
Supplied	1863
Rev. Thomas Little	1864
Rev. Benjamin Cox	1865–1866
Rev. A. H. Honsinger	1867–1868
Rev. O. M. Boutwell	1869–1870
Revs. J. Halpenny and G. W. A. Wood	1871
Rev. J. H. Wallace	1872
Rev. H. H. Bennett	1873
Rev. R. Sanderson	1874
Rev. R. H. Barton	1875
Rev. Jas. Hale	1876–1878
Rev. W. W. Wilder	1879–1880
Rev. Clarke Wedgeworth	1881–1882
Rev. M. P. Bell	1883–1885
Rev. W. H. Hyde	1886–1887
Rev. W. R. Puffer	1888
Rev. W. E. Douglass	1889–1891
Rev. R. L. Nanton	1892–1894
Rev. J. H. Wallace	1895–1897
Rev. M. S. Eddy	1898–1903
Rev. P. A. Smith	1904–1908
Rev. W. T. Best	1909–1922
Rev. Wm. J. McFarlane	1923–1928
Rev. I. A. Ranney	1929–1932
Rev. Lawrence Larrows	1933–

Morristown Soldiers in the Civil War

Alexander, Freeman R.	13th Regt., Co. "E." Enlisted Sept. 8, 1862; mustered out July 21, 1863; buried in Lake View Cemetery.
Allen, Ephraim E.	13th Regt., Co. "E." Enlisted Sept. 8, 1862; mustered out July 21, 1863; buried in LaPorte Cemetery.
Backum, David A.	7th Regt., Co. "E." Enlisted Jan. 30, 1862; re-enlisted Feb. 15, 1864; deserted Sept. 27, 1864.
Bailey, George	6th Regt., Co. "B." Enlisted Oct. 4, 1861; discharged for disability June 16, 1863.
Baker, Freeman	9th Regt., Co. "H." Enlisted June 2, 1862; killed in action Sept. 29, 1864.
Barry, Thomas	11th Regt., Co. "M." Enlisted Sept. 19, 1863; died of disease Nov. 8, 1864; buried at Arlington, Va.
Bassett, William H.	17th Regt., Co. "C." Enlisted Feb. 15, 1864, as musician; died July 1, 1864, of wounds received June 7, 1864; buried at Arlington, Va.
Bingham, Fenno	17th Regt., Co. "C." Enlisted Feb. 13, 1864; discharged for disability June 12, 1865.
Bingham, Lucian	17th Regt., Co. "C." Enlisted as Corp. Dec. 16, 1863; died May 28, 1864, of wounds received May 6, 1864; buried at Arlington, Va.
Biscorner, Jeremiah	13th Regt., Co. "H." Enlisted Sept. 8, 1862; mustered out July 21, 1863; buried in Randolph Cemetery.
Biscorner, Oliver	5th Regt., Co. "D." Enlisted Aug. 29, 1861; died of disease June 21, 1862.
Blanchard, Andrew J.	3rd Regt., Co. "E." Enlisted as Capt. May 24, 1861; resigned Oct. 28, 1861.
Blanchard, Charles	2nd Baty. Lt. Arty. Enlisted July 28, 1864; transferred to 1st Co. Hvy. Arty. Mar. 1, 1865.
Boardman, Chas. W.	5th Regt., Co. "D." Enlisted as Corp. Sept. 16, 1861; re-enlisted Dec. 15, 1863; promoted Sgt. Oct. 17, 1864; mustered out of service June 29, 1865.
Bridge, George A.	11th Regt., Co. "M." Enlisted Sept. 1, 1863; promoted Corp. Nov. 24, 1864; promoted Sgt. Mar. 1, 1865; transferred to Co. "D" June 24, 1865; mustered out Aug. 25, 1865.
Brown, David D.	3rd Regt., Co. "C." Enlisted Feb. 6, 1865; mustered out June 24, 1865; buried in Wheeler Cemetery.
Brown, Dexter I.	3rd Regt., Co. "C." Enlisted Feb. 6, 1865; mustered out June 24, 1865.
Brown, Josiah	7th Regt., Co. "E." Enlisted Dec. 2, 1861; died of disease Apr. 22, 1864.
Bugbee, Carlos	3rd Regt., Co. "E." Enlisted June 1, 1861; discharged Jan. 15, 1863, for disability; re-enlisted as Sgt. in 17th Regt., Co. "C," Sept. 2, 1863; promoted to 2nd Lieut. July 10, 1865; mustered out July 14, 1865; buried in Riverside Cemetery.

APPENDIX 293

Burnett, Abram	17th Regt., Co. "C." Enlisted Jan. 5, 1864; mustered out July 14, 1865.
Burnham, Edwin R.	3rd Regt., Co. "E." Enlisted June 1, 1861; killed in action May 5, 1864.
Butler, Andrew	5th Regt., Co. "D." Enlisted Aug. 15, 1861; discharged for disability Apr. 19, 1863.
Butler, Elisha	5th Regt., Co. "D." Enlisted Aug. 15, 1861; discharged for disability Feb. 20, 1863.
Butler, William B.	5th Regt., Co. "D." Enlisted July 14, 1862; discharged for disability Jan. 4, 1863.
Capron, William W.	17th Regt., Co. "C." Enlisted Oct. 14, 1863; mustered out July 14, 1865; buried in Riverside Cemetery.
Champaigne, Charles	8th Regt., Co. "A." Enlisted Aug. 8, 1864; mustered out June 28, 1865.
Champeau, Alexander	3rd Regt., Co. "E." Enlisted June 1, 1861; discharged for disability Sept. 25, 1862.
Chaplin, Joseph M.	13th Regt., Co. "E." Enlisted as Corp. Sept. 8, 1862; wounded July 3, 1863; discharged July 21, 1863; re-enlisted in 17th Regt., Co. "C"; wounded May 12, 1864; taken prisoner July 30, 1864; paroled Feb. 22, 1864; transferred to Vet. Res. Corps Apr. 13, 1865; discharged July 26, 1865; buried in Mountain View Cemetery.
Cheney, Carlos E.	13th Regt., Co. "E." Enlisted as Sgt. Sept. 8, 1862; mustered out July 21, 1863; re-enlisted as 2nd Lieut. Mar. 24, 1865; in Co. "M" Front. Cav.; promoted 1st Lieut. Apr. 6, 1865; mustered out June 27, 1865.
Cheney, Charles B.	Front. Cav., Co. "M." Enlisted Jan. 3, 1865; mustered out June 27, 1865.
Choate, Orville	13th Regt., Co. "E." Enlisted Sept. 8, 1862; mustered out July 21, 1863; re-enlisted Jan. 1, 1864; discharged Oct. 12, 1865.
Churchill, Lyman N.	13th Regt., Co. "E." Enlisted Sept. 8, 1862; mustered out July 21, 1863.
Clark, Carlos S.	8th Regt., Co. "A." Enlisted Nov. 6, 1861; re-enlisted Jan. 5, 1864; wounded Sept. 19, 1864; discharged June 1, 1865.
Clark, Reuben	5th Regt., Co. "D." Enlisted Aug. 15, 1861; promoted Corp.; died of disease Mar. 7, 1864.
Clark, Samuel B.	17th Regt., Co. "C." Enlisted Dec. 20, 1863; wounded May 12, 1864; mustered out July 14, 1865; buried in Lake View Cemetery.
Clark, Seth L.	3rd Regt., Co. "H." Enlisted July 2, 1861; discharged for disability May 2, 1862.
Clement, James H.	8th Regt., Co. "A." Enlisted Sept. 24, 1861; died of disease Jan. 10, 1863; buried at Chalmette, La.

APPENDIX

Cleveland, Charles A.	6th Regt., Co. "H." Enlisted Aug. 14, 1861; deserted June 28, 1862; transferred to Vet. Res. Corps Mar. 15, 1864; transferred back to company Nov. 5, 1864; mustered out Jan. 24, 1865.
Cole, Horace H.	13th Regt., Co. "E." Enlisted as Sgt. Sept. 8, 1862; mustered out July 21, 1863; buried in Mountain View Cemetery.
Collins, Ambrose C.	13th Regt., Co. "E." Enlisted Sept. 8, 1862; mustered out July 21, 1863.
Daniels, Jonathan W.	13th Regt., Co. "E." Enlisted Sept. 8, 1862; wounded July 3, 1863; mustered out July 21, 1863; buried in Riverside Cemetery.
Davis, Charles	3rd Regt., Co. "E." Enlisted June 1, 1861; mustered out July 27, 1864; buried in Mountain View Cemetery.
Davis, George	Unassigned recruit. Enlisted Jan. 5, 1864; discharged Aug. 18, 1865.
Davis, John T.	5th Regt., Co. "D." Enlisted Aug. 15, 1861; killed in action June 29, 1862.
Demas, George W.	3rd Regt., Co. "H." Enlisted June 1, 1861; deserted July 24, 1861.
Dickey, William G.	3rd Regt., Co. "K." Enlisted July 10, 1861; transferred to Vet. Res. Corps July 1, 1863; discharged July 16, 1864.
Dike, Ebenezer	5th Regt., Co. "D." Enlisted Aug. 13, 1861; discharged for disability Jan. 5, 1863.
Doty, George W.	2nd Regt., Co. "F." Enlisted May 7, 1861; promoted Corp. Oct. 1, 1861; wounded Dec. 13, 1862; transferred to Vet. Res. Corps Sept. 1, 1863; discharged June 29, 1864; buried in Pleasant View Cemetery.
Drown, George W.	3rd Regt., Co. "E." Enlisted June 1, 1861; re-enlisted Dec. 21, 1863; promoted Corp.; promoted Sgt. Dec. 27, 1864; wounded June 3, 1864; mustered out July 11, 1865; buried in Riverside Cemetery.
Dunham, Edward J.	11th Regt., Co. "D." Enlisted July 14, 1862; mustered out July 11, 1865; buried in Riverside Cemetery.
Dunham, Guy B.	11th Regt., Co. "D." Enlisted Jan. 4, 1864; promoted Corp. Dec. 17, 1864; mustered out June 23, 1865.
Dunham, William G.	11th Regt., Co. "D." Enlisted as Corp. Aug. 4, 1862; promoted 2nd Lieut. Dec. 28, 1863; promoted 1st Lieut. Sept. 2, 1864; mustered out June 24, 1865.
Dyke, Lorenzo	6th Regt., Co. "I." Enlisted Sept. 9, 1861; discharged for disability Jan. 22, 1863.
Earle, William B.	6th Regt., Co. "G." Enlisted Aug. 10, 1863; wounded Oct. 19, 1864; mustered out May 22, 1865; buried in Riverside Cemetery.

APPENDIX 295

Eaton, Joseph — 5th Regt., Co. "D." Enlisted Sept. 9, 1861; promoted Corp.; discharged Nov. 21, 1862, for wounds received June 19, 1862.

Eaton, Ransom — 8th Regt., Co. "A." Enlisted Nov. 14, 1861; died of disease May 26, 1863.

Eaton, Samuel C. — 11th Regt., Co. "L." Enlisted June 15, 1863; promoted Corp. Dec. 23, 1864; promoted Sgt. June 23, 1865; wounded June 23, 1864 and Sept. 19, 1864; transferred to Co. "C" June 24, 1865; mustered out Aug. 25, 1865; buried in Mountain View Cemetery.

Edwards, Ira V. — 11th Regt., Co. "L." Enlisted as wagoner June 1, 1863; promoted Corp. Oct. 27, 1863; promoted Sgt. Mar. 23, 1864; promoted 2nd Lieut. May 13, 1865; transferred to Co. "C" June 24, 1865; promoted 1st Lieut. June 26, 1865; mustered out Aug. 25, 1865.

Fisher, Jonas G. — 9th Regt., Co. "H." Enlisted June 4, 1862; discharged for disability Mar. 20, 1863; buried in Mountain View Cemetery.

Flanders, John W. — 7th Regt., Co. "K." Enlisted Dec. 31, 1861; died of disease Sept. 23, 1862; buried in Chalmette, La.

Fontaine, Louis — 9th Regt., Co. "H." Enlisted June 21, 1862; deserted Jan. 11, 1863.

Fullington, Charles B. — 8th Regt., Co. "A." Enlisted Oct. 2, 1861; discharged Nov. 25, 1862, for promotion in U. S. Colored Troops.

Gates, Amasa O. — 17th Regt., Co. "C." Enlisted as Sgt. Jan. 22, 1864; transferred to Vet. Res. Corps Feb. 22, 1865; mustered out May 28, 1865; buried in Pleasant View Cemetery.

Gates, William P. — 5th Regt., Co. "D." Enlisted as musician Aug. 19, 1861; discharged by order of the president Nov. 12, 1863; re-enlisted in Co. "M" of the Front. Cav. Jan. 3, 1865; mustered out June 27, 1865.

George, Harrison B. — 11th Regt., Co. "L." Enlisted July 21, 1863; promoted Corp. Dec. 27, 1863; promoted Sgt. Mar. 1, 1865; promoted Co. Q.M.-Sgt. June 23, 1865; transferred to Co. "C" June 24, 1865; promoted 2nd Lieut. June 26, 1865; mustered out Aug. 25, 1865; buried in Mountain View Cemetery.

Gerry, Orlando F. — 13th Regt., Co. "E." Enlisted Sept. 8, 1862; mustered out July 21, 1863; re-enlisted in the 17th Regt. Sept. 25, 1863; wounded May 6, 1864; mustered out July 14, 1865.

Gile, Eli B. — 13th Regt., Co. "E." Enlisted Sept. 8, 1862; mustered out July 21, 1863; buried in Mountain View Cemetery.

Glines, James — 17th Regt., Co. "C." Enlisted Dec. 31, 1863; promoted Corp. May 28, 1864; wounded May 12 and June 18, 1864; died July 30, 1864, of wounds; buried in Arlington, Va.

Gobar, Albert	8th Regt., Co. "K." Enlisted Jan. 20, 1862; discharged Mar. 4, 1862.
Gokey, Francis S.	17th Regt., Co. "C." Enlisted Jan. 11, 1864; wounded May 6, 1864; transferred to Vet. Res. Corps; mustered out July 20, 1865.
Goodell, Ransom B.	13th Regt., Co. "E." Enlisted Sept. 8, 1862; discharged for disability Feb. 15, 1863; buried in Riverside Cemetery.
Guyer, Guy H.	9th Regt., Co. "H." Enlisted as 1st Lieut. June 27, 1862; promoted Capt. Jan. 6, 1863; resigned Feb. 13, 1863; re-enlisted as 1st Lieut. in 17th Regt., Co. "C," Feb. 24, 1864; killed in action June 17, 1864; buried in Riverside Cemetery.
Hadley, Charles L.	5th Regt., Co. "D." Enlisted Sept. 2, 1864; mustered out June 19, 1865.
Harper, Nelson	Enlisted in 2nd Baty. Lt. Arty. July 28, 1864; mustered out July 31, 1865.
Hill, Welcome	7th Regt., Co. "H." Enlisted Feb. 1, 1862; re-enlisted Feb. 16, 1864; mustered out Aug. 24, 1865.
Hogan, Charles P.	7th Regt., Co. "E." Enlisted Dec. 30, 1861; promoted Corp. Mar. 1, 1863; mustered out Aug. 30, 1864.
Howard, George C.	3rd Regt., Co. "E." Enlisted as Sgt. June 1, 1861; transferred to Co. "C"; promoted to 2nd Lieut. Sept. 22, 1862; resigned Feb. 14, 1863.
Hoyt, George H.	3rd Regt., Co. "H." Enlisted June 1, 1861; discharged for disability Nov. 26, 1862.
Hull, Zura J.	9th Regt., Co. "H." Enlisted June 2, 1862; died of disease Oct. 28, 1863; buried at Hampton, Va.
Jenne, Samuel F.	2nd Regt., Co. "F." Enlisted Aug. 26, 1863; transferred to Vet. Res. Corps Dec. 7, 1864; discharged Aug. 22, 1865.
Kelley, William	13th Regt., Co. "E." Enlisted Sept. 8, 1862; mustered out July 21, 1863.
Kenfield, Frank	13th Regt., Co. "E." Enlisted as 2nd Lieut. Sept. 8, 1862; promoted 1st Lieut. June 4, 1863; wounded July 3, 1863; mustered out July 21, 1863; re-enlisted as Capt. of Co. "C," 17th Regt.; wounded May 6, 1864; taken prisoner July 30, 1864; paroled Mar. 1, 1865; discharged May 15, 1865; buried at Pleasant View Cemetery.
Kimball, Joseph O.	8th Regt., Co. "A." Enlisted Dec. 9, 1861; killed in action May 27, 1863.
King, Christopher	5th Regt., Co. "D." Enlisted Sept. 2, 1861; discharged for disability Dec. 3, 1862.
Kiser, Harvey O.	8th Regt., Co. "A." Enlisted as Sgt. Oct. 3, 1861; discharged for promotion in the U. S. Colored Troops Sept. 14, 1863; 1st Lieut. 89th U. S. Colored Infantry; resigned Mar. 25, 1864.

APPENDIX

Kusic, Richard	8th Regt., Co. "A." Enlisted Dec. 10, 1861; re-enlisted Jan. 5, 1864; mustered out June 28, 1865.
Ladeau, Frank	11th Regt., Co. "D." Enlisted Aug. 7, 1862; mustered out June 24, 1865.
Ladeau, John	11th Regt., Co. "D." Enlisted Aug. 7, 1862; wounded May 18, 1864; mustered out June 24, 1865; buried in Riverside Cemetery.
Ladeau, Joseph	11th Regt., Co. "D." Enlisted Dec. 1, 1863; transferred to Co. "C" June 24, 1865; mustered out Aug. 25, 1865.
Ladu, Peter, Jr.	9th Regt., Co. "H." Enlisted June 21, 1862; promoted Corp.; wounded June 4, 1863; died Feb. 1, 1865; buried at City Point, Va.
Lapoint, Henry	9th Regt., Co. "H." Enlisted Dec. 11, 1863; transferred to Co. "C" June 13, 1865; mustered out Dec. 1, 1865.
Laraway, James	17th Regt., Co. "C." Enlisted Jan. 5, 1864; wounded May 12, 1864; mustered out July 14, 1865.
Laraway, Philip	17th Regt., Co. "C." Enlisted Jan. 5, 1864; promoted Corp. July 1, 1865; mustered out July 14, 1865.
Lovely, Solomon	2nd Baty. Lt. Arty. Enlisted July 28, 1864; transferred to 1st Co. Hvy. Arty. Mar. 1, 1865; mustered out July 28, 1865.
Luce, Daniel A.	17th Regt., Co. "C." Enlisted Sept. 15, 1863; wounded May 6, 1864; wounded and taken prisoner Sept. 30, 1864; died at Richmond, Va., Dec. 9, 1864, of wounds.
Luce, Simon D.	5th Regt., Co. "D." Enlisted Aug. 14, 1861; transferred to Vet. Res. Corps Sept. 30, 1863; discharged Nov. 18, 1865; buried in Riverside Cemetery.
Mathews, Harrison	4th Regt., Co. "D." Enlisted Aug. 26, 1863; mustered out July 13, 1865.
Matthews, James M.	7th Regt., Co. "E." Enlisted Nov. 28, 1861; died of disease Nov. 14, 1862.
McClintock, William G.	17th Regt., Co. "C." Enlisted as Corp. Jan. 1, 1864; taken prisoner July 30, 1864; paroled Oct. 17, 1864; mustered out May 23, 1865; buried in Pleasant View Cemetery.
Meeher, Cyrus E.	3rd Regt., Co. "K." Enlisted Mar. 1, 1862; discharged for disability Oct. 4, 1862; promoted Corp.
Merrill, Samuel	11th Regt., Co. "D." Enlisted Aug. 9, 1862; transferred to Vet. Res. Corps Nov. 25, 1864; mustered out July 8, 1865.
Moulton, Napoleon B.	17th Regt., Co. "C." Enlisted Nov. 10, 1863; wounded May 12, 1864; transferred to Vet. Res. Corps Oct. 8, 1864; mustered out July, 1865.
Murphy, Eugene C.	7th Regt., Co. "K." Enlisted Feb. 3, 1865; taken prisoner Mar. 31, 1865; receipted for Apr. 21, 1865; mustered out May 18, 1865.

APPENDIX

Niles, Albert A. — 9th Regt., Co. "H." Enlisted June 1, 1862; promoted Corp. Jan. 27, 1863; promoted Sgt. Feb. 1, 1864; mustered out June 22, 1865; buried in Pleasant View Cemetery.

Niles, Porter S. — 9th Regt., Co. "H." Enlisted June 20, 1862; died of disease Oct. 17, 1863; buried at Hampton, Va.

Noe, Charles — 3rd Regt., Co. "C." Enlisted Feb. 7, 1865; mustered out July 11, 1865; buried in Pleasant View Cemetery.

Norton, William — 8th Regt., Co. "A." Enlisted Dec. 10, 1861; died of disease Mar. 21, 1864; buried at Chalmette, La.

Ober, Aaron S. — 1st Regt. Cav., Co. "I." Enlisted Sept. 19, 1861; taken prisoner Sept. 5, 1862; paroled Sept. 13, 1862; taken prisoner again Apr. 1, 1863; paroled Apr. 7, 1863; wounded July 6, 1863; transferred to Vet. Res. Corps Mar. 29, 1864; discharged Nov. 19, 1864.

Partlow, George W. — 11th Regt., Co. "L." Enlisted Oct. 12, 1863; died of disease Aug. 21, 1864; buried in Riverside Cemetery.

Peake, Delos M. — 11th Regt., Co. "L." Enlisted May 5, 1863; transferred to Co. "C"; mustered out May 22, 1865; buried in Mountain View Cemetery.

Peck, Orrin D. — 13th Regt., Co. "E." Enlisted Sept. 8, 1862; mustered out July 21, 1863.

Phelps, Buel — 2nd Regt., Co. "G." Enlisted Sept. 14, 1861; discharged for disability Dec. 20, 1862; re-enlisted in 11th Regt., Co. "M," July 24, 1863; promoted Corp. Aug. 1, 1864; taken prisoner Oct. 19, 1864; paroled Feb. 17, 1865; transferred to Co. "D" June 24, 1865; mustered out July 7, 1865; buried in Riverside Cemetery.

Powers, George R. — 3rd Regt., Co. "E." Enlisted as Corp. June 1, 1861; died of disease Feb. 1, 1862; buried in Riverside Cemetery.

Rand, Gilman S. — 8th Regt., Co. "A." Enlisted as 2nd Lieut. Nov. 13, 1861; died of disease July 22, 1862; buried in Riverside Cemetery.

Rand, Joseph A. — 3rd Regt., Co. "E." Enlisted June 1, 1861; re-enlisted Dec. 31, 1863; promoted Corp. June 21, 1865; wounded May 10, 1864; mustered out July 11, 1865.

Rider, Charles H. — 11th Regt., Co. "D." Enlisted July 14, 1862; mustered out June 24, 1865.

Roe, John — 3rd Regt., Co. "D." Enlisted June 1, 1861; taken prisoner Apr. 16, 1862; paroled May 11, 1862; discharged May 22, 1862.

Rollins, William — 8th Regt., Co. "A." Enlisted Nov. 25, 1861; discharged for disability Mar. 22, 1862.

Rowell, Harvey A. — 11th Regt., Co. "D." Enlisted Aug. 9, 1862; mustered out June 24, 1865.

APPENDIX 299

Safford, Darius J.	11th Regt., Co. "D." Enlisted as 1st Lieut. Aug. 12, 1862; promoted Capt. Co. "L" July 11, 1863; promoted Maj. May 23, 1865; taken prisoner June 23, 1864; escaped; wounded Sept. 19, 1864; promoted Lieut. Col. July 10, 1865; mustered out Aug. 25, 1865; buried in Riverside Cemetery.
Safford, Joseph P.	3rd Regt., Co. "E." Enlisted June 1, 1861; died of disease Sept. 15, 1862.
Sanborn, Seth C.	13th Regt., Co. "E." Enlisted Sept. 8, 1862; wounded July 3, 1863; mustered out July 21, 1863; re-enlisted in 17th Regt., Co. "C," Dec. 25, 1863; mustered out July 17, 1865.
Sawyer, Moses	3rd Regt., Co. "H." Enlisted June 1, 1861; died Sept. 11, 1862, while attached to Co. "F," 5th U. S. Arty.
Sawyer, Thomas F.	3rd Regt., Co. "H." Enlisted June 1, 1861; died of disease Nov. 9, 1862.
Scribner, Alonzo E.	5th Regt., Co. "D." Enlisted Aug. 12, 1861; re-enlisted Dec. 15, 1863; mustered out June 29, 1865.
Scribner, Charles P.	5th Regt., Co. "D." Enlisted Aug. 13, 1861; re-enlisted Dec. 15, 1863; promoted Corp.; promoted Sgt. Jan. 1, 1865; mustered out June 29, 1865.
Sheldon, Cornelius P.	11th Regt., Co. "L." Enlisted June 20, 1863; transferred to Co. "C" June 24, 1865; mustered out June 19, 1865.
Shiatt, Francis	2nd Baty., Lt. Arty. Enlisted July 28, 1864; transferred to 1st Co., Hvy. Arty., July 28, 1864; mustered out July 28, 1865.
Shippy, Gardner R.	3rd Regt., Co. "E." Enlisted Feb. 7, 1865; mustered out July 11, 1865; buried in Wheeler Cemetery.
Sleeper, James W.	5th Regt., Co. "D." Enlisted Sept. 2, 1861; discharged for disability Feb. 6, 1863.
Smith, Calvin W. H.	8th Regt., Co. "A." Enlisted Nov. 14, 1861; discharged for disability Feb. 21, 1863.
Smith, Harvey L.	8th Regt., Co. "A." Enlisted as Corp. Sept. 26, 1861; discharged Nov. 25, 1862, for promotion in the U. S. C. T.; 2nd Lieut., 3rd La. Native Guards; resigned Mar., 1863.
Smith, William H.	8th Regt., Co. "A." Enlisted Oct. 30, 1861; re-enlisted Jan. 5, 1864; mustered out June 28, 1865.
St. John, Francis	2nd Baty., Lt. Arty. Enlisted Aug. 1, 1864; mustered out July 31, 1865.
Stone, Edgar H.	3rd Regt., Co. "K." Enlisted Mar. 1, 1863; deserted Apr. 10, 1863.
Stone, Ozro P.	11th Regt., Co. "L." Enlisted as Corp. May 1, 1863; died June 18, 1864, of wounds received June 1, 1864; buried in Alexandria, Va.

APPENDIX

Story, Herbert H.	11th Regt., Co. "L." Enlisted June 24, 1863; transferred to Vet. Res. Corps Apr. 27, 1865; discharged Sept. 15, 1865.
Story, Irving L.	3rd Regt., Co. "E." Enlisted July 2, 1861; re-enlisted Dec. 21, 1863; mustered out July 17, 1865.
Stowe, Albert A.	8th Regt., Co. "A." Enlisted Nov. 13, 1861; re-enlisted Jan. 5, 1864; mustered out July 7, 1865.
Taylor, Henry C.	11th Regt., Co. "L." Enlisted June 1, 1863; taken prisoner June 23, 1864, and died at Andersonville, Ga., Aug. 23, 1864.
Terrill, Benjamin F.	13th Regt., Co. "E." Enlisted Sept. 8, 1862; mustered out July 21, 1863.
Tift, George H.	3rd Regt., Co. "E." Enlisted June 1, 1861; discharged for disability Sept. 28, 1861.
VanCor, Henry	2nd Regt., Co. "G." Enlisted Feb. 1, 1865; mustered out July 15, 1865.
Vincent, Noah W.	1st Regt. Cav., Co. "C." Enlisted Dec. 13, 1861; mustered out Dec. 13, 1864.
Warner, Leonard K.	3rd Regt., Co. "E." Enlisted July 2, 1861; re-enlisted Dec. 21, 1863; promoted Corp.; wounded May 18, 1864; discharged June 14, 1865, for wounds received June 3, 1864.
Wellsworth, Horace W.	17th Regt., Co. "E." Enlisted Mar. 25, 1864; killed in action July 30, 1864.
West, Henry E.	2nd U. S. Sharpshooters, Co. "E." Enlisted Oct. 28, 1861; discharged for disability Mar. 22, 1862.
Westover, William G.	8th Regt., Co. "A." Enlisted Nov. 14, 1861; discharged for disability Nov. 25, 1862; 1st Lieut., 3rd La. Native Guards, Nov., 1862; resigned Dec., 1863.
Wheeler, Charles	3rd Regt., Co. "C." Enlisted Feb. 8, 1865; mustered out July 11, 1865.
Wheeler, William C.	11th Regt., Co. "L." Enlisted May 27, 1863; transferred to Co. "I" July 13, 1863; discharged for disability Apr. 13, 1864.
Whipple, Morillo M.	11th Regt., Co. "L." Enlisted July 1, 1863; promoted Corp. Mar. 1, 1865; promoted Sgt. June 23, 1865; wounded June 1, 1864; transferred to Co. "C" June 24, 1865; mustered out Aug. 25, 1865.
Whipple, Moses T.	3rd Regt., Co. "E." Enlisted as Sgt. June 1, 1861; discharged for disability Jan. 25, 1864.
White, Amos	3rd Regt., Co. "E." Enlisted as Corporal June 1, 1861; promoted Sgt.; died June 4, 1864, of wounds received May 5, 1864; buried in Arlington, Va.
White, James C.	3rd Regt., Co. "K." Enlisted Aug. 19, 1863; deserted Sept. 24, 1863.
White, Peter	11th Regt., Co. "D." Enlisted Aug. 2, 1862; wounded June 23, 1864; mustered out June 24, 1865.

APPENDIX 301

Whitman, Seth — 3rd Regt., Co. "E." Enlisted Aug. 14, 1862; killed in action May 4, 1863.

Wilder, William F. — 3rd Regt., Co. "E." Enlisted June 1, 1861; discharged for disability Dec. 31, 1862.

Wilkins, Austin — 5th Regt., Co. "D." Enlisted as Sgt. Co. "D" Aug. 15, 1861; discharged Nov. 24, 1863, for wounds; buried in Pleasant View Cemetery.

Wilson, George J. — 11th Regt., Co. "L." Enlisted Oct. 12, 1863; transferred to Co. "C" June 24, 1865; discharged Sept. 1, 1865; buried in Pleasant View Cemetery.

Wilson, Stephen R. — 3rd Regt., Co. "E." Enlisted June 1, 1861; discharged for disability Oct. 12, 1861; re-enlisted 2nd Lieut. July 11, 1863; died July 6, 1864, from wounds received June 1, 1864; buried in Mountain View Cemetery.

Wilson, Warren J. — 6th Regt., Co. "K." Enlisted July 20, 1863; mustered out June 26, 1865; buried in Mountain View Cemetery.

Wing, Charles — 11th Regt., Co. "L." Enlisted May 8, 1863; taken prisoner June 23, 1864; paroled Dec. 6, 1864; transferred to Co. "C" June 24, 1865; mustered out Aug. 25, 1865.

Wood, Charles G. — 8th Regt., Co. "A." Enlisted Oct. 30, 1861; discharged Feb. 17, 1863, for promotion to 1st Lieut. in 4th La. Native Guards; resigned June, 1865.

Woodbury, Herbert E. — 3rd Regt., Co. "E." Enlisted Feb. 6, 1865; wounded Mar. 27, 1865; mustered out June 29, 1865.

Woolcutt, Ahial C. — 13th Regt., Co. "E." Enlisted Sept. 8, 1862; promoted Corp. Mar. 1, 1863; wounded July 3, 1863; mustered out July 21, 1863; buried in Riverside Cemetery.

Woolcutt, Hiram C. — 13th Regt., Co. "E." Enlisted as Corp. Sept. 8, 1862; died of disease Jan. 18, 1863.

Worthen, Samuel A. — 13th Regt., Co. "E." Enlisted Sept. 8, 1862; mustered out July 21, 1863.

Morristown Soldiers in the World War

Amsden, Ernest A. — Inducted: Aug. 28, 1918, Hyde Park.
Organization: 151st Dep. Brig., Camp Devens to disch.
Discharged: Dec. 4, 1918, Camp Devens, Mass.

Amsden, Leon B. — Inducted: Feb. 19, 1918, Hyde Park.
Discharged from the draft Feb. 23, 1918, by reason of physical disability.

Andrews, Foster I. — Inducted: Sept. 18, 1917, at Hyde Park.
Organization: Baty. "C," 302nd Fld. Arty., to disch.
Grades: Sgt., Nov. 1, 1917.
Overseas: July 16, 1918 to Apr. 26, 1919.
Discharged: Apr. 30, 1919, at Camp Devens.

APPENDIX

Badger, Harold C.
Enlisted: May 4, 1917, at Ft. Slocum, N. Y.
Organization: 2nd Rec. Co. to July 1, 1917; Baty. "F," 8th Fld. Arty., to disch.
Grades: Corp., June 4, 1918.
Overseas: Aug. 18, 1918 to disch.
Discharged: May 6, 1919.

Bates, Arthur G.
Inducted: Feb. 12, 1918, Hyde Park.
Organization: Co. "E," 59th Inf., to disch.
Grades: Corp., May 28, 1918.
Overseas: May 5, 1918 to June 29, 1919.
Slightly wounded in action July 22, 1918.
Discharged: July 1, 1919, at Camp Devens.

Bates, Clarence A.
Inducted: Oct. 15, 1918, at Potsdam, N. Y.
Organization: Stud. Army Train. Corps, Clarkson College, Potsdam, N. Y., to disch.
Discharged: Dec. 4, 1918, Potsdam, N. Y.

Bates, George L.
Called into active service: Aug. 10, 1917.
Organization: Medical Corps, 313th San. Tr., to disch.
Prin. Sta.: Ft. Benj. Harrison, Ind.; Cp. Grant, Ill.
Grades: 1st Lieut., Med. Corps, Aug. 10, 1917; Capt., Nov. 6, 1917; Maj., Feb. 25, 1919.
Overseas: Aug. 17, 1918 to June 4, 1919.
Discharged: June 12, 1919, at Camp Devens.

Battye, Harold J.
Enlisted: June 4, 1917, Ft. Ethan Allen.
Organization: Co. "C," 1st Vt. Inf., to Aug. 23, 1917; Co. "D," 102nd Mach. Gun Batn., to disch.
Overseas: Oct. 10, 1917 to Apr. 17, 1919.
Discharged: Apr. 29, 1919, at Camp Devens.

Bedell, Olie A.
Inducted: Oct. 15, 1918, Potsdam, N. Y.
Organization: Stud. Army Train. Corps, Clarkson College, Potsdam, to disch.
Discharged: Dec. 4, 1918, Potsdam, N. Y.

Best, J. Heber
Enlisted: Apr. 9, 1917, Ft. Ethan Allen.
Organizations: Co. "K," 1st Vt. Inf.; Hq. Co., 57th Pion. Inf., to discharge to accept commission.
Grade: 1st Sgt.
Commissions: 2nd Lieut. Inf., June 9, 1918; 1st Lieut., Sept. 20, 1918.
Organization: 57th Pion. Inf., 326th Inf. to disch.
Prin. Sta.: Cp. Wadsworth, S. C.; Cp. Merritt, N. J.; A. E. F.
Overseas: Sept. 28, 1918 to May 29, 1919.
Discharged: June 20, 1919.

Bidwell, James M.
Inducted: Oct. 2, 1917, Hyde Park.
Discharged from the draft Oct. 7, 1917, Camp Devens; no War Dept. record.

Bidwell, Wilmer H.
Inducted: Aug. 29, 1918, Hyde Park.
Organization: 152nd Dep. Brig., Camp Upton, N. Y., to disch.
Discharged: Dec. 3, 1918.

APPENDIX 303

Boardman, Dennis
: Inducted: Sept. 18, 1917, Hyde Park.
Organization: Baty. "C," 302nd Fld. Arty., to disch.
Overseas: July 16, 1918 to Apr. 26, 1919.
Discharged: Apr. 30, 1919, Camp Devens.

Boardman, Winfield H.
: Enlisted: Jan. 6, 1918, Camp Devens.
Organizations: 3rd Offi. Train. Camp, Camp Devens, to Apr., 1918; Co. "H," 301st Inf., to disch. to accept commission.
Commission: 2nd Lieut. Inf., June 28, 1918; 1st Lieut. Feb. 14, 1919.
Organizations: Co. "E," 301st Inf., to Jan. 23, 1919; Co. "I," 159th Inf., to Feb. 7, 1919; 151st Dep. Brig. to disch.
Prin. Sta.: Camp Devens; France.
Overseas: July 6, 1918 to Apr. 5, 1919.
Discharged: May 6, 1919, Camp Devens.

Bridge, Ellis C.
: Inducted: July 15, 1918, Hyde Park.
Organization: Rep. Unit 307, Motor Trans. Corps to disch.
Overseas: Oct. 20, 1918 to June 25, 1919.
Discharged: July 5, 1919.

Brooks, Gordon A.
: Enlisted: Dec. 15, 1917, at Ft. Constitution, N. H.
Organization: 5th Co., Coast Arty. Corps, Ft. Stark, N. H., to Aug. 9, 1918; Hq. Co., 38th Arty. Brig. Coast Arty. Corps to disch.
Grades: Corp. June 30, 1918; Sgt. Dec. 5, 1918.
Overseas: Oct. 5, 1918 to Feb. 18, 1919.
Discharged: Mar. 11, 1919, Camp Devens.

Burnham, Gideon S.
: Inducted: Feb. 8, 1918, Hyde Park.
Organization: Co. "E," 20th Engrs., to Dec. 4, 1918; 10th Co., 20th Engrs., to disch.
Grades: Corp. Sept. 12, 1918.
Overseas: Feb. 26, 1918 to June 1, 1919.
Discharged: June 11, 1919.

Burroughs, Eugene W.
: Enlisted: June 20, 1916, St. Johnsbury.
Entered Fed. Serv. Apr. 5, 1917.
Organizations: Co. "D," 1st Vt. Inf., to Aug. 30, 1917; Co. "B," 102nd Mach. Gun Batn., to Oct. 29, 1918.
Grade: Mechanic, July 10, 1917.
Overseas: Sept. 23, 1917 to Oct. 29, 1918.
Died of wounds Oct. 29, 1918.
Buried in Mountain View Cemetery, Morristown.

Call, Almon F.
: Inducted: Aug. 14, 1918, Hyde Park.
Organizations: Mech. Det., Tufts College, to Oct. 12, 1918; Coast Arty. Corps, Ft. Monroe, Va., to disch.
Discharged: Apr. 17, 1919, Camp Devens.

Carera, James
: Inducted: July 22, 1918, Quincy, Mass.
Organizations: 151st Dep. Brig. to Sept. 27, 1918; Q.M. Corps, Camp Devens, to disch.
Discharged: Dec. 6, 1918.

APPENDIX

Chase, Howard S. — Inducted: May 10, 1918, at Springfield, Mass.
Organization: Troop "B," 312th Cav., to disch.
Discharged: Nov. 18, 1918.

Chevalier, Emile J. — Inducted: May 24, 1918, Hyde Park.
Organizations: 151st Dep. Brig. to June 29, 1918; San. Squad. 2, Med. Dept., to July, 1918; San. Squad. 50 to disch.
Overseas: July 4, 1918 to June 22, 1919.
Discharged: June 30, 1919, Camp Devens.

Child, Frederick R. — Inducted: May 16, 1918, Hyde Park.
Organizations: Mech. Det., Univ. of Vt., Burlington, to Oct., 1918; Stud. Army Train. Corps, Univ. of Vt., Burlington, to disch.
Discharged: June 25, 1918.

Cleveland, Dennis E. — Inducted: May 24, 1918, Hyde Park.
Organizations: 151st Dep. Brig. to June 15, 1918; Co. "E," 302nd Inf., to Oct. 15, 1918; Co. "G," 307th Inf., to disch.
Overseas: July 5, 1918 to Apr. 30, 1919.
Discharged: May 10, 1919, Camp Devens.

Cleveland, Fred E. — Inducted: May 2, 1918, Hyde Park.
Organizations: 18th Co. Coast Arty. Corps, Ft. Witherell, R. I., to Aug. 28, 1918; Co. "A," 59th Am. Train, to Dec. 5, 1918; 18th Co., Coast Arty. Corps, Ft. Witherell, R. I., to disch.
Discharged: Dec. 21, 1918, Ft. Witherell, R. I.

Drowne, I. Allard — Enlisted: May 23, 1918, Ft. Revere, Mass.
Organizations: 17th Co., Boston Coast Arty. Corps, to Sept. 2, 1918; Ft. Revere, Mass., Sept. Autumn Replacement Draft, to Oct. 24, 1918; Baty. "B," 54th Arty. Co., Coast Arty. Corps, to disch.
Grade: Corp., July 16, 1918.
Overseas: Sept. 23, 1918 to Mar. 6, 1919.
Discharged: Mar. 13, 1919.

Drowne, Ralph E. — Inducted: Oct. 23, 1918, Hyde Park.
Organization: Stud. Army Train. Corps, Univ. of Vt.
Discharged: Nov. 23, 1918, Burlington.

Eaton, Everett T. — Inducted: Oct. 23, 1918, Hyde Park.
Organization: Stud. Army Train. Corps, Univ. of Vt.
Discharged: Dec. 13, 1918, Burlington.

Ellis, L. Raymond — Enlisted: Apr. 14, 1917, Ft. Ethan Allen.
Organizations: Hq. Co., 1st Vt. Inf., to Jan. 18, 1919; Hq. Co., 8th Inf., to disch.
Grades: 2/c Musician, June 29, 1917; Pvt., Dec. 11, 1918; 3/c Musician, Feb. 1, 1919.
Overseas: Sept. 29, 1918 to June 27, 1919.
Discharged: July 3, 1919, Mitchell Fld., N. Y.

APPENDIX 305

Emmons, Edward J. Enlisted: Apr. 19, 1917, Ft. Ethan Allen.
Organizations: Co. "D," 1st Vt. Inf. (Co. "B," 102nd Mach. Gun Batn.), to disch.
Overseas: Sept. 23, 1917 to Apr. 17, 1919.
Discharged: Apr. 29, 1919, Camp Devens.

Fairbanks, Bliss A. Inducted: Oct. 23, 1918, Hyde Park.
Organization: Stud. Army Train. Corps, Univ. of Vt.
Discharged: Dec. 14, 1918, Burlington.

Fisher, Harold H. Called into active service: Dec. 15, 1917.
Organizations: 306th Am. Train to Apr. 4, 1919; 1st Replace. Dept. to disch.
Prin. Sta.: Camp Jackson, S. C.; Camp Mills, N. Y.; A. E. F.; Camp Upton, N. Y.
Grades: 1st Lieut., Dec. 15, 1917; Capt., May 31, 1918.
Overseas: Aug. 7, 1918 to May 6, 1919.
Discharged: May 27, 1919, Camp Upton, N. Y.

Foss, Earl J. Inducted: May 16, 1918, Burlington.
Organizations: Mech. Det., Univ. of Vt., to July 13, 1918; 152nd Dep. Brig. to July 17, 1918; Co. "C," 312th Am. Train to disch.
Grades: Corp., Oct. 4, 1918.
Overseas: July 27, 1918 to Mar. 5, 1919.
Discharged: Mar. 17, 1919.

Freer, Hermon B. Inducted: Sept. 4, 1918, Davenport, Iowa.
Organizations: 163rd Dep. Brig. to Oct. 23, 1918; Hq. Co., 87th Inf., to disch.
Discharged: Jan. 27, 1919, Camp Dodge, Iowa.

Gamblin, Jay S. Enlisted: June 29, 1916, Ft. Ethan Allen.
Entered Fed. Serv. Apr. 2, 1917.
Organizations: Sup. Co., 1st Vt. Inf., to Oct. 7, 1918; Co. "E," 49th Inf., to disch.
Grades: Wagoner, Aug. 18, 1916; Corp., June 9, 1918.
Overseas: Sept. 29, 1918 to Jan. 16, 1919.
Discharged: Feb. 21, 1919, Camp Devens.

Gates, Whittier B. Enlisted: Apr. 27, 1917, Ft. Ethan Allen.
Organizations: Hq. Co., 1st Vt. Inf., to June 14, 1917; Co. "H," 1st Vt. Inf.; Co. "F," 101st Am. Train, to disch.
Grades: Sgt., Apr. 28, 1917; Sup. Sgt., Apr. 28, 1917; Color Sgt., June 2, 1917; 1st Sgt., June 7, 1917.
Overseas: Oct. 3, 1917 to Apr. 23, 1919.
Discharged: May 29, 1919, Camp Devens.

Godfrey, Erton E. Inducted: Aug. 28, 1918, Hyde Park.
Organization: 151st Dep. Brig. to disch.
Discharged: Dec. 4, 1918, Camp Devens.

Greaves, Clifton M. Enlisted: June 30, 1917, Burlington.
Organization: 301st Aux. Rmt. Dep., Q.M. Corps, to disch.
Grades: 1/c Pvt.; Corp., Aug. 27, 1918; Sgt., Nov. 1, 1918; 1/c Sgt., Mar. 1, 1919.
Discharged: May 15, 1919.

Griswold, Percy L. Enlisted: June 30, 1917, Ft. Ethan Allen.
Organizations: Co. "C," 1st Vt. Inf. (Co. "B," 101st Mach. Gun. Batn.), to disch.
Grades: Wagoner, Aug. 27, 1917; Pvt., Apr. 1, 1918.
Overseas: Oct. 10, 1917 to Apr. 7, 1919.
Discharged: Apr. 29, 1919, Camp Devens.

Hartley, Ralph M. Inducted: May 16, 1918, Burlington.
Organizations: Mech. Det., Univ. of Vt., to July 13, 1918; 152nd Dep. Brig. to July 17, 1918; Baty. "B," 336th Fld. Arty., to disch.
Grade: Wagoner.
Overseas: Aug. 27, 1918 to Mar. 5, 1919.
Discharged: Mar. 25, 1919.

Hersey, George R. Enlisted: June 30, 1917, Burlington.
Organization: 304th Co., Motor Trans. Corps, to disch.
Grade: Corp., June 30, 1917.
Overseas: Dec. 4, 1917 to June 30, 1919.
Discharged: July 9, 1919, Camp Mills, N. Y.

Hilliker, William H. Enlisted: Feb. 18, 1918, Camp Greene, N. C.
Organizations: Co. "E," 59th Inf., to Sept. 28, 1918; 360th Serv. Pk. Unit to disch.
Overseas: May 5, 1918 to Aug. 3, 1919.
Slightly wounded in action, July 20, 1918.
Discharged: Aug. 15, 1919, Camp Devens.

Hines, Charles F. Inducted: Feb. 22, 1918, Camp Greene, N. C.
Organizations: Co. "G," 39th Inf., to Apr. 8, 1918; Co. "B," 12th Batn., U. S. Guards, to disch.
Discharged: Sept. 9, 1918, by reason of physical disability.

Hutchinson, Wilkie S. Inducted: Aug. 5, 1918, Hyde Park.
Organizations: 325th Guard and Fire Co. to Nov. 18; 326th Guard and Fire Co. to disch.
Discharged: Sept. 10, 1919.

Isham, Frank S. Inducted: July 29, 1918.
Discharged from the draft Aug. 22, 1918, by reason of physical disability.

Jackson, Wayne E. Inducted: July 24, 1918, East Hartford, Conn.
Organization: 247th Amb. Co., 12th San. Troop.
Discharged: Jan. 21, 1919.

Jenkins, Friend H. Inducted: Oct. 25, 1918, Hyde Park.
Organization: Stud. Army Train. Corps, Univ. of Vt.
Discharged: Dec. 11, 1918, Burlington.

Jenkins, George R. Enlisted: Feb. 25, 1918, Camp Greene, N. C.
Organization: Co. "F," 39th Inf., to disch.
Overseas: May 10, 1918 to Dec. 31, 1918.
Discharged: Jan. 15, 1919.

APPENDIX 307

Jenkins, Merrill L.
: Enlisted: Jan. 17, 1916, Newport.
Entered Fed. Serv. Apr. 3, 1917.
Organizations: Co. "L," 1st Vt. Inf. (101st Am. Train), to disch.
Grades: 1/c Pvt., May 1, 1916; Wagoner, Apr. 1, 1918; Pvt., Nov. 4, 1918; Corp., Nov. 4, 1918.
Overseas: Oct. 3, 1917 to July 27, 1919.
Discharged: Aug. 1, 1919.

Jones, Walter D.
: Inducted: July 15, 1918, Hyde Park.
Organizations: Mech. Det., Univ. of Vt., to Sept. 9, 1918; Cas. Co. "A," Tank Corps, to Dec. 21, 1918; 819th Co., Motor Trans. Corps, to disch.
Grades: 1/c Pvt., Dec. 22, 1918; Corp., June 30, 1919
Overseas: Oct. 27, 1918 to Aug. 9, 1919.
Discharged: Aug. 18, 1919, Camp Devens.

Kahn, Oscar
: Inducted: Sept. 4, 1918, Hyde Park.
Discharged from draft Sept. 7, 1918, by reason of physical disability.
Inducted: Oct. 2, 1918, Hyde Park.
Organization: Inf., unassigned to disch.
Discharged: Dec. 9, 1918.

Keeler, Harold C.
: Inducted: May 24, 1918, Hyde Park.
Organization: Baty. "E," 302nd Fld. Arty., to disch.
Overseas: July 15, 1918 to June 10, 1919.
Discharged: Sept. 6, 1919.

Kelley, Maurice L.
: Enlisted: Dec. 15, 1917, Ft. Andrews, Mass.
Organization: Hq. Co., 2nd Batn., 55th Arty., Coast Arty. Corps, to disch.
Grades: 1/c Pvt., Jan. 1, 1918; Corp., Mar. 8, 1918; Radio Sgt.
Overseas: Mar. 25, 1918 to Jan. 22, 1919.
Discharged: Feb. 12, 1919.

Kinney, Terry
: Enlisted: June 30, 1917, Ft. Ethan Allen.
Organizations: Co. "C," 1st Vt. Inf., to Aug. 23, 1917; 101st Mach. Gun Batn. to disch.
Overseas: Oct. 9, 1917 to Mar. 20, 1919.
Discharged: May 17, 1919.

Knapp, Herbert
: Enlisted: June 30, 1917, Ft. Ethan Allen.
Organizations: Co. "C," 1st Vt. Inf., to Aug., 1917; 5th Co., 101st Am. Train, to Mar. 30, 1918; 3rd Co., 101st Am. Train, to Jan. 21, 1919; Co. "E," 101st Am. Train, to disch.
Overseas: Oct. 3, 1917 to Apr. 23, 1919.
Discharged: Apr. 29, 1919, Camp Devens.

Kramer, Karl B.
: Inducted: July 15, 1918, Burlington.
Organizations: Mech. Det., Univ. of Vt., to Sept. 15, 1918; Tank Corps to Oct. 5, 1918.
Died of disease, Oct. 5, 1918, Camp Colt, Pa.
Buried at Riverside Cemetery, Morrisville.

308 APPENDIX

Laird, Perley E.
: Enlisted: June 30, 1917, Ft. Ethan Allen.
Organizations: Co. "D," 1st Vt. Inf., to Aug. 30, 1917; Sup. Co., 102nd Inf., to Dec. 9, 1917; Co. "M," 102nd Inf., to disch.
Overseas: Sept. 16, 1917 to Apr. 7, 1919.
Discharged: Apr. 29, 1919.

Law, Linwood B.
: Inducted: Oct. 5, 1918, Middlebury.
Organization: Stud. Army Train. Corps., Middlebury College, to disch.
Discharged: Dec. 12, 1918.

Manthorn, Fred
: Enlisted: June 27, 1916, Ft. Ethan Allen.
Entered Fed. Serv. Apr. 2, 1917.
Organizations: Troop "C," 1st Vt. Cav., to July, 1916; Sup. Co., 1st Vt. Inf. (Sup. Co., 49th Inf.), to disch.
Grade: Wagoner, Aug. 18, 1916.
Overseas: Sept. 29, 1918 to Jan. 21, 1919.
Discharged: Mar. 4, 1919.

Mason, Earl R.
: Inducted: Sept. 3, 1918, St. Albans.
Organization: 151st Dep. Brig. to disch.
Discharged: Oct. 16, 1918, Camp Devens; surgeon's certificate of disability.

McDermott, Owen N.
: Inducted: Sept. 6, 1918.
Discharged from draft Sept. 8, 1918; surgeon's certificate of disability.

Meacham, William M.
: Inducted: May 24, 1918, Hyde Park.
Organization: Hq. Co., 302nd Fld. Arty., to disch.
Overseas: July 16, 1918 to May 3, 1919.
Discharged: May 7, 1919, Camp Devens.

Mercia, Ernest W.
: Enlisted: June 30, 1917, Ft. Ethan Allen.
Organizations: Co. "C," 1st Vt. Inf., to Aug. 27, 1917; Co. "D," 101st Mach. Gun Batn.; Co. "D," 103rd Mach. Gun Batn., to disch.
Overseas: Oct. 10, 1917 to Apr. 17, 1919.
Slightly wounded in action July 18, 1918.
Discharged: Apr. 29, 1919, Camp Devens.

Merritt, Francis L.
: Inducted: July 15, 1918, Hyde Park.
Organizations: Mech. Det., Univ. of Vt., to Nov. 11, 1918; Cent. Officers Train. School, Camp Lee, Va., to disch.
Discharged: Nov. 23, 1918, Camp Lee, Va.

Merritt, Mark S.
: Inducted: Oct. 26, 1918, Hyde Park.
Organization: Stud. Army Train. Corps., Univ. of Vt.
Discharged: Dec. 14, 1918.

Moffatt, Donald H.
: Inducted: May 24, 1918, Hyde Park.
Organizations: 151st Dep. Brig., to June 15, 1918; Co. "F," 302nd Inf., to Oct. 16, 1918; Co. "B," 1st G. H. Q. Batn., Mil. Pol. Corps, to disch.
Overseas: July 4, 1918 to July 10, 1919.
Discharged: July 16, 1919.

APPENDIX 309

Montgomery, Daniel J. — Inducted: Aug. 14, 1919, Hyde Park.
Organizations: Mech. Det., Tufts College, Medford, Mass., to Oct. 13, 1918; Cas. Det., Coast Arty. School, Ft. Monroe, Va., to disch.
Discharged: Dec. 18, 1918, Camp Upton, N. Y.

Moore, Harold F. — Inducted: Oct. 15, 1918, Potsdam, N. Y.
Organization: Stud. Army Train. Corps, Clarkson College, Potsdam, N. Y., to disch.
Discharged: Dec. 6, 1918, Potsdam, N. Y.

Morey, Ralph B. — Enlisted: June 30, 1917, Ft. Ethan Allen.
Organizations: Co. "C," 1st Vt. Inf., to Aug. 23, 1917; Co. "D," 103rd Mach. Gun Batn., to Nov. 25, 1918; 152nd Dep. Brig. to disch.
Overseas: Oct. 10, 1917 to Jan. 19, 1919.
Discharged: Jan. 30, 1919.

Morrill, Aaron W. — Enlisted: June 4, 1917, Ft. Ethan Allen.
Organizations: Co. "C," 1st Vt. Inf., to Aug. 20, 1917; Co. "C," 101st Mach. Gun Batn., to disch.
Grades: 1/c Pvt., July 1, 1917; Pvt., Oct. 3, 1917; Corp., Aug. 3, 1919.
Overseas: Oct. 10, 1917 to Aug. 23, 1919.
Slightly wounded in action Oct. 23, 1918.
Discharged: Aug. 28, 1919, Camp Devens.

Morrill, Erle J. — Enlisted: June 4, 1917.
Organizations: Co. "C," 1st Vt. Inf. (Co. "C," 103rd Inf.).
Overseas: Sept. 27, 1917 to Apr. 5, 1919.
Wounded in action July 30, 1918.
Discharged: Apr. 28, 1919, Camp Devens.

Mould, Charles E. — Inducted: Sept. 7, 1918, Hyde Park.
Organizations: 31st Ser. Co., Sig. Corps, College Park, Md., to Sept. 21, 1918; 3rd Ser. Co., Sig. Corps, Yale Univ., to disch.
Discharged: Dec. 11, 1918, New Haven, Conn.

Mould, Willis P. — Enlisted: May 11, 1917, Ft. Ethan Allen.
Organizations: Co. "C," 1st Vt. Inf., to Sept. 7, 1917; Co. "E," 101st Am. Train, to disch.
Grades: Sgt., May 26, 1917; Pvt., Sept. 10, 1917; Sup. Sgt., Sept. 18, 1917.
Overseas: Oct. 3, 1917 to Apr. 23, 1919.
Discharged: Apr. 29, 1919, Camp Devens.

Niles, Logan A. — Enlisted: Nov. 16, 1917, Westfield.
Organizations: Hq. Co., 1st Vt. Inf., to Dec. 26, 1917; Co. "C," 1st Vt. Inf., to Oct. 30, 1918; Co. "H," 330th Inf., to disch.
Discharged: Feb. 20, 1919.

Norton, LeRoy M.	Enlisted: June 27, 1916, Burlington. Entered Fed. Serv. Apr. 3, 1917. Organizations: Co. "C," 1st Vt. Inf., to July 5, 1918; 330th Inf., to Dec. 15, 1918; Co. "A," 54th Inf., to Jan. 31, 1919; Co. "E," 53rd Inf., to disch. Grades: Sgt., May 26, 1917; 1st Sgt., Nov. 9, 1917. Overseas: Sept. 29, 1918 to June 12, 1919. Discharged: June 19, 1919, Camp Devens.
Ober, Harold F.	Enlisted: June 30, 1917, Burlington. Organization: 304th Co., Motor Trans. Corps, to disch. Grade: Sgt. Chauffeur, June 30, 1917. Overseas: Dec. 4, 1917 to June 30, 1919. Discharged: July 9, 1919, Camp Mills, N. Y.
Paine, Harry H.	Enlisted: Dec. 8, 1917, Ft. Slocum, N. Y. Organizations: Q.M. Corps, Ft. Sam Houston, Tex., to Jan., 1918; 401st Co., Motor Trans. Corps, to Oct. 7, 1918; 678th Co., Motor Trans. Corps, to Feb. 4, 1919; 390th Co., Motor Trans. Corps, Mar. 8, 1919; 304th Repl. Unit, Motor Trans. Corps, to disch. Discharged: June 3, 1919.
Parker, Alban J.	Inducted: Jan. 12, 1918, Hyde Park. Organizations: Ordn. Train. School, Cp. Hancock, Ga., to Apr. 23, 1918; Mach. Gun School, Cp. Hancock to June 27, 1918; Ordn. Train. Corps, Cp. Hancock, to disch. to accept commission. Appointed July 13, 1918. Organization: Ordn. Dept. to disch. Prin. Sta.: A. E. F., Cp. Devens; Washington, D. C.; Detroit, Mich. Grades: 2nd Lieut., Ordn., July 13, 1918. Overseas: July 30, 1918 to Jan. 23, 1919. Discharged: Oct. 25, 1919, Governors Island, N. Y.
Parker, Benjamin	Enlisted: June 18, 1917, Ft. Ethan Allen. Organizations: Co. "C," 1st Vt. Inf., to Aug 23, 1917; Co. "D," 103rd Mach. Gun Batn., to disch. Overseas: Oct. 19, 1917 to Apr. 17, 1919. Slightly wounded in action June 16, 1918. Discharged: Apr. 29, 1919, Camp Devens.
Parker, Hugh H.	Enlisted: July 18, 1917, Ft. Ethan Allen. Organization: Co. "E," 1st Vt. Inf. (Hq. Co., 103rd Inf.), to disch. Overseas: Sept. 25, 1917 to Apr. 5, 1919. Discharged: Apr. 28, 1919, Camp Devens.
Patch, Harold C.	Inducted: Aug. 29, 1918, Hyde Park. Organizations: 152nd Dep. Brig., to Oct. 4, 1918; Co. "L," 124th Inf.; Co. "K," 330th Inf., to Jan. 10, 1919; Hq. Co., Dist. of Paris, to disch. Overseas: Oct. 17, 1918 to June 16, 1919. Discharged: June 21, 1919.

APPENDIX 311

Patnoe, Felix J.	Inducted: Apr. 1, 1918, Hyde Park. Organizations: Co. "K," 304th Inf., to Aug. 1, 1918; Co. "L," 163rd Inf., to Aug. 7, 1918; Co. "H," 39th Inf., to disch. Grades: Corp., July 8, 1918; Pvt., Nov. 27, 1918. Overseas: July 8, 1918 to Aug. 6, 1919.
Powers, Horace H.	Attended Train. Camp, Plattsburgh, N. Y., May 15, 1917 to Aug. 15, 1917. Called into active service Aug. 15, 1917. Organizations: Mach. Gun Co., 301st Inf., to Nov. 15, 1917; Coast Arty. Corps to termination of appointment. Prin. Sta.: Cp. Devens; Ft. Monroe, Va. Grades: 2nd Lieut., Inf., Aug. 15, 1917; 2nd Lieut., C. A. C. Reg. Army, Nov. 15, 1917; 1st Lieut., C. A. C., Feb. 27, 1918. Appointment terminated Apr. 9, 1918, Ft. Monroe.
Robinson, Lloyd C.	Called into active service Sept. 18, 1918. Organization: Det. Med. Dept., 151st Dep. Brig. Prin. Sta.: Camp Devens. Grade: 1st Lieut., D. C., Sept. 18, 1918. Discharged: Jan. 25, 1919, Camp Devens.
Ryder, Harold S.	Inducted: Nov. 21, 1917, Hyde Park. Organization: 303rd Rep. Unit, Motor Trans. Corps, to disch. Overseas: Jan. 17, 1918 to June 9, 1919. Discharged: June 14, 1919.
Sacks, Isaac H.	Inducted: May 24, 1918, Hyde Park. Organizations: Co. "E," 303rd Inf., to July 1, 1918; Med. Dep., Base Hosp. 39, to disch. Discharged: Mar. 8, 1919, Long Beach, N. Y.
Shattuck, Edward H.	Inducted: Aug. 5, 1918, Hyde Park. Organization: Syracuse Rec. Camp, N. Y., to disch. Discharged: Oct. 5, 1920, Staten Island, N. Y.
Silloway, Carroll L.	Enlisted: June 30, 1917, Ft. Ethan Allen. Organizations: Co. "C," 1st Vt. Inf.; Co. "C," 103rd Inf., to disch. Grade: Corp., Sept. 21, 1917. Overseas: Sept. 27, 1917 to Apr. 28, 1919. Discharged: May 13, 1919.
Silloway, Charles W.	Inducted: Oct. 15, 1918, Potsdam, N. Y. Organization: Stud. Army Train. Corps, Clarkson College, Potsdam, N. Y. Discharged: Dec. 6, 1918, Potsdam, N. Y.
Slayton, William T.	Commission: Capt., Med. Corps, Nov. 8, 1918. Organization: 154th Dep. Brig. Prin. Sta.: Camp Meade, Md. Discharged: Dec. 23, 1918, Camp Meade.

Smalley, Ray L.	Inducted: Oct. 23, 1918, Hyde Park. Organizations: Stud. Army Train. Corps, Univ. of Vt., to Oct. 31, 1918; Fld. Arty., Cent. Offi. Train. School, Camp Taylor, Ky., to disch. Discharged: Jan. 28, 1919, Camp Taylor, Ky.
Stancliff, Ralph S.	Inducted: Aug. 14, 1918, Hyde Park. Organizations: Mech. Det., Tufts College, to Oct. 12, 1918; Cas. Det., Coast Arty. Sch., Ft. Monroe, to Nov. 25, 1918; Det. Coast Arty. School, Camp Eustis, Va., to Feb. 8, 1919; 672nd Motor Trans. Co. to disch. Discharged: Apr. 14, 1919, Camp Eustis, Va.
Stancliffe, Reginald E.	Enlisted: Mar. 17, 1918, Ft. Slocum, N. Y. Organizations: Hq. Co., 57th Pion. Inf., to May 30, 1918; Co. "G," 1st Pion. Inf., to disch. Overseas: July 8, 1918 to July 7, 1919. Discharged: July 14, 1919, Camp Devens.
Stancliffe, Rufus W.	Enlisted: Mar. 17, 1918, Ft. Slocum, N. Y. Organizations: Hq. Co., 57th Pion. Inf., to May 30, 1918; 1st Pion. Inf. to Dec. 19, 1918; Co. "K," 318th Inf. Overseas: July 9, 1918 to May 27, 1919. Discharged: June 9, 1919, Camp Devens.
Stewart, Alexander T.	Inducted: July 29, 1918, Hyde Park. Discharged from the draft Aug. 25, 1918, on surgeon's certificate of disability, Syracuse, N. Y.
Stewart, Arthur C.	Enlisted: Oct. 17, 1917, Ft. Slocum, N. Y. Organization: Med. Dept. to disch. Grades: 1/c Pvt., Dec. 28, 1917; Corp., July 8, 1918; Sgt., Mar. 7, 1919. Discharged. Sept. 8, 1919, Camp Devens.
Stewart, John E.	Inducted: May 24, 1918, Hyde Park. Organizations: Co. "F," 302nd Inf., to Oct. 20, 1918; Hq. Co., 319th Inf., to disch. Overseas: July 5, 1918 to June 2, 1919. Discharged: June 9, 1919, Camp Dix, N. J.
Stewart, Max E.	Inducted: Oct. 23, 1918, Hyde Park. Organization: Stud. Army Train. Corps, Univ. of Vt. Discharged: Dec. 14, 1918.
Stockwell, A. Frank	Attended Train. Cp., Cp. Taylor, Ky., Oct. 4, 1918 to Nov. 7, 1918. Commissioned 1st Lieut. (Chaplain), Nov. 7, 1918. Prin. Sta.: Gen. Hosp. 4, Ft. Porter, N. Y., to disch. Discharged: Oct. 28, 1919.
Stiles, Morton H.	Inducted: Sept. 21, 1917, Elizabeth, N. J. Organization: Co. "A," 311th Inf., to Nov. 1, 1919. Grade: Sgt., Apr. 5, 1918. Overseas: May 19, 1918 to Nov. 1, 1918. Killed in action Nov. 1, 1918. Place of burial: Grave 8, Row 9, Block B, Meuse, Argonne, Amer. Cemetery, Romagne-sous-Montfaucon, Meuse, France.

APPENDIX

Sweet, Irving E. — Inducted: July 15, 1918, Hyde Park.
Organizations: Mech. Det., Univ. of Vt., to Sept. 13, 1918; Cas. Co., Tank Corps, to Sept. 17, 1918; Co. "A," 336th Batn., Tank Corps, to Dec. 20, 1918; 816th Motor Trans. Co. to disch.
Grade: Corp., July 1, 1919.
Discharged: Aug. 14, 1919.

Sweetser, Percy A. — Enlisted: June 2, 1917, Ft. Ethan Allen.
Organizations: Co. "C," 1st Vt. Inf., to Aug. 23, 1917; Co. "C," 102nd Mach. Gun Batn., to disch.
Grade: Bugler.
Overseas: Sept. 23, 1917 to Jan. 23, 1919.
Wounded in action Oct. 24, 1918.
Discharged: Feb. 20, 1919, Camp Devens.

Taylor, Clarence W. — Enlisted: June 4, 1917, Ft. Ethan Allen.
Organization: Co. "C," 1st Vt. Inf. (Co. "C," 103rd Inf.).
Overseas: Sept. 27, 1917 to Apr. 5, 1919.
Discharged: Apr. 28, 1919, Camp Devens.

Temporelli, Antonio — Inducted: Oct. 2, 1917, Hyde Park.
Organizations: Baty. "E," 302nd Fld. Arty., to Feb. 5, 1919; Hq. Troop, 2nd Army, to Apr. 21, 1919; Dep. Sup. Co. 40, Army Serv. Corps, to disch.
Overseas: July 16, 1918 to June 20, 1919.
Discharged: July 16, 1919, Camp Mills, N. Y.

Thomas, Bradley A. — Inducted: June 10, 1918, Akron, Ohio.
Organizations: Troop "A," 310th Cav., to Oct. 28, 1918; Baty. "A," 58th Fld. Arty., to Nov. 7, 1918; Fld. Arty. Cent. Offi. Train. School, Camp Taylor, Ky., to disch.
Grades: Sgt., July 1, 1918; Sup. Sgt., July 4, 1918.
Discharged: Dec. 2, 1918, Camp Taylor, Ky.

Thonet, George M. — Enlisted: June 28, 1917, Jefferson Bks., Mo.
Organization: Sup. Co., 2nd Cav., to disch.
Overseas: May 10, 1918 to June 29, 1919.
Grades: Clerk, Jan. 15, 1918; Mess Sgt., Oct. 14, 1918; Sgt., Mar. 8, 1919.
Discharged: July 8, 1919, Camp Devens.

Van Cor, Edwin W. — Inducted: Oct. 15, 1918, Hyde Park.
Discharged from the draft Nov. 23, 1918; surgeon's certificate of disability.

Ward, Ernest R. — Enlisted: June 30, 1917, Ft. Ethan Allen.
Organization: Co. "C," 1st Vt. Inf. (Co. "C," 103rd Inf.).
Overseas: Sept. 27, 1917 to July 20, 1918.
Killed in action July 20, 1918.
Place of burial: Pleasant View Cemetery.

Ward, William M.	Enlisted: June 30, 1917, Ft. Ethan Allen. Organization: Co. "C," 1st Vt. Inf. (Co. "C," 103rd Inf.). Overseas: Sept. 27, 1917 to Apr. 27, 1919. Severely wounded in action July 20, 1918. Discharged: May 13, 1919, Camp Devens.
Warren, Raymond M.	Inducted: Oct. 23, 1918, Hyde Park. Organization: Stud. Army Train. Corps, Univ. of Vt. Discharged: Dec. 11, 1918.
Warren, Smith M.	Inducted: Feb. 18, 1918, Camp Greene, N. C. Organization: Co. "E," 59th Inf. Overseas: May 5, 1918 to July 19, 1918. Killed in action July 19, 1918. Place of burial: Pleasant View Cemetery.
Wedge, John W.	Inducted: Aug. 5, 1918, Hyde Park. Organization: 325th Guard and Fire Co. Discharged: Sept. 10, 1919.
Whippen, Charles W.	Inducted: Sept. 18, 1917, Hyde Park. Organizations: Baty. "C," 302nd Fld. Arty., to June 27, 1918; Cent. Offi. Train. School, Camp Taylor, Ky., to disch. to accept commission. Grade: Corp., Nov. 1, 1917. Commission: 2nd Lieut., Fld. Arty., Aug. 17, 1918. Organization: Co. "B," 4th Reg. Fld. Arty., Repl. Draft. Prin. Sta.: Camp Jackson, S. C.; Ft. Sill, Okla.
Whittemore, Robert D.	Enlisted: June 4, 1917, Ft. Ethan Allen. Organizations: Co. "C," 1st Vt. Inf., to Sept. 7, 1917; Mach. Gun Co., 103rd Inf., to disch. Overseas: Sept. 27, 1917 to Mar. 19, 1919. Slightly wounded in action Nov. 9, 1918. Discharged: Apr. 4, 1919.
Wodkewiz, Josef	Inducted: May 24, 1918, Hyde Park. Organizations: 151st Dep. Brig. to June 15, 1918; Co. "E," 303rd Inf., to Aug. 2, 1918; Co. "K," 162nd Inf., to Aug. 14, 1918; Co. "D," 28th Inf., to disch.
Woodbury, Erwin L.	Enlisted: June 2, 1917, Ft. Ethan Allen. Organizations: Co. "C," 1st Vt. Inf., to Sept. 7, 1917; Co. "E," 101st Am. Train, to Sept. 14, 1918; Hq. Co., 103rd Fld. Arty., to disch. Overseas: Oct. 2, 1917 to Apr. 10, 1919. Discharged: Apr. 29, 1919, Camp Devens.
Wright, Herbert E.	Inducted: June 25, 1918, Hoboken, N. J. Organization: Med. Dept., Fox Hills, N. Y., to Feb. 5, 1919. Grade: Sgt., Nov. 2, 1918. Died of disease Feb. 5, 1919, Staten Island, N. Y. Place of burial: Essex Ctr.

Morristown Sailors in the World War

Allan, Everett L.
U. S. N.
Enlisted: Jan. 2, 1914, New York, N. Y.
Stations: *U.S.S. Nashville,* Apr. 6, 1917 to June 7, 1917; *U.S.S. Pennsylvania,* to June 11, 1917; *U.S.S. Utah,* to Jan. 1, 1918.
Discharged: Jan. 1, 1918, *U.S.S. Utah.*
Re-enlisted: Feb. 26, 1918, Burlington.
Stations: Rec. Ship, Boston, to Mar. 15, 1918; *U.S.S. Shawmut,* to Nov. 11, 1918.
Grades: Seaman, 179 days; Coxswain, 350 days.
Discharged: Sept. 8, 1919, as 2/c Boatswain's Mate, *U.S.S. Prinz Friedrich Wilhelm.*

Best, William A.
U. S. N.
Appointed from Morrisville, June 20, 1917.
Stations: Under instr., Naval Pay Officers' School, Washington, D. C., July 31, 1917 to Sept. 29, 1917; Asst. Sup. Officer, Navy Yard, Philadelphia, Oct. 4, 1917 to Feb. 26, 1918; Sup. Officer, Rec. Ship, Liverpool, England, Mar. 16, 1918 to June 17, 1919.
Grades: Asst. Paymaster, Ens., June 20, 1917; Ens., June 20, 1917; Lieut., Mar. 30, 1920.

Campbell, Elmer D.
U. S. N.
Enlisted: July 29, 1918, Burlington.
Stations: Nav. Train. Sta., Newport, R. I., to Oct. 15, 1918; Rec. Ship, Boston, to Nov. 11, 1918.
Grades: App. Seaman, 78 days; 2/c Seaman, 27 days.
Discharged: Apr. 14, 1919, Hq., 1st Naval Dist., Boston.

Gilbert, Neil S.
U. S. N. R. F.
Enrolled: May 3, 1917, New Haven, Conn.
Active duty: Sept. 29, 1917.
Stations: Sect. Base No. 6, Bensonhurst, L. I., N. Y., to Nov. 3, 1917; Hq., 3rd Nav. Dist., N. Y., to Nov. 11, 1918.
Grades: 2/c Seaman, 455 days; 3/c Storekeeper, 102 days; inactive duty, July 7, 1919, as 2/c Storekeeper, *U.S.S. Santa Cecilia,* N. Y.

Kellogg, Perrin N.
U. S. N.
Enlisted: Mar. 3, 1917, Burlington.
Stations: Nav. Train. Sta., Newport, R. I., Apr. 6, 1917 to Apr. 16, 1917; *U.S.S. Arizona* to May 9, 1917; *U.S.S. Missouri* to May 25, 1917; *U.S.S. Arizona* to May 28, 1917; Rec. Ship, New York, N. Y., to June 6, 1917; *U.S.S. Birmingham* to Nov. 11, 1918.
Grades: App. Seaman, 10 days; 2/c Seaman, 39 days; 2/c Fireman, 494 days; 1/c Fireman, 41 days.
Discharged: Aug. 21, 1919, Dist. Detail Office, Boston.

APPENDIX

Lander, Allan W.   U. S. N.
Enlisted: Dec. 6, 1917, Burlington.
Stations: Naval Air Sta., Bay Shore, N. Y., to Feb. 6, 1918; Naval Air Sta., Pauillac, France, to Mar. 10, 1918; Naval Air Sta., Arcachon, France, to Nov. 11, 1918.
Grades: Lds. Qm. A., 57 days; 2/c Qm. A., 273 days; 1/c Qm. A., 10 days.
Discharged: July 26, 1919, Dist. Detail Office, Boston.

Newcomb, Everett S.   U. S. N. R. F.
Enrolled: Dec. 21, 1917, Pelham Bay Park, N. Y.
Active Duty: Mar. 21, 1918.
Station: Naval Train. Camp, Pelham Bay, N. Y., to Nov. 11, 1918.
Grades: 1/c Musician, 325 days.
Inactive duty Jan. 4, 1919, Nav. Train. Camp, Pelham Bay.

Patnoe, Charles E.   U. S. N.
Enlisted: June 21, 1917, Burlington.
Stations: Rec. Ship, New York, to July 5, 1917; *U.S.S. Connecticut* to July 21, 1917; *U.S.S. Illinois* to Aug. 31, 1917; Rec. Ship, New York, to Oct. 6, 1917; *U.S.S. Arcturus,* S. P. 593, to Nov. 11, 1918.
Grades: 3/c Fireman, 314 days; 2/c Fireman, 194 days.
Discharged: June 12, 1919, Rec. Ship, Boston.

Screvens, George W.   U. S. N.
Enlisted: May 1, 1917, Burlington.
Stations: Nav. Train. Sta., Newport, R. I., to July 26, 1917; *U.S.S. Vermont* to Nov. 11, 1918.
Grades: App. Seaman, 86 days; 2/c Seaman, 402 days; Seaman, 71 days.
Discharged: Oct. 9, 1919, Rec. Ship, New York.

Stephen, Edward A.   U. S. N.
Enlisted: Dec. 11, 1917, Burlington.
Stations: Nav. Train. Sta., Newport, R. I., to July 29, 1918; Nav. Train. Sta., Norfolk, Va., to Nov. 11, 1918.
Grades: 2/c Hosp. App., 202 days; 1/c Hosp. App., 123 days; 3/c Ph. M., 10 days.
Discharged: Sept. 9, 1919, as 2/c Ph. M., *U.S.S. Virginia,* Boston, Mass.

Stone, Robert S.   U. S. N.
Enlisted: Dec. 15, 1917, Burlington.
Stations: Nav. Train. Sta., Newport, R. I., to Apr. 27, 1918; *U.S.S. Louisville* to June 30, 1918; Rec. Ship, New York, to Nov. 3, 1918; Nav. Hosp., N. Y., to Nov. 8, 1918; Rec. Ship, N. Y., to Nov. 11, 1918.
Grade: 3/c Fireman, 331 days.
Discharged: July 1, 1919, Rec. Ship, Boston.

Sweetser, Minnie	U. S. N. R. F. Enrolled: May 15, 1917, Boston, Mass. Stations: Mach. Div., Navy Yard, Boston, to May 25, 1918; Hull Div., Navy Yard, Boston, to June 30, 1918; Dist. Detail Office, Boston, to July 1, 1918; Navy Yard, Boston, Mass., to Nov. 11, 1918. Grades: 2/c Yeoman, 412 days; 1/c Yeoman, 133 days. Discharged: Oct. 29, 1920, Hq. 3rd Naval Dist., New York.
Thayer, Harrison S.	U. S. N. Enlisted: May 11, 1917, Washington, D. C. Stations: Rctg. Sta., Washington, D. C., to May 12, 1917; Rec. Ship, New York, to Sept. 30, 1917; Rctg. Sta., Washington, to Oct. 20, 1917; *U.S.S. Michigan* to Apr. 26, 1918; *U.S.S. St. Louis* to May 6, 1918; *U.S.S. Konigen Der Nederlanden,* Canal Zone, to Nov. 11, 1918. Grades: Lds. Yeoman, 38 days; 3/c Yeoman, 122 days; 2/c Yeoman, 75 days; 1/c Yeoman, 70 days; Aptd. Ens. (S. C.) Prov., Mar. 13, 1918; Lieut. (J. G.) (S. C.) Prov., July 1, 1918. Inactive Duty: Aug. 11, 1919, *U.S.S. Konigen Der Nederland.*
Towne, Ballou L.	U. S. N. R. F. Enrolled: Oct. 9, 1918, Burlington. Active Duty: Oct. 23, 1918. Station: Naval Unit, Univ. of Vt., to Nov. 11, 1918. Grade: App. Seaman, 33 days. Inactive Duty: Dec. 20, 1918, Naval Unit, Univ. of Vt.
Wells, Lee E.	U. S. N. Enlisted: Feb. 27, 1917, Burlington. Stations: Nav. Train. Sta., Newport, R. I., Apr. 6, 1917 to Apr. 15, 1917; *U.S.S. North Dakota* to May 2, 1917; *U.S.S. Solace* to May 23, 1917; Nav. Hosp., Washington, D. C., to June 15, 1917; Rec. Ship, Philadelphia, Pa., to June 19, 1917; *U.S.S. Von Steuben* to Aug. 12, 1917; Nav. Hosp., Philadelphia, to Aug. 29, 1917; *U.S.S. Von Steuben* to Nov. 11, 1918. Grades: App. Seaman, 9 days; 2/c Seaman, 575 days. Discharged: Oct. 28, 1919, as 3/c Ship's Cook, Rec. Ship, Boston.

Worshipful Masters of Mount Vernon Lodge

Thomas Taylor	Dec., 1812-	Dec., 1814
C. Huntington	1814	1815
Thomas Taylor	1815	1816
J. P. Hadley	1816	1817
Joseph Waterman	1817	1818
Abner Flanders	1818	1820
Joshua Sawyer	1820	1821

APPENDIX

Joseph Sears	Dec., 1821-	Dec., 1822
Thomas Waterman	1822	1823
James Tinker	1823	1824
Joshua Sears	1824	1826
Charles Meigs	1826	1827
Joseph Sears	1827	1828
Johnathan Merrill	1828	1829
Abner Flanders	1829	1830
Joseph Sears	1830	1850
Francis Smalley	1850	1852
Lewis Wakefield	1852	1853
Francis Smalley	1853	1856
Charles H. Heath	1856	1858
A. J. Blanchard	1858	1861
S. M. Pennock	1861	1866
H. H. Powers	1866	1868
D. J. Safford	1868	1870
Philip K. Gleed	1870	1872
C. W. Fitch	1872	1874
C. M. Peck	1874	1876
Austin Wilkins	1876	1879
A. P. Smalley	1879	1881
F. H. Carner	1881	1883
Harrison B. George	1883	1884
George W. Doty	1884	1887
O. A. Edgerton	1887	1888
E. E. Foster	1888	1890
Carlos A. Gile	1890-	Apr., 1893
C. C. Rublee	Apr., 1893	1895
Smith B. Waite	1895	1896
George M. Powers	1896	1898
E. W. Webster	1898	1900
C. B. Greene	1900	1902
W. M. Clark	1902	1903
J. Arthur Robinson	1903	1904
Calvin A. Spiller	1904	1906
Fabius L. George	1906	1909
Charles H. Raymore	1909	1911
Willis H. Terrill	1911	1913
Andrew C. Sulham	1913	1915
J. Henry Atchinson	1915	1918
James H. Eaton	1918	1920
Morris B. White	1920	1922
Ernest W. Gates	1922	1923
Charles E. Mould	1923	1924
Herbert E. Farnham	1924	1925
Walter D. Jones	1925	1926
George G. Morse	1926	1927
Fred Timmerman	1927	1928
Roy B. Woods	1928	1929
Ai N. Hall	1929	1931
Willard K. Sanders	1931	1933
Guy Kneeland	1934	

PHOTOGRAPHS

Below and on pages 320-22 and the top left of page 323 are reproduced 13 of the total of 20 photographs in the original Mower work. Space limitations were one consideration in not using them all but the main one was the difficulty of getting good quality reproduction from the photos as they were printed in the book. Thus, used where possible was an exact original photo, and in one case (Copley Hospital) a close equivalent original photo. Used for the others was a copy photograph of the Mower text print. Titles of Mower photos not used here at all are: Green Mountain Range From Elmore Mountain Road (the frontispiece); View [of Lamoille River] From Bridge Street; Lake Lamoille; Pulpit Rock; Lower Main Street In Late '60's; Peck's [Drug Store] Corner In Late 60's; and Wheeler's [Pharmacy] Corner In Late 70's.

The other added photos are credited as follows: Name of photographer, if known / Donor or other source (in both cases, all are of Morrisville unless otherwise indicated). All photographers' and donors' names are given in full, except for two frequently-cited sources. They are abbreviated as follows: Jones: Robert S. Jones; and MHS: Morristown Historical Society.

And for a comprehensive contemporary photographic record of Morristown, see *Morristown Photo Archive, 1976-1980* by Robert L. Hagerman. Sets of the Archive are available to the public at the Morristown Centennial Library and the Vermont Historical Society. — RLH

/ MHS

A Portland & Ogdensburg Railroad train at the Morrisville depot in or about 1874. Note that the locomotive was a woodburner.

Top: Second Peoples Academy building and the original half of the present Graded School, in the early 1900's. Middle: Copley Building, Peoples Academy, about 1930. Bottom: Upper Main Street, looking east, about 1935; First Congregational parsonage and church are at left.

Top: Covered bridge at about the site of the present iron bridge at the Morrisville power plant, pre-1886. Middle: Upper Main Street in the 1860's, at the intersection, to left, of what is now Park Street and was then called Wolcott Street; the first Peoples Academy is at left and the Christian Church, now Advent Christian Church, is at right. Bottom: Morristown Centennial Library, about 1930.

Alexander H. Copley

George W. Hendee

George M. Powers

H. Henry Powers

First Copley Hospital, about 1943.

323

Top left: First Peoples Academy, probably in the 1860's. Top right: Work is underway on restoration of the steeple of the First Universalist Church about 1930; men of the steeplejack firm, Hall Bros. of Burdick(?), Me., stand high aloft. Bottom: Teacher Katherine Hodges (back row, second from left) and her charges at the Morristown Plains School, No. 7, about 1920.

Top: Former President Theodore Roosevelt, the Bull Moose Party's Presidential candidate in 1912, appeared with full political regalia at the Lamoille Valley Fair on Aug. 30 that year. Middle: Morristown's last veteran of the Civil War, George A. Bridge, stands tall near Academy Park as a guest of honor at the dedication of Vermont Rt. 15 as the Grand Army of the Republic Highway on July 25, 1937. Bottom: Piled up near Academy Park in 1942 were the results of Morristown's successful World War II scrap metal drive; note the decorative streetlights, gift of Alexander H. Copley.

325

Walter D. Jones / Jones

Charles L. Grandey / Charles L. Grandey / Madeline Smilie

Top Left: The Puffer United Methodist Church, about 1964; this was built in 1888 and torn down in 1970 to make way for the present church. Top Right: The First Congregational Church sanctuary (which preceded the present church) as it was probably in the early 1890's. Bottom: The town hall on Main Street, torn down in 1968-69, as it was about 1965 (the crowd is gathered for what is believed to have been a Morrisville Fire Department benefit of some kind); the Harry Foss home is at left.

326

/David W. Mudgett

Arthur L. Cheney / Jones

Arthur L. Cheney / Jones

Top: Management and staff of H.A. Smalley & Co. posed for the camera in 1939 at the Smalley premises on Brooklyn Street; two principals and one longtime office employe are in the back row, from left: Oscar H Mudgett, Herbert A. Smalley, and Teresa Rasetti. Middle: The Holy Cross Church soon after its construction in 1913-14. Bottom: Interior of the First Universalist Church, about 1914.

327

Arthur L. Cheney / Jones

Clayton Fuller, Montgomery / Billie Goeltz, Stowe

T.H. Sweetser / MHS

Top: Making clear that the newfangled car was more trouble than it was worth was this spoof put on about 1908 by the horse-dealing firm of H.A. Smalley & Co. (the firm, of course, later sold cars!). Middle: Archery on the croquet court as seen at the Samoset Colony Club, about 1930. Bottom: This view of the rampaging waters of the Lamoille River in the 1927 flood is upstream at what used to be River Street (south off Bridge Street); most of the street was left a gully and never rebuilt.

Walter D. Jones / Jones

/ George H. Paine

Arthur L. Cheney / MHS

Top: One of Morrisville's long-time prominent citizens and a real "character" was James M. Kelley; victim of his golf prowess here on the Copley Country Club course in the late 1930's was Dr. Frederick L. Wells. Middle: Local landmark eatery from 1950 to 1965 was Paine's Restaurant on Vermont Rt. 15 at Needle's Eye Road. Bottom: Looking up Portland Street about 1915 at three prominent buildings, now all gone, from left: Randall Hotel, Centennial Block, and part of the Warren Block. Note that street-paving had not yet arrived in Morrisville.

329

Frederick G. Fleetwood / Richard C. Sargent

Willard K. Sanders / Robert L. Hagerman / Morristown Photo Archive

Thomas C. Cheney / MHS

Clifton G. Parker / Richard C. Sargent

H.E. Cutler / MHS

Homer L. Bentley / MHS

/ Madeline Smilie

Anna L. Mower at different stages in life, from left: Peoples Academy graduate, 1893; teacher at Peoples Academy, 1908-1912; in her 80's in 1962.

330

Walter D. Jones / Frances L. White

Walter D. Jones / Billie Goeltz, Stowe

T.H. Sweetser / MHS

/ MHS

Top: Two views, up and down, of the exciting toboggan run built on Kelley Point by the Lamoille Valley Winter Sports Club the winter of 1936-37. Middle: The Morrisville Fire Department in or about 1924 in front of the old firehouse on Union Street with the Department's first two motorized fire trucks: at left, a 1924 Maxim (still held by the Department), and a 1923 Ford "mongrel" truck. Bottom: Members of the Morrisville Fire Department about 1950 with their three trucks in front of the then new firehouse on Main Street (that burned in 1968).

Top: Trotters come around the turn in this harness race at the Lamoille Valley Fair in the late 1930's; view is to the south. Middle: Looking north at the Lamoille Valley Fair facilities about 1910. Bottom: The Morrisville Military Band in front of the firehouse on Union Street on November 11, 1942; from left are: Bernard F. Howard, Ai N. Hall, Burns Hutchins, Jack S. White, George Griggs, Grafton Miller, Don A. Sanders, James O. Reed, Glenn A. Wilkins, Jr., Warren H. Farnham, Gerald W. Tripp, Richard Griggs, Willard K. Sanders (the leader), and Robert J. Sparks.

Frederic M. Greene / Greene family   Homer L. Bentley / MHS   / Peoples Academy   / Francis M. Clark

Top Left: It's not certain if they were associated with Peoples Academy but Frank Harris, left, and Hugh Cushman are said to be the only known fencing team ever organized in Morrisville; that was about 1902. Top Right: Definitely associated with PA was the 1980-81 Student Council; clearly with no "hang-ups" are, from left: Patrick Hanifin, president; Jane Phelps, secretary-treasurer; and John Tague, vice president. Bottom Left: Long-time Morristowner Paul Cornell, now of Cabot, with the handsome 8-point buck which he shot in 1949. Bottom Right: Robert (Bob) St. Jock, Jr., Morristown's second licensed airplane pilot who went on to fame in the 1930's as a stunt flyer and racer.

More About Morristown, 1935-1980

ROBERT L. HAGERMAN

Morristown: A Capsule Description Of Four Municipalities In One

Town of Morristown

Origins: Chartered by Republic of Vermont August 24, 1781
Boundaries: Original bounds defined in the town's charter; part of town of Sterling annexed in 1855; part of town of Hyde Park annexed in 1899 (in exchange for part of Morristown annexed to Hyde Park)
Governing Bodies: Board of Selectmen and largely autonomous Pleasant View Cemetery Commission
Present Principal Municipal Departments and Services: Highway Department, Fire Department, Police Department, sanitary landfill (through private contractor), Health Program (special services), Recreation Program, Ambulance Service, planning and zoning (on joint basis with Village), and land and vital records.
Present Principal Facilities Owned: Town Building (town clerk's and other offices), Public Safety Building, fire station, Highway Department garage, Town Forest, Town Clock, Pleasant View Cemetery, Morristown Centennial Library, Copley parking lot, and Ambulance Service building.

Morristown Town School District

Origins: Established April 1, 1893 under No. 20, Laws of Vermont, 1892
Boundaries: Same as Town of Morristown
Governing Body: Board of School Directors
Present Principal Municipal Services: School system for grades 1-12
Present Principal Facilities Owned: All school facilities and related land: Graded School (probably including Academy Park), Morristown Elementary School, and Peoples Academy complex, *except* the Copley Community Memorial Building (gymnasium) and possibly the Copley Bandshell

Village of Morrisville

Origins: Incorporated June 13, 1890 (date of local acceptance of charter act: No. 214, Laws of Vermont, 1884)
Boundaries: Altered from time to time, now as defined by No. 243, Laws of Vermont, 1947
Governing Bodies: Board of Trustees and largely autonomous Water and Light Commission
Present Principal Municipal Departments or Services: Street Department, Water and Light Department, sewage collection and treatment system, refuse collection, and planning and zoning (on joint basis with Town)
Present Principal Facilities Owned: All water and electric system facilities including Morrisville and Cadys Falls generating stations and Green River Reservoir, sewage treatment plant, Street Department garage, Village Forest, Clark Park, Noyes House (leased to Morristown Historical Society), Copley Community Memorial Building (gymnasium), Copley Country Club

Morristown Fire District No. 1

Origins: Incorporated Sept. 10, 1980 by Town selectmen under general law
Boundaries: A small area in the Pinewood Estates Development as defined in the selectmen's incorporation certificate
Governing Body: Prudential Committee
Present Principal Municipal Service and Facility: Water system

Special Note: Cadys Falls, Morristown Corners and (if you can find it) Mud City are all unincorporated villages with no local government.

Chapter 1

Boundaries, Natural Landmarks, And Weather

TOWN LINE, CADYS FALLS ROAD

MUCH MAY HAVE CHANGED about Morristown since 1935 but not the town's boundaries. Miss Mower mentioned two such changes which occurred in the 19th century, about one of which she makes a slight error. These are deserving of additional explanation (and see Map No. 1).

The first change was the addition of a portion of the town of Sterling. This town was never heavily settled and what residents it had were faced with severe difficulties in administration of town affairs because of the way mountain ranges separated the pockets of settlement. In 1828 Vermont's General Assembly authorized the annexation of a two-mile-by-six-mile strip of Sterling to the town of Cambridge. In 1855 the Legislature abolished the town by dividing the remaining portion among Johnson, Stowe and Morristown; that act was amended the following year, making a few changes in the division. The portion annexed to Morristown measures some 6,120 acres.

A fluke in the location of the original Morristown-Hyde Park town line and in where settlement subsequently occurred in the latter town led to a significant change in those towns' shared boundary. And this change was marked by considerable controversy.

Hyde Park's key hamlet, later the incorporated Village of Hyde Park, established itself on high ground north of the Lamoille River near the town's southwest corner. The village's main thoroughfare was roughly parallel to, and only a few hundred yards from, the Morristown line. Clearly any growth of the village to the south and west would quickly spill into that "foreign" town.

The problem first came into focus in the late 1860's when construction began on the Lamoille Valley Railroad, part of what later became the St. Johnsbury & Lake Champlain Railroad. As the route was laid out,

336   MORE ABOUT MORRISTOWN, 1935-1980

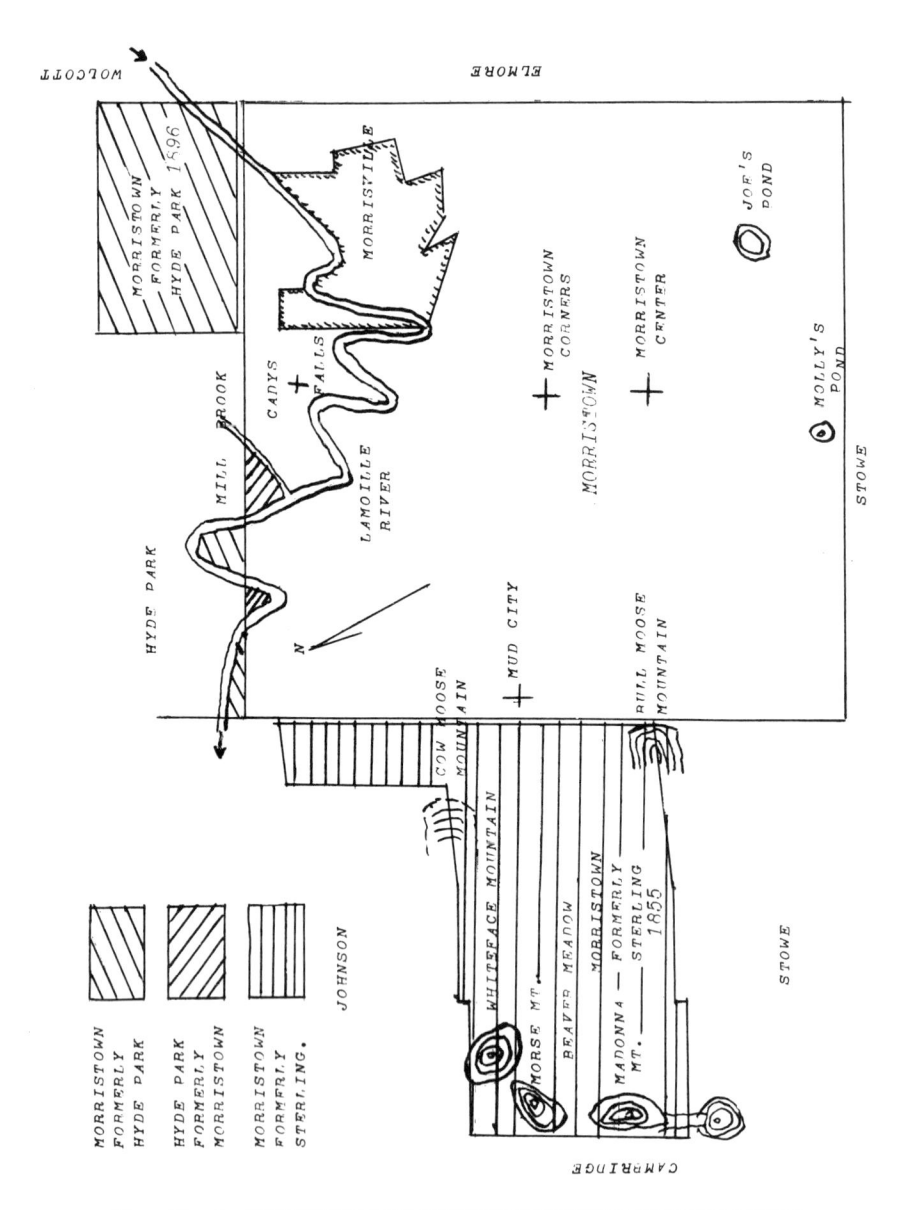

Map No. 1 - CHANGES IN MORRISTOWN'S BOUNDARIES

Map by Willard K. Sanders from his booklet, *A Brief History of the Town of Morristown, Vermont*, published by Morrisville Woman's Club in 1974 and used here by permission. The exchange of land with Hyde Park, which includes both "Morristown Formerly Hyde Park" and "Hyde Park Formerly Morristown," actually occurred in 1899, not 1896.

the Hyde Park station and much of the approaching railroad track wouldn't be in that town at all, but in Morristown! The situation bothered enough Hyde Park residents that they got the Legislature to pass a law in 1870 transferring at least some of this critical area from Morristown to Hyde Park. The annexation was, however, contingent upon approval of voters of both towns. It's not known what happened in Hyde Park, but in Morristown the issue never came to a vote and thus died.

The matter lay dormant for nearly a quarter-century. When it did revive, a major new element besides the railroad station was involved. That was the large calf-skin processing industry of Hyde Park's most prominent citizen, Carroll S. Page. While Page's operations initially were located in Hyde Park village, he subsequently built a larger complex of facilities across the line in Morristown. As a result it was Morristown, not Hyde Park, which derived property taxes from the complex.

Thus when it was announced the summer of 1898 that Hyde Park would again seek legislative action to have that critical area transferred to its jurisdiction, Morristowners immediately raised a hue and cry opposing the change. Their major concern was that loss to the Town's grand list. But it was also claimed that persons living in the area to be transferred wanted to remain Morristown residents.

In the end the controversy was resolved by a land trade. Annexed in 1899 from Morristown to Hyde Park was an area of about 183 acres westerly of Mill Brook (now more generally known as the Centerville Brook) and northerly of the Lamoille River; this abutted the Hyde Park village area (but never actually became part of the incorporated village). Annexed from Hyde Park to Morristown was a much larger area — 1,113 acres — in the former town's southeast corner. While the acreage differential was substantial in Morristown's favor, Hyde Park gained a significant edge in the trade-off of combined grand list valuations — real estate, personal property and polls.

Morristown's total area is 53.4 square miles or 34,176 acres (a correction of the figure given by Miss Mower). That consists of three parts: (1) the original town as chartered, about 6½ miles on a side giving 42½ square miles or about 27,040 acres; (2) the addition from Sterling, about 6,120 acres; and (3) the exchange with Hyde Park, a net addition of 930 acres.

The town is still mostly dry land, with just the three notable bodies of water which Miss Mower described — and three she didn't. The former are Molly's Pond, Joe's Pond and Lake Lamoille. The latter are Ward Pond, Boardman Pond and Luna Pond.

Molly's Pond is very small, measuring only about two acres. But while small in size, it is now large in stature as part of the important natural area known as Molly's Bog. In 1973 that was added to the National Registry of Natural Landmarks, a program of the National Park Service of the U.S. Department of the Interior. It achieved this distinction by being "a beautiful classic example of a small early successional, absolutely unspoiled cold northern bog." Miss Mower has noted (page 21) some of the interesting plants which grow on and near the floating mat of sphagnum moss which surrounds the open water of the pond. Others include the pitcher plant and two species of sundew, both carnivorous plants. There is also said to be a small colony of southern twayblade, a plant found in only one other place in Vermont.

The pond and bog lie on the west side of the LaPorte Road just north of the Stowe-Morristown line (a correction of the location given by Miss Mower). In 1962 James W. Marvin acquired most of the bog property on behalf of the Vermont Bird and Botanical Club, of which he was then president. The Club, via Marvin, in turn conveyed the 110-acre tract to the University of Vermont (UVM) "so that it may be preserved undisturbed for scientific and educational purposes." In acquiring the bog, the Club used a $500 bequest for that purpose which it had received from the late Harold C. Rugg, a long-time librarian at Dartmouth College, Vermont antiquarian, and an amateur botanist. Rugg made the bequest in his wife's memory so Marvin's deed to UVM specifies that the tract "be known as the 'Julia Hager Rugg Sanctuary'." But that name has been little, if ever, used, at least in published information about Molly's Bog.

Across the LaPorte Road from, and a little north of, Molly's Pond (and Bog) is Joe's Pond. Ten acres in size and 40 to 50 feet deep at its deepest, the pond has grass pickerel, horned pout and suckers growing in its waters. Area residents go fishing and swimming there but the access is limited. For around three sides of the pond is an extended boggy area, like Molly's Bog. Only the east shore and nearby land is more elevated, dry and stable.

The pond itself and some of the bog lie on the farm of Lawrence Stancliffe, property long in that family. In the late 1950's the State, through its Department of Forest and Parks, acquired about 30 acres of the bog just south of the pond, and two rights-of-way out to LaPorte Road. The purpose of this acquisition for about three years was to harvest sphagnum moss, a good medium in which to pack and ship tree seedlings from nursery beds to planting sites. Now the Morristown Bog Natural Area, as the property is identified, is managed by the Forest and Parks Department so as basically to leave it undisturbed in its natural state.

As Miss Mower notes (page 38), Indian Joe and Molly are the namesakes for these ponds as a tribute to their friendly aid to Jacob Walker, Morristown's first resident, and other early settlers in the Lamoille Valley. Morristown's Joe's Pond is particularly notable in this regard because here were found the remains of a dugout canoe presumed to have been used by Indian Joe himself. In 1956 the Stancliffes removed it from the pond and presented it to the Morristown Historical Society. It has since been a prized exhibit at the Society's Noyes House museum.

Molly's and Joe's Ponds are Morristown's only natural bodies of water while Ward Pond and Lake Lamoille are both artificial. Actually, the town has many other artificial ponds — 53 as of 1978. Most are farm ponds but others, generally created in recent years, are for recreational purposes associated with individual vacation homes or vacation home developments. In contrast, Ward Pond, by far the oldest artificial pond in Morristown, was created for an industrial use. Way

BOUNDARIES, NATURAL LANDMARKS

back in 1845 or 1846 Henry Carter built a log dam across Boardman Brook and established a sawmill near the five- or six-acre pond that was created. The mill, pond and adjoining land were subsequently owned by other parties until Walter C. Ward and his wife, Emma, acquired the property in 1903. That was the start of three generations of Wards who operated the sawmill for the next 60 years — the senior Ward until 1917 (and possibly later), a son, Leon E., until 1960, and Leon's son, Malcolm W., from 1960 to 1965, the mill's last year of operation (it was eventually torn down by a later owner).

Deserving of mention here is Boardman Pond, another artificial pond once located a half-mile or so south of Ward Pond and a short way upstream on the eastern of the two main tributaries which join to form Boardman Brook. The pond, like the brook, took its name from Harvey C. Boardman and later his son, Milton H., who operated a sawmill there for many years. It was closed down in 1930. The laid-up stone dam and some concrete walls remain but the pond is now brush and swampy field (T1).

And there's also Luna Pond. This tiny body of water — about three-quarters of an acre — rests in an old gravel pit above Peoples Academy. It reached some prominence in 1967 when the Lamoille County Jaycees, a young men's service organization, developed plans for using the pond for swimming as part of a larger recreation area. Unfortunately, the project sank rather than swam and never came to reality.

As for Lake Lamoille, the most notable change there since 1935 was the fading and ultimate closing in 1957 of the Samoset Cottage Colony on its west shore. A full history of that distinctive resort enterprise is given elsewhere. But contributing to Samoset's decline was the decline of the 153-acre lake itself. That has been officially characterized as eutrophic, which is to say it has been and is receiving certain dissolved nutrients, notably phosphorous, at a rate far in excess of normal. In less polite terms, some would call the lake dead.

Much of the problem has, of course, been the fact that for most of the years since the lake was created in 1907 it was receiving all of Morrisville's raw sewage, both human and industrial. The lake has also provided a settling basin for much of the silt and debris carried into it by the Lamoille River. Because of all the resulting shallow water, motorboating on the lake is said to be hazardous. As for fishing, it has been poor for some time.

Having touched on the names of several of Morristown's waterways and bodies of water, this is an appropriate place for a bit more information about the name "Lamoille," and more particularly that expression, "Spunky Lamoille." The term was, as Miss Mower relates (page 18), applied to those who worked hard to get Lamoille County established. But more than that, it has been used from time to time to express praise for any county resident or organization which has shown skill and determination in attaining some desirable end. It has also been used as a call to arms to rouse Lamoille Countians to action.

One example of the latter occurred in 1931. Long-time Morrisville newspaperman Arthur B. Limoge reported in an editorial that outsiders were commenting favorably on the new cement streets which Morrisville had just constructed. But, he went on, besides those and a little pavement in Johnson village, there were no other cement roads in all of Lamoille County. This, according to Limoge, was an unacceptable situation because increasing automobile traffic certainly warranted better highways. Then came the pitch: "This county received its name as "Spunky Lamoille" many years ago by fighting for its rights. It has become a tradition. Now the county should assert its rights and demand more consideration from the state in the building of high type roads."

Lake Lamoille is, of course, a "fat place" on the Lamoille River, Morristown's major and certainly best-known waterway. Two significant changes in the river have occurred since 1935. One is the uses made of its waters. Gone before 1935 were the water-powered industries once

---

SNOWMAN, ANYONE?

Take a lot of good packing snow, some child labor, and you're in business — at least that's how Helen Wasgatt started.

She sold (1) snowman this past week to a traveling photographer who had need of one. It was most amusing to see this snowman loaded onto a truck and carted away.

If you doubt this story, Helen has a receipt to prove it. The going price is $5 for an average size. It will be funny to see how she accounts for this on her income tax.

Helen Barton, Morrisville
Letter to the Editor
News & Citizen, February 24, 1966

---

sited at Morrisville and Cadys Falls. The Water and Light Department continues, however, to generate hydroelectric power at those two places. Otherwise the river now serves more for recreational than utilitarian purposes. More on that shortly.

The other change is not so readily apparent: the Lamoille River's waters are much cleaner. This improvement came and continues to come as a result of "classification" of the Lamoille River Basin. That is a regulatory procedure authorized by State law and administered by the Water Resources Board (WRB). The WRB's classification order for the Lamoille Basin was approved February 13, 1970. Responsible for guiding implementation of the WRB's classification order is an allied agency, the Water Resources Department, also part of the Vermont Agency of Environmental Conservation. In 1976 it adopted a water quality management plan for the Basin. As a result of various municipal treatment plants, including Morrisville's, and other pollution control measures, the water quality of the Lamoille River Basin has improved significantly.

The Lamoille River Basin drains 706 square miles of Vermont, or about 7.5% of the state's area. Rising in the southeastern part of Orleans County, the main river flows 84.9 miles, and descends 1,200 feet in elevation before reaching Lake Champlain at the town line between Colchester and Milton. About nine of those miles of main stream lie in Morristown and almost all of Morristown lies within the Lamoille

River Basin. The principal exception is the town's southwest corner where the Sterling Brook flows south into Stowe and the Winooski River Basin. Morristown's main tributaries of the Lamoille are Boardman Brook, Ryder Brook, Kenfield Brook and Jacob Brook.

The Lamoille River Basin has been described by Vermont's Fish and Game Department as "one of the best watersheds in Vermont for trout," a fact to which many Morristown anglers can attest. In this regard, the F&G Department in the 1960's acquired 68.5 acres of streambank property along the Lamoille and one of its tributaries, Kenfield Brook. Purpose of the acquisition was twofold: to assure public access to these waters for fishing, and to permit streambank improvements to control erosion and to improve fish habitat. But because of the expense, little of the latter has been done to date.

This is as appropriate a place as any to note that Morristown has one other tract of State-owned land within its boundaries, this one substantial. That's the 1,000 acres or so of the Mt. Mansfield State Forest along the Sterling Range at the extreme western side of the town. Within this area or very close to it are the summits of three principal mountains of that range: Madonna Peak, 3,640 feet high; Morse Mt., 3,380 feet; and Whiteface Mt., 3,715 feet. The latter is the highest point in Morristown. The lowest elevation is about 520 feet above sea level; that's where the Lamoille River exits the town.

Back on the Lamoille, one other piece of public property on its banks is of special interest. Once known as Clark Park, the tract is situated just downstream of the Morrisville dam where a scenic stretch of the river merges into Lake Lamoille (V1). Within its bounds is the natural landmark, Pulpit Rock.

On January 1, 1904 George W. Clark, a prominent local resident, conveyed the 12- to 14-acre parcel to the Town to be "a public park." For reasons unknown, however, the Town apparently didn't learn about the gift until 1912, when the deed was recorded and townspeople voted to accept Clark's donation. While Clark's gift was to the Town, he required that its administration as a park be by the Village, *not* the Town. That confusing condition and the limitation on its use was eliminated in 1926 by an appropriate change in the deed through Clark's heirs (he died in 1924). That made the Village the owner of the land.

Until this time little had been done with the property to establish it as a park. Access to the property was via River Street, which then reached from its present western stub all the way to the Morrisville power plant (it was also connected to Bridge Street by an extension to the south of Brooklyn Street). Early in 1927 the *Morrisville Messenger* called for more improvements at the park. Something happened, but not what was expected. It was the Flood of 1927. As Miss Mower reported (page 279), the rush of waters overflowed the Lamoille River's banks just upstream of the Morrisville dam, destroyed the above-mentioned streets, and carved a great gash across the Clark property and neighboring land closer to Bridge Street. The streets were never rebuilt, and Clark Park was abandoned. Today it is a little-known patch of brushy woodland, very rough and rock-strewn at the flood-damaged east end, but quite pleasant at the more elevated west end.

Fishing has been mentioned as one recreational activity on the Lamoille River. Another which has seen definite growth in recent years is canoeing. The river has been mentioned in several canoeing guides and other publications as a good place for both day and overnight trips. And from 1974 through 1979 part of the Lamoille in Morristown was the scene of the "Lamoille River Ramble." Held in spring each year, that's a more-fun-than-formal canoe race sponsored by the Morrisville Rotary Club, which moved the site to Johnson in 1980.

Turning from the pleasantness of water recreation on the Lamoille to tragedies which have occurred there, the river has claimed at least five victims in Morristown since the early 1930's: 61-year-old Mira Rodgers Heath in 1933; Philip Jones, 14, in 1947; Constance Draper, 2, in 1954; Randall Ward, 2½, in 1965; and Gaylord Moffatt, 30, in 1980.

As Miss Mower reported (pages 278-79), the Flood of 1927 caused major damage here but took no lives. Vermont and the Lamoille Valley

---

A YEAR OF DROUGHT, 1959

Above the confluence of the Green and Lamoille rivers, the stream was practically dry, and some of the best stands of alfalfa in the county sprang up in the bed of the river. It is a tribute to the honesty of our local real estate agents that no building lots were sold in this dry river bed. Fishermen reported that the under-sides of the fish which they caught were all worn raw from rubbing on the bottom of the creek.

Willard K. Sanders, Superintendent
Morrisville Water and Light Department
1959 Annual Report

---

have experienced three other major floods since that time, though Morristown itself escaped really serious damage in all of them. Those occurred March 18-19, 1936, June 30-July 1, 1973 and April 1, 1976.

As for violent weather of other kinds, a memorable event was the New England hurricane of September 21, 1938. According to the *Morrisville Messenger*, the storm's heavy rain and high winds "raised havoc" here. The electric system was shut down overnight, the statue on the Soldiers Monument at Academy Park was blown down, and roofs were ripped off several buildings. And then there was the devastation to trees, both individuals and in groves.

On August 9-10, 1976 Hurricane Belle (the National Weather Service was now naming each such storm) gave its last gasp over this area. There were high winds and flash flooding but damage was not nearly as severe as the devastation which occurred to the south.

As for the weather generally, Morrisville has had at least two residents keeping their eyes on it every day for long periods of time. Which is to say, they observed and recorded key data about temperature, precipitation and other elements. Charles A. Sanders was such an observer for nearly 40 years from 1866 to 1905. Doing the same thing for a similar span of years was Howard N. Terrill. He began about 1933 and continued until his death in July, 1975. The local official observer from November that year until late 1980 was E. Brewster Buxton (there has been no observer since then). The Morrisville Water and Light Department has, however, been keeping careful track of one weather element, precipitation, since 1940.

As for what kind of weather we have here, lifelong Morristowner Willard K. Sanders provided this observation back in 1974: "Morristown lies in Longitude 72° 35' west, and Latitude 44° 32' north and but for the fact that it is thirty five miles too far south, would be equidistant from the equator and the north pole. The weather sometimes indicates a much nearer proximity to the latter than is indicated on the map." If the reader is already nodding his head (with a smile) he most likely will continue doing so with Buxton's description: "Morristown experiences almost every type of weather found anywhere in the world — though fortunately not the extremes which occur at some places."

As for specific data about Morristown's climate, an official "normal" has not yet been established because the records kept by Terrill and Buxton are still about three years short of the 20-year period which the National Climatic Center requires for such calculations. But Buxton has provided the following averages of data recorded near the center of Morrisville for 1962-1979:

Monthly precipitation has varied from a low of .18 inches in February, 1978 to a high of 6.98 inches in May, 1973. Annual precipitation has varied from 32.28 inches in 1965 to 46.66 inches in 1976 for an average since 1962 of 41.16 inches. Total snowfall varies considerably from year to year between about 100 inches to about 170 inches.

As for temperatures, monthly averages have ranged from a low of 5.7°F in February, 1979 to a high of 69.8°F in July, 1963. The annual average has been 41.6°F. The last frost in spring averages out to come on May 27, with the earliest on May 8, 1972 and the latest on June 11, both 1971 and 1972. The first autumn frost averages out to be September 17, with the earliest 32°F reading on August 31, 1976 and the latest on October 8, 1977. The average span of frost-free days for Morrisville has been 112 days.

As for the overall extremes since 1962, it was -37°F on February 13, 1967 and 97°F on July 3, 1966. For those going "Pshaw! — I know it's been much colder than that," you may be right. Though it was unofficial, what the *Morrisville Messenger* described as "the coldest day ever recorded in this vicinity" was -48°F at 7 a.m. December 30, 1933.

> For more about some of this chapter's subjects including a proposed boundary change with Elmore, Indian Joe and Molly, and "Spunky Lamoille," see the "first draft" of *More About Morristown, 1935-1980*; details about what and where that is are in the Foreword.

Chapter 2

Town And Village: Which Is What And How They're Governed

"YES, VIRGINIA, there is a Morristown. Many outlanders, and even a few local residents, either don't know or have forgotten that fact. They keep wanting to call the town Morrisville. And perhaps it's not surprising because poor Morristown has never had the public mention and attention that Morrisville, the village within the Town's bounds, has had. Think about it. The Town's main commercial center and all its schools lie within Morrisville; Morrisville is the name of the post office; Morrisville was the name of the railroad station in the days of passenger trains on our local railroad; and Morrisville is the name which appears most prominently on most road maps. So when folks talk about, or reporters write about, anything local, it tends to get identified as a Morrisville matter, even when it's the whole Town, not just the Village, that's involved. Can you imagine, Virginia, a newspaper headline which announces, "Morrisville Selectmen Vote On Zoning"! It's happened. Of course, it's Morris*town* which is governed by selectmen, not Morris*ville*, which has trustees. Confusing, isn't it?

"But yes, my young friend, there is a Town of Morristown as well as a Village of Morrisville. And if you'll be patient, we're now about to explain and describe the two municipalities, how each is governed, and the services which each provides and has provided (as you will see, the Town has taken over several services which only the Village used to

TOWN AND VILLAGE

provide). And we'll even tell how Morristown and Morrisville officials have talked about a complete merger. If that ever happened, the latter government would disappear altogether. Wouldn't that be something, Virginia — no Morrisville at all!?"

And so with a play on the famous *New York Sun* editorial of 1897 to little Virginia O'Hanlon about the existence of Santa Claus do we introduce Morristown's distinct yet superimposed and inter-related municipal governments. And at the outset we should note that there are not just two of them but actually three, the Morristown Town School District being the third. After some background information, we'll review the basic governance of each and then, in the following chapters, the various public services for which each has been responsible.

Historically, the town has been Vermont's basic local unit of government, with certain exceptions to be noted shortly. For the most part, towns operate under certain provisions of the Vermont Constitution and the State's general laws. The Town of Morristown is one of those so governed. As such it experiences that much lauded element of grass-roots democracy, the town meeting. Morristowners hardly need to be reminded that at their annual meeting the first Tuesday of March, they gather to elect officers, create new offices on occasion, approve or disapprove special appropriations, levy their local taxes, and cuss, discuss and vote upon assorted other questions. What they may not be aware of is how special in Western society is the phenomenon of the town meeting. The town or township as a kind of municipality takes various forms throughout the United States, but only in Vermont and the other New England states do town voters assemble to participate directly in making decisions on policies, programs and finances. In towns elsewhere such decisions are made almost exclusively by elected governing boards and/or administrators.

In addition to towns Vermont has two other local units of government which, with towns, predominate in the state's system of municipal government. They are the city and the incorporated village. There are nine of the former and about 50 of the latter. Like towns, they are creatures of the state but in contrast, each of their charters not only creates the particular municipality but also spells out its particular powers and how it is to be governed. Beyond that similarity, the city and incorporated village have important differences.

The city, like the town, is a distinct and integral political unit which is established to provide a broad range of municipal services, but which does so under one or another of several city forms of government (a description of these is beyond the scope of this work).

The incorporated village, however, is generally a densely populated area *within a town* which is set off as a municipality within a municipality. Its charter empowers it to provide certain services within the village boundaries, which cannot be provided or have not been provided by the town but which the village residents want or need. And to establish and carry on those special or additional services, incorporated villages are necessarily empowered to raise their own property taxes. As a result, a resident of an incorporated village pays not only village taxes but also town taxes. He or she is also both a village voter *and* a town voter. All of which is curious and sometimes confusing.

The final type of municipality to be mentioned in this brief review is the school district. In keeping with the above complexities, Vermont has two kinds of local, as distinguished from union, school districts: the town school district and the incorporated school district. Like the town, the town school district basically operates under general statutes. That is, it is not specially chartered. While its boundaries are exactly those of a particular town, it is legally a distinct municipal corporation with its own governing board, it's own tax rate, and legally, if not literally, its own meeting of voters. Such is the Morristown Town School District.

The incorporated school district is roughly comparable to the incorporated village: it gets a special charter from the General Assembly to operate schools for a defined geographic area usually within a particular town school district. The latter itself continues to operate schools in the area *outside* the incorporated district's boundaries.

TOWN OF MORRISTOWN

Under Vermont's system of town government, Morristown voters, as noted, make many decisions at their annual meeting each March. Between meetings the Town's governing or legislative body is its board of selectmen. The board has overall responsibility for various Town services, notably highways and bridges, refuse disposal, police and fire departments, and ambulance service. Until 1978 Morristown's board of selectmen had always had three members, one selectman elected each year for a three-year term. But under a statutory option open to them, voters that year expanded the board to five members.

The Town's other elective officers are, or have been, the following (except as noted, all are elected to one-year terms):

— Moderator

— Clerk and Treasurer: At least since well back into the 19th century Morristowners have regularly elected the same person to these two distinct positions. The terms of both officers were one year until 1972, when voters, under a new statutory option, changed them to three-year terms.

— Listers: This is generally a board of three members, each elected in staggered years to a three-year term. But on at least one occasion (and there may have been others), Town voters in 1972 and 1973 authorized and elected two additional listers for one-year terms to assist in a comprehensive reappraisal of properties making up the Town's grand list.

— Collector of Delinquent Taxes

— Auditors: A board of three members, each elected in staggered years to a three-year term.

— Road Commissioner: This has been both an elective and appointive post at different times since 1892 when the General Assembly established this town office. Until 1911 State law made it strictly an elective post. Under a new law beginning that year, Morristowners

TOWN AND VILLAGE

had the choice of either electing the road commissioner themselves or authorizing selectmen to fill the post by appointment. They have switched back and forth a couple of times but since 1955 have had it an appointive post.

— Overseer of the Poor: As of October 1, 1968 a State law passed the previous year abolished this long-established town office. Abolishment of the post was part of the General Assembly's directive that the State take over administration of general assistance to the poor, something which previously had been a local responsibility. The new law also provided, however, that each town's selectmen appoint a "town service officer" to assist the Vermont Department of Social Welfare in that administration.

The author presumes that Morristowners are generally familiar with the duties of the above elective Town officers. But he suspects that the duties of other elective offices which follow are a mite unfamiliar, and possibly even downright mysterious!

— Pleasant View Cemetery Commissioners: This is a board of five members, each elected on a staggered basis to a five-year term. See the chapter about the Town's cemeteries for information about the commission's responsibilities.

— Constables: Vermont law requires all towns to elect at least one constable and provides the option, which Morristown has used for many years, of electing another one — hence the Town's first and second constables. Until recently, one significant of various statutory duties for constables was the *first* constable's service as presiding officer at the Town's polling place in election of State and Federal officers. In that capacity he supervised arrangement of the polling facilities, selection of election clerks, security of ballot boxes, and counting of the votes. But a new election law in 1978 transferred that responsibility to the town clerk. The first constable continues to oversee the voting at town meetings, however, though this is a result of local custom, not law.

The law, however, does give constables broad law enforcement and court administrative powers, notably in the arrest of criminal suspects and the service of writs in civil cases. The degree to which these powers have been exercised has, however, varied considerably among individual constables in recent years.

— Grand Jurors: Grand jurors are a town's equivalent of the county state's attorney — they prosecute crimes, generally those of a "minor" sort, such as breach of peace. The jurisdictions of the town and county prosecutors overlap, however, and for some time now the Lamoille County state's attorney has handled virtually all prosecutions relating to crimes committed in Morristown. Thus the office, here at least, is hardly an active one.

The town grand juror, incidentally, should not be confused with members of a *county grand jury*. The latter may be convened by the county court's judges to hear evidence and determine if an indictment should be issued formally charging an accused person with committing a crime. In Lamoille County such a grand jury is composed *not* of the town grand jurors elected by the ten county towns but of 18 persons selected at random from a list of county residents.

— Town Agent To Prosecute And Defend Suits: The town agent to prosecute and defend suits officially represents the Town (or Town School District) in the prosecution or defense of suits in which the Town is a party. As the agent need not be an attorney, he almost certainly would use the services of Morristown's designated town attorney, should any suit occur. The position's duties have hardly overburdened its incumbent, at least in recent times. So far as the author could learn, neither the Town or Town School District has brought suit or been sued in many, many years.

— Trustee of Public Funds: Morristown has such an officer but the writer is not sure he's legal! Vermont law provides that a town's voters may establish and elect a board of *three* trustees of public funds to manage "real and personal estate ... held by a town in trust for any purpose," unless the grantor has specified otherwise. This option has been on the books since 1888 but not until 1950 did Morristowners exercise it (previously selectmen served *ex-officio* as such trustees). Voters, however, that year authorized only one, not three, trustees and designated the Town treasurer as that trustee. They've been doing the same thing every year since.

According to Treasurer Sydney C. Mander, he has but two trust funds to manage. One is the Copley Agricultural Fund, a trust fund of $10,000 established in 1946 by Morristown's well-known benefactor, Alexander H. Copley. This is described in more detail elsewhere. The other is the Thomas C. Cheney Senior Improvement Prize Fund. Cheney, a prominent Morristown citizen, in 1957 established a fund of $500. From its earnings $10 was to be — and has been — awarded each year to the senior student at Peoples Academy showing the most improvement. The fund has actually earned significantly more than $10 a year with the result that in 1979 it had grown to $841.23.

— Justices of the Peace: A special category of local elective office is justice of the peace. It is special because the election of justices does not occur annually at town meeting, but rather biennially as part of the State's general election in November. While for many years Vermont's justices of the peace presided over the lowest courts in the State's judicial system, since 1974 they have had only the following three duties and powers: administration of oaths, solemnization of marriages, and membership on a municipality's board of civil authority. The latter, whose membership includes certain other municipal officers besides the justices, involves far and away the most significant of a justice's duties. This board has broad responsibilities in regard to elections, including preparation of a municipality's checklist of eligible voters, conduct of elections, and canvassing of voting results. The board of civil authority also serves as an appeals board for any property owner who questions listers' appraisal of his or her property, and for any person who questions the inclusion of his or her name on the list of poll (or head) taxpayers. Finally, the board of civil authority, with certain other town officers added, acts as a board of abatement for local taxes.

These statutory powers and responsibilities all are borne by Morristown's justices of the peace. The number of justices varies from

TOWN AND VILLAGE

five to 15 among Vermont's towns, depending on population. Morristown has 12.

In addition to these elective positions, a number of other Town officers are appointed by selectmen. These appointive officers have changed to some extent over the last 40 years, reflecting social and technological changes. The once-elected-now-appointed road commissioner has been discussed above. Other appointive Town officers are or recently have been the following:

— Inspector Of Lumber, Shingles And Wood: The inspector of lumber, shingles and wood shall, at the request of any interested party, "examine and classify the quality of lumber and shingles, measure

---

RESIGNATION OF WILLARD SANDERS AS TREE WARDEN

Dec. 1, 1945

Selectmen, Town of Morristown
Morristown, Vt.

Gentlemen:

Herewith, I tender my resignation as Tree Warden of the Town of Morristown, which I am informed I was recently appointed.

I find upon a careful study of the law that the possibilities, ramifications, and intentions of the law as relates to this important office are exceedingly complex and could lead to something, properly handled.

A well known bard has said that only God can make a tree and I have no intention nor inclination to compete with the almighty; neither can I spend much time in removing these things which He has made.

Your thoughtfulness and trust in imposing upon me this important office are appreciated but I felt that I must forego the pleasure of serving in this capacity.

Yours very truly,

W.K. Sanders

---

lumber, shingles and wood and give certificates thereof." But recently at least there haven't been very many interested parties seeking the inspector's services — except to check a quantity of firewood, something now seeing much increase in use.

— Fence Viewers: This town office, from time to time the subject of good-natured humor, dates back to Colonial days. A town's board of three fence viewers is empowered to resolve disputes between property owners over the legal adequacy of an existing fence, where a new division should go, and/or the responsibility between propertyowners for the construction of a new or replacement fence. They have no authority, however, to establish disputed property boundaries.

— Pound Keepers: In Morristown this office has gone to the dogs —

literally. Town pounds, which go way back in history, are places where stray animals can be taken, pending determination of the owner and the return to same. It is also the place where, if necessary, the town might place an animal found to have been maltreated by its owner. Vermont statutes prescribe certain responsibilities — and fees and charges — for a town's one or more pound keepers.

As recently as the mid-1970's Morristown had four pound keepers. Under an informal arrangement, two of them were pounds for the usual larger farm livestock — cows, horses, goats and sheep. But no critter ever wandered or was brought in for their care. That presumably reflects the significantly fewer farms and livestock in Morristown compared to earlier years, and probably better fences which today's farmers do have for their livestock.

It's a different story with another of man's long-traditional domestic animals — the dog. Morristown has plenty of wandering canines and, since 1977, two pound keepers to pick up, care for and dispose of them. One is Emery F. Foss, Jr., owner of the Lamoille Landfill and Salvage Depot, which serves several area towns (including Morristown) with dog pound facilities. The other pound keeper is Brian Kellogg, one of Foss's employees.

— Fire Warden: The Town's fire warden, who is appointed by the State forester with the approval of selectmen, has a number of responsibilities in the prevention and control of forest fires. Among other things, anybody planning to burn brush or rubbish in or near any woodland must, with certain exceptions, get a permit from the fire warden.

— Health Officer: The Town's health officer, who is appointed by the State board of health on recommendation of selectmen, has broad responsibilities and powers for maintaining healthful conditions and correcting unhealthy conditions in the Town.

— Energy Co-ordinator: Acting under an option provided by a new law in 1976, Town voters in 1977 authorized selectmen to appoint an energy co-ordinator. They subsequently did. Under the law, this officer "shall co-ordinate existing energy resources in the town and cooperate with the municipal planning commission and with those federal, state and regional agencies of government which are responsible for energy matters." The co-ordinator also "may study and evaluate sources of energy which are alternatives to those presently available with a view toward the more efficient and economical utilization of existing and potential energy resources."

— Civil Defense Chairman: Under a State law on the books since 1951 Morristown has had a civil defense chairman from time to time but not continuously. The law provides that such chairman heads up "a local organization for civil defense [established] in accordance with the state civil defense plan and program." The term "civil defense" incorporates power blackouts, civil disturbances and natural disasters, as well as classic civil defense in case of war, and nuclear attack in particular.

— Tree Warden: Finally, from time to time in the past Morristown has had a tree warden, but more recently has been without one for some years. This officer is responsible for protection and preservation of existing shade trees along public ways and for planning and implementing a program "of shading and beautifying public ways and places by planting new trees and shrubs."

MORRISTOWN TOWN SCHOOL DISTRICT

The principal elective officers of the Town School District of Morristown are, of course, its school directors. Together as the district's legislative body, they are charged with overall responsibility for policies, operations and finances of the Town school system.

Morristowners also annually elect a Town School District moderator — invariably the same man as the Town moderator. As for other key officers, the law provides that the town clerk, town auditors and town treasurer automatically hold those same offices for their town school district.

VILLAGE OF MORRISVILLE

To expand a bit on Miss Mower's account of the establishment of the incorporated Village of Morrisville (page 246), the original Village comprised what was then the Town's School District No. 1. On February 24, 1885 voters of the District rejected a charter act (No. 214) approved by the 1884 General Assembly. Then, with one curious exception, the matter lay dormant for five years until June 13, 1890, when District No. 1 residents voted "almost unanimously" to accept the 1884 act. The exception was the fact that the Legislature of 1888 had passed *another* charter act (No. 255). This differed from the 1884 law in only a few ways, the most significant being a precise description of the village-to-be's boundaries. No local vote was ever taken on this, and why it was passed, or why it was not the one to be voted on, is a mystery.

Morrisville's charter was subsequently amended five times, specifically in 1894, 1898, 1902, 1904 and 1906. A major change occurred with No. 313 of the laws of 1910. That provided a comprehensively-revised charter for the Village, and is the act to which all subsequent amendments have applied. There have been nine of these, in 1912, 1917, 1925, 1935, 1937, 1945, 1946, 1947 and 1973.

It's the author's impression that the powers granted to the Village of Morrisville in its original charter were not actually very extensive. Authorized municipal services were limited to streets, fire-fighting, and some, but not comprehensive, water system facilities. Only with the charter amendment of 1894 was the comprehensive water system, plus electric and sewer services authorized, all three adding significantly to the validity of forming the incorporated village in the first place.

Another broad area of special powers granted to the Village which were not available under the general statutes governing towns was that of controlling or regulating a variety of matters. These included different commercial enterprises, recreational activities, and certain citizen responsibilities. The original charter defined some areas for such controls and the comprehensive charter revision of 1910 broadened these considerably. Among other things, that charter amendment authorized the regulation of "disorderly and gaming houses," "immoderate riding or driving [of horses] in the streets," and even "the time and place of bathing within any of the public waters in said corporation"! At a special meeting September 17, 1902 Village voters approved a comprehensive set of bylaws, and various bylaw changes and additions occurred in subsequent years. Unfortunately, there currently is no up-to-date compilation of bylaws now in force.

The area comprising the Village of Morrisville has grown a number of times over the years by changes in its official boundaries. The principal expansion, which occurred in several stages, has been to the north in the area along the Lamoille River south of the Morrisville Drive-In Theatre, and extending east beyond Brooklyn Street. A very curious feature of the boundary in this area is a "shoestring" extension of the line. This includes within the Village a special boundary extension for the road which leads from Brooklyn Street to the Pratt-Read manufacturing plant (formerly Atlas Plywood). The road, however, remains a private road, that is, it is not maintained by the Village. The

---

REGULATING ROOSTERS

The high spots of the [Village's 1931 annual meeting] ... [included] passing over the article to instruct the trustees to restrict or regulate the keeping of roosters within the village limits. While the article was sponsored by substantial citizens, it failed to pass, apparently from a lack of faith on the part of the voters in the ability of trustees to regulate the crowing of said roosters.

Morrisville Messenger, April 15, 1931

---

last enlargement of the Village occurred in 1946 with the addition of a small tract in the Jersey Heights area. The Village's charter actually empowers it to alter its boundaries on its own initiative. But the changes which have occurred have been incorporated from time to time by appropriate charter amendments which give new boundary descriptions. The last of these was No. 243 of the laws of 1947.

With one major exception the Village is governed and managed by its board of trustees. That board has five members, each elected to a five-year term on a rotating basis. The board's chairman has traditionally been the trustee with the longest tenure. The exception is the board of water and light commissioners, each of whose members similarly is elected to a five-year-term on a rotating basis. This body governs the Village's Water and Light Department, subject only to such bylaws as Village voters may enact.

Other current elective Village officers are its clerk and treasurer — traditionally the same person as the Town clerk and treasurer; collector of taxes; board of three auditors; and an agent to convey real estate. All are elected to one-year terms. And, oh, yes, a presiding officer at Village meetings, the moderator. Or is it the Village president? Historically there's some confusion on this point, but since 1979 it's been a moderator who voters have selected.

TOWN AND VILLAGE

Finally, ever since the incorporated Village was established, voters annually elected a chief engineer and two assistant engineers for their fire department. Until 1968, that is. That year the Town took over responsibility for the fire department and since 1969 the department's volunteer firefighters have been electing their own officers, with confirming appointments by the selectmen.

With occasional exceptions, persons holding offices have not been mentioned by name in the above descriptive roster. In the Appendix, however, will be found lists of certain key municipal officers.

One other exception is of special interest. That's the increasing, though still very limited, frequency of women serving in municipal offices. Until 1921 Morristown and Morrisville were definitely male-dominated, men holding all local elective offices to the total exclusion of females. Though no special note was taken at the time, the "break-through" came that year with the election of Anna L. Mower as a member of the board of school directors, a position to which she was re-elected four times, serving until 1935. Except for the period 1955 to 1959, the Town school board has since had at least one and sometimes two female members. But so far, women have never been a majority of the five-member board. Those other female school directors have been Laura Morse, 1935-1944; Marguerite Woods, 1944-1947; Madge Churchill, 1947-1955; Norma Wakefield, 1959-1965; Dorothy Sargent, 1962-1971; Betty L. Blowers, 1971-1980; Mary West, 1977-present; and Mary Ann Wilson, 1980-present.

Atty. Helen Anair was the Town's first female grand juror, being first elected in 1928 and serving until 1933. That same year the Village's all-male board of trustees was breached for the first time by a distaff member. With her candidacy promoted by the Morrisville Woman's Club, Marguerite S. Chapin defeated Morris B. White, 85 to 68, in her election to a five-year term on that board. The one other female trustee since then has been Mary Kunstman; she was elected in 1977 and is still serving her five-year term.

Janice I. Edson was the Town's first woman lister; she served just a single year, 1958-59. The one other female lister has served much longer. Roberta M. Stafford was appointed in 1964 to complete the unexpired three-year term to 1965 of Richard F. Snow. She has been re-elected five times since then and is presently still serving in this important Town office.

The Town and Village's first woman tax collector was Lefa N. Brown, who served from 1946 to 1949. The two municipalities' first female clerk and treasurer was Winona S. Sawyer. She was first elected in 1953 and served until her death on June 21, 1966. And the above-mentioned Mary Kunstman is also the Town's first woman to serve as auditor. She was appointed in 1976 to fill the unexpired term of George Campbell, at his death, and subsequently served until 1979.

> For more about several of these municipal officers and descriptions of two not mentioned here at all — trustee of public money and weigher of coal, see the "first draft" of *More About Morristown, 1935-1980*; the Foreword describes what and where that is.

Chapter 3

Schools

I can see no good that would result from [the town school system] that cannot be attained quite as easily and more cheaply under the present [district] system.

SUCH WAS THE COMMENT in the town report of 1886 provided by its superintendent of schools, George M. Powers, later to be one of Morristown's most prominent citizens but then a young man only a few years out of college. His was hardly a minority view for, as Miss Mower reported, Morristowners were strongly opposed to giving up the district system of schools. But the remark provides a good point of departure for describing the major changes which Morristown schools have undergone since that time: the town system *has* replaced the district system; all the small outlying "district" or rural schools have long since passed into history; and all education now occurs in a greatly expanded central complex of school buildings.

Miss Mower has described Morristown's earliest public schools and mentioned briefly the town's division into 19 school districts. As a bit more background, after some early divisions of the town into districts, Town voters in 1838 approved a comprehensive new arrangement of 15 districts (see Map No. 2). Various changes, additions and deletions subsequently occurred. When, on April 1, 1893, the mandatory town school district law went into effect, the number of districts was back at 15. Fourteen of them and their respective schoolhouses lay outside District No. 1 with Peoples Academy and its associated graded school.

Beginning almost immediately, one or more of those 14 rural schoolhouses — as we shall hereafter refer to them — was not actually used, though which ones were closed changed from year to year. The number in operation held fairly stable — 11 to 14 — until 1930-31, when only nine rural schools were in use. The number declined to three by 1943-44, where it held for eight years, then dropped to two in 1951-52, and to only one in 1952-53 and 1953-54. That was the school at Morristown Corners, the old District No. 2. Doris Russ had been teaching there several years, for four of which her number of students had actually increased from 19 to 29 and then to 31 in 1954-55. But that was the last year of operation for the last of Morristown's old rural schools.

One of those not in use, North Randolph, burned on November 4, 1936 (T66). Then in 1939 the Town School District began selling off the idle schoolhouses to private owners, a process which continued until 1958 before the last one was disposed of. Two of the schools have since been lost: Lamson Hill (No. 8) to sheer decrepitude and eventual razing about 1971 (T63), and Tyndall Hill (No. 16) to fire about 1961 (T64). With two exceptions — Cadys Falls (No. 2), which has been used for storage, and Morristown Plains (No. 7) (T7), which became a horse barn — all the other schoolhouses were converted to dwellings. And two of the structures were moved, one of them right out of town! That was the Billings Mill School (No. 19) (T65), which went to Stowe. The other was the Plains School, which was moved a short way from its original site.

The other rural schoolhouses which became and still are dwellings are: Morristown Corners (T2), South Randolph or Campbell (T4), South LaPorte (No. 5) (T5), Sand Hill (No. 6) (T6), Cole Hill (No. 10) (T8), North LaPorte (No. 13) (T9), Cheney Hill (No. 14) (T10), and Mud City (No. 15) (T11).

So let us now return to District No. 1, which owned and operated both Peoples Academy and the Morrisville Graded School. Miss Mower has traced the history of these schools, at least up to 1935. But one matter in this early period bears special examination before moving on to the years since then.

That occurred shortly after that important law of 1892 made mandatory the town system of schools. The law meant the new Morristown board of school directors managed not only all those outlying rural schools, but also the two schools in the Village. However, some Villagers apparently didn't like to lose control of their facilities. So in 1894 they obtained from the General Assembly an act authorizing formation of what would be an incorporated school district separate from the town school district. Boundaries of the new district, to be known as "The Peoples' Academy and Morrisville Graded School," would be the same as those of the incorporated Village of Morrisville, which by that time was in its fifth year of existence. The enabling act required, however, that voters in the proposed district approve its establishment. That never happened. What apparently was the only vote on the question was held February 26, 1897; on that occasion the proposal wasn't actually defeated but was tabled and then never revived.

During the mid-1930's the Town's school population wavered around the mid- to upper-500's. After that, it spurted for a few years, dropped again to a low of 563 in 1944, then began a long, sustained increase which by the 1951-52 school year had reached 713. Between 1936 and 1944 the number of rural schools had dropped from nine to three. Each closing meant, of course, more youngsters attending the Graded School. Those additions coupled with the general increase in school population meant that that school was, by the late 1940's, carrying 330 students, 80 more than its rated capacity. So at their annual meeting in 1951, Town voters heeded the school board's urgings and authorized bonds of upt to $192,000 for a new "intermediate" building (final cost was about $190,000). Constructed at the same time was a new gymnasium, officially the Copley Community Memorial Building, using funds which Alexander H. Copley had given the Village of Morrisville (this and Copley's other gifts to the Town and Village are described in more detail elsewhere). The new gym took the place of the gymnasium housed in the lower two floors of the Copley Building of Peoples Academy. The construction and condition of that, according to the school board, made it very unsafe for continued use.

The intermediate building and gymnasium were built just to the north of, but separate from, Peoples Academy. The former housed eight classrooms and related facilities for grades 5 through 8, grades 5 and 6 being transferred from the Graded School (or Elementary School as it was then being called) and grades 7 and 8 from Peoples Academy. This expansion of school facilities in the Village permitted closings of the remaining rural schools. The last, as already noted, was that of the Morristown Corners School at the end of the 1954-55 school year.

Some other highlights in the history of the Morristown school system during the years 1936-1952:

− Curriculum content at Peoples Academy changed in several ways during these years, particularly in the school's vocational offerings, though the history of these is a little imprecise. In 1935 there were three basic courses of study leading to a high school diploma: college preparatory, social science, and commercial. The latter in particular included specific vocational subjects. In 1937 vocational home economics and agriculture were added to these basic offerings. The latter was apparently dropped several years later, but was re-established in 1947.

− Music and physical education became integral parts of the PA curriculum beginning in 1936-37. Related to the former was the revival of a Peoples Academy band in early 1949. The school band had been established in 1930 and was subsequently directed for several years by Willard K. Sanders. But its sounds had faded from PA's halls in the late 1930's.

− A regular feature during this period was a weekly chapel at PA. Students were key participants in these exercises, which generally consisted of a flag salute, Scripture reading, recitation of the Lord's prayer, anthem by the glee club and a special speaker. The student gatherings, later called assemblies, have continued to the present time, on a weekly basis until the early 1970's and every two or three weeks since then. A key change occurred in 1963 or 1964 when the Lord's Prayer and Bible reading were dropped from the assembly program. This was the result of certain U.S. Supreme Court decisions

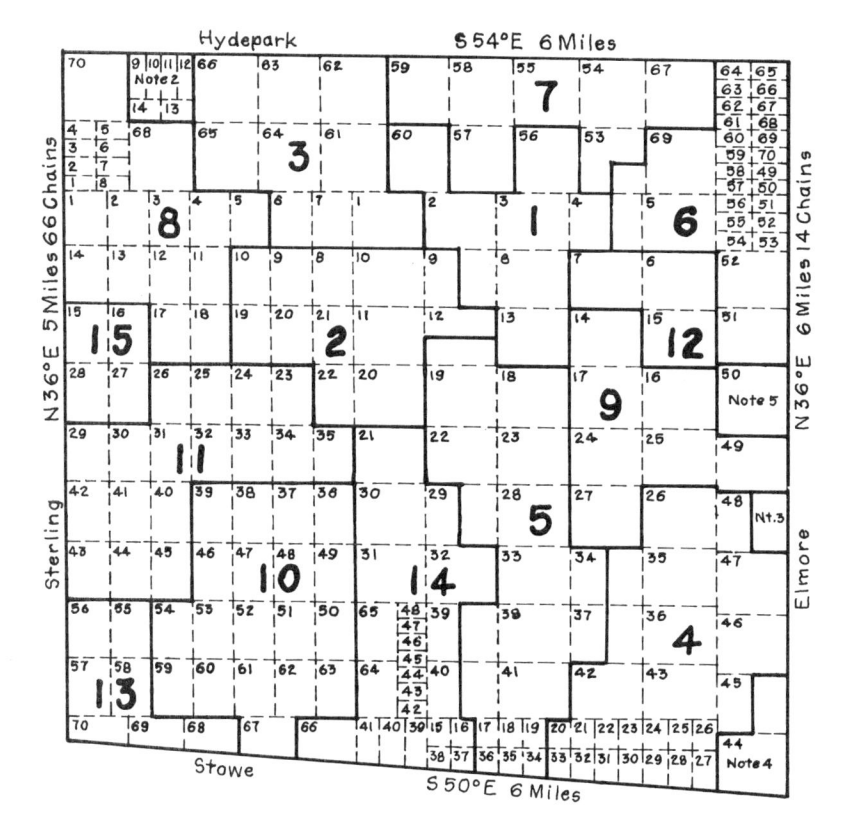

Map No. 2 - MORRISTOWN ORIGINAL LOTTING AND SCHOOL DISTRICTS ESTABLISHED IN 1838

Map by Robert L. Hagerman, 1980

LEGEND:　　`64` `- -` Lot Line　　——— School District Boundary

NOTES

1. General Information: "Lotting" was the procedure by which a town was divided into equal portions among its original proprietors and certain "public rights." A "division" was a portion of a town's total area, usually established by a rating of its value. By a drawing of lots, each proprietor got one lot within each division. Lots in Morristown's three divisions can be distinguished by their relative size: First Division - 105 acres; Second Division - 210 acres; and Third Division - 28 acres. As for school districts, the 1838 division shown here was a comprehensive new plan which replaced earlier divisions; it was the foundation for later changes. The boundaries of each district were defined by the original lots.

2. It is unclear if this area was part of District No. 3 or No. 8.

3. This area was made part of District No. 2, Elmore.

4. This area was made part of District No. 6, Elmore.

5. This area is part of District No. 12, Morristown.

6. In 1848 all of Lots 12, 18, 19, and 22, the eastern quarters of Lots 10 and 20, the western half of Lot 9, and the northern half of Lot 23, all in the Second Division, were removed from Districts Nos. 2 and 5 and recombined to form District No. 19. What areas comprised Nos. 16 (early), 17 and 18 is unknown.

TEACHING ON TYNDALL HILL

During my seven or so years of teaching at the Tyndall Hill School I averaged about 12 youngsters, with 16 the most for any one year. They generally ranged in age from 7 to 16 years old (in my first year of teaching at the Lamson Hill School one student was actually older than I; I was only 16 and he was 20!).

The Tyndall School had no belfry with a bell as several of the other rural schools had. But I did have a hand bell which I rang to call the students in at the beginning of the school day, after the 15-minute recesses in the morning and afternoon, and after the lunch hour. School let out at 4 p.m.

In addition to teaching I was also the janitor for the school. I had to clean the place and also get there early in the morning during the cold weather months to start a fire in the stove. When the students were inside, I began each day by calling and recording the roll. That was followed by a Bible reading and salute to the flag. Beyond that, the days varied quite a bit, though there was a pattern for teaching children whose ages ranged as much as they did (my one year at the Cadys Fall School I had 32 students spanning all eight grades!). Basically, while I was teaching a particular subject to youngsters in one age grouping, the others were occupied with something they could do on their own. For example, I might spend 20 minutes with the third and fourth graders on reading. I'd often start by asking what we had read the day before; that tested their understanding and recall. Then I'd have different students read aloud from their books. When somebody hit a tough word, I'd explain its meaning or pronunciation. Now while this was going on, the younger children would be doing what I called "busy work" — like practicing writing the letters of the alphabet or coloring in a coloring book. The older ones would be preparing for their next lesson in something, like doing arithmetic problems or composing a paragraph in English.

There was also a good bit of overlapping. If I was teaching history to seventh graders, the sixth graders would often listen in and learn a lot that way. And a good older student would sometimes sort of serve as an assistant teacher by helping a younger one with reading.

As for discipline, I never really had a problem. Just one time in my 51 years of teaching did I have to take a student to see the principal. I do remember once putting a boy across a chair and using a geography book on him where he felt the warmth. And Jimmie Palmer tells me he remembers my pulling his ear when he misbehaved. But mostly I just used stern words when the occasion required them. The children knew by the look in my eye that I meant business.

> Grace A. Tyndall
> Teacher, Tyndall Hill School, 1920's
> Recollection, 1978

SCHOOLS

in 1962 and 1963 which ruled against such religious exercises in public schools.

— And graduation time in June, 1948 was PA's Centennial Commencement! Highlights of the celebration marking the Academy's 100th anniversary included a student pageant dramatizing the Academy's history and the publication of a booklet containing a comprehensive roster of Academy principals, instructors and graduates.

Ralph A. Eaton served as principal of Peoples Academy for 13 years of the 16-year era covered here. He was appointed in 1936 to succeed Merwin B. Forbes, who had held the post since 1934. Eaton, a native of Waterbury, was a graduate of Norwich University. He subsequently did some graduate work at the University of Southern California, then returned for a master's degree at the University of Vermont. He left PA in 1949 to become principal at Middlebury High School. He served in that position and as the local superintendent of schools for many years and in 1978 was living in retirement in Middlebury.

Succeeding Eaton was Norman R. Hartfiel, a native of Farmington, N.H. Following graduation from Keene Teachers College, he had earned his master's degree in education at the University of New Hampshire. He had then gained 15 years experience as teacher and principal before coming to Peoples Academy. He was principal here until 1952.

Continuing the sustained growth begun in 1944, enrollment in the Morristown schools increased from the 713 of 1951-52 to 979 in 1966-67. Additional construction, both to meet the enrollment pressure and to improve educational facilities, came in two stages.

Completed in 1958 was a major addition to the Peoples Academy complex. Total estimated cost was $188,000.

One part of the addition, since called the east wing, included seven classrooms for the junior high grades and office space for the school nurse. This wing extended beyond a new locker room area added to the rear of the Copley gym. The effect of the added space, with its relief of the enrollment pressure, was a realignment of classroom usage in the existing facilities. The intermediate (north) wing now served grades 4-6 (previously 5-8) and the old Graded School now served grades 1-3 (previously 1-4). The remainder of the addition included a large room for home economics instruction and a connecting corridor which closed the gap between the original Copley Building and the Copley gym.

Completed in early 1967 at a cost of about $284,000 were further additions and improvements to the Peoples Academy facilities. There were two distinct additions to the school plant. One consisted of two classrooms, one of them for science, at the east end of the junior high (east) wing. The other, since called the south wing, included an industrial arts shop, drafting room, music room and associated practice rooms, and a combination kitchen-cafeteria and multi-purpose room.

Several changes to the Copley Building itself also occurred during this period. One was a complete renovation in 1953 of the auditorium. In 1964 the old two-story gymnasium was floored over halfway up to provide a study hall and improved library on the basement level, and a storage area below it in the sub-basement. These and changes for certain other support services facilities were completed in 1965. The new kitchen-cafeteria completed in 1967 permitted the conversion that same year of the old kitchen-cafeteria in the basement of the Copley Building to two study halls and a teachers room. The abovementioned library-study hall in turn became solely a library.

As it had in the mid-1930's, Peoples Academy continued during this period to offer three basic courses of study leading to a high school diploma: college preparatory; commercial, which included vocational courses in stenographic and business skills; and general, which included several distinct vocational offerings, initially agriculture and home economics and later industrial arts. A noteworthy new feature of

---

THE WOOD SHED

The woodshed building behind Peoples Academy played an important part in the general character building of the school's students during the 1930's and early 1940's. The boilers which heated the building were then wood burners. They burned many, many cords of wood, preferably very heavy rock maple. The cords were solid cords, not running cords. As punishment for minor discipline problems, students had to load many wheelbarrow-loads with wood, then push same to the chute at the side of the main building, remove the cover there, and slide the wood into the boiler room beneath the agriculture classroom. While two or more boys were wheeling wood from the wood shed, the custodian-fireman, Roy Wells, could start his after-school sweeping with the knowledge that his fuel supply was being properly replenished. An inspection of the Academy's cellar quickly revealed the students' behavior pattern of the preceding day or two: a big woodpile indicated major problems; a small pile indicated things had been going smoothly for everyone — except Roy!

Ralph A. Eaton
Principal, Peoples Academy, 1936-1949
Recollection, 1978

---

a PA education during this period was the 5,000-or-more-word essay which every senior had to prepare before he or she could graduate.

Robert E. Hasseltine, another long-time principal of the Academy, held the post from 1952 to his "retirement" in 1970. A native of Bristol, he was a graduate of the University of Michigan and a combat veteran of World War II. After teaching one year in Ann Arbor, Mich., he served at three other Vermont high schools before assuming the PA principalship. Following that "retirement," he taught one year at Lamoille Union High School before rejoining the PA faculty as a teacher and, from 1976 to 1980, as coach of the PA girls basketball team.

As for other historical highlights during this period, driver education was instituted at PA in 1953. That same year saw the establishment of an important support service for the whole school system: a guidance program.

In 1955 Town School District voters approved expansion of their

SCHOOLS

board of directors from three to five members, a number which has since been maintained.

In 1938 the superintendent of schools had urged that a school nurse be added to the local staff. A school nurse didn't happen but beginning that year and continuing at least until the early 1950's a public health nurse did serve a district encompassing the towns of Morristown and Stowe. Her duties included some health services to school children. Then beginning in 1954 a school nurse *was* engaged to serve the three town school districts of Morristown, Stowe and Elmore, which together comprised the Lamoille South Supervisory Union.

This is an appropriate place to review the history of that union. Under enabling legislation passed by the Vermont General Assembly in 1906, Morristown, Stowe and Elmore formed a union to share the services — and expense — of a full-time salaried superintendent of schools. Those are the same three towns which presently (1980) comprise the union. But it hasn't always been that way. In 1910 some Elmore citizens wanted to withdraw that town but in the end did not. In September, 1922 Hyde Park and Wolcott were added to the Union. But the expansion was short-lived, the original three-town union being re-established only a few months later. A longer-lived addition was that of Worcester, which remained a member of the Union from 1935 to the early or mid-1940's.

Superintendents of schools serving the Lamoille South Supervisory Union since its founding have been: Frank K. Graves, 1907-1910; Leonard F. Cole, 1910-1912; Carlton Howe, 1912-1922; Leonard Smith, 1922-1930; Ralph E. Noble, 1930-1932; Lee W. Thomas, 1932-1936; Edward L. Clark, 1936-1937; Milton G. Moore, 1937-1947; Rupert J. Spencer, 1947-1952; Charles P. Boright, 1952-1966; and Alfred W. Hurley, 1966-present.

The last of our somewhat arbitrary triad of periods for reviewing the history of Morristown's public schools is the years 1967 through 1980. It has been a period of significant changes, some of them representing major departures from well-established local educational trends, practices, or traditions.

As significant as any was a reversal of that long-sustained growth in Morristown's school population. Enrollments continued to grow from the 979 of 1966-67 to a peak of 1,117 in 1972-73. Student numbers have since generally declined to 942 at the beginning of the 1980-81 school year. The decline is interesting because it occurred at the same time that overall Town population was growing. A key factor which explains the apparent contradiction is that the Town's birth rate had declined, a characteristic currently common to both the state and the nation.

While the construction completed in 1967 relieved enrollment pressure in the upper grades, pressure continued to grow in the facilities for the lower grades. At this stage, Morristown joined Elmore, Wolcott and Stowe in studying the possible formation of a comprehensive union school district for kindergarten through grade 12. But the idea came to naught in 1968, leaving Morristown to go it alone on a needed new elementary school (the *supervisory* union remained intact, however). An important step came before any construction proposal was presented. That was Town School District voters' approval that same year of the purchase of several contiguous tracts of land totalling 50-plus acres adjacent to the approximately 25 acres already owned "on the hill." But voters first rejected the school board's proposal for a new school, then approved the necessary bonding in a second vote on the $1.2 million project. Construction began in late 1970 and was completed in early 1972.

Core facilities of the Morristown Elementary School, as it is known, include administrative offices, teachers room, library-learning center, area for special instruction, and multi-purpose room (the learning center was named in honor of Dorothy D. Sargent, who died in 1971; she had been an active member of the school board since 1962 and its chairman since 1965). These are designed to serve as many as 700 students, twice the opening and present capacity of about 350 (more classroom space can be added to the building). Attached are two major wings, or teaching areas. One is for six classes of youngsters, the other for eight classes. There are, however, no solid walls between the individual "classrooms!" That open arrangement — a feature in sharp contrast to Morristown's other school facilities — was designed to provide great flexibility in changing "classroom" sizes and facilities and to allow for use of a variety of teaching techniques. It was also cheaper to build than a comparable closed-classroom design. Appropriate sound-insulation materials — including rugs on the floor, which some voters thought was an extravagant luxury! — counteract potential noise interference between adjacent class areas.

While original plans called for transfer of Grades 3-6 to the new school, only grades 3-5 were actually shifted. That relieved overcrowding at both the north wing of the Peoples Academy complex and at the Graded School. Classrooms in the former have since been used for Grade 6 students and for teaching various high school subjects, while the latter has housed Grades 1 and 2.

Peoples Academy has continued to offer several courses of study leading to its high school diploma, namely, college preparatory, business education (formerly termed "commercial"), and general, the latter including various vocational offerings. A basic change from previous years is that beginning with the class of 1981: credit, course and skills requirements for a diploma are somewhat stiffer than those for preceding classes. A key reason for the change was the State-mandated requirement that all students demonstrate "basic competency" in the classic skills of reading, 'riting and 'rithmetic. Other specific changes in graduation requirements were the dropping of the senior essay in 1970 and of physical education about 1975. The latter was, however, added as a requirement on the elementary level.

As for curriculum, the early 1970's saw the first of a number of changes. Where all courses had been full-year courses, students were offered certain semester-length courses, a change which broadened their choices. Under the so-called Work-Study elective, a student can now combine some on-the-job training in the "outside world" with his or her classroom studies. And Title IX, a Federal law of 1975 which barred sex discrimination in public school courses, has had a definite effect on PA. Girls have since been taking previously all-boy industrial arts courses and boys have been taking previously all-girl home economics courses. Boys and girls also join in what previously were separate physical education classes.

As for vocational courses of study at PA itself, agriculture ended with the 1980-81 school year, but the home economics course con-

---

THE BOYS' HOME ECONOMICS COURSE

Last fall some senior boys asked Miss [Irene] McAlister this question, "May we take a course in cooking?" Mr. [Robert E.] Hasseltine [the principal], being a family man, understood and granted his permission. Soon eleven senior boys had signed up for a nine-weeks' cooking class, which was to be held during the Activity Period under the direction of Miss McAlister. ...

Donned in neat spotless aprons, the boys arrived at the kitchen the first day, all ready to enter that mysterious world of cooking. Now it was Miss McAlister's job to teach those eager beavers the art of baking, frying, boiling and roasting. ...

The class cooked cookies, cream puffs, cakes, doughnuts and pies. The food was edible even though the pies were low in the middle. ... The boys really enjoyed mixing the ingredients, but from the time the food was put into the oven, they waited with eager anticipation until the dish was taken out.

The recipes were always given to the boys the day before, thus they had plenty of time to study them. One day a certain member was detected searching the icebox. When asked "What are you looking for?", he answered, "I'm looking for the cream. This recipe says to cream the sugar and the shortening."

Bob [Peck] and Jimmy [Palmer] were the famous cake bakers. Stanley [Baker] topped these cakes with delicious frosting. Another specialty was Wayne's [Williams] doughnuts. These could be really enjoyed if you ate only the hole in the middle.

1953 *Peopleonian*

---

tinues. Vocational offerings have, however, broadened considerably as a result of a "shared time" program started in 1971 (and possibly earlier) with the Lamoille Area Vocational Center at Lamoille Union High School in Hyde Park. Courses there include food trades, machine shop, auto mechanics, building trades, graphic arts and child care.

Bernard C. Sheltra became principal of Peoples Academy in 1971, succeeding David I. Driscoll, Jr., who had served only one year, from 1970 to 1971. Sheltra, a native of Johnson where he still resides, graduated from Johnson State College in 1960. After some graduate work at Colgate University, he attended the University of Vermont and earned a master's degree. He joined the PA staff in 1963, serving first as a mathematics teacher and later as assistant principal before his elevation to the principalship, which continues at this writing.

And there have been these other significant developments for Morristown schools during this last period of review:

— The Morristown-Elmore Teachers Association was organized in 1970 as a result of a 1969 state law establishing a framework for labor relations with public school employees. The META represents the teaching staff in negotiations with the Morristown board of school directors for contracts regarding salaries, fringe benefits, grievance procedures and other matters.

— While no notice was taken at the time, the 1972 *Peopleonian* marked the publication's golden anniversary. Beginning in December,

---

STUDENT COUNCIL PROMOTES SCHOOL SPIRIT

The Student Council has been busy with several activities during the first semester. One big event was the Christmas Ball which was held December 18th. Couples dressed in holiday outfits danced to the music of [the] Hourglass [band].

One of the Student Council's main goals for the year is to promote school spirit. In order to meet this challenge, the council has planned several spirit events. Each class, grades 7 - 12, will be competing throughout the year to earn spirit points. The class with the most points at the end of the year will have their year of graduation engraved on the Spirit Plaque.

Two Spirit Events have already taken place. Points were awarded to the "loudest cheering" class at a Pep Rally last month. The juniors proved to be the class with the "Big Mouths"!!! They won first place in the contest. Green and Gold Day was the second spirit event. Students dressed in the traditional school colors gained points for their class. Faculty members wearing Green and Gold earned five points which they could designate to the class of their choice. The event was very successful; it was great to see such participation and spirit!!!!!! ...

By student Laurie Wilkins in *Peoples to People* (Vol. III, No. 2, February, 1980), newsletter to local citizens published by Peoples Academy

---

1922 as successor to another school publication, *The Scribbler*, the *Peopleonian* originally and for some years was a three-times-a-year literary publication of the senior class which contained fiction, poetry, school news and humor (and it cost only 20 cents an issue!). Later, and continuing to 1949, it was published twice a year, in December and June, with the latter issue taking on the characteristics of the classic senior class yearbook. The shift to that once-a-year appearance and format occurred with the 1950 *Peopleonian* and has continued to the present time.

— 1973 was another anniversary year for Peoples Academy. Arranging a celebration to mark the high school's 125th year was the Peoples Academy Alumni Association, itself now 81 years old.

— A very special piece of scientific equipment at Peoples Academy

SCHOOLS

was lost to thieves on September 19, 1974. They broke into the Grout Observatory and stole the brass casing of the fine Bausch and Lomb telescope mounted there. That, along with the observatory itself, had been given to the Academy in 1931 by George G. Grout. The observatory was designed by Morrisville's Morris C. Greene and built by his firm, the Morrisville Foundry Co. The telescope, apparently stolen for its high salvage value, was replaced by a "twice-as-powerful" one in 1975, thanks to the donated labors and skills of Arden Magoon of Stowe, an advanced amateur astronomer and telescope builder.

— Four months later the Academy was the victim of a horrendous incident of vandalism. Early in the morning of January 18, 1975 two teenagers got into the school and wreaked havoc, among other things by turning on fire hoses and flooding the place. The mess was eventually cleaned up and repaired — at a cost of more than $30,000.

— Following voter authorization at the 1975 town meeting, both the Town and Town School District changed their fiscal years from the calendar year to a July 1-June 30 year. After an 18-month transition period covering all of 1975 and half of 1976, the first of the new fiscal years was July 1, 1976 to June 30, 1977.

— Morristowners in 1975 again voted down a proposal to establish a kindergarten in the Town school system. It was the last of a series of defeats for the proposal at various town meetings going back to at least 1967. The matter has not been voted on since.

— On April 5-7, 1978 Peoples Academy students presented their 20th annual "Melody Minstrels," a stage variety show complete with interlocutor, end men, jokes, songs, dances and assorted high-jinks and climaxed by the leg-stretching strutting of the classic kake walk. Participation in this major extracurricular activity had grown from 40 or 50 students in 1959 to more than 100.

— 1977-78 and 1978-79 were bright years for PA sports and it was the girls who made it so. They won five state championships and had one near-miss in the two-year period. That compares to only two championships in all the rest of the school's history. The first of the earlier victories was in 1936 when the girls basketball team became state champions. And in 1955 the boys basketball team became champions of what was then the Class B division. The modern-day victory record began the fall of 1977 when the girls field hockey team reached the semi-finals of the Class I state championship play-offs. Then in 1978 both the girls basketball team and the girls softball team made it all the way to the top. Not only that but in 1979 both the latter teams repeated history by again winning the Class I girls titles in their respective sports. A key player on all these teams was Carol Kelly. In the spring of 1979 she added one more laurel for herself and PA by winning the state schoolgirls golf tournament.

> For more about Morristown's schools including individual histories of each of the old rural schools, see the "first draft" of *More About Morristown, 1935-1980*; details about what and where that is are in the Foreword.

THE RED BRIDGE

Chapter 4 - Roads And Bridges

WHO HAS BEEN RESPONSIBLE for how you get from here to there in Morristown? Which is to say, who has built and taken care of the Town's 90 or so miles of roads and assortment of bridges?

Operating under Vermont's general statutes relating to towns, the Town of Morristown itself, through its selectmen, basically had sole responsibility for local roads for the Town's first hundred years or so. The Town still takes care of most of them but in the second hundred years there have been several significant changes, notably in how the Town exercises that responsibility and in the shift of some Town roads to other government units.

Until 1892 the Town had been divided into highway districts, each with its own "surveyor." The surveyor was responsible for upkeep of the roads therein, using Town taxes allocated to his particular district. Residents could pay their highway tax, or at least part of it, by "working it off." Selectmen, however, retained basic responsibility for laying out, building, and maintaining Town roads. In 1892 a new law did away with the long-established district/surveyor system and established the position of road commissioner. Morristowners' record of sometimes electing and sometimes having selectmen appoint their commissioner has been described in Chapter 2.

The Town's first road commissioner, elected at the 1893 March meeting, was Isaac N. LeBaron. Others since then have been: Gilman A. Barrows, 1894-1911; E.E. Hadley, 1907-08 (Hadley served concurrently with Barrows; this was the only year that Morristown had two road commissioners); E.H. Eggleston, 1911-12; G.R. Currier, 1912-13 and 1915-16; L.M. Munson, 1913-14; Lee S. Allen, 1914-15, 1916-20 and 1930-56 (Allen is far and away the man with the longest tenure in this Town office); Delbert H. Welch, 1920-21; Guy S. Campbell, 1921-30; Wenzel C. Spear, 1956-63; and Rudolph C. Ward, 1963-present.

The year 1890 saw the first shift of some local roads away from exclusive Town responsibility. As recorded elsewhere, that year was marked by establishment of the incorporated Village of Morrisville, which took over maintenance of all the roads — now called streets — within its boundaries. Until 1907 Village trustees managed directly all street-building and maintenance operations. That year Morrisvillians created the post of superintendent of streets, to be appointed by the trustees. The first man to so serve proved to be the longest-term incumbent so far. That was Dana N. (Dane) Hutchins, who remained in the post until about 1929, or 20-plus years (Hutchins Street was named after him). Others since then have been Leon Lapalme, 1928(?)-44; Carroll R. Wheelock, 1944-50; Milford Denton, 1950-52; Rudolph C. Ward, 1952-72; Roger G. Cote, 1972-77; and William Moulton, 1977-present.

Two other laws in 1892 marked the start of the State's involvement with town roads. One created the Vermont Highway Commission, predecessor to what eventually became the Vermont Department of Highways. Another raised a special tax, revenues from which were used by the towns for their highways. A full history of State-town relations regarding roads is beyond the scope of this work. Suffice it to say that one or another systems for classifying town roads has since been used. And in varying amounts based on these classifications, the State has provided funds (both its own and Federal monies) to help pay for their rebuilding and improvement.

While the towns retain both ownership and responsibility for these "State-aid" roads, various town roads have, since 1931, been taken over completely by the State. State highways established in Morristown that year were portions of Route 15 and 100, just under 8½ miles altogether. As part of a final paving program for Rt. 15 in 1941, its original route into and back out of the center of Morrisville was shifted to the present route on the north side of the Lamoille River. But the stretch of the original route out Park Street and across Tenney Bridge remained part of the State highway system as Vermont Rt. 15A.

Even before it got its official number, Vermont Rt. 15 had an official name. In 1919 it became the Ethan Allen Trail in honor of Vermont's anti-New York and Revolutionary War hero. The special name remained for about ten years but then Rt. 15 lost it to another Vermont road. On September 20, 1930 U.S. Rt. 7 on the west side of the state became (and still is) the Ethan Allen Highway. Rt. 15 managed to get along without a name for about seven years. Then on July 25, 1937 it was dedicated (in Morrisville) as the Grand Army of the Republic Highway in honor of the well-known Civil War veterans organization, and has since been so known.

Vermont Rt. 100, a mid-state north-south route, was, like Rt. 15, established as a State highway in 1931. The stretch in Morristown, which was paved by 1936, follows, of course, what has long been known locally as the LaPorte Road. But on October 3, 1967 it, too, received an official State-designated name. That's the 43rd Infantry Division Memorial Highway, which name honors the U.S. Army unit which included many Vermonters and which served with distinction in World War II.

The last 2¼ of the present 12¼ miles of state highway in Morristown were added in 1956 or 1957. That's the stretch of main road between Morrisville and the Elmore town line which became part of what was first known simply as the Montpelier-Morrisville State Highway and, in 1966, became Vermont Rt. 12.

As for Morristown's town roads, one key element to their story for the last 50 or so years is the modest decline in total mileage. In 1931, the first year of State highways, all roads in Morristown totalled about 95 miles, of which about 8¼ miles were state roads and 86¾ were town roads. From then until 1960, town road mileage dropped more than 12 miles, the result of additional transfers to the State highway system and the conversion to "trails" of various back roads which became deserted as outlying farms were abandoned (the Town still owns the right-of-way of trails but is not obligated to maintain them). By 1978, however, town road mileage showed a slight net increase of about 2½ miles, the total being just over 76 miles. This resulted from the Town's rehabilitation of some former trails plus the addition of some wholly new roads to the town road system.

Two other major developments relating to Morristown's roads for the last 50 years can be stated briefly but are of great significance. One has been the general upgrading in the quality of the roads. This includes both their basic construction — improved width, grades, foundation, culverts and ditching — and that particular sign of modern times, pavement. In 1931 no town roads were paved; in 1979 about 27½ miles are hard-surfaced. The second development is the increased use of mechanized equipment, which over the years has become both more powerful and more sophisticated.

Before 1928 the Town stored its then mostly non-motorized road equipment, notably big snow-rollers, in sheds just off Brooklyn Street on Veneer Mill Road (MS34). That year the Town acquired property at the south end of Maple Street in the Village and, using timbers from the flood-destroyed Tenney covered bridge, constructed a new Town garage (or Town shed as it has also been referred to) (V2). Subsequently, that building was enlarged and other structures added to the complex. Then in 1978 the Town used a grant of Federal funds to build a new and much larger garage on Cochran Road (T12). The old Town garage promptly became the new Village garage, details of which transaction are given below.

Telling somebody how to find a back-road farm or residence was made a whole lot easier in 1977 when new wooden road-name signs were erected for all Town roads — something the roads apparently had mostly never had before. Morristown has, incidentally, close to a hundred different roads and each has an official town highway number. But a road name seems a lot nicer than a number and is probably easier to remember. Most of the signs have since been standing tall on their wooden posts, but more than a few have had run-ins with a snowplow or vandals.

Roads, or rather streets, in the Village of Morrisville have seen

ROADS AND BRIDGES

the same basic changes as the Town's highways, though the mileage itself has remained quite stable over the last 50 years: about one mile of State highway and about ten miles of Village streets (like the Town's roads, Village streets are eligible for varying amounts of State funds, depending on their classification).

As for pavement, Morrisville voters took an ambitious step in June, 1929. They voted to carry out an extensive program of concrete streets, curbings and new sidewalks for the several main thoroughfares in the central business district, specifically some or all of Bridge, Portland, Main, Congress and Park Streets and Copley Avenue. This apparently was the first street-paving to be done in the Village, though there previously had been some concrete sidewalks. The work was completed in 1931 and for some years thereafter Morrisville proudly advertised its "cement streets" as the mark of a vigorous, progressive community. By 1952 very nearly all Village streets had been paved.

At this point we might take note of that remnant of the horse-and-buggy days which gives Watering Trough Hill its name. The fancy six-foot-long granite trough on lower Main Street, carved to resemble a log and standing on stone "stumps," was made in 1906 at the local stone sheds of Mould and Davis. The Morrisville Woman's Club sponsored the community project and gave "liberally" to meet the costs; the Town and Village also "chipped in substantially." Water for the trough came not from the Village water system, however, but from a spring under East High Street just above it.

By 1966 mighty few horses were getting water at the trough — but a number of area residents were! Unfortunately the spring water had become highly polluted, so in October that year Water and Light Superintendent Willard K. Sanders announced that the trough would be disconnected from its source. "Henceforth," he said, "it will be used as a container for flowers and shrubbery." That eventually happened, but not for six years. In 1972 Morrisville's Girl Scout Troop 454 made care and beautification of the trough a project of the troop until it disbanded a few years later. The Scouts cleaned up the area and planted flowers in the old granite landmark. Several other organizations and individuals subsequently carried on the project. Then, contrary to Sanders' prediction, the trough underwent a reversion in 1980: it has since had water running through it — this time safe to drink. Village Street Superintendent William Moulton cleaned out the granite log and connected it to a Village water system main on East High Street. So far, however, we don't believe any horse has wandered by to refresh itself.

The story of Morrisville's street signs is given elsewhere in these pages. But it might be noted here that at least three of today's streets had different names in years gone by. Washington Highway was originally South Street. Bridge Street was Cottage Street before the bridge there was built (a different Cottage Street now runs off Randolph Road). And Congress Street started out by that name in 1879 when the first part of it from Main Street to Harrison Avenue was built. Then on Arbor Day in May, 1887 local residents planted elm trees along the street and for a short while it was called — what else? —

Elm Street. But a reversion to Congress Street occurred in 1889 when the street was extended southward.

And who knows where Main Street ends and Elmore Street begins? The change of name occurs at the first and main curve of Main Street as it leads out of the Village's business center (see the little dashed line marked on the street in the map of the Village). It seems that the early road to Elmore went straight at that point past the present Gerald Tripp home, continued to Tenney Bridge, and from there joined the present Elmore Road at what is now the Earle Welch (round barn) farm (T41). When the new and present road to Elmore was built in 1845, it initially "branched off" Main Street, a stub of the old road remaining in use for some years. The new road was thus called Elmore Street. So the Tripp home is the last one on Main Street and the former and long-time Wakefield home which is now owned by David Lowe is the first on Elmore Street.

While Morrisville does have street signs, one thing it *doesn't* have is parking meters. Some years ago Village trustees did think from

---

MORRISVILLE'S FIRST DUMP TRUCK

I can recall vividly seeing the Village street superintendent, Dana Hutchins, at work in the 1920's with his horse-drawn gravel wagon. He'd fill the wagon with a few inches of gravel, then drive it to the spot to be filled or graded. The bottom of the wagon was just heavy planks laid in place. Hutchins would first loosen and pull out one of those, and then the rest of the planks. Out spilled the gravel right where he wanted it. I guess you could say that was the Village's first dump truck.

Walter M. Sargent, Jr.
Recollection, 1979

---

time to time about that urban device for controlling parking (and producing revenues) but always rejected the idea.

As noted above, equipment, tools and supplies of the Morrisville Street Department are now housed in the former Town garage on Maple Street, which the Village purchased in 1978 (V2). For the Village the move represented a consolidation of three previously separate buildings and storage sites. The main and best known of these was the old Morrisville Fire Department stationhouse on Union Street (V3). The Village garage had been in the back part of that building until 1948. It expanded into the firehouse portion at the front when a new fire station was built on Main Street (C24). In 1978 the old Village garage was sold to a small industry, Clayhill Resources, Ltd., the history of which is given in Chapter 14.

Bridges are integral parts of roads and streets and, because they usually last many years, the larger ones at least become familiar local landmarks. Some basic history about each of Morristown's main bridges thus seems appropriate. First, however, what will probably be a confusing note needs to be made about whose bridges they are.

ROADS AND BRIDGES

Under a combination of general State law and the Morrisville village charter, the Town owns and maintains *all* bridges within its boundaries. That includes those within the Village even though, as noted above, the Village has full responsibility for its streets. A key exception in the area outside the Village is Tenney Bridge on Vermont Rt. 15A; as part of the State highway system, the State itself owns and maintains that. But what about Bridge Street Bridge within the Village? — Vermont Rt. 100 passes over that. True, but under State law, where a State highway passes through an incorporated village, the village retains basic control of that highway as a village street. Yet, as just noted, within *our* village, the Town still owns the bridges. So Morristown is responsible for Bridge Street Bridge, even though a State highway passes over it (we said this would be confusing).

Let's begin with Morristown's one remaining covered bridge, the Red or Chaffee or Sterling Brook Bridge over the stream by that name on the Cole Hill Road (the Chaffee name came from a long-established family living in that area). The Red Bridge, as it is now best known, is about 65 feet long with a five-foot overhang at each end. The truss of wooden beams is none of the classic kingpost, queenpost, Howe or Town trusses but a special one, apparently of local design, which is strengthened with iron rods. It has a metal roof and its board siding is painted the color which gives it its name (T13).

The bridge, originally without the iron rods, was built in 1896, but by whom is unknown. Early on, it had a brush with disaster but came out of it stronger than before. On October 16, 1897 the town was battered by "a gay old gale," as the *News & Citizen* described it. That left the bridge "badly out of gear." John Orville Reed, a resident of the area, was engaged to put things aright and it was he who installed the iron rods.

In 1968 the bridge's west end was discovered to have shifted. The old wooden structure was in poor condition in other ways so with help from the Vermont Department of Highways, the Town in 1971 carried out a major rehabilitation, replacing the west abutment and installing a wholly new steel and concrete span to support the wooden superstructure. As Town Clerk Sydney C. Mander described it at the time, "If the wind blows the covered bridge down, you will still have a bridge to drive over." Finally, Morristown's Red Bridge, along with all of Vermont's other picturesque and historic covered spans, was added in 1974 to the National Register of Historic Places, a program of the Heritage Conservation and Recreation Service of the U.S. Department of the Interior.

Many Morristowners may be surprised to hear this, but there is actually a *second* existing covered bridge within the Town's boundaries. It's for pedestrians only, however, and was built just a few years ago. Sited well up the Sterling Valley Road, the bridge is part of a luxurious six-story residence known as "Snow Palace." This was built in 1973 for Gar Anderson of Stowe as a summer-winter vacation home. From a parking lot just off the road, residents and visitors reach the house itself on the other side of Sterling Brook via the little covered bridge.

Morristown has had at least six other covered bridges, one of them a railroad, not highway, bridge. The latter preceded the local railroad's present steel bridge over the Lamoille River just upstream of the Bridge Street Bridge in the center of Morrisville. The covered bridge was built in 1890-91 as a replacement for an earlier wooden span. It lasted until 1934 when it was torn down and the present bridge constructed (V4).

One of the highway covered bridges carried Mud City Loop Road over Kenfield Brook. Little is known about the bridge except that it was torn down in 1939 and the present 80-foot-long concrete and steel bridge constructed in its place (T14). It is known as Putnam Bridge, after the long-time nearby farm of the Mayo Putnam family. Another covered bridge carried the LaPorte Road over Ryder Brook about a mile and a half south of Morrisville. It was one of the Town's 15 bridges and culverts which were carried away in the flood of 1927. It was replaced by the present concrete bridge (T15).

Three of today's well-known steel bridges over the Lamoille River each took the place of a wooden covered bridge. They were:

— Tenney Bridge: Miss Mower relates (pp. 279-80) how this landmark bridge was built in 1833 and was destroyed in the flood of 1927. The approximately 113-foot span was swept about a mile downstream. It was "recovered" but not as a bridge. Its beams instead were used in 1928 to construct a new Town garage at the south end of Maple Street (V2). Some time prior to his death in 1943 Dr. Walter G. Bridge of Massachusetts, a native Morrisvillian, built a beautiful and precise model of the Tenney Covered Bridge. Since 1959 that has been on exhibit at the Morristown Historical Society's Noyes House Museum. A classic steel-girder bridge replaced the historic wooden span, the new bridge opening for traffic on March 23, 1929 (T16).

— Cadys Falls Bridge: The covered bridge here was built about 1834. Apparently it was a simple truss of some kind because in 1895 a timber arch was added to strengthen it. This bridge was also destroyed in the flood of 1927. The present 120-foot steel girder span which took its place was constructed the following year by the American Bridge Co. of Albany, New York. The bridge has served since then but the years and elements have taken their toll, major repairs being made in 1970 and 1980.

— Power Plant Bridge (and Bridge Street Bridge): This little steel bridge across the great falls of the Lamoille River in Morrisville (V5) leads to the Village's power generating station there, where it dead-ends (before the flood of 1927 the road continued on as described elsewhere in these pages). Hence it is little seen by local residents, which is too bad. That's because it is quite a dramatic setting with the dam upstream and the river gorge downstream.

The 85-foot bridge was constructed in 1900 by the Vermont Construction Co. of St. Albans. Cost? Just under $1,500. The covered bridge which had previously stood on a site very near this one had been washed out by high water on April 1, 1886. After debating a few weeks about rebuilding there, the Town voted instead to build a "replacement" bridge farther upstream on the site of the present Bridge

ROADS AND BRIDGES

Street Bridge (V6).

The first bridge there was built of iron and was financed in part by private subscriptions from local residents. By 1925 it was badly deteriorated. So in 1926 the present steel and concrete bridge was constructed. Major planned rehabilitation work was carried out in 1974, and in July, 1975 a bit of *unplanned* rehabilitation was needed when a Vermont Department of Highways paint truck snagged itself on the bridge and sprayed paint over it instead of on the centerline of a road.

Morristown has had two other significant steel bridges, one now gone, the other soon to follow. Both were built in 1907 for part of a new road between Morrisville and Cadys Falls. That was needed to replace the old road flooded out by the damming of the Lamoille River to create Lake Lamoille.

The bridge over the Lamoille River at the end of Bridge Street (V7), long known as the Long Bridge, was indeed that: 264 feet, which at the time made it Vermont's longest one-span bridge north of Brattleboro. The concrete abutments for the 37-foot high trusses rested, and still rest, on solid rock on both ends. And solid the bridge remained for some years, among other things surviving the 1927 flood. But time and the elements had their effects. While major repairs were made in 1969 and 1970, selectmen in 1977 declared the bridge unsafe and closed and barricaded it. Construction of a replacement bridge is now scheduled for 1982.

The so-called Lake Lamoille Bridge, or Little Bridge, or Samoset Bridge, which crosses the lake's southwestern bay, was 61 feet long (T18). Time also took its toll there and by the 1970's its posted weight had dropped to 6,000 pounds. That a 6,000 pound bridge cannot hold up 50,000 pounds was demonstrated beyond doubt when a loaded logging truck collapsed the bridge on April 14, 1976 and plunged into the lake. Whether or not to replace the bridge sharply divided Town selectmen, but in the end, two of the three of them voted to rebuild. A local firm, Contractors Crane Service, was general contractor for the new steel and concrete bridge; it was dedicated in October, 1977.

Finally, a major new highway project for Morristown scheduled to begin in 1985 or 1986 is construction of a 1.8 mile bypass of Vermont Rt. 100 around Morrisville's central business district, this to relieve traffic congestion along the present Rt. 100 through the Village. The new limited access highway will leave the present Rt. 100 a few hundred yards south of the Union Carbide Corporation building on Jersey Heights (V31a), cross the Lamoille River on a new bridge just upstream of the Village sewage treatment plant, and connect with Vermont Rt. 15 opposite the Sunset Motel (MS17) a few hundred yards west of the present Rts. 15-100 intersection.

> For more about Morristown's roads and bridges including an account of the "Dugway" road controversy not mentioned here, see the "first draft" of *More About Morristown, 1935-1980*; details about what and where that is are in the Foreword.

Chapter 5 - Morristown Fire Department

"... the community's fire protection is second to none. The fire in the Centennial Block was not the first time that the Morrisville Fire Department had shown what its men were capable of doing, nor will it be the last. ... This small group of men are a dedicated lot who put their duty to the community above all else, sometimes even at the risk of their lives. ..."

SO EDITORIALIZED the *News & Citizen* following the disastrous fire of February 24, 1972 which destroyed a landmark building in the center of Morrisville. At one time or another probably most Morristowners have paid similar mental tribute to the Town's hardy volunteer firefighters who are willing to leave their bed, board or bath at a moment's notice to go face fierce heat, smelly smoke, sometimes freezing water — and frequent danger while they fight a fire.

And *Town* firemen they are, though their unit is still usually called the Morrisville Fire Department and its equipment and firehouse is so marked. The shift of this municipal firefighting service from a Village to Town function is perhaps the most significant change affecting the Department in the last 40-plus years. Other important developments since 1935 have been participation in formal mutual aid agreements with other municipalities, and three different fire stations to house trucks and equipment. Let's take a closer look at those, beginning with the last.

As of 1935, what was then the Morris*ville* Fire Department was located in the front part of the long and large wood-frame building which still stands on the north side of Union Street about midway between Congress and Summer Streets (V3). The building actually consists of three basic parts, the middle portion having a particularly interesting history which goes back well over 150 years. It began as a schoolhouse on Randolph Road in 1822 and was in three other locations before it got where it is now!

The third move and fourth site came the summer of 1897 when the building was shifted to its present site, being set back from Union

Street with a view to its expansion as the firemen's facility. The first addition to the building was made that same year — a hose tower on the east-front corner. Three years later a large two-story addition was built at the front. The big frame structure remained solely a firehouse until probably 1924, when the Morrisville Street Department moved into the schoolhouse portion. The present addition at the rear was constructed that year to provide additional space.

On September 22, 1949 a new fire station on Main Street was dedicated (C24). Measuring 40 feet wide by 70 feet long, the one-story structure had concrete block walls faced with red brick. The rear 18 feet were set off for the firemen as a "club room" for meetings, training sessions and social activities. Completed in 1950, the firemen themselves did the finishing work here and paid for the construction materials and furnishings.

It can't help but seem somewhat amusing when a fire department's own fire station house burns down. In early 1968 that's just what happened here but there was nothing funny about it. This is how Water and Light Superintendent Willard K. Sanders described the sad event in his 1968 annual report: "For the Irish, Sunday March 17, 1968 may have been a great day, but for the Morrisville Fire Department it was a stinker, for soon after noon the fire horn announced an alarm and the firemen arrived at the fire station to find it a raging inferno, and were scarcely able to save their new rescue wagon and old water truck, the other equipment being lost despite the heroic efforts to save it. It was a heart-breaking scene; there was a hydrant right in front of the fire station but all the hose was burning. ..."

The construction of a new fire station involved a basic question this time: should the fire department continue to be a Village responsibility or should it become a Town responsibility? In the end, Morristowners approved overwhelmingly — 224 to 69 — bonding by the Town of up to $150,000 for a new firehouse and equipment. With Morrisville's Oneal Demars, Jr. as the general contractor, construction of a new fire station proceeded during 1968 and on December 7 an open house marked its completion. The main part of the wood-frame-with-brick-veneer building measures 70 by 74 feet. At its southeast corner is a 32-by-40-foot meeting and social room for the firemen. This, too, was built and paid for mostly by the firemen themselves. The new firehouse (C26) is named the William Towne Memorial Building in honor of the man whose service as chief of the Morrisville Fire Department spanned three decades (and see roster below).

While Village trustees, at Town selectmen's request, continued to oversee Fire Department operations for a short time, 1968 represented the turning point for the Department as a Town rather than Village responsibility. The Town takeover was, however, more of a final step in a long-developing pattern of Town involvement — financial, if not administrative — in the Village fire service. As Elmore today pays Morristown for fire protection services, Morristown for many years had been paying Morrisville for its services in fighting fires located in the area of the Town outside the Village limits. Help to Morrisville for purchases of fire equipment was another major element of

Town aid over the years, specific appropriations for that purpose being made in 1924, 1948 and 1951.

One significant change involved in the Town's takeover of local fire services was the method of choosing top officers for the Department. Under Village administration Village voters themselves annually elected both the chief and two assistant engineers. Under Town administration, selectmen appoint the chief and two assistants but the appointments have been confirmations of the men elected to those offices by the firemen themselves.

The following is a roster of chief engineers since 1890, the year the incorporated village was established: C.A. Gile, 1890-91; George W. Doty, 1891-92 and 1900-06 (Doty also served as fire chief of Morris-

---

TRAVELING BY TRAIN

Word by phone from Johnson [about 8 p.m. June 20, 1895] told of the fire at the Buck steam sawmill two miles below. ... Morrisville firemen hustled their "Old Capitol No. 1" [engine] and hose to the depot, anxious to render any aid to Johnson if it might be possible to do so. The outfit was with some difficulty mounted on a flat car, and after a delay of nearly half an hour ... the "Swanton Special," a freight engine [and cars] ... was ordered to rush the fire apparatus to Johnson. Reaching the scene of the fire, it was with great difficulty that the machine was [put into service pumping water] ... but "she played beautifully" ... and very material aid was given in preventing the further spreading of the flames. ... It was a wild ride, indeed, going down with that apparatus held as it was by the men on an open flat car. Rushing on into the darkness they went at a terrific speed, the men crouched and swayed back and forth as they whirled along the curves. Cinders and soot spattered on their backs like hail, but they "got there just the same" and returned [about six hours later], ... a pretty tired and hungry group.

News & Citizen, June 27, 1895

---

town Fire District No. 1 forces for many years before Morrisville's incorporation, making a total of nearly 30 years in all, according to one source); E.W. Webster, 1892-1900; George F. Stevenson, 1906; E.M. Davis, 1906-07; William H. Towne, 1908-41 (yes, that's 33 years, the longest term of service for any Morrisville fire chief); Otto E. Blodgett, 1941-48; Louis D. Gilbert, 1948-49; Herbert H. Strong, 1949-55; Gideon S. Burnham, Sr., 1955-66; Robert B. Page, 1966-77; Raymond P. Hamel, 1977-80; and Wayne R. Camley, 1980-present.

Brief reference was made above to certain fire trucks purchased for the Morrisville Fire Department. The quantity of motorized equipment held by the Department has generally increased over the years, though with one reduction in the mid-1960's. From 1924 to 1949 there were two trucks; and in 1981 there are eight trucks. Space limitations prevent a detailed account of each of these but one that's certainly deserving of record here is the Department's 1924 Maxim pumper truck.

That was acquired new for $9,000 in 1924. Its color was red, and it had a 500-gallon-per-minute pump with hose. It was also originally equipped with a chemical extinguisher tank behind the cab. Following the Flood of 1927 the truck was called into extraordinary service, first in Johnson pumping out cellars in that hard-hit community, then for three weeks in Waterbury pumping out tunnels at the Vermont State Hospital complex buildings (Morrisville fireman Gideon S. Burnham, Sr. served with the truck during this trying period). Because of wear and tear which pumping all that muddy floodwater produced, the truck was returned to the factory in 1928 to have the pump rebuilt and a small (120 gallons) water tank installed in place of the chemical tank. The truck continued in active service until 1963 when Village voters decided to replace it. Though retired, it was not sold, however, and thus was still around at the time of the 1968 firehouse fire. Being stored in a barn some distance from the fire station, it escaped damage and subsequently was returned to active duty for several months until a new pumper truck replacing that lost in the fire arrived in Morrisville. That same year the firemen themselves bought the Maxim from the Town and during 1972 and 1973 they carried out a full restoration of the now-antique truck, spending about $2,000 in the process. The firemen have since showed off "the lady" (as they now affectionately call the truck) in ceremonial functions, local parades and at firemen's conventions around the state. In 1979, however, they voted to limit to about 20 miles the distance it could be driven under its own power to such events. Finally, the 1924 Maxim has attained the distinction of being the oldest piece of motorized fire equipment in Vermont which is still in the hands of the original fire department to purchase it.

Fire trucks, of course, don't themselves fight fires. Firemen do, which in our case means members of the Morrisville-cum-Morristown Department. Authorized size of the Department for many years was 22 members, *not* including the three chiefs who Village voters then were electing. About 1970, that is, after the Town took over the Department, that was expanded to 30 members, not including the chiefs. Since the Department was established, the minimum age for members was 21 but that changed to 18 in 1974 or soon thereafter (that was the year Vermont lowered its age of majority to 18). Throughout the Department's history members have been exclusively male. They also have been mostly, but not exclusively, native Morristowners. Related to this is the fact that local family tradition has been a significant factor in the character of the Department's membership, various pairs of fathers and sons or sons-in-law having both been members.

While they are volunteer firefighters, the Morristown firemen are paid for their time on duty. A complete record of their rates of pay over the years is not available but in 1954 Village trustees authorized a raise from $1.00 to $1.50 per hour of service fighting fires, from $1.00 to $1.50 for each summer practice attended, plus $.50 for each winter meeting attended. In 1981 the men are receiving $4.00 per hour for fire calls and $4.00 for each summer practice and winter meeting which they attend.

While paid for official services, members of the Morristown Fire Department are more than a number of men who come together "just" to fight fires. As a group they also have elements of a fraternal order and service organization. A measure of the first is their various social get-togethers. These include dinners at the firehouse which start off their monthly winter meetings. For some years the firemen also have had a family day each summer and a dance each spring (the latter in 1979 became an autumn event). As a service group they have regularly

---

LAUGHS WITH A LIFENET

Considerable amusement was created last evening ... on Portland Street when the firemen, out for a drill, tried out the new life net. Many young men and two heavyweights ascended a ladder to the roof covering part of the walk and jumped into the net below, which was held up on the shoulders of the men. All went well, however, until Dennis Cleveland, a 200-pounder, jumped and when he landed into the net some of the firemen bent low under the pressure, while others were heard to grunt.

Morrisville Messenger, August 27, 1924

---

donated time and effort to raise funds for, and to repair or improve, Fire Department equipment.

And here is a good place to mention the Department's Auxiliary, though it now no longer exists. Formed in 1966, the Auxiliary had its origins when some of the firemen's wives turned out to make and deliver hot coffee and sandwiches to the men serving at an extended winter fire. As an organization, they continued that support service, which also included cleaning and drying the firemen's clothing. To help the Fire Department in purchasing equipment or for other needs, they also had their own fundraisers. But in 1981 the Auxiliary dissolved, though some of the firemen's wives have continued their support services in an informal way.

A relatively recent development for the Fire Department has been the Town's involvement in so-called mutual aid agreements with other municipalities. Fire departments in neighboring communities in Vermont have long helped each other out on an informal basis in time of need. Informal arrangements, however, have sometimes breeded difficulties about the nature and extent of mutual aid obligations and related costs to the municipalities involved. To ease this problem, the General Assembly in 1968 passed a law which provided the basis for formal mutual aid agreements for fire services.

The first such system to take advantage of the act was the non-profit Capital Fire Mutual Aid System, Inc., which was chartered in September, 1970. This was intended to associate fire departments in a broad area around Montpelier, and a number subsequently did so. In March, 1972 Morristown selectmen decided to join the Capital system on a trial basis — a "trial" which continued to 1978 when the Town withdrew. A few years earlier there had been some difficulties with the towns of Hyde Park and Wolcott over fire services. A resolution came in 1976 when Morristown joined those towns in a closer-to-home mutual aid agreement. In 1978 that was succeeded by the present broader-based Lamoille County Mutual Aid Association, Inc. It is comprised of Morristown's and the six other municipal fire departments currently functioning in the county: Hyde Park, North Hyde Park, Stowe, Cambridge, Johnson and Wolcott. The agreement sets out arrangements under which each participating fire department can either request help from or be called upon to provide help to, another department or departments.

Fighting fires. That's what the Morristown Fire Department is mostly all about. We've mentioned the burning of the Department's own fire station as a fire of a very special sort. The following is a roster of some of the other major fires for Morristown since 1935.

On April 6, 1937 George C. Cole was killed when he fell from a fire truck on its way to assist fighting a fire in Stowe. He is the only local fireman who has been killed in the line of duty.

On March 1, 1947 fire destroyed the upper two stories of the Ferris Block on Main Street. Ray Sweetser, 29, jumped from the second-story apartment where the fire began; he was badly burned and other-

---

BAD NEWS FOR A FIREMAN'S SHOES

Today, for both insurance and safety reasons, a fireman absolutely has to be wearing his full uniform of hat, coat and boots or he can't serve at a fire. But a few years back things were more informal. Sometimes a man got to the station late without any of those things. But he'd hop on the truck and go to the fire anyway because he could wear some of the extra gear we usually carried along. And that's what happened one time with Wyvis Wells. It was back on May 4, 1963 when there was a bad fire at one of Bob Houle's chicken barns down on the Stowe Road. The alarm had sounded and Wyvis showed up in his street clothes — wearing a brand new pair of shoes. But off we went with Wyvis aboard and at the fire he got a coat and hat, but no boots. He helped us get the fire down, though we couldn't save the barn, only the nearby buildings. Of course, slopping around in the water and mud wasn't doing Wyvis's shoes much good. But what really did them in was this: when he steps inside the barn to hose down the last of the fire, he sank up to his knees in two feet of soggy chicken manure!

Alan J. Hayford
Assistant Chief Engineer
Recollection, 1979

---

wise injured and died later that day. Nine families were left homeless and a government agency office and two businesses on the ground floor received heavy smoke and water damage. One of the latter was the dry-cleaning business of Louis Ferris, owner of the structure, who rebuilt two years later (west end of Building C4, which is actually two adjoining blocks).

For loss of life the single worst fire in Morristown's history occurred early January 19, 1965 when a family of six all died in the blaze which destroyed their home on Bridge Street. Killed were Theodore F. Corey, his wife, Mary, and their four daughters ranging in age from one to four years.

The fatality in a fire on January 18, 1971 had a very personal association for Robert B. Page, then chief engineer. Destroyed was a two-story four-apartment building on East High Street at the intersection with Main Street. Mrs. Elsie Page, 75, mother of Chief Page, who with his wife owned the building, was overcome by smoke in her apartment and died of suffocation.

In what has surely been the Town's and Village's most serious conflagration in recent times, fire destroyed the Centennial Block at the corner of Main and Portland Streets (C57) early February 24, 1972. The blaze broke out in the third-floor apartment of Albert E. Styles, 19, at the north end of the block. He died when flames forced him to jump from his window overlooking Portland Street. Four ground-floor businesses were lost and 30 or so residents of apartments on the second and third floors of the three-section brick-facade block were left homeless.

A fire-related death was that of a prominent Morrisvillian, 71-year-old Ernest H. Clegg, on March 19, 1976. Fire struck and destroyed the large wood building behind his home on Wabun Avenue where he housed his monument business. The former police chief, constable, tax collector and cemetery commissioner suffered a fatal heart attack while watching the blaze. Clegg, incidentally, had presented as a gift to the Town the cornerstone for the fire station built in 1968.

As most any fireman will tell you, no fire is a good fire and the best fire is no fire at all. Though it hasn't been much publicized recently, Morristown Fire Department personnel for some years have done some work in the field of prevention, notably in conducting, when requested, fire safety inspections of local homes and businesses.

> For more about the Morristown Fire Department including individual histories of each of its fire trucks, see the "first draft" of *More About Morristown, 1935-1980*; details about what and where that is are in the Foreword.

Chapter 6

Morristown Police Department

CAN YOU BELIEVE this community once had 35 policemen? Not only that but it happened some 90 years ago when the Village was administering local police services, not the Town, as has been the case for the last ten years or so. Yes, very soon after Morrisville was incorporated on June 13, 1890 its trustees appointed 35 policemen to serve within the Village area. They didn't have uniforms and they didn't get paid. But then they also didn't have any training for their jobs and didn't serve regular hours. Mostly they were empowered to make arrests, which presumably occurred on a happenstance basis or when they were called out for a particular emergency.

The small army of Village policemen apparently lasted only a short time, because in 1894 trustees appointed just four policemen. The record is not clear but while these men were paid for time on duty, the amount of that duty was again apparently limited only to special times of need. In 1896 trustees appointed five police officers and this time they also designated one man as chief of police. That was Edgar H. Stone, who thereby became the Village's first person to have that title.

The year 1894 saw another significant development for law enforcement in the Village — it got itself a jail! Purchased for about $300, according to *News & Citizen*, was "an iron cage of two compartments ... [with] two berths in each compartment ..., giving a capacity for four prisoners." It seems, however, that there was actually mighty little iron in the jail. While sturdily built, it was a classic wood-frame structure. The entrance was a heavy timber door at one end and there were two windows. Across them were the jail's only iron bars.

The lock-up was first located behind the town hall on Main Street (C21). Then in 1903 it was moved to the back area of the Morrisville Fire Department stationhouse on Union Street (V3). The jail remained in this location until 1927 when Village trustees sold it for the lucrative sum of $20. (the structure was actually used for non-jail purposes for some time before its sale). The original purchaser subsequently conveyed it to Town and Village Clerk Ralph L. Barrows, who got it moved to Barrows' farm home on the Elmore Road (T44). There he converted the jail to a garage and it still serves that function.

Apparently the Village continued to have paid policemen on and off over the years — but mostly off. At a special Village meeting in 1934, however, Morrisvillians approved a proposal to hire two policemen — one full-time and a part-time assistant. Trustees subsequently appointed Ernest H. Clegg and Wallace Strong to the two positions, the former full-time, the latter part-time. Strong remained on the job only a few months but for Clegg it was the start of his subsequent many years as Morrisville's first *full-time* chief of police.

Clegg served continuously until 1953, then returned to the office in 1964 and served until his retirement February 1, 1969. Other Village chiefs of police have been: Earl A. Magoon, 1953-56; no regular police officer engaged, 1956-58; and Delmar L. Magoon, 1958-64. The Town has had one chief of police so far, note of which will be made shortly.

While Clegg was Morrisville's chief of police, he was, for the most part, chief of a one-man department — himself. But occasionally the Village engaged other police officers for part-time duty and Clegg supervised them.

The evidence is skimpy but it's the writer's impression that Morrisville (and by implication Morristown) saw relatively little serious crime in the late 19th and early 20th centuries — public intoxication getting the most regular mention in the local newspapers. Perhaps for a time before World War II, and certainly after the war, motor vehicles and all the frailties and misdeeds of their drivers — accidents and traffic and parking violations — became a principal concern of Clegg and his successors.

During this post-war period and continuing through the early 1960's there were also certainly some "minor" crimes — breach of peace, vandalism and petty larceny, and even some "major" crimes — grand larceny and burglary or breaking and entering. However, according to annual police department reports which began in 1959, the numbers of these crimes, particularly in the latter case, were generally very low, that is, only one to four a year. But during the latter 1960's the local crime rate took a major jump and has generally continued to increase ever since. Three comparisons bear this out: there were three burglaries in 1959 and an average of 37 for 1970 through 1978; for grand larceny, principally auto thefts, none were reported in 1959, while an average of 24 occurred over most of that same span of recent years; and where there were but two or three cases of vandalism each year in the early 1960's, the number of incidents — including some very serious ones — has averaged 50-plus a year so far in the 1970's, with a high of 100 in 1978 alone.

As for crimes of violence, Morristown managed to get through nearly two centuries of existence without a killing among its populace. When that did happen, the town experienced not just a single, but a double murder. Found dead on March 26, 1979 by Morristown police were Clifford N. (Junior) Manosh, 49, and Mrs. Earlene Camley, 33. The scene was Bridge Street Road across Kelley Point of Lake Lamoille. Both persons had been shot in the head with a revolver, with Manosh's body found lying across the front seat of Mrs. Camley's car and her body found in the woods a short distance from the car. Subsequently arrested and charged with two counts of first-degree murder was Seth W. Camley, 37, who was Mrs. Camley's estranged husband. He pleaded innocent and his trial, shifted under a change of venue to the Orange County Superior Court, was held in December.

While admitting to the killings, Camley's defense was that he shot Manosh in self-defense in the belief he had a shotgun with him, and that he shot his wife "in the heat of passion" after seeing her and Manosh engaged in a sexual act when he found them together in the car. Deciding he had acted with both malice and premeditation, the jury on December 20 found him guilty of first degree murder in Manosh's death. In Mrs. Camley's death the seven women and five men convicted him of second degree murder on the basis he had acted with malice but not premeditation. He was subsequently sentenced to life imprisonment for the Manosh murder and 15 years to life for the murder of his wife. Then in a major turn of events in early December, 1981, the Vermont Supreme Court overturned both convictions. In a unanimous decision, the Court ruled that the trial judge had improperly instructed the jury. While awaiting the appeal, Camley has been imprisoned at the St. Albans Correctional Facility. He may well face a new trial, but that was not certain at this writing.

To deal with Morristown's increase in crime, the one-man police department of Ernest Clegg has long since been left behind. And with the department's growth also came a change from Village to Town administration. It was not a simple one.

Very briefly, beginning in April, 1967 there were actually *two* distinct municipal police departments: Town selectmen hired Lawrence C. (Bud) LaClair, Jr. as their one-man department, who worked in conjunction with the Village's one-man department, Ernest Clegg. The following year selectmen and trustees effectively created a single police department, Town and Village each bearing half the expense. In late 1969 (by which time Clegg had retired) there were three officers, with LaClair the chief (technically, at that point, the "officer in charge").

But supervision remained a joint Village-Town affair — and that proved troublesome. In addition, serious policy and personnel problems developed over the next several years. The upshot of these assorted difficulties was trustees' acceptance of selectmen's offer to take over the police department as an exclusive Town responsibility, beginning November 1, 1975. It has been that ever since.

LaClair has continued to serve as chief of the Morristown Police Department. The number of regular officers under him was varied between four and five, plus two or three special officers.

A significant step to curb public drinking and the rowdy behavior of local young people with which the drinking was associated was taken by Village trustees in August, 1977 by adopting two ordinances. One, the so-called "open bottle law," prohibits the drinking of, and even carrying an open container of, any intoxicating beverage in certain defined "public areas." The second, the "breach of peace ordinance," makes unlawful certain behavior tending to provoke or make likely a public disturbance. Town selectmen adopted almost identical ordinances in September, 1979.

As for police headquarters, after some earlier locations, an office for the department was established in early 1968 on the second floor of the Town building on Main Street (C48). Then about May, 1971 the office was moved to the ground floor of a building at the extreme west end of Main Street. The approximately 9-by-18 foot office, small by any terms, soon proved miniscule for the by now significantly enlarged Morristown Police Department. Resolution of the problem took the form of a little manna from the Federal heavens — a grant of $256,000 from the Economic Development Administration with which was constructed the Morristown Public Safety Building (C2). But not without a major controversy along the way.

Initially, the building was, with minor exceptions, to serve the Police Department exclusively. But then, with construction well underway based on a design by Nelson Paus Zilius Architects of Hyde Park, selectmen developed a proposal to move all the Town offices to the new building (after which the existing Town building would be disposed of). But at a special town meeting May 8, 1978 Town voters overwhelmingly rejected the proposal, 53-289. General contractor Oneal Demars, Jr. promptly resumed construction, basically following the original plans. The structure was dedicated on November 4, 1978 as the Ernest H. Clegg Building.

As a result of other action at that special town meeting, a special Police Study Committee scrutinized another proposal by selectmen, this "for contracting out the work of the Morristown Police Department." Concerned over mounting costs of the Department, they believed the Lamoille County Sheriff's Department could be a viable but less costly alternative. But in the end, the Study Committee voted unanimously that the Town continue its own police department and not contract out for such services.

> For more about the Morristown Police Department including information about other crimes of violence, and about the one-time jail and police court here, see the "first draft" of *More About Morristown, 1935-1980*; the Foreword describes what and where that is.

MORRISVILLE DAM AND POWER PLANT

Chapter 7

Morrisville Water And Light Department

AS A MUNICIPAL PUBLIC SERVICE, that furnished by the Morrisville Water and Light Department has direct impact on probably more people than any other service of either the Town or Village. Water is supplied to nearly all Villagers plus a fair number beyond the Village boundaries, particularly on the north side. Electric service is far broader, extending throughout most of Morristown and into five other towns.

The capital facilities of the Department's electric and water systems have expanded significantly over the years since 1935. These changes will be detailed below but first a look at some general aspects of the Department.

As noted elsewhere, the Water and Light Department is governed by a board of five elected water and light commissioners with terms of office of five years on a staggered basis. A roster of the commissioners since the Department was formed in 1895 appears in Appendix 1. But note should be taken here of the lengthy tenures of certain of the commissioners, all of it true public service for no remuneration was ever received by any of them (or any other commissioners). Those serving 30 or more years have been: George M. Powers, 44 years (1895-1939); Levi M. Munson, 43 years (1917-60); Charles H. Slocum, 40 years (1895-1935); Charles H.A. Stafford, 35 years (1902-37); and James O. Reed, 30 years (1934-64).

Under Morrisville's charter the commissioners have broad authority for managing the Water and Light Department. But they must get approval of Village voters for long-term borrowing and otherwise are subject to such bylaws as voters may enact. There have been relatively few of these and their status is now somewhat uncertain. But among other things they empower the commissioners to change electric and water rates. For the former, however, they can only propose rates which are subject to a final determination by the Vermont Public Service Board (earlier known as the Public Service Commission). As for water rates, the Water and Light Board, so far as is known, has always proposed rate changes to voters for their approval.

Until 1904 all Morrisville electricity was produced solely for Village residents. While others could buy Morrisville power after that year, Villagers continued to benefit in another way: they paid less for their juice than the "outsiders" did. That favorable discrepancy for Morrisvillians, which had prevailed in earlier rate schedules, was formally justified on the basis that they and their property were at some risk for any Village indebtedness incurred for the electric system. But one suspects it was really more of a fringe benefit for Villagers as owners of that system. In any event, the Public Service Board formally frowned on the practice in its 1972 order authorizing a rate increase which began late that year. The lower rates for Morrisvillians continued, however, until a new rate schedule effective on July 3, 1979 ended the longstanding discrepancy.

While those outsiders were paying more for their electricity, both they and Morrisvillians themselves for many years were paying bargain rates. The Village's very first electric rates of 1895 were said to be "as low as any known in the United States." The later record is somewhat uncertain but definitely in 1915 and 1942 and probably for all the years between and a few years beyond, the rates were the lowest in Vermont, at least for residential customers. More than that, in 1942 the residential rates were the lowest in all of New England. In 1951, when higher rates went into effect, Morrisville apparently lost that distinction but its rates have continued to be lower than those of most other utilities in Vermont.

Even while Morrisville's electric rates were so pleasantly modest, the Water and Light Department most years was still making a "profit," which is to say, net income remaining after deduction of operating expenses, debt retirement, and at least some capital improvements. As such, it sort of became the Village's "sugar daddy," voters regularly appropriating portions of the surplus for different purposes instead of raising taxes to do so. Throughout these pages note is made of the various ways those profits were used. But the ultimate came in the years 1934 through 1945 when Water and Light Department profits paid for *all* Village expenses and Villagers levied no taxes on themselves at all. The situation changed when, in 1972, the Public Service Board effectively ended the free-for-all disbursement of Water and Light Department profits. In determining an allowable electric rate increase which began late that year, the Board limited to $7,500 a year what the Department could (and still can) transfer to the Village treasury. That has represented a payment in lieu of Village taxes on the Department's own property in the Village.

The Water and Light Department's office was in several different places until 1911. That year it moved to the building just north of

WATER AND LIGHT DEPARTMENT

the present Ben Franklin Block on Portland Street (the northeastern portion of Building C83), where it remained for 12 years. Then in December, 1923 it moved across the street to the Fisk or Warren Block (C58), where it remained for 25 years (that building was torn down in 1972). In early May, 1948 it moved to the front room of the Masonic Temple at the corner of Portland and Brigham Streets (C62). That was supposedly a temporary move, the Water and Light Board and staff anticipating a move to another site. But those plans never developed and 31 years later the office is still there. An addition to the office on the building's north side was constructed in 1976.

Since its founding in 1895 the Department has had but four superintendents, three of them with very long service. The first was Fred Dow, who served from 1895 to 1900. Succeeding him that year was Calvin A. Slayton, who proceeded to serve for the next 40 years. Slayton played a major role in the Department's various expansion projects during that period, most of them described on pages 247-56 of Miss Mower's history.

Joining Slayton's staff on August 11, 1924 had been Willard K. Sanders, a native Morrisvillian who had graduated from Peoples Academy only a year earlier. It was the start of what proved to be Sanders' lifetime career with the Water and Light Department. He succeeded Slayton as superintendent and treasurer in 1940 and served in both posts until March 5, 1973. He stepped down then as superintendent but continued on a part-time basis as treasurer and advisor until July 1, 1977, when he fully retired after 53 years of service. Like Slayton, he also was involved in various capital projects and general expansion of both water and electric services. Details of these are provided below.

As Superintendent Sanders had earlier joined his predecessor's staff, so his successor joined Sanders' staff. That was Robert B. Page, who though not a native Morristowner, was about as close as you can get, being born and brought up in neighboring Stowe. He joined the Department in July, 1950 and was appointed assistant superintendent in 1964. He succeeded Sanders as superintendent in March, 1973 and continues to so serve at this writing.

Sanders was a knowledgeable, and at times, ingenious, engineer and a generally able administrator. But today he is certainly most remembered for his annual published reports. For they became a grand local institution and from time to time brought Sanders himself and Morrisville into state, even national, prominence via various publications. These include articles in *Yankee* and *Vermont Life* magazines and several pages in Ralph Nading Hill's book, *Yankee Kingdom*. His reports were in large measure straightforward, factual accounts of each year's projects and activities (much of this history has been drawn from these). But they were also liberally laced with reminiscences, anecdotes, witticisms and jovial comments on everything from kids to kilowatts. Samples of those writings appear here and there throughout this chapter.

Let's now take a look at the basic facilities of the Village's water and electric systems, picking up from their status as of about 1934.

Taking the former first, at that time the Village was drawing its water from two places. One was the so-called Bugbee Springs on the north side of Vermont Rt. 15 about a mile and a half east of the intersection with Vermont Rt. 15A, the other a group of springs on the north side of Elmore Road in the area opposite Elmore Mt. Road. Water from the latter ran into the reservoir off Elmore Street in the Village (V35). Water from the former reached the Village via a pipeline through the Dugway and along Park Street. Pumps in the basement of the Town Hall (C21) distributed the water or, when demand was low, pumped it to the reservoir.

Because of the risk of fire at the Town Hall, these pumps were moved in 1934 to a new concrete pump house at the end of Park Street. Apparatus to chlorinate the water was also installed at this time, a first for the water system.

By the end of the 1930's demand was nearing or exceeding the 285 or so gallons-per-minute flow of the abovedescribed springs (plus one other smaller one down hill from the Elmore Road springs). So in 1940 the Water and Light Board set about to find a new source of supply — this time to be a well. The site finally selected was the so-called

---

A SANDERS SAMPLER: GETTING THE WORK DONE

The transformer, 20 feet tall, 10 feet square, weighing some 40,000 pounds and costing about 75 cents per pound, was landed near its permanent site and after three days of tugging, lifting, straining and freezing it was finally landed on its foundation. The men of our line and water crews are to be complimented upon bringing this work to a successful conclusion under conditions which were most discouraging. ... Several winch cables and one or two of the Ten Commandments were broken during the process. (1956)

Brigham Meadow, part of the farm of Melville and Bernice Brigham along Vermont Rt. 15A just downstream from Tenney Bridge. Water from a drilled well and its new pumphouse began flowing to the Village via the Bugbee Springs main on February 6, 1943.

At that time the Elmore Road springs were sold and use of the Bugbee Springs ended. Though held in reserve, the latter, with a few brief exceptions, have never since supplied the Village (several residents and businesses in the immediate area of the springs do, however, draw water from them under a special lease arrangement). The transmission main from the springs is still in place, including its crossing of the Lamoille River, but it is disconnected from the rest of the system just beyond the river. In 1969 the Water and Light Board proposed that the springs and 110 acres of surrounding land be sold but voters defeated the proposal. So the Village still owns the property.

While the Bugbee water was generally healthful and the collection system adequate, it seems there had been problems from time to time. Or so Sanders indicated when he wrote in his 1969 report that "it will be recalled ... that in the 'Good old days' when we were using the

Bugbee springs water, Russ Graves one day had a robust frog emerge from his kitchen faucet, and Ed Edson had a full blown salamander exit from his."

Though the Brigham water was also good water (and without any indigenous wildlife), it *was* different from the Bugbee Springs water. Among other things, the former was (and still is) very slightly acidic, while the latter was strongly alkaline. And the Brigham water is soft, though less so than the Bugbee water. As for the purity of the new water, at least some Villagers were convinced they were drinking seepage from the far-from-pristine Lamoille River. But the river and the water-bearing subsurface stratum are separated by a thick and impervious layer of clay. And the water has invariably passed tests for purity conducted by the Vermont Department of Health.

The site of the Village's first well proved to be a significant one: three other wells, both new and replacement, have since been established there. In 1952 a new well, No. 2, was sunk about 250 feet upstream of the first. It began service in early 1953. But problems developed with this well. So in 1962 it was abandoned after a replacement well was sunk only about eight feet away.

By 1969 Sanders was reporting that Well No. 1 was "showing signs of giving out." So Layne New England Corporation of Arlington, Mass., which had done all the previous well prospecting and drilling, was engaged to drill and install a third well, this one about 200 yards downstream from the first. Well No. 3 was basically completed during 1973. This third well was one step in other major developments for the system. Before describing those, however, one other significant matter might well be noted here.

In 1970 Village voters approved fluoridation of their water. The equipment was installed that year and has since been operating. In describing the proposal in his 1969 report, Sanders noted that improved dental health was expected to be one result but added that "those with store teeth will not benefit to any great degree." That is still true but a study in 1977 showed that fluoridation was helping those with real teeth: local schoolchildren in grades 1-3 were experiencing 57% fewer cavities.

As for those major developments, in 1945 the Water and Light Department purchased a mile-and-a-quarter right-of-way for a second water main connecting Brigham Well No. 1 directly to the reservoir near upper Elmore Street. And in 1943 the Department purchased a portion of what was known as the Hale farm, several hundred yards out Center Road from its intersection with Vermont Rt. 15. That was to be the site for a second reservoir. However, it was 20 years before the first happened and 35 years before the second happened!

The Village water system faced two related problems. What Sanders referred to in 1964 as the Village's "Model T reservoir in a jet age" held (and still holds) about 500,000 gallons. As has been noted, the reservoir was supplied with water via a pipeline through the Dugway from Bugbee Springs and later from the Brigham Meadow wells. One of the two problems was that only so much water could be pumped through that six-inch main. As water usage mounted, there were increasing occasions, and at least one real crisis in 1964, when the reservoir was emptying faster than it could be filled. Of equal, if not greater, concern was the true emergency which would result should the Dugway pipeline ever rupture or give way — a prospect that landslides in that area made more than a remote possibility.

The first problem was resolved in 1965 and 1966 when a new 10-inch cast iron pipe was laid between the Brigham wells and the old reservoir. Resolution of the second took another 12 years. After assorted complications and defeats by voters of certain early funding proposals, a major Federal grant was received. That in combination with State funds paid for the complete water project. Not a drop of local funds was needed.

In addition to a 1,500,000 gallon, 110-foot-diameter, 30-foot-high, wire-reinforced concrete reservoir at the Hale farm site, the project included the laying of a 16-inch/12-inch main between the new reservoir and the existing Village system, and a 12-inch main from Brigham Well No. 3 to the other new main. Work began in late 1976 and was successfully completed in early 1978. At that time, noted Superintendent Page with his own touch of annual report humor, "A malfunction in an altitude valve at the reservoir gave us some trouble but after some rather uncomplimentary urging decided to open."

Since completions of the new mains and reservoir, water has come exclusively from Well No. 3, with Wells No. 1 and No. 2 held in reserve. And all pumping is done at the wells with the Park Street pumps now by-passed. Here it might be noted that the length of all mains in the Village system from 16-inch to one-inch has gone from 11.63 miles in 1952 (no 16-inch mains then) to 20.96 miles in 1978.

"We now [turn] to the Electric Department with its constant historical repetition of development, expansion, redevelopment, more expansion, and still more redevelopment to enable it to take care of its ever-increasing demand for power." So wrote Willard Sanders in a history he prepared in 1951 of the Water and Light Department's first 55 years. While local demand for power has continued to increase substantially since then, how the Department has met that growth has changed significantly. Instead of developing new or expanded facilities to produce locally the additional needed electricity, the Department basically has been purchasing it from other sources. More on that shortly but first let's review the Department's major capital projects since 1935.

In 1943 to 1945 the Lake Lamoille dam and some of the facilities at the Cadys Falls power plant (T47) were completely rehabilitated. The 1906 concrete dam, which is 371 feet long, had apparently been constructed in fairly rudimentary fashion and was leaking badly. And various improvements were made in 1946 and 1947 at the Cadys Falls plant. Among them was construction of a 26-by-30-foot brick and concrete addition on the north side of the original powerhouse structure. Housed in this was a new 700 kilowatt generator and appropriate waterwheel and related facilities. With the 600 kilowatts of the original generator, that more than doubled the plant's generating capacity to its present 1,300 kilowatts.

While important, this project was far overshadowed by another one taking place in the hinterlands northeast of the hamlet of Garfield in Hyde Park and extending into southeast Eden, areas long known respectively as the Lower and Upper Diggins. That was construction of a large dam and sizable dike to create the Green River Reservoir.

Development of the wilderness area's power potential had been on the mind of its several owners since early in the 20th century. But no power project ever came to reality (the U.S. Army Corps of Engineers also considered the area for a time as the site for a flood control project). The area was mostly timberland which had been heavily lumbered until the early 20th century. It was cross-hatched by several streams (including the Green River itself) and seven bodies of water with the following assortment of names: Great, Clear, Dead, Long, Round, Hyde and Half Pound Ponds.

For eight years the Water and Light Department studied the idea in conjunction with the Public Electric Light Company of St. Albans (later to become part of the Central Vermont Public Service Corpora-

> **A SANDERS SAMPLER: OPERATIONAL PROBLEMS**
>
> The usual cats were removed from our poles during the year, the bucket of the new line truck capably serving to assist in this project; some of the cats were as hot to handle as an energized transmission line. One raccoon also felt the need to crawl between a pole and a transformer for warmth, and upon getting across the primary terminals, created his own illumination, and the last time I saw him, appeared to have been somewhat overheated. (1968)

tion). That utility owned and operated hydro-generating facilities at Fairfax and Milton on the lower Lamoille River and thus could benefit greatly by controlled additional flow in the river. The upshot was a contract signed in 1945 under which the Village would own and develop the project, and the Public Light Company and the Village would share the expense over a 36-year period (beginning in 1950) on the basis of benefits to the respective parties. That year the Village bought nearly 6,000 acres of land and an assortment of rights: water, penstock, powerhouse and transmission. Cost: $190,850.79.

There were three major elements to the project. One was the clearing of some 600 acres of the main flowage area. Another was the 248-foot-long, 20-foot-high earth dike at the Reservoir's easternmost point. This plugs the only low spot in the hills surrounding the Reservoir (other than the Green River outlet itself). And the third was, of course, the dam and related facilities. Those include two gate-houses and a weir just downstream. That's a concrete structure which controls erosion by dampening the force of water discharging from the dam. The arched dam, made of 10,300 yards of concrete, is 320 feet long, 110 feet high, 40 feet thick at the base and seven feet thick at the top. Sanders once described it as "flood-proof, earthquake-proof and water-proof."

Basic function of the dam is to impound water for controlled release when needed downstream, both at Morrisville's two generating plants and those of the Central Vermont Public Service Corp. As one might expect, one usual period of draw-down is July through September, when flow in the Lamoille River is generally very low. But another, which actually drops the Reservoir much more dramatically, is generally January through March. That's the time of year of greatest electricity demand by customers.

Charles T. Main, Inc. of Boston did the engineering and supervised the construction. The O.W. Miller Company, Inc. of Ludlow, Mass. was general contractor for all three phases, subcontracting construction of the dike to Derrick DeGroot of Jericho.

Work began in April, 1946 and by June the dike was completed. Pouring of concrete for the dam began on August 20, 1946 and continued until December 14, at which time it was about two-thirds complete. Other work in the dam area and the clearing carried through much of the winter, construction of the dam proper resuming in May, 1947. Then, as Willard Sanders reported in the *News & Citizen* of August 7, 1947: "Saturday morning, Aug. 2, without fanfare or ceremony, the last section of the Green River dam was poured. It had at last become a concrete structure, not only literally but abstractly: a thing of beauty, and, we hope, a joy forever, or at least for 200 years." Finally, in October one of Lamoille County's largest civil engineering projects was complete. Total cost, including real estate: $848,675.67.

When full, the Reservoir contains 758 million cubic feet of water with a maximum depth of 90 feet. It covers 625 acres with some 16½ miles of shoreline, all this at an elevation of 1,220 feet above sea level. That makes it the nineteenth largest of the more than 500 lakes and ponds in Vermont including the state's two boundary giants, Lakes Champlain and Memphremagog.

The Reservoir itself abounds in fish, notably pickerel (some of monumental size!), perch, sunfish and bullheads, and its surrounding woodland is wholly undeveloped. This serves as a public recreation area for boaters and canoeists, snowmobilers, hunters and fishermen. The Water and Light Board has not promoted such recreational use, but it does permit, even welcomes, it.

While many have indeed made good use of the area for recreational pursuits, tragedy has come to one angler. That was 60-year-old Clyde W. Jewett of Morrisville, who drowned on August 12, 1956 while fishing on the Reservoir.

In 1952 (and possibly as early as 1948), the Lamoille County forester of what was then the Vermont Forest Service began applying professional forest management techniques to Morrisville's 5,400-plus acres surrounding the Reservoir. In 1959 what has since been known as the Morrisville Village Forest was, under a state law, designated a municipal forest — the largest in the state (it actually includes other woodland property of the Water and Light Department, notably Bugbee Springs, the Cadys Falls dam area, and the Hale farm property, bringing the total to about 5,500 acres). Under the designation, the Village agrees to manage the forestland in accordance with approved forestry principles.

Since completion of the Reservoir, the Water and Light Board has made two significant additions to its land (and water) holdings in that area, both to the east of the "big pond." In 1950 it purchased 300-plus acres, part in Hyde Park, part in Wolcott. The tract includes several ponds, the largest being Zack Woods Pond (the other major ones: Perch, Mud and Little Mud Ponds). And in 1958 the Board acquired Little Clear Pond and a two-rod strip of surrounding forestland. This served for "protection of our water and flowage rights," according to Sanders' report that year.

A related development concerning the Green River real estate was the Department's suit in 1968 against the Town of Hyde Park. The Department claimed that that town's assessment of its property for tax purposes was "excessive" (under Vermont law, a municipality can levy property taxes on another municipality for any land, but not improvements, which the latter owns within the former's boundaries). While a Vermont Supreme Court decision in 1970 and subsequent lower-court

---

A SANDERS SAMPLER: TOPICAL AFFAIRS

Observation of the Hula-Hoop fad this past summer has led us to speculate that if all the energy expended in the manipulation of these hoops by our young people could have been harnessed, synchronized, and integrated, we would have had, for the time being, at least, an unrivaled supply of cheap, tax-free electric energy ... (1958)

---

action provided a basis for settlement, the matter is again under litigation at this writing (1981).

So that basically is the story of the Green River Reservoir project. One significant element not noted above, however, is the fact that the project's original plans included provision for one generating station at the dam and others downstream on the Green River. More on that shortly but first a look at two other major capital projects.

One was a new penstock connecting Lake Lamoille to the Cadys Falls plant. Constructed in 1906, the 1,000-plus-foot-long original penstock had been worn thin by the constant flow of water, and otherwise was badly deteriorated. So in 1961 a new steel penstock, 1,150 feet long, was fabricated by Vermont Structural Steel, Inc. of Burlington and installed by a local contractor, Blow and Cote, Inc.

Among other things, the project involved an extended draining of Lake Lamoille, the third, and possibly the fourth, time this had happened since the lake's creation in 1907. During the one-month dry spell the lake's bed "sprouted a luxuriant growth of swamp grass," a circumstance which confounded at least one seaplane pilot. He expected to land on Lake Lamoille but couldn't find it and ended up putting down on Lake Elmore.

One other facility of the Water and Light Department continues to be its dam of 204-acre Lake Elmore and the associated water rights. This serves a similar role as the Green River Reservoir, though on a much smaller scale and under a key restriction not applying there: the water won't be drawn down between June 1 and Labor Day, the summer camping season. By 1943 the old dam was leaking so badly that it was completely rebuilt that year. The old wooden gatehouse was retained but after "a playful zephyr" blew that down in 1945, the present gatehouse of brick was built.

This list of capital projects properly should also include a full description of the Village's transmission and distribution lines, both original and larger replacements, with all their substations, transformers and assorted other gadgetry which makes the whole electric system work. Suffice it to note the expansion and present status of the system with a few statistics. About two miles each of transmission and distribution lines in 1895 had grown to slightly over 29½ miles of transmission lines and 110 miles of distribution lines by 1952, and to about the same transmission mileage and about 175 miles of distribution lines as of the end of 1978. The 60 or so charter customers grew to 1,312 by 1952 and in 1979 numbers some over 2,500.

A SANDERS SAMPLER: LOCAL HISTORY

The [incandescent] light in the "square" by the [Randall] hotel was named "Jacob Walker" after the first settler in Morristown, it being the consideration of a deed of right-of-way for a pole line across Josh Merriam's farm, now under Lake Lamoille, that the light be so named. Of course, this light was taken down when the new [mercury vapor lights] were put up last summer, and inasmuch as we later purchased the entire Merriam farm and flowed it, we do not feel that we have jeopardized our holdings in so doing. Unlike Deacon Walker, who was a model of temperance, his electrical namesake was lit every night for 57 years. (1952)

They are distributed throughout the Village's service area, which for some years has included, besides the Village itself, most of the outside Town (the area generally west of Tyndall Hill is served by the Vermont Electric Co-operative of Johnson), and parts of the towns of Elmore, Wolcott, Stowe, Hyde Park and Johnson.

One change in the character of Department operations and revenues came in 1946. The Water and Light Board decided that year to end the Department's long-standing practice of providing house-wiring installation and repair services and of selling and renting various electrical appliances (that, the Board felt, was better left to the private sector). For example, in 1907 it was renting out electric flatirons for $1.00 a month plus ten cents a week for power used.

Another change was the end some years ago of Morrisville's sales to wholesale customers, mostly municipalities. So served at different times were the Waterville Light and Power Company and the Villages of Stowe, Johnson and Hyde Park. The latter was the last wholesale customer, its final purchase contract ending in 1969.

In contrast to the Department's now-absent wholesale power sales has been its long-increasing power *purchases*. Morrisville's first purchase contract was in 1928 with the Green Mountain Power Corporation (GMPC). It has been buying some of its power ever since, both from the GMPC and a number of other sources. Those include some St. Lawrence Seaway power via the Power Authority of the State of New York (beginning in 1958) and Vermont Yankee atomic power (beginning in 1972). The percentage of purchased power remained very low through the 1930's and into the 1940's. But by 1955 it had reached one third, by 1964 it was about half and in 1978 it was about three quarters (31.6 million kilowatt-hours purchased out of a total load of 42.1 million kilowatt-hours).

This continued growth of the amount of purchased power *and* its ever-increasing costs has been a key factor in financial woes for the Department in recent years: it had deficits in five of the seven years, 1972-78, and again in 1980.

Morrisville has recently taken two significant steps in this regard. One is participation in the Vermont Public Power Supply Authority (VPPSA), which was created by a 1979 state law. Through it, certain of Vermont's municipal utilities and certain electric cooperatives are joined together in developing generating facilities and/or bargaining for purchased power from available suppliers.

The other is very much a local step to reduce the amount of power Morrisville has to purchase. Now planned are significant additional generating facilities, these to be built in two stages. The new facilities will bring to reality those long-ago plans at the Green River Reservoir. Constructed at the Reservoir dam will be one 1,800 kilowatt generating plant. This is scheduled for completion by early 1983 at a cost of about $3.2 million. Another 1,800 kilowatt generating plant will be established on the Green River about a mile and a half from the Reservoir and just below the hamlet of Garfield. This is expected to be completed in 1985 at a cost of about $3.6 million.

Also underway at this writing (September, 1981) is resurfacing and other rehabilitation of the 250-foot concrete dam at the Morrisville generating station (V33). Cost: about $250,000. The capacity of this plant's two generating units is 1,800 kilowatts.

Power from the new facilities is expected to be generated primarily during peak period needs, from 4 to 8 p.m. weekdays during the wintertime. This will produce the greatest economic benefits for Morrisville system customers because purchased peak power is substantially more expensive than base power.

Finally, the reader might wonder why the Green River generating facilities were not built sooner than is now to be the case. It was a question of economics. When power demand accelerated in the 1950's the Water and Light Board didn't develop those facilities because by that time and continuing for some years, it was cheaper to buy power elsewhere than to build more local hydro-generating facilities.

For assorted other details about all aspects of the Morrisville Water and Light Department, see the "first draft" of *More About Morristown, 1935-1980*; the Foreword tells what and where that is.

LAMOILLE LANDFILL AND SALVAGE DEPOT

Chapter 8 - More Town And Village Services

They've dammed her up in Morrisville;
  Made a little lake;
Old folks sit around her,
  Their pleasure to take.
The trout would like to live there,
  But the taste is much too strong;
One drink of Lake Lamoille, and they'd
  All be dead and gone.

They're cleaning up our river,
  Sterilizing our stream.
It will be the purest
  That you've ever seen.
You can run it in your bath-tub,
  Even drink it, too.
They're changing the Lamoille
  From dirty brown to blue.

SUCH IS ONE VERSE and the chorus of Rev. John Nutting's comical-topical "Lamoille River Song" which he wrote about 1965.*
It's comical for obvious reasons and topical because of efforts then underway in Vermont to halt and reverse years of pollution of the State's waters, the Lamoille River among them. A principal control step at this time was the "capture" and treatment of municipal sewage. With major injections of State and Federal funds, various Vermont communities were moving to construct new sewage collection systems and treatment plants. Among them was the Village of Morrisville.

Its project consisted of two basic elements. One was a *partial*

---

*Copyright 1974 John Nutting, Used by permission.

separation of collection systems for sewage and storm water runoff. Previously a single system of underground pipes collected both sewage and storm water — and dumped it all, untreated, into the Lamoille River. For the new arrangement, some 15,000 feet of new storm sewer lines were installed, leaving the existing pipes to carry sewage only. In addition, some 16,000 feet of sewage interceptor lines were installed. These carried the sewage to the project's other basic element, a sewage treatment plant (V9), or in the official phrase, water pollution control facility. The project began in 1972 and was completed in 1974.

The plant is situated along the Lamoille River on the south side of Bridge Street. The system of treatment is known as "extended aeration." The raw sewage first passes through several mechanisms for removal of rags and other large floating debris, and of heavier materials, mostly grit and stones but also an occasional pair of false teeth! After then passing through a grinder to break up sewage's most familiar ingredient, it reaches one or the other of two aeration tanks. Rotors churn the sewage to add oxygen, an element essential to "digestion" of the organic material by certain bacteria which are a key part of the whole system. The aerated sewage then passes into settling tanks. Here the bacteria-laden sludge settles out. Other steps follow but the nearly-clear effluent, after treatment by chlorine to kill harmful micro-organisms, passes into the Lamoille River — a whole lot purer than what entered the system.

It might be emphasized here that it is the Village, not the Town, which owns and operates the sewage collection and treatment facilities. Village taxpayers are paying part of the capital costs of the project through Village bonds. But the expenses of maintenance and operation of the system are financed by a user's fee, a schedule of which was first established by Village trustees in September 1974. Earlier that year the Village board had also adopted regulations governing use of the public sewage system. Owners of property lying beyond a specified distance of the public system are required to install a private sewage disposal system of some type. Requirements for those are spelled out in a set of health regulations which serve both the Village and the outside Town. They were jointly adopted by Village trustees and Town selectmen in February, 1973.

Having described how one form of human waste is handled locally, let's look at another. That is rubbish. Its history involves, like assorted other municipal services, both the Town and Village.

What presumably was the Village's first public dump was situated well out what is now known as Farr Avenue off Washington Highway (V10). It is uncertain when that was established but it was definitely functioning as of 1935. That year Morrisville voters authorized municipal rubbish and garbage collection for themselves. There may have been a break in that service about 1941 but in 1942 voters reauthorized the service. It has been operating ever since with Village trustees contracting from time to time with a private operator to do the work.

In 1958 trustees established a new dump off Trombley Hill Road on the Village-owned Hale farm property (T19). But drainage problems forced an early abandonment of that.

At this point the Town entered the picture. Trustees and selectmen agreed on arrangements for joint operation of a new dump to serve both municipalities. The site for that was, and still is, property owned by Foss, Phelps and Fagnant, Inc. a short way out the Garfield Road (T20). And a classic dump it was, with no fancy procedures like what were later to be the case.

But it was not to last, for in 1970 the Town assumed full responsibility for the dump — or rather sanitary landfill. Under mandate of new State regulations, the Town had to apply new techniques to control pollution and protect public health. Basically, these have involved concentrating deposits of debris in a systematic way, then compacting each day's accumulation and covering it with a layer of fill. Thus the name "sanitary landfill."

Finally, in 1973 the operation assumed a significant new status, one which has since remained in force. Selectmen began paying a private contractor to operate the landfill. That was Lamoille Landfill and Salvage Depot, Inc., a corporation formed and managed by Emery F. Foss, Jr.

Another public service long a responsibility of Morristown and all other Vermont towns is no more. That is care of the poor. As reported in Chapter 2, the State in 1968 took over administration of welfare aid. But for many of the years that Morristown did have that responsibility it used a poor farm as major means for housing and feeding the needy. Miss Mower has provided some information on this but let's take a closer look.

The Town's first poor farm, the one jointly owned and operated with Johnson and Stowe, was located on the west side of LaPorte Road about a mile and a half north of the Stowe town line. On September 19, 1895 all buildings on the farm were lost in a fire reported as "evidently of incendiary origin." Because of various problems there was no rebuilding and this joint poor farm was sold in 1897, the three towns going their separate ways.

Morristown subsequently bought and sold several of its own poor farms. The last, previously the M.H. Boardman farm on Randolph Road, was acquired in 1933 (T21). A number of small cottages (apparently ten or more) were subsequently constructed for individual residents. By 1954, however, poor people were no longer being supported at the farm and in 1955 Town voters authorized its sale.

Though general care of the poor by the Town ended, one relatively little-known Town "agency" has long provided certain special services to such persons. That's the Morristown Health Committee. Voters created it in 1945 to administer a local appropriation to aid needy youngsters with eye examinations plus eyeglasses and sometimes eye surgery. Later the program expanded to include dental, hearing and speech examinations and appropriate therapeutic services. For a time in the early 1970's the Committee also sponsored pre-school children's health and immunization clinics, until the State set up a program of so-called "well-child" clinics.

In sharp contrast to these services to the poor has been the modern-day development of Town involvement in a wholly different public service. That is recreation. The record is a bit uncertain but with one interesting exception, support of a recreation program with local tax monies began in 1949. More on that in a moment but first a look at the exception.

The 1930's marked the start of what today is a major element of Vermont's economy, the ski industry. America's first ski tow began operation in 1934 in Woodstock. Three years later the first tow in Stowe began pulling skiers up Mt. Mansfield's slopes. The success of Stowe entrepreneurs led residents in other Lamoille County towns to try the same thing.

A number of prominent Morristown citizens were among those who in 1936 established the Lamoille Valley Winter Sports Club (LVWSC). The club sought to develop and promote local winter sports facilities. Participation by local residents was strongly encouraged but the principal purpose of the effort clearly was to boost the local economy by attracting tourists.

A major — even monumental — endeavor of the Club was construction and operation for the 1936 winter of a long toboggan chute on the south side of Bridge Street Road on Kelley Point. As *The Vermonter* magazine later described it, "[The workers] went over and over the slide with their watering pots until it was coated with glare ice. Boy, how a toboggan would go down that chute ... 1800 feet in 11 seconds. It levelled off across a long field and they had to leave loose snow for the last 200 feet to keep riders from going to Kingdom Come."

When the LVWSC's private effort faltered, a new organization got Village voters to appropriate funds in 1938 for the toboggan chute (and certain other winter sports facilities) as part of "a system of Public Recreation," that is, something for local residents, not visitors. But the chute lasted only that year and the Village recreation appropriation only about two more years.

After what appears to have been a nine-year absence of any municipal recreation program, the Town school system established one in 1949. It's uncertain how long this arrangement lasted but in 1957 Town voters created the Morristown Recreation Committee to continue or re-establish such a program for local pre-high-school-age youth. For the first two years the program was limited to summertime. This consisted of both morning and afternoon sessions, the former providing a variety of supervised activities — games, crafts, sports, and the latter swimming instruction at Lake Elmore. Apparently beginning the winter of 1959-60 the program became bi-seasonal with re-establishment of a skating rink across from Academy Park at the intersection of Copley Avenue and Park Street. With certain additions, that has been the basic pattern ever since.

One addition actually began before the Town recreation program did. That was Little League Baseball. First established in 1955, it has grown to a major summer program for both boys and girls, with teams from a number of Lamoille County towns participating. The local teams and local program have been managed for some years by the Morrisville Baseball Association, an organization of volunteers separate from the Morristown Recreation Committee.

Along the way, there has also been a significant capital project for recreation. Based on plans developed by the Recreation Committee and built in 1973 were two tennis courts directly behind Peoples Academy, and a playing field and other recreation facilities on a

---

TOWN AND VILLAGE: SO WHO'S CONFUSED? - #1

To clear up the confusion which exists in the mind of some voters in regard to Town and Village sharing the cost of some worthy proposed project, it is to be remembered that two-thirds of the Grand List of the Town is concentrated within the Village limits. Take, for example, the [special health] appropriation which we agree is money well spent for the benefit of all the children and adults residing both within and without the Village limits and which benefits the whole Town. In checking your Town and Village reports you will find that the bulk of this load is carried by the Village taxpayer and results as follows: For this project the Town appropriates $400.00 of which you people within the Village limits pay two-thirds, or $267.00, plus your own Village appropriation of $778.00 (amount requested from Village by State this year), of which, if voted, you will pay 100 percent, making a grand total of $1,045.00 which you will pay in taxes, leaving only $133.00 of the $1,178.00 for those of the Town, residing outside the Village limits, to pay. Therefore, it is well to remember when voting at Town Meeting that you bring not only unequal, but double taxation upon yourself unintentionally through the confusing Village-Town taxation setup when you agree to share any part of the cost of a beneficial Town project in this manner. In other words, projects that benefit the entire Town population, which includes the Villagers, should be provided 100 percent in Town Meeting and projects that are a distinct benefit to the Villagers only should be dealt with at Village Meeting.

Morrisville Annual Report, 1949-50

---

site off Elmore Street well above the Academy.

Morristown and Morrisville are changing and today two forms of municipal regulation are shaping what and where that change is occurring. One is an official plan, the other is zoning bylaws. They were some time in coming and started out in reverse order from that normally prescribed.

Zoning bylaws (or regulations or an ordinance, as they are variously called) divide a municipality into different zones and prescribe what uses — basically residential, agricultural, commercial and industrial — may be made of land within the zones. They also set out particulars for such authorized uses, for example, the size of allowable lots and the distances of a permitted structure from the boundaries of its lot. Such regulations not only control the use of land but can serve a variety of other purposes: stabilizing or reducing the costs of public utilities and services, enhancing public health and safety, and controlling visual appearance.

Local consideration of zoning began in 1953 and continued off and on until 1968, by which time there was general realization that appropriate zoning would be difficult without first having a "master plan" for the Town and Village. That year Town and Village voters in 1968 approved formation of a joint planning commission. With both funding and technical assistance from the Lamoille County Development Council, which also serves as Lamoille County's regional planning commission, and with the services of a consultant, the Morrisville-Morristown Planning Commission created a municipal development plan for the Town and Village. Selectmen and trustees in late 1972 adopted the proposal as the official municipal plan. The plan was amended in

---

TOWN AND VILLAGE: SO WHO'S CONFUSED? - #2

Note: Additional expenses of $4,875.63 were shared on Police Department expenses. Use of Town equipment amounts to $1,103.23, making a total of $5,978.86 due the Town. The Village sold its grader to the Town for $1,500.00 and the Town would have paid over to the Village a share of [State] highway money amounting to $3,810.65 — making a total of $5,301.65. Deducting the $5,310.65 the Town owed the Village from the $5,978.86 the Village owed the Town leaves $668.21. This figure is reported under Miscellaneous Expenses under the heading, "MISCELLANEOUS."

Note at end of "Summary of Orders Drawn by Trustees," Morrisville Annual Report, 1969-70

1976, and further amendment is under consideration at this writing (1981). The plan deals with past and projected population, highways, and — the largest item — land use, both existing and proposed. Different uses are defined in the text by different zones and delineated on accompanying maps.

Well before adoption of the Town/Village plan, both selectmen and trustees had, in May, 1971, adopted something authorized by Vermont statutes: "interim zoning." Basically, this provides a means for some control of land use pending adoption of permanent zoning bylaws. For the Village those came in 1973 and for the Town in 1976. In 1978 both Town selectmen and Village trustees adopted several amendments to each of the two municipalities' respective zoning bylaws. They are still in effect at this writing.

The two zoning ordinances are certainly one significant element of municipal regulation which has come to Town and Village. But it is by no means the only one. Mention was made earlier of certain "police" ordinances (one defining breach of peace, the other prohibiting open alcoholic-beverage containers on public property) and of sewer-use and health regulations. There are others as well.

Adopted by Town selectmen in December, 1973 (with an effective date of February 10, 1974) was a "Housing Maintenance and Occupancy Ordinance." This, which covers all of the Town, including the Village, specifies conditions of space, sanitation, light, heat, ventilation and safety which the owner of any dwelling for one or more families must provide and maintain for its inhabitants.

And last but not least is a local legal leash on loose or loud canines. The Town has such an ordinance. The first version, adopted by selectmen in 1975, was notable for its brevity: exactly four sentences. The second, adopted in June, 1976, is more elaborate. It prescribes that any and all Morristown canines must be collared and licensed, can't run at large, and can't "disturb the quiet of any ... person by barking, howling or biting or in any other manner." Violations mean that the owner can be fined and/or the dog can end up in the hoosegow, that is, the dog pound. But the dogs also get some protection: the ordinance prohibits cruelty to them.

Finally, to close out this chapter we might note the obvious: the local public services described above have been a mighty — and sometimes confusing — mixture of Town and Village services. Several have always been one or the other. Others have involved Town and Village either in some joint fashion, or in the shift of services from the latter to the former. This complexity has led in recent years to two studies of — but no final action on — a basic question: wouldn't a single local government make more sense than two? Or more specifically, shouldn't the Village of Morrisville simply dissolve and merge back into the Town of Morristown. A number of other Vermont towns and incorporated villages have done so, either by a special act of the General Assembly or under general statutes which provide for local adoption of a "plan of merger."

In 1966 Morristown and Morrisville voters authorized creation of a committee to study the matter. In April, 1968 the committee issued a report of its findings but little appears to have come of that.

Then in 1974 and 1975 a committee of the Morrisville-Morristown Joint Planning Commission studied the question again. In a preliminary report the committee listed advantages and disadvantages of a merger (there were many more of the former than the latter). But while it continued to meet for a time, the committee eventually dissolved without any final report or recommendations. Since then there has been no further active consideration of the merger matter.

> For some, but not substantial, additional information about these municipal services, see the "first draft" of *More About Morristown, 1935-1980*; the Foreword describes what and where that is.

Chapter 9 - Other Town Facilities

THE TOWN AND VILLAGE SERVICES described so far have often involved municipally-owned property in some way. It was, however, the services themselves, rather than the property, which was generally in the forefront. A number of other municipal functions — all Town-sponsored — remain to be described in which land and/or buildings have a particularly distinctive role.

Town Hall

The first is no more. That's the town hall, which stood on the south side of Main Street near Academy Park (C21). For over a hundred years that's where Morristowners gathered for their annual and assorted special town meetings. Marking the shift of the Town's center of gravity from Morristown Corners to Morrisville, the new hall was constructed in this new location in 1854-55. Originally a single-story structure, it was "severely simple in line, but substantial in form," according to a history of the hall written by Willard K. Sanders. Then in 1869, as Miss Mower recorded, a second story was added by the local Masonic lodge. As for the Town-owned first floor, in 1899 it underwent a major rehabilitation plus the construction of a 17-foot addition on the rear end to provide space for a stage and related facilities, including a classic drop curtain.

As for other uses of the town hall, Sanders records that "the old hall [was] the locus of many gatherings of all kinds, aside from those relating to the business of the Town: lecture courses, concerts, fairs, promenades, dances, local talent plays, travelling troupes, religious conventions, war-bond rallies, Peoples Academy commencement exercises and that perennial, admission-free attraction, White's Medicine Show ..."

1951 was the beginning of the end for the town hall when a recreation program for teenagers was shifted to the newly-constructed gymnasium and other facilities at the Peoples Academy complex. There were other starts and stops along the way but in 1967, for the first time, Morristowners held their annual meeting at the auditorium of Peoples Academy. Then in 1968 the old town hall was torn down, the land being divided and sold to the two neighboring home-owners.

The PA auditorium continued as the place for town meetings through 1974. Then in 1975 the meetings were moved to the Copley gymnasium, where they have been held ever since.

Town Office

Another important Town facility has always been that housing the town clerk's office. We should say the town *and* village clerk's office because the person serving as Morristown's clerk has almost always served as Morrisville's clerk. And that same person for a long time has also been treasurer of both municipalities.

We don't have a full record by any means, but in 1912 the Town office (as we shall call it) was established in rented space on the ground floor at the north end of the Centennial Block (C57). A vault for records was constructed at the rear of the building at that time. When, in 1939, the Union Savings Bank & Trust Company was constructing a new home-office building on Main Street (C49), its previous quarters next door, constructed in 1892, became available (C48). Town voters subsequently authorized purchase of the brick structure and the town clerk's offices were moved there about May 1, 1940. They have been there ever since. The Town has leased the second floor to various parties, the school superintendent's office of the Lamoille South Supervisory District being housed there since about 1970.

Two significant additions to the building occurred in 1973, the year following destruction by fire of the Centennial Block. A new, additional vault for Town records was built on the east side of the building. This was interlocked with the new building constructed for Lucien and Hazel Renaud on a portion of the Centennial Block site (C47). Also constructed that year was a two-story addition at the rear of the Town building. That gave more space on the first floor to the town clerk, listers and other local officials, while the school superintendent has used the extra space on the second floor.

Cemeteries

Another Town facility is its eight cemeteries, which Miss Mower described (pages 280-83). Pleasant View Cemetery, the newest of the eight, remains the largest. With two additions since 1893, it now covers about 20 acres, some of which is wooded and/or on steep ground not suitable for burial sites. One other major change since 1935 was a new brick holding vault constructed in 1963. It replaced the original vault, which had to be abandoned because of limited capacity and drainage problems. That first vault was built in 1894.

Administration of the cemetery is divided between the Pleasant View Cemetery Commission and the Pleasant View Cemetery Association. The former, composed of five commissioners who are elected by Town voters to five-year terms on a rotating basis, serves as the Town's

OTHER FACILITIES

agent in owning the property. It is the Commission which sells lots, and which acquired the additional land for enlarging the grounds. It also handles purchases of capital equipment for care of the cemetery.

The Pleasant View Cemetery Association (PVCA), a non-profit corporation, is responsible for maintenance of the cemetery grounds. It employs the sexton and his staff and pays for supplies, equipment repair, etc. How the PVCA finances the upkeep changed significantly in 1978, with the change also reflecting how the Commission and PVCA are interlinked.

At the risk of oversimplification, under the earlier system, an annual fee paid by lot owners produced the income to pay for PVCA's upkeep of the cemetery (some lots were, however, endowed for that purpose). Today any new lot purchased must, in effect, be endowed at the outset. Specifically, a person now pays the Commission $75 for a single cemetery lot. The Commission retains $25 of that (for its capital expenses) and transfers the other $50 to PVCA as endowment for perpetual care of the particular lot. The PVCA invests the $50 principal (with other endowment funds), and uses only the income for maintenance expenses.

Two other notes about PVCA: Its officers are chosen by the lot-owner members at their annual meeting in April. As for income, the PVCA for most of its years has also received an appropriation by the Town. The amount has increased from time to time over the years, being $2,000 in 1980.

Combining what the Pleasant View Cemetery Commission and Association do for that cemetery, the Morristown Cemetery Association (MCA) serves as both owner and maintainer of the Town's seven other cemeteries. In 1978 it established a funding system very similar to PVCA's. The only difference is that relating to the $75 which a purchaser pays for a lot: $10 is for the lot itself and $65 is for the perpetual-care endowment. Town voters traditionally have also appropriated funds for the MCA; the amount has also increased from time to time, standing at $2,500 in 1980.

The MCA differs from the PVCA in certain other respects. Anybody interested in the organization, and not just lot-owners, may become a member. And when those members meet annually, also in April, they choose the usual officers *plus* a board of trustees. There are seven of the latter and by tradition each "represents" one of the seven cemeteries. The following is a brief review of notable changes at, or other information about, each cemetery:

Wheeler Cemetery (T26) — About one third of an acre in strips along the south and west sides was added to this cemetery in 1974.

Mountain View Cemetery (T27) — With its high open elevation the name of this cemetery remains very appropriate. About a half-acre was added along the southwest side in 1961. A monument of particular interest here is that of Jacob Walker, Morristown's first settler. In 1957 the Morristown Historical Society, with appropriate ceremony, marked Walker's grave and monument in a distinctive way with a special metal sign. That is still in place.

Greenlawn or Plains Cemetery (T28) — In 1965 a one-rod-wide strip was added along the east end of this smallest of the Town's cemeteries. Part of this cemetery has been set off for burial of the poor.

Randolph and LaPorte Cemeteries (T29 and T30) — There have been no significant changes in either of these. The LaPorte Cemetery also has some space set off for burial of the poor.

Lake View Cemetery (T31) — This cemetery also remains basically unchanged since 1935, with one exception: trees grown up around it now block off any real view of Lake Lamoille, the source of its latter-day name. Also, lots are no longer available in this cemetery, though burials continue to be made in lots previously purchased.

Riverside Cemetery — Like Lake View, all lots in this cemetery have been sold, with only an occasional burial in a previously-acquired family plot occurring from time to time. The ornamental, black-painted arched iron gateway at the entrance was acquired by the Morristown Cemetery Association in 1923 at a cost of $213.15. Sadly, this cemetery has been hard hit by vandals on several occasions, with gravestones being broken or knocked over. Other of the cemeteries, notably Wheeler and Pleasant View, have also been damaged by vandals in recent years.

Town Forest

Some Town property which the author suspects few residents are aware of is our municipal forest. The Town Forest, not to be confused with Morrisville's vast Village Forest surrounding the Green River Reservoir, consists of two separate tracts of woodland. They are located on the west side of Morristown, the area which formerly was part of the town of Sterling.

The larger tract, totalling an estimated 393 acres, consists of three parcels acquired by the Town in 1958 and 1959, two because of a special circumstance. It seems that a bad storm washed out part of Town Road 43. That led to the farm where Robert Sulham and his family were living in what were already difficult circumstances. Faced with a major expense to rebuild the road, selectmen were able to buy the 173-acre Sulham farm, for $1,700, having arranged for the family's resettlement on other property north of Morrisville. That was early in 1958. About the same time the Town acquired, for $750, the 133-acre Jerome Smith farm farther out the same road. The Smiths, too, were living there at the time; they moved to another farm in the Mud City area. A year later, the Town acquired, for $1,500, a third, contiguous piece of about 87 acres. This is known as the Wells-Struthers lot, after Mrs. Agnes Struthers who, as guardian of owner Henry Wells, conveyed it to the Town.

The other tract has a somewhat intriguing background. Known as the Billings lot, this originally was Lot No. 31 of the Second Division of the town of Sterling. The charter of Sterling, issued by Governor Isaac Tichenor in 1805, required its proprietors to set off five "rights or shares" for "Public Uses," one each for the following: "an english school or schools" within the town, a college within the state, a county grammar school, the first settled minister, and "the support of the ministry in said town." These rights, as with charters of other Vermont towns, were so-called leaselands. The owner was actually a leaseholder and paid an annual rental to the specified beneficiary (that "english school" was the local public elementary school, the college was the University of Vermont, and the grammar school, meaning a secondary-level school, became the one established at Johnson). When Sterling's proprietors went to dividing up the town among themselves and those "Public Uses," Lot No. 31 of the Second Division became the lot for the support of the ministry in that division. The author traced its history only to the point of knowing that as of 1889 the lot was held by the Town of Morristown.

On February 9 that year selectmen leased the 100-acre lot to James J. Billings, a prominent and well-established local lumberman. He was granted the right "to cut and remove all timber, wood and lumber, and all trees of every and all kinds, both hard and soft ..." And that he did, having earlier set up a sawmill and carrying on an extensive lumbering operation for some years in the Sterling Valley.

Certain characteristics of the Billings lease, which need not be detailed, can't be fully explained. Suffice it to say, that while the lease ran only until 1894, the Town seemed to treat it as a "live account" for many years after that. In any event, income from the Billings lease, along with rents from other lots for "support of the ministry," went into the Town's so-called ministerial fund. That was divided each year among the town's several established churches.

Selectmen's interest in the Billings lot was joined to their interest in the Sulham-Struthers-Smith tract when they considered and then established all this Town-owned acreage as official municipal forest. They made that designation for part of the land in 1958 and the balance in 1959. The action occurred under a 1951 state law relating to establishment of municipal forests. Among other things, the law requires that such forest be managed under direction of the State forester, a key official of the Vermont Department of Forests, Parks and Recreation. That has since been the case for Morristown's municipal forest.

Lamoille County Forester Arlo K. Sterner, who for some years carried the actual responsibility for managing municipal forests in the county, initially had a lot of trouble just *finding* the Billings lot! As will be seen from the map of the Town, the lot lies on high elevation land just east of Madonna Peak and no road comes anywhere near it. While Sterner found marketable timber there, its remoteness and the nature of the terrain have so far precluded any harvest.

In contrast, several things have happened with the Sulham-Struthers-Smith tract. First some description. While part of this property was well-established woodland when it was acquired, much was in a state of transition: land once cleared and actively farmed was at various stages of reversion to forestland, from still-open to well-brushed-over. Town Road 43, though no longer maintained for vehicular travel, leads to this property; other old Town roads branch off from that within the tract.

Management activities here have included the planting of some 30 acres of open land to white and red pine and Norway spruce, this in 1958-61; harvests of sawlogs, pulp and firewood; and the clearing of more than two miles of snowmobile trails, mostly over those old Town roads across the property. Related to the latter was the selectmen's lease in 1973 of the former Sulham house and 15 acres of land to the Lamoille County Sno-Packers. The rental is $1 a year and the club has the right of first refusal on sale of the land, should the Town get an offer to purchase it. The club has fixed up the old house in rustic fashion and uses it as a headquarters for winter snowmobile outings. The trails are also used by snowshoers and cross-country skiers and occasionally by hikers.

Town Clock

The last Town facility which we'll describe here is our Town Clock. That is mounted in the steeple of the former First Universalist Church, now the Lamoille County Senior Citizens Center (C15). As mentioned briefly by Miss Mower (page 57), the clock was given to the Town by Samuel M. Pennock, a former Morristowner then living in Massachusetts. Pennock's letter offering the eight-day clock, which arrived here in early December, 1882, prescribed that it be placed in the Universalist Church "with consent of the church and society." On Christmas Day that year, the pew owners of the Universalist Meeting House Society voted to permit the Town to use the church tower.* And the following day, Town residents at a special meeting voted unanimously to accept the clock. To meet Pennock's conditions for the gift, voters directed selectmen "to do all things necessary to prepare the tower ... for the reception of the clock" and "at all times to keep the same in proper repair and running."

It took a little time but apparently about June, 1883 the clock was in the tower and broadcasting the time by sight and sound. Its placement there extends over three levels. The brass and iron clockworks, made by Geo. M. Stevens & Co. of Boston, stand on a 5½-by-7-foot wooden platform a short way above the base of the tower. The clock itself and the bell-sounding mechanism are each powered by a large wooden crate filled with stones which hangs at the end of a wire cable (and more about the bell cable below). The bell itself is mounted on a platform about eight feet above the clockworks. It was cast by Henry Hooper & Co. of Boston in 1867 and acquired by the Universalist Church that year. Finally, the four 68-inch clock faces on the outside of the tower are another eight or ten feet above the bell and are serviced from a platform at that level. The hands of each are wooden and point to large Roman numerals, also wooden, which mark each hour.

Note might be made here of the special community service which the church bell provided for some years around the turn of the century — a fire alarm. It's not certain when such service began but during at least part of the 1890's and continuing into the 20th century, the bell was used to rouse members of the Morrisville Fire Department. Then in 1910 a new two-step alarm system went into operation: telephone "central" was notified of a fire and relayed the call to the

---
*Local "common knowledge" has it that the Town actually came to own the tower. But the author doubts such a conveyance ever occurred.

Warren Leather Co., which sounded the alarm on its steam whistle. That system lasted until 1923, when an electric siren went into use.

To keep the Town Clock going, it has its official winder. About once a week he climbs into the tower and using a crank, winds up the two rock-weighted cables on separate metal drums. Other maintenance duties include repairs of any malfunctions, replacement of any burned-out light bulbs which light the clock faces, and resetting the minute and hour hands on a clock face which have been frozen in place by ice or snow.

Town selectmen appoint the clockwinder. Since 1883 they have been, with a few uncertainties, the following: 1883-88, Hiram Safford; 1888-89, C.A. Gile; 1889-90, E.M. Brown; 1891-92 (?), Isaac N. LeBaron; 1892-93, John Daniels; 1894-1916, Isaac N. LeBaron; 1917-24, Raymond E. Darrah (A.R. Campbell may have been clockwinder for a few months in 1916-17); 1924-40, John Ovitt; 1941, no record; 1942-66 (25 years, the longest term of any clockwinder), Leland E. Ring; 1967-73, Richard Vize; 1974-80, E. Brewster Buxton; and 1980-present, David E. Lowe. Annual salary of the clockwinder has gone from $25 in 1883 to $100 in 1980.

In addition to the regular maintenance performed by the clockwinder, the clock from time to time has undergone certain significant repairs and improvements or other changes. A few highlights:

— In 1895 electric lights were installed in the church, but it was not until 1916 that an electrical circuit for lighting the interior of the clock tower and the clock faces was added.

— In 1959 the clock's bell was silenced for a time in response to a complaint by operators of a nearby guest home that the sound was keeping them and their patrons awake at night. But at the 1960 town meeting Morristowners ended the silence by ringing up a vote that their clock "should be kept wound and wound to strike the hours."

— In 1968 the Universalist Church Society, which had become inactive in the early 1960's, conveyed the church property as a gift to the non-profit Lamoille County Civic Association, Inc., which converted it to the Lamoille County Senior Citizens Center.

Finally, 1978 was a significant year for the Town Clock, thanks to the interest and efforts of clockwinder E. Brewster (Bux) Buxton. When he assumed the job in 1974, the clock's bell was working erratically because the weight would sometimes stick in the wooden chute down which it was guided. Buxton was also concerned about the safety of the senior citizens then using the old church: it seems the bottom of the chute had become a broom closet! So about 1975 he silenced the bell by no longer winding it. Then after several years of wondering how to correct the problem and who could do it (the clockworks also needed attention in other ways), Buxton engaged the services of Tower Clock Specialists of Waltham, Mass. The firm solved the bell problem in the following way: the chute for its weight was eliminated for much of its length by introducing a new pulley arrangement for the weight's cable; that shortened considerably the actual vertical distance which the weight dropped. On April 19, 1978 the bell began again to sound the hours — the first time in some three years.

MORRISTOWN CORNERS

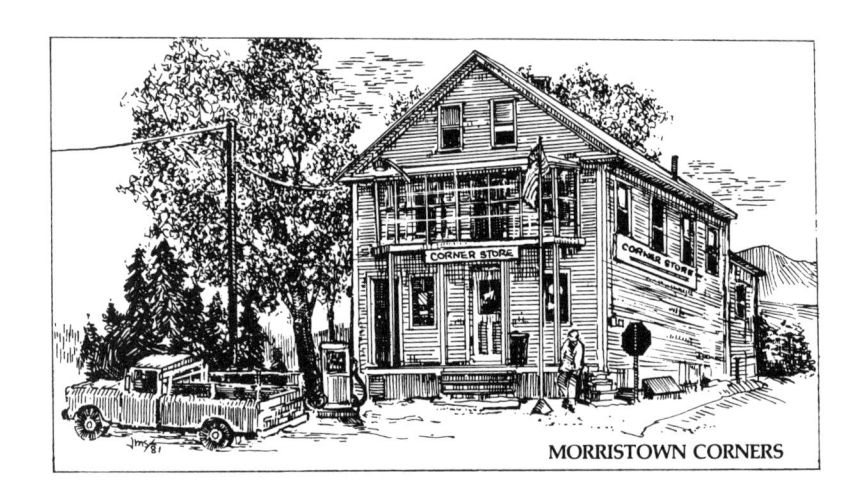

Chapter 10 - Other Public Services, High And Low

ONE LEVEL UP from municipal facilities and services are those on the county level. In Vermont's system of local government, county services are limited to operation of certain parts of the State's court system and to law enforcement and court-related administrative duties of the county sheriff. Since Lamoille County was created in 1835, Hyde Park has been the county's shire town, that is, the place for the county courthouse, jail and related facilities. On several occasions, however, other towns, including Morristown, have attempted to wrest away county seat status from Hyde Park.

A series of such attempts occurred in the 1850's when bills were introduced in the Vermont Legislature seeking such a change. But none was ever passed. One other significant effort at change came in 1910 following a fire on April 17 that year which destroyed all the county buildings in Hyde Park. A group of Morristown citizens launched an effort to get the shire moved here, among other things raising a substantial sum to help pay for the new facilities. But they encountered heavy criticism for proposing such a low blow to Hyde Park in the midst of its crisis, and their proposal came to naught.

One level down from municipal services of Morristown and Morrisville are those existing in certain outlying hamlets and developments, notably Cadys Falls and Morristown Corners. More importantly, this is an appropriate place to review how those rural communities have changed since 1935.

Miss Mower provides many details about Cadys Falls — its several industries, post office, schoolhouse and church building. All those have been gone, or at least closed, for many years. And some of the farms in the immediate area are no longer operating. But the cluster of some 25 houses remains largely intact and the community has added a distinctive enterprise which has long made Wednesday a special day in Cadys Falls.

The schoolhouse was closed in 1944 but still stands, the property now in private hands. As for the old church building, it continued an

OTHER PUBLIC SERVICES

active life for some years as a community hall under the management of the Cadys Falls Hall Society mentioned by Miss Mower (page 71). But then it fell into disuse and eventually was torn down in 1975.

Cadys Falls is not, of course, an incorporated village, though some residents talked about doing that back in 1895. But for some years the community has had at least one "municipal" service, water. That was established back in 1904 by Carroll G. Mudgett. He installed appropriate piping to bring and distribute water from a good spring he acquired about a half-mile to the east. The system subsequently passed to other private owners but by 1946 it was in serious disrepair. So in 1947 a new non-profit co-operative, Cadys Falls Co-operative, Inc., took over and has since owned and operated the system.

As for Wednesday in Cadys Falls, that is special because it is auction day at the community's long-standing commercial enterprise, Morrisville Commission Sales. On that day cars and trucks fill the yard in front of the barn and other buildings on the north side of the road at the west end of the village (T22). First and long-known as Hicks Commission Sales, the business was started on a small scale in 1946 by Willis G. Hicks, a Cadys Falls native, and Ernest Goodwin of Hyde Park. The two built the business on a combination of honest dealings, good management — and Hicks's entertaining auction style. Goodwin retired in 1964 and Hicks continued as sole owner until he

---

SOME WILLIS HICKS CHATTER

Heard from Hicks at an auction in Morrisville in August, 1972:
— Inviting an opening bid on a box of miscellaneous dishes: "I'm going to set somebody up in housekeeping for $1.75."
— Holding up a metal trivet: "Now there's a brand-new antique if I ever saw one."
— To the man who bought a grass-trimmer: "Your wife can use that while you're sleeping."
— Right after the same man bought an electric clock for fifty cents he asked Hicks, "Does it work?" Hicks's response: "What do you care — you don't get up on time anyway."
— And while holding up a slip of paper after just bidding off a small metal safe to somebody: "I sold you the safe, not the combination, so I guess I can throw this away."

RLH

---

sold the business in 1969. It subsequently passed through several hands, one owner changing the name to Morrisville Commission Sales in 1973. Owner since 1976 has been Morrisville Commission Sales, Inc.

Morristown Corners, like Cadys Falls, has certainly changed since 1935. It remains an essentially rural community though it now has far fewer active farms than was the case back then. As noted in Chapter 3, the Morristown Corners school closed in 1955, the Town's last rural schoolhouse to do so. The building has since served as a private residence. Also still very much there is the hamlet's long-standing general store, known as The Corner Store (T23). It has been owned and operated by Gerard and Cecile Valcour since 1977.

The Corners also has a community water system, the history of which is very similar to that at Cadys Falls. It was established in 1908 and 1909 by George I.A. Smith, who used several springs about three quarters of a mile west of the Corners proper. By 1948, after passing through several other private hands, the system was in poor condition. Taking it over that year and since restoring, operating and expanding the system has been another non-profit co-operative, the Morristown Corners Co-operative, Inc.

They aren't really villages like Cadys Falls and Morristown Corners but Morristown has two other "community" water systems besides the major Morrisville system. One is that at the Pinecrest Park for mobile homes on Cochran Road (T24). This was established in 1968 as Sunset Park by Everett and Theresa Lowe. It has since been owned by others, one of whom changed the name to Pinecrest Park in 1971. The water system itself serves the 37 or so mobile home sites in the park.

The other water system is that of the recently-established Morristown Fire District No. 1. This began as a private system for owners of the approximately 20 homes in the Pinewood Estates development off Needles Eye Road (T25). That was established in the early 1970's. But the system's source of supply proved inadequate, particularly in dry periods. To resolve the problem, some, but not all, homeowners petitioned selectmen to include them in a fire district, a special municipal corporation authorized by Vermont law. Selectmen did just that on September 10, 1980. Since then the fire district has arranged financing and is now awaiting construction of transmission lines which will connect the district's 16 or so members to Morrisville's municipal system.

And now on to Mud City — surely Vermont's greatest understate-

---

MUD CITY MINUTES

Some of the latest news items from that prosperous section known to fame as "Mud City" were given to us a few evenings since by "Mayor" Chaplin ... Joseph says he cannot afford to sling the style he has to as chief official of the municipality on his present salary; either the style must come down from its lofty perch or the salary must be elongated and elevated to a perch more in keeping with the demands of the public. He claims that under his administration a cooper shop is about to be started by Chas. Merrill, that a nearby bridge site is to be capped with an iron bridge this fall, and that every citizen of the city has, following his own example, displayed the American flag. Alongside of the regular flag he will put out a suitable headquarters or Mayor's flag this week.

News & Citizen, August 24, 1898

---

ment of a metropolis! The name goes back to 1898 when Joseph M. Chaplin, a farmer in that remote west Morristown area, began identifying himself in fun as the "mayor of Mud City." Chaplin took the

OTHER PUBLIC SERVICES 413

name from Mud Brook, which runs through the area. For the next year or so the *News & Citizen* carried occasional items about doings up in Mud City — including word of the defeat by Chaplin's "constituents" of his proposal to change its name to Maple Hill! That wasn't very much time but it was enough to forever implant the colorful name on the Morristown scene. Among other things, of course, the road serving that area is called Mud City Loop.

We'll conclude this chapter by continuing Miss Mower's review of that oldest Federal service of all, the United States Postal Service. First to correct a couple of points in her record: At the Morristown

---

MAIL DELIVERY, EARLY STYLE

Mr. Gilbert, "Uncle Daniel" as he was commonly called, was a quaint old New England character full of original ideas. One of his hobbies [as Morrisville postmaster, 1853-61] was to deliver mail from his high silk hat. When through sorting the incoming mail, Mr. Gilbert would fill his high crowned hat with mail and go for a stroll up the street, raising his hat only to those who had mail therein, sort it out and deliver it on the spot as he met people.

Morrisville Messenger, January 25, 1928

---

post office at Morristown Corners, James Hill continued as postmaster until 1907, when he was succeeded by Martin W. Carleton. Carleton served until the post office was discontinued on March 15, 1914 (both were owners of the store there). And rural free delivery is reported to have started in Morristown on February 15, 1902, not in 1901.

As for the Morrisville post office, plans for a new building were first talked about in 1962 but it was several years before they came to fruition. In the meantime, as of October 1 that year the post office left its site of over 60 years in the Drowne Block (C83) and moved to the building at the corner of Brigham and Portland Streets (C61). There it remained until the new and present post office (C8) opened for service on January 24, 1966.

As for the postmasters, the last mentioned by Miss Mower, John E. Stewart, continued in the post until 1947. He was succeeded by: Ballou L. Towne (acting postmaster), 1947-49; Dayton J. Wakefield, 1949-1955; Ballou L. Towne, 1955-68; and Joseph A. Yacovone, 1968-75.

An unhappy experience marked Yacovone's service. Upon his conviction of petty larceny for shoplifting at a local supermarket, he was suspended as of October 24, 1975. Though pardoned in 1976 by Governor Thomas P. Salmon, Yacovone did not return to the postmastership or other postal employment. Several men supervised the local office for nearly three years before Leo Gendron became postmaster on May 6, 1978. The interim "officers-in-charge" were Glenn A. Wilkins, Jr., October 25-December 5, 1975; Bernard Allaire, December 6, 1975-June 30, 1976; John Quinn, July 1, 1976-November 17, 1977; and Leon Andrus, November 18, 1977-May 5, 1978.

Chapter 11 - Morristown Centennial Library

OUTWARDLY, THE HANDSOME BRICK BUILDING which houses the Morristown Centennial Library has maintained its familiar form, with hardly a change since 1935. But inside, services have increased, the number and variety of materials available to patrons has grown considerably, and the building itself has expanded — downwards!

Details of these changes shortly, but first a look at a basic facet of this public library which also remains as it always has been. That's the fact that while the land and building are owned by the Town, the library is actually operated by a private, non-profit public-service corporation. That's the Morristown Centennial Library Association, Inc. (MCLA). Its membership and form of organization are essentially as Miss Mower described them (page 118).

Though not a Town service, the Town has long provided financial support in two ways to supplement the MCLA's income from endowments and miscellaneous sources. The most significant is the annual appropriation made by Town voters. As Miss Mower notes (page 119), such appropriation began in 1911 to meet a condition of the Carnegie Library Foundation grant. The amount has increased several times from the original $500 to the present $3,060. For some years the Village made its own annual appropriation, but that ended in 1950.

And as Morristowners have long seen in the annual town report, the Town continues to pay the $60 in interest on the $1,000 note established as a permanent obligation to the library at the time of its founding in 1891. And indeed it is permanent. The resolution adopted on January 3, 1891 specified that "the town shall pay the annual interest [on the one thousand dollars] to said Association on the first day of each January so long as the Association is in existence."

As Miss Mower noted, the library's first quarters were on Portland Street in the north end of the present Ben Franklin Store Block

MORRISTOWN CENTENNIAL LIBRARY 415

(C83). In 1892 it moved to the second floor of what is now the Town building on Main Street (C48). There it remained until completion of the present building in 1913 (C39).

Various changes and redecoration of the building have occurred from time to time over the years. But all were of a relatively minor nature compared to those which occurred in 1960. That year the basement was completely fitted out to provide a large reading room, magazine room and other facilities. This major improvement was made possible by Thomas C. Cheney, a prominent Morrisville attorney who died October 13, 1957. His bequest to the library of $10,000 constituted "a joint memorial gift" with his wife, May Terrill Cheney, who had died ten years earlier, on October 25, 1947.

In 1962 large bronze letters spelling "LIBRARY" were mounted above the columns of the front entrance portico. In 1975 a parking lot for patrons and library staff was constructed on part of the lawn adjacent to Richmond Street. Finally, in 1979 a maple sapling was planted in the center of each half of the front lawn.

When the library opened on April 19, 1891 it had 850 volumes in its collection and by the end of its first year had a circulation of 5,081. The library was then open only two days a week. Since then, those figures have all grown enormously, and the variety of available materials and services has greatly expanded. As of 1979, catalogued volumes numbered 17,594 and circulation was 30,131.

In addition to basic fiction and non-fiction books for both recreation and research, the library circulates paperback books, magazines, pamphlets, maps, phonograph records (both classical and popular), and picture puzzles. To supplement the library's permanent collection the librarian every two months borrows an additional selection of books from the Regional Library in St. Albans which is operated by the Vermont Department of Libraries. And through a prevailing system of interlibrary loans, the Morristown library can obtain books for local patrons held by libraries many miles away. It also provides special materials and services for shut-ins and the visually-handicapped, and certain reading programs for the children.

A special resource of the library is a detailed card index to certain newspapers published in Lamoille County since 1860, major holdings of which the library has. These include the *Lamoille Newsdealer, Lamoille News, News & Citizen, Morrisville Messenger, Transcript,* and *Lamoille County Weekly.* Beginning in 1968, the index was compiled by Robert L. Hagerman in his spare time as a community project. Mrs. Elsie West has continued the indexing since 1978.

Many individual Morristown citizens have supported the library with donations of time, money, reading materials and furnishings (and see below). Of special note here are members of the Board of Trustees of the Morristown Centennial Library Association, who serve on a volunteer basis. But the institution's basic services have been furnished by a salaried librarian and/or assistant librarian. Particularly noteworthy for her long tenure was Anna L. Mower, librarian from 1913 to 1955.

A full roster of librarians and/or their assistants is somewhat uncertain, at least for the early years. Frederick G. Fleetwood is listed by some sources as the librarian from 1891 to 1913. But he appears to have been the titular librarian, while an "assistant" or "acting" librarian actually managed the library's day-to-day operations. Those assistants were: 1894, Melvina M. Slayton; 1895-98, no record; 1899-1900, Mrs. Ernest (Jessie) Gates; and 1910-13, Oella Thompson.

Following her assumption of the librarianship in 1913, Miss Mower appears to have had no full-time assistant until 1946. But beginning in the late 1930's she had limited part-time assistance from student helpers. Later librarians have also followed that practice. In any event, the following is a roster of the full-time library staff, beginning with Miss Mower: Librarians: 1913-55, Miss Anna L. Mower; 1955-59, Miss Glendora Hall; 1959-81, Mrs. Evelyn H. Shanley; and 1981-present, Mrs. Betty Chalifoux; Assistant Librarians: 1946-48, Miss Glendora Hall; 1948-55, Mrs. Florence Mould; 1955-60, no regular assistant; 1961-73, Mrs. Florence Mould; 1973-75, Mr. Robert L. Hagerman; 1975-81, Miss/Mrs. Jane Boyce (Mitchell); and 1981-present, Mrs. Jane Nuse.

Scattered here and there on the main floor of the library are a number of works of art and special memorabilia which serve as decorative, functional or educational resources. All were gifts of friends of the library. Three of special note are the following.

Apparently the oldest of these gifts is one of the library's most familiar fixtures. That is an old grandfather clock, the pendulum of which ticks away the minutes while its charming bell sounds the hours. It is the library's only clock. Dr. Willard H. Stowe, a Morristown native then living in Massachusetts, presented this in 1891, the year the library was founded. He did so in memory of Mrs. Susan W. Tenney of Morristown, who had earlier given it to Dr. Stowe.

A lovely marble statue atop a matching marble pedestal near the check-out desk depicts the legendary Lorelei, a beautiful siren. Dwelling at a stretch of rapids and whirlpools on the Rhine River in Germany, she lured boatsmen to their doom with her sweet singing. The statue, completed in 1869, was by C. Voss of Rome. Mrs. J.C.T. Slayton presented it to the library in 1930.

Finally, of several gift paintings adorning the library's walls the picture of greatest significance to the library itself is certainly the large fine oil painting which hangs over the fireplace. It portrays Laura J. Gleed, founder of the Morristown Centennial Library Association. And though she died before its completion, Mrs. Gleed also obtained the Carnegie grant which paid for construction of the library's permanent home. The portrait was painted in 1884 by Mrs. Lillian Fisk Thompson, formerly of Morrisville. It was presented to the library in 1951 by Mrs. Frederick Gleed Fleetwood, daughter-in-law of Mrs. Gleed.

For more about the Morristown Centennial Library, notably information about other of its works of art and memorabilia, see the "first draft" of *More About Morristown, 1935-1980*; details about what and where that is are in the Foreword.

LANGDELL FARM COWS AND MORRISVILLE PLAZA

Chapter 12 - Population, Land Use And Economy

FOR NATIVE AND LONG-TIME Morristowners it won't come as any surprise to say that their town has changed considerably in years since 1935. The population is larger and the character and use of the land is different in many areas, particularly in the outside Town. And while the elements which make up the local economy have remained about the same, the proportion of each has altered significantly.

As for population, the numbers of Morristown and Morrisville residents have been as follows (the Village population figure subtracted from that of the Town produces the number of persons in the "Outside Town"):

Year	Morristown	Morrisville	Outside Town
1930	2,939	1,822	1,117
1940	3,130	1,967	1,163
1950	3,225	1,995	1,230
1960	3,347	2,047	1,300
1970	4,052	2,116	1,936
1980	4,448	2,074	2,374

Thus Morristown has maintained the steady, though moderate, growth in population which Miss Mower had noted for all its earlier years (page 287). Most of the increase of the last 20 years has come, however, in the outside Town, the growth there being far greater than in the Village. That actually declined between 1970 and 1980.

As for changes in land use, any long-time Morristowner can surely tell you how much more active farmland there was in the 1930's than is now the case. Aerial photographs taken in 1941 and 1974 reveal dramatically the change in proportions of open and forested land, the result principally of abandoned farms with their reversion of open pasture and crop land to trees and brush. In 1941 about 41% of Morristown's approximately 34,176 acres was cleared land; in 1974 open acreage had dropped to about 18%.

The decrease in the amount of land used for agriculture is borne out by the major change over the last 50 years in the number of individual farms and in the livestock holdings of dairy farms, the principal kind in Morristown and Lamoille County. In 1929 there were 178 farms here with four or more cows one year or older for an average of 19.3 cows per farm (there were also another 89 farms with fewer than four cows). In 1978 there were only 41 farms (with *five* or more cows) with a total of 2,314 cows or 56.4 cows per farm.

While cows and farms have grown fewer over the years, the numbers of both have basically stabilized since the late 1960's. Thus dairying in Morristown, while certainly much less a part of the Town's economy than it once was, is still a significant element.

As noted, dairying is by far the dominant type of agriculture in Morristown, there being very few farms of other types such as beef cattle, sheep, fruit or truck. One small but significant exception has been the Town's several commercial chicken farms since the 1930's. Very briefly, the principal of them were: Ernest H. Clegg, Wabun Avenue, eggs and fresh butchered chickens, late 1940's to mid-1960's; Raymond Lanpher, Elmore Street, eggs, 1940's to about 1965; Maurice L. Jacobs, Cote Hill Road, layers and eggs, 1940's to about 1965; Ernest and Faith Godfrey, Cote Hill Road, layers initially, broilers later, about 1951 to about 1966; and Robert Houle, LaPorte Road, eggs, hatching chicks, broilers and capons, started in Stowe in 1943, in Morristown 1946-64 (Michael Hill then carried on the business for some years before closing it down).

The only major poultry farm now in Morristown is one that's been here many years. That was established in 1952 by McDonald and Marjorie Miller on a former dairy farm on Cadys Falls Road (T49). Converting and then expanding the facilities over the years, the Millers produced broilers for about two years. They then shifted to raising breeder chickens and selling the hatching eggs. In 1974 they sold the business but when problems developed for the new owners, the Millers re-acquired the property in 1978.

Morristown has also had its share of those engaged in that classic Vermont enterprise, maple-sugaring — though the number is now quite small. Basic information is limited but in 1964 the Town had 26 sugarbushes (out of 156 in Lamoille County), and in 1976 six operating and four potential sugarbushes (out of 99 operating and potential bushes in the county). Of special interest in this regard is that the Vermont Maple Sugar Makers Association was founded here on January 16, 1893 with Morristowner Frank Kenfield as its first president.

Other basic elements of Morristown's economy, both now and in the 1930's, have been manufacturing, retail trade and commercial services, tourism, and institutional or human services. Let's now look at them.

Morristown is hardly an industrial town but manufacturing has certainly had a significant place in the Town's history. While it is a crude measure, the number of manufacturing firms gives some indication of changes in this element of the local economy. From 1934 to

POPULATION, LAND USE AND ECONOMY

1958, that number varied from 17 to 12 firms and from 1959 to 1968 it held steady at nine or ten firms. It rebounded to about 12 firms through 1974, then dropped significantly to a low of six firms by 1977. In 1978 a turn-around began with the establishment of two new manufacturers.

Details of the history of at least the larger and/or longer-established of these Morristown industries appears in the next chapter. Suffice it to note here that wood products, both lumber and manufactured items, have constituted the most dominant type of local industry. One or more processors of milk products have been another continuing, though less substantial, element of the local manufacturing scene. One other significant factor in this regard is the shift of local manufacturing facilities away from Morrisville proper, notably those once sited along the Lamoille River and near the railroad tracks off Portland Street. Most industries are now in the outside Town north of the Village, specifically at the end of Stafford Avenue and along Harrel Street.

The area of the Town north of the Village has been the scene of another major change in land use and economic make-up of Morristown. That is, of course, the establishment of what is now a large commercial area essentially separate from the long-standing central business district of the Village. For convenience we will call it the Morrisville Suburb (and see map of same). Much of this development has occurred since 1965 but many businesses appeared — and some disappeared — well before that. Space limitations permit only some highlights.

To begin with, a major commercial enterprise of sorts which operated for many years on the west side of Brooklyn Street in this area was the Lamoille Valley Fair (MS36). Its history is given elsewhere in these pages. Carrying out the initial dispersal to other uses of the fairground property following the fair's closing in 1942 were Everest and Cordelia Pouliot, and later their son, Archil (Archie). The former acquired the property in 1944. A key reason: to use the lumber in some of the fairground buildings to replace their dairy barn in Essex which had burned!

Apparently the first "real" business in this area was the combination gasoline station and small grocery store of Hector Bailey on the southwest corner of the Rts. 15/100 intersection (MS22). Established in the late 1920's, Bailey continued the business, at least on a limited basis, until his death in 1968.

In 1946 Archie Pouliot established a combination dance hall and roller skating rink, constructed in part by using one of the former Lamoille Valley Fair livestock barns. That was moved to Pouliot's site on Brooklyn Street (MS31). Subsequent owners and uses of the structure have been: c. 1948 to 1960, Harry T. Stackpole, Sterling Motors auto agency; 1962-72, Robert Stearns, Stearns Supply Co. (bottled gas and appliances); and 1972-present, Francis J. Gillen and family, Gillen Lincoln and Mercury, Inc. auto agency.

The automobile was also the moving force in the next three businesses in our chronology. The first was the Veterans Service Station on Brooklyn Street, which was founded in 1947 by Raymond A. Cleveland. It was operated by him and his three sons until Cleveland's death in 1963. Since 1964 the property has been the State's District 6 highway maintenance garage. The present main building there was constructed in 1968 (MS33). What is now the Auto Care, Inc. business of Ralph and Martha Wiltshire (MS18) began as a service station in 1949 by Kenneth Warren. He operated it until his death in 1959. And back on Brooklyn Street right where the fairground racetrack used to be, the Morrisville Drive-In Theatre opened for business the summer of 1949 (MS32). Its history is given elsewhere.

On July 15, 1950 brothers George and Roland Paine founded Paine's Dairy Bar on Rt. 15 opposite Warren's Service Station. Roland left a short while later and George, with his wife, Irene, continued what became Paine's Restaurant, a local landmark eatery until 1965. Other owners followed and in recent years it has been the gift shop of Mr. and Mrs. Raymond Overton (MS19).

Blow and Cote, Inc., the longstanding local construction contractor, was founded by Denis Cote and Richard Blow in 1949 or 1950 at the end of Goodell Avenue (MS27). For one of their buildings they converted a Lamoille Valley Fairground barn. Since 1963, when the firm moved to the intersection of Harrel Street and Vermont Rt. 15,

Map No. 3 - MORRISVILLE SUBURB, 1980

The following is a roster of building/landmark identification numbers which are used in the text as keys to this map, together with their respective names or uses. Names in roman type are current; those in italic type are former names or uses.

MS1 - H.A. Manosh, Inc.
MS2 - Northgate Plaza
MS3 - Shell gas station
MS4 - Northgate Car Wash
MS5 - Morrisville Lanes
MS6 - Morrisville Plaza (6a: P&C Supermarket; 6b: Ames Department Store)
MS7 - Franklin-Lamoille Bank
MS8 - Top Gas gas station
MS9 - *Terry's Snack Bar*
MS10 - McMahon Bros., Inc.
MS11 - A. Brown Auto & Home Store
MS12 - Stop and Shop store
MS13 - Lamoille County Agricultural Center
MS14 - Sanel Auto Parts/*Goldberg's Auto Parts*
MS15 - Grandey Insurance and Real Estate Agency
MS16 - Charlmont Restaurant
MS17 - Sunset Motel
MS18 - Auto Care/*Warren's Service Station*
MS19 - Overton's Gift Shop/*Paine's Restaurant*
MS20 - Ted's Gas Service
MS21 - Stewart's Television
MS22 - Morrisville Bottle Redemption Center/*Hector Bailey Store*
MS23 - Jack's Body Shop
MS24 - *Addie Cheney home and business*
MS25 - Wayne Blaisdell home/*first Ernest Bailey home*
MS26 - *Second Ernest Bailey home*
MS27 - Joseph L. Trombley truck terminal/*Blow and Cote*
MS28 - Hutch Concrete
MS29 - Vermont Industrial Products
MS30 - Lamoille Valley Railroad
MS31 - Gillen Lincoln & Mercury/*Stearns Supply Co./Sterling Motors*
MS32 - Morrisville Drive-In Theatre
MS33 - State garage
MS34 - *Morristown Highway Department shed*
MS35 - *"Little Laguardia" landing strip*
MS36 - *Lamoille Valley Fairground*

POPULATION, LAND USE AND ECONOMY   421

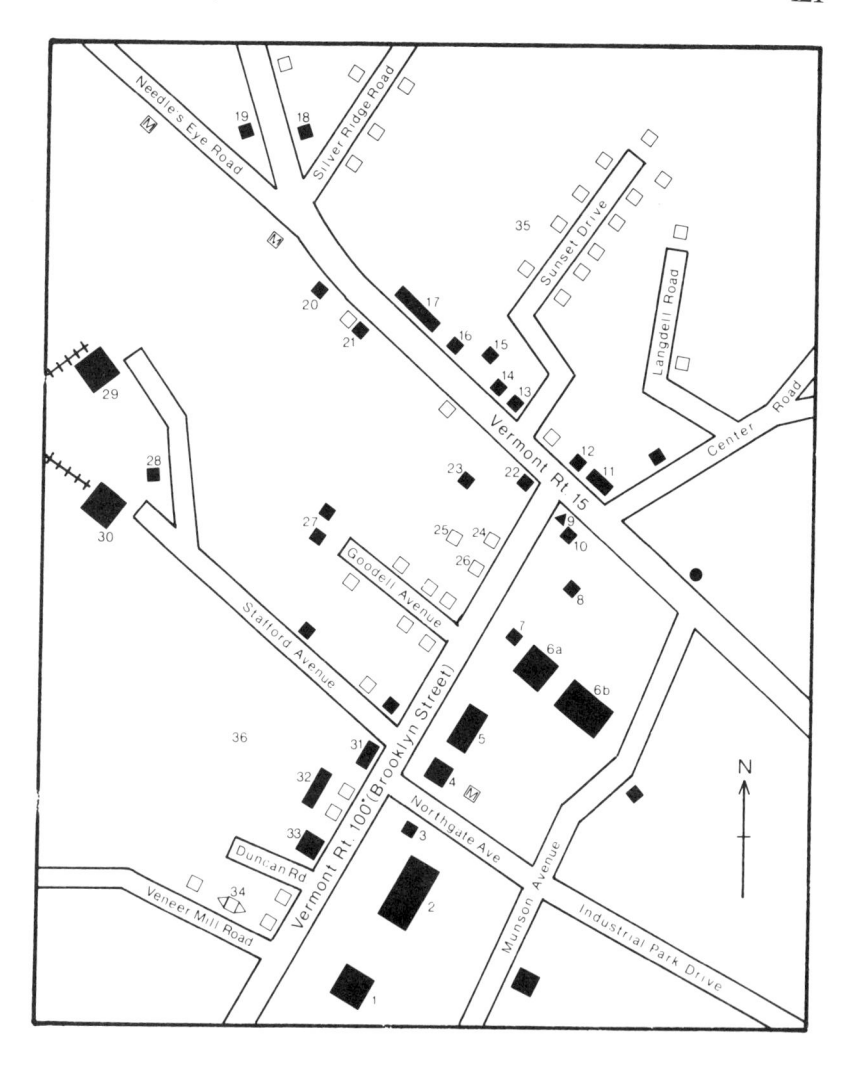

Map No. 3 - MORRISVILLE SUBURB, 1980

Map by Robert L. Hagerman, 1980

LEGEND

■ Commercial or Industrial Building　　　Ⓜ Mobile Home
▲ Commercial Building No Longer Existing　● Farm
☐ Residence　　　　　　　　　　　　　+++ Railroad Track

the property has been owned and used by Joseph L. Trombley for his milk-hauling and other trucking business.

In 1960 Louis J. Ferris built the structure at the intersection of Rts. 15 and 100 which he has leased ever since to McMahon Bros., Inc., the auto dealer (MS10). In 1960 Mr. and Mrs. Robert Houle established the Sunset Motel on Rt. 15 (MS17). Details of both these enterprises appear later.

In 1961 the present A. Brown Auto and Home Store, one of a major chain, was established on Rt. 15 opposite the intersection with Rt. 100 (MS11). In 1963 a branch store of Goldberg's Auto Parts of St. Johnsbury began operation on Rt. 15 (MS14). In 1970 Sanel Auto Parts, Inc. acquired the business and is still operating there. Also in 1963, Oneal Demars, Jr. constructed an office building at the intersection of Rt. 15 and Sunset Drive for lease to the Vermont Extension Service and other agencies and organizations. It has since been known as the Lamoille County Agricultural Center (MS13).

And finally in 1964 one more building appeared on the north side of Rt. 15. That was the Charlmont Restaurant (MS16), a sister enterprise of the Houles' motel which was owned and operated by their son and daughter-in-law, Philip and Phyllis Houle. In 1971 Edward and Mary Ann Wilson acquired the property — and lost it to fire on April 23, 1976. But they rebuilt the restaurant and associated cocktail lounge, dance-hall and meeting facility along lines very similar to the original, and continue its operation at this writing.

That, of course, was not the "final" new commercial building in this area but it provides a convenient break-off point for this accounting. These various enterprises together constituted a substantial degree of commercial development. But what certainly solidified that development was the establishment of not just one but two shopping centers in 1971, each with its modern supermarket as a major drawing-card for traffic. The Northgate Plaze (MS2) was the creation of Howard A. Manosh. It has housed several different businesses over the years but retains its original big-time grocer, the Grand Union Co. That large chain for some years had had its store in the central Morrisville business district.

The Morrisville Plaza (MS6) was developed by a St. Johnsbury firm, Murphy Realty Co. Originally occupying its two major buildings were a Giant department store (MS6a) and a Big Save supermarket (MS6b). They were succeeded several years later by the present similar businesses, respectively, Ames and P&C.

Briefly, other principal commercial structures in this area and the year each began are:

East side of Brooklyn Street: MS1, headquarters of H.A. Manosh, Inc., the well-drilling and excavating business of Howard A. Manosh of North Hyde Park, 1967; MS5, Morrisville Lanes bowling alley, built in 1964 and operated about five years (until his death) by Harry F. Grant, owned and operated by others since then; MS7, branch office of Franklin-Lamoille Bank, opened in 1971.

North side of Rt. 15: MS15, Grandey Insurance and Real Estate Agency, relocated by owners Philip Houle and Paul Nesky in 1978 to

POPULATION, LAND USE AND ECONOMY

this new building from the agency's former site on Main Street in Morrisville (C20), where Charles L. Grandey founded the business in 1960.

South side of Rt. 15: MS21, Stewart's Television Sales and Service, built in 1965 for Arthur Stewart, who moved his enterprise from its former location on Elmore Street in the Village; MS23, Jack's Body Shop, 1971, auto body repair shop named for and managed by Jack Downer, a new business in a new building owned (with the whole corner property) by Body Beautiful, Inc., a corporation controlled, initially principally and later wholly, by Adrian A. West.

And Stafford Avenue: MS28, Hutch Material and Supply Corp. of Montpelier, local concrete batch plant, new facility, 1972; MS29, Vermont Industrial Products, Inc., 1978; and MS30, Lamoille Valley Railroad, Inc., the lessee of this combination office, engine house and repair facility built in 1969.

Among the various Morrisville Suburb merchants are or were several who moved their respective enterprises from previous sites in Morrisville's central business district. Those relocated businesses, in combination with the other wholly new businesses, certainly have had a depressing effect on the Morrisville commercial area, which for many years has had 60 or so businesses. However, it's hard to say how much. But one indication of such ill effect was the formation in 1973 of a merchants group known as the Morrisville Village Association. Its purpose was to identify and correct problems such as traffic flow and parking in the existing business area and to attract appropriate new businesses. But the organization lasted only about a year.

Another such effort is now underway. Aided by a State grant and operating through the new, non-profit Morrisville Action Corporation, existing merchants and others are developing plans to improve the appearance of and otherwise revitalize the Village commercial area.

Tourist-related enterprises have always been a very limited part of the Town's basic economic base. The single major resort-type business here was the Samoset Cottage Colony on Lake Lamoille, which lasted from 1908 to 1957. And a few Morristown hostelries have offered special recreation facilities and activities to attract tourists (see Chapter 16 for details about these). A related element of the local economy is the vacation homes which a number of people have here. In 1973 there were 56 such "second" homes and more have undoubtedly been built since then. But compared to the other Lamoille County towns and many other Vermont towns, Morristown ranks very low in this economic element.

The contrast is major, however, when one looks at the role of institutional or human services. Hyde Park, as the shire town, has the Lamoille County Courthouse, and Johnson has Johnson State College. But for nearly all other public services, Morristown is the place to come. These agencies together have certainly represented a fast-growing element of Morristown's economy, particularly in the last 15 years.

One measure of this is employment. In 1935, Town and Village services (including schools), the Extension Service and the Copley Hospital were the only public service agencies with offices or facilities here. Total employment: about 65. In 1980 there are 28 agencies or programs, several with two or more departments or divisions. Total employees: just under 500!

Another thing affected is the Morristown Grand List. A few of these agencies own their facilities, and that property is exempt on the Grand List. Most of the others, however, lease space in privately owned buildings which *are* on the Grand List, and thereby share in the local tax burden.

The following are capsule descriptions of these public service agencies and organizations. They are given in roughly chronological order of their establishment here.

Extension Service — This service (MS13) provides a wide variety of information, advice and assistance to farmers on crops, livestock and related agricultural techniques, and to rural families on all aspects of homemaking. Key related activities are the Extension Service's work with Home Demonstration Clubs for women and 4H Clubs for young people. Initially sponsored by the Farm Bureau, a farmers organization, the Service for some years has been administered by the University of Vermont in co-operation with the U.S. Department of Agriculture.

Soil Conservation Service (SCS) — This agency of the U.S. Department of Agriculture provides information and technical services to land planners, farmers and other landholders to help them conserve, protect and make best use of soils and related natural resources, including water. There was some SCS activity in Lamoille County in the late 1930's and early 1940's. Then in 1945 the Lamoille County Soil Conservation District was organized to administer the service in this area. That later became the Lamoille County Soil and Water Conservation District and in 1968 was renamed the Lamoille County Natural Resources Conservation District (MS13).

Agricultural Stabilization and Conservation Service (ASCS) — This is another agency of the U.S. Department of Agriculture. Established in 1939, its county office here (MS13) administers Federal cost-sharing programs for conservation and timberstand improvement, emergency assistance in times of flood or drought, and incentive payments for certain agricultural products.

Lamoille County Forester — This is the local representative of a State agency which began as the Vermont Forest Service and is now the Department of Forests, Parks and Recreation of the Vermont Agency of Environmental Conservation. Over the years the county forester has provided information and technical services relating to forest management, and, more recently, advice on a variety of related environmental matters. Out of its headquarters in Montpelier, the Vermont Forest Service first provided services in the county in 1945, and in 1946 stationed its first county forester here (MS13).

Copley Hospital — A detailed history of this institution, founded in 1932, is given in Chapter 18.

Vermont Department of Employment Security — This State agency provides help to employers in finding qualified employees and help to the unemployed in finding suitable jobs. An office was initially maintained on Portland Street from 1945 to 1954 (C77). Then in 1970 what was now known as the Vermont Job Service re-established an office here, this time on Pleasant Street (C94). In 1975 the department also opened a full-time unemployment compensation office in the same location.

State Police — In 1947 Vermont established a state police force, something it had not had before. Administered by the Department of Public Safety, a state trooper "outpost" was established here beginning that year. Since late 1978 a larger complement of state police personnel have been working out of leased office space in the Morristown Public Safety Building (C22).

Vermont Agency of Transportation — This agency carries out summer and winter maintenance of the State highway system. As noted above, in 1964 facilities for its District No. 6 were established here on Brooklyn Street (MS33).

Lamoille County Development Council (LCDC) — Founded in 1962, this non-profit corporation stimulates economic development in the county, acts as the county's regional planning commission, and assists the county's ten towns and several incorporated villages in solving municipal problems and in obtaining grants of funds for a variety of purposes (MS13). Closely associated with LCDC has been a separate non-profit industrial development corporation, the Association to Boost Lamoille Enterprises, Inc. (ABLE). More information about that appears in Chapter 14.

Lamoille County Mental Health Service (LCMHS) — Established in 1966, this non-profit corporation provides a variety of direct and consultation services for the prevention and treatment of mental illness, including those related to alcohol and drug abuse. It is presently in its own building near Copley Hospital (V20).

Central Vermont Community Action Council (CVCAC) — The regional agency provides a variety of services — information, referral and advocacy — for low income people in Orange, Washington and Lamoille counties. CVCAC is a non-profit corporation which is basically financed by Federal funds. Since 1966 it has had a Lamoille County "outreach office," which presently is in Morrisville (C67).

Department of Forests, Parks and Recreation, Vermont Agency of Environmental Conservation — Headquarters for what is now District No. 4 of this department were established in 1967 in the Lamoille County Agricultural Building (MS13). The office manages State forest and park lands and various municipal forests within the district. It also deals with a variety of related environmental matters including forest fires and disease control.

Social Welfare Department and Social and Rehabilitation Services Department, Vermont Agency of Human Services — This State agency established headquarters here for these departments' Morrisville District in September, 1968. It is now located in part of a commercial building on Harrel Street built and owned by Oneal Demars, Jr. (V26).

Lamoille County Senior Citizens Center — This facility for the area's elderly was established in 1968 in the former First Universalist Church (details are given elsewhere). The Center (C15) serves senior citizens as both a social and recreation center and as a site for obtaining information and services on taxes, Social Security, and health and nutrition needs. Many of the latter have been provided by the Lamoille branch office of the Central Vermont Area Agency on Aging. That has been located in the Center since 1973.

Lamoille Home Health Agency — This non-profit corporation provides nursing, therapeutic, and related health and homemaking services to area residents at their own homes. Founded in 1971, its office since 1980 has been in a converted house just east of Copley Hospital (V20).

Planned Parenthood of Vermont (PPV) — This non-profit corporation provides information and services to both men and women about birth control, family planning, and related health and social matters. A Lamoille County chapter formed in 1972 now operates out of the Health Center Building.

Champlain Valley Work and Training Program — This is another non-profit public service corporation, one principally financed by Federal funds. It provides employment and training services, work programs, and counseling to the jobless and unskilled. A Morrisville office was established in 1973 and is now located in the former Drowne House (C45).

Northern Vermont Resource Conservation and Development Project — This is another agency sponsored by the U.S. Department of Agriculture. It serves one of two "project areas" in Vermont, this one covering the state's six northern counties. It provides technical and financial assistance to eligible recipients on conservation-related problems and projects, including those of erosion, flooding and recreation. Becoming operational in 1974, its office has always been in the Green Mountain Pharmacy building (C47).

Retired Senior Volunteer Program (RSVP) — This Federally-funded program makes arrangements for interested senior citizens to do volunteer work in a variety of public service agencies and organizations, the former thereby assisting the latter as they remain active in community life. A county RSVP unit was established in 1974 and is now housed at the Lamoille View Apartments on Park Street (C123).

Adult Field Services Division, Department of Corrections, Vermont Agency of Human Services — This division, formerly and long known as the Probation and Parole Division, works with the State court system in supervising probation and parole programs for individual convicted criminals, and in conducting pre-sentence investigations relating to new convictions. Since 1975 the Lamoille County office has been housed at the Demars Building on Harrel Street (V26).

Lamoille Area Health Council (LAHC) / Lamoille Family Center (LFC) — Closely associated are these two non-profit organizations. The first, which was organized in 1975, plays a role in a basic statewide health planning program now administered by the Vermont Health Policy Corporation. An additional specific LAHC action was its sponsorship of the Lamoille Family Center, which was established in 1976. The Center provides information and services on all aspects of bearing and rearing children. The LAHC and the LFC share staff and office space in the rear of Adrian's Store (C79).

POPULATION, LAND USE AND ECONOMY 427

Department of Health, Vermont Agency of Human Services — This department provides two basic services. One is general public health information and nursing services. Here since 1977, this division's office is in the Demars Building on Harrel Street (V27). Much longer established is the department's administration of a special Federally-funded program of health and nutrition information plus actual foods for pregnant and nursing mothers, infants and children up to age 5. Established here in 1974, the so-called WIC Program joined its sister Public Health Nursing office in the Harrel Street building in 1977.

Farmers Home Administration (FmHA) — Another unit of the U.S. Department of Agriculture, the Farmers Home Administration loans money for municipal water and sewer projects, for rental housing, and to individual low and middle income families who cannot afford other financing to purchase homes, farms, cattle and equipment. First established here in 1975, the FmHA office moved in 1978 to the Demars Block (C82).

Lamoille County Diversion Program — This is a special citizen-run government-funded program which provides an alternative to formal court prosecution for first-time offenders charged with certain misdemeanor offenses. Established in 1978, the county program's one-person staff is now located in the Morristown Public Safety Building.

Adult Basic Education — This program, operating since about 1965, provides home tutoring, classes, and related educational services to area residents deficient in basic skills of speaking, reading, writing and mathematics. Since 1979 its office has been on Park Street (C37).

United Cerebral Palsy, Inc. — This private non-profit organization's headquarters were established here in 1980 at the Northgate Plaza (MS2). It assists cerebral palsy victims and their families, and carries on advocacy and public education programs about the debilitating condition which affects nerves and muscles.

Community College of Vermont — In 1980 this State educational "institution" established one of two administrative offices for its Northwest Region in the Sherman Block on Portland Street (C64) (the other office is in St. Albans).

Finally, one agency whose services are not of a health or social nature is the National Guard Armory on Washington Highway; its history is given elsewhere. And at least three other agencies have come and gone from Morrisville. They are, in brief: Vermont Legal Aid, Inc., early 1970's, legal services to low income persons; Project to Advance Veterans Employment, Inc., about 1977; and a Community Artist program funded by the Vermont Council on the Arts, 1979-80.

> For other details about Morristown's economy and various of its businesses and institutional and human service agencies, see the "first draft" of *More About Morristown, 1935-1980*; the Foreword describes what and where that is.

Chapter 13 - Industries

AS DESCRIBED IN CHAPTER 12, the Morristown industrial scene has changed in several general ways since 1935. As for changes in specific industries, they are pretty much what would be expected over 40-plus years: some long-established firms closed, some new ones were started but didn't last, and others were started and continue to the present time. Let's begin by looking at the various industries mentioned by Miss Mower and other principal ones established before the previously-mentioned "turn-around" year of 1978.

Vermont Tanning Corp.

The Vermont Tanning Corp. continued the tannery here (V11) until 1935 or 1936, when financial problems apparently led to its closing. The St. Johnsbury & Lake Champlain Railroad purchased the property in 1940 and the buildings were subsequently torn down.

Morrisville Foundry Company / Greene Corporation

The first name is what it was for nearly a century but now it's the Greene Corporation. Under the two names combined, it is Morristown's longest-established, continuously-operating manufacturing business. And while it has been owned and managed by three generations of the Greene family, that notable characteristic is drawing to a close.

To fill out Miss Mower's history a bit (page 263), Channing B. Greene and Carl A. Gile gained control of the company in 1902 when they purchased nearly all its stock. Channing's brother, C. Porter Greene, joined the firm in 1905 and served as pattern-maker for the foundry operation for most of the years until his death in 1949. Channing Greene served as president and manager until his death on March 20, 1913. His widow, Frances, became president of the company at that time, serving until her own death May 20, 1942. Their son, Morris C. Greene, who had been manager for some years, continued in that role and also succeeded his mother as president. In 1914 Gile had sold his stock-holdings to Morris Greene, leaving the company wholly-owned by that family.

Morris Greene remained president and manager until his death July 10, 1951. He was succeeded by a member of the family's third generation to guide the business: his son, Frederic M. Greene. Fred Greene had joined the company in 1945, following military service in World War II. In 1967 he closed down the business's foundry operation. That had been the foundation of its manufactured products, including the well-known Eureka and Uncle Sam plows. It was also, of course, the Morrisville Foundry Company's namesake. Reflecting the change, the Greenes changed the name in 1968 to The Greene Corporation.

The firm has provided a diverse array of products and services at its Foundry Street facilities (C72). Those plows were made and sold until about 1950. Other foundry products have been stoves, machine parts, waterwheel parts, and assorted kitchen flatware including griddles, frying pans and muffin tins. About 1902 the firm began making one-cylinder horizontal gasoline engines, casting the engine-blocks at the foundry. Farmers were the big buyers of these, using them to chop corn, cut firewood, etc. The machine shop, which has long been a principal part of the business, was established in 1897.

And the Foundry put Morrisville in the forefront of the automotive age in other ways: it became Lamoille County's first auto repair garage in 1905, and even sold Buick cars for a time around 1913 and Harley-Davidson motorcycles around 1915. (Harvie M. Rich appears to have been Morristown's first automobile dealer, selling Pope, Cadillac and Buick cars as early as 1906.)

From time to time, various Greenes besides those mentioned here have served as directors and/or officers of the company. And for some years, Fred's wife, Jane, has played a direct role in the business by doing the bookkeeping and other administrative tasks. But the old order changeth. Fred Greene died November 12, 1980. Before that, he and other family members had set in motion plans to sell their stock in the company to Gene M. Blake, Jr. — a transaction still pending in mid-1981. Blake has been with the firm since about 1972 and its president since 1979.

Two special notes about the Morrisville Foundry Company are in order here to close out its history. One is actually about another local industry in which Morris Greene was involved, and which made what was then a rather unusual product.

In 1921 Greene and Frederic Timmerman and his wife, Celema, formed the Timmerman-Greene Corporation. Timmerman had the key product ideas and managed the business while Greene, who had the Foundry to look after, provided general support and mechanical expertise. For shop space the company used a barn behind the Timmerman home, now gone, on Pleasant Street (C85). The company's first major product, an automotive tool, was not a success. But there was recovery and a new product, this time that marvel of the airwaves, the radio. Timmerman developed and produced several different models, all operating on DC current, including one marketed as the "Timmerman Special."

The year production began is uncertain but it was probably 1923 or 1924. Manufacturing radios in Morristown at this time was amazing enough, but it was made more so by the fact that not until 1922 did anybody actually own a radio here! That year A.L. Huntley became what apparently was the first Morristowner to have a "wireless apparatus." Others purchasing sets that same year, but after Huntley, were George P. Drowne, Dr. Lloyd Robinson and Walter Jones.

But it was not to be. When AC sets were developed by the big companies, Timmerman-Greene could not compete and by 1927 the little manufacturer closed down — this time for good.

The other special note is that the old foundry was reactivated in

---

LAKE LAMOILLE LAUNCH

When navigation again opens upon Lake Lamoille it is quite probable that the center of attraction will be the new motor boat, now under process of construction at the Morrisville Foundry, the builders and owners being Channing B. and C. Porter Greene. The boat is 22 feet long with a six foot beam, and when completed will be a handsome one and will carry at least twenty people. The power will be furnished by a six horse power, four cycle, two cylinder oppose gasoline motor, which has been made entirely by the Greene Brothers. It is a great improvement over the ordinary motor boat power and, while it is much more complicated, works perfectly.

News & Citizen, March 18, 1908

Yes, they did indeed launch that boat and operate it on Lake Lamoille, though for how many years I have no idea. Of course, they had to have proper officers for their craft, and you know how they decided who would be which? Under naval regulations a ship's captain couldn't be colorblind. But that's just what my grandfather Channing was. So he became the engineer, while Great Uncle Porter became the captain.

Frederic M. (Fred) Greene
Comment on news item, 1980

1978. Doing business as White Heat Foundry, Christian (Chris) Ransom acquired the long-idle foundry building from the Greene Corporation (C72A), and has since been operating there.

George A. Morse Company / Morrisville Lumber Company

What used to be the George A. Morse Lumber Company, Inc. has long been the Morrisville Lumber Company, Inc., though with some significant differences between the old and the new.

As Miss Mower noted (page 264), the former established a major mill here in 1907. That was located about in the area of the Morrisville Lumber Company's present facilities (C73 plus area to the west and north). For many years the Morse company produced both dressed hardwood lumber and flooring, but later produced only the flooring. For 40 years the firm was a partnership of founder Morse, his son, George G. Morse, and a son-in-law, Charles H. Raymore. Forming the abovenamed corporation in 1933, the trio expanded the manufacturing business to include a retail business as well. That was selling what became a varied line of building materials. Following the senior Morse's death in 1934, his son guided the company.

In 1946 City Lumber Co. of Bridgeport, Inc., a Connecticut corporation, bought the George A. Morse Co., then conveyed it about a year later to another Connecticut corporation, the Morrisville Lumber Company, Inc. Bruno A. Loati, who moved here from Connecticut, was the company's first president — and still is 34 years later (by 1962 he owned all stock of the company). Morrisville Lumber's present sales motto, "Everything For Building Anything," was established in 1947.

Disaster struck August 25, 1949 when fire destroyed the dressing mill and all the auxiliary buildings except the office and a garage. Loati promptly rebuilt the retail sales facilities and subsequently a finishing mill, but not the main lumber mill. He has since expanded the Morrisville facilities several times, and in 1976 opened a branch outlet in Stowe.

Atlas Plywood Corporation / Pratt-Read Corporation

Atlas Plywood is a name no longer part of the Morristown manufacturing scene, though a new owner of the facilities (V27) continues to serve as an important local industrial employer. The Boston-based Atlas Plywood Corporation was a major industry, at one time owning some 40 wood-products mills across the country. Weakening in the 1950's, the company began closing, selling or converting these properties until the Morristown plant was its last plywood operation (plywood shipping containers was the main product). Then, as a result of several corporate changes, the Morrisville operation was, by 1969, the Atlas Plywood Division of North American Philips Corporation. Various setbacks, including a fire which destroyed the local plant's sawmill, led North American to sell the property in 1974 to a new industrial concern.

That was Pratt-Read Corporation of Ivoryton, Conn., a major producer at its plant there of wooden piano parts. It makes some of those here plus a variety of other hardwood items. In 1980 employment had reached about 100, not far below the 120 to 150 that prevailed during Atlas Plywood's better years here.

C.H.A. Stafford and Sons, Inc.

Charles H.A. Stafford's two sons, who figured so prominently in this important Morristown industry, were Guy C. and Roy C. Stafford. In addition to its mainstay product, last blocks for the shoe industry, the company manufactured rolling pins and bowling pins. After the death in 1937 of both C.H.A. and Roy Stafford, Guy Stafford carried on the business until his own death in 1947. Operations continued for a while, then were closed down and the company's properties dispersed. The factory buildings themselves and land went in 1953 to the first of various companies which have owned and operated the asbestos mines in Eden and Lowell. Since 1975 that has been Vermont Asbestos Group, Inc. The Morristown property (V28) serves as a warehouse and shipping depot.

United Farmers Cooperative Creamery Association & Other Dairy Industries

United Farmers Cooperative Creamery Association, Inc., born in Morrisville in 1919, has grown to enormous size since 1935. But ironically it no longer has any production facility here.

The United Farmers' plant in Morrisville referred to by Miss Mower was constructed in 1925 off Railroad Street (C89). At that time it was described as the "most up-to-date creamery in Vermont, if not all New England." The plant was enlarged and modernized in 1940. Its products during the early years were very diverse, including condensed and evaporated milk, cottage cheese, buttermilk, powdered skim milk, casein, ice cream and ice cream mix.

In addition to the other plants mentioned by Miss Mower, the Co-op in 1937 acquired and made major improvements to a creamery plant in

---

WORLD SERIES SOUND SYSTEM, TIMMERMAN-STYLE

One of my distinct memories from [about 1923] was the scene during the World Series. Dad [Frederic Timmerman] had built an amplifier, and if radio reception was unusually good, he hooked it up to a set with a speaker directed out the back window of the shop [on Pleasant Street] — and relatively large numbers of mostly males gathered to listen to the game! When the reception was poor, either Dad or Herb Strong would listen with earphones, and repeat the commentary over what we would now call a P.A. system — that is, using a microphone and the amplifier. I distinctly recall fifty or more folks sitting around the back yard listening to the game.

Dr. Frederick W. Timmerman
Letter to Frederic and Jane Greene
December, 1979

Randolph. And by 1944 it had established eight retail dairy bars and ice cream parlors in the Boston area in addition to the major processing plant described by Miss Mower. This direct link to retail markets was seen as the Co-op's particular strength in terms of improved returns to its farmer-members, the milk producers.

The first of three major mergers involving the original United Farmers Co-operative Creamery Association, Inc. occurred in 1947. The result of that was the United Farmers of New England, Inc., with 2,500-plus members. Big grew bigger, initially with the acquisition of other smaller creameries by United Farmers, and then with another merger in 1972. The resulting new 6,000-member milk-marketing cooperative, New England's largest, was Yankee Milk, Inc.

The year of that merger, however, also saw the closing of the Morrisville plant, which by this time was serving as only a transfer point for fluid milk. Also closed in 1972 was the farm products store which United Farmers had operated for many years in a building off Pleasant Street (C91).

Finally, in 1980 Yankee Milk was one party in the creation of a complex — and controversial — new corporate entity known as Agri-Mark, Inc. The huge milk-marketing co-operative will control about half of the six billion pounds of fluid grade milk produced in the New England and eastern New York area. Believe it or not, it all began in Morristown.

And deserving mention here was the notable role of one Morristown man in that beginning. He was Earl Gray, who for some years operated a farm on what is now known as Earl Gray Road. Gray was a charter member of the original United Farmers co-operative, and for 41 years served as its president, retiring in October, 1960 at age 76. He continued as President Emeritus until his death on September 30, 1962.

The only milk products industry now in Morristown is Cabot Farmers Co-op Creamery Co., Inc. It operates a plant off the end of Wabun Avenue (V29). And the abovementioned H.P. Hood Company (earlier H.P. Hood & Sons) operated a milk transfer station here from about 1949 to 1962. That was located in the Morrisville yard of the St. Johnsbury and Lamoille County Railroad.

Finally, there are, of course, Morristown's various dairies, businesses which combine roles of manufacturer, i.e. processor, and retail and wholesale merchant. As of 1935, about five small commercial dairies were operating in Morristown. From two of them came today's long-standing Morse's Dairy, though technically that is no longer a Morristown business.

One predecessor was the dairy of the Douglass family on Jersey Heights (V30). Howard and Maude Douglass bought the farm and related business in 1928 from Frank and Orpha Strong. Following Howard's death in 1930, his widow and children carried on the enterprise until 1946, when Maude sold out. Buying the processing equipment was Dwight W. Griggs, who had recently acquired a farm and dairy business on Randolph Road previously owned by other family members. He established a small plant and sales outlet in the center of Morrisville. After operating the business for only two years, he and his wife Beatrice (now incorporated as Griggs Dairy, Inc.) sold out to Leslie J. and Gwendolen Craigie in 1948. Craigie, building his own processing plant back out on Jersey Heights (V31b), ran the business for the next 14 years. In 1962 Howard and Martha Morse purchased the dairy from their long-time friends, the Craigies. The Morses and later their son, Douglass, have carried on the business ever since, incorporating as Morse's Dairy, Inc. in 1977.

There have been two significant changes in the business along the way. In 1969 the Morses stopped doing their own processing. Since then they have been solely distributors, buying their dairy products — still with the Morse's Dairy label — from other suppliers. And in 1977 Morristown actually "lost" Morse's Dairy! That year it moved from the Jersey Heights building to a new building on Center Road in Hyde Park just across the Morristown line. From that location the firm continues to make both retail/home and wholesale deliveries throughout Lamoille County, except Stowe.

Two post scripts: One is that Martha Morse is one of the

Douglasses' children and she and her husband helped run the family enterprise for a time before it closed. The second is that the Douglass farm, after passing through several other hands, proved to be the last operating farm within the Village of Morrisville. Closing it down in July, 1980 were its then-lessees, Emery F. Foss, Jr. and his son, Jeffrey.

One other long-established Morristown farm enterprise was Greaves Dairy on Washington Highway (T50). That was started in 1928 by Clifton M. Greaves and later continued by sons Mahlon and Martin until they sold out to the Mansfield Dairy of Stowe in 1973. The family has since continued the farm and while some of their hay and corn is grown within Morrisville's boundaries, none of the farm's buildings are there.

Finally, in 1977 a Morristown farm family made a bit of history for the Vermont dairy industry. That year Bernard and Ruthe Sinow and their sons, Matthew and Marc, started the Homestead Farm Dairy, said to be the first new family-owned milk processing plant in Vermont "in recent memory." The Homestead Dairy, both production facilities and store, is housed in a new barn-style building at the Sinow farm on LaPorte Road (T51). The Sinows offer whole and skimmed milk, ice cream, various related dairy products, and other farm products like maple syrup.

Union Carbide Corporation

This is a huge industrial concern indeed but its facility here (V31) *stores* things instead of *manufacturing* them. In 1951 what was then Union Carbide and Carbon Corporation acquired about 16½ acres of land on Jersey Heights between LaPorte Road and the Lamoille River. The building there which had housed C.C. Miller's garage and Pontiac auto dealership became the site for its corporate records center. Throughout the years the records center has had about four employees.

Concord Manufacturing Corporation

This manufacturer of pajamas and other men's and women's garments is now Morristown's biggest industrial employer. Playing a major role in getting the firm established here was Robert Houle, a successful local building contractor and entrepreneur, who at the time was a Morristown selectman. Concerned over the high unemployment and the number of Morristowners then on poor relief, he set about to attract some new industry to Morristown and thereby get some of those people back to work. The result was Concord Manufacturing Corporation. Houle himself financed and constructed the initial 6,000-square-foot building on Harrel Street (T33). He leased the property to Concord Manufacturing until 1973, then sold it to the company. Since late 1965, when it opened, the plant has been enlarged four times, to over 32,000 square feet, and employment has grown from an initial 25 to 175 in 1979, most of them women stitchers.

Research Engineering Corporation

Here is another Morristown industry which has grown dramatically since its establishment in 1967. Originally known as North American

Metals, Inc., the Harrel Street business was founded by F. William Alley, a member of the United States team in the 1960 Summer Olympics and a one-time world-record holder in the javelin. In 1970 Alley established Research Engineering Corporation as a direct outgrowth of North American Metals.

Early basic products were precision metal tubes, which were used, among other things, for golf club shafts and javelins. Broadening its technical capabilities, the firm has since manufactured a number of other products. These include a variety of weighing, measuring and testing devices for track and field events, many items of sophisticated equipment for the medical industry, and production machinery of different kinds. A major development for the firm in the mid-1970's was making tubular forms from woven graphite, a material stronger than steel but lighter than aluminium. Specific products again are various kinds of sports equipment including golf club shafts and flyrods.

In mid-1977 Research Engineering entered into a relationship with Johnson Wax Associates, Inc., a wholly-owned subsidiary of S.G. Johnson & Son, Inc. of Wisconsin, a major American industry. This included joint acquisition of H.L. Leonard Rod Co., a manufacturer of fly fishing equipment.

Since its establishment, North American Metals/Research Engineering has enlarged its original Harrel Street plant three times and constructed a second building there as well (T34). In 1979 it acquired a small vacant manufacturing plant in Stowe for production and sale of H.L. Leonard products. Also reflecting the firm's growth is its number of employees. That has gone from three in 1967 to 42 in 1979.

Hutch Concrete

It's not really a manufacturer but it certainly produces a product. That's Hutch Material and Supply, Inc. of Montpelier which makes concrete here. In 1972 it established a branch concrete-preparation facility at the end of Stafford Avenue (MS28) and ever since has been mixing and delivering Hutch concrete to area construction projects.

Before describing the several local industries established in very recent years, note should be taken of the county organization which played a major role in attracting and establishing them here. Actually, there are two organizations, though they are closely related. The first is the Lamoille County Development Council (LCDC). This was founded in 1962 by local citizens as an outgrowth of the Rural Area Development Committees program of the Extension Service. LCDC became a non-profit corporation in 1964, hired a part-time executive secretary for a while and then a full-time administrator beginning in late 1966. Provided in Chapter 12 was a general description of the organization's functions, a principal one being economic development for the county. While tourist promotion has been one element of that effort, LCDC has concentrated more on industrial development in recent years.

For legal and financial reasons it sponsored formation in late 1968 of a separate but related non-profit corporation for that specific purpose. That was the Association to Boost Lamoille Enterprises, Inc. (ABLE). After limited activity for five years, ABLE was revived in 1973 and has taken several major actions since then.

One was its role in resolving the threatened abandonment of the St. Johnsbury & Lamoille County Railroad in the mid-1970's. That troublous time for the railroad is described in Chapter 17. It also aided in securing Pratt-Read Corporation as the purchaser of the Atlas Plywood plant as mentioned above.

And it played a third significant "recovery" role during 1974 and 1975 in the transfer of the long-established asbestos mining and milling operations in Eden and Lowell from the GAF Corporation of New York City to the newly-formed Vermont Asbestos Group, Inc. (VAG). Led by John Lupien, employees themselves bought most of the company's stock. That made VAG probably the nation's largest employee-owned industrial operation. Some of the company's property is in Morrisville,

---

MODERN MILK AT THE DOUGLASS DAIRY

It was 1944 or 1945 when the Douglass Dairy purchased and installed pasteurizing equipment for its milk. Local folks were, of course, very used to raw milk and we knew other dairies had found out their customers didn't much like this new-fangled milk, when they first started getting it. So we introduced our pasteurized milk pretty careful. For about three weeks we bottled the new milk in the usual way but labeled it with the old, familiar raw-milk labels. Then one day we switched to new labels. Well, there were some pretty unhappy customers who claimed the pasteurized stuff didn't taste right and wasn't any good. But they couldn't say much when we told them they had actually been drinking it for the last three weeks!

Howard E. Morse
Recollection, 1980

---

specifically storage and shipping facilities at the end of Wabun Avenue (V28).

A wholly new industry for Morristown was a direct offshoot of the successful rehabilitation of the asbestos operations by VAG. Sparked by Lupien, a process was developed for production of a new type of fireproof wallboard. Established in 1976 by VAG to manufacture the wallboard was a wholly-owned subsidiary, Vermont Industrial Products, Inc. (VIP). In 1978 it completed a $2 million, 22,400-square-foot plant off the end of Stafford Avenue (MS29). The 15-acre site was purchased from Howard A. Manosh, whose firm, H.A. Manosh, Inc. of Morristown, was also the general contractor. As of early 1980, however, the plant was still operating on a trial production basis.

It might be noted here that VAG's turn-around soon sparked interest of other investors. After some extended turmoil of various stock-purchase offerings, the abovementioned Howard Manosh gained control in 1979, thereby ending the company's employee-controlled status.

Returning to ABLE, its single largest undertaking was its purchase

INDUSTRIES

in 1976 of 37 acres of land on the north side of Harrel Street for what became its Lamoille Industrial Park (T35). The first manufacturer established there was Decart, Inc., subsidiary of DEKA-Textilfarben of West Germany. Decart purchased a four-acre site for a 12,000-square-foot new plant. Production began there in 1980. The 60-year-old parent firm manufactures various high-quality paints and dyes used in the arts and crafts field for coloring fabrics, leather, metal, wood, glass and ceramics. A closely-related product is hobby kits for making batik, stained glass and other craft items.

Second occupant of the Lamoille Industrial Park is Hearthstone Corporation, an industry originally established in 1978 at the Northgate Plaza (MS2). It manufactures an airtight, wood-burning cast iron and soapstone stove, the design for which was created by the company's founders, Alan B. Shute and Peter Von Conta. In 1980 Hearthstone acquired and occupied with its then 41 employees an industrial shell building in the Lamoille Park. This had been constructed in 1978 on a speculative basis by ABLE so that it would have manufacturing space readily available to an industrial prospect.

By early 1981 ABLE had sold several more lots in its industrial park, though at this writing no construction of additional industrial commercial facilities is underway. But with that success, the industrial development organization decided "to put more of its energy into the rest of the county," the towns of Johnson and Cambridge being the most likely focal points. Symbolic of this change was ABLE's move from offices in the Lamoille County Agricultural Building (MS13) to a building in Hyde Park, the county seat.

Finally, two other recently-established manufacturers, both small, round out Morristown's current industrial scene. One is Concept II, a business established in 1977 by two brothers, Richard and Peter Dreissigacker. Operating in a barn on LaPorte Road (T32), the Dreissigackers designed and are producing graphite fiber-fiberglass rowing oars for crew events.

The other small industry is of special interest for two reasons: it is the first new industry in a long time to be established within the Village of Morrisville, and it gives new life to a landmark building on Union Street (V3), the long-time former firehouse and Street Department garage. Taking over the building in 1978 was Clayhill Resources, Ltd., a Vermont corporation established that year by Allan Barshaw and William R. Cox of Johnson, and John Pierce of Morrisville. The business deals in and processes semi-precious stones and gems. Since its founding, the firm has employed about five people.

> For other details about these principal Morristown industries — plus information about lesser ones not mentioned here, see the "first draft" of *More About Morristown, 1935-1980*; the Foreword describes what and where that is.

WEST SIDE OF PORTLAND STREET

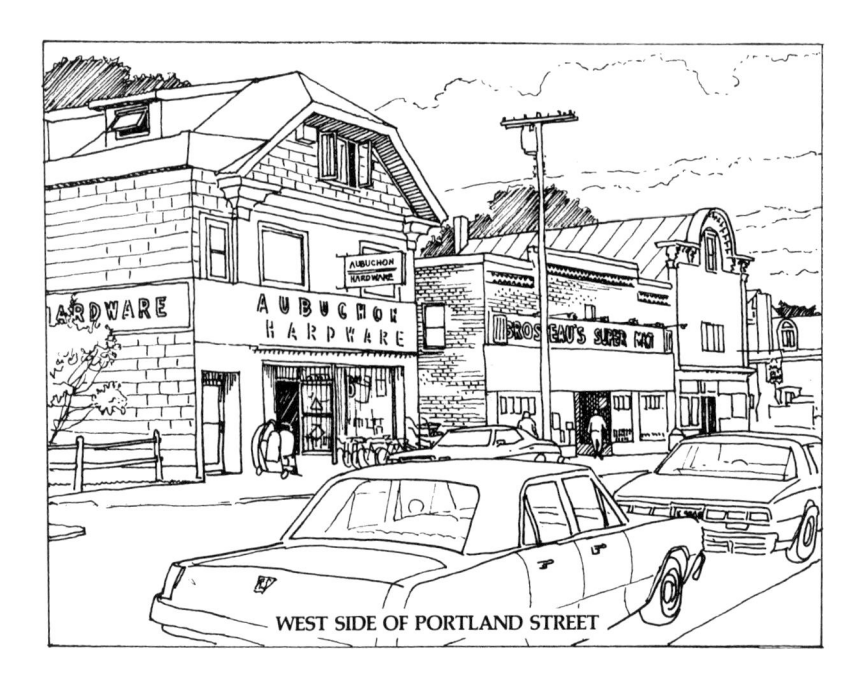

Chapter 14 - Morrisville Businesses

IN ITS REVIEW OF CHANGES in Morristown's economy, Chapter 12 provided a chronology of many of the businesses so far established in the major new commercial area north of Morrisville, the so-called Morrisville Suburb. But it gave only a brief overview of the history of the Village's long-established central business district. Let's now return there and take a closer look at its individual businesses.

Or at least some of them. This review will be limited to businesses of particular prominence or longevity. We'll begin with the few mentioned by Miss Mower (page 265) and then go on to others in the merchandising field. We'll next focus on enterprises in other particular fields, including automobile agencies, banks, movie theatres and newspapers (a few of them actually outside the Village). Then, still looking at commercial endeavors but now for the whole Town, Chapter 15 will deal with public houses and Chapter 16 will describe enterprises in two other fields, transportation and communication.

H.A. Slayton & Co. / Lamoille Grain Co.

Henry A. Slayton, founder of this firm, died February 20, 1932 and, as noted by Miss Mower, his son, Albert H. (Allie), succeeded him as proprietor and manager. In the 1930's the firm was dealing in much more than the feed and grain mentioned by Miss Mower. There were also seed, cement, lime, plaster, brick, coal, farm implements, and such food commodities as flour and sugar.

After leaving Slayton hands in 1951, the business premises on lower Portland Street (C71) became an outlet for a major out-of-state feed and grain distributor. Then in 1968 Roger Gilman and Milford

MORRISVILLE BUSINESSES

Guy bought the business and renamed it Lamoille Grain Company. Guy died in 1969 and Gilman in 1977. In 1980 Guy's widow, Carmen, and Gilman's son, Kenneth E., each own a 50% interest. The latter manages the business.

The firm's line of goods presently consists of livestock feeds, mostly for dairy cows, plus garden and farm seed, fertilizer, pet food, and small tools and supplies for farmers.

The Munson Store

The brick building which so long housed the Munson Store is still standing solidly, but the store itself which Harlan P. Munson founded in 1888 is no more. In 1904 he constructed that three-story structure to house his growing business (C51). While he didn't handle food, his merchandise included just about everything else: clothing, hardware, building supplies, feed and grain, fertilizers, seed, and farm machinery. Munson died July 19, 1914.

Carrying on the business was his only son, Levi M. Munson, a lifelong Morrisville resident who subsequently held several important Village offices for many years. With two associates, Munson in 1939 formed a corporation, The Munson Store, Inc. In 1955 he sold the store property and his by then controlling interest in the corporation to Oscar Churchill. Munson died in 1963.

Except for farm machinery which had been dropped some years earlier, Churchill continued the business with relatively few changes until 1972. Late that year he closed it down and sold the property to Country Properties, Inc. The building has since housed that firm's own real estate business plus the Barrows, Mercia & Rollins insurance office.

C.T. Morrill & Sons - The Wrong End Store

In 1923 C.T. (for Carroll Tenney) Morrill acquired from A.G. Small the two-story wood-frame building on lower Portland Street (C76). Small had been operating there since about 1897. At that time the commercial attractiveness of the lower end of Portland Street was apparently much less than the upper end. Turning disadvantage to advantage, it was Small who coined the phrase, "The Wrong End of Portland Street," and successfully promoted it for his enterprise.

Morrill retained the "Wrong End" name but where Small had been operating more of a general store, Morrill narrowed the line to men's, women's and children's clothing and related dry goods and accessories. A few years before his death in 1944, C.T. brought his two sons, Erle J. (Ex) and Robert Donald (Don), into the business as partners. Don died in 1957 with Ex subsequently becoming sole proprietor of the family business. In 1972 he and his wife, Ann, then in their 70's, closed out the business and sold the property, which has since been used for other enterprises.

A particularly colorful aspect of the business's history was the Morrills' advertisements in local newspapers. These featured several fictional characters, the first of whom, Lem Simpkins, was introduced on January 16, 1924. Lem had dropped in for a visit and while seated in front of the stove on the main floor, he was whittling — and keeping count of the customers by slicing off one shaving for each person who entered the store. After a few paragraphs describing the store's

> ## LEM IN ACTION
>
> Lem, Deb, Hank Green and Boob gathered around the old box stove to have a friendly discussion on politics. The boys drew cuts to see who would wait on the customers. Deb was hanging up the NEW HART SCHAFFNER & MARX and CURLEE SUITS and OVERCOATS that just arrived when, with a loud crash, the shelving in the back room, loaded heavy with JOHNSON WOOL PANTS and JACKETS, fell down and covered up the BALL BAND RUBBERS and RUBBER BOOTS. During the confusion the truckman backed up and dumped three cases of HEAVY WOOL and PART WOOL SHIRTS. Hank got the FLEECE LINED UNION SUITS mixed up with the 50 PERCENT WOOL ONES and Deb got sore and called him a Republican nut. This made Hank madder'n a hatter and he called Deb a Democratic bum.
>
> A battle royal followed. The air was full of WORK SHOES from $1.25 to the best Wolverines. By the time they got to the SHEEP SKIN COATS they were pretty well warmed up. After the scrap they found Hank's dog asleep on a pile of DOUBLE BED BLANKETS, 70X80 size, for which THE WRONG END IS FAMOUS.
>
> The boys were busy putting out WHITNEY and SHIRTCRAFT DRESS SHIRTS, BOTANY TIES, BOSTONIAN HATS and BATES SHOES. The PAJAMAS are so beautiful they would make a man want to walk in his sleep. INTERWOVEN HOSE sold well and the HEAVY WORK SOX kept the cash drawer smoking.
>
> It was Boob's turn to wait on a lady customer. She wanted to see SILK DRESSES and he showed her RAINCOATS. She was quite indignant and slapped Boob's face. Lem rushed to her assistance, saying "Don't mind him, lady, he's a Republican." Lem sold her a pair of SUEDE SHOES, a pair of GORDON HOSE, some SILK UNDIES, a new POCKETBOOK and an UMBRELLA.
>
> But whether the Republicans or Democrats win, THE WRONG END boasts the LARGEST LINE OF INFANTS' WEAR ever shown in a country store. Don't forget the place.
>
> C.T. MORRILL
> "Wrong End" of Portland Street
> Morrisville, Vermont
>
> Advertisement
> *Morrisville Messenger*
> October 21, 1936

spirited sales, the ad closed by noting with a straight face that "if any of you folks want to interview Lem, you will find him here — buried in shavins."

Green Mountain Pharmacy

This business had its beginnings when the Centennial Block was built in 1891 at the corner of Main and Portland Streets (C57). A.L. Cheney established a drugstore there and carried it on until Elwyn J. Wheeler purchased it in 1921. Among their offerings was a classic American soda fountain dispensing ice cream and carbonated beverages in various forms and combinations. In 1941 Wheeler and his wife, Lucy, incorporated the business as Green Mountain Pharmacy, Inc.

In January, 1953 the Wheelers sold the business to Lucien (Boss) and Hazel Renaud, formerly of Hardwick. In 1969 they completely remodeled the store, among other things removing the old soda fountain. Then tragedy struck on February 24, 1972 when fire destroyed the Centennial Block. The Renauds, who owned about half the block site in addition to the pharmacy business itself, immediately built the present two-story structure (C47) and have been operating there since.

Peck's Pharmacy

The first drugstore on the opposite corner of Portland Street goes back at least 25 years earlier. A different building stood there then. Owned principally by attorney H. Henry Powers, the structure housed Amasa O. Gates' drugstore (the law offices of Powers and his partner, Philip K. Gleed, were on an upper floor). On March 1, 1869 fire destroyed the building. Powers and Gleed rebuilt that same year on the same site (the structure has long been known as the Fleetwood Building after another Morrisville attorney, Frederick G. Fleetwood, who later owned the building for some years and had his own law offices there). Beginning with A.O. Gates, a druggist seems to have been a ground-floor tenant there ever since.

Successors to Gates are not all known but purchasing the business in 1930 was Fred C. Peck, a native Morrisvillian. A son, W. Wallace, took over the enterprise with his wife, Jean, when the senior Peck died in 1939. They operated the business until 1972 when they sold it to Donald Paritz and his wife, Ann. Retaining the Peck's Pharmacy name, they continue its operation at this writing.

Ben Franklin Store / Adrian's

In 1930 Rethel C. West and his father, Otis, rented the second floor of the Kelley Block on Portland Street (C79) and began selling boots and shoes, and other clothing and household items. Two years later the Wests expanded into the lower part of the building when that became available. From the outset of their enterprise they were affiliated with the Ben Franklin Store chain, the well-known national variety store concern. About that same time Rethel purchased a store in Hardwick. Otis managed that until shortly before his death in 1942.

In 1949 Rethel acquired the Drowne Block on Portland Street (C83). The two-story brick structure had been built in 1902 by George P. Drowne. On the ground floor Drowne for many years carried on his own clothing and dry goods business and rented space for other uses, including the Morrisville Post Office. That had moved there when the building was constructed. West renamed the store "Adrian's" after his son, who subsequently joined in management of the two Portland Street businesses in 1959. All the "soft goods" — clothing, accessories, linens, fabrics — went to Adrian's, while "hard goods" — housewares, toys, toiletries, candy — remained at the Ben Franklin Store.

A major change occurred in 1961 and 1962 when the two stores switched places! The "new" Ben Franklin Store not only used the existing store space in the Drowne Block but expanded into the portion on the north side of the building which was vacated by the Post Office in 1962. That expansion was followed by another in 1968, when a single-story wood-frame addition was constructed on the north side of the brick structure.

Rethel West died July 5, 1972. The two Portland Street business blocks in 1980 were still part of his estate but managed by his widow, Edith, and son, Adrian. Under the Wests' sustained ownership, Mor-

---

THE CANDY CASE

My father [Rethel C. West] got this very nice new wood and glass candy case for the Ben Franklin Store just before World War II. It originally was one long case which we later divided into two parts and stacked one on top of the other. The different kinds of sweets — candy corn, mints, jelly beans and so forth — were stored there and measured out by weight for bulk sales.

My sister, Rethel, and I worked there as kids. It was where we first learned to wait on customers and to make change. And we also learned something about merchandising — the way my father practiced it. "Always use the scoop, not your hands," he'd say. And when filling an order, you were supposed to keep *adding* a bit more candy to the bag to bring it up to the desired weight. If you ever put in too much and then had to take some out again, that made the customer feel bad. So you always gave them the extra, if you did go a bit overweight. And if a customer showed some interest in a particular candy, you'd give him or her a free sample. "Give 'em a piece, and they'll buy a pound," my father would say.

Adrian West
Recollection, 1980

---

risville's Ben Franklin Store has long been the chain's oldest store under continuous ownership by the same family.

Jones Jewelry Store

This business was founded in 1911 by Homer J. Edmunds in the Wilson building on lower Portland Street (C75). Edmunds was an optometrist, so fitting and selling glasses was his principal endeavor. But jewelry and watches were important sidelines. In 1914 a young Morrisville native fresh out of Peoples Academy became Edmunds' employee. That was Walter D. (Bug) Jones, whose specialty became watch repairing. It was the start of his life-time association with the business.

About 1920 Edmunds moved to new quarters in the Portland Street building which has housed the business ever since (C81). Following Edmunds' death in 1952, Jones and his wife, Hazel, acquired the business, renaming it Jones Jewelry Store. Jones himself died in 1957. Managing the enterprise since that time have been his widow and son, Robert. The latter has carried on the watch-repairing skills learned from his father. Walter Jones' name remains particularly familiar to Morristowners through the many black and white photographs which he took of local scenes, buildings and activities during much of his later years.

Towles Hardware

We're not sure how long this Portland Street building (C80) has housed a hardware store but in 1922 Harry Graves bought the business from Charles W. McFarland. Graves handled what was described a few years later as "the largest and most complete stock of hardware between St. Johnsbury and Burlington." In 1947 he sold the property and business to his son and daughter-in-law, C. Russell and Ethelda Graves.

Then in 1967 what had been Graves Hardware for 45 years became Towles Hardware. Purchasing the block and business was Towles, Inc., the family enterprise of Everett and Ramona Towle and their son and daughter-in-law, Eldon and Joyce Towle. The hardware business actually represented an expansion of the local plumbing and heating business which the senior Towle had been operating for over 25 years. Finally, in late 1974 the Everett Towles sold their 50% interest in the enterprise to Lawrence (Larry) and Carolyn Hale.

White's Funeral Home

Morris B. White added his name in 1911 to the local undertaking business which had been started here about 1855. About 1920 White moved the business from its previous site on Main Street to the basement and ground floor of the Kelley Block on Portland Street (C79). In 1931 White and his wife, Zora, acquired the former George F. Earle "home place" on Brooklyn Street and subsequently housed the funeral service there, where it has been ever since (V13). About 1941 White also established a florist shop in the north end of the Centennial Block (C57). Managed by his son, Jack S. White, that continued until the senior White's death in 1963.

In 1947 Morris White had incorporated the two businesses as White's Inc., doing so in conjunction with his two sons, Jack and Leon M. White. Since Morris's death, the business, now limited to funeral services, has remained in the family, with Jack as manager (Leon died in 1981).

Arthur's Department Store

The predecessor to Arthur's Department Store was a clothing and dry goods business operated since about 1942 by George Gillen. In 1972 Arthur A. and Theresa D. Breault, through their corporation, Breault Enterprises, Inc., rented the so-called Ferris Block property

(C4) and established Arthur's Department Store. In 1975 the Breaults, through another corporation, aTa Realty, Inc., purchased the Ferris Block, actually two buildings, and a third building to the immediate east (C5). That paved the way for a major expansion and remodeling of their store. They now handle a complete line of men's, women's and children's clothing and accessories.

Lamoille County Food Co-operative

It is neither long-established nor especially prominent. But contrary to our opening statement, we here include mention of the Lamoille County Food Co-operative because it is not a business in the usual sense, which is basically to make a profit for its owners. In contrast, a co-operative is basically an enterprise owned by and operated for the benefit of those using its services. A food co-operative in particular provides an "instrument" for its members' joint wholesale purchase of foodstuffs, at resulting lower individual costs compared to normal retail purchases. An additional benefit is that of getting special foods, such as those grown organically, which are not usually available in the typical supermarket.

The local co-operative had its beginning in 1973 as the Morrisville Food Co-op. It was sort of a "branch" of the parent Plainfield Food Co-op. Then in 1975 members in this area established the independent Lamoille County Food Co-operative through a non-profit corporation of similar name.

With the new organization came a notable change in operation. Instead of members pre-ordering their individual needs, the co-operative established a store and stocked it with merchandise for members to buy in the more usual retail fashion, but at special members' prices. The first store was located in the former United Farmers store building off Pleasant Street (C91). In March, 1976 it moved to the Foss Block on Portland Street (C82) and in August, 1977 to its present location on lower Main Street (C3b). The Lamoille Co-op now serves about 100 member households, or 300 to 400 people.

Lamoille Valley Farmers Market

Another Morrisville merchandising operation of a very special nature is the Lamoille Valley Farmers Market. Like other of several such small-scale markets which appeared in Vermont in the 1970's, it provides a central, organized, retail outlet through which local growers of fruits and vegetables and local producers of handcrafts can market their offerings.

Sparked by the abovedescribed Morrisville Food Co-op, the first farmers market here began operations in 1975. Its site was the sidewalk and alleyway area near the Foss Block on Portland Street (C82). But after initial modest success it faltered, then faded in 1977. Reactivated in 1978, the market has been operated since then by the non-profit Lamoille Valley Growers Association, Inc.

Its site has been Academy Park. Each Saturday morning during the summer and early fall, ten to 15 retailers have set up their stands on the little green to market their vegetables and fruits, baked goods, crafts, and other items. As part of the event's promotion, each market day has generally featured some special attraction. These have included musical groups, demonstrations of some agricultural practice (like milking a goat), and such antic events as a turnip-throwing contest.

Morristown has had a number of automobile sales and service agencies over the years. H.M. Rich, believed to be the first, and Morrisville Foundry Company, another very early auto dealer, were mentioned in Chapter 13. Others located in the commercial area north of Morrisville were described in Chapter 12. Morrisville itself has had at least two auto dealers which have come and gone. One was Prunier Motors, which handled Pontiac and American Motors cars. Located on outer Jersey Heights (V33), it was founded in 1954 by Fred A. Prunier and carried on by him and other associates until his death in 1978. It closed in 1980. The other was Ward's auto agency on Elmore Street (V39). Originally the family business founded by Walter Ward handled appliances, and later John Deere farm equipment. Then in 1964 principals George D. Ward (Walter's son) and his son, George D. Jr. (Dewey), also began selling Plymouth cars, later adding the Chrysler line. But the business faltered, then closed in early 1976.

The remaining three automobile businesses are all long-lived. Two have always been in Morrisville proper, while the third was in the Village for many years before "movin' north."

Mudgett-Smalley Motors

This long-established automotive enterprise actually began in the horse-and-buggy days — and sold those very things. Herbert A. Smalley and Walter M. Sargent, Sr. founded the business in 1907 as partners. Using an existing stable on the Brooklyn Street tract of land purchased at that time, they sold horses imported from the west, cattle, farm machinery, sleighs and harness. The firm began selling automobiles in 1913 and during its early years was agent for many different makes of cars. In 1932 it stopped dealing in Western horses, and shifted entirely to automotive sales and service. Dodge cars and trucks subsequently became its principal line and, as of 1980, still is. It has also handled other makes from time to time.

Two key changes in the business's structure and personnel occurred in 1928. A corporation was established, H.A. Smalley & Co., Inc., with Sargent and Smalley continuing as owners and top officers. And Oscar H. Mudgett joined the staff as a salesman and account collector. Subsequently, those three men, their sons and/or their spouses divided ownership and management positions in different ways at different times (Sargent died in 1958, Smalley in 1959, and Mudgett in 1968). Current manager and part owner, as he has been for some time, is Mudgett's son, David. And in 1970 the corporation changed its name to Mudgett-Smalley Motors, Inc.

As for the company's long-familiar Brooklyn Street facilities (V32), the big wood-frame main building was constructed in 1925 to the immediate north of the original horse barn. The latter was remodeled in 1937 to provide additional space for storing cars. It remained in active use until 1978, when it was torn down. The present 14-bay, concrete-block auto repair building on the north side of the main building was constructed in 1972.

McMahon Bros.

Brothers Raeburn R. and Harold C. McMahon founded this business in their home town of Stowe in 1913. In 1924 they moved it to Morrisville, their main site there being a converted livery stable on Congress Street. In 1960 the firm left Morrisville proper and moved to leased quarters in a new building at the intersection of Vermont Rts. 15 and 100 (MS10).

In the earliest years of their business the McMahons sold and serviced Fords. Then in late 1931 or early 1932 the firm became an agent for Chevrolet trucks and cars, later adding, Buicks, Oldsmobiles and Jeeps to its line.

The two McMahons initially operated as partners, then incorporated as McMahon Bros., Inc. in 1931. The business subsequently passed to Raeburn's sons, Cornelius T. and Edward R. McMahon. The latter has managed the firm since then, at least through 1979.

Lakeside Garage

Another long-time auto agency is Lakeside Garage on lower Bridge Street (V12). It takes its name from its proximity to Lake Lamoille. The firm was founded in 1916 by James O. Reed and Fred C. Peck, with Reed buying out Peck two years later. For about 25 years Lakeside serviced and repaired cars, but did not sell them (though it did sell auto parts and tires). Then in 1940 it became a Ford dealer, and has remained so ever since. In 1957 the business was incorporated as Lakeside Garage, Inc. When James Reed died in 1972, the business passed to his son, Rupert J. (Rip) Reed, who continues to manage it at this writing.

Banks

For the last few years two banks have been operating in Morristown. But only one was founded here and that, of course, is The Union Bank. A full-service bank, it has come a long way since it began business as the Union Savings Bank & Trust Company on July 27, 1891.

The bank's first home mentioned by Miss Mower was in a part of the law offices of its first vice president, George W. Hendee, (and his partner, H.C. Fisk). Those were located in the Warren Block on Portland Street (C58). The bank promptly began construction of the two-story brick building on Main Street mentioned by Miss Mower, and opened its doors there in 1892 (C48). In 1940 work was completed on a new building next door (C49). That has been the bank's headquarters ever since, though the building has seen several changes. Completed in 1958 were a number of improvements including a one-story addition on the east side.

When it comes to construction, 1971 represents a major milestone for the bank. Work was completed that year on new buildings for its branches in Jeffersonville and Stowe. Both branches were established in 1919. Also started in 1971 and completed in 1972 was a two-story addition at the rear of the Morrisville headquarters building. This included, among other things, facilities for drive-in window service.

As for its chief executives, the bank's first president was not George Hendee as Miss Mower reported, but rather Carlos G. Noyes. Noyes served until 1898 and was succeeded by the following: Hendee, 1898-1907; Charles H. Stearns, 1907-36; Frederick G. Fleetwood, 1936-38; Walter M. Sargent, Sr., 1938-57; Albert H. Slayton, 1957-58; Wayne T. Burt, 1958-70; Edward J. Welch, 1970-75; Walter M. Sargent, Jr., 1975-79; and W. Arlen Smith, 1979-present.

In 1974 the Union Bank and Trust Company made its informal name its official name, "The Union Bank." Both legal necessity and simplification of the bank's own multifarious uses of its name were reasons for the change.

Other banks have been operating for many years in Lamoille County but until recently the Union Bank was the only one in Morristown itself. That situation changed in 1973 when the Lamoille County Bank of Hyde Park built a drive-in branch office at the Morrisville Plaza shopping center (MS7). The building was enlarged in 1980. Between those times the Lamoille County Bank had, in 1974, merged with the Franklin Bank of St. Albans to become the Franklin-Lamoille bank. Responding to this competition in its backyard, to the growing commercial activity in the Morrisville Suburb, and to increasing traffic congestion around its Morrisville headquarters, the Union Bank in late 1979 completed its own drive-in branch at the Northgate Plaza (MS2).

Newspapers

In the course of his research, this author uncovered a number of facts which enrich (and in a few cases, correct) the history of Lamoille County newspapers which Miss Mower outlined so carefully (pages 234-39). For most of those, however, we refer the reader to our first draft and instead basically pick up here where Miss Mower left off.

As of 1935, Arthur B. Limoge was proprietor and editor of the so-called Messenger-Sentinel List. That consisted of the *Morrisville Messenger*, the *Johnson, Wolcott* and *Stowe Messengers*, and the *Jeffersonville* and *Cambridge Sentinels*. They all had exactly the same editorial and advertising material. Only the masthead name was different to give each paper an obvious hometown ring for subscribers in the respective communities. In 1942 Limoge acquired the *News & Citizen* from Arthur A. Twiss, adding it to the Messenger-Sentinel List (one other acquisition had been the *Cambridge Transcript* in 1927).

But that list didn't last. A Post Office Department ruling in 1943 required that Limoge have at least one-sixth of the material in each of the separate papers different from that in the others in order to retain second class mailing privileges under the individual newspaper names. Such a change, Limoge abruptly announced, was "entirely out of the question." Thus on June 3 that year only the *News & Citizen* issued from the Morrisville press, while the array of seven other newspaper names passed into oblivion.

With his wife, Mable, and son, Clyde, Arthur Limoge incorporated the business in 1945 as News & Citizen, Inc. Since his death in 1958, the newspaper and related printing business has remained a Limoge family enterprise. Clyde has managed the business since that time and served as editor for many of those years, while a daughter, Mrs. Frances (Frankie) White, handled most office functions from 1958 until her retirement in 1979. Clyde's son, Bradley, joined the business in 1973 and eventually will assume full control.

In 1963 the old press shop building on Main Street (C7) was given up to make way for a new Post Office, and the business moved to a new building on Brooklyn Street (V14).

Two additional significant changes occurred in 1973. One was the start of a second weekly publication, *The Transcript*; this is distributed free throughout Lamoille County and several neighboring towns on a postal patron basis (the *News & Citizen* continues to be sold, both individually and by subscription). The second was the acquisition of a new offset press for printing the two newspapers and other work. Playing a key role in these developments was Lewis R. Nichols, who

---

OLD NEWS IS NO NEWS

Send in your items of news when they are fresh. We don't like to publish a birth after the child is weaned, a marriage after the honeymoon is over, a death after the widow is married again, nor a notice of an entertainment after the job work is done elsewhere and the editor is charged for admission.

L.H. Lewis, Editor
News & Citizen
September 6, 1899

---

served as editor of both the *News & Citizen* and *Transcript* from that time until early 1977. Other editors since Nichols have been Dennis A. Redmond, 1977-79; Leslie Gee, 1979; Thomas M. Sargent, 1979-80; James Naples, 1980; Sargent again, 1980-81; and Laura McKeon, 1981-present.

Movie Theatres

Morristown has had three movie theatres in the approximately 80 years that cinema has been a major factor in American entertainment. One, the Tegu, came and went. A second, the Morrisville Drive-In Theatre, has a fair record for longevity but is nonetheless a relative newcomer. The third, the Bijou, is nothing less than a Morrisville institution. That's partly because it has been around so long and partly because a single family name, Emmons, has been connected with the business almost continuously since the theatre's founding.

It was in 1902 that Leon C. Emmons and his partner, W.C. Laird, established the first Bijou theatre in one of the store spaces of the Randall Hotel building (C9). Emmons subsequently bought out Laird and in 1909 moved his "theatorium" to the building at the south corner of Portland and Brigham Streets (C61). But bigger things were afoot. In July, 1910 Emmons opened his theatre in a newly-constructed wood-frame building at the corner of Portland and Bridge Streets.

For several years, however, Emmons actually leased the theatre to other individuals for its operation. Then during a particularly unsettled period for the Bijou around 1920, Emmons and his wife, Augusta (Gussie), first sold, then repurchased the theatre. They also took over its direct management, with Gussie playing the major role in that.

In the Bijou's early days movies were the silent kind, of course, and the theatre followed the standard practice of hiring a pianist to provide appropriate musical accompaniment. By 1930 "talkies" had arrived and in August that year the Emmonses had sound equipment installed, one of the first threatre operators in Vermont to do so.

On April 25, 1936 Leon Emmons died. A year later, his widow, Gussie, found herself faced with major competition for the local entertainment dollar — the opening of another movie house, the Tegu

---

16-PAGE LANDMARK

Many businesses, and many people, have so-called "Firsts" in their careers. The *News & Citizen* is no exception. This week for the "First" time in its 91 years of bringing the news of what goes on in the area, the *News & Citizen* brings to the people of Lamoille County its FIRST 16-PAGE EDITION.

We are quite proud of this accomplishment. It is a far cry from the not too distant years past when it was sometimes necessary to go through the waste basket and pick out discarded copy to fill an eight-page edition. ...

Clyde A. Limoge, Editor
News & Citizen
December 2, 1971

(pronounced Tee'-gue).

John and Andrew Tegu of St. Johnsbury were the principals of what was known as the Tegu Theatre Circuit. In early 1937 they bought the Burke Block on Portland Street, tore that down and on September 10 opened a brand new theatre (C60). For the next nine years the 650-seat brick building was billed as "Vermont's Little Radio City," a rather immodest reference to New York City's famous Radio City Music Hall.

But Gussie Emmons had not been idle. Months before the Tegu was to open, she launched her own building program, a program extraordinary for the fact that it was accomplished without missing a single day's movie showings. It was done this way. While the outer walls of a new brick and concrete block building were constructed completely around the existing wood-frame building, movies continued to be shown in the latter. Then during the several weeks that it took to demolish the old building and construct the new interior, Mrs. Emmons rented the town hall on Main Street (C21) to continue the

Bijou movies. The new building (C66) had about 500 seats on the ground floor and another 150 in the balcony. The construction race with the Tegu came right down to the wire. The new Bijou won by opening September 6, 1937 — four days before the Tegu!

Competition between the two theatres was keen: a mix of bidding to get the better films and using promotional devices like raffles to draw the patrons. Both theatres offered an attraction familiar to numerous Morrisville area youngsters during the 1930's, 1940's, and 1950's: Saturday afternoon matinees with their irresistible adventure serials.

When one theatre finally did go, it was the Tegu. That was some time in June, 1957 when, without prior announcement, the Tegu Circuit's theatres apparently all closed simultaneously. The Tegu property here subsequently became a First National Store, one of the national grocery chain, and today is Brosseau's Super Market.

Back at the Bijou, on May 21, 1963 Gussie Emmons died at the age of 87. She was then the oldest independent theatre exhibitor in New England. Beginning some years before that and since, ownership of the business passed, via a corporation, first to her three sons and one daughter, and following their deaths, to the sons' respective widows. They are Blanche, Margery, and Helena Emmons, all of Morrisville. Blanche Emmons has served for some years as manager.

The closing of the Tegu in 1957 had certainly been some relief for the Bijou. It was not total, however, because a strong summertime competitor for the previous eight years had been the Morrisville Drive-In Theatre. That opened August 5, 1949 on part of the former Lamoille Valley Fairgrounds on outer Brooklyn Street (MS32).

Owner of this newest example of the open-air, auto-oriented entertainment facilities which had been sweeping America was Green Mountain Drive-In Theatres, Inc. The following year the company became a "two-link" theatre chain by opening the Derby-Port Drive-In just outside Newport city in the town of Derby. Organizers of and early investors in the new enterprise were all Morrisville area residents. Only recently did the theatre change hands. In 1980 Howard A. Manosh, a prominent local entrepreneur, acquired the business.

The drive-in's first season was a pretty noisy one. The sound system, it seems, was two loudspeakers mounted on top of the screen and, according to one report, "at times the voices of actors and actresses could be heard in Cadys Falls." Things quieted down the following spring when in-car speakers, such as are in use today, were installed.

The theatre accommodates about 300 cars. Its other facilities include a play area and benches for children in front of the cars near the screen, and a snack bar-projection building. Each year since its opening the theatre has operated about 20 weeks from the last week of April to the middle of September.

> For details about various of these local businesses — plus information about a few others not mentioned here at all, see the "first draft" of *More About Morristown, 1935-1980*; the Foreword describes what and where that is.

Chapter 15 - Public Houses

MORRISTOWN'S PUBLIC HOUSES since 1935 have certainly been diverse in character — a classic center-of-the-village hotel, three main-highway motels, and even a few enterprises catering mainly to tourists. We'll begin our review with one of the latter, and then record the others in roughly chronological order.

Samoset Cottage Colony

Founder of this major resort-type enterprise was Dr. William T. Slayton. He called it Dreamwold, a romantic name for the summer recreation community he began establishing in 1908 on the western shore of newly-created Lake Lamoille. Beginning with his own former-farmhouse home there, Dr. Slayton proceeded over the next five or so years to build and equip 20 guest cottages for summertime "camping." The lake, of course, offered fishing, swimming and boating. Other recreational facilities on the 40-acre complex included a nine-hole golf course, tennis courts, archery range, bowling green, croquet court and bridle paths for horseback riding.

Each cottage was given the name of a Pilgrim woman — Humility Cooper, Rose Standish and Desire Minter, to name a few. In 1913 that led Dr. Slayton to rename his resort more appropriately as Samoset-on-Lake-Lamoille, Samoset being the Indian chief who had been friendly to the Pilgrims upon their arrival at Plymouth in 1620.

The lake resort, which operated from late May through Labor Day, appears to have been a complete success under Dr. Slayton's ownership and management. But in 1924 he sold the development to George W. Munsey of Haverhill, Mass., who altered the name to Samoset Cottage Colony. While business remained brisk, attendance did decline during the 1930's, presumably in part because of the Depression. In an effort to reverse that trend, Munsey in 1937 expanded and diversified by taking guests in the wintertime. He initially offered ice-skating, sleigh rides, sledding, and tobogganing. And for the 1939-40 season he provided a rope tow for skiers.

Apparently that didn't work because Munsey sold Samoset in 1941. The new owner then and one subsequent owner experienced continuing problems and in 1957, the Samoset resort passed into history.

Randall Hotel

And the walls came tumbling down in 1956. The walls of the Randall Hotel, that is, which with a prominent place opposite the head of Portland Street was so long Morrisville's centerpiece commercial structure (C9).

Miss Mower has noted (page 244) how the hotel's founder, Carroll F. Randall, remained its proprietor and manager for more than 30 years. It was Randall's death on May 14, 1925 which ended that long tenure. In appropriate fashion, his funeral was held at the hotel.

A nephew of Randall, Frederick Child, Jr., then managed the 50-room hotel for about a year before the property was sold to Mr. and Mrs. F.L. Burbank, former hotel-keepers of Montpelier. Two years later, on May 15, 1928, they suffered a major setback when fire destroyed much of the hotel's third story and the upper part of its original distinctive six-story tower. The former was replaced but the tower got shortened three stories in the rebuilding.

The property changed hands three more times over the next 25-plus years, each new owner renovating and altering the structure in various degrees, some of them major. The last owner to actually operate the hotel was Erwin D. Miller. In 1956 he sold it to Edward R. McMahon of Stowe, who razed the structure to make way for other use of the site.

Farm Motor Inn & Country Club / The Farm Resort

"How To Keep 'Em Down On The Farm: Make It A Golf Course." Such was the headline for a story in a national golf publication in early 1972 which described the dramatic new use which a Morristown family had made of its long-established farm.

That farm was the LaPorte Dairy of Mandoza and Edna Couture, 280 acres along the LaPorte Road three miles south of Morrisville (T40). About 1956 the Coutures began taking in guests at their farm home. In 1962 they expanded their overnight accommodations by converting their chickenhouse to a motel with both single rooms and efficiency apartments. They named it the Farm Motel. Then in 1963 the Coutures sold off all their Holstein cows but continued raising and selling hay. Several years later they set about converting pasture, hay meadow and former cornfields to recreational instead of agricultural use.

Completed in 1971 was a beautiful 18-hole, par-3 golf course. Concurrently, the Coutures' classic big red barn was converted to a restaurant and lounge, and a pro shop for the golf course. Subsequently added were a swimming pool and tennis courts.

The Coutures called the complex the Farm Motor Inn and Country Club. Guests were attracted to stay at the motel by the various recreational facilities, and especially the golf course (the latter was also open to the general public, both on a club membership basis and for a daily greens fee). In the wintertime the resort facility catered to winter sports enthusiasts: alpine and cross-country skiers, snowshoers, ice skaters, and snowmobilers.

Playing a major role in the enterprise with the senior Coutures were their two sons: Norman, who was superintendent of the golf course, and Henri, who with his wife, Ann Marie, managed the motel, restaurant and related facilities. Tragedy struck the family, however, in 1972 when Mandoza died from injuries suffered in an automobile accident.

The first of several major changes in the facility itself and its ownership and management came in 1975. That year the Coutures leased the premises to another party and in 1977 sold them to Farm Resort, Inc. The principal stockholder of that was Richard T. Willis of Richmond. A major change in the facility under Willis came in 1978 when the golf course was changed to a regulation 9-hole course.

But Willis encountered serious difficulties. They finally ended in June 1980 with foreclosure of his mortgage and reversion of the property to Edna Couture (who in 1977 had been remarried, to Leo Gagner of Jeffersonville). Operating only the golf course itself, Mrs. Gagner has since had the property on the market.

Mountain View Cottages

Located on Vermont Rt. 15 about a half-mile from the Wolcott town line, the Mountain View Cottages tourist court was established by Claude W. and Arlie T. Lambert (T36). In 1957 they acquired the farm property of Mr. and Mrs. Rolland Choquette. The property, which fronts on the Lamoille River, offers views of both Elmore Mountain and the Sterling Range. Hence the name for what became the Lamberts' summer-autumn seasonal business.

Over the next two years they built two cottages themselves. Then in 1960 they "imported" five others from what had been a tourist camp in Cambridge.

In 1963 they purchased a single "creamy" machine and built a small stand for serving the frozen confection. Thus was born the Mountain View Snackery — the last word of which was also the Lamberts' contribution to the English language! Business was good and over the next three or four years the family added more pieces of "fast food" equipment, expanded the snackery building, and increased the staff several times.

In 1971 the Lamberts sold the combined businesses to the first of several subsequent owners. In 1981 Kelsey and Mary Brandt own the snackery (and original farmhouse) and Paul and Ruth Goudet own the Mountain View Cottages. The latter facility was earlier expanded to include a campground for tourists with trailers or tenting equipment.

Sunset Motel

Robert Houle, long-established Morristown entrepreneur and construction contractor, was both the founder and builder of the Sunset Motel, which opened July 4, 1960 (MS17). Located on Vermont Rt. 15 a few hundred yards west of the intersection with Vermont Rt. 100, the motel initially included 12 units. Houle subsequently expanded it several times. In 1964 he constructed right next door what became known as the Charlmont Restaurant. For some years that was owned and operated by a son and his wife, Philip and Phyllis Houle.

In 1971 the senior Houle sold the motel, now numbering 34 units, to another son, Robert, Jr., and his wife, Jean. They in turn sold it to William and Eva Shafer in September, 1974. The Shafers operated it only about a year before selling to Kenneth and Madeline Bourgeois, the present owners.

Monette's Lodge

This Morristown lodging place was a fairly substantial one which had interesting origins. But it lasted only a few years, at least as a place for overnight accommodations.

Its founders, Leo and Irene Monette, had gone into farming in 1946 on the former Tyndall farm far out on what is now called Cote Hill Road (T37). Having decided to give up farming, they converted their barn in 1963 to what became Monette's Lodge. Operating year-round, their basic facilities included 13 rooms for some 46 guests, a restaurant, bar and dance hall, with dances held every Saturday night at the latter. In 1965 the Monettes sold the lodge and related property, including their long-time family home, to Dr. David Bryan of Stowe. But they continued to manage the facilities for him. Then in 1968 Dr. Bryan conveyed the property to other interests and Monette's Lodge came to an end.

A notable subsequent lessee in the early 1970's was the Free State of the Ark, Inc. That was a commune founded in 1971 by Donald A. Frederiksson but which came to an unhappy end only a few years later. Finally, in 1977 the old Monette's Lodge building and some land were sold to the Full Gospel Christian Assembly, Inc., a new Morristown church, the history of which is provided in Chapter 20.

Crimson King Motel

The Crimson King Motel is located on the west side of Vermont Rt. 100 near the Stowe town line (T38). It is a small motel which was operated as a retirement enterprise by Leamond (Lee) and Dora Perkins until they sold it in mid-1981 to Dan and Alice Desmond. Formerly residents of Connecticut, the Perkinses had acquired land for the project in 1967 and over the next three years built the present facilities.

They named their motel after the Crimson King maple tree, a favorite of theirs in Connecticut. It is a special tree, each unit of which consists of a scion of the patented Crimson King species grafted to the stock of Norway maple. Sadly for the couple, however, they had great difficulty growing their namesake tree on their property.

> For other details about Morristown's public houses — plus some information about several small guest houses not mentioned here at all, see the "first draft" of *More About Morristown, 1935-1980*; the Foreword describes what and where that is.

MORRISVILLE RAILROAD YARD

Chapter 16 - Transportation And Communication

TWO OTHER ELEMENTS of any community's social and economic life are its transportation and communication facilities. In Morristown's case we'll basically view these through separate histories of the individual enterprises or facilities, both public and private, which have provided such services here.

Lamoille Valley Railroad

The long-familiar railroad track is still there — the ribbon of steel which follows the original roadbed through the scenic countryside of northern Vermont. But much, much has changed with the old St. Johnsbury & Lake Champlain Railroad since Miss Mower completed her brief history (page 123). Before reviewing those changes, however, a few modifications of her account need to be made.

As originally conceived, the Portland & Ogdensburg Railroad was to be a major trunk line connecting the Atlantic coast at Portland, Maine with the Great Lakes at Ogdensburg, New York. Two portions of this line were in fact built and operated: the Eastern Division through Maine and New Hampshire, and the Vermont Division. Some planning was also done for the Western Division across upper New York State (and into Canada) but none was ever built.

The Vermont Division itself was composed of three separate Vermont railroad corporations: the Essex County Railroad between Lunenberg on the Connecticut River and St. Johnsbury; the Montpelier & St. Johnsbury Railroad between St. Johnsbury and Danville (as its name indicates, this line was originally to have run to Montpelier); and the Lamoille Valley Railroad between Danville and Swanton (not between Hardwick and Cambridge Junction, as Miss Mower has it). While each of these maintained a separate corporate existence, the three were managed together by an "executive committee of the joint companies composing the Vermont Division." The St. Johnsbury & Lake Champlain Railroad was organized in 1880 after the P&O's Vermont Division collapsed in 1877.

Following bankruptcy proceedings for the StJ&LC initiated in 1945, a reorganization plan was worked out under which a new company, the St. Johnsbury & Lamoille County Railroad, Inc., took control on January 1, 1949. (Having the same initials for the new line's name

---

MIXED-UP MILK TRAIN

Those were the days, circa 1940, when the railroad used our water to fill their locomotives. Usually in the summer when the water was low, we, with the use of an electric pump, filled the railroad tank with water from the river. It so happened that just prior to the last time we used this river water, the [United Farmers] creamery began to discharge skim-milk into the river just above the intake of this pump.

One day, just after this pump had been put in service, Engineer Charlie Johnson and Locomotive 1485 and two cars came up the pike with the morning mail train and stopped at Morrisville to fill the tender, as was their usual custom, which being accomplished, he set out for a routine and uneventful run to St. Johnsbury, expecting to arrive on the advertised.

Everything went alright until he whistled for the crossing west of Wolcott, when, instead of the usual strident blast of the whistle, it gave a very wet warble, not unlike a child's bird whistle. Then things began to happen.

The boiler began to foam, skim-milk began to bubble from the stack at each exhaust until the jacket of the locomotive was white with the residue, and the air pumps began to falter, letting the air brakes leak-on and drag. The cylinder cocks were opened and each stroke of the pistons sent a cloud of skim-milk way out of the right-of-way, the electric generator gave up the ghost and the injectors, mercifully, failed to pick up.

Stopping somewhat short of the Wolcott Station, Charlie and the fireboy went to pulling the fire to prevent burning the crown-sheet, while the conductor ran for the nearest phone to call St. Johnsbury for another engine. In due time the train proceeded, several hours late, the 1485 was towed to St. Johnsbury where its boiler was drained, some flues had to be renewed, and orders went out to take water at either Cambridge Jct., or Greensboro Bend, but DO NOT USE ANY MORE MORRISVILLE WATER.

Willard K. Sanders, Superintendent
Morrisville Water and Light Department
Annual Report, 1969

---

prevented what would have been a major expense for changing its identification on all its rolling stock!) Among the stockholders was Lewis A. Putnam, who served as president.

A key to the line's revitalization was a conversion from steam to diesel locomotives carried out by the new management. Freight revenues increased but, after years of decline, passenger service ended

TRANSPORTATION AND COMMUNICATION

on June 30, 1956.

Late that same year an agreement was made to sell a controlling share of the company's stock to Murray M. Salzberg, Meyer P. Gross and Morris H. Snerson, operating as the H.E. Salzberg Co. of New York City. It was not until early 1960, after much controversy and lengthy litigation before the Interstate Commerce Commission (ICC) and the Federal courts, that the Salzberg group finally assumed control.

But times were not good for the StJ&LC. In 1965 the Salzberg interests filed an application with the ICC for permission to abandon the line. The regulatory agency held hearings on the application but never made a decision because in early 1967 Samuel Pinsly of Boston, a successful owner-operator of other short lines, purchased the StJ&LC. Pinsly inaugurated a number of capital improvements and changes in

---

RETURNING THE FAVOR

Some time in August, 1950 Extra No. 37 West took siding for No. 74 East at Morrisville. Due to a heavy switch-list, brakeman Jack Crafts was on top of a car three cars from the head-pin. Jack was built like the old Morrisville water tower and was respected by other St. Jay hands both for that physical size and for his integrity and years of experience. A thunderstorm was closing in but the rain had not started. Suddenly there was a terrific flash and crash. The engineer looked back, thinking the depot building had been hit. That was all right but he could not see Jack on top. Then he spotted him on the ground beside the line of moving freight cars. The hogger yelled and blew the whistle in the danger call and brought the train to a halt. The crew promptly reached Jack and took him to the depot where the operator, Joe Stone, called an ambulance. On arrival at the Copley Hospital, Jack was alive and it was soon clear he would survive, and he did. As he regained consciousness, Jack asked who had hit him on the back of the head. He said he wanted to return the favor. The old rounder was then informed that he had been struck by lightning.

Adapted from a story told by
Warren G. (Rick) Fancher, 1973

---

operations, but traffic declined instead of increased as Pinsly had expected. Worse was the deterioration of much of the StJ's roadbed — a condition which contributed to at least 37 derailments in 1972. The upshot was Pinsly's own application in late 1972 to abandon the line.

The StJ's rescuer this time was not other private interests but the State of Vermont. In 1973 the State acquired the line from Pinsly and leased it for operation to a group of Lamoille County businessmen headed by Bruno Loati of Morrisville. During this troublous period the entire line was actually closed down for about four months beginning in late 1972, and the stretch from Morrisville east was idle for another one-and-three-quarters years. Federal funds made possible a program of rehabilitation begun in 1974, and on January 4, 1975 a special train made a festive inaugural run between Morrisville and St.

Johnsbury to mark reopening of the entire 99-mile line.
But not until 1978 did a measure of stability return to the local railroad. And that came only after two more changes both in the management and the name of the line.

More on that momentarily but first it might be noted that one key effect of the StJ&LC on Morrisville occurred in 1959 when the line's headquarters were established here for the first time (they had been in Montpelier since 1949 and, before that, in St. Johnsbury). Used for offices was the old passenger depot building (C74), the original part of which had been built about 1872. Under Pinsly's ownership, a large new office building and equipment repair shop was built in 1969 at the end of Stafford Avenue north of the Village (MS30).

In 1976 the State's lease arrangement with the Loati group ended in controversy. As a result, the St. Johnsbury and Lamoille County Railroad name and the nearly century-old StJ&LC initials passed into history. The successor lessee-operator — but only for a year — was the Northern Vermont Railroad Company, a subsidiary of Morrison-Knudsen, Inc. of Idaho. The Vermont Transportation Board then almost gave up on finding a long-term operator before reaching agreement on a ten-year contract with a new corporation effective January 1, 1978. That was the Lamoille Valley Railroad Company (LVR), which used the history-repeats-itself name of part of the original trans-Vermont line. The new company is basically controlled by shippers along the line plus the Central Vermont Railway.

Earlier, in 1977, the Vermont General Assembly had authorized $7.2 million in bonds which, in conjunction with additional Federal funds, was to be used for further major rehabilitation work on the railbed. That project, which lifted authorized operating speeds from a dismal 8 mph to 25 mph, was completed in late 1979.

For its part, the LVR management has made a number of improvements in the railroad's operations and rolling stock. An interesting recent development was the successful inauguration of passenger excursion trips over the line in mid-1981. In any event, traffic has generally been building since 1978 and both the company itself and the Vermont Transportation Agency are optimistic about the Lamoille Valley Railroad, at least for the near future.

For some years before these recent major developments the local line had attained almost legendary status among rail buffs as a one-of-a-kind country-bumpkin railroad. The nostalgic days of steam and regular passenger trains may be gone but most local residents would also surely miss the wail of a diesel horn as a Lamoille Valley freight train rolls out of Morrisville late in the evening.

Morrisville-Stowe State Airport

Information about the early days of air transportation in Morristown appears in Chapter 19. Described there are the town's first aviators and its first "airport." That was the Copley Airfield, which was noteworthy because its two landing strips were also fairways for a golf course! The Morrisville-Stowe State Airport is noteworthy for another significant, though not so colorful, reason: it is the first air facility in Vermont to have been constructed and owned by the State itself.

Details in a moment but first a note about another Morristown "airfield." That was a turf landing strip located in a field north of Vermont Rt. 15 (MS35). Principal user of the strip was the Morrisville Squadron of the Civil Air Patrol (CAP), which was organized in

---

SANTA RIDES THE RAILS

Yes, for the last two years Santa Claus himself has been riding the rails on the Lamoille Valley Railroad. His appearance has been the result of a co-operative effort of the railroad's employes and management. Beginning in 1978, we have run a special train over the whole line — between St. Johnsbury and Morrisville the third Saturday before Christmas, and between Morrisville and Swanton the second Saturday.

The train has consisted of a locomotive, flat car and caboose. The people in the shop decorate them all up using evergreen trees and branches which the section men cut and bring in. The flat car carries an old sleigh, which is filled with Christmas packages. That's Santa's, of course. The Morrisville Water and Light Department loans us one of its big, lighted decorative bells. That goes on the front of the locomotive — along with a set of deer antlers to suggest Santa's reindeer!

Well, very early the first Saturday we all get over to St. Johnsbury to finish up the decorating. Then off we go, stopping at each station along the line. And who is the engineer? Why Santa Claus, himself, of course — at least Santa as played by our general manager, Dave Snyder. It's really something to see him in his beard and costume as he leans out the window of the locomotive, waving and pulling on the diesel horn as the train comes into a station.

When the train is stopped, Santa moves from the locomotive to the caboose. The local children climb up the steps at one end and go inside where they can see and talk to Santa and tell him what they want for Christmas. Then after they receive some candy, they go out the other end. Helping Santa with all this are some of his elves! They are our female office employes, who have made their own costumes.

Folks along the line really seem to enjoy the whole thing and appreciate it a lot. We receive many letters of thanks and the

Edward A. Lewis, Business Manager
Lamoille Valley Railroad, 1980

February, 1959. Local CAP members and other users called the landing strip "Little Laguardia," a humorous reference to what was then New York City's major air facility, Laguardia Airport. The strip was used only in 1959 and early 1960 while the new airport was being built.

Under plans developed by the Vermont Aeronautics Commission (in 1960 renamed the Vermont Aeronautics Board) the State built what initially was a gravel landing strip on the site which it purchased east of LaPorte Road about two miles south of the Morrisville business center. With Governor Robert T. Stafford, himself a pilot, on hand, the facility was dedicated on August 4, 1960.

The new runway was 2,100 feet long by 75 feet wide with about 90-foot safety strips along both sides. In November, 1961 the runway was extended 150 feet to the north. And in 1963 it was extended another 650 feet to the south, and a 50-foot-wide by 2,700-foot-long landing surface plus an apron and taxiway were paved. That gave the airport a capability of handling planes up to small twin-engine size. At this time the VAB also acquired sufficient additional land to permit an eventual extension of the runway to 4,000 feet. In August, 1965 a lighting system was installed. That consisted of both approach beacons and runway lights.

The first name of the new air facility was actually the Morrisville State Airport. In 1963, however, the VAB changed the name to Morrisville-Stowe State Airport. This was both to recognize existing use and to promote new use of the airport by Stowe residents and patrons of that town's resort and recreational facilities.

Described so far have been the basic physical facilities at the State-owned airport. As for its management, that has been kind of an on-again-off-again affair, at least initially. For several years, and the first year in particular, service at the new airport was downright primitive! While the VAB carried out some housekeeping duties from Montpelier, David W. Mudgett of Morrisville served as the airport's first "manager," a job which he performed as a public service. "The State needed somebody whose phone number they could list in a directory," he told the author, "and mine was it." And a flier really *needed* to call somebody if he landed there low on gas — because there wasn't even a gas pump at the airport when it first opened! That lack was corrected in 1961.

Concurrent with installation of the gasoline pump was the State's construction of the first building at the airport. That was a small A-frame structure which served as headquarters for the Morrisville CAP Squadron, a place to house radio equipment, and an "office" for airport services, such as they were.

Since 1964 the airport's management has been more formalized. Beginning that year, though with gaps from time to time, the State entered into leasing or other agreements with private firms for that purpose. Each has generally sold and rented planes, offered charter services and flight instruction, and provided varying degrss of aircraft maintenance services. The following is a roster of those managers.

 — 1964-1970: Walter B. Hoblin and his company, Vermont International Airways, Inc. Hoblin built the airport's first hangar (later removed) and promoted the sport of gliding.

 — 1972-73: David Fosgate and his Highgate-based Swangate Air Service, Inc.

 — 1973-75: Montair Flight Service, Inc. of Burlington.

 —1975-present: Mansfield Aviation, Inc. This began as the company of Norris LaClair and his wife, Kitty, who lived right at the airport. A special service of theirs was scenic flights. In 1978 they sold their interest in the corporation to Stephen S. Fried of Plymouth, Mass. and his company, Yankee Aviation, Inc. Fried has employed several men as on-site managers. He has promoted a revival of the airport as a center for the sport of gliding, or soaring, as current parlance has it. Under his management the airport was also established in 1981 as a "commercial drop zone" for sport parachutists. And in late 1979 Fried had a new hangar constructed.

The Morrisville-Stowe Airport is, according to a Vermont Aeronautics Department staff member, "as safe as any airport of its size." What accidents have occurred have generally been caused by problems with the plane itself or by pilot error, rather than by any characteristics of the airport itself and/or the surrounding terrain.

And there have been accidents, 13 of them as of early 1978. Two produced fatalities. The first of those occurred on October 22, 1966. Involved were a glider and its pilot, Roger S. Brown of Syracuse, N.Y., as they were being towed into flight. At take-off, Brown was still attempting to fasten his canopy. When his glider was released by the tow plane about 1,000 feet beyond the south end of the runway, it spun out of control and crashed, killing Brown.

Four Massapequa, N.Y. residents died when their single-engine aircraft crashed while preparing to land at the airport on October 26, 1977. Killed were the pilot, Joseph C. Buehl, and three passengers: Buehl's wife, Elizabeth, and William F. Lambui and his wife, Mary. After an initial landing approach was too high, the plane was circling the airport when it crashed near Ryder Brook just east of the runway.

The story of the Morrisville-Stowe State Airport is not complete without a more detailed history of the organization briefly mentioned above, the Morrisville Squadron of the Civil Air Patrol (CAP). The CAP is an auxiliary of the U.S. Air Force (USAF) through which civilian pilots are organized to aid in search and rescue efforts for lost planes and people. The USAF does furnish local CAP units with aircraft and fuel for search missions but members serve on a volunteer basis and each squadron must raise its own funds for all other equipment, fuel and supplies.

With David W. Mudgett and Henry B. Mould as principal movers, the Morrisville Squadron was organized on February 11, 1959. After some initial difficulties, the Squadron has generally maintained a stable membership of about 20. Mudgett was its first commander, a position he held until 1973 or 1974. Bruce Wilder served as commander from then until January, 1978. He was succeeded by Wayne Perry of Stowe, the present commander. The Squadron has generally met weekly at the airport for training sessions and practice searches, minor maintenance of the squadron plane, planning of fund-raising events — and plenty of "hangar-flying" conversation.

"Little Laguardia" was, as noted above, the squadron's first base of operations. Landing there June 14, 1959 was the first airplane assigned to the squadron by the USAF, a Piper L-4B. In mid-1961 that was exchanged for an Aeronca L16. Both these planes lacked electrical systems and so had to be hand-cranked. For that reason they also lacked radios. That meant, in Mudgett's understatement, that to communicate with anybody on the ground "you had to shout pretty loud." Desiring the modern flying amenities which electricity provided, the squadron in 1968 obtained its present plane, a Piper PA-8 Super-Cub.

The Morrisville Squadron's first search operation occurred in August, 1960 and it has aided in a number of other such missions since then. They are definitely not pleasure flights: hours of careful watching in tight search flight patterns are involved. On at least one search, that for Herbert Sachs of Stowe in 1967, it was a Morrisville CAP member, Carroll Page of Hyde Park, who spotted the wreckage of Sachs's plane on Mt. Abraham in Lincoln.

And for a final note on air facilities here, Morristown has one other "airfield." That's the private landing strip which Real E. Perras established in 1979 at his farm on Earl Gray Road. At this writing Perras does not have a plane of his own. Using the strip instead is another Morristown resident, Adrian West, for his aircraft.

Buses and Taxis

Morristown's roads and bridges described in Chapter 4 are mostly used, of course, by vehicles of one sort or another to get people and materials from here to there. Many individuals do this in their own vehicles, but others depend on public highway transportation, that is, buses and taxis.

Still well remembered by older Morristowners for his services in this field is A. Clovis (Coutch) Couture. Couture in 1922 acquired from Leon C. Emmons the long-established Morrisville-Stowe stage line, which carried passengers, mail and freight. Couture initially continued its operations with horses but within a year entered the automotive age by purchasing what was called "a new Ford bus." It looked more like a truck, however, with passengers seated in a closed compartment behind the driver's cab.

In 1924 Couture really made a name for himself with what must have been the area's first snowmobile. It was an adaptation, with skis, of the Ford bus. For two or three winters Couture made regular runs to Stowe in that unusual vehicle.

Also beginning in 1924, Couture's "stage" became the Red Bus Line, and his route was extended to Waterbury. Later and until shortly before his death in 1947, he operated as the Mount Mansfield Bus Line. A major part of his business was transporting skiers between the Waterbury railroad station and Stowe, and between Stowe village and the ski slopes on Mt. Mansfield.

Couture was also one of about a half-dozen different contractors who bussed students for the Morristown Town School District. That practice continued until 1952 when Clarence C. Miller became the sole school bus contractor. He continued the service until 1972, when Richard R. Godfrey, the present contractor, took over.

The record of those providing taxi service in Morristown following Couture's passing is somewhat uncertain. But this much is known. Operating one service for a couple of years in the late 1940's were Omer and George Morway. Much longer established was Alton R. (Peavine) Graves and his City Cab. He began about 1949 and continued until 1965. Operating another taxi service from 1962 to 1969 was Sidney Bartlett. He sold out to Red Lowell, who in turn was succeeded in 1971 by Fred and Peggy Pierce. They are still operating their service at this writing.

Telephones

Alexander Graham Bell invented the telephone in 1876. We don't know who Morristown's telephone pioneers were but only four years later the *Lamoille News* reported from Morrisville that "Telephones are creating quite a sensation in town. There are a number up in running order and 'more to follow'." The first local inter-town telephone communication came in 1882 when, as Miss Mower noted (page 128), a line went up between Morrisville and Hyde Park village, connecting several businesses, offices and homes in both communities.

The history of telephone companies subsequently providing service

---

WEATHER ON THE PARTY LINE

A rather special service I remember giving local patrons was, believe it or not, the weather report. This was in the late 1920's. I and the other telephone operators would give one long ring on each of the rural lines. There were ten or so parties on a rural line at that time. That ring would tell all of them to pick up. We would then give the weather forecast, which the office had obtained from Burlington. We always did this right at noon time. I think some people set their clock by the time of that call.

> Pearl Cote
> Long-time Morrisville operator
> Recollection, 1980

---

in Morristown is a bit complicated, and uncertain in some particulars. Briefly, two companies initially were operating here. Each had its own switchboard and circuitry and its own list of subscribers (those who wanted service from both companies had to have two different telephone instruments to do so!). One was the Vermont Telephone and Telegraph Company (VT&T), which was chartered in 1884. Its switchboard, initially located in the Fleetwood Building (C46), was moved in 1898 to the third floor of the Centennial Block (C57). The other was the Citizens Telephone Company, which was chartered in 1896. The location of its switchboard is not known.

Though some details are unclear, both companies by 1931 had been acquired by or merged into the New England Telephone & Telegraph Company (NET&T), a corporate unit of the massive Bell system. A key step along the way was the consolidation of the Citizen switchboard with that of the VT&T in 1903. Then in early 1909 new and larger switchboard facilities necessitated a move from the third to the second floor of the Centennial Block. There the telephone office remained for the next 34 years.

It was from this place, of course, that local telephone patrons would hear the familiar "Number, please?" from operators on duty at Central. In addition to handling basic local and long distance calls, the Morrisville operators provided a number of special services. Particularly well remembered is their handling of calls to report fires, and subsequent actuating of the Village fire alarm system.

Subscribers serviced through the Morrisville exchange (which besides Morristown, includes Elmore and most of Hyde Park and Wolcott) have grown from 602 in 1918 to 2,884 as of June 1, 1979.

Other milestones under NET&T management are the following:

— In 1943 the switchboard and office moved from the Centennial Block to a room in the Randall Hotel block (C9).

— On December 15, 1948 the Morrisville exchange went to a dial system. Housing the intricate circuitry and switching equipment was a new brick building constructed on Union Street (V17). Operators continued to serve at a switchboard there (the Randall Hotel office was closed) but not for local calls. They now handled only long-distance toll calls, not only for the Morrisville exchange but also the Jeffersonville, Johnson and Stowe exchanges.

— On June 26, 1971 the Morrisville exchange went to direct dialing for long distance calls.

— And finally, on July 26, 1979 the era of local telephone operators came to an end as the Morrisville telephone office went to fully automatic operation.

Odds and Ends and EMCO

No commercial radio or television station has made Morristown its headquarters. But a special television antenna installed here has brought the space age to the town in a very real way. That antenna is part of the cable television system of EMCO CATV, Inc. of Manchester. Founded in 1960, the company in early 1979 began installing its 12-channel cable system in Morristown and Hyde Park. As of May, 1980 it had 374 subscribers on its 14 miles of transmission lines.

As for other kinds of electronic communication, note was made in Chapter 13 of the first commercial broadcast radios which appeared in Morristown in 1922. The earliest *known* commercial television set here was the 17-inch Motorola purchased in 1949 by Arthur C. Stewart.

EMCO's first subscribers here were Mr. and Mrs. Norman Black — and for a special reason. The company leased part of the Blacks' farm on Frazier Road as the site for its antenna facilities (T39). It made the first connection to their home as part of the arrangement.

Two of the three current reception units consist of high wooden poles with various individual antennae mounted on their tops for receiving signals from earthbound television transmission stations in the Northeast and Canada. The third, installed in late 1979, is a rather special 6-meter-wide dish antenna on the ground. It receives signals transmitted via a satellite orbiting some 22,300 miles in space!

> For other details about these transportation and communication facilities and enterprises, see the "first draft" of *More About Morristown, 1935-1980*; the Foreword tells what and where that is.

Chapter 17 - Alexander Hamilton Copley

We should not hesitate to impute to him the noblest motives of generosity. What has he not done for us? And remember when you make out a list of things, you are assessing not just fortunate possessions but a man's character and spirit. ...

Here was a man regarded in metropolitan parts of commerce as a hard bargainer, a shrewd manipulator not too sympathetic or generous or careful about public esteem. ... Yet here was a man I know who in his secret heart had a wistful desire to be accepted in some community of men and women and children as a good neighbor and friend.

SO SPOKE REV. GEORGE E. GOODLIFFE, pastor of the First Congregational Church, at funeral services here for Alexander Hamilton Copley, who died on May 22, 1948 at his home in Milton, Massachusetts. The 91-year-old Copley had been in failing health for several years and was almost totally deaf and nearly blind when death came. But for more than 20 years before his end, much of Copley's time and energy had been devoted to assessing the needs of Morrisville and Morristown and using substantial parts of his substantial fortune to fill those needs, both present and future. Such was the "list of things" to which Rev. Goodliffe referred. Some of Copley's gifts have been described by Miss Mower but the roster of benefactions has grown considerably since the Mower history was published. And because of certain trusts which Copley established, that roster presumably will continue to grow forevermore. It thus seems appropriate to provide as complete a record as possible of the fruits of that generosity to date. But first a bit more about the man himself to supplement that provided by Miss Mower (page 97).

Rev. Goodliffe touched on some aspects of Copley's character and to those we can add some impressions of a longtime Morrisvillian, Eloise Stafford. She had a number of contacts with Copley through her father, Charles H.A. Stafford. He served as something of an agent for Copley by overseeing construction of two of the institutions which he funded, a new Peoples Academy building and the original Copley Hospital. In 1977 Miss Stafford remembered Copley as "a very pleasant, very precise, quiet and somewhat odd man. He moved very slowly, dressed very nicely and was vain but in a nice way. He wanted my father to scrutinize every bill for the school construction; he didn't really trust the school board to spend his money right and so paid for the school directly himself and didn't give the town a lump sum for the purpose. For most people he was a kind and generous man but he really was very tight in the way he spent his money."

And Atty. Clifton G. Parker, who was associated with the implementation of several of Copley's gifts and in the settlement of his estate offered these recollections of Copley in his later years:

"Mr. Copley was not a large man and always dressed in a business suit. Walking down the street, he was not someone who would particularly attract anyone's attention. He used a cane when walking, not for support, I think, but mostly to aid him in his poor vision — testing the height of a curb, that sort of thing. Of his bad vision, I remember that when he needed to sign something, his long-time secretary, Amy Wade, would rule a very heavy ink line and help him get his pen over it in the right place so he could follow the line. I believe his terrible loss of hearing really affected all his social contacts. ... As for his many gifts to Morristown and Morrisville, there were some tax considerations — he much preferred giving his estate away himself for charitable purposes rather than have the government taking it in taxes and then doling it out. And he didn't wish to be famous or desire a lot of publicity because of his gifts. I think he was truly and sincerely desirous of just being generous to his old hometown."

Unfortunately, that Copley munificence apparently did not extend to his Massachusetts hometown. Or so it would seem from the report of one Milton resident who said in 1962 that "here he is remembered as a typical 'Scrooge,' both in disposition and money matters!" Be that as it may, the Copley generosity is well known and gratefully remembered in Morristown. The following are what that generosity has produced to date, given in roughly chronological order.

Peoples Academy - Copley Building

Miss Mower has sketched the history of this (pages 97-98). The so-called Thomas lot which Copley gave as a site for the new school measured about 15½ acres. He had purchased this in 1901 for his wife, Lucy,* as the location for what was to have been a summer home for the couple. But Lucy died in 1906 so that a Copley home in Morrisville was never built. In 1941 Copley added to the high school site by giving the Town School District another 13 acres of land with

---

*Lucy Frances Page, daughter of Mr. and Mrs. Charles R. Page of Morristown. They were married February 18, 1886 in Morrisville. Both are buried in the Page family lot in the Pleasant View Cemetery.

its house. This bordered the original school property on the east.

As noted above, Copley paid directly for the new school's construction; he gave out no figure of the total cost, but one report describes it as being "more than $250,000."

In early 1930 the Morristown School Board announced it had "recently received" a gift of $10,000 from Copley. Apparently this Copley grant was separate from the basic construction project but what other school purpose it served is uncertain.

Music Awards

The *Morrisville Messenger* of September 20, 1933 carried an announcement that Copley was offering prizes of $100 each to the Peoples Academy band and glee club "for meritorious work." There is no record, however, that any prizes were ever awarded.

Streetlights

A project closely related to that of the school itself was the construction in 1929 of concrete-paved Copley Avenue, which connected the new school with "downtown" Morrisville. The Village paid for that but Copley apparently helped meet some of the expense, perhaps for landscaping. He certainly paid for another striking feature of the avenue, its series of 24 ornate streetlights. These consisted of wrought-iron "basket" fixtures, each fitted with Belgian leaded glass lights and standing atop a reinforced concrete standard.

Because of very high maintenance costs brought on largely by vandalism, this significant element of Copleyana was replaced in 1962 by five modern mercury luminaire lights on high metal standards. Clarence C. Miller subsequently bought the ramshackle lights, restored some of them, and then resold them.

In 1981 two lights still remain, though not working, in their original positions on West High Street. They were erected there by Copley to illuminate the area near the Patch house (now gone) where he used to stay. Two more, which are not actually streetlights, are those standing on either side of the front entrance to the Copley Building of Peoples Academy; they *are* still working.

Copley Bandshell

Many a Morristowner has walked or driven up to the Peoples Academy grounds at eventide on Thursday to hear a concert by the Morrisville Military Band. The Band is, of course, playing in the bandshell provided by Copley in 1931 (V37). Little can be added to Miss Mower's account (page 233) except to note that beginning in 1972 (and possibly earlier), the bandshell has been, when weather has permitted, the site for Peoples Academy's graduation ceremonies.

First Universalist Church

Copley made a number of significant donations to Morrisville's First Universalist Church, certain of which had a major impact on the church's continued functioning. Details appear in Chapter 20.

Copley Country Club and Airfield

Again, Miss Mower has sketched the beginnings in 1934 of what became the Copley Country Club and early Morrisville airfield (pages 128-29). A full history of this community facility appears in Chapter 19.

Copley Hospital

Miss Mower describes the establishment of Copley Hospital in 1932 (pages 176-77). Its history since that time follows in Chapter 18.

Street Signs

In the spring of 1935 handsome street signs appeared at various intersections in Morrisville, another gift from Copley. The signs themselves were of enamel — white letters on a blue background, each set into a metal framework and mounted on a metal post. Time, the elements,* and vandals took their toll and in 1972 the Copley signs were replaced by new green and white metal signs.

Community Building

In 1938 Copley established a fund of $50,000 to be used by the Village of Morrisville for construction of a new community building. His initial gift (he later added another $50,000) apparently was made as something of an incentive grant because at Morrisville's annual meeting in 1938, Village voters approved an appropriation of $75,000 to be combined with Copley's $50,000 for purposes of constructing an appropriate building. Envisioned was a structure housing an auditorium, municipal offices and possibly a fire station.

With several false starts and certain complications, it was not until 1948 that a formal plan was finally developed to use the special Copley fund in that manner. Acquired by the Village as a site was the Noyes House property at the west end of Main Street (C1). The house was to be torn down and constructed in its place would be an elaborate new structure complete with municipal offices (but no firehouse), auditorium-gymnasium, club rooms for various organizations, and even a rifle range! So what happened? At a special meeting September 30 that year Village voters effectively killed the proposal.

Less than a year later a different plan took shape for a new gymnasium adjoining Peoples Academy. There was some strong opposition on grounds that this did not match Copley's intentions. But Village voters eventually approved the proposal in 1951.

The gym, officially named the Copley Community Memorial Building, was completed in 1952, its construction taking place in conjunction with that of the new north wing to the Academy. Of interest is that the gym building and the land on which it stands is Village, *not* Town School District, property. And reflecting, at least in part, the broad community use intended by Copley, it has echoed to the sounds of various activities besides physical education classes and basketball games. Town meetings, high school dances, and children's Halloween

---

*These signposts are said to have been so attractive to dogs as targets for urinating that many of them deteriorated to the point where they had to be replaced.

programs are just a few.

Copley Agricultural Fund

In 1946 Copley established a trust fund of $10,000 for Morristown to be known as the Copley Agricultural Fund. Income from the Fund (the principal was to remain intact) was to be used "for the purpose of maintaining, in whole or in part, instruction and educational facilities ... for a high school course in agriculture ..." (the trust includes provisions for the Fund's transfer to another Copley fund if it is not used for that specified purpose). In 1947 a course in vocational agriculture was established at Peoples Academy which apparently was financed, at least in part, by the Fund. It is difficult to trace how the Fund has since been used, but in recent years at least, the annual income (now about $600) has simply gone into the town school system's general fund.

Agricultural Scholarship

About 1946 Copley established another fund, the estimated $200 in annual income from which was to provide scholarship aid to students going on to further study in the field of agriculture. While at least one such scholarship grant was apparently given in 1948, what happened to the fund after that has been lost to history.

Amy Wade Fund

This benefaction to Morrisville began as Copley's benefaction to his long-time secretary, Amy Wade. He provided her with a life tenancy in a one-family house which he had acquired in Brockton, Mass. Upon her death, the property was to revert to the Village of Morrisville. Wade died in February, 1961 and at the Village's annual meeting that April, voters authorized their trustees to sell the property. They also stipulated, according to the brief official record, that "The proceeds [are] to be held until another meeting." Those proceeds came to $12,000 but 19 years went by before voters decided what to do with them.

By 1979 the Amy Wade Fund had grown, with interest earnings, to nearly $21,500. Sparked by the interest of Trustee Richard C. Sargent, Village voters in 1980 directed that "the interest from the Amy Wade Fund [be used] to purchase and plant trees and shrubs and for other beautification of Village streets and other Village property, and if not needed for those purposes, to defray other expenditures ..."

Trust Funds

Copley established two other special, and very substantial, trust funds to provide local benefits, one known as The Copley Fund, the other The Alexander Hamilton Copley Fund. Details about those follow this basic review of the various Copley gifts.

Miscellaneous Notes

In addition to the funds which he provided for these numerous social and municipal improvements, Copley also gave several antique artifacts to the Town. One was a "handsome, old-fashioned desk." This is now on display at the Morristown Historical Society's Noyes House Museum.

Another remembrance of Copley is a handsome portrait owned by the Copley Hospital which was painted by Ruth Greene Mould in 1966. Commissioned by the Copley Hospital Auxiliary, she executed her oil painting on canvas using a large sepia photograph of Copley as a basic "model." The portrait now hangs in the patient solarium.

The Copley Fund

The Copley Fund is a trust fund created by Alexander H. Copley in 1942 for the purpose of establishing and maintaining a home for elderly women in Morristown and Morrisville. The trust's erratic history has included actual ownership of real estate, a major boost from another benefactor, a court judgment, and several fights with the Internal Revenue Service. After all that, the home for elderly women has not been established. And it, or any comparable facility, is not likely to be established, as matters now stand.

Copley established The Copley Fund with a letter of trust in 1942, and an amendment to that in 1945. Named as original trustees were Atty. Clifton G. Parker and Levi M. Munson. The Fund was initially quite small but Copley added to it at various times before his death in 1948 so that in early 1949 it amounted to $102,760.49.

In his trust Copley directed that when trustees had decided the Fund was large enough, all its principal and accruals of income were to be used for establishing and operating the Alexander H. Copley Home for Elderly Ladies. Here, he prescribed, "elderly women may receive care and maintenance on a fee basis or upon the conveyance of their property to said Home conditioned on their life support and maintenance ..." Whether or not a home operated on this basis constituted a charitable purpose later came into dispute, as will shortly be noted.

Under direct and indirect stimulus by Copley himself, the Fund in its early years came to own several large residential properties in Morrisville. They were the Gov. Hendee or Valleau House on Main Street (C40), the Whipple or Patch house on West High Street (now gone), and the so-called Hardy house at the end of West High Street. Each was a prospective site for the home for elderly ladies — at least in Copley's view. But in the end, trustees sold them all off, the Hendee house in 1947, the others in 1952. They did so partly because they felt each of the structures was not wholly suitable, and partly because they believed that the Fund at that stage was simply not large enough to do what Copley envisioned.

While Munson and Parker continued some study of the matter, the Copley Fund for some time lay in limbo, except for regular increases resulting from earnings produced by the Fund's investments. Then in 1963 a dramatic development occurred. Munson himself died on January 16 that year. Under his will, the residue of his substantial estate was to go to the Copley Fund, though it could be used under somewhat less restrictive terms than Copley's own letters of trust. The Munson estate took several years to settle and over that time the Copley

Fund saw a series of major increases in its principal, culminating in 1968. At the end of that year the Munson bequest stood at $562,118.68 and the Copley Fund itself at $191,307.93, for a grand total of $753,426.61.

Well before that time, however, Parker and Walter M. Sargent, Jr., Munson's successor as trustee, had launched a new effort to dispose of the Fund. On January 7, 1965 they sent a memorandum to trustees of the Copley Hospital in which they proposed that the Fund be used to construct an "extended care facility for deserving elderly persons" which would be operated by the hospital on a contract basis with the Fund's trustees. It would be built in conjunction with other expanded facilities which the hospital board was considering.

But what seemed like an eminently suitable use of the Fund was never realized. Frustrating the trustees were two tax challenges by the Internal Revenue Service (IRS). Parker and Sargent eventually won both but the second victory in particular saw a distinct alteration in the status of the trust. That involved warding off an IRS assessment of income taxes by establishing clearly that The Copley Fund was a charitable trust. To accomplish that, trustees sought, and on February 16, 1970 obtained, a *cy pres* decree from Judge Rudolph J. Daley as chancellor of the Lamoille County Chancery Court. While the order established the charitable purpose of the Fund, it also permitted the trustees — and this is of equal importance — to use the Fund somewhat differently than Copley had specified, that is, for something other than a home for elderly ladies.

Daley ruled that although Copley's letters of trust and the Munson bequest manifested "a general intention to devote the property to charity," the purpose specified had "become impossible or impracticable of enforcement." He then prescribed the following: "That the trustees shall use all of the funds and other property [of the Copley Fund and of the Munson bequest] ... exclusively for the purposes of providing and maintaining an extended care facility for the care and support of elderly persons, male or female, residing in Morristown, Vermont, or adjacent areas, who are in need of such care and who are deserving of financial assistance for or towards such care at such facility."

At the time, trustees Parker and Sargent characterized the decree as "a long-awaited step towards actual realization of use of the [Copley and Munson] funds." In fact, however, the decree was too late. The hospital had long since gone ahead with its own building program.

The Copley Fund trustees rested on their oars but a new Federal tax matter put them to rowing again. The Tax Reform Act of 1969 effectively required that a charitable trust annually use the income which it had accumulated the previous year. In other words, it couldn't let the income accrue, something the Copley Fund had been doing for some time. But how to spend that income, particularly in view of the use which the *cy pres* decree had specified for the Fund?

Parker and Sargent did not seek a change in the decree though it presumably will be necessary at some point. Instead they developed what they termed an "interim plan" for distribution of Fund income directly "to elderly deserving persons resident in the several towns of Lamoille County." Beginning in 1972 and continuing each year since, the trustees have distributed the Fund's annual income by issuing checks to each of 134 persons, one for every 100 persons in Lamoille County's 1970 population of approximately 13,400. A specified number of beneficiaries was allocated to each town according to its proportional share of the county population, specifically: Belvidere, 2; Cambridge, 15; Eden, 5; Elmore, 3; Hyde Park, 14; Johnson, 19; Morristown, 41; Stowe, 24; Waterville, 4; and Wolcott, 7. For selection of the "deserving" recipients in each case, the trustees have relied basically on recommendations which they obtain from each town's selectmen and other local officials. All recipients must be 65 years or older. None, however, are identified in any public way. The amount per person distributed each year has been $300 to $400.

At the end of 1974 Clifton G. Parker and Walter M. Sargent, Jr. resigned as trustees of the Fund. The passing of the Copley (and Munson) baton was, however, very much a family affair. Appointed by the Lamoille County Probate Court as successor trustees were the two men's sons, Dr. Robert C. Parker and Atty. Richard C. Sargent. At this point it should be noted that the trustees receive no income for their services; it is wholly a volunteer effort.

The younger Parker and Sargent have continued the program of annual distributions set by their seniors — though a major development gave them pause in 1977. A local committee sought their approval of a plan for something approaching Copley's original idea: use the Fund's principal ($908,445.02 at the end of 1980) to establish a homelike retirement facility for ambulatory elderly men and women who, while needing some financial help, could pay something for their care from their own resources. Trustees Parker and Sargent assisted with the committee's study but in the end rejected its proposal.

The Alexander Hamilton Copley Fund

The Alexander Hamilton Copley Fund is probably familiar to more Morristown residents than the Copley Fund just described, though the similarity of names makes it easy to confuse the two. The former, however, is more familiar for two reasons. The first is that two important municipal improvements have been funded by it in recent years. The second is that Copley took certain steps to keep local residents aware of the fund.

The AHC Fund (as we shall abbreviate it) was established as a trust by Copley in his will, the final version of which he executed in March, 1937. A curious feature of the trust provisions is Copley's seeming confusion of the Village of Morrisville and the Town of Morristown.

Paragraph Eleventh of Copley's will, as amended, opens as follows: "... I give, devise and bequeath to the TOWN OF MORRISTOWN, Vermont, all the rest and residue of my property of every nature remaining in the hands of my Trustee, the same to be held as a permanent charitable trust fund to be known as the ALEXANDER HAMIL-

TON COPLEY FUND, and the net income only to be used for creating works of public utility and beauty for the use and enjoyment of the inhabitants of the Village of Morrisville in the said Town of Morristown, Vermont, and to be confined to localities within the area of said Village or to purposes specifically benefitting its residents. It is my intention that no part of said income, however, shall be used for religious, political, educational or any purpose which it shall be the duty of the said Village of Morrisville or the said Town of Morristown, Vermont, in the ordinary course of events, to provide."

Note that while the Village and its inhabitants are quite clearly the beneficiaries of the AHC Fund, it is the Town which is actually to hold the Fund. Not only that but Copley then provides that the Fund be governed by a board of trustees consisting of the three (later five) Town selectmen (*not* Village representatives) plus two other trustees which Copley himself named. (He first appointed Attys. George M. Powers and Frederick G. Fleetwood, then after they had both died, Levi M. Munson and Atty. Clifton G. Parker.)* Copley underlines his intent with the following confusing statement: "As this is a public charitable gift for the Village of Morrisville, Vermont, it is my intention that said Town shall at all times be officially represented by a majority of the Board of Trustees charged with [the gift's] management." Copley then also requires that the Town provide office facilities and record-keeping personnel to aid in management of the Fund. More significantly, he also requires that the Town be responsible for ongoing maintenance of each project carried out with monies from the Fund. It all seems somewhat contradictory: the Village is supposed to get all the benefits but Town officials control decisions on those benefits, and the Town has to pay for their upkeep.

Be that as it may, Copley included other stipulations concerning how the Fund was to be administered and used. The more important ones: (1) "I direct that [the Fund's] income shall not be anticipated or pledged beyond the amount actually in hand, but it may be accumulated for any purpose within the scope of the gift, and successive accumulations may be applied to the same object. Any work or works established from the Fund may be improved, enlarged or added to from time to time ...;" (2) "I also direct that no part of said income shall be mingled with other funds or applied in joint undertakings, but that each work established under this gift shall be separate and distinct, and shall always bear in a conspicuous place a suitable inscription identifying it as erected or established from said ALEXANDER HAMILTON COPLEY FUND;" and (3) Copley makes clear he doesn't want the AHC Fund to be used "for small and comparatively unimportant needs which might be ... technically within the scope of the trust;" rather, it should be left to accumulate and used "only for important civic improvements." Local residents who think some needed facility or program could be paid for by the AHC Fund should keep in mind that Copley's instructions, taken together, certainly limit how his Fund can be used.

*Edward J. Welch subsequently succeeded Munson, and Atty. Richard C. Sargent succeeded Parker, as the two appointed trustees.

As for that basic provision of Copley's will that AHC Fund projects be "for the use and enjoyment of the inhabitants of the Village of Morrisville," the two projects paid for to date, and one of them especially, appear to require a very liberal interpretation of that restriction. More shortly but first a look at the size of the Fund.

Copley's estate included considerable real estate holdings in eastern Massachusetts. Trustees liquidated those during the three years following Copley's death in 1948. Proceeds from that ultimately brought the principal of the Fund to $257,451.83, an amount now fixed.

The first project, a major one, to be financed by the AHC Fund was the large public parking lot in the center of the Morrisville business district. This involved the purchase of about 153,000 square feet of property between Portland and Pleasant Streets and bordering on Hutchins Street on the north. That was then cleared of existing buildings, storm sewers were put in, pavement was laid, parking spaces were marked for 100 to 125 cars, and lighting was installed. Before the construction itself went ahead in September, 1966, Morristown voters met a requirement of Copley's trust by voting to have the Town "maintain, operate and provide for the future current expenses of such facility from town funds and means." When the project was finally closed out in 1970 (complete with the required identification monument), the AHC Fund had spent $128,320.80, $98,500 of which was for real estate. That was deeded to the Town on May 27, 1972.

The one other project which the Alexander Hamilton Copley Fund has financed so far is the building and equipment for a local ambulance and rescue service. While this project surely provides an enormously valuable public service, it should be noted that it has, from the beginning, been wholly identified with the Town, not the Village, which Copley specified as the beneficiary of his trust. And those receiving the services can be considered the general public, not just Village, or even Town, residents.

In August, 1974 Town voters approved the recommendations of a previously-authorized Town study committee for an appropriate rescue service facility. They also committed the Town to maintaining the building and equipment. A plot of land was then acquired by the AHC Fund on Washington Highway across from the Copley Hospital. A building was constructed by a local contractor, O'Neal Demars, Jr. A nonprofit corporation, Morristown Ambulance Service, Inc. (MAS), was established to manage the service. MAS crew members are all volunteers and services are provided free of charge. Members, however, have to undergo extensive training before handling any medical emergencies. Service began June 1, 1975 and on November 17 that year the AHC Fund trustees transferred title to the facility to the Town. The $81,717.20 in capital costs which the Fund paid for included $4,000 for the land, about $50,000 for the building, and about $16,000 for a new ambulance.

Finally, one other proposal was considered, but rejected, by AHC Fund trustees in 1980. That was to purchase two rundown tenement blocks in Morrisville, raze them and convert the lots to small parks.

Chapter 18 - Copley Hospital

MUCH HAS HAPPENED to the Copley Hospital since its opening in 1932 (pages 176-77). A large new building has taken the place of the original little "cottage" hospital, and that itself has undergone two major additions and a number of interior changes. Perhaps more significantly, the hospital's role in providing health services in the Lamoille County area has expanded considerably, particularly in recent years.

To return to the hospital's beginning, Miss Mower has noted (page 176) that Addison P. Wheelock had built the impressive structure which was converted to that purpose. That occurred in 1896. As for the conversion, there appears to be no record of how much money Alexander H. Copley donated in establishing the hospital. And in addition to those funds, he subsequently paid for a variety of new equipment and new facilities, some of which are noted below.

Articles of association for the original private, non-profit Copley Hospital, Inc. were signed on January 25, 1930 by ten subscribers including Copley himself. There was, and still is, no capital stock and the hospital is "owned" by the corporation's corporators, in 1980 a group of about 200 area residents. The corporators are a self-perpetuating body which chooses its own additions and replacements. The corporators in turn choose most of the members of the hospital's governing board of trustees (these elected members all serve without pay).

The hospital (V19) officially opened for service on October 3, 1932. Its first patient was 95-year-old Mrs. Lucy Bean of Morrisville, who was admitted for treatment of a fractured hip. The hospital's first live birth was that of Charles James King, son of Mr. and Mrs. Philip King of Morrisville, who arrived on November 6, 1932 (sadly, one stillbirth had preceded the happier event).

Shortly after the hospital's opening, its medical staff of eleven doctors formally organized and chose Dr. George L. Bates as their first president. The doctors also worked out a system under which they took turns being "on call" for emergency needs at the hospital

— a system which prevailed for many years.

The hospital's first two years were surely fraught with difficulties. The patient census was apparently higher than expected. And money in those Depression days was, of course, tight. As a result, the hospital had a long list of overdue accounts. Mrs. Vivian Greene Isham, the hospital's first superintendent, also had a number of serious problems with equipment and the building itself. These included a shortage of patient beds, short-comings with the X-ray system, cramped quarters for the laundry and kitchen, and an expensive heating system.

Many, if not all, of these structural problems were alleviated by some major changes financed by Copley. Completed in 1935 was a conversion of the Wheelock carriage house at the rear of the hospital to a dormitory for its nursing staff. The nurses had previously been housed in the hospital itself and that area was converted to nine additional beds, raising the hospital's capacity to 28 (plus five bassinets). The kitchen and laundry were enlarged and the hospital's furnace was converted from oil to coal, the latter resulting in a major reduction in fuel costs.

An interesting development of the hospital's early period was how it served an educational function by helping to train future doctors — a function not since repeated. From 1935 to 1938 seniors at the University of Vermont Medical School each spent a month at the Copley Hospital in a program of on-the-job training. They were known as "junior internes."

To help make ends meet during the Depression period in which it was founded, the hospital appealed for and received donations of various things from area residents. Those included some hard cash but food was far and away the item most frequently given. And payment in kind for hospital services was accepted in many instances: noted Mrs. Isham in her annual report for 1938-39, "We have been able to get most of our wood [for the furnace in the nurses' dormitory] on bills, where we have been unable to collect any other way."

On another front, the hospital received a substantial financial boost from the Village of Morrisville. At their annual meeting in 1933 Village voters approved an "appropriation" in the following form: Village trustees were authorized to issue a promissory note of $15,000 to the hospital, with 5 percent interest payable to the hospital out of Water and Light Department profits. The principal was also to be paid if and when the Water and Light Department treasury permitted. The Village subsequently issued the promissory note and paid the interest on it for some years. But the author has not been able to determine what finally happened to it.

Much clearer is the record of other help which Village taxpayers provided the hospital for 27 years. This was free water and electricity. When first approved in 1936, the contribution was worth about $500. By 1964, when a year's worth of power and water for the hospital had climbed to over $4,000, Village voters decided it was too much. By a count of 46 to 30, they turned off the hospital's faucet and pulled its electric light switch. It has paid for those utilities ever since.

Returning to those early years, a key development elsewhere in Lamoille County had its first real impact on Copley Hospital in the late 1930's and early 1940's. That was the establishment of Mt. Mansfield and Stowe as a major ski resort. The winter of 1940-41 the hospital treated 126 ski accident victims and has been doing more of the same every winter since then.

In her annual report of 1946 Supt. Isham told her board of trustees that "No one knows better than I how desperately we need more

---

THE EARLY YEARS

The following is a sampling of items which appeared in various of the annual reports submitted during the 1930's by Superintendent Vivian Greene Isham to the hospital's board of trustees:

Our nursing staff has been changed many times, due mostly to marriage. We have been most fortunate in having a very excellent staff of registered nurses, and I believe we owe a great deal of our success to these young women. [Report of 1933-34]

It has been with great satisfaction that we have watched the increasing interest of the Public in the Copley Hospital. It is now becoming our Hospital and show place to bring visitors, instead of a "White Elephant." People in this Community are slow to accept innovations, but when they do, they are most loyal. [Report of 1935-36]

An Insurance inspector advised [that we install] a door in the roof of the elevator. He advises something new every year, however, I don't quite see how that will benefit us. [Report of 1936-37]

The Cemetery Association donated a plot of land on Washington Highway facing the hospital. We are in hopes to set out trees on this land, obviating the rather gruesome effect it would have on patients, if used as intended. [Report of 1936-37]

This is my seventh report to you. Every year I have spoken of Mr. Copley's great generosity and his interest in the institution. I am at a loss for new words of appreciation to express the deep gratitude, love, and respect we (who are in such close touch with Copley Hospital) feel for him. [Report of 1939-40]

---

space." It took a while but on November 23, 1958 a new two-story brick structure was dedicated about two hundred yards east of the original hospital (V20). In addition to 38 patient beds (including ten in the maternity and surgical wing), the new building provided an enlarged and more sophisticated operating area plus a maternity section, more substantial X-ray facilities, laboratory, doctors' quarters, and business office.

As for the old hospital building, it became another important health-care facility in Morristown. In 1960 Maude Cline, R.N. acquired the property and converted it to what she called the Dumont Nursing Home. Since 1963 the facility has been owned and operated by Carl

Paisner and Herbert Kaufman of Framingham, Mass. Initially doing business as Morrisville Nursing Home, Inc., they have made several changes in the structure in addition to general remodelling. One was a six-bed addition constructed in 1966, which brought the capacity to about 45 beds.

Then in 1972 the company established a new, modern 80-bed health care facility on Harrel Street (V21), since known as Dumont Nursing and Convalescent Center (a short while later a new corporation of that name succeeded Morrisville Nursing Home, Inc.). With completion of that facility, the Dumont Nursing Home was renamed Dumont Manor and has since served basically as a retirement home for the aged, that is, for those not requiring intensive medical care. In 1973 what had been the nurses' residence for the original Copley Hospital was, after long idleness, refurbished and reopened as a residential home for elderly persons requiring minimal supervision. Capacity of The Annex, as it is known, is 11 residents, plus the "house mother." Finally, the Dumont Nursing and Convalescent Center itself was enlarged in 1979.

Returning to the hospital, its governing board in 1966 announced plans for a major addition to the "new" structure. The basic problem was overcrowding. Construction of a new wing to the rear of the original building began in 1967 and on November 2 and 3, 1968 an open house was held to mark its completion. The new wing included 21 additional beds, nine of them in private rooms of which there had previously been none. Also provided were special patient bathroom-shower facilities, a post-operative recovery room and a patient solarium-lounge.

In 1971 a number of changes were carried out in the original wing. These included relocation of the laboratory and doctors' lounge, and major revision and remodeling of the business offices and reception area, all on the ground floor, plus establishment of a small, second operating room on the second floor. In 1975 an enlarged, more comprehensive maternity wing was established on the second floor along with improvements to the nurses' station in that area.

Before reviewing another major building program just recently completed, let us first look at several organizations which have supported Copley Hospital in various ways. We'll also examine how the hospital's health care role has changed in recent years and some of the manifestations of that change.

The Copley Hospital Auxiliary has been around almost as long as the hospital itself. As recorded by Miss Mower (page 177), the Auxiliary was formed in 1933 as a volunteer organization to support the hospital in various ways. While its membership has always been open to both men and women, the latter have certainly predominated.

For many years the Auxiliary's main mission was making and mending hospital linens, towels, and patient garments. By 1979, when the sewing services ended, they had become just one of several functions of the Auxiliary.

Another is fund-raising. From the beginning, the organization held various benefit events to earn monies to pay for materials and other expenses of the linens project. Since 1970, however, the Auxiliary has been sponsoring one or more major fund-raisers each year to help pay for special capital needs of the hospital. The monies donated have grown ever more substantial: from about $7,000 in 1975 to about $20,000 in 1979. These events and projects have included dances, auctions, stage shows, and, most recently, a thrift shop. The shows, known as *The Copley Follies*, were produced from 1975 through 1978. The shop, started in 1978, is known as Second Chance. Established in the former Gates home (C113) on Brigham Street, it serves as a sales outlet for secondhand merchandise offered at "bargain" prices.

A third major Auxiliary function has been its provision of a number of direct volunteer services. But the story of those really begins with another group of hospital volunteers. That was a special service unit of the Lamoille County Chapter of the American Red Cross, and was known as the Gray Ladies. Beginning in 1959, the 25 or so women members of the Copley unit did such things as handle patients' various personal requests, distribute mail, reading material and flowers to patients, and entertain children patients.

But the Gray Ladies dissolved about 1968, and the Auxiliary subsequently assumed responsibility for those basic volunteer patient services. In 1975 the organization expanded its role still further by establishing an information-reception desk for patients and visitors in combination with a small refreshment and gift center in the hospital's lobby. That same year it also established a junior volunteer program under which 14-year-old boys and girls (or about that age) perform some of the patient services.

The Auxiliary's administration of various volunteer services at the hospital ended in June, 1980 (the Second Chance shop continues, however, to be wholly operated by volunteers). Since that time the hospital itself has had a salaried Volunteer Coordinator who recruits, trains, schedules and supervises volunteers for different tasks.

In closing it should be noted that in 1964 the Copley Hospital Auxiliary formally incorporated itself as a non-profit corporation.

Another key hospital organization is what was originally known as the Copley Hospital Nursing Circle but which in 1974 underwent a change of name to Copley Hospital Circle. Its membership from the beginning has basically been all hospital employes. Formed in February, 1957, the organization serves a variety of functions. It has sponsored social and educational programs for the staff, has explored and developed improved methods of hospital administration and patient care, and provides services to its employe-members such as gifts to newly-weds and personal visits to those who are ill. It also donates funds to pay for needed hospital equipment and facilities. One such key project was a fund established in 1960 in memory of Dr. Oscar Calcagni, a long-time member of the hospital medical staff. That was eventually used for the patient solarium-lounge that is part of the new wing completed in 1968.

The original Copley Hospital was both small and limited in the services which it provided. And those services were restricted almost exclusively to inpatients, that is, those actually admitted to the hospital. In recent years, however, the hospital has greatly expanded its health care role for the area. Growth of outpatient services both at the hospital itself and at facilities outside of Morrisville has been a major development. But there have been others as well. In rough chronological order they have been the following.

In 1968 the Health Care Building adjacent to the hospital was constructed to provide attractive office facilities convenient for physicians on the hospital's medical staff and their patients (in its first years some space was also rented to other health and social service agencies).

From 1973 to 1975 the hospital and Johnson State College jointly operated a so-called "satellite clinic" in Johnson village. This provided health services for both the college and surrounding communities.

Beginning in 1974, the hospital played a major role in co-operation with the Cambridge Area Chamber of Commerce in developing plans for what became known as the Cambridge Regional Health Center. Construction of the Center in Cambridge village began in 1976 and was completed in 1977. The Center, with support services from the hospital, offers medical and dental care to residents of Cambridge, Waterville, Belvidere and Johnson in Lamoille County, Underhill and Westford in Chittenden County, and Fletcher in Franklin County.

As direct support of a related health service, the hospital in 1973 deeded about one-half acre of its then 6½ acres of Washington Highway property to the Lamoille County Mental Health Service, Inc. as the site for construction of its own mental health clinic building. That was completed in early 1975. Founded in 1966, LCMHS is a private, non-profit, tax-supported organization which provides a variety of services in the mental health field. It was originally housed in the hospital itself, then moved to the Health Center Building when that was completed.

Also completed in 1975 just across Washington Highway from the hospital grounds was a new building housing the Morristown Ambulance Service (V32). That was described in Chapter 17.

Since the mid-1960's Americans have seen many changes in how health care is delivered and paid for. Various of these have led more and more people to seek outpatient treatment at their local hospital, instead of through their personal physicians. For residents of Lamoille County and beyond* that has been the Copley Hospital. Just consider: in 1955, when the hospital was still in its original building, it served 1,173 outpatients. In 1975 it served 24,919 outpatients — a 20-fold increase!

Outpatient services, which includes emergency service, usually involve the attendance of a physician. The system at Copley for pro-

---

*The hospital's service area for some years has been considered to be all ten Lamoille County towns plus Lowell, Craftsbury and Greensboro in Orleans County and Hardwick in Caledonia County.

viding that coverage on a round-the-clock basis has changed significantly in the face of the ever-increasing demands. While several transitional stages were involved, the responsibility basically shifted from individual physicians who took turns providing the necessary coverage, to physicians who are employes of the hospital and serve on regular shifts.

But while the hospital provided physicians to treat the greatly increased number of outpatients, its physical facilties and equipment by 1976 had become woefully inadequate, both for the direct outpatient services and for certain new support services such as a medical library. Additional patient beds were not required but another distinct need was improvements in certain fire and safety features of the building.

Before construction began on a major expansion and modernization

---

LAUGHS IN THE LAB

It's hard to believe but the laboratory at the new Copley Hospital in 1958 began with only about $100 worth of equipment. There was a $25 used microscope, a waterbath worth about $40, an old refrigerator, and a couple of pipettes. It was also a one-horse laboratory — me. Today our equipment is worth probably $200,000 and we have a staff of ten.

Now, of course, 99.99 percent of the requests for tests and examinations which we have processed over the years have been for real. But with the help of some of our more comical doctors, there have been a few lighter moments. One physician asked me to do certain tests on some blood. That turned out to be from his dog. Another requested some tests on the contents of a standard urine container. It turned out it was urine which he had made with an old tea bag!

                         Francis G. Favreau
                         Laboratory technologist since 1957
                         Recollection, 1980

---

program, the hospital for a time actually faced a possible close-down. This arose out of the fact that because of so-called Life Safety Code deficiencies, the Vermont Department of Health would not grant the hospital a permanent license to operate beyond the end of 1978. Under a review process carried out by certain other State agencies, a modified $2.8-million project was eventually approved. That in turn paved the way for issuance of the license to operate. Construction began in late 1978 and was completed in 1980.

The multi-faceted project included major rearrangement, renovation and improvements of portions of the original building plus construction of 13,000 square feet of additional floor space, the latter in two-story wings. One of these, with a new main entrance, is at the northwest side or front of the original structure. The other is on the original building's northeast side. Among the resulting major improvements were a wholly new emergency room and outpatient complex and a new centralized surgery complex.

Basic purpose of the project was, of course, to better meet area health needs. A related, and very real, spur was that at least some of the improvements had been mandated by the Joint Commission on Accreditation of Hospitals if Copley Hospital was to continue to receive JCAH accreditation. Such accreditation, which Copley had held continuously since September, 1967 — and which, with construction underway, was renewed in October, 1979, certifies that the hospital is providing up-to-date, high-quality health-care services based on standards set by the JCAH.

The Copley Hospital complex has continued to grow in other ways. In 1980 the hospital acquired the former Volney Farr residence to the immediate east. This was converted to offices for lease to the Lamoille Home Health Agency, which previously had its offices in the Health Center Building.

A major project still pending at this writing (1981) is a housing complex for the elderly and handicapped on Washington Highway across from the hospital. Administered by a separate non-profit corporation, Lamoille Area Housing Corporation, plans call for construction of five two-story wood-frame buildings with a total of 38 living units. Aided financially by certain Federal programs, the complex will be known as Copley Terrace.

Finally, to close out this history of the Copley Hospital, two additional bits of information seem appropriate. One is a roster of the hospital's chief administrators, who have been the following: Mrs. Vivian Greene Isham, 1932-1947; Clyde Brumm, 1947-48; Mrs. Lefa Nay Brown, 1948-1963; James Treloar, 1963-1964; Thomas J. Dowd, 1964-1966; Earl S. Smith, 1966-1972; John R. Whitcomb, 1972-1977; and David E. Speltz, 1978-present.

The other is a few statistics which will illuminate to some degree the growth and changes in the hospital during its 50 years of existence and 48 of actual operation: number of patients admitted: 1932-33, 277, and 1979, 1,937; number of beds: 1932, 19 beds and 5 bassinets, and 1980, 54 beds and 6 bassinets; number of employes: 1932, about 7, and 1980, about 200; and cost per day of patient care: 1932, $3.69, and 1980, $133.

> For additional information about the Copley Hospital and its various structures, see the "first draft" of *More About Morristown, 1935-1980*; the Foreword describes what and where that is.

Copley Country Club
MORRISVILLE   VERMONT
Frank Stockwell

Chapter 19 - Copley Country Club And Airfield

Any day now when you want a little golf you can hop in your plane (if you have a plane), fly over to the Copley Country Club at Morrisville and land right on the fairway. No, not next to the golf course, right on it. So far as is known, Morrisville has the only combined airport and golf course anywhere, the only municipally owned course in the state and the lowest membership fee in the country, a season membership ... costing only five dollars.

THOSE ARE A LOT of potent adjectives but that's the way the *Burlington Free Press* described what Morrisville was indeed able to claim for several years as a unique facility. The full story in a moment but first a few preliminary notes about Morristown's entrance into the air age.

The first mention of any airplane in the skies over Morristown was a one-sentence report of the local sighting of an "aeroplane" which appeared in the *Morrisville Messenger* of June 30, 1915. About four years later planes were sufficiently numerous around these parts to provoke the *Messenger's* editor, Lewis P. Thayer, to register this complaint: "Mr. Aviator: — When passing over this town kindly dispense with dropping those 'dead soldiers' [i.e. empty beverage bottles] as we have a great sufficiency down here now." And by that time or soon thereafter, an air strip had apparently been established on the field on the east side of outer Brooklyn Street.

Morristown's first aviator was Ralph S. Stancliffe, who received his pilot's license in 1928. Close behind him were the town's second and third fliers, Robert St. Jock, Jr. and Walton Waite. All went on, for some years at least, to earn their respective livings in aviation, though well beyond the borders of Morristown. St. Jock, who was born in Elmore in 1910 and graduated from Peoples Academy in 1928, did so in truly spectacular fashion. While he trained other fliers and handled many utilitarian flying assignments from several different bases, he took up stunt flying and racing, eventually achieving celebrity status as an "internationally known acrobatic flyer and racer." One of his specialties was upside-down flying. On August 12, 1942 St. Jock met his death in Arkansas — while flying, but not stunting.

So Morristown had some of its own aviators in those early years of the air era. But the town's facilities for doing very much right here were pretty limited. Alexander Copley decided to change that.

In February, 1934 he deeded to the Village of Morrisville about 38 acres of land on the plateau east of Maple Street (there were some later small additions). Thinking of both economic development for the community and its recreational needs, Copley prescribed that his gift of land be used for "a public park, aviation field [and/or] golf course." The deed also has this interesting provision: that "if not used for all or any of such purposes such lands shall revert and pass to the Copley Hospital, Inc."

Concurrent with Copley's gift, application had apparently been made to a Federal agency for funds to aid in development of the airfield; $9,000 was ultimately received from this source to help pay for the $21,000 project. Plans for the golf course itself were developed by two local residents, Levi M. Munson and James M. Kelley, the latter of whom supervised the actual construction. The Village provided some direct help to the project, installing utilities (sewer, water and electricity) and building the access road. Copley apparently paid for all the capital costs not otherwise provided as described. These included a clubhouse building for the golf course, which continues in service to this day. More about the golf course shortly but first a closer look at the airfield.

Its two runways were both 1,800 feet long. One, which was actually oriented roughly east-southeast by west-northwest, was generally referred to as the east-west runway. The other was the so-called north-south runway, though it was similarly skewed from those actual compass headings. Local pilots also usually thought of the east-west strip as the shorter of the two, apparently because large trees and a boundary fence near its east end shortened the *effective* length for takeoffs and landings. Trees also grew near the other three ends of the two runways, particularly the north end of the north-south runway.

The two landing strips intersected at a point about two thirds of the length of both of them. At the intersection was a 100-foot circle formed by a three-foot-wide blacktopped strip which was painted bright yellow; this made the airfield easy to spot from the skies. At the ends of the runways were similar asphalt strips, also painted yellow (some remnants of those still remain in 1980). An air sock was mounted on a tower near the clubhouse but there was no gasoline pump, hangar or other support facilities at the field.

For fliers the Copley Airfield had a number of hazards. Among others, there were those trees to avoid on take-offs and landings. And there was some concern for pilots about the effects of an accident when taking off in a westerly direction — right over Maple Street and the populated area of Morrisvile. According to David W. Mudgett, who received his pilot's license in 1953, the Copley Airfield was, from a safety standpoint, "poor at best." Happily, however, no serious airplane accident apparently ever occurred there.

Official opening of the airfield was marked with a big air meet on June 6 and 7, 1936. Another noteworthy event there (and by some accounts the *only* other one) was the first — and apparently the only — direct air mail delivery and pick-up at Morrisville. The occasion was the U.S. Postal Service's (USPS) commemoration of the 20th anniversary of air mail service. As part of the week-long observance, the USPS arranged for six special flights to be made in Vermont on May 19, 1938. These provided air mail service to 14 communities, including Morrisville, which had never had it before. There was appropriate fanfare when no less than Ralph Stancliffe landed his "sleek yellow monoplane" at the Copley Airfield to pick up and deliver some mail.

No precise data exists of how much the Copley Airfield was used by fliers. But long-time local residents contacted by the author generally recalled that that use was very limited. In any event, by 1946 whatever limited use the Copley Airfield had received in its early years had apparently faded to an absolute minimum. About that time the newly-established Vermont Aeronautics Commission issued a report on airport needs in the state. To begin with, the report's listing of existing airports did not include the Morrisville airfield. The report then described areas in the state lacking air facilities and, as Stage 1 of a Vermont Airport Plan, recommended construction of facilities in five places especially needing them. One was Morristown.

That gap was not actually filled until 1960 when the new Morrisville-Stowe State Airport was completed (see Chapter 16 for an account of that). In the meantime the Copley Airfield continued to be used on rare occasions. The last flight from its once-famous fairways apparently occurred on May 3, 1959. The newly-established Morrisville Squadron of the Civil Air Patrol provided airplane rides for a number of its members (for many, it was their first flight). According to the *News & Citizen*, "although quite windy and bumpy, everybody had a very enjoyable ride." And so the Copley Airfield passed into history.

Returning now to the golf course, it opened for play in early May, 1936, and dedication ceremonies were held on July 23. As originally laid out, the 9-hole course measured 2,514 yards. Par was 34. A number of changes have since occurred in tees, fairways, greens and numbering of holes (see Map No. 4). Today the course measures 2,748 yards and par is 35.

Robert (Red) Reynolds set two course records on this layout. His first was a 31 scored in September, 1974. Then in July, 1975 he beat his own record with a 30. That still stands.

While many country clubs offer other sports facilities, usually tennis courts and a swimming pool, Copley is for golfers only. In the early days, however, members had the special facilities needed to indulge themselves in one other sport, a now somewhat unusual one — lawn bowling. A green for that game was built in 1937 in the area behind the present pro-shop building. The first such green in Vermont, it was the inspiration of James M. Kelley, the man who played a major role in the establishment and subsequent management of the Copley golf course and related Club facilities and activities. The bowling green lasted until the early or mid-1960's when it was converted to the present-day practice putting green.

Standing on the center high point of the golf course is the Copley Country Club's clubhouse. It is a single-story, irregularly-shaped wood-frame building which measures about 40 by 40 feet. While the interior has been altered and added to on several occasions over the years, the exterior remains relatively unchanged.

As noted above, the Village of Morrisville helped in some aspects of the original construction of the airfield and golf course. And as villagers did with the Copley Hospital, they also approved continuing financial support to this other Copley facility. From 1936 to 1962 the Village paid the golf-course/airfield's water and light bill, and

---

SATURDAY SOCIAL

One of the most enjoyable parties of the season [at the Copley Country Club] was held Saturday nite, Sept. 12, [1936]. Over 80 members and friends were present.

At 8:15 a large Bingo game was started at one penny a card. Half of the winnings went to the Copley Hospital Auxiliary. At 9:00 P.M. a blind auction was held. "Jim" Kelley was the auctioneer. Due to "Jim's" original and humorous remarks the bidding developed into real competition, and also gave the guests many hearty laughs.

Refreshments were ice cream and cookies.

The rest of the evening was spent in dancing and card playing.

Frances M. Limoge, Secretary
House Committee, Copley Country Club

---

beginning somewhat later, the costs of fire insurance. In the latter year the golf club corporation began paying those expenses.

To manage and operate the golf course The Copley Golf Corporation was formed in February, 1935. A non-profit corporation, its members choose the officers and board of directors. The first membership drive in 1936 ended 29 short of its goal of 250. The number of members has fluctuated over the years since then. In 1979 there were 294.

In financing construction of the golf course, Copley made clear his feeling that low income should not be a bar to anybody's use of the facility. By one account at least, he prescribed that membership dues should be no more than $5.00. That's what they were for many years — and as such, the lowest membership fee of any golf course in the United States! The first dues increase came in 1944 (to $7.50) and they have gone up several more times since, reaching $80 in 1980.

A number of golf tournaments have been established and played over the years at the Copley Country Club. Among the more important:

— The first tournament on the course was held June 28, 1936. It was between the married men and single men among the Club's members (the former swamped the latter, 10½ to 1½).

— The oldest local tournament actually began before the Copley Country Club was even established! That is the annual Page Cup tourney, a handicap match for the Club's male members. It was established in 1925 at the Lamoille Country Club of Hyde Park. The name comes from Hyde Park's prominent citizen, former governor and U.S. senator Carroll S. Page, who donated the "beautiful silver loving cup" to the Lamoille Club. That closed some years ago and in 1964 the cup was donated to the Copley Country Club. The tournament was re-established there in 1965 and has been held each year since.

— The Club men's championship has been held every year since 1938. The women's championship began in 1942 but has not been held regularly, at least in the early years.

— And finally, there is — what else — but the Alexander Hamilton Copley Tournament. An 18-hole handicap tournament for both men

---

COPLEY CAPSULES, 1962-63

The most powerful golfer of the year so far is Barb Jordan. She broke the cement Tee Box Marker on #9 with a potent drive. The ball ended behind her in the corn field. Pat Fitts drove her pointed golf carrier thru her foot and ended up on crutches. The woes of playing golf. (*News & Citizen*, July 19, 1962)

Sand traps have been added on five holes. It's been said that there is more sand on the golf course now than there is on the shores of nearby Lake Elmore. (*News & Citizen*, May 16, 1963)

The men had an Inter Club Match with Stowe Sunday. Morrisville placed second. It was a very hot day, the greens were too fast, the cups were too small and unfortunately the Stoweites were too good. (*News & Citizen*, August 1, 1963)

---

and women Club members, this event honors the memory of the Club's benefactor and namesake. It began in 1979.

In addition to golf, the Copley Country Club over the years has been the scene of a variety of social activities, some wholly separate from golf itself, others in conjunction with the game. Among the former are socials, card games, potluck suppers, dances and dinner-dances. Most notable among the latter is the Twilight League, at which male members of the Club gather in the late afternoon and early evening for a round of golf followed by card-playing and socializing at the clubhouse. This event was established in 1949 and has continued ever since, initially on Thursday evenings but for most of its years on Wednesday. In the early 1960's women members established their own day of golf at the Club, initially on Tuesday, and later and presently on Thursday. A special event of the men's twilight gatherings is their annual Fish Chowder Night. Chief chowder chef since its beginning in the early 1950's has been Walter M. Sargent, Jr.

For other information about the Copley Country Club and Airfield — including an account of the colorful Ponzi Gang of golfers, see the "first draft" of *More About Morristown, 1935-1980*; details about what and where that is are in the Foreword.

FORMER FIRST UNIVERSALIST CHURCH

Chapter 20 - Churches

NO EASY SUMMARY STATEMENT can be made about religious life in Morristown since 1935. Of the several churches and religious groups described by Miss Mower as existing at that time, three no longer exist. Some of the others have experienced a fairly steady increase in membership while the remainder have had mixed records of growth and decline. Finally, several wholly new churches have become established here over the last 45 years. The following is the history of each of these, presented in roughly chronological order of their founding.

First Congregational Church, United Church of Christ

Highlights of the history of the First Congregational Church since 1935 include one addition to, and several changes and renovations in, the interior of the church building and its facilities on Main Street (C41). It has also become part of a new denomination.

Let's begin, however, with a few basics, one of them the church's number of members. That initially declined, then generally increased fairly steadily between 1935 to about 1965, when it stood at about 380. Since the latter year there has been a fairly steady decline to the 240 members of 1979.

A continuation of Miss Mower's roster of pastors for the church (page 290) begins with Rev. George E. Goodliffe, who became the longest-serving pastor in the church's history. His pastorate began on January 5, 1919 and ended with his death on February 27, 1952 — more than 33 years. Other pastors since Rev. Goodliffe have been: Rev. Fred R. Manthey, Jr., August 1952, to December, 1955; Rev. Walter L. Cooley, June 1956 to May, 1960; Rev. Earl A. Vincent, September, 1960 to April 15, 1969; Rev. Robert C. Langtry, September, 1969 to December 1, 1979; and James Missroon (not yet ordained), July, 1980 to present.

As for major changes in the church facilities, a new wing to the Sunday School rooms was constructed at the east end of the vestry in 1949. In 1957 the chancel underwent major change and renovation. A new choir loft, half on each side, was established, a new or remodeled retable and reredos were provided, and a new pulpit and lectern were installed.

In 1965 the church's 1885 pipe organ, which was built by the George S. Hutchings Company of Boston, underwent a major program of restoration and improvement. This included an increase in the number of pipes from 503 to 783 and a conversion from mechanical to electrical operation. Also at this time the high reredos on the chancel was replaced by a much lower one.

In 1971 a major program of repairs and improvements to the church structure included the installation of metal reinforcement rods to halt a "spreading" of the structure which had developed.

And as a final note about the church structure, the enlarged and remodeled building of 1875 was not destroyed when the present sanctuary building was constructed in 1896. The 1875 structure, one end of which originally stood close to Main Street, was moved back, turned at right angles, and became the vestry for the new church.

A very familiar part of the church not mentioned by Miss Mower is its bell. The *Lamoille Newsdealer* of November 4, 1863 carried the brief report that "The Congregationalists have ... raised money to put a bell in their church." They apparently got a used bell because an inscription on the bell itself dates its casting as 1844. The maker was Andrew Meneely of West Troy, N.Y.

One of the pleasanter sounds in Morrisville is the result of a long-standing tradition among its three (and originally four) churches on Main Street. At 9:30 each Sunday morning, the bells at the Puffer Methodist, First Congregational, and Advent Christian Churches each sound in turn with a simple double ring. The "answering" of the bells is then repeated. Finally, a general tolling follows for a minute or two. Before its decline and final closing in the 1950's, the bell at the First Universalist Church was also involved.

Other significant developments for the church:

Beginning in 1945 and continuing nearly every year until 1981, the First Congregational Church and Puffer United Methodist Church shared an exchange of union services during the summer months. Under this, one church "closed" in July, the other in August, with joint Sunday services being held at the alternate church in each case. In this way, each church's minister was provided a month's vacation from his pastoral duties. In 1981, however, both churches held their own respective services during both summer months.

January 1, 1957 marked the establishment of a new corporate body for the church. That was (and still is) the First Congregational Church of Morrisville, Vermont, Incorporated. While significant in and of itself, the new corporation was also something of an historic landmark. For it involved the dissolution of not one, but *two*, long-established earlier governing bodies comprising the church. One was the First Congregational Church of Morristown. The other was the First Congregational Society of Morristown, apparently a descendant of the "Ecclesiastical Society" which Miss Mower reported as being founded in 1823 (page 41).

The history of both is a bit uncertain and complex. Suffice it to say that these separate but related bodies reflected a basic characteristic of the Congregational denomination. The church organization was constituted of adherents of the Congregational faith who were official members of the local corporate body which observed that faith. The ecclesiastical society was constituted of both members and non-members of the church itself. Its larger interest was in seeing that the community had some physical facility where religious services could be held. It thus saw to the financing and construction of a meeting house for such services. In the early days those might well have been led by non-Congregational as well as Congregational preachers. But the meetinghouse generally came to be used only by the local Congregational church. The related ecclesiastical society continued to exist, however, overseeing the physical property and, later, the financial affairs of the church. The church organization meanwhile was basically responsible for all spiritual matters of the church and its members.

Over time, this division of responsibilities apparently got blurred, and became more of a hindrance than a help to orderly administration of a church's affairs. So since about the turn of the century, individual Congregational churches one by one replaced the two related but distinct governing bodies with a single body. Though there is some uncertainty, that is basically what happened here.

Also in 1957, the First Congregational Church joined the Puffer United Methodist Church in sponsoring a non-denominational kindergarten. Details appear in the history of the Methodist church below.

At the church's annual meeting on January 15, 1961 members unanimously approved a resolution to ratify the constitution of the United Church of Christ. The new denomination represented a union of the Evangelical and Reformed Church with the General Council of Congregational Christian Churches. The origins of the Morristown church have, however, been retained in its formal name, the First Congregational Church, United Church of Christ.

First Baptist Church

Except for a brief period from about 1977 to 1979, there apparently has been no sustained organized unit of the Baptist denomination in Morristown since the dissolution of the early Baptist Church described by Miss Mower (pages 50-52). During that time the Hallmark

Baptist Church of Greenville, South Carolina sponsored a mission here, which was called the First Baptist Church. Possibly from the beginning and certainly for most of its existence, religious services and other gatherings were held at the Lamoille Grange hall on Pleasant Street.

Puffer United Methodist Church

Before reviewing the history of this church since 1935, let's first take a closer look at its name and denomination.

In 1895, seven years after completion of the building described by Miss Mower (page 54), it was decided to name the new church "Puffer Methodist Episcopal Church." This was in honor of Rev. William R. Puffer. He was pastor during the construction period and "overcame many discouraging obstacles" in the building of the church. Rev. Puffer had continued his pastorate here until 1889. He retired from the ministry a year later and subsequently became a resident of Richford. He died there July 27, 1900 at 71 years of age.

The present denominational name evolved in two stages. In 1939 the Methodist Episcopal Church combined with the Methodist Episcopal Church South and the Methodist Protestant Church to form the Methodist Church. Then in 1968, the Methodist Church combined with the Evangelical United Brethren Church to become the United Methodist Church.

Membership of the local church generally increased throughout the late 19th century and well into the 20th century. In 1888 there were 160 members and in 1965, 493. That was the peak year (or near to it), with membership dropping off to 406 in 1979.

And to continue Miss Mower's roster of pastors (page 291), the following have so served since 1935: Rev. Lawrence E. Larrowe, 1933-36; Rev. Bailey G. Lipsky, 1936-43; Rev. Loren G. Heaton, 1944-48; Rev. Melvin R. McGaughey, 1949-56; Rev. Wilfred J. Fillier, 1956-69; Rev. Albert T. Strobel, 1969-80; and Rev. Oren J. Lane, 1980-present.

As for the church's physical facilities, the most significant change is, of course, the new church building which was constructed in 1970 and consecrated on February 7, 1971. Prior to that, the 1888 structure had undergone a number of changes and additions over the years. But in 1968 it was found to have many structural problems, and the decision was made to completely replace the old church rather than attempt to correct those problems.

Among items transferred from the old to the new structure were the handsome weathervane and the church's bell. The creator of the former is unknown but it was installed at the top of the higher of the 1888 church's two steeples when that was built. The bell was given to the church in 1891 by Moses Weld Terrill, the former Morristowner who became a successful industrialist in Middletown, Connecticut. The bell, with its fittings, weighed about 1,200 pounds. It was manufactured by Clinton H. Meneely of Troy, New York. As noted above, this bell plays a part in a local bell-ringing tradition.

An earlier major project was the construction in 1961 of a large wing for Sunday School classrooms and other support facilities. This was named the Wesley Parish Building. At that time the existing kitchen was completely done over and other portions of the vestry and parlor were renovated (the parlor and some adjoining area, it might be remembered, constitute the original chapel built in 1874).

As for the church's parsonage, since 1902 it was the house on the south side of Harrison Avenue at its intersection with Summer Street. That was succeeded by the present parsonage on Main Street adjacent to the church (C43). It was purchased in 1954.

Completion of the abovementioned Wesley Parish Hall provided new quarters for a non-sectarian educational enterprise in which the Puffer church had been involved for several years. That was the Jack and Jill Kindergarten. The Morristown public school system was not offering pre-elementary education (and, as noted in Chapter 4, still doesn't). So beginning in 1947, the Methodist and Congregational churches jointly sponsored a public kindergarten. For the first four years it was held at the Congregational church's Sunday School rooms, before moving in 1961 to the new Methodist facility, where it has continued ever since. About 1969 formal sponsorship shifted from the two churches to a parents' co-operative, its present status. Tuition continues to be charged as it has from the beginning but in addition, one parent of each enrolled child must donate some time as an assistant to the teacher.

First Universalist Church

The first Universalist Church building on Main Street in the center of Morrisville (C15) remains the Village's and Town's highest and most distinctive structure. It no longer houses the religious group which it so long served, however, but does continue an active life of public service. More on that shortly but first a review of the history of the church for the period since 1935.

The apparent good health of the church in the 1920's and 1930's was reflected in the announcement by its officers in mid-1931 that it had cleared a remaining long-term debt of about $1,200.

Contributing a significant $500 to that fund-raising effort was Alexander H. Copley, Morristown's major benefactor. Earlier, in 1928, Copley had also conveyed to the First Universalist Society a handsome three-story frame house and, in 1933, financed its preparation for subsequent service as a parsonage. In 1937 he donated what was identified as "a very substantial sum of money" to the church, and for many years had also made regular annual contributions. He was not, however, an active Universalist himself but apparently made his gifts in recognition of his mother, Jane M. Copley, who had played a major role in the church's functioning, and possibly in remembrance of his wife as well.

Though still incomplete for the years before 1865 and with a few minor uncertainties for the years since then, the following is a more complete roster of the church's pastors than Miss Mower was able to provide: Rev. B.H. Fuller, 1832 and 1834; Rev. Eli Ballou, 1837; possibly Rev. J.M. Magoun, 1840; Rev. J.W. Ford, 1842; Rev. William Parker, 1844; Rev. Hollis (?) Sampson, 1846; Rev. J.S. (John?) Palmer, 1851; Rev. S.C. Eaton, 1853; Rev. Lester Warren, 1864; Rev. G.W.

Bailey, 1865-75; Rev. I.P. (for Isaac Phillips) Booth, 1876-81; Rev. G. Foster Barnes, 1881-83; Rev. Frank Healey, 1884-89; Rev. Myra Kingsbury, 1889-92; and Rev. Alfred E. Wright, 1892-93 (Rev. Wright and his wife were *both* ordained in Morrisville, in 1893).

Also, Rev. I.P. Booth (the same as above), 1893-1904; Rev. Otto S. Raspe, 1905-10 (ordained here in 1906); Rev. John E. Porter, 1911 (ordained here); Rev. R.D. Cranmer, 1912-16 (ordained here in 1913); Rev. Frank A. Stockwell, 1917-18 (ordained here in 1917); Rev. George F. Fortier, 1918-22; Rev. Edward Ellis, 1922; Rev. George F. Morton, 1923-25; Rev. Donald K. Evans, 1926-30 (ordained here in 1927); Rev. Charles Easternhouse, 1930-32; Rev. William J. Metz, 1936-39; and Rev. Milton E. Muder, 1939-43. For the next eight years the church had no regular pastor and held services only during the summer of some, and perhaps all, of those years. Then in 1951 Rev. Frank Stockwell, the same man who had been ordained here, was engaged again as pastor. He was the last to so serve, doing so until 1956.

Major decisions that year reflected the church's by now definite decline. In May, members voted to sell the parsonage, and in February they had closed down the church for the balance of the winter due to lack of funds. At that time hope was expressed that the church would have at least summer services. It's not certain those were held in 1956, but another former pastor, Rev. Metz, did lead services for five weeks during the summer of 1957. The ebb in church membership was reflected in the attendance figures for those services: an average of only 36 (membership and attendance had once been well over a hundred and perhaps even higher). The gathering on August 18 appears to have been the last service of and at the First Universalist Church.

On September 27, 1962 13 members gathered in the church parlor to discuss, as long-time Clerk Mary D. Gates recorded it, "a matter which saddened everyone, namely disposing of the church and its furnishings, as we can no longer maintain it." After some time and consideration of other possibilities, members voted in May, 1968 to give the church building to the Lamoille County Civic Association, Inc. (LCCA). That is the non-profit sponsor of what was to become the Lamoille County Senior Citizens Center. The church also contributed a savings account of some $13,000 to LCCA, which has since held it in trust to provide income for upkeep of the building.

More in a moment about the Center but first an additional note about the 1962 meeting. That really represented the church's finale. And yet one decision at that meeting has kept it in existence, though not functioning. That was unanimous approval of a motion "that the Universalist Society be perpetuated as long as there are three members left to perpetuate it." At this writing (1979) there are at least ten surviving members: Erle and Ann Morrill and Erle's sister, Mrs. Gertrude Morrill Griggs; Mrs. Isabel Towne; Mrs. Doris Jenney; Harold Eaton and his sister, Mrs. Leone Eaton Marshall; Miss Roberta Stafford; George Hersey; and Mrs. Marjorie Emmons.

The church officially began its new life as the Lamoille County Senior Citizens Center on November 6, 1968. To prepare the way, pews from the sanctuary had been removed and sold, and the structure renovated, remodeled and refurnished in various ways. The church has since been serving a "congregation" of those 60 years or older as a place for social get-togethers, entertainment and recreation, and services. The latter are both services which the seniors receive — transportation, health, meals and financial advice, to name a few — and volunteer services which they provide to others. These have included repairs of linens for the Copley Hospital and vocal concerts by the Center's long-established Lamoille County Entertainers.

The Center does not have a formal membership but there are a 100 or so regular participants in its activities and services. Through their own organization separate from the LCCA, the seniors elect officers and make decisions about activities and programs and the raising of funds to support them.

Until 1974 the Center operated principally with Federal and State funds, the latter provided through the Vermont Office on Aging (for several years VOA has maintained a branch office at the Center). Since 1974 the Center has been basically self-supporting, raising its own funds in various ways. These have included donations, sponsorship of an annual Harvest Supper, and the selling of craft items which the seniors make.

The LCCA retains responsibility for the building itself and oversees hiring a director of the Center and a basic operating budget.

Advent Christian Church

While smaller in membership than several other of Morristown's churches, the Advent Christian Church here is certainly one of the town's stable religious bodies. Membership figures over the years since 1935 are not available but the 85 members in 1976 have grown to 98 in 1980. Other evidence of the church's strength are the several additions to, and changes in, its physical facilities since 1935.

A review of those momentarily but first a continuation of Miss Mower's roster of the church's pastors (page 290): Rev. Alice Bennett, October, 1930-April, 1937; Rev. William H. Brusby, May, 1937-June, 1943; Rev. Edwin P. Chapman, February, 1944-April, 1947; Rev. William Flewelling, September, 1947-October, 1952; Rev. William H. Brusby, June, 1953-October, 1960; John Carpenter, January, 1961-April, 1964 (a student during much of his pastorate here, Carpenter was ordained at the Morrisville Advent Church); Rev. David Crook, May, 1965-August, 1969; Rev. George S. Stone and his wife, Rev. Doris N. Stone, June, 1970-June, 1978; Rev. Robert Leonard, interim pastor, May 6-June, 1979; and Rev. James Jensen, September, 1979-present.

The church acquired its first parsonage in 1944 at 24 Maple Street. This was sold in 1959 in exchange for the house at 3 Maple Street just around the corner from the church on Main Street (C29).

In 1960 a major program of remodeling the church interior was carried out. This project not only enlarged the worship area and seating capacity but also included installation of new pews and flooring.

In 1967 the church purchased the house (C30) right next to the church at the corner of Maple and Main Streets. Established here was a large fellowship hall, classrooms and three rest rooms. The building is also used for prayer meetings, youth work, mission meetings, fellowship suppers, and wedding receptions.

Several things happened in 1974. Of particular interest was the erection of a new steeple atop the belfry of the church. This replaced the original which had been taken down some years earlier (apparently in the early 1950's). The interesting bell here, already described by Miss Mower (page 58), participates in the abovedescribed little Sunday-morning bell-ringing tradition shared by Morrisville's Main Street churches.

Finally, a major project carried out in 1977 was construction of a connecting link between the church and educational wing. This provided a large central entrance area and two new classrooms.

Holy Cross Church

Major developments for Morristown's Roman Catholic church since 1935 have included its change from a mission to a parish, major growth in the number of Catholics served, and substantial development of the church's site on Brooklyn Street.

A full review in a moment but first a few additional details about the church's early years. The original church structure was dedicated June 10, 1914. In 1931 a 39-by-32-foot addition was constructed at the rear of the original church, which itself was remodeled. The enlargement doubled the seating capacity of the church, bringing it to a little less than 400.

During the early years of the Morrisville church, it was a mission of the parish church in Hyde Park, St. Teresa's. Pastors during this period were: Rev. William P. Crosby, the first, 1911-15; Rev. John M. Kennedy, 1915-17; Rev. Peter Boivin, 1917-37; Rev. Valmour Desautels, 1938-43; and Rev. Francis E. McDonough, 1943-46.

On July 3, 1946, following the assignment of the Rev. Gerard Buckley as the first resident pastor, Holy Cross Church was elevated from a mission to a parish. It has been that ever since. As a parish, it became wholly independent of St. Teresa's Parish. Membership records for the parish are very limited but apparently it has seen a steady increase over the years since 1946. As of 1980 there were 315 families and over 1,000 parishioners. The Holy Cross Parish includes all of Morristown, Elmore and Wolcott plus a small portion of Hyde Park.

Pastors of the church since it became a parish and highlights of their respective tenures are the following.

Father Buckley's service here was brief, lasting only until March, 1947. He initially lived at the Hyde Park rectory until the first rectory in Morrisville was purchased later in 1946. That was the former Denis Couture house (V31b) located on the west side of LaPorte Road just outside the Morrisville village limits.

Father Buckley was succeeded in 1947 by Rev. Francis E. McDonough, who, as noted above, previously served at the church while it was still a mission. Under his direction, the Blessed Sacrament Church in Stowe was constructed in 1949. There had been a Catholic mission in that town since 1900. Initially it was under the jurisdiction of St. Andrew's Parish of Waterbury but was transferred to the Holy Cross Parish when that was established in 1946. The Stowe church continued as a mission until 1954, when it, too, became a parish.

Father McDonough also oversaw construction of a new rectory. In 1951 Union Carbide and Carbon Corporation (later and presently Union Carbide Corporation) wanted to acquire the original rectory property as part of a larger tract for its present records center. The money that it paid for this ($22,000) made possible construction of the house adjacent to the church which has since been the rectory.

As a parish priest, Father McDonough was especially interested in a more active participation by the laity in the Liturgy, and so anticipated by many years what is now general practice in Roman Catholic worship. It might also be noted that he had a keen interest in railroading and was a licensed locomotive engineer. That interest led to the acquisition of a rather special bell for the church. With the help of parishioner Joseph L. Stone, a long-time employe of the St. Johnsbury & Lake Champlain Railroad, Rev. McDonough prevailed upon the railroad's management to donate the bell from one of its "fleet" of steam locomotives which it was then in the process of scrapping for replacement by diesel locomotives. This was about 1950, and the church's belfry was built at that time to house the old railroad bell for its new, religious mission.

Father McDonough was succeeded in March, 1953 by Rev. Omer Dufault. In the fall that year he organized the Holy Cross Kindergarten, which is still in operation. The kindergarten has been open to any child regardless of religion.

And sparked by Father Dufault, the Holy Cross Parish Credit Union was chartered on June 24, 1955. In the beginning only members of the parish were eligible to become members of the credit union. Then under a change in its charter on October 30, 1970, the name became Morrisville Credit Union and membership eligibility was expanded so that anybody residing or regularly employed in Lamoille County could join. The charter membership of 18 grew to 478 members in 1976 and in 1980 stood at about 740. Also under Father Dufault's leadership the church structure in 1958 underwent what was later described as a "complete renovation."

He was succeeded in February, 1960 by Rev. Francis Candon. Father Candon organized the women of the church into a parish unit of the Vermont Council of Catholic Women. That subsequently dissolved. He also organized a unit of the Knights of Columbus for the Catholic men of the area. Known as Father Boivin Council #5041, it, too, became inactive but was re-established in 1980.

Rev. Peter Rosseau succeeded Father Candon in February, 1963. A major development during his tenure was the construction in 1966 of the Monsignor William Crosby Center. The two-story wood-frame structure has a large hall for meetings and social activities, five classrooms and other related facilities.

Rev. Bernard Couture succeeded Father Rosseau in September, 1969. Following church decisions which grew out of the Second Vatican

CHURCHES

Council of 1962-65 to increase the role of the laity in parish governance, Father Couture organized the first local parish council in 1965. Members of the parish elect members of the council, which serves as an advisory group to the pastor on matters which concern operation of the parish.

Rev. Donald J. Ravey became the seventh pastor of Holy Cross Parish in January, 1977 and is still so serving. In 1978 he oversaw a major building program which included both changes to, and the refinishing of, the church's interior. Among other things, a new doorway with ramp was constructed in the north wall near the west end to provide access to the interior for the elderly and physically handicapped.

Episcopal Mission

"His one hope and ambition was to erect a chapel on Bridge Street and nearly all the funds he received were used for that special work, but the project was not completed." Such was the appropriate "epitaph" which appeared in the obituary of Rev. Frederick William Burge, for many years priest of the Morrisville Episcopal Mission, who died December 27, 1949 at the age of 77.

Miss Mower has described (page 62) his acquisition in 1931 of a building on Bridge Street and the conversion of two of its rooms to serve as a "temporary" Chapel of the Resurrection. "Temporary" because Rev. Burge (rhymes with "merge") had grand plans to build a new, permanent and very substantial church nearby (V23).

Construction didn't actually begin until August, 1937 and continued off and on — mostly off — for the next ten years. Rev. Burge's congregation was very small and finding funds to pay for the new church was apparently a big and continuing problem for him. But on June 5, 1947 an achievement of sorts was realized when a first service was held, according to a local news item, in the "permanent but still very incomplete" structure. That was an understatement if there ever was one: the wall of the church's apse was all that had been completed.

And so it remained until Rev. Burge's death. The property subsequently passed into new hands and the apse was razed.

Morristown has continued to have only a few Episcopalians and they have attended churches elsewhere, notably St. John's in the Mountains in Stowe and the recently-established St. Francis of Assisi Church in Johnson.

Mormon Church

Morristown for some years has been a center of activity for members of the Church of Jesus Christ of the Latter-day Saints, or Mormons as they are generally known. Before summarizing that story, however, it is necessary to provide some description of how the church governs itself, particularly on the local level. The following terms represent different levels of local organization; they are given in *ascending* order of their degree of self-governing status: "Sunday school," "branch," and "ward." Each lower level is generally "dependent" on a next higher level unit in its area until it reaches that next higher level itself; a key factor for a change in status is the size of the local unit's membership.

According to Mrs. George (Gladys) Godfrey, a lifelong Morristown resident, her grandfather, William Hadlock, joined the Mormon Church in 1894. He was then living in Jay but moved in 1910 to a farm in Morristown on LaPorte Road. It was at his home there that meetings of Mormons in this area were first held. Hadlock subsequently moved to a farm at Morristown Corners, the homestead of which is the so-called Tinker House (T42). The Mormon meetings moved there as well.

Initially the group was a Sunday school. With subsequent varying levels of membership over the next 60 or so years, it alternated between that and branch status several times. As a Sunday school, it was initially dependent on the church's Burlington branch, and later, on the Barre branch. The latter was subsequently elevated to, and presently is, the Montpelier ward.

In November, 1979 a Morrisville branch was re-established. A key difference from the earlier branches here is that the present one has independent status. That is, it is basically *not* dependent on the Montpelier ward for financial and leadership support as was previously the case.

Membership currently numbers 73, of which about 35 are active. In addition to Morristown, the members reside throughout central and eastern Lamoille County, some neighboring towns of Franklin County, and the Hardwick area in Caledonia County. Except for about a year in 1977-78, when gatherings took place at Stowe High School, the local Grange hall has, since the 1950's, been this religious group's main meeting place.

And for most of the time since about 1960, the parent church has assigned two missionaries to the Morrisville Sunday school or branch. These are pairs of young men or women, or sometimes an older married couple, who donate two years to church work. Their principal function here has been to seek and attract new members to the Mormon religion.

Christian Science Society

After the beginnings described by Miss Mower (page 63), the Christian Science Society of Morrisville continued as an active body through the 1920's and 1930's. But by the early 1940's its membership had declined greatly. As a result of this inactivity, the Mother Church, the First Church of Christ, Scientist in Boston withdrew its recognition on December 6, 1944. During its existence, the local society had continued to meet over "the old Brick Store" (C53).

Seventh-day Adventist Church of Morrisville

There was some early organized activity by adherents of this faith in Morristown. This included several camp meetings in the late 19th century and the organization of a church in 1900. But that lasted only a short time and the foundations of the present church were actually laid in three communities outside of Morristown. They were North Wolcott, North Hyde Park and Johnson, at each of which a small Seventh-day Adventist church was established.

For some time, representatives of the three churches felt it would be well to unify into a single unit. That happened in 1948 when a new church, with 59 charter members, was organized. Playing a prominent role in these proceedings was Richard A. Mitchell, the man who had been serving as pastor of the three merging churches.

Beginning immediately and continuing over the next two and a half years, plans were discussed for a church building in Morrisville. Finally purchased was a site on the east side of Best Street (V24). Construction of the new church itself extended over another three and a half years. In the meantime, services were generally being held each week at the Lamoille Grange hall. Then on January 1, 1955 the congregation moved into the new building (the structure was not dedicated until August 2, 1958, by which time it was free of debt).

Pastors during this period (succeeding Mitchell) were W. Richard Lesher, October, 1948 to August, 1952; Carroll Perry, October, 1952 to January, 1953; Leighton (Leigh) Whitcomb, January, 1953 to May, 1954; and Gerald B. Smith, who began serving in August, 1954. The latter two men supervised the construction with church members contributing much of the labor.

Since the establishment of the Morrisville church, its membership has remained quite steady at about 50. In addition to the church's regular Saturday sabbath services, it has held a Vacation Bible School nearly every year and carries out much welfare work. The church has also served the larger community in various ways. Such service has included a cooking school, several five-day programs to stop smoking, and several series of evangelistic meetings and Bible study groups.

Gerald Smith continued his pastorate until March, 1957. Other pastors since then have been: Allen T. Bidwell, June, 1957-October, 1959; Louis DeLillo, May, 1960-July, 1967; Christof Kober, August, 1967-September, 1970; Milton W. Hallock, September, 1970-September, 1973; David Greenlaw, December, 1973-July, 1976; Raymond O. Richardson, September, 1976-December, 1979; and Ray Nelson, March, 1980-present.

Kingdom Hall, Jehovah's Witnesses

Organizers of the first group of Jehovah's Witnesses to meet regularly in Lamoille County were Mr. and Mrs. Perley L. Reynolds of Jeffersonville. They became interested in the denomination's teachings in 1936 after studying several books published by the Watchtower Bible and Tract Society, the Witnesses' parent organization. The Reynoldses, with help of personnel sent by the Watchtower Society, subsequently organized what became the denomination's first regular Bible study group in the county. That was about 1940.

Bible study meetings were subsequently held in Cambridge Village. Here, in mid-1941, the participating Witnesses were seriously harassed at several of their meetings by ruffians. The Lamoille County Sheriff's Department apparently finally took some action to control the problem after being urged to do so by the American Civil Liberties Union.

The violence against the Witnesses, some of which also later occurred in Morrisville, was prompted basically by the Witnesses' refusal to salute the American flag. That action, or non-action, which is based on their religious belief against idolatry, rankled many Americans as being distinctly *un*American. But the U.S. Supreme Court had found it legal under the denomination's Constitutional rights.

Several families on the west side of Lamoille County continued to meet for Bible study during the 1940's. Late in that decade the small congregation (about 15) moved to Morrisville for a time, meeting in private homes. Then from about 1950 to 1958 the group met at the home of two members in Johnson village, returning to Morrisville the latter year or thereabouts. For the next few years the group rented space for its meetings in the building on Bridge Street (C67) next door to the Bijou Theatre. Then in 1960 a major development: the church's newly-incorporated Morrisville Congregation of Jehovah's Witnesses, Inc. bought a building on Bridge Street several hundred feet down from the Brooklyn Street intersection. Kingdom Hall, as the structure is known, has since been located there (V25).

The former store has gone through two major remodelings to serve church needs, one initially, the other in 1971. And reflecting continuing membership growth, a major addition to the rear of the original structure was completed in 1976. Members of the congregation did the bulk of all of this construction work.

In the mid-1970's the parent church reduced significantly the territory served by the Morrisville church. Despite those changes, average attendance at the local Kingdom Hall has held its own, in 1980 standing at between 100 and 120 with peaks of 160 at times.

Jewish Faith

If Morristown has had any Jews living here in the first 175 years of its settled existence, there is no record of it. This publication will change that by providing at least a brief account of Jews in Morristown since 1964.

In November that year Bernard and Ruthe Sinow and their five children — Marc, Morissa, Matthew, Mona and Marcia — settled here on the so-called Ryder farm located at the corner of Vermont Rt. 100 and Morristown Corners Road. They were then probably the only Jewish family in Morristown. Today, by the Sinows' estimate, there are about ten Jewish families in Morristown itself and others in neighboring towns where 15 years ago there had been few, if any. Matthew Sinow said the family had encountered considerable anti-Jewish animosity when they moved in 1960 to Monkton, Vermont from their previous home base of North Haven, Connecticut. They had also "had some scrapes in Morristown but not as bad."

For a combination of reasons — the sheer small number of Jews and differences in religious views among those few — there is no synagogue or other organized Jewish activity in Morristown or any nearby town. The Sinows themselves regularly attend services at the Beth Jacob Synagogue in Montpelier and in addition maintain an actively religious family life.

One interesting public notice of the Sinows' faith is the large white Hebraic letters which were painted in two places on the farm's

CHURCHES 501

red barn in 1966 or 1967. Each set of letters says "Shalom," a word of salutation or welcome. "It means 'Come in any time'," Matthew Sinow said, "and we've had lots of Jews rap on the door as a result — at any time, too!"

Full Gospel Christian Assembly / The Church In The Mountain

This church, one of Morristown's newest, is the first in many years to have its meeting place outside the limits of the Village of Morrisville. Home of the Full Gospel Christian Assembly, Inc., a non-profit Vermont corporation established in late 1974, is the former Monette's Lodge on Cote Hill Road (T37).

The church, which is wholly independent of any national church organization, was founded by Rev. Vincent F.J. Circello, an ordained Southern Baptist minister. Church activities at present include a Bible school and worship service on Sunday morning, a Youth Fellowship meeting on Monday evening, and a Family Prayer and Bible study gathering on Thursday evening. These are all held at what the church's 35 or so active members now call The Church In The Mountain, a name derived from a Biblical passage, Micah 4:1.

In December, 1977 Rev. Circello ended his pastorate to undertake the establishment of another Full Gospel church in Williston. Rev. Eldred A. Marston, an ordained Advent Christian minister, has been pastor since that time. He had been serving as the Morristown Full Gospel church's associate pastor since January, 1976.

Christian Life Center

The Christian Life Center, a non-denominational full-gospel fellowship of Christians, began holding services in Morrisville on July 8, 1979. Organizer and pastor-teacher of the group is Rev. Robert Leonard. He is a former interim pastor of the Advent Christian Church of Morrisville, who left that pastorate amidst controversy about his appointment on a regular basis.

An ordained elder with the United Evangelical Churches, Rev. Leonard told the author that the Christian Life Center is something of a home mission of that interdenominational organization of churches, ministries and clergy. A primary focus of the Center is the Bible and its understanding. The Center's participants, originally about 35 and now (1980) about 70, come from different church backgrounds, including Catholic, Baptist, Pentecostal, Methodist and Advent Christian. The latter is represented by several former members of the Morrisville Advent Christian church who left to support Rev. Leonard in formation of the new religious group.

For its meetings, the Christian Life Center rents space at the Seventh-day Adventist Church on Best Street (V24). It has no other affiliation with that church.

For other details about various of Morristown's churches, see the "first draft" of *More About Morristown, 1935-1980*; the Foreword describes what and where that is.

MORRISTOWN HISTORICAL SOCIETY'S NOYES HOUSE MUSEUM

Chapter 21 - Organizations

MORRISTOWN IS certainly well organized! Which is to say, it is the home of a large and diverse array of organizations, individual histories of which are provided here. At the outset it might be noted that members of most of them are not exclusively Morristowners by any means. Each, however, is distinctly related to Morristown in some way, either by name or historic background, by the ownership of property here, or by the fact that this is where it regularly holds its meetings.

Most of the organizations described by Miss Mower (Chapter XIII) still exist. Of the others described below, a few have come and gone since 1935, while those remaining have been established at different times since then and are still functioning. Rather than describe them in the same order as Miss Mower, we have, for convenience sake, grouped them into several categories. We'll begin with fraternal orders.

The Masons and Related Masonic Orders

Mount Vernon Lodge, No. 8, of the Free and Accepted Masons, Morristown's longest-established organization, and its three affiliated Masonic orders have, with one exception, remained active throughout the years since 1935.

The lodge's temple remains the building at the corner of Portland and Brigham Streets (C62). The most significant change relates to the front of the structure. As noted in Chapter 7, this area since 1948 has been rented to the Morrisville Water and Light Department for its offices.

The three affiliated Masonic orders of which there have been local units are: Coral Chapter, No. 16, Order of the Eastern Star; Tucker Chapter, No. 15, Royal Arch Masons; and Lamoille Commandery, No. 13, Order of Knights Templar.

The last no longer exists, having surrendered its charter on September 25, 1967. Miss Mower mentioned the service of one of its members, Thomas C. Cheney, as grand commander of the state Order of Knights Templar (page 215). One other member to so serve was Willard K. Sanders in 1945.

The Order of Eastern Star was established in 1855 so that female near-relatives of Master Masons could share, at least in part, in the benefits and knowledge of the all-male Masonic order. Members, however, are both male and female, the others eligible for membership being Master Masons themselves. The Coral Chapter had 104 members in 1969 and 116 members in 1979.

Tucker Chapter, No. 15, Royal Arch Masons continues to function but in recent years its strength has faltered. Its membership has fallen from 84 in 1969 to 40 or so in 1980, and those have not been very active.

New England Order of Protection

Adding to and correcting somewhat Miss Mower's brief account of this organization (page 220), Lamoille Lodge No. 317 of the New England Order of Protection (NEOP) was established in Morrisville on July 18, 1898. The order, later described as "one of the strongest financial fraternal organizations in the state," was itself founded in 1887.

Beginning soon after its chartering and continuing for many years, the Lamoille Lodge had quarters on the third floor of the Darling/Woodbury Block on Portland Street (C82). Later, meetings were held at the Lamoille Grange hall. The lodge's membership for many years in the early part of this century was well over 100. Still very active until at least 1952, the lodge faded from the local scene some time after that.

Lamoille Grange, No. 233

Before reviewing the "recent" history of the local unit of this well-known national fraternal organization, some amplification of Miss Mower's sketch of its beginnings (pages 220-221) is in order.

Malvern Grange, No. 24, was organized here on September 9, 1873. While it remained strong enough to build its own hall in 1877, it seems to have faded out not long after that. Lamoille Grange, No. 233, was organized on February 7, 1893.

A landmark step was the Grange's acquisition in late 1924 of the building on Pleasant Street which had been the original Peoples Academy (C90). For some years the structure had served as a feedstore and was then owned by Carroll E. Lanpher. Lanpher leased back the first floor of the building and continued his store there, while the Grange settled into the second floor for its meeting hall. Then in 1938 Lanpher closed his business and the Grange took over the whole building, making major alterations in the interior at that time.

In 1977 Lamoille Grange completed a major two-year project in observance of the combination American and Vermont Bicentennials in 1976 and 1977. That was the restoration of the exterior of the building to a close representation of its appearance as the original Peoples Academy. Of particular significance was the construction and placement of a replica of the school's original bell tower over the front gable. Mounted there was no less than the school's original bell. Cast in 1850 by Henry N. Hooper & Co. of Boston, it had been purchased as a gift for Peoples Academy by Col. E.B. Herrick. The bell had passed to the second Peoples Academy when that was built, and then removed, but preserved, when it was torn down in 1929.

Concurrent with its acquisition of the Lanpher property, the local Grange incorporated in late 1924 as Lamoille Grange Number 233, Inc. For reasons unknown, that first corporation was dissolved as of March 1, 1932. But in 1960 a second (non-profit) corporation was formed. This was and still is Lamoille Grange No. 233, Inc.

In addition to its ritualistic work and other regular social and educational meeting activities, the Lamoille Grange has carried out several public service projects. One is the attractive picnic area which members built in 1950 in a grove of white pine trees on LaPorte Road just south of the intersection with Stancliffe Road. Grangers continue to maintain that at the present time. And while it does produce a modest income through donations, the Lamoille Grange has long provided a sort of "public service" by making its hall available for use by others. As a result, it's safe to say that no other meeting place in Morristown has been used by so many organizations, churches and other groups.

During the 1950's and 1960's this organization saw a steady and significant decline in membership numbers. There has, however, been some recovery since 1970. But today the Lamoille Grange and the Gihon Valley Grange of North Hyde Park are the only ones remaining of the 11 or more Granges which have operated at different times in Lamoille County.

Our next category is patriotic and veterans organizations.

Daughters of the American Revolution

The Jedediah Hyde Chapter of the National Society of Daughters of the American Revolution (DAR) continues to function in this area, though with increasing difficulty because of reduced membership. That now numbers about 30, only some 20 of which are active. And geographically, the residences of current members extend well beyond Morristown, a few living as far away as St. Albans and Williston. Membership, incidentally, is open to any woman who is a direct descendant of any person who supported the American Revolution, either as an actual military combatant or as a civil patriot providing moral, political, or financial support.

Gathering monthly at individual members' homes, meetings of the local chapter include both education about, and discussion and action on, patriotic and community service projects. One of the latter has been the gathering of local vital records data to add to the DAR's genealogical resources. But best known is the annual DAR Good Citizenship Awards. A national program in which the local chapter has participated since 1937, the award goes to the senior at various area high schools (including Peoples Academy) who most displays "qualifications of Leadership, Dependability, Service and Patriotism to an outstanding degree." Until 1976, the award was for females only but since that time, boys have also been eligible for selection.

Grand Army of the Republic

The final passing of Morristown's post of this notable Civil War veterans organization occurred with the passing of that last surviving member in 1935 who was mentioned without identification by Miss Mower (page 217). He was George A. Bridge, who died November 26, 1937 at age 90.

An interesting memento was left behind by Bridge at his death. In 1915 Glenn A. Wilkins, son of Morristown Civil War veteran Austin Wilkins, presented the James M. Warner GAR Post with a special cane. Made with an ebony shaft and an appropriately-inscribed gold-plated head, the cane was to be carried by the post's oldest surviving member until his death. At that time it was to pass to the next oldest member until his death, and so on.

The first of seven men (not all Morristowners) to carry it was Joseph M. Chaplin, the colorful "mayor" of Mud City mentioned in Chapter 11. It subsequently passed from man to man until it reached Bridge in 1933. Shortly before his death, Bridge disposed of the cane in a special way. He gave it to Glenn A. Wilkins, Jr., son of the donor, who later presented it to the Morristown Historical Society.

Woman's Relief Corps

While Morristown's unit of the Grand Army of the Republic has long since passed, its sister organization still exists, though in weak condition. That's the James M. Warner Woman's Relief Corps, No. 57 (WRC).

Membership is about 40, but "it's a struggle to keep going," according to Mabel Twombly, president in 1980. At their monthly meetings members observe some ritual and deal with the organization's patriotic and public service activities. These have included the occasional presentation of an American flag to a local school, church or other institution and, until fairly recently, the decoration of Civil War veterans' graves.

For some years the Morristown WRC continued to meet in its quarters mentioned by Miss Mower (page 218), the former Masonic Temple in the Town Hall (C21). Since the early 1950's meetings have been held elsewhere, with the Lamoille Grange hall the usual place since 1961.

One other Morristown woman who was a state WRC president was Mrs. Allen Phillips. We don't have the exact year but it apparently was in the early 1950's.

Sons of Union Veterans Auxiliary

Morrisville's G.W. Doty Camp of the national Sons of Union Veterans organization dissolved many years ago. But its Auxiliary is still functioning, though not as strongly as in former years.

Expanding a bit on Miss Mower's brief mention (page 220), the Auxiliary was organized in March, 1911. Numbered No. 8 of those in Vermont, it is now one of only five such units still active in the state. It presently has about 25 members, but rarely do more than ten turn out for its monthly meetings at the Lamoille Grange hall.

In addition to ritualistic work at the meetings, members deal with the organization's now limited patriotic and public service activities. Of particular interest among its records are maps of each cemetery in Morristown on which are identified the graves of the town's Civil War veterans buried here. The Auxiliary used to decorate these graves with small American flags for Memorial Day.

Post No. 33, American Legion and American Legion Auxiliary

This veterans organization with its auxiliary unit has, with occasional faltering, remained active throughout the years since 1935.

At the outset it might be well to note that membership in the Legion is open to persons, both men and women, who have served in the American armed forces during any part of a time period specified for each of the wars in which the United States has been involved since and including World War I. The time period for that war is April 6, 1917 to November 11, 1918. The others are: World War II, December 7, 1941 to December 31, 1946; Korean War, June 25, 1950 to January 31, 1955; and Viet Nam War, December 22, 1961 to May 7, 1975. Service can be on either American or foreign soil.

Post No. 33 membership has grown from about 50 when it was organized in 1919 to about 150 at present. Membership in the Auxiliary unit is actually open to any member — male or female — of the family of a Post member. But the Morristown Auxiliary has always been exclusively female. It currently numbers about 100. Many members of both units are non-Morristown residents. In 1975 Morristown Post No. 33 and its Auxiliary incorporated as a non-profit corporation.

In 1961, Barracks 3104 of World War I Veterans was established in association with the local Legion post, and a World War I Veterans Auxiliary was organized in 1965. Though the ranks of these old veterans are "thinning fast," the eight or ten who remain continue to meet monthly. The Auxiliary is also still active.

Either individually or jointly, the Post and Auxiliary over the years have sponsored a variety of community service projects and programs. Foremost on the patriotic front has been participation in arranging and conducting local observances on Memorial Day, Independence Day, and Veterans (formerly Armistice) Day. The two Legion units have also shared in sponsoring certain of the patriotic objects at Academy Park; details of these are described in Chapter 22.

During the 1940's and 1950's the Post sponsored various sports programs including baseball, basketball, wrestling, and boxing. For some years the Post and Auxiliary have participated in the state Legion department's sponsorship of the Green Mountain Boys and Girls State. That is an annual gathering at which boy and girl delegates from different high schools (including Peoples Academy) conduct separate simulated legislative sessions. And since 1968 the two organizations have co-ordinated a major annual fund-raising effort for the so-called France Project. For the first four years the money made it possible for two Peoples Academy students to travel to and live with

ORGANIZATIONS

individual French families during the summer. Then, beginning in 1973, members of the French III and Latin III classes have traveled in Europe during the school's spring vacation.

Fund-raising Bingo games and various Post and Auxiliary meetings and other activities are held at the local Legion barracks in the building (C13) off Main Street behind the former First Universalist Church. The following information will supplement the very brief mention of this interesting structure given by Miss Mower (page 218).

Back in the 1890's interest developed in having a community gymnasium in Morrisville. In early 1897 the Morrisville Gymnasium Association (MGA) was organized and led by a group of prominent local citizens. First site of the Association's facilities was leased space on the third floor of the Darling Block (now the Demars Block, C82). This 40-by-60-foot space was fitted out with all kinds of bodybuilding and exercise equipment. Around the outside of the room was a running track (it took 34 trips to make a mile!).

The MGA managers promised that "It will be [our] aim and determination ... to conduct a quiet, orderly place." Orderly it may have been, but quiet it wasn't. Many signed up to use the facility, and the noise and vibration which they created proved to be a big annoyance to tenants on the first two floors.

In response, the MGA decided to build its own structure. In 1898 the present large wood-frame building was completed. Measuring 42-by-72-feet and nearly 25 feet high, the ground-level floor was large enough for a basketball court, with the exercise equipment mounted around the outside walls. There were also two bowling alleys and a raised running track. The gym was open from November to May and local residents paid an annual fee for the privilege of using the facility. Peoples Academy was also using it, at least for basketball games.

The record is sketchy but private operation of the gymnasium faltered some years later. Whatever the reason, in 1913 Morristown voters appropriated $500 to acquire the structure for use for Peoples Academy athletic activities and other local functions.

Because Peoples Academy's new Copley Building (completed in 1929) had a gymnasium, the Main Street structure was no longer needed for school athletic purposes. So in 1930 the Town sold the old gymnasium building to Legion Post No. 33 and its Auxiliary. Of interest is the fact that the Town conveyed the property "on condition that the premises granted are to be used for the charter purposes of the grantee and if the said premises are used for other purposes, this deed shall become void and the premises revert to the said town of Morristown."

While the exterior of the building has remained largely unchanged, the interior has seen several major changes under Legion ownership. Of particular significance was one of a number of alterations which occurred between 1975 and 1979. That was the installation of a new low ceiling. That completely closed from view the raised running track and original high gymnasium ceiling.

An unusual activity for the gymnasium came in 1954. Alfred E. Hitchcock, the famous movie producer and director, built a set there for filming part of one of the more humorous of his classic mysteries, *The Trouble With Harry*.

Veterans of Foreign Wars, Post 9653, and Auxiliary

A unit of this other major American veterans organization, the Veterans of Foreign Wars (VFW), also has a home in Morristown. Details of its history in a moment but first it might be well to note how its membership qualifications differ from those for the American Legion. Eligible to join the VFW is any veteran of the American armed forces who served *overseas* during time of war and qualified for an appropriate campaign ribbon for that service. Until 1979 it was a male-only organization but since that year, female veterans, otherwise qualified, have also been eligible for membership. So far, however, the local post has had no female members.

Lamoille County's first post was the Ward-Warren Post No. 2571. It was organized in May, 1932 in Morrisville. Its name is a combination of the last names of two Morristown soldiers, and so honors them for giving their lives in World War I. They were Ernest Raymond Ward and Smith Millard Warren. But the new post apparently lasted only a short while.

Then on April 15, 1951 Lamoille County Post No. 9653 was established here. There were 44 charter members. By 1980 that had grown to 492 members. In 1954 the Post incorporated as a non-profit corporation. On May 21, 1953 an Auxiliary to the post was formed. The 19 charter members have since grown to 195 members in 1980. The Auxiliary basically consists of the wives of Post members, though certain other close relatives are also eligible to join. It provides important support to various Post activities and projects.

After using several different meeting places in its early years the Post in early 1955 acquired the E.W. Bailey & Company grain business property on Pleasant Street (C92). That, with various additions and improvements, has been the VFW hall ever since.

In addition to its use for membership activities the hall is also the site of two regular public events which provide entertainment to participants as they raise funds for the Post. One is the Bingo games held weekly since the early 1960's. The other is the annual cribbage tournament which began in 1965.

Post 9653 and/or its Auxiliary have also carried out a number of public service projects and programs over the years. These include: a Christmas party for children; snowmobile and bike safety programs; and co-sponsorship of a hunter safety course. As another service, the Post makes its hall available for use by other organizations at no charge. Many have done so. And the Post has helped carry out observances of patriotic holidays and has provided various of the patriotic and memorial objects at Academy Park. Details are presented in Chapter 22.

Several Post and Auxiliary members have achieved prominence on both the state and national levels of the VFW organization. Most notable has been Philip R. Gowen of Hyde Park. He served as commander of the Vermont department in 1962-63, and has held several posts

ORGANIZATIONS

on the organization's regional and national levels. Two other state commanders from the local post have been Sidney Bartlett of Morrisville, who was chosen in 1973 but died in office on August 1 that year, and Wayne R. Camley of Morrisville, who served 1979-80.

On the distaff side, two local Auxiliary members have served as state presidents of that organization: Priscilla Bartlett of Morrisville, 1972-73, and Margaret Thompson of Hardwick, 1974-75.

Then we have the so-called service clubs, both men's and women's.

Morrisville Rotary Club

The Morrisville Rotary Club, No. 2673 of the well-known international men's service club, has generally been going strong ever since its founding in 1927 (page 221). Members are drawn from various business, industrial, service and professional fields throughout Lamoille County. Membership a few years ago was 30 but has recently dropped off to 20 or 21.

The club's weekly luncheon meetings were held on Wednesdays until 1946 and have been held on Mondays ever since. There have been just three meeting places: the Randall Hotel (C9) from 1927 to some time in the early 1950's; Paine's Restaurant (MS19) from then until 1965 (or soon thereafter); and the Charlmont Restaurant (MS16) since then. The meetings provide social exchange, discussion and action on Club projects and other business, and education through guest speakers on various topics.

The club has rendered public service on many fronts over the years, including the following: help to needy individuals and families; sponsorship of a Boy Scout troop at different times; and in the early 1950's, a special project on Potash Brook to provide trout fishing for local youngsters.

There are two recreational programs which the club founded and is still carrying out. One, already mentioned in Chapter 1, is the Rotary Ramble canoe races on the Lamoille River. The other is sled dog races which have been held in Elmore each year since 1976.

Rotarians have raised funds for their service projects in various ways over the years. One which has occurred every year or two since 1968 has been the Morrisville Rotary Home Show. Held at the Morrisville Armory (V18), area merchants, equipment dealers and other exhibitors each have a display booth to promote and/or sell their wares or services.

Lamoille County Jaycees

This local organization was a chapter of the national organization formally known as the United States Junior Chamber of Commerce, from the initials of which the term "Jaycees" derives. While membership is limited to men 21 to 35 years old, it is open to such young men in all walks of life.

The Lamoille County chapter, which proved to be short-lived, was organized in September, 1964 and had 30 to 40 members during its prime years.

While the organization enjoyed a variety of social activities, a principal purpose was to develop leadership among its members in carrying out community service projects. One in 1967 focussed very much on Morristown — though it proved unsuccessful. That was an effort to establish a public recreation area around tiny Luna Pond on high ground to the east of Peoples Academy.

Interest faded, however, and the Lamoille County Jaycees dissolved in the early 1970's. Before that time, however, one member, John Stevens of Morristown, had gone on to become president of the state Jaycees organization. That was in 1969.

Morrisville Woman's Club

The oldest local club for women is the Morrisville Woman's Club (MWC), the first 40 years of which Miss Mower described.

Except for 1906, when the club considered dissolving itself, it

---

UPLIFT CLUB: SOME EARLY DOIN'S

The second annual meeting of the Club was held [in November, 1916] at the home of Mrs. Bliss. The ladies came in the afternoon for the business meeting and election of officers; the husbands came in the evening and a picnic supper was served, followed by a sale of fancy articles and candy, and the auctioning of a quilt which had been made by the Club members. Music for the evening was furnished by the Peoples Academy orchestra.

It was about this time that the Club became interested in the Red Cross. A Red Cross chairman was appointed, and the members did much to help, both financially and in making garments. It was also voted to not serve refreshments at the regular meetings for the duration of the war.

The meeting held on July 17th [1917] at the home of Mrs. Bertie Boardman took the form of an old-time "Last Day of School". The members came dressed as children, and brought their lunch in lunch pails.

A few months later, the members of the Club began to get hungry again, and voted to rescind the "no refreshments" vote, and decided to serve light refreshments at the meetings, but the records show that much good work was done.

Myra Gould in her "A History of the Uplift Club of Morrisville, Vermont, 1914-1961"

---

has generally remained a strong and active organization, though membership has dropped off in recent years. Those members, while primarily Morristowners, also include residents of other nearby Lamoille County towns (except Stowe, which has its own women's club). Meetings of the club are held once a month, October through May. They have been held since 1978 at the Lamoille Grange hall, and since about 1950 at one or another meeting room at the Peoples Academy complex. Before that they took place at individual members' homes.

Education and the enrichment of social lives of members plus service to others continue as the principal functions of the organization. The public service projects since 1935 have been many and diverse. Among them are the following:

Actually completed in 1935 was its sponsorship of the publication of Anna L. Mower's *History of Morristown, Vermont*. The club's involvement had begun eight years earlier when it approved a proposal made by one of its members to support preparation of a town history. The member? Miss Mower herself.

In 1958 the club undertook several beautification projects in Morrisville. One which is still carried out is the planting of flowers in the triangle in front of Academy Park.

During the 1960's the MWC played an active role in the creation of three local social service agencies: the Lamoille County Mental Health Service in 1966, the Lamoille County Senior Citizens Center in 1968, and the Lamoille Home Health Agency in 1969. All remain well established today. And each year since 1978 it has seen to the placement and lighting of a Christmas nativity scene in the Union Bank's small "park" on Portland Street.

For a few closing odds and ends, the colors of the Morrisville Woman's Club are yellow and white. The club remains a member of both the General and Vermont Federations of Women's Clubs. And one of its members, Mrs. Dayton (Norma) Wakefield, served as the state president, 1955-57.

Uplift Club

Another long-established club for women but one that is no more is the Uplift Club. It was actually founded in Elmore but particularly in its later years Morristown was the site of many, if not most, of its meetings and activities, and many, if not most, of its members were Morristowners.

Founder and first president of the club was Mrs. Leo A. (Myra) Gould, whose farm home in Elmore was on the Elmore Mt. Road about a half-mile south of the intersection with the Lower Elmore Mt. Road. On November 19, 1914 eight women met at Mrs. Gould's home to form what they decided should be called the Uplift Club. Other women subsequently joined as charter members and the membership eventually grew to about 30.

The club served a variety of functions — social, educational and community service. Activities in the first category included periodic "Gentlemen's Nights" for the members' menfolk, plus picnics, wedding and baby showers, and celebrations of birthdays and wedding anniversaries. Principal among the second function was the club's role as a Home Demonstration Club under the University of Vermont's Extension Service Program.

The club provided community service in various ways. During World War I it was very active in carrying out programs of the American Red Cross. Later the club made "cancer pads" for those needing them and mended garments for the Copley Hospital. In 1924 it organized and for several years directed a "junior club" for girls, apparently the first member of the Vermont Federation of Women's Clubs to do so (it had joined the Federation in 1920).

By its 50th anniversary in 1964 the club had apparently weakened considerably, and not long after the death of founder Myra Gould on August 19, 1965, it dissolved.

Morrisville Junior Woman's Club

Much younger than the Uplift Club but fading from the Morristown scene about the same time was the Morrisville Junior Woman's Club (MJWC). It was organized in October, 1938 and subsequently had 25 to 30 members. The Morrisville Woman's Club actually played a major role in getting the new club organized. There was no formal age distinction, but as its name indicates, the Junior Club was intended to attract women younger than those in the "senior" club, and it did so.

One of the MJWC's earliest community service endeavors was getting Morrisville voters in 1942 to approve re-establishment of a weekly rubbish pick-up service in the Village. Carried out in 1951 was a successful drive to raise funds to construct a sturdy chain-link fence around the playground in front of the Graded School. And in 1962-63 club members unsuccessfully campaigned to get Morristown voters to approve funding for a kindergarten.

That setback, in combination with a general fall-off of members' interest in the club, led to a decline in the MJWC's vitality. By the mid-1960's it had dissolved.

Green Mountain Business and Professional Women's Club

This is a new chapter of what is really quite an old national organization. The Green Mountain Business and Professional Women's Club was organized on December 5, 1979. It is a member of both the Vermont and National Federations of Business and Professional Women's Clubs, the latter of which was formed in 1919.

The approximately 20 members, who mostly reside in Lamoille County towns, basically consist of women who work outside the home, part-time or full-time. And surprise — not all members are female! National federation rules permit male members so long as they support the organization's objectives; as a result, the Green Mountain chapter has two male members.

Overall objective of the organization is to provide support in various ways to working women. Offered at individual meetings or through special courses are training and education in public speaking, self-assertiveness, proper dress, job-related problems with alcohol and drugs, domestic violence, and retirement planning.

One special event is the group's naming of a local "Woman of the Year." The first, selected in 1980, was Theresa Breault of Morrisville. She was honored for her major role in owning and operating Arthur's Department Store in Morrisville with her husband, Arthur. In addition, she has been an active member of various organizations.

Each of the next five organizations has some sport or recreation as its principal interest.

ORGANIZATIONS

Sterling Section, Green Mountain Club

The Sterling Section is one of the local or regional chapters of Vermont's well-known hiking organization. The Green Mountain Club (GMC) was founded in 1910 and subsequently established — almost totally with volunteer labor — the 263-mile Long Trail (LT). This "Footpath in the Wilderness" runs along the main spine of the Green Mountains from the Massachusetts line to the Canadian border. Part of the LT along the Sterling Range passes through Morristown. The GMC's sections, 15 of them in 1980, each sponsor hikes and other outdoor pleasure activities and also provide a continuing volunteer service to the hiking public by maintaining a portion of the LT system.

There were two early GMC sections in Lamoille County, but both were short-lived. For many subsequent years, however, a Morrisville man was sort of a one-man Sterling Section before the present section was formed. That was Fred W. Mould, a long-time GMC member. Among other things, Mould built or helped build part of the Long Trail between Smuggler's Notch and the Lamoille River, and several shelters on or near this stretch of LT. One of particular interest, which Mould and others established in 1913, was located near the prominent beaver meadow area at the base of the Sterling Range in west Morristown. It was first known as Shattuck's Lodge, after the man who had used it as a logging camp. Later it was called Mould's Lodge, after Fred Mould himself. He died on June 9, 1950, at age 71 — while out hiking.

Before his death, however, Mould had seen the formation of the Sterling Section. This was organized on January 27, 1946 with Henry B. Mould, one of Fred's sons, as its first president. Spark for the section's formation was a plan to build a replacement lodge for what by that time was a somewhat bedraggled Mould's Lodge. Throughout the warm weather months of 1946 12 to 15 Sterling Section stalwarts (including Fred Mould on some of the trips) turned out almost every Sunday to help erect a sturdy log cabin. It became known as Beaver Meadow Lodge (T35) after the nearby beaver meadow area.

The Sterling Section remained active for the next 10 or 12 years but then went through two cycles of doldrums and reactivation. The last active period began in 1970. Paid-up membership has fallen off since then from a high of about 75 in 1971 to about 40 in 1980. Throughout this time, however, an active core of members had made a sustained effort to return to generally good condition the approximately 13 miles of Long Trail system for which the section is responsible. This includes Whiteface Shelter in Morristown (T36) and French Camp in Johnson as well as Beaver Meadow Lodge. The section has also generally maintained a regular schedule of day hikes at roughly two-week intervals during the summer and fall, plus several snowshoe hikes during the winter.

Lamoille Valley Fish and Game Club

The Lamoille Valley Fish and Game Club was organized at a meeting in Morrisville on May 13, 1957. It became a non-profit corporation in 1961.

The club first leased, then acquired in 1960, about 90 acres of back-country land on Garfield Road in Morristown for a clubhouse and related facilities. Construction of the clubhouse continued for some time before it was basically completed in 1962. Developed in stages over the next 18 years was what has recently been described as "one of the finest shooting ranges in the state."

These facilities are the scene of the club's long-standing annual Chicken Shoot, a competitive *target-* rather than chicken-shooting event. Other regular events have been an annual sugar-on-snow party at the clubhouse and a venison dinner. The former continues today but the latter, long held at the Lamoille Restaurant in Morrisville, ended about 1975.

As part of the club's efforts to promote safe gunhandling and sportsmanlike hunting, it conducted an annual Hunter Safety Course for boys and girls from about 1965 to about 1978. A different event

---

HAM AT A CHICKEN SHOOT

The Lamoille Valley Fish & Game Club had a successful chicken shoot on its Club grounds last Sunday [September 23, 1962].

Top winners in the various events were Cedric Demeritt on the pistol ... Al Robarge on the running deer ..., and Norm St. Pierre of Burlington ... .

On the bull[seye] target with open sights Paul Irish took both strings shot with his right hand wrapped in bandages. Norm Keith and Blake shared honors for the scoped [i.e. rifle mounted with a scope] bull target.

Probably the fastest moving event of the afternoon, the ham shoot, was won by Brad Limoge. No, you don't shoot at a ham. The ham is hung on a string and then shooters take turns attempting to break the string. ...

News & Citizen, September 27, 1962

---

for younger youngsters is the club's annual Fishing Derby. Held since about 1961 at one or another farm ponds in the Morristown area, children compete for prizes by fishing for trout which have been stocked in the pond for the occasion.

The club in 1980 has about 135 members, a significant drop from the high of 330-plus members in the late 1960's.

Lamoille Riding and Driving Club

This organization of people who find sport and recreation in riding on top of or driving behind horses was formed on August 30, 1960 at a meeting at Peoples Academy. Later that same year the club incorporated as a non-profit corporation, with Morristown designated as its principal office. Since its establishment, the club has sponsored various horse-related events and activities. These include trail rides, both pleasure and competitive, gymkhanas, and horseshows. The latter event has been held each year since 1961, and since about 1966 has been accredited by the Vermont Horse Show Association as an official point show.

ORGANIZATIONS

Site of the first horseshow was the Erwin Miller stable and show ring (later owned by Wendell Jones) in the area on Harrel Street where the Dumont Nursing and Convalescent Center is now situated (V21). It remained there several years, then was held for several subsequent years at a farm in Hyde Park. Beginning in 1972 the show was back in Morristown, being held at the Ryder Brook Stables on LaPorte Road until that closed in 1978. Since then it has been held in Johnson.

The club has also carried out several public service projects and programs. One is its sponsorship for the last several years of a 4H Club which has the care and training of horses and the equestrian art as its special interests. And while the Club remains an active organi-

---

A RIDE ENJOYED BY ALL

The trail-ride of the Lamoille Riding & Driving Club, held on Oct. 13th [1963], started with 17 riding horses, one team and last, but not least, "Mr. Mule," a pony-mule owned by Leroy Langdell. Along the way six more riders joined the group, to make a total of 24 riders and one team drawing 5 spectators, lunches, halters, ropes, and belongings. The group stopped for lunch on a mountain meadow next to Hershel Robson's property [in west Morristown], which commanded a beautiful view of the Sterling mountains.

Except for a few incidentals such as ripped trousers, dumped riders, lost tourists, forgotten lunches, stuck car drivers, the day went smoothly with lovely weather, scenery and a ride enjoyed by all. ...

A bit of humor shows us that horses aren't so archaic and useless after all. During the trail ride a red-faced automobile driver went off into the soft dirt at the side of the road as he peered back over his shoulder at the trotting Blacks and bright wagon. Yes, it was the same trotting team that pulled his helplessly stuck "machine" out! ...

News & Citizen, October 24, 1963

---

zation, the size of its membership has dropped from about 150 in its early years to the present 35 or 40.

Lamoille County Sno-Packers

This organization of snowmobiling enthusiasts was formed in early 1968. It was the first to organize of what are now eight such clubs in the county.

It might be noted here that under Vermont law, membership in a snowmobile club carries special significance. To operate a snowmobile over somebody else's property, a snowmobiler must either obtain his own individual written permission and carry it with him or he must be a member of a club to whom the landowner has granted a blanket permission. The latter course clearly is much more convenient for most snowmobilers.

The Lamoille County Sno-Packers Club holds various snowmobiling outings, both on its own and in conjunction with other snowmobiling groups. It also serves to foster responsible snowmobiling practices among its members and others. And it has worked to establish and maintain snowmobiling trails and related facilities in this area. A major project was the Sno-Packers' construction in 1973 of an 160-foot suspension bridge across the Lamoille River about a half-mile downstream from Tenney Bridge. This was widened in late 1980.

Two other major developments for the Sno-Packers occurred in late 1973 and early 1974. The latter was the Club's incorporation as a non-profit corporation. The former was its lease from the Town of 15 acres of the Morristown Town Forest together with an old house on the property. Members fixed this up in rustic fashion to serve as a clubhouse. The lease from the Town (at $1 a year) has continued ever since. Its terms include the following provision relating to use by others of the Town-owned property: "The ... land and building shall remain as public property and be subject to use by the general public under the jurisdiction of the Board of Selectmen and the Lamoille County Sno-Packers."

Lamoille River Swingers

Square dancing is what this active organization is all about. The club was formed on January 2, 1975. One organizational feature is that it has always had a husband and wife serve as co-presidents, instead of one person as the usual single president. The membership, numbering 92 in 1980, extends well beyond Lamoille County, and ranges in age from 18 to the 70's.

The club each year offers classes for both beginners and experienced square dancers. These practice sessions are held at the multipurpose room at the Morristown Elementary School. Periodic dress-up pleasure dances are held at the cafeteria at Peoples Academy.

Our final two organizations carry an association with Morristown that is far closer than any of the others.

Morrisville Military Band

The Morrisville Military Band (pages 229-33) continued to flourish until World War II years. From 1942 to 1946 its membership was significantly reduced but it continued to play concerts and in Memorial Day and Armistice Day parades.

In 1946 Mrs. Mary Sanders Mitchell became the first woman to join the previously all-male organization. The fact that she was "well-chaperoned" by her father, Don A. Sanders, her brother, Willard K. Sanders, and her husband, Leslie Mitchell — all members of the Band — soon overcame objections by some of the older members. In 1952 several other women joined the Band and now, with Women's Liberation in full swing, female members are hardly an unheard-of event.

Note might be made here of the long and devoted service which those three members of the Sanders family made and have made to the Band. All, of course, played regularly (and Mary still does) and in addition served in various official capacities. Particularly notable was Willard Sanders. He played with the band a total of 57 years and was its leader from 1933 to about 1951 and then again from about 1953 to

1968. Sanders also did some composing and two of his works are of special significance here. One was the *Peopleonian March*, composed in 1935 and dedicated to his father, Don, a charter member of the band. The other was the *Morrisville Military Band March*, composed about 1950.

A present member with exceptionally long service is Gerald W. (Gunboat) Tripp. He joined the Band in 1927.

In 1949 Band members launched a campaign to raise money for new uniforms. A major fund-raiser, in March and April, 1950 was their "Muddy River Minstrels," which played to capacity audiences in Morrisville and Stowe. Lovely blue and gold uniforms were purchased and used until abandoned in 1965. Informal dress has been the custom since then.

Since 1935 the Town has continued to appropriate funds for support of the Band, though in varying amounts. Until 1978 the Village also usually made an appropriation. Each player receives a small sum

---

MT. MANSFIELD MUSIC

Labor Day, in 1922, found the [Morrisville Military Band] once more entrained in its truck, this time under the ownership of Mr. Andrews, headed for the top of Mt. Mansfield to help dedicate the new automobile road up the mountain [to the Summit House hotel]. We made the summit eventually but only after everyone got out on the curves and steep hills and pushed the truck up by hand. ... We alternated with the Stowe band in playing martial music and took time to climb the Nose. We had dinner in the Hotel at which time Erwin Woodbury expressed his fondness of tomatoes which were served. Erwin was accordingly awarded some 20 dishes of this vegetable from the other band members and he consumed them all. ...

Willard K. Sanders
Recollection, 1950

---

for his or her services and the remainder, if any, has been used for upkeep of instruments, purchase of music and miscellaneous expenses.

Membership of the Band has fluctuated through the years, but the average has been about 30 members per season. Players have come not only from Morristown but also from Stowe, Wolcott, Hyde Park, Johnson and Cambridge.

During Sanders' "leave of absence" as director from about 1951 to about 1953, Robert Sparks led the Band. Other directors have been: George Bedell, 1968-70; Charles Miller, 1972-74; Harl Hoffman, 1975-77; Glory Douglass, 1978-80 (the first female to do so); and the current director, Roxanne Van Vechten. During 1971 the Band had no leader but gave concerts during that summer in spite of this handicap.

The Thursday-evening summertime concerts of the Morrisville Military Band in recent years have been given for about eight weeks from late June or early July through most of August. In this modern automotive age most of each audience come in their cars, parking them in two or three lines in front of the Copley Bandshell. Sometimes a few of those listeners plus occasional music-lovers who arrive on foot settle on blankets on the lawn near the shell. During a concert, listeners in the cars applaud each number by honking their horns!

Morristown Historical Society

As we noted at the outset of this chapter, almost all the local organizations to be chronicled here were actually related to a larger geographic area than just Morristown. But one organization which is true-blue Morristown in make-up and activities is the Morristown Historical Society.

The organization's first meeting was held March 19, 1947 at the Morristown Centennial Library. In 1949 a constitution was adopted and in 1952 the Society incorporated as a non-profit corporation.

A moving force in establishing the organization and its first and long-time president was Anna L. Mower. Others playing major early and continuing roles were Eloise Stafford, Blanche Adams, Rev. Frank A. Stockwell and Jean Pinney.

Early meetings of the Society were generally held at the Library. Much of its activity for the first few years was compiling information about various elements of the town's history. The young organization also began to accumulate memorabilia of the town, both artifacts and documentary material. Miss Mower stored these early holdings at the Library. But it was soon clear that the Society needed a home elsewhere, if it was going to collect very much.

The answer came through a different community project, already described in Chapter 17. That involved the Village's acquisition in 1947 of the Noyes House property at the west end of Main Street (actually 1 West High Street). This was originally to have been the site for a new Community House paid for by a special fund established by Alexander H. Copley. But in the end the Copley fund was used to build the Copley Community Memorial Building (gymnasium) at Peoples Academy. So in 1952 the Village leased the Noyes House to the Morristown Historical Society for use as its headquarters.

With its prominent location, the old, sturdy and handsome brick house with frame ell and attached barn was ideal for its new function. The house was built by Jedediah Safford. He was the son of John Safford, who, as Miss Mower reported (page 71), settled in 1796 in the area of Morristown that was to become Morrisville — the first person to do so. Just when the house was built is uncertain, but it must have been some time prior to 1833, when Jedediah sold the property to another member of the Safford family. It remained in Safford family hands until 1860. After two other owners had held the property, Carlos S. Noyes, prominent businessman, purchased it in 1875. That was the start of 73 years of Noyes ownership, first by Carlos and later by his son, Arthur C. Noyes.

Between 1952 and 1959 the Society carried out a major rehabilitation of the structure and conversion to a museum. As the *News & Citizen* later described the project, "... With rotting porches, peeling paint, plugged chimneys, falling plaster, leaky pipes, and inadequate wiring, it seemed an impossible task to make the repairs and fill the cavernous halls with displays and furniture, particularly since the Society had no dues and no money. Through the Herculean efforts of a few dedicated souls, the repairs were made, the building equipped, and converted to the present pleasant premises." Key elements of the restoration were the razing of a large veranda, removal of dreary yellow paint from the brick walls, and the re-opening of a classic 19th century fireplace with its bake-oven, crane and other metal fittings.

A whole lot more was also going on during this time. Regular meetings were being held, usually monthly. A number of these featured special programs such as an "Old-time Singing School," "Old-time District School" and "Old-time Lyceum." In 1952 the Society inaugurated what became its annual "Come and See Party," a day-long open house at the Noyes House with special exhibits and programs as added features.

On another front, three sturdy metal historic markers were set out in the mid-1950's: one, in 1955, at the site of Jacob Walker's first log cabin on Stagecoach Road south of Morristown Corners (T43); a second, in July, 1957, at Jacob Walker's grave in Mountain View Cemetery (T27); and a third, also in July, 1957, at the site of the town's first church, the large but ill-fated brick structure constructed in 1823 at Morristown Corners (T55). (All but the latter were still there in 1980.)

And a key reason for establishing the Society was also being fulfilled: the gathering in of historical records and artifacts (more than 2,500 items by 1960). These included items of both a general nature like early clothing and household utensils, and those specifically related to Morristown. Individual items in the latter category, such as the remains of what supposedly was Indian Joe's log canoe, are mentioned here and there throughout this text. So that the public could see all this, the museum was open Monday through Saturday from 2 to 5 p.m. Volunteers served as hosts and hostesses.

Since the 1960's the vitality of the Society has definitely slackened, particularly in recent years. Special programs continued to be offered, but only occasionally. In the last few years none of these has been held and meetings of the Society generally have been few and far between. The annual Come and See Party continued to take place through 1980, but was not held in 1981. And openings of the museum went from the six-day schedule to a three-day weekend and then, in 1981, to only several occasional openings.

As for the Noyes House, one significant development was the discovery that the brick walls were spreading (one very serious crack appeared near the middle of the rear wall). To correct the problem, metal brace rods were installed in 1971. A decorative touch was added to these in the form of a large metal "M" at the end of each rod on the outside of the front wall.

Finally, the Society's one current major project has been sponsorship of the preparation of this updated history of Morristown.

> For other details about various of Morristown's organizations, see the "first draft" of *More About Morristown, 1935-1980*; the Foreword describes what and where that is.

Chapter 22
Military Record

SOLDIERS MONUMENT, ACADEMY PARK

ONE OF THE TOWN'S most familiar landmarks is the Soldiers Monument at Academy Park in the center of Morrisville. Embedded in the ground in front of the monument are several other war memorial stones which are described in detail below. Together these permanently honor those Morristown men and women who served — and particularly those who died — in the Civil War and subsequent armed conflicts in which America has been involved.

The author regrets that he is not including, as Miss Mower did for the Civil War and World War I, a full roster of Morristown's veterans of World War II, the Korean War, and the Viet Nam War. Morristown men who were *casualties* in World War II (and one casualty in the Korean War) are, however, listed below.

As for the home front, older Morristowners will remember the various war-support activities of World War II: the defense bond sales (and defense stamps sold in Morristown's schools); the appointment of Civil Defense officials; the Victory Gardens; the saving of used cooking grease for production of munitions; gasoline rationing; and paper and metal scrap drives.

Local national defense activities have waxed and waned since World War II. There were active Civil Defense organizations here during the 1950's and early 1960's, and at least a town Civil Defense Chairman in recent years. And from 1955 through 1958, part of the Cold War period with Russia, there was a Ground Observer Corps post functioning here. Volunteers manned a spotting station to watch the skies for possible Russian bombers.

A significant military activity in Morristown began in 1947 with the establishment here of a unit of the Vermont National Guard. That was Company I of the 172nd Infantry Regiment of the 43rd Infantry Division. The unit's supply room was on the third floor of the Foss Block on Portland Street (C82). Training exercises also took place there, while drills were held during the winter at the American Legion barracks (C13) and on the Peoples Academy grounds in the summer.

Company I's first active duty came on August 9, 1949 when its men fought a forest fire in Elmore for part of that day. (Assistance in disasters — fire, flood, storm — and in the control of civil disturbances are among the missions of the National Guard.) Then early in the Korean War period, Company I was called up in August, 1950 for 21 months of active *military* duty. But the company did not go to Korea. It trained at Camp Pickett, Virginia and then served in Munich, Germany until mid-1953, when the tour of duty ended.

A major development for the local Guard unit was getting its own home. Constructed in 1956-57 was the present State armory, the large brick structure on Washington Highway in the Village (V18). The Morrisville Memorial Armory was dedicated to those Morristown men who were casualties in World War II and the Korean War. They are:

— Robert Guy Baker, killed in action, Italy, December 15, 1944.
— Howard S. Bumps, died August 12, 1944, France.
— Wilbert L. Conrad, Jr., died of wounds, Guam, April 15, 1945.
— Gordon Lee Jacobs, killed in a vehicle accident, Osaka, Japan, January 28, 1949.
— Roger Gates Kellogg, killed in an airplane accident, Rapid City, South Dakota, May 22, 1943.
— Raymond M. Kneeland, killed in action, Philippine Islands, June 5, 1942.
— Cedric C. Laraway, killed in action, France, November 17, 1944.
— Willie L. Laroche, killed in action, Guadalcanal, December 25, 1942.
— Hector A. Lefebvre, wounded, November 14, 1944.
— Ellis L. Macie, died, Oklahoma, October 17, 1942.
— Reginald L. Putnam, killed in action, Germany, February 27, 1945.
— Orrin E. Russell, died, Sampson, New York, March 17, 1945.
— Donald G. Sherman, killed in action, Europe, May 24, 1945.
— Walter S. Ward, killed in action, February 3, 1945.

The one Korean War casualty inscribed on the dedication tablet at the Armory is Lester R. Keith (details are not given). And not listed on the Armory tablet are at least two other Morristown men known to be World War II casualties: Raymond S. Gates (a native of Morrisville but a resident of Barre at the time he entered the service), killed in action, Peleliu Island in the western Pacific Ocean, November 17, 1944; and Albert B. Goss, died of wounds, July 31, 1944.

The Armory has since been the site for the National Guard unit's drills and training exercises, and the assembly point for out-of-town training missions, including an annual trek to Camp Drum, New York.

In 1959 what had been Company I of the 172nd Infantry Regiment became Company C of the 1st Battle Group of the 172nd Combat Arms Regiment, and in 1964, Company C of the 1st Battalion of the 172nd

Armored Regiment. Translated, that means the local unit was changed from an infantry company to a tank company.

Finally, on at least two other occasions the Morrisville National Guard Unit has been called into active duty. One was related to a labor dispute in Burlington in 1969, the other was to provide flood assistance in Lyndonville in 1973.

Backtracking momentarily at this point, we've learned that, contrary to Miss Mower's report (page 145), at least one Morristown man saw Army service, though no combat, in the Spanish-American War. That was Dell L. Sanders, who served from May to October, 1898.

Let's now return to Academy Park and trace the changes in this landmark. The name comes, of course, from the area's former close relationship to Peoples Academy. It is the place where Morristown has long focussed its tributes to military veterans, both with physical patriotic objects and with annual ceremonies, notably that on Memorial Day. The little green has also been the site of other structures and activities which are not military or patriotic in character.

In 1909 Morristown's well-known Civil War memento, the large cannon known as Black Betsy, was given a place of honor in the Park. It was displayed on a large two-tiered cement foundation. Over time, the wooden wheels and carriage rotted and were eventually removed. But the cannon remained in place — at least until July 3, 1940. That night vandals blew it to pieces with dynamite.

Brief mention is made in Anna Mower's work of different bandstands in the Park (pages 229-233). The first was built in 1883. What happened to that is not known but another was built in 1895. Made of wood, the fancy octagonal band platform, which was encircled by a decorative balustrade, stood on sturdy posts a good six feet off the ground. The *News & Citizen* provided this wry descriptive note: "The band stand is done, all but the electric wiring to provide illumination to enable the [Morrisville Military Band] boys to distinguish a possible fly from an impossible note in the music."

The next major change for the Park was the completion in 1911 of the Soldiers Monument, a fine account of which Miss Mower has provided. Two details are worthy of addition: A "time capsule" with assorted local memorabilia was placed in the foundation of the monument, and a circular cement walk was laid around the monument, intersecting the walkway which then led to Peoples Academy (that's all gone now).

At this time the 1895 bandstand was moved — in modified form — from the north side of the walk to the south side. By 1919 it had become unfit for use and was replaced by a temporary stand built at the foot of the park.

Then in August, 1921 the Morrisville Military Band sounded forth at a dedication concert for a new concrete bandstand in the Park. Trumpeted the *News & Citizen*, "It truly is a thing of beauty that will be a joy forever." "Forever" lasted only about ten years, however. As noted earlier, Alexander H. Copley in 1931 provided his gift of a new bandshell on the grounds of Peoples Academy (V37).

The author is uncertain if there were any other non-patriotic observances or activities at the Park in succeeding years, at least until 1978. Beginning that year, the Lamoille County Farmers Market has used the Park during the summer and early fall as the site of its Saturday market days. This was described in more detail in Chapter 14.

Returning to our chronology, 1921 saw the appearance of another patriotic item, near but not at Academy Park. That was the bronze tablet which is mounted to one side of the front entrance at the Morristown Centennial Library. It pays tribute to Morristown's veterans of World War I.

Another veterans memorial, this one also at the Library, appeared in 1945. At town meeting that year voters approved and appropriated funds for what was termed a "temporary memorial" to Morristown's veterans of World War II. Produced was a large wooden, glass-covered, cabinet-type structure. This initially was mounted on posts in the center of the lawn on the west side of the Library. W. Leon Conrad, whose son, Wilbert L., Jr., died of wounds received in the war, was chairman of the committee which saw to the memorial's design and construction; he also watched over its maintenance for many years. Two local committees subsequently considered ideas for a *permanent* memorial but no project was ever carried out.

Just when is not known, but probably some time in the 1950's the wooden Roll of Honor was moved to its present position on the front wall to the left of the Library's front entrance. In 1976 and 1977 Boy Scout Richard Thayer carried out a major restoration of the memorial as an Eagle Scout project. Post 9653 of the Veterans of Foreign Wars (VFW) sponsored the project

Returning now to Academy Park, a granite memorial to servicemen who were killed in America's wars was installed in front of the Soldiers Monument in 1961. It was a gift of the VFW Post 9653 and American Legion Post 33. About this same time it is believed the two organizations also erected near the new monument a flagpole for the American flag.

In 1978 the VFW and American Legion posts replaced the single flagpole with two flagpoles, the second for Vermont's state flag. Also in 1978, John Clegg, a local dealer in cemetery monuments, donated and installed four ground-level memorial stones to supplement the existing monuments. Standing just behind the VFW/Legion stone, the four are inscribed, respectively, "WW I," "WW II," "KOREA," and "VIET NAM."

Still standing tall as the centerpiece of Academy Park is the Soldiers Monument. Over its 70 years it has been worn and torn to some extent by the elements. The most serious encounter was with the famous New England hurricane of September 21, 1938, when the bronze statue of the soldier was blown off its base. Fortunately, it was returned intact.

In 1979 the monument underwent a major cleaning and rehabilitation. John Clegg did the work, charging only for his costs, which were paid by the local VFW post.

> For additional information about Morristown's military record and various related memorials, see the "first draft" of *More About Morristown, 1935-1980*; details about what and where that is are in the Foreword.

Chapter 23

Politics
And
Social
Issues

POLITICS AND SOCIAL ISSUES are subjects not touched on at all by Miss Mower but together they certainly represent one element of Morristown's character and history.

At the outset it might be noted that elections of local officers — Town selectmen, Town School District directors, and Village trustees, etc. — have always been non-political. Which is to say, candidates for those offices have never identified themselves as Republican or Democrat or with any other political party.

The one "local" office where such political affiliation is a factor is the Town's justices of the peace. Technically, as noted in Chapter 2, that is a county, not town, office. More to the point, justices of the peace carry political identification in their election and service because this has some bearing in their administration of local elections as members of the Town's board of civil authority.

One other element of local political activity is the existence of town committees for political parties, notably Republicans and Democrats. Under Vermont law, local voters of those respective political persuasions are to caucus and organize biennially (in the odd-numbered years). Republicans have certainly done so regularly in Morristown, though the turnout for such caucuses has fallen off in recent years. Organization of Democratic town committees at appropriate caucuses has occurred, but more sporadically.

As for Morristown's political record in state and national elections, the town can fairly be called "staunchly Republican." In fact it has voted for Republican candidates more heavily and more frequently

POLITICS AND SOCIAL ISSUES

than the state as a whole. That has, of course, traditionally been a Republican stronghold, though the tradition has weakened in recent years. On two occasions, but only two, Morristown has left the Republican majority fold.

The first was in 1964 when Morristown, the state, and the nation chose Democrat Lyndon B. Johnson of Texas for President by a large margin over Republican Barry M. Goldwater of Arizona. That's the only time either the state or town has ever favored a Democrat for the nation's highest office.

The other exception came in a gubernatorial contest and needs a bit more background. For over 100 years Vermonters had been electing Republicans to the state's highest office. In 1962, however, they chose Democrat Philip H. Hoff by a narrow margin over the incumbent Republican, F. Ray Keyser, Jr. But Morristown stuck with the Republican by a 3 to 2 margin. Hoff was re-elected in 1964 and this time Morristown swung in his favor by a large margin: 778 votes for Hoff and 585 for his Republican opponent, Ralph A. Foote. But in 1966, when Hoff was again re-elected, Morristown once again preferred the Republican nominee, Richard A. Snelling, 713 to 547.

Let's now shift closer to home and the election of the local representative in the House of Representatives of Vermont's General Assembly. Until 1965, Morristown, like all Vermont towns and cities, had had its own representative. Since that year, under a new apportionment of the Vermont House, Morristown has been part of a representative district. Details of this change and a roster of the local representatives are given in the next chapter. Pertinent here, however, is the fact that with one exception, Morristown has always elected a Republican as its own or the district representative. The exception came in 1962 and 1964, when Morristowners elected Karl R. Manning, a Democrat, as their town representative.

Since we've been reviewing election results, we might record here where Morristowners have cast their ballots in state and national elections. Until 1965 the polling place was the town hall (C21). Locations since then have been: 1966 and 1968, the auditorium at Peoples Academy; 1970-78, the Lamoille County Senior Citizens Center (C15); and 1980, the activities room in the north wing of the Peoples Academy complex.

And we might also note in passing Morristowners' action on a certain electoral procedure. That's the so-called Australian Ballot for local elections of Town and Town School District officers. Use of the Australian Ballot involves several elements: a formal nominating procedure; the use of printed ballots on which only the names of properly-qualified nominees appear; and the voting at polls which are open throughout a specified period on town meeting day. This compares with the longstanding much more informal procedure in which nominations are made from the floor at the annual meeting and voting, when there is a contest, is by a much less formal written ballot. In this procedure voters can participate only if they are on hand at the time any particular election occurs. On three occasions — 1967, 1970 and 1973 — a proposal for use of the Australian ballot was put to Morristown voters. It was soundly defeated each time.

Turning to social issues, over the years since 1935 a number of these have become ballot questions as a result of one or another state laws. In some cases Morristown's vote had significance only as part of the statewide total on each question. In others, the local vote had a direct local effect.

Taking the former category first, the following are the more significant or interesting of several statewide referendum questions:

— In 1936 the question was whether or not Vermonters wanted a scenic highway, known as the Green Mountain Parkway, to be constructed along or near the main range of the Green Mountains. The project would have been financed in large measure by the Federal government. In what has since been often viewed as a manifestation of Vermont's independent character, the proposal, with its Federal largesse, was defeated statewide by a substantial margin, 30,897 to 42,318. Mor-

---

PEAVINE'S LIQUOR DELIVERY SERVICE

Yes, "Peavine" Graves and his City Cab. Many people will certainly remember him for his rather special delivery service. That was in the early 1950's when Morristown was still "dry" for hard liquor. Peavine used to make regular trips in his taxi to Waterbury to meet the trains stopping there. That also happened to be the closest town to Morristown which was "wet" and which had a State liquor store. So Peavine obtained the official liquor price list and people here would tell him what they wanted — say, a fifth of Seagram's whiskey at $3.75. They'd pay him the money for that, plus 25 cents a bottle for picking it up and delivering it. Now that was all perfectly legal — he wasn't selling you liquor, only charging you for its transportation.

During the holiday season, things got downright busy for Peavine. He'd make three or four trips a day just filling liquor orders. He had this little taxi office at the west end of Main Street. At times that would be filled with cases of liquor which he had "taxied" up from Waterbury. I sometimes used to think there was more liquor there than there ever was at the liquor store.

Clyde A. Limoge
Recollection, 1980

---

ristowners, however, strongly *favored* the idea, 427 to 296.

— In 1960 Vermonters were asked to approve wagering at horse races using the so-called pari-mutuel system. A majority said "yes" but Morristowners didn't like the idea very much, registering a 459-829 negative vote.

— And in 1976 a referendum asked Vermonters if "the General Assembly [should] consider enactment of a Vermont lottery to supplement state revenues." They said it should, and by a nearly three to one margin, 127,001 to 49,447. In what would seem to be a change of heart on the matter of gambling, Morristowners registered a definite, though not quite so substantial, favorable vote, 927 to 502. The Legislature, incidentally, did establish a Vermont Lottery, which has been operating since 1978.

POLITICS AND SOCIAL ISSUES

As for votes on social issues which had direct local impact, one series, which is now probably little-remembered, related to certain Sunday amusements. Under two related state laws passed in 1939, each town's voters could vote to allow or prohibit any or all of three particular activities on Sundays: the playing of baseball, "concerts and lectures," and "moving pictures." In 1939 Morristowners approved the first two by substantial margins but voted against the showing of movies, 143-254. In 1940 and 1941 they approved all three, though the vote was fairly close on the movies the first of those years. Under a change in the law, the only vote in 1942 was on Sunday movies. More Morristowners were now apparently hooked on the silver screen and voted 398-217 to permit their showing that day. That was, however, the last vote on any of these "regulated" Sunday amusements.

"Wet" or "Dry." That has been one measure of Vermont towns since the repeal in 1933 of the famous Prohibition amendment of the U.S. Constitution. For Vermont's system of control of intoxicating beverages, the Legislature passed a law in 1934 which provided for local option: each town and city's voters could decide if they wished to permit the sale of either or both of two basic kinds of intoxicants: "malt and vinous beverages" and "spiritous liquors." Each year there was a new vote on both categories, a procedure which continued until 1969. Under a change in the state law, each town and city's vote that year was to remain "final" until such time as it voted otherwise.

Morristown began the annual ritual in 1934 by voting "wet" on both kinds of intoxicants. By the following year, however, voters' feelings had changed significantly because the Town voted dry both ways by substantial margins. It remained dry on beer and wine until 1942, and then switched back and forth on that several times until 1950. That year it voted wet on beer and wine and continued to do so without further lapses through the 1969 final vote.

It was somewhat tougher going for "spiritous liquors." For another nine years Morristowners continued to vote against allowing their sale. Then in 1960 the switch came, "wets" outvoting "drys," 242 to 231. Booze had come to stay in Morristown.

Under that 1934 law, Vermont itself got into the liquor business, selling bottles of the "hard stuff" through two types of outlets: State liquor stores, which the State itself operated, and State liquor agencies, which were private vendors operating on a commission basis under agreements with the Vermont Liquor Control Board. (Malt and vinous beverages were and still are licensed to be sold either of two ways by individual retail vendors: by the drink, and in the bottle for consumption off the premises; except for those who operate a state liquor agency, private vendors can sell spiritous liquors only by the drink, when licensed to do so.)

Morrisville became the location of Liquor Agency No. 14 in 1965. On July 8 that year the agency opened on the ground floor of the "Old Brick Store" on lower Main Street (C53). The liquor outlet, under several different licensees, has been there ever since.

> For some, but not substantial, additional information about politics and social issues here, see the "first draft" of *More About Morristown, 1935-1980*; the Foreword tells what and where that is.

ROUND BARN AT WELCH FARM

Chapter 24 - Prominent People And Buildings

THIS CHAPTER IS BASICALLY an extension of Miss Mower's Chapter XVIII, "Morristown In Public Affairs." But in addition to biographical notes about certain very prominent Morristowners, we will provide at least brief histories of the notable homes with which each was associated. Beyond that we will make note of both a number of other prominent citizens, without reference to their homes, and of a limited selection of houses and other structures which are of special historic or architectural interest.

We'll begin with George W. Hendee, the only Morristowner to have served as Vermont's governor (pages 268-70). His distinctive home is the Victorian-style, three-story, mansard-roofed, white-clapboarded building (C40) which stands just west of the Morristown Centennial Library. Construction of the home began the spring of 1877 and was completed in 1878.

Following Gov. Hendee's death on December 6, 1906, the home was owned by two other parties until it was purchased in 1911 by Dr. and Mrs. A. (for Archibald) J. Valleau. The Valleaus remained residents there for over 25 years.

The record is uncertain but the Valleaus apparently were the last for which the impressive structure was basically a private residence. For the next ten years the status of the property was very uncertain, it being successively owned by the Village of Morrisville (for a possible community house), the Copley Fund (for a possible home for elderly ladies), and the First Congregational Church. Details of these changes were provided in Chapter 18. During this time the building was converted to offices and apartments, uses which continue at present (Dr. Valleau had, however, established his medical offices there earlier). With the exception of a fire escape from the third floor which was constructed in the 1970's, the exterior of the building, which is nicely maintained, remains essentially unchanged from its original form — including the granite steps which cost Gov. Hendee $125!

PEOPLE AND BUILDINGS 529

The second Morristowner described by Miss Mower who achieved high prominence was H. Henry Powers (pages 270-73). His Morrisville residence for the last 27 years of his life was the three-story white-clapboarded frame structure on the north side of Park Street which is now a portion of the Lamoille View Apartments (C123). This was constructed for Powers and his wife in 1885-86, after their earlier home on the same site was moved therefrom.

For some years following Powers' death in 1913 the home was in other hands. Then beginning in 1935, the house was known for more than 40 years as the home and office of Dr. David A. Walker, Morrisville's popular veterinarian. At the time of his retirement, Dr. Walker and his wife, Lucy, sold the house and its approximately four acres of grounds in 1979 to The Housing Group, a partnership comprised of Kenneth and Alfred Lunde of Barre. Along with construction of a large new building to the rear, they converted the Powers / Walker home to government-subsidized housing for the elderly and handicapped. Called Lamoille View Apartments, the project was completed in 1980.

Another Morristowner described by Miss Mower who attained high public office was Frederick G. Fleetwood (pages 275-76). Not specifically mentioned by Miss Mower was Fleetwood's term as Congressman. That was 1923-25, when he was U.S. Representative for Vermont's First District. It might also be noted here that he was born September 27, 1868 and moved to Morrisville in 1886. He died January 28, 1938.

His long-time residence was the fine, Queen-Anne-style, three-story frame house on the south side of Park Street, in 1980 the home of Mr. and Mrs. Paul Nesky (C124). Fleetwood had inherited that from his mother, Laura F. Gleed, upon her death in 1912. The house was built in 1885-86 for her husband and Fleetwood's step-father and legal mentor, Philip K. Gleed.

The final prominent Morristowner chronicled by Miss Mower was George M. Powers, long-time Chief Justice of the Vermont Supreme Court (pages 276-77). Here and there in earlier pages we have provided other information about the man.

Powers continued as Chief Justice until his death on June 24, 1938. Many Vermont newspapers joined Morrisville's own *Messenger* in honoring the man. The following year his family presented the State with an oil portrait of Powers painted by Harold Dunbar. It continues to hang outside the Supreme Court chambers in Montpelier. On that occasion the new Chief Justice, Sherman R. Moulton, observed that Powers' "opinions, and the influence of his keen mind will always remain a tradition with the court, and have left an indelible imprint on the jurisprudence of his state."

Powers' wife, Gertrude, a daughter of one of Vermont's governors, Urban A. Woodbury, died December 30, 1962. Only one of his four children, Roberta F. Powers, is still living (1981). She makes her home in Somerset, N.J., where, among other things, she is writing a biography of her father.

Morrisville still has the distinctive home which was closely associated with George Powers. It is the large, two-story frame house on the northeast corner of Congress and Union Streets (V34), owned since 1967 by Mr. and Mrs. Robert Moran. Following their marriage in 1893, George and Gertrude Powers first lived in a suite of rooms at the Randall Hotel. In early 1895 they leased the fine home set well back on the north side of lower Main Street (C114). That was built for Charles M. Peck in 1883-84.

Then in early 1899 the couple acquired the Congress Street lot. A few months later, construction of their new home began, and early in February, 1901 the family moved in. The George Powers home is closely related both by family association and in architectural style to the abovedescribed H. Henry Powers house. Architect for the former was probably the same as the latter: A.B. Fisher & Son of Burlington.

Two other Morristowners who achieved high public office, that of Attorney General of Vermont, were Alban James Parker and Clifton Goodrich Parker.

While Alban Parker was born here (March 21, 1893) and graduated from Peoples Academy (1911), his subsequent life was all spent elsewhere, with Springfield his principal home town. So we will note here only that he was Attorney General from 1941 to 1947 and that he died, in Springfield, on May 10, 1971.

Clifton Parker was born in Wolcott on October 2, 1906, the son of Mr. and Mrs. H. Alton Parker. He was educated in Wolcott public schools and at Hardwick Academy. He studied law in St. Johnsbury and was admitted to the Vermont Bar in October, 1932. He moved to Morrisville and opened a law office in the Drowne Block on February 1, 1934.

On March 1, 1936 he entered into partnership with Morrisville's long-time and prominent attorney, Frederick G. Fleetwood, moving his offices to those of Fleetwood on the second floor of the Fleetwood Building (C46). The partnership continued until Fleetwood's death in 1938. Thereafter Parker maintained a solo practice until January 1, 1970 when he established a partnership with Attorney Richard C. Sargent. That continued until Parker's retirement on December 31, 1972.

Like Alban Parker, Clifton Parker entered public office as a state's attorney soon after he began his legal career. He served in that post for Lamoille County from 1936 to 1941. During this period he also served as First Assistant Clerk of the Vermont House of Representatives in the 1939 and 1941 sessions. The latter year Attorney General Alban Parker appointed Clifton Parker as his deputy, a position he held until 1947. And continuing some overlapping of State jobs, Clifton served as Clerk of the House of Representatives from 1943 to 1947. In 1946 he was elected Attorney General and was re-elected for two successive terms, serving in all from February 1, 1947 through December 31, 1952 (he resigned on that date to pave the way for an early appointment of his elected successor).

Throughout his political career he was a Republican. He also served for many years in two important local offices: as Town moderator from 1946 to 1966 and as a Village water and light commissioner, 1939-50 and 1951-60. On November 6, 1926 Parker married Florence Simmons in Johnson. The couple have six children.

This seems to be as appropriate a place as any to continue Miss

PEOPLE AND BUILDINGS   531

Mower's roster of Morristown members of the Vermont General Assembly.

Town representatives were: Frank J. Allen, 1935-37; Roy C. Stafford, 1937-39; Erwin W. Terrill, 1939-41; Raeburn R. McMahon, 1941-43; Erwin H. Olmstead, 1943-47; J. Harold Hill, 1947-51; W. Leon Conrad, 1951-59; Willie (Will) C. Davis, 1959-63; Karl R. Manning, 1963-65; and Madelyn C. Manning, 1965. (Karl Manning resigned in early 1965 following his re-election in 1964 to a second term. His wife, Madelyn, was appointed January 28, 1965 to fill his vacancy. She was the first woman, and so far the only woman, to represent Morristown in Vermont's House of Representatives.)

In 1965, as a result of court-ordered reapportionment, the General Assembly's House of Representatives ended its one-town / one-representative composition. Instead, it was divided into representative districts so that each of its now 150 representatives (previously 246 representatives) represented approximately the same population. In this reapportionment Morristown was joined with Stowe and Elmore to form District 20, a two-member district. The first election for the new House of Representatives was held November 23, 1965. District 20 representatives were: 1965-67, Max B. Davison of Morristown and Frederick E. (Fred) Westphal of Elmore; 1967-69, Giles W. Dewey of Stowe and Westphal; 1969-71, 1971-73 and 1973-75, Dewey and George H. Paine of Morristown.

Under a new apportionment of the House of Representatives in 1974, Morristown became part of a new two-member district. That is the Lamoille-2 District, which also includes Elmore, Hyde Park, Eden and Belvidere. Lamoille-2 District representatives have been: 1975-77, Paine of Morristown and Ernest J. (Stub) Earle of Eden; 1977-79 and 1979-present, Earle and McDonald Miller of Morristown.

As for the Vermont Senate, Morristowners have represented Lamoille County from time to time but by no means all the time. While Lamoille County was created in 1835 by the Vermont Legislature, it was not apportioned a senator until 1841 when a new apportionment of the Senate was carried out based in part on the 1840 census. Morristown men who have been the county's* senators are: 1844-46, David P. Noyes; 1853-55, Horace Powers; 1857-59, Thomas Gleed; 1864-66, Samuel M. Pennock; 1866-69, George W. Hendee; 1872-74, H. Henry Powers; 1880-82, Philip K. Gleed; 1888-90, Henry C. Fisk; 1894-96, Frank Kenfield; and 1906-08, Charles H.A. Stafford.

Also, 1919-21, Melville P. Maurice; 1921-23, William Taft Slayton; 1929-31, Roy C. Stafford; 1933-35, Gustin E. Smith; 1943-47, Raeburn R. McMahon; and 1965-69, Samuel R. Loomis (Loomis also served two earlier terms while a resident of Elmore).

And finally, to continue Miss Mower's roster of Morristown lawyers who have served as state's attorney for Lamoille County (page 168), the following have so served since 1935: 1936-41, Clifton G.

*And it was *just* Lamoille County until 1974. Under a reapportionment of the Senate that year, the town of Craftsbury in Orleans County was added to Lamoille County's ten towns to create what has since been the Lamoille Senatorial District.

Parker; 1947-53, George A. King; 1953-61, Robert A. Magoon; 1976-80, P. Scott McGee; and 1980-81, Joseph J. Wolchik.

Gates House, Noyes / Slayton House, Old Brick Store

Returning now to other historic or otherwise significant structures in the town, various of these have already been described in different special contexts in preceding chapters. Among those not so mentioned are three in the center of Morrisville. They are closely related in their origins by the fact that all were constructed for the same original owner. Two are the two brick structures on the north side of lower Main Street: the "Old Brick Store" (C53) and the so-called Noyes/Slayton House (C54). The third is the Gates House on Brigham Street (C113).

The Gates House — the name derives from two generations of Gates who lived there for nearly 75 years — is believed to be the oldest existing structure in the Village. It's not known, however, just when it was built. What is known about its age is closely related to the history of the Noyes / Slayton House, so we'll turn to that.

In 1816 David P. Noyes acquired one and three-quarters acres of land which is believed to be the site for what became the Noyes/Slayton House. However, Noyes first built a frame house there, presumably in the year or so after the land's acquisition. Then when he decided to construct the fine two-story, granite-silled brick home, he moved the frame structure farther back on the lot. The brick house was apparently constructed in 1835, though that is not certain.

In 1842, when Rev. Septimius Robinson moved to Morrisville from Morristown Corners to help establish the First Congregational Church in its new home here, he needed a place to live. Noyes donated the original frame house to him. Rev. Robinson, having then purchased a lot on Brigham Street, had the house moved to that site, where it has remained ever since.

In 1906 Leo Gates acquired the home. It remained in that family's hands through a daughter, Mary, until her death in 1978. Not long after that the property was acquired or leased by the Copley Hospital Auxiliary as the site for its Second Chance thrift shop.

As for the Old Brick Store, Noyes also built that two-story structure, about 1820. He then sold both the brick home and store in 1866 to George J. Slayton and Charles M. Peck. Peck sold out his interest to Slayton in 1873. The property remained in Slayton family hands for the next 70 or so years. In 1910, under ownership of Henry A. Slayton, George's son, the house underwent general refurbishing while a frame addition at the rear was torn down and the present ell constructed.

Following Henry Slayton's death in 1932, Dr. Oscar Calcagni acquired the house from his estate in 1941. He both lived and carried on his practice there until his death in 1958. After several subsequent owners, Lyle and Rachel Miller purchased the house in 1979 and converted it to a boarding home for elderly persons.

As for the Old Brick Store, it apparently continued as a general store through the 1930's. From 1943 to 1964 it housed a freeze-locker business and since 1965 has been the site of the local State liquor agency and related beverage store.

Jacob Walker Houses

Moving now out of the Village, there are two houses a short way south on LaPorte Road which are probably of very special local historical significance. That's because both are believed to be houses which Jacob Walker, the town's first settler, built and lived in during his later years here. One is the single-story small frame house on the west side of LaPorte Road which is now the home of Mrs. Edith Dodgen (T60). The other is the brick house next south of the Dodgen home which is presently owned by Mr. and Mrs. Neal Graham (T61).

The association of both structures with Jacob Walker was described in 1940 by Morristown's prominent citizen, Thomas C. Cheney: "After a few years Deacon Jacob Walker built a new and more commodious loghouse east of his old one [on the road south of Morristown Corners, T43], just west of LaPorte Road ... He had, in the meantime, erected a saw mill and oil mill on the so-called Ryder Brook, near this new home. ... His second home ... was built in 1801. He lived in this second house until he erected the brick house just south of the same in 1820, where he lived until his death, July 24, 1843, aged 77 years."

Are the two present houses the original Jacob Walker houses? Cheney certainly said as much, and they probably are. But there is some uncertainty.

One immediate question is raised by Cheney's description of Walker's second house as a "loghouse." That suggests, of course, the classic pioneer structure with walls made of logs laid up on top of each other. The Dodgen house, which is definitely the same structure which Cheney was referring to, does not have such walls. It is nonetheless a very old house of frame construction with hand-hewn timbers, including ground floor joists which *are* half-round logs.

As for the Graham house, it almost certainly is Jacob Walker's 1820 house. Strong supporting evidence is the definite early 19th century character of its orientation, basic design and handmade bricks. The main reason for doubting that the present house was built in 1820 rests on certain pieces of printed matter which Graham found in the house. One was fragments of an 1853 newspaper which were imbedded with the lath underlying the plaster near the house's one fireplace. This suggests that the present house was built that year or some time following. If that did happen, it immediately raises assorted questions about what happened to Jacob Walker's 1820 house. But the contrary argument is that only the plastering itself was done at the later date.

While the house's original exterior and some of its interior structural characteristics and finish detail remain intact, the interior has undoubtedly undergone assorted changes over the years. The Grahams themselves have done a number of things since their acquisition of the property in 1975. Most significant was their construction in 1979 of a major two-story addition on the west side of the brick house.

Tinker and Kenfield Houses

Two places of special interest in the Morristown Corners area are the so-called Tinker House and Kenfield House.

The first is the large two-story brick home in the northeast quadrant of the Corners intersection (T42). This was built for Morristown's prominent early physician, Dr. James Tinker (pages 170-71). Just when is uncertain but one undocumented source puts it at 1828.

Since 1967 the two-story house with its extended frame ell has been the home of Peter and Alexandra Heller and their family. Since 1975 Mrs. Heller has also been operating a store for used books in several of the structure's ground floor rooms.

The Kenfield House (T57) at the start of Cote Hill Road just west of Morristown Corners is another brick home, though significantly smaller than the Tinker House. Alas, its time of construction is also uncertain, though the owners since 1950, Ernest and Faith Godfrey, are sure that it was built before the Tinker House, probably 1825 to 1828. The Godfreys, who raised four sons and a daughter in the home, built the frame addition at the rear of the single-story structure in 1956 or 1957.

The Kenfield name derives from Capt. Frank Kenfield, a prominent member of that prominent early Morristown family which Miss Mower described (pages 27, 136-39) (Kenfield Brook derives its name from this family). He owned the home for some 20 years before his death in 1914.

Spaulding House

Moving to the other side of town, we'll next consider the house at the corner of the Elmore Road (Vermont Rt. 12) and Elmore Mountain Road. That has long had the reputation of being Morristown's oldest two-story house (T58). According to one undocumented but probably reliable source, it was constructed in 1812.

Of particular significance about the structure's early history is that the farm of which it was a part was the home base of Amasa and Maria Spaulding for at least the 40 years between 1830 and 1870 (we thus designate the home the Spaulding House).

The farm subsequently passed through many hands. Silas H. Jewett and his wife, Frances, the last owners who *also* farmed it, held the property from 1945 to 1964. Owners since then have planned it for building lots. The Spaulding House itself, the nearby barn, and 2½ acres of land have been owned since 1971 by Richard and Pamela Ryder.

Welch Round Barn

A particularly well-known historic structure of special character is the round barn on the farm of Mr. and Mrs. Earle Welch on the Elmore Road (T41). "Round" really is an appropriate adjective but technically the yellow-painted structure is an icosagon, or twenty-sided. The barn is interesting, not only for its unusual construction but also for its long association with the Welch family — an association which includes one downright romantic happening.

PEOPLE AND BUILDINGS

Earle's grandfather, William S. Welch, built the barn in 1916. He and his oldest son, Delbert, first logged out and cut enough lumber to begin construction. Two carpenters, Will Goodrich and Irving LeBaron of Morrisville, were hired and they boarded on the farm while the work proceeded.

The barn is 240 feet in circumference. In the center is a silo, 12 feet in diameter and 40 feet high. Around this silo is a hay bay 14 feet in width and 40 feet deep. The rationale of the design, which is said to have originated with the Shakers in Hancock, Mass. in 1824, is that it is more efficient than the traditional rectangular barn with its attached silo(s). The feeding of cows in a circle from a central storage point for both hay and silage is the key.

That "romantic happening" occurred by reason of those two carpenters who boarded at the farm while the barn was being constructed. Mark Pendergrast, in an article about this rare Vermont structure in the *Burlington Free Press* in 1978, provided this account: "Because of the extra cooking and housekeeping, William [Welch] hired Shirley Parker to help his wife Grace. During the course of the busy summer days, young Delbert and Shirley had occasion to see quite a bit of each other, and by the time the barn was finished, a wedding was planned. They were married in December of 1916."

When William died in 1934, Delbert took over the farm. Three years later his and Shirley's only child, Earle, was born. Earle grew up on the farm and continued working it with his father until late 1957, when Delbert died. Earlier that year Earle had married Arlene Compagna. Their son, Dean, is the fourth generation of Welches on the round-barned farm.

Favreau Garage

Our last structure is hardly what one would call prominent. But it is special by virtue of being the town's only building whose walls are constructed of stone. It is the garage which stands near Washington Highway behind the long-time Volney Farr residence (V38) which is now owned by the Copley Hospital.

The garage was built some time in the 1920's by Alphonse Favreau, who from 1921 until his death in 1934 owned and farmed what was then a substantial tract of land with the house. Favreau was also a well-known and accomplished mason, among other things laying thousands of bricks in Peoples Academy's Copley Building when that was constructed.

The stone garage has an interesting — even amusing — form of construction. It is comparable to the practice of some Vermont farmers who paint only the front end and sides of their barns. They don't paint the back end because nobody ever sees that! Favreau used smoothfaced pieces of handsome granite for the front and sides of the garage. But for the back wall he used common old field stones!

> For additional details about various of these prominent persons and buildings — plus one or two of the latter not mentioned here at all, see the "first draft" of *More About Morristown, 1935-1980*; the Foreword describes what and where that is.

Chapter 25
Odds
And
The End

JACOB WALKER MONUMENT

THIS, THE FINAL, CHAPTER is our catchall department. Here are items which didn't seem appropriate for any of the previous chapters.

Place Names

Three areas or neighborhoods of the Village have distinctive names, though one of them is now little used.

The two very familiar ones are Jersey Heights and Brooklyn. The first is on the high ground along Vermont Rt. 100 southwest of the business district. The second is the area along Brooklyn Street in the northwest part of the Village. Both names go well back into the 19th century, local newspapers carrying references to "Brooklyn" as early as 1878 and to "Jersey Heights" as early as 1885. It's wholly conjecture but the author presumes that Morrisvillians at that time had some fun likening their village to New York City by adopting two familiar geographic names associated with that metropolis.

The third area is Dorchester Heights, the high ground along Washington Highway just above the intersection with Maple Street. Prominent there is the Dumont Manor retirement home (V20). As recorded in Chapter 19, that was previously the Copley Hospital and originally the grand private residence built in 1896 for Addison P. Wheelock. Wheelock, as Miss Mower reported (page 176), was a resident of Dorchester, Mass., the well-known suburb of Boston. The name, Dorchester Heights, derives from that association.

Two areas of the outside Town also have distinctive names, though we believe neither is in common use today. One is Morristown Plains, or simply the Plains. That is the generally level area north of the

ODDS AND THE END

Lamoille River from the intersection of Harrel Street with Vermont Rt. 15 on the east to where Needle's Eye Road beings its drop toward Cadys Falls about a mile and a half to the west. There used to be the Morristown Plains School, and we still have the Plains (or Greenlawn) Cemetery (T28). And Harrel Street used to be called Plains Road.

The other special place name is Egypt or Little Egypt. That's how Morristowners referred to the area along the Lamoille River west of Morrisville before it was flooded over by what is now Lake Lamoille. Origin of this marvelous name is, however, unknown.

Fair And Field Days

To Anna Mower's comprehensive account of the Lamoille Valley Fair (pages 178 ff.) we can add but little and that is the following.

Beginning in the 1880's baseball games were held between local teams, in 1893 bicycle races were introduced, in 1914 a motorcycle Motor-Drome was featured, and in 1922 airplane rides were offered for the first time. And Miss Mower mentioned two years when there was no fair, 1890 and 1900. Another was 1917 because of an epidemic of infantile paralysis.

It was World War II which brought the end of the fair. In 1942 its management decided to close for the duration to help in the national effort to conserve gas, rubber, oil and other needed resources. They pledged to reopen after the war, but it never happened.

Note was made in Chapter 12 how the fairground property (MS36) was dispersed. The area across Brooklyn Street, now well filled with assorted commercial buildings, was a hayfield in the days of the fair where those visiting airplanes landed and rides were sold. Ironically, that field became one site of a revived, though somewhat different, form of country fair institution.

That's the Lamoille County Field Days. It was born on August 12, 1961 at the Peoples Academy grounds as the "first annual Tractor Rodeo." Co-sponsors were the school's Future Farmers of America chapter (FFA) and the Morrisville Young Farmers Association (YFA). The affair consisted mostly of several competitive events for tractor drivers and their machines: backing ability, an obstacle course, time to hook to a set of plows, and a classic weight-pulling contest.

In 1963 what was now advertised as the Lamoille County Tractor and Field Day moved to the Ivan Maxham farm on LaPorte Road (that "Field Day" designation represented the addition of such events as a couple of greased pigs for the kids, a cross-cut saw competition for the men, and a rolling-pin throwing contest for the women). The following year, the FFA, YFA and other local agricultural organizations supporting the event joined forces in a single organization. That was the Lamoille County Field Days, Inc., the non-profit corporation which has been the sponsor ever since.

In succeeding years the Field Days expanded both in time (generally two days) and in scope of activities. These have included pony and ox-pulling contests, lumberjack events, livestock and pet shows, and judging of farm crops, vegetables, maple products, homemade food and crafts.

Later sites for the event were as follows: 1965 and 1966, the Maxham farm; 1967 and 1968, field opposite the old fairgrounds; 1969-75, the Silver Ridge Pavilion in Hyde Park; and 1976-80, the so-called Demars field at the east end of what is now the Lamoille Industrial Park (T48). Then in 1981 this Morristown-born event apparently left town forevermore. Lamoille County Field Days, Inc. bought some land along Vermont Rt. 100C in Johnson as their new and presumably permanent home.

Celebrations

And to close things out on a happy note, Morristown since 1935 has held or participated in three notable historical celebrations: its own Sesqui-Centennial in 1940, America's and Vermont's joint Bicentennials in 1976 and 1977, and the town's own Bicentennial in 1981.

The Sesqui-Centennial observance, a major local event, marked the 150th anniversary of the town's settlement in 1790 by Jacob Walker. It began Sunday evening, June 30, 1940, with the dedication of a monument to Jacob Walker and a special Sesqui-Centennial service at the First Congregational Church. The monument, composed of a bronze tablet mounted on a granite stone, stands in the middle of the little island at the intersection of Main and Park Streets. At the top of the tablet are the years 1790 and 1940. At the bottom is the message, "In Grateful Memory of Jacob Walker, First Settler Of Morristown. Erected By Its Citizens July 4, 1940." In between is an inscription in Latin: *Et Majores Vestros Et Posteros Cogitate*. According to the *Morrisville Messenger*, "The Inscription ... was suggested by Fred E. Steele, III [English instructor at Peoples Academy]. The English translation of the Latin phrase is 'Think of your forefathers, think of your descendants,' and was taken from a speech by John Quincy Adams at Plymouth in 1802 and quoted by [Vermont author] Dorothy Canfield Fisher in 'Seasoned Timber'."*

On the evening of July 3 a banquet sponsored by Coral Chapter, No. 16, Order of Eastern Star, was held at the Masonic temple. That was followed by a Sesqui-Centennial Ball at the American Legion barracks. On Independence Day there was a big parade and a sort of field day at the Peoples Academy grounds. The grand finale came that evening at the Lamoille Valley Fairground. With thousands of people packing the grandstand and grounds, the program included an address on the history of Morristown by G. Noyes Slayton, a concert by the Morrisville Military Band, and an historical pageant depicting major events in the town's history. With apparent full justification, the *Morrisville Messenger* headlined its extensive coverage of all this with "Morristown's Sesqui-Centennial Is A Grand Success."

One other memento of the Sesqui-Centennial (besides the monument) is a musical one. That's the song, "Our Morristown." While it was given a community sing at least three times during the celebration, the author suspects it has rarely, if ever, been played, sung or heard since that time. The music was composed by Morrisville's

---

*The translation as given in the book actually reads: "Think of your forefathers! Think of your posterity!".

lifelong resident, Willard K. Sanders. The lyrics were written by Leon E. Daniels. He had spent some of his years as a child here, graduating from Peoples Academy in 1893. He had then lived all of his adult years elsewhere, achieving some prominence as a poet and as a teacher of languages and music. The following is one verse of Daniels' "ode":

> Hills that of old looked down,
> Guard still our Morristown,
> From lovely Stowe to where
> Pent Lamoille thunders.
> Elmore, thy challenge throw
> O'er the broad vale below,
> Westward where Sterling the
> Blue skyline sunders!

In contrast to Morristown's concentrated observance of its own Sesqui-Centennial, its participation in the national and state Bicentennial was more diffuse, though there were certain major events and projects which highlighted the doings here.

Some particulars in a moment but first a bit of background. The national Bicentennial, culminating on July 4, 1976, marked, of course, the 200th anniversary of the adoption of America's Declaration of Independence from England. Vermont's Bicentennial in 1977 marked the 200th anniversary of the state's own declaration of independence from England's New Hampshire and New York Provinces and the creation of the independent Republic of Vermont (it didn't become one of these United States until 1791).

The Morristown Bicentennial Committee, in co-operation with other local organizations, developed a list of possible Bicentennial projects and programs. It was an ambitious list and in the end many of the proposals never came to reality. But those that did include:

— The sponsorship by the Morrisville Woman's Club of several sturdy plank benches at different points in the Village, including two at Academy Park.

— Development of a house-numbering system for the Village. While the *system* was established, it's the author's impression that many individual houses do not have them.

— Restoration of the original Peoples Academy building to a close approximation of its original form, including the construction of a bell tower to house the Academy's original bell. As noted in Chapter 21, this project was carried out by the Lamoille Grange, which has long used the building as its hall.

— And oh yes, the publishing of an updated history of Morristown (five years late!).

In any event, the Morristown effort was sufficient to qualify it for designation in 1976 by the American Revolution Bicentennial Administration as an official Bicentennial community.

As for events, Morristown marked the national Bicentennial with a variety of them during June and July, 1976: a concert at Peoples Academy, a special Children's Day Service at the First Congregational Church, a Bicentennial Dance at the American Legion barracks, and a special "Come and See Day" at the Noyes House Museum by the Morristown Historical Society.

Saturday, July 3, saw a mammoth parade through Morrisville. Among the numerous bands, marching units, fire trucks, stiltwalkers and assorted floats was a former Vermont governor, Deane C. Davis. Dressed as an early Methodist preacher, he was riding one of his Morgan horses. Another unit in the parade was a 500-pound Bicentennial birthday cake drawn on a pony cart. With "Happy Birthday, America" emblazoned in its icing, the cake included, among other things, 45 pounds each of flour and sugar and 245 eggs! The parade was followed by a field day or rides, games and other activities at the Demars field on Harrel Street. That concluded with a talent show and a big display of fireworks.

And finally, there was Morristown's Bicentennial in 1981. Unlike the earlier Centennial and Sesqui-Centennial which celebrated the 100th and 150th anniversaries of the *settlement* of the town, the Bicentennial commemorated the 200th birthday of the town's *chartering*. That charter, as Miss Mower recorded (pages 5-7), was issued by Governor Thomas Chittenden on August 24, 1781. The celebration was inspired and organized by Town Clerk Sydney C. Mander with major assists from his wife, Ida, and Joyce Leonard.

On August 22 there was a parade led by Attorney General John J. Easton, Jr. and the Vermont National Guard's top-flight 40th Army Band (a major usual local parade element was lost when five minutes before this one began, most of the Morristown Fire Department's fire trucks were called out to a serious fire!). That was followed by a "mini-midway" of games, musical numbers and dance performances, kiddie rides, bake sales and hot-dog stands at the Copley Memorial Parking Lot and elsewhere in the Village.

And on the evening of August 24 the Peoples Academy auditorium was the scene of a colorful Morristown Bicentennial Pageant of skits and musical numbers. These were related to different landmark structures located in the Village. Ida Mander was organizer, director, scriptwriter and a member of the cast of this.

Sydney Mander, who narrated the show, concluded it with a quotation about Morristown from an earlier prominent local citizen, H. Henry Powers. And we shall do the same for this updated history of the town: "We have much to be proud of and more to be hopeful for."

> For additional details about these various odds and ends plus others not mentioned here at all — Butternut Island, SOS Children's Village / Morehaven, Morristown's centenarians, local developments relating to current energy problems, and the changing Morristown social scene, see the "first draft" of *More About Morristown, 1935-1980*; the Foreword describes what and where that is.

APPENDIX

Principal Officers Of Town Of Morristown, Morristown Town School District And Village Of Morrisville

The following rosters of principal local municipal officers cover somewhat different periods of time, as follows:

— Town of Morristown: Names are provided of selectmen, listers, clerk and treasurer, and moderator since 1900. That is pretty much an arbitrary starting point but it was also somewhat convenient because of the readier availability of these officers' names for the 20th century period (*and* it avoided the necessity of collecting an additional 104 years' worth of names since the Town's organization in 1796!).

— Morristown Town School District: Names are provided only for the school directors. But in this case the beginning point is 1893, which is the year the town school district system began.

— Village of Morrisville: Names are provided of trustees, clerk and treasurer, and water and light commissioners. The three former are since 1890, the year the incorporated village was established, and the latter is since 1895, when the first board of water and light commissioners was established and elected.

Note: The word "present" in the years of service given for certain individuals means that the person was still serving as of the end of 1980.

TOWN OF MORRISTOWN

Selectmen, 1900-1980

E.E. Brigham: 1897-1902
Harlan P. Munson: 1897-1902
A.B. Smith: 1897-1902
E.E. Harris: 1902-04
Milton H. Boardman: 1902-03
O.W. Chaffee: 1902-05, 1909-13
W.S. Welch: 1903-04
N.B. Blair: 1904-07
H.H. Small: 1904-07
G.H. Terrill: 1905-06
A.J. Bartlett: 1906-07
George W. Doty: 1907-08
C. Leo Gates: 1907-14
Clement F. Smith: 1908-11, 1913-16
Fred A. Gilbert: 1908-09
G.I.A. Town: 1911-12
R.J. Caswell: 1912-14
Ernest W. Gates: 1913-19
Guy S. Campbell: 1914-21
Gustin E. Smith: 1919-31, 1933-39
Roy C. Stafford: 1916-23
F.A. Strong: 1921-33
H.D. Neuland: 1923-29
Earl N. Gray: 1929-32, 1939-42

Clyde L. Wood: 1931-34
Carroll E. Lanpher: 1932-41, 1945-53
Hayden Turner: 1934-38
G.E. Smith: 1935-39
Morris B. White: 1938-45
H.E. Earle: 1941-43
Erwin W. Terrill: 1942-46
Will C. Davis: 1943-46, 1952-61
H.H. Campbell: 1946-53
Leroy Langdell: 1947-52
Oscar Churchill: 1952-56
Lawrence E. Gregory: 1954-68
Emery F. Foss, Jr.: 1956-65
Robert J. Houle: 1961-67
George H. Paine: 1965-74, 1975 [1]
Charles A. Bailey: 1967-73, 1979-present
Joseph L. Trombley: 1969-78
William H. Moulton: 1971-75 [1]
Laurie R. Gray, Sr.: 1974-present
Gordon D. Lewia, Sr.: 1975-79
Brian R. Greenia: 1978-present
Leo R. Trombley: 1978-present
Adrian A. West: 1978-present

1. Moulton resigned January 24, 1975; Paine was appointed to fill the vacancy until the 1975 town meeting.

Town Clerk and Treasurer, 1900-1980

Albert A. Niles: 1900-18
E.S. Robinson: 1918-19 [1]
Ralph L. Barrows: 1919 [1]-53
Winona M. Sawyer: 1953-66 [2]
Sydney C. Mander: 1966 [2]-present

1. Robinson died in office July 2, 1919; Barrows was appointed to fill the vacancy until the 1920 town meeting, after which he was elected.
2. Sawyer died in office June 21, 1966; Mander was appointed June 22, 1966 to fill the vacancy until the 1967 town meeting, after which he was elected.

Listers, 1900-1980

Oscar Sherwin: 1898-1901, 1902-03, 1905-06, 1907-11
George A. Cheney: 1900-01
J.H. Atchinson: 1900-02
T.J. Stewart: 1901-02
Harrison Dodge: 1901-02
H.D. Bryant: 1902-03, 1908-10
L.S. Small: 1902-03, 1908-11
I.N. LeBaron: 1903-08, 1910-11
Austin Wilkins: 1903-05, 1907-08
E.H. Eggleston: 1903-06, 1912-14
Hiram S. Keeler: 1906-07
George E. Mudgett: 1906-07
H. Henry Powers: 1908-10
F.A. Strong: 1908-09
H.S. Mathews: 1909-10
Dana N. Hutchins: 1910-30
J.R. Parker: 1910-15
A.J. Sherwood: 1911-12
C.H. Richardson: 1913-20, 1921-26
George H. Terrill: 1915-18
Harry Neuland: 1919-21
George W. Brown: 1918-19
James M. Kelley: 1920-22
F.R. Child: 1922-23
Will C. Davis: 1923-26
C. Leo Gates: 1926-28
Arthur H. Douglass: 1927-30
G.S. Stancliffe: 1928-35
J.E. Stewart: 1930-34
W.P. Smilie: 1930-31
Erwin W. Terrill: 1931-42, 1949-50, 1951-52
Frank Strong: 1934-35
Gerald Towne: 1935-43, 1950-59
Clyde Wood: 1935-36, 1946-58
Harold Parker: 1936-46
Arthur Stancliffe: 1942-45
Lawrence E. Gregory: 1943-46, 1971 [1]-77 [2]
Ernest Hadlock: 1945-46
Karl Manning: 1946-47, 1953-54
Adelbert R. Warren: 1946-48
Adelbert Magoon: 1947-50, 1960-62 [4], 1964-69
Silas H. Jewett: 1948-49
George H. Paine: 1950-51
C. Olin Harvey: 1952-53
George Godfrey: 1954-57
Carroll E. Lanpher: 1957-60
Roger G. Newton: 1958-59
Janice I. Edson: 1958-59
Ralph Hayes: 1958-59
H.H. Smilie: 1959-60
Richard F. Snow: 1959-64 [3]
Louis Gilbert: 1960-64
Gideon S. Burnham: 1962 [4]-69
Roberta M. Stafford: 1964 [3]-present
William H. Barker: 1969-75
Harold V. Baker: 1970-71 [1]
Ernest G. Godfrey: 1972-77
Clarence R. Whittier: 1972-73
Everett B. Lowe: 1973-74
Dayton J. Wakefield: 1977 [2]-present
Norman Black: 1977-78
Donald Fairbairn: 1978-79
Gordon D. Lewia, Sr.: 1979-80 [5]

1. Baker resigned September, 1971; Gregory appointed to fill the vacancy until the town meeting of 1972, after which he was elected.
2. Gregory resigned in 1977; Wakefield was appointed to complete his unexpired term until the 1978 town meeting and was elected thereafter.
3. Snow resigned in 1964; Stafford was appointed to complete his unexpired term to the 1965 town meeting and was elected thereafter.
4. Magoon resigned March 9, 1962; Burnham was appointed to complete his unexpired term to the 1963 town meeting and was elected thereafter.
5. Lewia resigned in late 1980; Heber A. Shanley was appointed Jan. 1, 1981 to fill the vacancy until the 1981 town meeting.

OFFICERS

Moderator, 1900-1980

George M. Powers: 1888-1905, 1925-26
Frederick G. Fleetwood: 1905-12, 1923-24
Thomas C. Cheney: 1912-23, 1924-25, 1926-46
Clifton G. Parker: 1946-66 [1]
Robert A. Magoon: 1966 [1]-67
Lee A. Barrows: 1967-71
Gerald W. Tripp: 1971-present

1. Parker resigned and Magoon was appointed to fill the vacancy on May 31, 1966 until the 1967 town meeting.

MORRISTOWN TOWN SCHOOL DISTRICT

School Directors, 1893-1980

Charles H. Slocum: 1893-98
Amasa O. Gates: 1893-95
John M. Campbell: 1893-1903
George H. Terrill: 1895-1902
Thomas C. Cheney: 1897-1903, 1917-20
A.F. Whitney: 1901-04
George I.A. Smith: 1902-21
George F. Earle: 1903-12
E.E. Harris: 1904-05
George A. Morse: 1905-06
Calvin A. Slayton: 1906-18
Arthur L. Cheney: 1912-15
Dr. George L. Bates: 1915-17
George P. Drowne: 1919-20
Walter M. Sargent: 1918-19
Charles H.A. Stafford: 1920-37
Rev. George F. Fortier: 1920-29
Anna L. Mower: 1921-35
James O. Reed: 1929-32
Raeburn R. McMahon: 1932-45
Laura Morse: 1935-44
Rev. George E. Goodliffe: 1937-52 [1]
Marguerite Woods: 1944-47
J. Harold Hill: 1945-53
Madge Churchill: 1947-55
Halbert C. Stancliffe: 1952 [1]-60
Francis Marsceille: 1953-56
Heber Shanley: 1954-61
Oscar H. Mudgett: 1955-59
Edward J. Welch: 1955-61
Howard E. Morse: 1956-61
Norma H. Wakefield: 1959-65
Dr. Richard E. Pease: 1960-63 [3]
Francis A. Clark: 1961-62
Wells C. Woodard, Jr.: 1961-67
Lewis A. Putnam: 1961-67
Dorothy D. Sargent: 1962-71 [2]
Dr. Herbert P. Beam: 1963 [3]-66
McDonald Miller: 1965-present
Everett G. Towle: 1966-70
Lewis D. Mowry, III: 1967-71 [4]
Oneal H. Demars, Jr.: 1968-76
Paul L. Griswold: 1970-present
James H. Palmer: 1971-75
Betty L. Blowers: 1971-80
Philip Chiaravelle: 1975-80
Theodore Buker: 1976-78
Mary West: 1976-present
Maryann Wilson: 1980-present
Joseph J. Wolchik: 1980-present

1. Rev. Goodliffe died in office February 27, 1952; Stancliffe was elected at the 1952 Town School District meeting to complete the unexpired term and was re-elected thereafter.
2. Sargent died in office July 26, 1971.
3. Dr. Pease resigned in 1963; Dr. Beam was appointed to fill the vacancy until the 1964 Town School District meeting and was elected thereafter.
4. Mowry resigned November 3, 1971; Palmer was appointed to fill the vacancy until the 1972 Town School District meeting and was elected thereafter.

VILLAGE OF MORRISVILLE

Village Trustees, 1890-1980

Philip K. Gleed: 1890-92
Seymour Harris: 1890-92
A.F. Whitney: 1890-92, 1894-98
Harlan P. Munson: 1890-93, 1907-15
Amasa O. Gates: 1891-92
George W. Hendee: 1892-94
G.A. Barrows: 1892-94
Charles H.A. Stafford: 1892-93, 1895-97, 1898-1905, 1907-15
Elmer E. Harris: 1892-94
A.R. Campbell: 1893-95, 1898-1905, 1913-18
Arthur L. Cheney: 1893-95, 1905-06
George W. Doty: 1894-95, 1907-14
Dr. Elmore J. Hall: 1894-95
J.W. Spaulding: 1895-97
George W. Clark: 1895-98
W.W. Peck: 1895-97
Carlos A. Gile: 1897-98
Henry Waite: 1897-98
James M. Jackson: 1897-98
George A. Morse: 1898-1905, 1907-17
H.M. Rich: 1898-1905
Dana N. Hutchins: 1898-1907
A.H. Boynton: 1905-06
F.J. Smalley: 1905-06
L.L. Camp: 1905-06
O.F. Crowell: 1905-06
George F. Earle: 1906-07, 1914-29
George M. Tillotson: 1906-07
Walter M. Sargent, Sr.: 1906-07, 1940-49
D.L. Sanders: 1906-07
Frank Kenfield: 1907-13
J.R. Parker: 1912-18
Levi M. Munson: 1914-48
George G. Morse: 1916-31
F.C. Peck: 1917-27
W.F. Churchill: 1918-28
Dr. William M. Johnstone: 1927-32
Marguerite S. Chapin: 1928-33
Gustin E. Smith: 1929-39 [1]
Hayden E. Turner: 1931-38 [2]
Guy C. Stafford: 1932-47 [3]
Morris B. White: 1933-48
Walter D. Jones: 1939-46
Ralph H. Terrill: 1946-51
Francis A. Clark: 1948-55
Henry E. Jenney, Jr.: 1948-57 [4]
Carroll E. Lanpher: 1948-57
Walter M. Sargent, Jr.: 1949-54
Leon M. White: 1951-61
C. Russell Graves: 1954-58
Dr. William P. Guthmann: 1955-60
Clarence C. Miller: 1956 [4]-63
Earle C. Dunham: 1957 [5]
Emile R. Couture: 1957 [5]-62
Robert B. Page: 1959-64
Oscar E. Churchill: 1960-65
Lyle L. Chaffee: 1961-66
Robert J. Sparks: 1962-67
Dr. Harry C. Foss: 1963-68
Joseph L. Trombley: 1964-69
Elroy Towle: 1965-70
Donald Anderson: 1966-71
Robert M. Bourne: 1967-72
Dr. David U. Walker: 1968-73
Arlo K. Sterner: 1969-74
Robert J. Levis: 1970-75
Denis Cote: 1971-76
Robert Hasseltine: 1972-77
Adrian A. West: 1973-78
Eldon E. Towle: 1974-79
Frederick T. Bird, Jr.: 1975-80
Richard C. Sargent: 1976-present
Mary Kunstman: 1977-present
Duane B. Sprague: 1978-present
Andrew A. Jensvold: 1979-present
Richard Shanley: 1980-present

1. Smith died in office September 22, 1939.
2. Turner died in office July 19, 1938.
3. Stafford died in office November 3, 1947.
4. Jenney died in office January 17, 1957; Miller was appointed to fill the vacancy until the Village's 1957 annual meeting and was elected thereafter.
5. Dunham resigned during 1957; Couture was appointed to fill the vacancy until the Village's 1959 annual meeting and was elected thereafter.

Village Clerk, 1890-1901

W.H. Robinson: 1890-99
Albert A. Niles: 1899-1901

Village Treasurer, 1890-1901

A.M. Burke: 1890-93
H.M. Rich: 1893-96
Frederick G. Fleetwood: 1896-1900
Albert A. Niles: 1900-01

OFFICERS 545

Village Clerk and Treasurer, 1901-1980

Albert A. Niles: 1901-18
E.S. Robinson: 1918-19 [1]
Ralph L. Barrows: 1919 [1]-53 [2]

Winona M. Sawyer: 1953 [2]-66 [3]
Sydney C. Mander: 1966 [3]-present

1. Robinson died in office July 2, 1919; Barrows was appointed to fill the vacancy until the Village's 1920 annual meeting and was elected thereafter.
2. Barrows resigned on March 5, 1953; Sawyer was appointed to fill the vacancy until the Village's 1953 annual meeting and was elected thereafter.
3. Sawyer died in office June 21, 1966; Mander was appointed June 22, 1966 to fill the vacancy until the Village's 1967 annual meeting and was elected thereafter.

Moderator / President, [1] 1890-1980

Frank Kenfield: 1890-91
Albert A. Niles: 1891-92
George W. Hendee: 1892-94
George M. Powers: 1894-98, 1912-13
Thomas C. Cheney: 1898-1912, 1913-17, 1919-23

Melville P. Maurice: 1917-19
Frederick G. Fleetwood: 1923-24
Levi M. Munson: 1924-47
Walter M. Sargent, Jr.: 1947-49
J. Harold Hill: 1949-53
Robert A. Magoon: 1953-present [2]

1. The title of the person who presides at Morrisville's annual and special meetings has varied over the years between these two terms.
2. At the Village's 1961 annual meeting the appropriateness of Magoon's service in this position was challenged on grounds that he was then living (and still is) outside the Village boundaries; he was re-elected nonetheless.

Water and Light Commissioners, 1895-1980

George M. Powers: 1895-1938 [1]
E.W. Webster: 1895-1901
George A. Morse: 1895-1914
Charles H. Slocum: 1895-1935
Henry A. Slayton: 1895-1902
Charles H.A. Stafford: 1902-37
Carlos A. Gile: 1901-17
Walter F. Churchill: 1921-34
Morris C. Greene: 1935-51 [2]
Levi M. Munson: 1917-60
James O. Reed: 1934-64
Herbert A. Smalley: 1937-59 [3]
Clifton G. Parker: 1939-50 [4], 1951-60 [5]
Edward A. Wing: 1952-67 [6]
Frederic M. Greene: 1960-70
Roger G. Newton: 1960 [4]-71
Rethel C. West: 1960-62, 1964-69

Lyle H. Hunt: 1962-67
Lewis A. Putnam: 1967-74 [7]
Lyle L. Chaffee: 1967-68 [8]
Louis Jordan, Jr.: 1968-73
Wilbert J. Patton: 1969-74
Porter C. Greene: 1970-72 [9]
Arlo K. Sterner: 1971-76
Robert M. Bourne: 1972-present
Merrill E. Edson: 1973-74 [10]
Richard R. Hill: 1974 [10]-present
William T. Dick: 1975-76 [11]
Earle Dunham: 1975-78
Dayton J. Wakefield: 1976 [11]-present
Charles L. Grandey: 1976-79
Howard E. Morse: 1978-present
Bruno A. Loati: 1979-present

1. Powers died in office June 24, 1938.
2. Greene died in office July 10, 1951.
3. Smalley died in office June 21, 1959.
4. Parker resigned November 1, 1950 to avoid a conflict of interest; he was elected again at the Village's 1951 annual meeting.
5. Parker resigned October 3, 1960; Newton was appointed to fill the vacancy until the Village's 1961 annual meeting and was elected thereafter.
6. Wing resigned November 9, 1967.
7. Putnam resigned April 8, 1974.
8. Chaffee died in office January 7, 1968.
9. Greene died in office February 3, 1972.
10. Edson resigned in 1974; Hill was appointed to fill the vacancy until the Village's annual meeting in 1975 and was elected thereafter.
11. Dick died in office June 21, 1976; Wakefield was appointed to fill the vacancy until the Village's 1977 annual meeting and was elected thereafter.

Map No. 5 - TOWN OF MORRISTOWN, 1958/1964

That this is a map of Morristown some 20 years ago is a case of happenstance rather than design. While Vermont's Agency of Transportation (VAT) has current "working" general highway maps for each town, including Morristown, the most recent *high-quality* highway map suitable for a base map of Morristown was the indicated 1965 map of the predecessor Department of Highways. The following are special notes relating to certain boundary lines.

1. The slight angle in the Morristown-Elmore line must be in error. As defined in Morristown's charter (and see Map No. 2) that line follows a single compass direction its full length.

2. Current VAT maps of Morristown show the lower part of Elmore Mountain Road which here straddles the Stowe line to now be *all* in Morristown. That apparently was the result of a resurvey of that line which Stowe and Morristown carried out jointly in 1975.

3. The boundary line of Morrisville as shown here is inaccurate in places. See Map No. 7 for a basically accurate rendering.

Roster of Building/Landmark Identification Numbers and Names

These identification numbers are used in the text as keys to this map. Names in roman type are current; those in italic are former names or uses.

T1 - *Boardman Mill*
T2 - *Morristown Corners School*
T3 - *Cadys Falls School*
T4 - *South Randolph School*
T5 - *South LaPorte School*
T6 - *Sand Hill School*
T7 - *Morristown Plains School*
T8 - *Cole Hill School*
T9 - *North LaPorte School*
T10 - *Cheney Hill School*
T11 - *Mud City School*
T12 - Town Garage (Morristown Highway Department)
T13 - Red Bridge
T14 - Putnam Bridge
T15 - Ryder Brook Bridge
T16 - Tenney Bridge
T17 - Cadys Falls Bridge
T18 - Little Bridge
T19 - *Second Village Dump*
T20 - Lamoille Landfill and Salvage Depot/*Morristown Dump/Landfill*
T21 - *Poor Farm/Boardman Farm*
T22 - Morrisville Commission Sales
T23 - Corner Store
T24 - Pinecrest Park
T25 - Pinewood Estates
T26 - Wheeler Cemetery
T27 - Mountain View Cemetery
T28 - Plains Cemetery
T29 - Randolph Cemetery
T30 - LaPorte Cemetery
T31 - Lake View Cemetery
T32 - Lowe Farm/Concept II
T33 - Concord Manufacturing Corp.
T34 - Research Engineering Corp.
T35 - Lamoille Industrial Park
T36 - Mountain View Cottages
T37 - Full Gospel Christian Assembly Church/*Monette's Lodge*
T38 - Crimson King Motel
T39 - EMCO CATV Antenna Site
T40 - Farm Resort
T41 - Welch Farm/Round Barn
T42 - Tinker House
T43 - Site of original Jacob Walker house
T44 - Former Morrisville jail
T45 - Beaver Meadow Lodge
T46 - Whiteface Shelter
T47 - Cadys Falls power plant, Morrisville Water and Light Dept.
T48 - *Houle's Farm*
T49 - Miller Farm
T50 - *Greaves Dairy*
T51 - Homestead Dairy
T52 - *Phelps, Foss & Fagnant sawmill*
T53 - *Grossman's of Vermont*
T54 - *Methodist/Baptist Chapel*
T55 - Town's first church
T56 - *Call and See House*
T57 - Kenfield House
T58 - Spaulding House
T59 - No landmark so numbered
T60 - Dodgen House (second Jacob Walker house)
T61 - Graham House (third Jacob Walker house)
T62 - Morehaven

MAP OF MORRISTOWN

T65 - *Billings Mill School*
T66 - *North Randolph School*
T63 - *Lamson Hill School*
T64 - *Tyndall Hill School*

Roster of Town Highway Numbers and Names

Listed are the present (1980) highway numbers with their respective names as established by selectmen in 1977 plus subsequent additions. Remember, however, that roads built since 1964 do not appear on this map. Town highway numbers missing from the list (below 106, that is) exist but those roads do not have official names, and so were omitted.

1 - Randolph Road
2 - Cadys Falls Road
3 - Bridge Street Road
4 - Center Road
5 - Stagecoach Road
6 - Samoset Road
7 - Cote Hill Road
9 - Griggs Road
10 - Terrill Road
11 - Needle's Eye Road
12 - Silver Ridge Road
13 - Trombley Hill Road
14 - Frazier Road
15 - Lanphear Road
16 - Harrel Street
17 - Lepper Road
18 - Garfield Road
19 - Cram Road
20 - Stearns Road
21 - Lazy Lane
22 - Darling Road
23 - Walton Road
24 - Babcock Road
25 - Fontaine Hill Road
26 - Ledge Road
27 - Patch Road
28 - Watanjay Farm Road
29 - Rooney Road
30 - Mud City Loop
31 - Call Road
32 - Magoon Road
33 - Morristown Corners Road
35 - Cottage Street
36 - Washington Highway
37 - Lower Elmore Mt. Road
38 - Towne Road
39 - Elmore Mt. Road
40 - Fitzgerald Road
41 - Earl Gray Road
42 - West Settlement Road
43 - Bryan Pond Road
44 - Beaver Meadow Road
45 - Tine McKee Road
46 - Hadlock Road
47 - Bull Moose Road
48 - Laroche Road
49 - Gallup Road
50 - Cole Hill Road
52 - Lyle McKee Road(?)
53 - Lyle McKee Road(?)
54 - Cochran Road
55 - Golf Course Road
56 - Goeltz Road
57 - Bliss Hill Road
58 - Neuland Road
59 - Churchill Road
60 - Sterling Valley Road
61 - Ross Road
62 - Ron Terrill Road
63 - Chaffee Road
64 - Sterling Brook Loop
65 - Children's Village Road
66 - Bedell Road
67 - Long Branch Circle
68 - Pumpkin Hollow Road
70 - Dr. Neal Road
71 - Lawrence Road
72 - Stancliffe Road
73 - Lawrence Stancliffe Road
74 - Elmore Mt. Road
75 - Elmore Mt. Road
76 - Elmore Mt. Road
77 - Sunset Drive
78 - Sand Ridge Road
79 - Davison Road
80 - Goddard-Nisbet Road
81 - Veneer Mill Road
82 - Duncan Road
83 - Stafford Avenue
84 - Goodell Avenue
85 - Munson Avenue
86 - Tamarack Hill Road
87 - Vanesse Road
88 - Demars Road
90 - Langdell Road
91 - Langue Road
92 - Manosh Road
93 - Pinewood Estates Road
96 - Campbell Road
97 - Tamarack Road
100 - Joe's Pond Road
101 - Northgate Avenue
106 - Industrial Park Drive

Map No. 6 - CENTRAL MORRISVILLE, 1980
By Robert L. Hagerman

This map is based on field surveys and a map, "Important Structures In Central Morrisville, Vt. For The Morristown Historical Society," prepared in 1978 by Susan Mulvey, a student at Johnson State College. Her map was based on maps made in 1955 by The Sanborn Company of Pelham, N.Y. (and used by permission) together with field surveys. Buildings existing in 1980 in the following areas are not shown: Bridge Street west of Lamoille River; extreme north end of Portland street; and East and West High Streets. Outlines and dimensions of buildings are approximate. No outbuildings are shown.

The following is a roster of building identification numbers which are used in the text as keys to this map, together with the respective names or uses by which they are referred to in the text. Names in roman type are current; those in italic type are former names or uses. The several breaks in continuous numbering for buildings in several areas resulted when certain buildings were added to those which were shown in the Mulvey map, such additions occurring *after* the numbering of the "original" buildings had been fixed. Numbered buildings without names do not appear in the list. But some of those *are* mentioned in the text by the number only; for applicable page references, see the Index under "Buildings, Central Morrisville" (a few buildings with names here but referred to by number only are indexed the same way). For a map of the central business district with the names of present businesses in the various commercial buildings see *The Transcript*, July 13, 1981.

C1	- Noyes House Museum
C2	- Morristown Public Safety Building
C4	- Ferris Block/Arthur's Department Store/*Gillen's Department Store*
C6	- *James Kelley House*
C7	- *News & Citizen office*
C8	- Post Office
C9	- *Randall Hotel*
C11	- Brooks Variety Store/*Grand Union Store*
C12	- *Tinker/Powers House (second site)*
C13	- American Legion barracks/*Morrisville Gymnasium*
C15	- Lamoille County Senior Citizens Center/*First Universalist Church*
C20	- *Grandey Insurance Agency and home*
C21	- *Town Hall*
C22	- Harry Foss House
C24	- *Morrisville Fire Department firehouse*
C26	- Morristown Fire Department firehouse
C29	- Advent Christian Church
C30	- Advent Christian Church education building
C33	- Graded School
C34	- *Second Peoples Academy*
C39	- Morristown Centennial Library
C40	- *Gov. Hendee House*
C41	- First Congregational Church
C42	- First Congregational Church parsonage
C43	- Puffer United Methodist Church parsonage
C44	- Puffer United Methodist Church
C45	- Drowne House
C46	- Fleetwood Building/Peck's Drug Store
C47	- Green Mountain Pharmacy block
C48	- Town Building/*Union Savings Bank & Trust Co.*
C49	- The Union Bank
C50	- Terrill's Texaco Service
C51	- *The Munson Store*
C53	- Old Brick Store/State Liquor Agency
C54	- Noyes/Slayton House
C55	- Parkview/Tift Block
C57	- *Centennial Block*
C58	- *Warren Block*
C60	- Brosseau's Super Market/*Tegu Theatre*
C62	- Masonic Temple/Morrisville Water and Light Dept. office

MAP OF CENTRAL MORRISVILLE

C64 - Community College of Vermont / Sherman Block
C66 - Bijou Theatre
C67 - Central Vermont Community Action Council
C69 - *H. Waite & Sons block*
C70 - Bourne's Service Station
C71 - Lamoille Grain Co. / *H.A. Slayton & Co.*
C72a - Greene Corp. / *Morrisville Foundry Co.*
C72b - White Heat Foundry / *Morrisville Foundry Co.*
C73 - Morrisville Lumber Co. / *George A. Morse Co.*
C74 - Station Restaurant / *Railroad Depot*
C75 - Village Cleaners / Wilson Building
C76 - *Wrong End Store*
C78 - Manor House / Hutchins Block
C79 - Adrian's / Kelley Block
C80 - Towle's Hardware
C81 - Jones Jewelry Store
C82 - Demars Block / *Foss / Woodbury / Darling Block*
C83 - Ben Franklin Store / Drowne Block
C85 - *Timmerman House*
C89 - *United Farmers Creamery*
C90 - Lamoille Grange hall / *First Peoples Academy*
C91 - *United Farmers store*
C92 - Veterans of Foreign Wars hall
C120 - Safford House
C123 - Lamoille View Apartments / *Dr. Walker / H.H. Powers House*
C124 - Nesky House / *Gleed / Fleetwood House*

Map No. 7 - VILLAGE OF MORRISVILLE, 1980

The following is a roster of building/landmark identification numbers which are used in the text as keys to this map, together with their respective names or uses. Names in roman type are current; those in italic type are former names or uses.

V1 - *Clark Park*
V2 - Morrisville Street Department garage / *Town garage*
V3 - Clayhill Resources / *Morrisville Street Department garage and Morrisville Fire Department firehouse*
V4 - Railroad Bridge
V5 - Power House Bridge
V6 - Bridge Street Bridge
V7 - Long Bridge
V8 - Boardman Brook "Bridge" (culvert)
V9 - Morrisville Sewage Treatment Plant
V10 - *First Village Dump*
V11 - *Vermont Tanning Corp. / Warren Leather Co.*
V12 - Lakeside Garage
V13 - White's Funeral Home
V14 - News & Citizen
V15 - Mudgett-Smalley Motors
V16 - *Prunier Motors*
V17 - New England Telephone Co.
V18 - National Guard Armory
V19 - Dumont Manor / *Copley Hospital / Wheelock House*
V20 - Copley Hospital
V21 - Dumont Nursing and Convalescent Center
V22 - Holy Cross Church
V23 - *Episcopal Mission*
V24 - Seventh-day Adventist Church
V25 - Kingdom Hall, Jehovah's Witnesses
V26 - Demars Building
V27 - Pratt-Read Corp. / *Atlas Plywood*
V28 - Vermont Asbestos Group / *C.H.A. Stafford & Sons*
V29 - Cabot Farmers Co-op Creamery
V30 - *Foss Farm / Douglass Farm*
V31a - Union Carbide Corp.
V31b - Union Carbide / *Morse's Dairy*
V31c - Union Carbide / *Holy Cross rectory*
V32 - Morristown Ambulance Service
V33 - Morrisville power plant of Morrisville Water and Light Dept.
V34 - *George M. Powers House*
V35 - Reservoir of Morrisville Water and Light Dept.
V36 - Grout Observatory
V37 - Copley Bandshell
V38 - *Favreau Garage*
V39 - Godfrey, Richard R. & Sons / *Ward's, Inc.*

INDEX

Because of space limitations, this index, while reasonably detailed, is not comprehensive, particularly for names. A major means of "condensation" relates to names with only one or two page references. Where possible, entries for these were combined under *a common last name*, as in "Bidwell name" or "Brigham name, other." (All such individual names in *More About Morristown* are, however, included in the comprehensive index to the "first draft" of that work; a supplementary index to the Mower work also appears there which lists many of the individual names excluded here.) Other names in the Hagerman work sometimes not indexed here include those thought to be relatively accessible through some appropriate subject heading, such as the name of a particular business for the name(s) of its proprietor(s), or the name of a particular public agency or municipal department for the names of its chief officer. Also not indexed here are: (1) names which appear in the roster of local municipal officers (Appendix, page 541), and (2) names of many buildings which appear on the rosters of same which accompany certain of the maps.

Abbreviations used: a page number in italics means a photo or drawing; an asterisk (*) following a page number means there is more than a single reference to that name or subject on that page; "DJ" means Dust Jacket; "F" means Foreword; and "PC" means Photo Credits.

ABLE (Association to Boost Lamoille Enterprises): 425, 435-37
Academy Park: General: 193, 194, 230, 233, 256, 445, 511, 520, 522-23, 539; Soldiers Monument: 107, 132, 183, 191-92, 216, 342, 520, 522-23
Accidents: airplane: 461, 462; *see also* Drownings; Fires, major
Adams name: 104-05, 194, 213, 518
Adrian's store: 426, 441-42
Adult Basic Education: 427
Advent Christian Church: 59, *321*, 489, 494-95, 501
Aging, Agency on: 426
Agricultural Stabilization and Conservation Service: 424
Agriculture: 264-65, 287, 417-18, 444-45, 452, 537; *see also* Dairying
Agri-Mark: 433
Alcoholic beverages: 187, 382, 383, 384, 394, 526, 527, 532-33
Alger name: 6, 81
Allen, Isaac: 74, 75, 81, 82
Allen name, other: 207, 290, 292, 366, 531
Alley, F. William: 435
Ambulance Service, Morristown: 474

American Civil Liberties Union: 500
American Legion, Post No. 33, and Auxiliary: 177, 183-84, 185, 219-20, 506-08, 523, 538, 540
American Mineral Co.: 253
American Observer: 76, 178, 234-35
Ames store: 422
Amsden name: 301*
Anair, Helen L.: 168, 353
Anderson, Gar: 371
Armistice Day: 156-57
Armory: 509, 521; *see also* National Guard
Arnold Granite Co.: 262
Arthur's Department Store: 444, 512
Arts and artists: F, 115, 116, 416, 427, 470
Atlas Plywood Co.: 264, 431, 436
Auctioneer: 411
Australian ballot: 525
Auto Care: 419
Automobile: 122, 128, 178, 242, 243, 245, 267, *327*, 370, 382, 447*, 515, 517-18
Automobile-related businesses: 419*, 422*, 423, 429*, 434, 445-46, 462-63
Aviation: 182, 184, 237-38, *332*, 393, 483-85, 537

Bailey, Rev. George: 118, 289, 292
Bailey name, other: 57, 190, 419, 508
Baker name: 101, 289, 292, 363
Baldwin name: 167, 193
Balloons: see Aviation
Bands and bandstands: 156, 181, 188, 211*, 228, 229-33, 356, 467, 522; see also Morrisville Military Band; Copley Bandshell
Banks: 77, 446-47
Baptist Church: 50-52, 78, 490-91
Barnes name: 6, 229*
Barrows, Ralph L.: 248, 382
Barrows name, other: 229, 366, 439
Bartlett, Sidney and Priscilla: 463, 509
Barton name: 92, 342
Baseball: 184, 190-91, 399-400, 432, 527
Bates, Dr. George L.: 174-75, 192, 193, 195, 220, 302, 475
Bates name, other: 148, 174, 302
Beaver Meadow Lodge: 513
Bedell name: 218, 302, 517
Beebe, William A.: 106-07, 185, 191*-92*, 194
Bells: 58, 408-09, 489, 491, 495, 496, 503-04
Ben Franklin Store & Block: 245, 387, 414, 441-42; see also Drowne Block
Bennett name: 59, 73*
Benton name: 103, 135
Best, Rev. W.T.: 54, 151*, 155, 192
Best name, other: 302, 315
Bicentennial, American / Vermont: 503, 539-40
Bicentennial, Morristown: 540
Bidwell name: 302*
Big Save supermarket: 422
Bijou Theatre: 448-50
Billings, James J.: 261, 406-07
Billings lot: 406-07
Bingham, Luther: 21, 30, 64, 289
Bingham name, other: 32*, 81, 136, 167, 292*
Biscormer name: 292*
Black Betsy: 183, 188, 189, 522
Blake, Gene M., Jr.: 429
Blanchard, Andrew J.: 94, 95, 104, 134, 196, 292, 318
Bliss name: 88, 103
Blodgett, Otto E.: 213, 376
Blow and Cote: 393, 420
Board of Trade: 54
Boardman Brook: 21, 262, 339*, 341
Boardman, Charles W.: 122, 133, 292
Boardman, Elisha: 13, 24, 27-28, 64, 65, 130, 242-43, 289
Boardman, Milton H.: 28, 243, 286, 290, 339, 398
Boardman Pond: 339
Boardman Tavern: 78, 284
Boardman name, other: 24, 27-28, 34, 56*, 67, 69, 168*, 280, 282, 289, 303*, 339, 510
Body Beautiful, Inc.: 423
Bogs: see Joe's Pond & Bog; Molly's Pond & Bog
Booth, Rev. I.P.: 57, 84, 289, 493
Boundaries: Town: 20, 68, 335-37, 343, 546; Village: 352, 550
Bowling, lawn: 451, 485-86
Boy Scouts: 151, 193, 509, 523
Boynton, L.B. (Bing): 30, 188, 244
Boynton name, other: 135, 157
Breault, Arthur & Theresa: 444, 512
Brick buildings: 25, 42, 74, 241, 259, 380, 404, 414, 439*, 442, 447, 449, 464, 518-19*, 521, 532*, 533, 534*; see also Copley Building, Peoples Academy; Old Brick Store
Brickmaking: 259, 261
Bridge, George A.: 292, 324, 505
Bridges: general: 279, 370-73; Tenney: 279*, 367, 372; Cadys Falls: 279, 280, 372; Red: 21, 31, 366, 371; Jones: 127; Bridge St.: 371, 372; Long: 373; Little (Samoset): 373; Power Plant: 320, 372, 385; snowmobile: 516; pedestrian: 371
Brigham, Elisha: 33, 34, 41
Brigham Meadow: 388, 389
Brigham, Melville: 32, 34, 388
Brigham name, other: 24, 32-33, 71, 75, 131, 281, 284, 286, 289
Brooklyn: 76, 536
Brooks name: 194, 303
Brosseau's Super Market: 438, 450
Brown, Lefa Nay: 353, 482
Brown name, other: 50, 68, 131, 292*, 409, 422
Bugbee springs: see Springs, Bugbee
Buildings: the following are page references to certain buildings referred to in the text partly or only by their respective identifying numbers instead of a particular building name (and see footnote to listing of maps in Table of Contents for reference to rosters of building names and numbers): Central Morrisville: C3b: 444; C5: 444; C37: 427; C40: 470; C45: 426; C47: 404; C48: 415; C53: 527; C61: 413, 449; C67: 425; C75: 442; C77: 425; C79: 443; C83: 414-15; C91: 444; C94:

INDEX 553

425; Morrisville Suburb: MS34: 368; see also Brick buildings
Bundy name: 115, 269
Burge, Rev. Frederick W.: 62, 497
Burke, Asahel: 76, 131, 164*, 246
Burke, Joseph: 24, 131, 164
Burke name, other: 31, 56, 79, 164*, 214*
Burnett, Calvin: 56, 72, 75*, 86, 88, 259-60
Burnett name, other: 56, 207, 293
Burnham, Gideon S.: 303, 376, 377
Burnt Ground Cemetery: 281
Burroughs, Eugene W.: 146, 147, 303
Burt name: 149, 447
Bus service: 462
Businesses: 419-23, 438-50, 451-54, 455-64, 548; see also individual business names
Butler name: 293
Butter tubs: 261
Butternut Island: 540
Buxton, E. Brewster: 343, 409*
Bylaws: see Ordinances
Bypass, Morrisville: 373

Cabot Farmers Co-op: 433
Cady, Orlo: 57, 67, 289
Cady name, other: 66, 68, 120-21
Cadys Falls: 34, 56, 61, 66-71, 185, 210, 242*, 243, 251, 255, 260, 261, 279, 282, 340, 410-11, 450
Cadys Falls Cooperative: 411
Cadys Falls Hall Soc.: 61, 71, 411
Calcagni, Dr. Oscar: 479, 532
Calkins name: 127-28, 248
Call-and-See House: 243
Cambridge, town of: 335, 379, 437, 447, 454, 480, 499-500
Camley, Seth and Earlene: 383
Camley, Wayne R.: 376, 509
Camp name: 87, 88, 219
Camp meetings: 54, 185-88
Campbell Jewelry Store: 265-66
Campbell name: 74, 84, 118, 128, 315, 353, 366, 409
Campfire Girls: 151, 193
Cannon: 183, 522; see also Black Betsy
Capron name: 59, 293
Carleton, Martin W.: 239, 413
Carner name: 214, 318
Carter name: 95, 131, 339
Catholic Church: see Holy Cross Church
Celebrations: 189-95, 538-40
Cemeteries: 280-83, 403, 404-06, 519; see also Pleasant View Cemetery; Morristown Cemetery Association
Census: see Population

Centenarians: 540
Centennial Block: 77, 128, 172, 328, 374, 380, 463, 464
Centennial, Morristown: 125, 189-91
Central Vermont Community Action Council: 425
Chaffee name: 31, 56, 109, 110
Champlain Valley Work and Training Program: 426
Chapin(pen) name: 6, 151, 155, 353
Chaplin, Joseph M.: 30, 147, 293, 412-13, 505
Charlmont Restaurant: 453, 509
Charter, town: 4-7, 540
Chase name: 59, 192, 304
Cheney, Arthur L.: PC, 172, 441
Cheney, Thomas C. and May: 35, 70, 88, 99, 114, 126, 148, 152, 156*, 168*, 215, 290, 329, 348, 415, 503, 533
Cheney name, other: 70, 227, 261, 289, 293*
Child(s) name: 24, 177, 304, 452
Choral Union, The: 228-29
Christian Church: 53, 58-59, 321
Christian Life Center: 501
Christian Luminary, The: 234, 268
Christian Science Society: 63, 498
Christmas: 459, 511, 526
Church in the Mountain: 501
Churches: general: 39-63; 488-501; at Morristown Corners: brick church: 42, 43, 51, 64, 65, 519; chapel: 51, 53, 59, 66; at Cadys Falls: 71
Churchill name: 181, 293, 353, 439
Civil Air Patrol: 459, 461-62, 485
Civil defense: 350, 520
Civil War: 71, 94, 132-44, 158, 208-09, 324, 505, 506
Clark, George: 118, 282, 290, 331, 341
Clark Park: 279, 341-42
Clark name, other: 70, 76, 293*, 318, 361
Clayhill Resources: 370, 437
Clegg, Ernest H.: 380, 382, 383, 384, 418
Clegg, John: 523
Clement name: 227, 228, 243, 293
Cleveland name: 73, 294, 304*, 378, 419
Climate: see Weather
Cline, Maude, R.N.: 477
Coal: see Energy
Cole Hill: 34
Cole name: 24, 33-34, 40, 42, 65, 75, 79, 122*, 130, 131*, 281, 285, 289, 294, 361, 379
Collins name: 169, 294
Commission sales: 411
Commune: 454

Community artist: 427
Community College of Vermont: 427
Concept II: 437
Concord Manufacturing Corp.: 434
Congregational Church, First: 40-49, 75, 77, 107, 116, 142, 150, 151, 158, 163, 172, 191, 224, 228, *320*, *325*, 488-90, 492, 528, 532, 538
Conrad, Wilbert Leon, Sr. & Jr.: 522, 523, 531
Contractors Crane Service: 373
Cook, Denison: 131, 132, 284, 285
Cooke, Jonathan: 75, 86, 131
Cooke, Samuel: 11, 29-30, 33, 40, 41, 130, 281, 289
Cooke name, other: 29-30, 32*, 33, 40, 41, 131
Cook's Brook: 259
Copley Agricultural Fund: 348, 469
Copley Airfield: 128-29, 458, 483-85
Copley, Alexander H.: 97, *322*, 465-74, 475, 477, 484, 487, 492
Copley Avenue: 256*, 369, *465*, 467
Copley Bandshell: 233, 467, 517, 522
Copley Building, Peoples Academy: *see* Schools, Peoples Academy
Copley Community Memorial Building (gymnasium): 356, 359, 404, 468, 518
Copley Country Club: 128-29, *328*, *483*, 484, 485-87
Copley Follies, The: 479
Copley Fund, The: 470-72
Copley Fund, The Alexander Hamilton: 472-74
Copley Golf Corporation: 486
Copley Hospital: 97, 176, 223, 256, *322*, 423, 470, 471, 475, 484, 511
Copley Hospital Auxiliary: 177, 470, 478-79, 486, 532
Copley Hospital Circle: 479
Copley, Jane M.: 177, 492
Copley Parking Lot: 474, 540
Copley streetlights: *324*, 467
Copley Terrace: 482
Cornell, Paul: *332*
Corner Store, The: *410*, 411-12
Corrections Dept.: 426
Cote name: 367, 420, 463
Court, police: 384
Couture name: 452-53, 462, 495
Craigie, Leslie & Gwendolen: 433
Cram name: 229*, 257
Credit union: 496
Crime: 285, 382-83; *see also* Vandalism
Crimson King Motel: 454
Currier name: 239, 366

Cushman name: 117, *332*
Customs: 283-85

Dairying: 264, 287, 418, 432-34, 534-35; *see also* Agriculture
Daniels name: 294, 539
Darling name: 31*, 32*, 289
Daughters of the American Revolution: 219, 504-05
Daughters of Zion: *see* Masons and Masonic orders
Davis name: 257, 294*, 376, 531
Davison, Max B.: 531
Decart: 437
Demars Block: 427, 507
Demars Building: 426, 427
Demars, Oneal, Jr.: 375, 384, 422, 474
Democratic Party: *see* Politics
Depot, Morrisville: *319*, *455*, 458
Depression: 256, 262, 263, 286, 451, 476*
Dewey, Giles W.: 531
District representatives: 531
Doctors: 169-76
Dodge name: 76, 133, 135, 218
Dodgen, Edith: 533
Dogs: 349-50, 402, 468, 481
Dorchester Heights: 536
Doty, George W.: 76, 144, 164, 180, 188, 189*, 191*, 216*, 218*-19, 241, 247, 248, 251, 257*, 282, 294, 318, 376
Douglass dairy and family: 433-34, 436
Douglass name, other: 79, 190, 239, 517
Dow name: 39-40, 69, 387
Dreissigacker name: 437
Drown name: 59, 70, 145, 230, 294
Drowne block: 241, 413, 442, 530; *see also* Ben Franklin Block
Drowne House: 426
Drowne name: 304*, 442
Drownings: 342, 392
Dugway: 373, 388, 389-90
Dumont Manor: 477-78
Dumont Nursing and Convalescent Center: 478, 515
Dumps: *396*, 397-98, 512
Dunham name: 24, 31, 81, 294*
Durett name: 31*
Dwight name: 48*
Dyke name: 73, 79, 294

Earle, Araunah Augustus: 236-38
Earle, George F.: 218, 241, 443
Earle name, other: 207, 281, 294
East Brook: 21
Eastern Magnesia Talc Co.: 255
Eaton name: 76, 91, 213, 241, 295*,

INDEX 555

304, 318, 359, 493
Edson name: 74, 80, 353, 389
Egypt: 537
Elderly: *see* Senior Citizens
El(l)sworth name: 133, 168*
Elmore Mt.: 21, 539
Elmore Street: 370
Elmore, town of: 67, 255, 343, 361, 370, 375, 394, 495, 509, 511, 531, 546
Elmore name: 76, 186, 261
EMCO CATV: 464
Emmons, Augusta L.: 449-50
Emmons, Leon C.: 449*, 462
Emmons name, other: 146, 305, 450*, 493
Employment Security, Dept. of: 424-25
Energy: general: 540; wood: 153-54, 360, 407; coal: 153-54
Entertainment: *see* Recreation
Epidemics: 181; *see also* individual diseases
Episcopal Mission: 61, 62, 497
Exchange Hotel: 244
Extension Service: 422, 423, 424, 435, 511

Fairbanks name: 189, 242, 305
Fairs: 178-83, 537-38; *see also* Lamoille Valley Fair
Fancher, Warren G.: 457
Farm Bureau: 424
Farm Motor Inn / Farm Resort: 452-53
Farmers Home Administration: 427
Farmers Market: 444-45, 523
Farnham name: 318, *331*
Farr name: 281, 482, 535
Farrand name: 6*
Favreau name: 481, 535
Felcher name: 43, 71, 81, 131, 282, 288
Fencing: *332*
Ferrin, John: 43, 75, 81, 289
Ferrin, W.G.: 162, 164, 268
Ferrin name, other: 81, 82, 289
Ferris Block: 379, 444
Ferris, Louis J.: 380, 422
Field Days, Lamoille County: 537-38
Fire alarm: 257, 409, 464
Fire Department, Morrisville and Morristown: 257-58, 232, *330**, 353, 370, 374-80, 382, 408, 437, 540
Fire districts: 376, 412
Fires, major: 210, 241, 244*, 245, 257-58*, 262, 374, 375, 379-80, 422, 431*, 441*, 452, 540
First National Store: 450
Firsts: settlement: 25; birth: 27, 288; church: 42, 43, 51, 64, 65; settled minister: 43; tavern: 27; school: 64; physician: 64; lawyer: 65, 159;

lawsuit: 65; death: 71, 288; merchant: 196; automobile: 128; marriage: 288; auto dealer: 429; radio: 430; television set: 464; airplane pilot: 483
Fisher name: 115, 193, 241, 295, 305
Fishing: 341, 392, 513-14
Fisk, Henry C.: 128, 165-66*, 238, 246, 263, 269, 289, 447, 531
Fisk name, other: 115, 166, 190*, 243
Fitch, Cordilla W.: 76, 77, 164, 189, 257
Fitch name, other: 214, 229
Flanders name: 226-27, 295, 317, 318
Fleetwood Bdlg.: 208, 441, 463, 530
Fleetwood, Frederick G.: 84, 98, 127, 148*, 168, 191, 192, 225, 275-76, 290, *329*, 416, 441, 473, 529, 530
Fleetwood, Louise S. (Mrs. F.G.): 219, 276, 416
Floods: of 1828: 67, 278; of 1869: 67, 278; of 1927: 126-27, 242, 254, 263, 278-80, *327*, 341-42*; of 1936: 342; of 1973: 342; of 1976: 342
Forbes, Merwin B.: 110, 359
Forests, municipal: Town: 406-08, 516; Village: 392
Forests, Parks and Recreation, Dept. of: 424, 425
Foss Block: 521
Foss, Emery F., Jr.: 350, 398
Foss name, other: 305, *325*
Foster, Ellis E.: 229, 262, 318
Foster name, other: 244
Four Corners: *see* Morristown Corners
Franklin-Lamoille Bank: 422, 447
Frederiksson, Dr. Donald A.: 454
Free State of the Ark: 454
French name: 88, 111-12, 126
Full Gospel Christian Assembly: 454, 501

Gates, Amasa O.: 84, 97, 127-28, 189, 230, 295, 441
Gates, C. Leo: 35, 241, 532
Gates, Mr. and Mrs. Ernest W.: 63, 213, 241, 318
Gates House: 479, 532
Gates, Mary D.: 35, 493, 532
Gates, Nathan: 67, 68, 130, 142, 259*, 282
Gates, S. Leo: 56, 243, 244
Gates name, other: 34-36, 56, 67, 72, 81, 87, 103-04, 142, 217*, 281, 289, 295, 305, 416
Geology: 1-3
George, Fabius: 66, 86, 231, 318
George, Harrison B.: 57, 295, 318
George name, other: 76, 210, 229
Giant store: 422

Gilbert, D., D.A., or Daniel: 72, 76*, 240-41, 413
Gilbert name, other: 76, 101, 229*, 315, 376
Gile, Carl A.: 230*, 231, 318, 376, 409, 428-29
Gile, Eli B.: 79, 231, 295
Gile name, other: 31*, 56
Gillen Lincoln & Mercury: 419
Gillen name: 419, 444
Gilman name: 270, 439*
Girl Scouts: 369
Gleed, Laura (Mrs. P.K.): 48*, 116-17, 194, 222, 223, 224, 416, 529
Gleed, Philip K.: 84, 88, 92, 96, 100, 105, 114, 117, 128, 144, 159, 161, 163-64, 166, 167*, 168, 185, 188, 189, 190, 246, 271, 275, 276, 286, 289, 318, 441, 529, 531
Gleed, Thomas: 102, 159, 161-62, 168, 236, 241, 268*, 270, 289, 531
Gleed name, other: 118, 162*, 185, 207
Goddard name: 175*, 267
Godfrey, Ernest & Faith: 418, 534
Godfrey name, other: 305, 462, 498
Goldberg's Auto Parts: 422
Goodale, Cyril: 40, 41, 42, 64, 288
Goodale name, other: 24, 28-29, 81, 130; see also Goodell
Goodell name: 111, 270, 296; see also Goodale
Goodliffe, Rev. George E.: 98, 213, 465, 488
Goodwin, Ernest: 411
Gould, Myra: 510, 511-12
Graham, Mr. and Mrs. Neal: 533
Grand Army of the Republic: 60, 63, 139, 166, 183, 189-90, 192, 193, 215-16, 218, *324*, 367, 505
Grand List: see Taxation
Grand Union Co.: 422
Grandey, Charles L.: DJ, 423
Grandey Insurance & Real Estate: 422-23
Grange: see Lamoille Grange; Malvern Grange
Granite sheds: 262
Grant, Harry F.: 422
Graves, Alton R.: 462-63, 526
Graves, C. Russell: 389, 443
Graves Hardware: 443
Graves name, other: 361, 443*
Gray Ladies: 479
Gray name: 115*, 433
Greaves Dairy and family: 305, 434
Greeley, Horace: 180-81
Green: see Academy Park

Green Mountain Business and Professional Women's Club: 512
Green Mountain Club, Sterling Section: 513
Green Mountain Parkway: 526
Green Mountain Pharmacy: 426, 441
Green Mt. Power Corp.: 254-55*, 395
Green River and Green River Reservoir: 255, 391-93, 395
Greene, C. Porter: 231*, 232, 233*, 263, 428, 430
Greene, Channing B.: 230, 231*, 263, 318, 428, 430
Greene Corp. (Morrisville Foundry Co.): 231, 263, 365, *428*, 428, 445
Greene, Diadama (Mrs. M.): 63, 224
Greene, Frederic M.: PC, 429*, 430
Greene, Morris: 263, 365, 428-29*
Greene name, other: 116, 428, 429
Griggs name: *331**, 433, 493
Gristmills: 65, 66, 68, 71, 259*, 261
Griswold name: 48, 197*, 198*, 306
Ground Observer Corps: 520
Grout, George G.: 263, 365
Grout observatory: 263, 365
Grout name, other: 95, 112
Gymnasium Association, Morrisville: 194, 219-20, 507-08; see also Copley Community Memorial Building

Hadley name: 198*, 227, 296, 366
Hadlock, William: 498
Hagerman, Robert: DJ, F, 415, 416
Hale farm: 389, 390, 392, 398
Hall & Cheney, druggists: 172, 174
Hall, Dr. Elmore John: 76, 77, 118, 171-72, 282
Hall name, other: 51-52, 171, 211, 289, 318, *331*, 416*
Hanifin, Patrick: *332*
Hardwick, town and village: 255
Hardy, V.M.: 48, 49, 84, 192, 195
Hardy name, other: 76*
Harris name: 73, 238-39, 246, *332*
Harrison Avenue: 189
Haskins name: 164, 282
Hasseltine, Robert E.: 360, 363
Hayford, Alan J.: 379
Health Center Building: 480*, 482
Health Cmte., Morristown: 398-99
Health, Dept. of: 426-27
Hearthstone Corp.: 437
Heath, Charles H.: 84, 92, 102, 162, 193-94*, 196, 270, 318
Heller, Peter & Alexandra: 534
Hendee, George W.: 77, 84, 88, 100,

INDEX

124*, 128, 154, 165, 166, 168, 183, 185, 188, 189, 190, 234, 263, 266*, 268-70, 289, 322, 447*, 531; house of: 470, 528
Hendee, Rev. Jehial P.: 86, 87, 234, 268
Hendee name, other: 268*, 269*
Herrick name: 98, 244, 282, 504
Hickok name: 144, 177
Hicks, Willis: 411
Hide business: 68, 337
Highway Dept., Morristown: see Roads, town
Hill name: 24, 206*, 239, 296, 413, 418, 531
Hinsdale, Joseph: 12*, 24, 27
History of Morristown, Vermont: 511
Hitchcock, Alfred: 507-08
Hogan, Charles P.: 88, 166-67, 296
Holy Cross Church: 60, 273, 326, 495-97
Homestead Dairy: 434
Hood Milk: 264, 433
Horses and horse-racing: 180*, 182, 242, 266-67, 269, 331, 445, 514-15, 526
Hotels: see Public houses
Houle, Philip & Phyllis: 422, 423, 453
Houle, Robert: 418, 422, 434, 453
Houle name, other: 453
House-numbering: 539
Howard name: 66, 296, 331
Howe name: 223, 361
Hulburd, Roger W.: 100, 113, 148, 155, 188, 194
Hunting: 188-89, 332, 392, 513-14
Huntington, Christopher: 197*, 198
Hurd name: 24, 281
Hurley, Alfred W.: 361
Hurricanes: 342-43, 523
Hutch Concrete: 423, 435
Hutchins, Dana N.: 367, 370
Hutchins name, other: 76, 331
Hyde Park, town and village: 255, 335-37, 361, 379*, 393, 394*, 410, 433, 437, 463, 464, 495*; see also North Hyde Park
Hyde name: 106, 186, 197*, 198, 219

Independent Order of Good Templars: 221
Indian Joe and Molly: 3, 18, 36-38, 72, 190, 338, 343
Industries: 66-68, 71-72, 418-19, 428-37; see also Sawmills; Tanneries; Gristmills, Iron-Making; Potash
Infantile paralysis: 537
Influenza: 157-58
Iron-Making: 66, 67
Isham, Vivian G.: 476*, 477, 482
Isham name, other: 31, 177, 306

Jack's Body Shop: 423
Jackson name: 192, 229, 306
Jacob Brook: 341
Jail: 246, 381-82
Jaycees, Lamoille Cty.: 339, 509-10
Jehovah's Witnesses: 499-500
Jenkins name: 306*, 307
Jenney, Doris: 493
Jennings name: 115, 118
Jersey Heights: 352, 433, 434, 445, 536
Jewett name: 392, 534
Jewish faith: 500
Joe's Brook: 21
Joe's Pond & Bog: 21, 38, 337, 338
Johnson, town and village: 255, 285-86, 335, 379, 394*, 437, 480, 498, 500, 538
Johnson name: 74, 456
Jones Jewelry Store: 442-43
Jones, Walter D.: PC, 307, 318, 430, 443
Jones name, other: F, PC, 6, 88, 342, 442, 443
Joslin (Joslyn, Gosslin) name: 24, 79, 131, 244, 266
Judd Hill: 80

Keeler name: 74, 307
Keiser name: 131*
Keith, Norm: 514
Kelley Block: 245, 441
Kelley, James M.: 148*, 149, 151, 152, 231, 328, 484, 485-86*
Kelley name, other: 220, 296, 307
Kelley Point: 330, 383, 399
Kellogg name: 48, 49, 315, 350
Kelly, Carol: 365
Kelsey, Hiram S.: 57, 69, 180
Kenfield Brook: 341*, 534
Kenfield, Frank: 136, 137-39, 189, 191, 192, 216*, 217, 246, 289, 296, 418, 531, 534
Kenfield House: 534
Kenfield name, other: 24, 27*, 137
Kibbey (Kibbie) name: 74, 282
Kimball, Robert: 131, 196, 289
Kimball name, other: 135, 282, 296
Kindergartens: 361, 365, 490, 492, 496, 512
King name: 213, 296, 475, 532
Korean War: 520, 521, 523
Kunstman, Mary: 353*

LaClair, Lawrence C., Jr.: 383-84
Lake Elmore: 254, 393*, 399, 487
Lake Lamoille: 173, 252-53, 338, 339, 340, 373, 390, 393, 394, 406, 430, 451-52, 537
Lakeside Garage: 446

Lambert, Claude & Arlie: 453-54
Lamoille Area Health Council: 426
Lamoille Area Housing Corp.: 482
Lamoille Country Club: 487
Lamoille County: 13-19, 339-40, 410, 480, 531
Lamoille County ...: Agricultural Center building: 422*, 437; Agricultural Society: 178-79; Bank: 447; Civic Assoc.: 409, 493-94; Development Council: 401, 425, 435; Diversion Program: 427; Entertainers: 494; Food Cooperative: 444; Grammar School: 96; Medical Assoc.: 176-77; Mental Health Service: 425, 480, 511; Natural Resources Conservation District: 424; Sheriff's Department: 384, 499-500; Sno-Packers: 408, 515-16
Lamoille Family Center: 426
Lamoille Grain Co.: 439
Lamoille Grange: 60, 62, 95, 219-20, 220-21, 491, 498, 499, 503-04, 505, 506, 510
Lamoille Home Health Agency: 426, 482, 511
Lamoille House: 244
Lamoille Industrial Park: 437, 538
Lamoille Landfill and Salvage Depot: 350, *396*, 398
Lamoille Newsdealer: 123, 180-81
Lamoille Publishing Co.: 238
Lamoille Riding & Driving Club: 514
Lamoille River: 3, 20, 66, 71-72, 246-47, 340-42, *385*, 389, 391, 396-97, 419, 539; *see also* Floods; Bridges
Lamoille River Swingers: 516
Lamoille South Supervisory Union: 361, 404
Lamoille Valley Fair and fairground: 166, 178, 180-84, 216, 266, 269, *324*, *331**, 419, 420*, 450, 537, 538
Lamoille Valley...: Fish and Game Club: 513-14; Pulp Co.: 262; Railroad: original: 123-24, 269; later: 423, 455-59 (*see also* Railroads); Winter Sports Club: 399
Lamoille Veterans Assoc.: 183
Lamoille View Apartments: 426, 529
Land use: 417-19
Landfill: *see* Dumps
Langdell name: *417*, 515
Lanpher, Carroll E.: 95, 503
LaPorte Dairy Farm: 74, 452
LaPorte Road and District: 43, 72, 74-75, 123, 243, 285, 367
Laraway name: 297*
Last blocks: 264, 431

Lawyers: 159-68
LeBaron, Isaac N.: 189, 289, 366, 409
LeBaron, W. Irving: 212, 535
Leonard name: 494, 501, 540
Leonard Rod Co., H.L.: 435
Lewis, Charles: 165, 168, 215, 217
Lewis, L. Halsey: 165, 238, 448
Lewis name, other: 67, 81, 459
Libraries: 116-19; *see also* Morristown Centennial Library
Lilley Wagon Co.: 68
Limoge name: 98, 239, 340, 447-49, 486, 514, 526
Lincoln, Abraham: 142, 185
Liquor control: *see* Alcoholic beverages
Little Laguardia: 459, 461
Little name: 24, 130*, 285
Livingstone, F.B.: 188, 289
Loati, Bruno: 431, 457
Long Trail: 20, 513
Loomis, Samuel R.: 531
Lots and lotting: 12, 357, 406-07
Lottery, Vermont: 526
Lowe, David E.: 370, 409
Lowe, Everett and Theresa: 412
Luce name: 181, 297*
Luna Pond: 339
Lupien, John: 436*

Madonna Peak: 341
Magoon name: 365, 382*
Main Street: 256, *320*, 370
Malvern Grange: 220, 503
Malvern Stock Farm: 97, 266
Mander, Sydney & Ida: 348, 371, 540
Manning name: 68, 525, 531*
Manosh, Clifford N.: 383
Manosh, Howard A. and H.A. Manosh, Inc.: 422*, 436-37, 450
Mansfield Aviation: 460-61
Maple Hill: 413
Maple sugaring: 418
Marshall name: 131, 493
Mason name: 159, 274, 308
Masons and Masonic orders: 177, 196-215, 218, 219, 241, 387, 403, 502-03, 538
Matthews name: 33, 97, 118, 189, 212, 244, 246, 297*
Maurice, Melville P.: 148, 156, 167, 168, 531
McAlister, Irene: 363
McDaniels, John: 18, 37, 197*, 198*
McKinley, Pres. William H.: 191
McMahon Bros.: 422, 446
McMahon, Raeburn R.: 220, 446, 531*

INDEX 559

McMahon name, other: 446, 452
Meacham name: 116, 308*
Meigs, Charles: 65, 159, 196, 318
Merger, Town and Village: 402
Merriam, E.B.: 114, 118, 263
Merriam name, other: 18, 114*, 152, 394
Merrill, Jonathan: 198, 205, 318
Merrill name, other: 197, 297
Merritt name: 308*
Metcalf name: 282
Methodist Church, Puffer United: 51, 52-54, 57, 75, 150, 166, 186*, 325, 489*, 490, 491-92
Mexico, War with: 132
Miles name: 184, 240, 241
Militia: 130-31, 132, 144, 149, 183
Mill Brook: 21, 259
Mill Village: 56
Miller, Clarence C.: 434, 462, 467
Miller, Erwin D.: 452, 515
Miller, McDonald & Marjorie: 418, 531
Miller name, other: 331, 517, 532
Minerals in Morristown: 21
Ministerial fund: 407
Minstrel shows: 365, 517
Mitchell name: 416, 499, 516*
Mobile homes: 412
Modern Woodmen of America: 221
Moffatt name: 308, 342
Molly's Pond & Bog: 21, 38, 337-38
Monette's Lodge: 454, 501
Montgomery name: 47, 118, 309
Moore name: 309, 361
Moran, Mr. and Mrs. Robert: 530
Morehaven / Morr-Haven: 540
Mormon Church: 497-98
Morr-Haven / Morehaven: 540
Morrill, Ann: 439, 493
Morrill, C.T. & Sons: 439-41
Morrill, Erle J.: 309, 439, 493
Morrill name, other: 309, 439
Morris name: 8*-9
Morristown and Elmore Agricultural Society: 179-80
Morristown Cemetery Assoc.: 283, 405, 406
Morristown Centennial Library: 77, 107, 116-19, 142, 222, 223, 321, 414-16, 523*
Morristown Center: 64-65, 71, 169, 243
Morristown Corners: 65-66, 85, 207, 239-40, 243, 255, 259*, 260*, 261*, 410, 411-12, 413, 498, 519, 534; see also Churches
Morristown Corners Cooperative: 412
Morristown Fire District No. 1: early: 376; later: 412

Morristown Historical Society: F, 338, 405, 470, 502, 505, 518-19, 540
Morristown Photo Archive: 319
Morristown Seminary: see Quimby School
Morristown, Town of: general: 344-46, 400, 401, 402, 517; annual meetings: 403-04; area of: 20, 337; capsule description: 334; fiscal year: 365; high and low points: 341; location in different counties: 13-19; name: 7-9; organization: 288; polling places: 525; song: 538; social scene: 540; see also Officers, local
Morristown Town School District: 334, 345-46, 348, 351, 365, 462; see also Schools; Officers, local
Morristown-Elmore Teachers Assoc.: 364
Morrisville Action Corp.: 423
Morrisville Credit Union: 496
Morrisville Drive-In: 420, 450
Morrisville Foundry Co.: see Greene Corp.
Morrisville House: 30, 77, 97, 184, 210, 240, 244
Morrisville Junior Woman's Club: 512
Morrisville Lanes: 422
Morrisville Lumber Co.: 430-31
Morrisville Messenger: 54, 238-39, 447-48
Morrisville Military Band: 182, 230-33, 331, 467, 516-18, 522*, 538; see also Bands & bandstands
Morrisville Plaza: 417, 422, 447
Morrisville Suburb: 419-23, 447
Morrisville, Village of: general: 71-77, 246-58, 344-46, 351-53, 400, 401, 402, 517, 518; boundaries: 352, 550; capsule description: 334; charter: 351-52, 385-86, 540; see also Officers, local
Morrisville Village Assoc.: 423
Morrisville Woman's Club: 117, 119, 176, 185, 221-25, 353, 369, 510-11, 512, 539
Morrisville-Stowe State Airport: 458-62, 485
Morse, George G.: 213, 318, 430
Morse, Howard & Martha: 433-34, 436
Morse Lumber Co., G.A.: 264, 430-31
Morse, Dr. Moses: 5, 7, 9-11
Morse Mt.: 341
Morse name, other: 11*, 152, 167, 186, 189, 264, 281, 353, 433
Morse's Dairy: 433-34
Mould & Davis: 262, 369
Mould, Fred: 262, 513
Mould, Henry B.: 461, 513

Mould, Ruth Greene: 116, 470
Mould name, other: 116, 309*, 318, 416
Moulton name: 76, 297, 367, 369
Mountain View Cottages: 453-54
Movie theatres: 178, 448-50, 527
Mower, Anna L.: DJ, F, *329*, 353, 415, 416, 511, 518
Mower, M.C.: 122, 189, 239, 260
Mt. Mansfield Electric RR: 123, 253
Mt. Mansfield State Forest: 341
Mud Brook: 413
Mud City: 355, 412-13, 505
Mudgett, David W.: 446, 460, 461-62, 484-85
Mudgett, Oscar H.: *326*, 445-46
Mudgett name, other: 21, 411
Mudgett-Smalley Motors (H.A. Smalley & Co.): *326*, 327, 445-46
Munson, Harlan P.: 48, 191, 246, 247, 251, 265, 439
Munson, Levi M.: 148, 149, 154, 265, 290, 366, 385, 439, 470, 471, 473, 484
Munson Store: 265, 439
Murder: 383
Murphy name: 297, 422
Music: 226-33; *see also* Bands

National Fibre Board Co.: 262
National Guard: 149, 427, 520-22; *see also* Militia; Armory
Nesky, Paul: 423, 529
Neuland name: 74, 290
New England Order of Protection: 220, 503
News & Citizen: 165-66, 447-48
Newspapers: 123, 234-39, 415, 447-48; *see also* individual newspapers
Newton name: 205, 206*, 207
Nichols, Lewis R.: 448
Niles, Albert A.: 95, 148, 166, 168, 183, 186, 192*, 194, 216, 298
Niles, Salmon: 166, 181, 186*
Niles name, other: 192, 217*, 298, 309
Noble, Ralph E.: 110, 361
No-Names: 184, 190
North American Metals: 435
North Hyde Park: 379, 498
Northern Vermont Resource Conservation and Development Project: 426
Northgate Plaza: 422, 427, 447
Norton name: 298, 310
Noyes, Arthur C.: 518
Noyes, David P.: 56, 69, 72*, 196, 289, 531, 532
Noyes House: *502*, 518-19
Noyes name, other: 72, 88, 96, 205, 241, 447, 518

Noyes / Slayton House: 532
Nursing services: 223
Nutting, Rev. John: 396

Ober name: 195, 227, 262, 298, 310
Officers, local: Town: DJ, 283*, 346-51; 353, 366-67, 376, 404, 525, 541-43; Town School District: 351, 543; Village: 352-53, 376, 385, 404, 544-45
Oil mill: 64
Old Brick Store: 63, 498, 532-33, 527
Olds, Comfort: 24, 25-26, 64, 78, 281
Olds name, other: 131, 239
Olmstead, Erwin H.: 531
Opera House: 223
Order of Eastern Star: *see* Masons and Masonic orders
Ordinances, regulations, bylaws: 351-52, 384, 385-86, 397, 400-02
Overton, Raymond: 420

P&C supermarket: 422
Page, Carroll: 462
Page, Carroll S.: 68, 111, 337, 487
Page, Charles R.: 76, 97, 266, 289*, 466
Page, Robert B.: 376, 380, 387, 390
Page name, other: 68, 97, 380, 462, 466
Paine, George H.: 420, 531*
Paine name, other: 131, 310, 420*
Paine's Restaurant: *328*, 420, 509
Palmer, James (Jimmie): 358, 363
Palmer name, other: 73*, 289
Parent-Teacher Association: 221
Park Street: 256
Parker, Alban J.: 310, 530*
Parker, Clifton G.: 168, *329*, 470ff., 473ff., 530, 531-32
Parker name, other: 310*, 472, 530*, 535
Parking & parking meters: 370, 474
Pastime Club: 213-14
Patnoe name: 311, 316
Patten name: 67
Paul name: 61, 230
Peck, Charles M.: 318, 530, 532
Peck, Fred C.: 441, 446
Peck name, other: 261, 297, 298, 363, 441
Peck's Pharmacy: 441
Pennock, Samuel M.: 57, 236, 289, 318, 408, 531
Peopleonian: 363, 364
Peoples Academy: *see* Schools
Peoples Academy Alumni Association: 99-100, 193-95, 364
Perras, Real E.: 462
Perry name: 24, 461
Pettingill name: 59, 67

INDEX

Phelps name: 180, 298, *332*
Phillips, Mrs. Allen: 505
Photographs: DJ, F, 319-32; *see also* Morristown Photo Archive
Pierce name: 437, 463
Pinecrest Park: 412
Pinewood Estates: 412
Pinney, Jean: 518
Pinsly, Samuel: 457
Pitkin name: 88*, 100-01, 109
Plains, Morristown: 259, 281*, 536-37
Planned Parenthood of Vermont: 426
Planning: 400-02
Pleasant View Cemetery, Association, and Commissioners: 280, 283, 347, 404-05, 406
Plumley, Frank: 88, 112, 192
Poland, Luke Potter: 88, 117, 158, 160-61, 162, 168
Police Department, Morristown and Morrisville: 381-84
Police, State: 425
Politics: 187-88, 195, 235-36, 240-41, 524-25
Ponds (not listed by name): 338, 393
Ponzi Gang: 487
Poor name: 75, 282
Poor relief: 285-86, 347, 398-99, 406, 425
Population: 24, 132, 287, 361, 417
Portland Street: 256
Postal Service: 65, 75, 239-42, 413, 442, 447-48*, 485
Potash Brook: 65, 259, 509
Potash-making: 64, 65, 122, 259, 261
Pouliot name: 419
Powers & Gleed: *see* Powers, H. Henry and Gleed, Philip K.
Powers, Caroline W.: 165, 270, 276
Powers, Frederic(k): 43, 75, 81, 86, 88
Powers, George M.: 84, 88, 98, 100, 105, 114, 126, 127, 148*, 154, 155, 167, 168, 181, 188, 195, 228, 233, 247, 251, 276-77, 289, 318, *322*, 354, 385, 473, 529-30
Powers, Gertrude W.: 195, 224, 228*-29, 277, 529-30
Powers, H. Henry: 7, 43, 57, 84, 88, 96, 100, 105, 114, 127-28, 159, 163, 166, 167*, 168, 171, 189, 190, 191*, 192, 216, 243, 270-73, 275, 276, 289, 318, *322*, 441, 529, 530, 531, 540
Powers, Dr. Horace: 53, 86, 144, 170-71*, 185, 236, 270, 531
Powers, Roberta F.: 277, 529
Powers name, other: 81, 134, 177, 277, 282, 298, 311
Pratt, Eunice: 64, 71, 78

Pratt-Read: 352, 431, 436
Probation & Parole Division: 426
Proprietors, original: 5-6, 9, 11-12, 284; *see also* Appendix 3 of the "first draft" of *More About Morristown, 1935-1980* for a roster of proprietors and their holdings
Prunier Motors: 445
Public houses: 27, 69, 77, 242-45, 451-54; *see also* individual names of hotels, etc.
Public Safety Bldg.: 384, 425, 427
Puffer United Methodist Church: *see* Methodist Church
Puffer, Rev. William R.: 54, 491
Pulp mill: 262
Pulpit Rock: 246-47
Putnam, Dr. David: 86, 87, 102, 171
Putnam name, other: 102, 372, 456

Quimby name and school: 85*
Quinn, John: 413

Radio: 178, 234, 242, 429-30
Railroads: 123-27, 186, *319*, 335-37, 423, 428, 433, 436, 455-59, 496
Rand name: 24, 28, 37, 49, 94, 122, 282, 298
Randall, Carroll F.: 244, 452
Randall Hotel: 77, 156, 232, 244, *328*, 394, 452, 464, 509, 530
Randall name, other: 177, 284
Randolph Road and district: 72, 74
Rasetti, Teresa: *326*
Rationing: 150-51, 153-54
Raymond name: 92, 145
Raymore, Charles H.: 290, 318, 430
Reapportionment: 531
Recreation: 178, 226-33, 339, 392, 399-400, 403*, 451-53, 461, 485-87, 506, 508, 509, 510, 513-18, 519, 537, 538-40; *see also* names of individual sports
Recreation Committee, Morristown: 399-400
Red Cross, American: 157-58, 193, 223, 280, 479, 510, 511
Reed, James O.: 232, 233, *331*, 385, 446
Reed name, other: 67, 371, 446
Referenda: 526-27
Regulations: *see* Ordinances
Renaud, Lucien & Hazel: 404, 441
Republicans: *see* Politics
Research Engineering Corp.: 435
Retired Senior Volunteer Program: 426
Revolutionary War, veterans of: 281, 282
Reynolds name: 107, 194, 485
Rich name: 6, 76, 241, 429, 445

Rights: *see* Lots and lotting
Ring name: 74, 409
River Street: *327*, 341
Road commissioner: 346-47, 366-67
Roads: Town: 120-22, 281, 366-68, 370, 373, 406, 547; State: *324*, 339-40, 367-68, 373, 419; *see also* Streets and Street Department, Morrisville; Bridges
Roberts name: 130, 210, 281
Robinson, E.S.: 48, 230, 242
Robinson, Rev. Septimius: 40, 43-45, 47, 86, 87, 88, 92, 189, 532
Robinson, Rev. W.A.: 118, 189, 190
Robinson name, other: 49, 88, 161, 219, 220, 230, 241, 246, 311, 318
Rockwell, Rev. Daniel: 41-42, 43, 64*
Roosevelt, Theodore: 182, *324*
Rotary Club, Morrisville: 127, 221, 232, 342, 509
Round barn: *528*, 534-35
Rowell name: 133, 298
Royal Arch Masons: *see* Masons and Masonic orders
Rubbish service: *see* Dumps
Rublee, Dr. Charles C.: 76, 172-73, 188-89, 246, 318
Rugg, Harold and Julia: 338
Ryder Brook: 21, 66, 341, 533
Ryder Brook Stables: 515
Ryder name: 36, 68, 311, 534

Safford, Darius J.: 118*, 135*, 139-42, 183, 188, 210, 299, 318
Safford, Jedidiah: 39, 71, 72, 75, 94, 282, 284, 518
Safford, John: 24, 39, 71-72, 259, 518
Safford, Joseph: 130, 282, 299
Safford name, other: 49, 71-72*, 247, 282, 409, 518
Samoset Cottage Colony: 173-74, 215, *327*, 423, 451-52
Sanborn name: 88, 103, 112-13, 118, 188, 299
Sanders, Charles A.: 23, 343
Sanders, Don A.: 229, 230*, 231, 232, 233, *331*, 516-17
Sanders, Willard K.: F, 196, 213, 232, 233, 318, *329*, *331*, 340, 343, 349, 356, 369, 387ff., 403, 456, 503, 516-17, 539
Sanders name, other: 516, 522
Sanel Auto Parts: 422
Sargent Dorothy D.: 353, 362
Sargent, Richard C.: 472, 473, 530
Sargent, Walter M., Jr.: 447, 471-72, 487

Sargent, Walter M., Sr.: 155*, 156, 445-46, 447
Sawmills: 64, 65, 66, 68, 71, 76, 259, 261, 264, 339, 407, 430-31
Sawyer, Joshua: 19, 67, 69, 317
Sawyer name, other: 123, 134*, 197*, 198*, 299*, 353
Schools: general: 72, 78-116, 354-65; Copley Building, Peoples Academy: 97-99, 359*-60, 404; Graded School: 96, 355, 359, 362; Elementary School: 362, 516; Peoples Academy and Peoples Academy complex: 43, 72, 86-116*, 166, 172, 190, 193-94*, 230, *320*, *321*, *323*, *332*, 348, 354, 355-60, 362-65, 403, 404, 466-67*, 468, 503-04, 507*, 510, 516, 521, 522, 537, 538; PA principals: 100-10, 359, 360, 363; school districts and rural schools: 70*-71, 72, 78-84, *323*, 354-55, 357, 358, 365, 374, 410; superintendents of schools: 361; *see also* Kindergartens; Lamoille South Supervisory Union; Morristown Town School District; Quimby School; Town system of schools
Scribner name: 299*
Searles name: 6*
Sears, Joseph: 64, 65, 81, 131-32, 205*, 207, 239, 243, 289, 318*
Sears name, other: 107-08, 318
Seaver name: 67, 68, 180
Second Chance shop: 479*, 532
Senators, State: 531
Senior citizens, and Senior Citizens Center, Lamoille County: 409, 425-26*, 471-72, 493-94, 511, 525, 532, 540
Sesqui-Centennial, Morristown: 538
Seventh-day Adventist Church: 498-99, 501
Sewer system and sewage treatment: 246, 256, 351, 396-97
Shanley, Evelyn H.: 416
Shaw Brook: 21, 259, 261
Shaw, Crispus: 24, 31, 40, 42, 64, 79, 130, 132, 281
Shaw, Ebenezer: 32, 55, 259, 282
Shaw Hollow: 31
Shaw, Leslie M.: 31, 188, 190, 273
Shaw name, other: 24, 31*, 32*, 40, 42, 64, 79, 132, 157, 273*, 274
Sheltra, Bernard C.: 363
Shire town: 410
Silloway name: 220, 311*
Silver Ridge Pavilion: 538
Simpson, Mary Jean: 108, 156, 194

INDEX 563

Singing schools: 226-27, 519
Sinow family: 434, 500-01
Skiing: 399, 452, 453, 477
Slayton, Albert H.: 212, 265, 438, 447
Slayton, George: 76, 123, 191, 532
Slayton, H.A. & Co.: 127-28, 232, 249*, 254, 265, 438-39
Slayton, Henry A.: 48, 63, 72, 192, 247, 249*, 251, 438, 532
Slayton, Dr. William T.: 148, 173-74, 213, 290, 311, 451, 531
Slayton name, other: 99, 112, 117-18, 154, 224, 387, 416*, 538
Sled dog races: 509
Slocum, Charles H.: 84, 95, 165, 212, 247, 251, 263, 282, 385
Small, William: 73*, 130, 282
Small name, other: 72-74, 132, 148, 282, 289
Smalley & Co., H.A.: *see* Mudgett-Smalley Motors
Smalley, Herbert A.: 267, *326*, 445
Smalley name, other: 267, 290, 312, 318*
Smallpox: 181, 281
Smith, Allen B.: 118, 124, 239, 286
Smith, Clement F.: 220-21, 289
Smith name, other: 168, 197, 198, 257, 299*, 361, 406, 412, 447, 482, 531
Snow Palace: 371
Snowmobiling: 392, 408, 462, 515-16
Snowroller: 122, 368
Social Welfare Dept.: 425
Society of Social Friends: 92-93
Soil Conservation Service: 424
Soldiers Monument: *see* Academy Park
Somerby, Joseph A.: 76*, 234-36
Sons of Union Veterans and Auxiliary: 218-19, 505-06
SOS Children's Village: 540
Spanish-American War: 145, 522
Sparks, Robert J.: *331*, 517
Spaulding, Barzilla: 130, 132, 282
Spaulding House: 534
Spa(u)lding name, other: 32*, 51, 56*, 81, 132*, 157, 230*, 241, 534*
Spear name: 74, 367
Spiller, Calvin A.: 212, 213, 318
Spiritualist Society: 61, 71
Springs: Bugbee: 248, 249, 250, 388*, 392; Elmore Road: 248, 250, 388*; other: 369
"Spunky Lamoille": 18, 178, 339-40, 343
Square dancing: 516
St. Jock, Robert, Jr.: *332*, 483-84
Stackpole, Harry T.: 419
Stafford & Sons, C.H.A.: 264*, 265, 267, 431-32
Stafford, Charles H.A.: 98, 177, 191-92, 212, 262-63, 290, 385, 466, 531
Stafford, Eloise: 466, 518
Stafford, Guy C.: 431
Stafford, Roberta M.: 353, 493
Stafford, Roy C.: 290, 431, 531*
Stancliffe, Ralph S.: 312, 483, 485
Stancliffe name, other: 312*, 338
State's attorneys: 168, 531-32
Stearns, Charles H.: 77, 188, 447
Stearns Supply Co.: 419
Steele, Fred E., III: 538
Sterling Brook: 21, 341, 371
Sterling Range: 20, 341, 513, 539
Sterling, town: 198*, 335, 337, 406*
Sterner, Arlo K.: 407
Stewart, Arthur C.: 312, 464
Stewart, John E.: 241, 312, 413
Stewart name, other: 248, 281, 312, 423
Stewart's Television: 423
Stockwell, Rev. Frank A.: F, 57, 152*, 312, 483, 493*, 518
Stoddard name: 131*
Stone building: 535
Stone, Edgar H.: 299, 381
Stone, Mason S.: 88, 100, 106, 152, 195
Stone name, other: 230, 299, 316, 496
Story name: 186, 227, 300
Stowe, town and village: 253, 255, 285, 335, 361*, 379, 394*, 431, 447, 462, 487, 495-96, 498, 531, 546
Stowe, Dr. Willard H.: 118*, 416
Street signs: 468
Streetlights: 246, 251, 252, 467
Streets and Street Department, Morrisville: 256, 367, 368-70, 375, 437; *see also* individual street names; Roads
Strong name: 31, 376, 382, 433
Sulham name: 318, 406
Sumner name: 24*, 131, 132, 281
Sunday amusements: 527
Sunset Motel: 373, 422, *451*, 453
Sunset Park: 412
Sweet & Burt: 160, 212, 213
Sweetser, Percy A.: 146, 220, 313
Sweetser name, other: 317, 379

Tague, John: *332*
Tanneries: 65, 66, 67, 72, 77, 257, 259*, 262-63, 428
Taverns: *see* Public houses
Taxation and Grand List: 78-79, 80, 256*, 265, 424
Taxis: 462-63, 526

Taylor name: 131, 197*, 198, 300, 313, 317*
Tegu Theatre: 449-50
Telephone: 127-28, 242, 463-64
Television: 423, 464
Temperance: see Alcoholic beverages
Templars, Independent Order of Good: 221
Tenney name: 49, 95, 113, 280*, 416; see also Bridges, Tenney
Terrill, Moses Weld: 70, 76, 190, 289, 491
Terrill name, other: 69, 70, 132, 186*, 242, 289*, 290, 300, 343, 531
Thayer, Lewis P.: 238-39, 483
Thayer, Richard: 523
Thomas name: 74*, 88*, 97, 115, 122, 313, 361
Thompson name: 113, 115, 168*, 416*
Tift block: 232
Timmerman name: 318, 429-30, 432
Timmerman-Greene Corp.: 429-30, 432
Tinker House: 170, 498, 534
Tinker, Dr. James: 41, 53, 65, 169-70, 171, 239*, 318, 534
Tinker, Dr. Ralph: 40*, 64, 169, 196
Tinker name, other: 170*, 171, 194, 207, 261
Tobogganing: 330, 399
Towle name: 443*
Towle's Hardware: 443
Town clock: 57, 408-09
Town hall: DJ, 27, 53, 54, 61, 64, 65-66, 185*, 232, 250*, 325, 388*, 403-04, 505
Town offices/building: 344, 384, 404, 415
Town representatives: 289-90, 531
Town, Samuel: 65, 68-69, 132
Town name, other: 68-69, 70, 79, 170, 243
Town system of schools: 84, 96, 354
Towne, Ballou L.: 317, 413*
Towne, William: 375, 376
Towne name, other: 257, 493
Tracy, Thomas: 76, 86*, 87*, 289
Transportation Agency, Vermont: 425; see also Roads, State
Trees: DJ, 349, 350-51, 407-08, 415, 454, 469
Tripp, Gerald W.: 331, 370, 517
Trombley, Joseph L.: 422
Twiss, Arthur A.: 238, 447
Twombly, Mabel: 505
Tyndall Hill and name: 115, 358, 394, 454

Union Bank, The and Union Savings Bank & Trust Co.: 77*, 118, 119, 157, 158, 269, 404, 446-47, 511

Union Carbide Corp.: 434, 496
Union House: 244
United Cerebral Palsy: 427
United Church of Christ: 490; see also Congregational Church, First
United Farmers Cooperative Creamery Assoc.: 265, 432-33, 456
United War Work Campaign: 156
Universalist Church, First: 52-53, 54-58, 75, 177, 273, 323, 326, 408, 409, 488, 489, 492-94
Uplift Club: 224, 510, 511-12
Utton name: 266*-67

Valleau, Dr. Archibald: 175, 528
Vandalism: 365, 368, 406, 467, 468, 522
Vendues: 284
Vermont Asbestos Grp.: 431-32, 436-37
Vermont Citizen: 186, 238
Vermont Electric Cooperative: 394
Vermont House: 244
Vermont Industrial Products: 423, 436
Vermont Legal Aid: 427
Vermont Public Power Supply Authority: 395
Vermont Sugar Makers' Assoc.: 139, 418
Vermont Tanning Corp.: 263, 428; see also Tanneries
Vermont Yankee: 395
Veterans of Foreign Wars, Post 9653, and Auxiliary: 508-09, 523
Veterans Service Station: 419
Viet Nam War: 520, 523
Vincent name: 49, 300
Virginia, Jack: 18
Voting: 347, 525

Wade Fund, Amy: 469
Waite name: 77, 182, 265*, 318, 483
Wakefield name: 318, 353, 370, 413, 511
Walker, Jacob: 24*, 25, 36, 40, 51, 64*, 79, 120, 122, 189, 243*, 259, 281, 394, 405, 519*, 533, 536, 538
Walker name, other: 24, 25, 56*, 288*, 529
Wallace name: 53, 217, 262*
War of 1812: 18, 131-32
Ward, Ernest: 147, 313, 508
Ward Pond: 338-39
Ward, Walter C. and Emma: 231, 339, 445
Ward name, other: 314, 339*, 342, 367*, 445*
Ward's, Inc.: 445
Warner, James M.: 215, 505*
Warner name, other: 184, 300
"Warning out": 284
Warren Block: 77, 241, 328, 387, 447

INDEX

Warren, Charles C.: 128, 165, 262; *see also* Warren Leather Co.
Warren Leather Co.: 128, 166, 263, 409; *see also* Tanneries
Warren, Smith M.: 147, 314, 508
Warren name, other: 132, 241, 314, 419
Water and Light Dept., Morrisville: general: 77, 246-56, 265, 343, 352, 385-95; commissioners: 385, 545; electric system: 246-47, 251-56, 342, 351, 386, 390-95; "profits," how used: 256, 257, 386, 476, 486; water system: 248-51, 256, 351, 386, 387-90
Water pollution: 248, 340-41, 396-97, 398. 456
Water systems, non-Village: 411, 412
Watering troughs and Watering Trough Hill: 222, 369
Waterman, George: 70, 93, 165, 194, 237
Waterman, Joseph: 197*, 198*, 317
Waterman, Vernon W.: 67, 69-70, 124, 165, 242, 289
Waterman name, other: 42-43, 113, 165, 181, 183, 197*, 270, 282, 318
Waterville Light and Power Co.: 254, 255, 394
Washington, George: 184, 185, 207
Washington Highway: 281
Weather: 21-23, 152-53, 340, 342-43, 371, 394, 463
Webster, Edward W.: 257, 262, 318
Webster, Wingate: 43, 75, 81, 82
Webster name, other: 282
Welch, Edward J.: 447, 473
Welch farm and family: *528*, 534-35
Welch name, other: 31, 366
Weld, Moses: 75, 130, 227, 281
Welfare: *see* Poor Relief
Wells name: 317, *328*, 360, 379, 406
West, A.G.: 58, 59, 244-45
West, Adrian A.: 423, 442, 462
West Brook: 21
West, John: 66, 87, 88, 180
West, Rethel C.: 441-42*
West name, other: 300, 353, 415, 441-42*
Westphal, Frederick E.: 531
Wheeler name: 81, 282, 300*, 441
Wheelock, Addison P. and home of: 176, 267, 475, 536
Wheelock, Edwin: 88, 92, 101, 190, 193
Wheelock name, other: 207, 367
Whipple, Wilbur F.: 48, 190, 227*-28, 229*-30
Whipple name, other: 229, 244*, 300*
White Heat Foundry: *428*, 430
White, Jack S.: *331*, 443-44

White, Leon M.: PC, 99, 443
White, Morris B.: 213, 318, 353, 443
White name, other: 134, 260, 300*, 443, 448
White's Funeral Home: 443
Whiteface Mt.: 20, 341
Whiteface Shelter: 513
Whiting Milk: 264
Whitney, A.F.: 54, 186, 246
Whitney name, other: 6, 31, 202, 281, 285
Wilder, Bruce: 461
Wilkins, Austin: 192, 301, 318, 505
Wilkins, George: 92, 180, 190
Wilkins, Glenn A., Jr.: *331*, 413, 505
Wilkins name, other: 74, 290, 364, 505
Willard, Samuel A.: 159-60, 240*, 282
Williams name: 24, 59, 270, 363
Wilson, Edward & Maryann: 353, 422
Wilson, Hollis S.: 105-06, 167, 276
Wilson name, other: 76, 139, 195, 244, 301*
Wiltshire, Ralph & Martha: 419
Wolchik, Joseph J.: 532
Wolcott, town: 361*, 379*, 394, 495, 498
Woman's Relief Corps: 213, 216, 217-18, 505
Women: first in various roles: 353, 516, 517, 531; home for elderly: 470-72; other: 144, 155, 156, 157, 179, 377, 378, 478, 487*, 505, 506
Wood: *see* Energy
Wood name: 49, 214, 260, 301
Woodbury, Gertrude: *see* Powers, Gertrude W.
Woodbury, Urban A.: 100, 111, 135, 190, 192, 211
Woodbury name, other: 103, 233, 301, 314
Woods name: 213, 318, 353
Woodward, Dr. George E.: 172, 174, 230
Woolcutt name: 301*
Worcester, town of: 361
World War I: 145-48, 158, 193, 212, 223, 232, 239
World War I Veterans: 506
World War II: *324*, 520-21, 537
Wright name: 6, 57, 147, 314
Wrong End Store: 439-41

Yacovone, Joseph A.: 413
Yankee Milk: 432-33
Young Men's Christian Assoc.: 151-52
Young Women's Christian Assoc.: 156

Zack Woods Pond: 393
Zoning: 400-01